Researching Communications

A Practical Guide to Methods in Media and Cultural Analysis

Second Edition

David Deacon, Michael Pickering,
Peter Golding, Graham Murdock

HODDER
EDUCATION
PART OF HACHETTE UK

For Jo, Karen, Jen and Barbara

First published in Great Britain in 2007 by
Hodder Education, part of Hachette UK
338 Euston Road, and London NW1 3BH

www.hoddereducation.com

British Library Cataloguing in Publication Data
A catalogue record for this book is available from the British Library

Library of Congress Cataloging-in-Publication Data
A catalog record for this book is available from the Library of Congress

ISBN 978 0 340 92699 4

2 3 4 5 6 7 8 9 10

Typeset in Adobe Garamond by Dorchester Typesetting Group Ltd
Printed and bound in Great Britain by the MPG Books Group

What do you think about this book? Or any other Hodder Education title?
Please send your comments to the feedback section on www.hoddereducation.com.

Contents

Preface to the First Edition

In recent years there has been a massive expansion in the numbers of students studying the media and communications. Though sometimes much derided in public debate, this field of study has clearly met a substantial demand for interdisciplinary understanding of what have become dominant features of everyday experience. Two unfortunate consequences of this expansion, however, threaten its essential vitality.

First, the twin lineage of, on the one hand, cultural studies, often rooted in the humanities and more recently anchored in debates drawn from psychoanalysis and philosophy, and on the other hand media studies, often rooted in the social and behavioural sciences, has bequeathed what sometimes seems a highly differentiated field of study. Students focused on media studies seem unfamiliar with much important work in cultural theory, while cultural studies students often bypass much research with social-science foundations. Second, the methods of research and inquiry encountered and used by students are themselves becoming detached from their roots in the humanities and social sciences. As cultural and media studies become ever more self-enclosed, so too the empirical techniques essential to understanding and extending their output become truncated and myopic.

One result of this development is to constrict many students' understanding of, and enthusiasm for, original research. Chary of anything smacking of numbers or data analysis, they begin to regard all research as suspect and unattractively mundane. Drawn to more qualitative methods, they soon become disenchanted with their imprecision, and what is often a mismatch between aspiration and output.

This book is the result of many years of discussion with students attempting to feel their way through these minefields. The authors collectively have nearly 100 years of teaching experience in research methods relevant to cultural and media analysis. We have taught between us in up to 20 different countries. From that background comes the conviction that researching communications is a means to understanding some of the most fundamental and critical areas of contemporary human activity, and that it can only be undertaken adequately by acquiring, in a very practical way, the techniques necessary for a comprehensive range of research methods, and by understanding the assumptions, strengths and weaknesses of all of them.

With that in mind the book sets out to explain and illustrate the entire range of methods necessary to research communications. We have organised the book around tasks and questions the researcher will face, rather than as a sequence of disconnected skills and techniques. Above all, we wish to stress the essential complementarity of so-called qualitative and quantitative methods, and the reader will find much in the book to both question and dilute this distinction. We also wish to show how these techniques can be made to work in practice. There is nothing worse than a textbook that smugly tells you how it should be done, but coyly ignores the essential messiness and intransigence of a stubborn reality. In presenting examples we have drawn on the real experience of our own research and on that of others, in order to show exactly how research works.

Preface to the Second Edition

The publication of the first edition of this book was received with gratifying support and approval. It seemed the continuing development of cultural and media research had created an appetite for guidance on empirical methods, especially one which went beyond simple distinctions between quantitative and qualitative approaches, as we had sought to do.

The feedback we have received has also helped us develop ideas for a revised version. In undertaking the revision we have introduced major changes to the content and examples provided, without departing from the central approach. In particular, we have made significant alterations to the sections on using archives and on using computers. We have added sections on the Internet as a resource for research, and also assessed carefully the advantages and disadvantages of on-line methodologies. In explaining observational techniques we have expanded our account to include observing online and 'blogs'. In the chapter on using computers for data analysis we have completely updated the material for current versions of SPSS and other relevant packages. We have provided new worked examples in the chapters on 'unpacking news' and 'interpreting images', some of which are contemporary and some historical. These examples from the past have not just been included for their intrinsic interest, but also to signal our conviction that media and cultural studies needs to develop a more historical perspective. A closed 'present-centred' viewpoint can too easily neglect how immediate events often have deep-rooted connections with the past.

The production of this second edition has not been possible without help from many people. For specific editorial assistance, we would like to thank Sarah Barnard, Vivienne Church, Ben Oldfield, Linda Ohlsen, and for the index to the new edition, Lyn Greenwood. Our thanks also to Matthew Sullivan and his colleagues at Hodder Arnold. More generally, we would like to express our thanks to: Jo Aldridge, Michael Billig, Georgina Born, Simon Cross, John Downey, Mike Gane, Alastair Gordon, Alan Jeffery, Emily Keightley, Thomas Koenig, Sharon Lockyer, Katie Macmillan, Jim McGuigan, Sabina Mihelj, Maggie O'Neill, Charles Oppenheim, John Richardson, James Stanyer, Ian Taylor, Alex Turner, Alex Wade, Dominic Wring, Lian Zhu and all our other colleagues in the Department of Social Sciences at Loughborough University, who have collectively provided the most stimulating of intellectual environments. In such a rich research context it is difficult not to think constructively about the business of doing research. Our students too, in many places and circumstances, have contributed much to our understanding of what helps and what does not, and have, over many years, assisted in the development of many of the ideas and illustrations presented here.

David Deacon
Michael Pickering
Peter Golding
Graham Murdock
Loughborough, May 2007

Acknowledgements

The authors and publishers would like to thank the following for permission to use copyright material in this book.

Ian Taylor, Loughborough University for Figure 4.1 (page 66); figures used in Figure 5.3 (page 98) © Crown copyright material reproduced with permission of the Controller of HMSO; American Society of Newspaper Editors for figures used in Figure 5.4 (page 98); Paris-Match/IZIS for Figure 7.1 (page 149); Daily Mail for Figure 8.1 and extract from 'Kassem hit by bullets in a Bagdad street' (pages 172–174); Figure 10.1 and extract from 'Death of a "campus bum"' (pages 218–220) © Mirrorpix / Courtesy of John Frost Newspapers; Figures 10.2 to 10.21 (pages 231–238) © BBC; Philip Schlesinger for extract from 'Between Sociology and Journalism' (pages 255–256); Richard Ericson for extract from 'Visualising Deviance – A Study of News Organsations' (pages 270–272); Figure 11.2 (page 275) Copyright 2007, Linden Research, Inc. All Rights Reserved; Figure 12.1 (page 304) © 2007 Members of the Audacity Development Team; Figures 14.2 to 14.13 (pages 333–344) from SPSS for Windows, Version 14. Chicago: SPSS Inc; Figures 14.14 to 14.21 (pages 345 to 354) NVivo 7 screen shots are reproduced with kind permission from QSR International and are subject to copyright. NVivo and NVivo 7 are registered trademarks of QSR International. www.qsrinternational.com.; American Sociological Association for extract from ethical guidelines of ASA (pages 369–371); British Sociological Association for extracts from 'Language and the BSA' (pages 372–376).

Every effort has been made to trace and acknowledge ownership of copyright. The publishers will be glad to make suitable arrangements with any copyright holders whom it has not been possible to contact.

chapter one

Approaching Research

Communications and contemporary life

Modern communications media have become a major focus for research for the simple reason that they are central to organising every aspect of contemporary life, from the broad patterning of social institutions and cultural systems, to intimate everyday encounters and people's personal understandings of the world and their sense of themselves. We cannot fully understand the ways we live now without understanding communications. This offers media researchers enormous opportunities to contribute to current knowledge and debate.

Institutions

Communications companies feature prominently among the world's largest firms and play a major role in economic and political life. Not only do they provide the specialised information and communication links that enable modern enterprises to coordinate production on a global scale and allow financial dealings to continue 24 hours a day, they are also pivotal to the orchestration of consumption. In addition to selling an ever-expanding range of their own goods and services, they are the main conduits for the avalanche of general advertising and promotion that oils the wheels of the consumer system as a whole. Their economic importance is matched by their role in the organisation of politics. In modern democracies, where political parties must compete for the support of floating voters and social movements continually press to have their views and concerns added to the political agenda, the mass media have become the major public spaces where images are massaged, policies promoted, events made sense of and issues debated.

Cultural systems

The promotion of products and political platforms is, in turn, part of a much more diverse and broadly based cultural system, in which competing views of the world are expressed through a proliferating range of expressive forms, from graphic arts and street styles to fiction and music. To reach a wider public, these productions, and the diverse ways of thinking, feeling and looking that they express, have to engage with the principal mass media of film, television, publishing and the music and computer industries. Exploring the patterning of the generalised public culture that is constructed by this activity, examining what stands at its centre and what is pushed to the margins, and investigating the way that particular cultural forms organise meaning, tells us much about the imaginative spaces we hold in common.

Understandings and identities

However, as we shall see in later chapters, when we look in detail at how to unpack the meanings carried by media imagery, texts and talk, we find that public communications seldom trade in simple 'messages' offering a unitary view of the world. Instead, they offer a range of mental maps which can be entered at different points and navigated in a variety of ways. Nor is it simply the 'contents' of media that mobilises meanings. Through their visual style and the promotion that surrounds them, media machineries – television sets, mobile phones, camcorders, iPods, satellite dishes – speak powerfully to their owners (and to us) about the kinds of people they are and would like to be. The interplay between understandings and identities grounded in people's everyday lives, and the generalised world views, structures of experience and images of self offered by the public communications system, is both complex and continually being renegotiated.

Patterns of everyday life

The public media also play a major role in organising the routines and rituals of everyday life. Television is a central presence in domestic and family life. Inviting friends to the house to listen to music or play computer games has become an important element for cementing teenage friendships. Reading the newspaper or listening to breakfast radio is an almost universal accompaniment to people's daily journey to work. In addition, many of the rituals marking important personal moments are bound up with media: photos capture our first halting steps or university graduation; going clubbing or to the cinema is central to courtship; weddings and family gatherings are increasingly captured on video.

Undisciplined study

Observing the growing centrality of media to these various dimensions of contemporary life, a number of writers have called for a new discipline of communications studies. How far you support this call depends in part on how you interpret that slippery term 'discipline'. Clearly, worthwhile research on communications needs to be rigorous and disciplined rather than impressionistic and haphazard; evidence needs to be collected, analysed and presented systematically. Showing you how to do this is our major aim in this book. But the great strength of communications as a field of study is that it is an *interdisciplinary* space, where a range of existing academic disciplines meets, bringing their own particular questions, concerns and intellectual traditions with them. Economists, political scientists and sociologists, for example, tend to focus on communications as an institutional system and its relations to economic and political life. Psychologists are more likely to be interested in the media's role in shaping people's beliefs and identities, while those coming from humanities disciplines, such as history, literary criticism and cultural anthropology, are more concerned with the role of communications in cultural systems and everyday life. The cross-fertilisation generated by these intellectual encounters is an essential source of intellectual dynamism and renewal, which prevents the study of communications becoming too self-referring. Drawing a boundary around the analysis of communications in the name of a new discipline has the opposite effect, making it more inward-looking.

Our view is that the study of communications should be undisciplined in this sense, and preserve its role as the primary arena where scholars from very different traditions can come together to puzzle out how best to make sense of the complex connections between communications systems, the organisation of contemporary social and cultural life, and our perceptions and understandings of the world around us. To do this, we need to pin down these links and detail how they work. Research is central to this enterprise.

At first sight, the range of available research methods looks like the inside of a mechanic's toolbox. Most of this book is devoted to telling you which methods can do which jobs, showing you how to use them, making clear what their limitations are and suggesting where they can be used together. But research methods are not just tools of the trade. They are ways of gathering the evidence required by competing definitions of what counts as a legitimate and worthwhile approach to the investigation of social and cultural life. In our view, many of the most interesting questions facing communications research are best tackled by combining different research methods. But this is not a universal view. Many writers insist that only certain methods are appropriate. To understand why, we need to look briefly at the main rival approaches to social and cultural investigation that underpin contemporary research in communication and media studies: positivism, interpretive approaches and critical realism.

The appliance of science: positivism

relations of cause + effect

Positivism developed in the mid nineteenth century as practitioners of the emerging social sciences struggled to distance themselves from speculation and personal commentary, and establish their credentials as 'scientists' on a par with those working in the natural sciences. Their case rested on a number of basic arguments, and although positivism has been modified several times since it was launched, it retains its core features.

Positivists begin by asserting that investigating the social and cultural world is no different, in principle, to investigating the natural world, and that the same basic procedures apply to both. From here, it follows that, as in the natural sciences, the only admissible scientific evidence consists of 'facts' established by systematic personal observation. Since people, unlike animals or rocks, can also talk to researchers, positivists add to their methodological armoury the process of asking simple, direct questions, but there is no place for extended encounters or personal involvement in their research practice. On the contrary, collecting usable 'facts' requires researchers to be 'objective', keeping their distance from their research subjects and not allowing their work to be influenced by their own values or subjective judgements. To further bolster objectivity and precision, positivists favour recording relevant 'facts' in terms of *quantities* or numbers that can be processed using statistical techniques. This preference draws its strength from the long-standing assertion that a 'science' of anything, including social and cultural life, must be based on *empirical data produced by direct observation*. (It does not necessarily follow from this that all such data has to be converted into numbers – qualitative research can also be empirical.)

The general argument in favour of empirical inquiry first developed during the Renaissance, when scientists separated themselves from theology and metaphysics by insisting that what they did was grounded solely in systematic observations of the material world and had no place for airy speculations about the hereafter or worlds beyond the reach of the five senses. Since then, this position has often been used to justify a militant *empiricism* that rejects any form of theory 'in favour of what it calls a practical concern with facts' (Filmer 1972: 43). However, it is important to remember that *not all empirical research or research using statistics is empiricist*. Empiricism is not a research style associated with particular methods. It is an attitude to the relations between theory and practical inquiry. Not all varieties of positivism are empiricist, but they do all have a particular view of what constitutes a valid theoretical proposition.

Positivists see the overall aim of scientific inquiry as developing generalisations about the relations between social 'facts' that establish basic connections of cause and effect. To achieve this, they insist that existing generalisations have to be tested continually against new evidence to see whether the specific predictions (hypotheses) they generate are supported (verified) or disproved (falsified). Testing requires the researcher to isolate the relations they are particularly interested in from other factors that may influence or interfere with them. Positivists argue that this is best done in a laboratory, where the researcher can control conditions. Where experimentation is not possible, for practical or ethical reasons, evidence can be collected by other methods, but confounding factors must be rigorously controlled (statistically) at the analysis stage. Positivists claim that these procedures produce robust predictions that enable social agencies to intervene more effectively to control the causes of social distress. For example, if it could be established beyond reasonable doubt that watching large amounts of screened violence caused teenage boys to behave more aggressively, there would be a strong case for greater censorship of film, video and television. This faith in science's 'positive' role in social engineering was written into positivism's title and its intellectual project from the outset.

Positivism, then, has strong views on what counts and does not count as legitimate and worthwhile research. These establish deep divisions. One of the most pervasive is between methods that produce *quantitative* evidence that can be expressed in numbers and those that generate *qualitative* materials, such as field notes or transcripts of interviews or group discussions. The current popularity of qualitative methods in studies of media audiences has prompted the Swedish communications scholar Karl Eric Rosengren to express his profound regret that so many researchers are missing out on 'the potentially rich harvest bound to come in once the necessary transubstantiation of valuable qualitative insights into quantitative descriptions and explanations based on representative samples…has been carried out' (Rosengren 1996: 140). He is adamant that a true 'science' of communication must trade in 'hard' numerical facts. Anything else, as Thomas Lindlof notes, is seen as 'too imprecise, value laden, and particularistic to be of much use in generating general or causal explanations' (Lindlof 1995: 10). Positivists do use qualitative methods, but only in the preparatory (or *pilot*) work for a study devoted to producing quantitative data. As the pioneering American communications researcher Robert Merton argued when he was investigating responses to military training films in World War II, although talking to soldiers raised interesting questions about their reactions, these speculations had to be 'tested' by more rigorous 'experimental research' (Merton 1956: 557).

This image of the experiment as the primary route to 'scientific' knowledge about social life and human behaviour is very much alive in present-day communications research. So much so that the distinguished psychologist Hans Eysenck maintained that research employing experimental methods produces the only evidence that can be used to settle the long-running argument as to whether or not there is a direct link between watching violence on film, television and video and behaving aggressively. He concedes that 'experimental designs are complex and difficult to make foolproof', and that 'statistical analysis often has to take care of the many unwanted variables that sneak into the experiment and may confound our data'. But he is adamant that 'nevertheless, when there is such an impressive amount of agreement [between available] studies…we may conclude that there is sufficient evidence in favour of the theory that…only the most prejudiced could reject all this evidence and call the case "unproven"' (Eysenck and Nias 1978: 12).

Even so, a number of researchers do reject the evidence Eysenck quotes (see Murdock and McCron 1979; Cumberbatch and Howitt 1989; Barker and Petley 1997). Two criticisms of the positivist approach to the media/violence debate are voiced particularly frequently. First, critics maintain that it works with a grossly oversimplified model of media effects, which casts audiences as passive victims. Instead of viewing films and television programmes featuring acts of violence as stimuli that prompt people to copy what they have seen or that trigger latent aggression, critics present them as complex imaginative worlds that people actively navigate their way around and make sense of. Second, they insist that the impact of media can be grasped properly only within the context of everyday life. Instead of conducting experiments in the artificial setting of the laboratory, or asking people narrowly based questions about their viewing habits and aggressive behaviour, research needs to examine the dynamics of social violence in the situations in which it naturally occurs – inside families, outside pubs and clubs on a Saturday night – and to explore the roles played by media imagery in forming the identities that people bring to those settings.

Making sense: interpretation

These criticisms stem from the second major intellectual tradition underpinning contemporary research on communications and media: the interpretive tradition. The central concern here is not with establishing relations of cause and effect, but with exploring the ways that people make sense of their social worlds and how they express these understandings through language, sound, imagery, personal style and social rituals. As the American anthropologist Clifford Geertz famously put it: 'Believing…that man is an animal suspended in webs of significance he himself has spun, I take culture to be those webs, and the analysis of it to be therefore not an experimental science in search of law but an interpretive one in search of meaning' (Geertz 1973: 5).

It is no accident that Geertz is an anthropologist. Advocates of **interpretive research** place particular emphasis on the ethnographic practices developed by anthropologists, where the researcher immerses herself in a particular social setting, getting to know the people intimately, observing how they organise their everyday lives and talking to them at length about how they see the world and themselves. As the French anthropologist Philippe Descola has noted, an ethnographer's

> laboratory is himself [*sic*] and his relationships with particular people, his own naiveté and cunning…the chance situations in which he finds himself, the role that he is made to play, sometimes unwittingly, in local strategies, the friendship that may link him to the person used as a principal informant, his reactions of enthusiasm, anger and disgust – a whole complex mosaic of feelings, qualities and occasions that give our 'method of inquiry' its own particular hue.

> (Descola 1997: 444)

Positivists talk about 'producing' research findings, as though the social 'facts' they are interested in were always there, waiting to be uncovered by the correct methodological procedures in their rational application. In contrast, interpretive researchers insist that all social knowledge is co-produced out of the multiple encounters, conversations and arguments they have with the people they are studying. A survey using closed questions – 'yes/no', 'when?', 'how often?' – is a one-way process. An ethnographic interview is a dialogue 'in which the analyst is herself caught up and examined, as much as the person she is submitting to investigation' (Bourdieu 1996: 18). We are all inescapably embedded in language and culture, and there is no Archimedean point outside where we can arrive at objective truth. This does not mean that cross-cultural communication and understanding is impossible; it simply means that communication and understanding operate within definite horizons, created by certain languages and cultures. Interpretive research is based on movement between the mutual horizons of those studied and those doing the studying. It depends on dialogue, not detachment. Methodological detachment is an illusion of the positivist paradigm.

This difference in research style is underpinned by a fundamental disagreement over what constitutes 'reality'. For positivists, social 'reality' is 'out there'. It consists of a network of forces and cause–effect relations that exist independently of anything that either researchers or the people they study might do or say. The job of research is to identify these forces, demonstrate how they work, and develop robust predictions that can be used as the basis for rational interventions. Interpretive researchers totally reject this view, arguing that far from existing apart from social action, the organising structures of social and cultural life are continually reproduced and modified through the myriad activities of everyday life. They claim there can be no 'social world independently of the social meanings that its members use to account it and, hence, constitute it' (Filmer 1972: 49). This position is sometimes called *constructivism*, since it insists that social realities are continually constructed and reconstructed through routine social practices and the conceptual categories that underpin them. For its supporters, the core task of research is an interpretive one: to make sense of the ways other people make sense of their worlds by continually 'guessing at meanings, assessing the guesses, and drawing explanatory conclusions from the better guesses' (Geertz 1973: 20). Analytical meaning is always provisional, never complete.

This style of research inevitably generates a wealth of qualitative materials, from transcripts of conversations and photographs and video recordings of everyday settings, to observational notes on particular situations. The aim is to develop what Geertz calls 'thick descriptions', detailing how people invest their world with meaning and negotiate and contest other systems of meaning. Where positivists look to the natural sciences as a touchstone, interpretive research allies itself with the humanities and views social life as a text whose various layers of meaning have to be teased out and interpretively deciphered. As Geertz explains, 'doing ethnography is like trying to read a manuscript – foreign, faded, full of ellipses, incoherencies, suspicious emendations, and tendentious commentaries' (Geertz 1973: 10).

The traffic between ethnography and textual or discourse analysis moves in two directions. Social action is approached as a living text whose layers of meaning and underlying organisation researchers have to illuminate. At the same time, cultural texts – newspaper stories, television programmes, films, advertising images and material objects – are seen as frozen moments in a continuous stream of social interactions, which embody the values and meanings in play within public culture in a particularly clear and compact way. As the German analyst Siegfried Kracauer noted (1952–53: 641), when we look at a text or item of discourse, 'every word vibrates' with the intentions and circumstances that produced it, and foreshadows many of the ways it will be read. This view of research as a process of 'reading' social and cultural texts is central to work in the cultural studies tradition, where it has produced a stream of novel and provocative insights.

In researching social action, however, it is not always possible to conduct a full ethnographic study. Researchers may be denied access to the settings they want to investigate; they may be allowed in for only a limited time; or they may lack the time and resources to spend a sustained period 'in the field'. In these situations they may work with a pared-down version of ethnography, borrowing the basic techniques of observation, open-ended interviews and group discussions, and using them, either singly or in combination, in a more concentrated way. As we shall see in the next chapter, in historical studies the difficulties of interpretive research are compounded by the need to rely entirely on the traces of these activities contained in available documentary sources.

The prevailing conception of interpretive work has led to a widespread rejection of any form of counting or calculating. The word has 'got about that no good qualitative researcher would want to dirty his or her hands with any techniques of quantification' (Silverman 1983: 204). Supporters of interpretive research claim that boiling people's thoughts and activities down to numbers ignores precisely the complexity and creativity of social and cultural life which research should be illuminating. However, a closer look reveals that they quite often support their arguments with assertions about how many people said or did something, and how often. Take, for example, the study of audience responses to a television drama-documentary about the IRA bombing of a pub in Birmingham, UK, conducted by Jane Roscoe and her colleagues (1995). The analysis uses verbatim quotations from the transcripts of 12 focus group discussions about the programme (a technique we examine in chapters 3, 4 and 12). At several key points, the argument is underlined by references to quantities, such as: 'there are *many occasions*…where participants drew on their classified group membership to inform their reading', and 'there were *many instances* of participants moving outside the particular "interest"…classifications used in this study as they made sense of the issues'

(Roscoe, Marshall and Gleeson 1995: 96, 98; emphasis added). These statements contradict each other, but we are not given the information that would allow for a resolution. We are not told how often each of these situations occurred, or whether they involved different participants or the same people at different points in the discussion. Some very simple counts of who said what, when and how often would have clarified the situation, and might have indicated patterns that suggested new directions for analysis and research.

This potential for revealing patterning is one of two basic reasons why research based primarily on qualitative materials might wish to employ some forms of counting or refer to existing statistics. Doing this does not necessarily compromise observation and interpretation; it simply makes approaches based on observation and interpretation more accurate and reliable. Words like 'often' and 'many' are not fixed measures, and clearly it does matter how much audiences draw on their own group category, or how much of a stake News International has in any particular company, for example. The second reason is that looking at the available statistics in the area you are particularly interested in can help to place your research on specific situations and settings in a broader context, and suggest possible lines for analysis. In the course of her statistical investigation of the general relationships between social conditions and cultural consumption in large American cities, for example, Judith Blau discovered that 'women constitute a primary source of market demand for music of all kinds' (Blau 1992: 132). Because it goes against the common-sense assumption that music, like many other cultural fields, is male-dominated, this 'finding' offers a provocative starting point for qualitative investigations of the different meanings of music in the lives of men and women.

What separates interpretive research from positivism is not *whether* figures are referred to, but *how* they are used. Positivists look to statistics to answer research questions. Interpretive researchers see them as a source of questions, a springboard for further investigation and analysis. They argue that 'facts' never speak for themselves, and that a 'statistical relationship, however precisely it can be determined numerically, remains…devoid of meaning' until it is interpreted (Bourdieu 1984: 18). What distinguishes a strong interpretation from a weak one, or a 'thick' description from a 'thin' one, is its comprehensiveness and elegance, together with its ability to explain the full range of relevant materials and incorporate other accounts as concisely as possible. Consequently, 'the more hints related to the mystery being solved' that are mobilised within a research project, including those produced by quantitative methods, 'the more the researcher and reader may trust the solidity of the interpretation' (Alasuutari 1995: 18).

The continuing refusal of many interpretive researchers to have anything to do with quantification is the mirror image of positivists' dismissive attitude to qualitative materials. Both box research into an unnecessary corner and close down the opportunities made available by *combining* different methods.

Choices and circumstances: critical realism

As we noted earlier, the contemporary media are central to the organisation of meaning at both a social and a personal level. Consequently, it is not surprising that interpretive approaches, with their focus on meaning-making, should have been taken up so enthusiastically by communications researchers. However, they are in competition with a second major alternative to positivism: **critical realism**.

Supporters of this position agree with interpretive scholars that 'the social world is reproduced and transformed in daily life' (Bhaskar 1989: 4). But they insist that everyday action cannot be understood properly without taking account of the broader social and cultural formations that envelop and shape it, by providing 'the means, media, rules and resources for everything we do' (ibid.). This argument rests on two core assumptions: first, that structures are always enabling (providing the conditions and resources for action) as well as constraining (placing limits on what is possible and feasible) (Giddens 1984: 25); second, that the relations between situated actions and general formations, local choices and prevailing circumstances are dynamic and two-way – that 'structures are constituted through action' at the same time as 'action is constituted structurally' (Giddens 1976: 161).

Both critical realism and positivism reject the philosophical idealism underpinning the interpretive argument when it claims that social reality exists only in the ways people choose to imagine it, and both pursue a realist philosophical position which accepts that there are social and cultural structures shaping people's options for action, but existing independently of their awareness of them. However, because positivism does not theorise structures in relation to the creativity of everyday practice, it can only think of their effects as a one-way process and cannot explain 'either how they change or how they can act as agents of change' (Fiske 1994: 195). Critical realism insists that unlike the structures that organise the natural world, social and cultural structures have traceable historical careers. They may be surprisingly resilient, but they are not permanent. They emerge at particular times, in a particular set of circumstances, and are continually modified by social action until they are eventually transformed into something else. Many social commentators argue that we have now reached exactly such a moment of transition, as the familiar organising structures of modern life, which emerged from the seventeenth century onwards and crystallised in the nineteenth century, are being replaced by new, postmodern forms (see Giddens 1990b).

Critical realists, then, argue for an understanding of the relationship between social and cultural structures and everyday activity 'that is based on a *transformational* conception of human activity' (Bhaskar 1989: 3; original emphasis). General structures generate a variety of possible responses, some of which may challenge and change prevailing circumstances rather than confirm them. However, because these underlying formations do not correspond with common-sense understandings, they usually remain invisible or opaque to people as they go about their daily business. The critical analyst's task is to bring them to light and explain how they work in order to encourage informed action aimed at eradicating barriers to equity and justice.

Take Karl Marx's famous analysis of capitalism, for example. When we look at capitalist societies, he argues, the first thing we notice is that they are market economies in which people are continually buying goods. This consumer system appears to be based on equal exchange. You pay a price you consider fair and you get something you want in return. But, Marx argues, if we examine the organisation of production, which pays the wages and salaries that support consumption, we find a world based on inequality and exploitation, systematically rigged to give employers a disproportionate share of the profits from labour. Not all critical realists would accept this particular analysis, but they would see it as a good general illustration of the analytical process at the heart of their enterprise.

Whereas positivism focuses on atomistic events (what people do or say in a particular situation, when in a laboratory or answering a questionnaire, for example), and interpretive approaches concentrate on the meanings people mobilise to make sense of their worlds, critical realism is concerned with the 'generative mechanisms underlying and producing observable events' and everyday meaning systems, and with the links between these levels (Bhaskar 1989: 2). This presents researchers with a formidable challenge. They must develop the capacity to 'range from the most impersonal and remote transformations to the most intimate features of the human self', 'from examination of a single family to comparative assessment of the national budgets of the world; from the theological school to the military establishment; from considerations of an oil industry to studies of contemporary poetry'. In every case of perspectival shift, this capacity also involves seeing 'the relations between the two' (Mills 1970: 13–14).

This agenda has several fundamental consequences for the organisation of research. First, it means that research aimed at producing comprehensive and convincing accounts of these relations must be interdisciplinary, drawing on insights from across the whole range of the social and human sciences. This is particularly important in communications research, since, as we noted earlier, the modern media now play a central role in every aspect of modern life, from the organisation of the global economy to the intimate textures of domestic life. Second, once researchers commit themselves to interdisciplinarity, or being undisciplined in the sense we have outlined, there is no reason in principle why they should not take advantage of the full range of investigative techniques produced by the various branches of the social sciences and humanities. As you will see as we work through them in the chapters that follow, all methods have particular strengths and weaknesses, and you need to know what they can and cannot do before you use them. But as you will also see, they can often be used together. When planning a research project, you should always consider whether a combination of qualitative and quantitative techniques might not produce a richer and more satisfactory account.

Mixing methods is central to critical realism: while it incorporates the kinds of work done by interpretive researchers, it also goes beyond them when they are confined to mundane operations within particular cultural systems. It is concerned with the underlying formations that organise meaning-making, as well as with how people make sense of their world on a day-to-day basis. This involves exploring how everyday communicative activity is shaped by differential access to three kinds of strategic resources:

- material resources – command over money, 'free' time and usable space;

- social resources – access to networks of support and confirmation of identity;

- cultural resources – competence in negotiating systems of language, representation and self-presentation (Murdock 1997b: 190–1).

Supporters of critical realism argue that it is only when analysis of underlying social and cultural formations is combined with research on the ways these structures are negotiated and contested on the ground that we can arrive at a comprehensive account of the organisation of meaning. As the Mexican anthropologist Néstor García Canclini, who works on the popular culture of Mexico City, has recently argued: 'The meaning of the city is constituted by what the city gives and what it does not give, by what subjects can do with their lives in the middle of the factors that determine their habitat, and by what they imagine about themselves and about others' (García Canclini 1995: 751).

Pursuing the critical realist project, however, is not just a matter of conducting more comprehensive research. It also involves a major commitment to developing more adequate theories of the way in which underlying social and cultural formations work to structure everyday action. The way we define situations and problems plays a crucial role in directing attention to some things rather than others. Take, for example, the idea that we now live in an 'Information Society', where the multiplication of media has generated unprecedented amounts of information, and where command over information has become a major asset in business, government and personal life. The problem is that this way of describing the situation fails to distinguish between information and knowledge. Information consists of atomised parcels of data about the world. Television news bulletins, for example, tell us about disasters, crimes, the activities of major politicians and the closing prices on the world's stock exchanges. They do not provide the conceptual frameworks that allow us to see patterns and connections, to understand what financial statistics tell us about the state of the economy and how this, in turn, might impact on levels of crime. These linking threads are the stuff of social knowledge, but they come from sources outside the news, principally the education system. So it is quite possible to have an information-rich society in the sense that there are more and more sources of isolated 'facts' about the world – new cable and satellite channels, CD-ROMs, podcasts – but where the majority of citizens remain knowledge-poor, first, because their education has not given them the conceptual armoury to make crucial connections between phenomena that appear to belong apart, and second, because they cannot afford to pay the prices demanded by the specialised communication sources that provide the missing links. Knowledge becomes valuable when it enables us to make connections across ostensibly disparate phenomena – when it turns information into understanding. Whether through critical realism or any other theoretical position, what is important is developing undisciplined knowledge and understanding in a disciplined way.

Interventions and responsibilities

Encouraging undisciplined research in a disciplined way is the purpose of this book. It introduces you to the major methods of research that can be used in communications and cultural inquiry, and takes you through the practical steps involved. As you work your way through it, bear in mind that research is never a self-sufficient activity. Theory is its conjoined twin. Both are crucial to the success of any inquiry. Theories tell us what to look for, how to describe the things we are interested in, and how a particular piece of research can contribute to our general knowledge and understanding of the social and cultural world. In this sense, a good theory is the most useful tool a researcher can have, but it should not be the only one you wield. There is always a danger of research being dictated to by theory, and of analysis being so governed by theory that opportunities for assessing its parameters through different sets of empirical data are wilfully ignored.

So, we might well ask, what is a 'good' theory? For critical realists, it is one that accounts for the full range of available evidence concisely and elegantly, and offers a more comprehensive and convincing account than rival theories. Advocates of interpretive approaches may agree with this aim, while at the same time insisting that any account must be based on subject–subject relations between researchers and whatever is researched, rather than on an isolated object of research separated off from its social and historical contexts, as in the positivist model. Theory is unavoidable; rationalist detachment and correct method based on the natural science model is not a possibility open to us in media and cultural analysis, for this always depends on some theoretical understanding of our topic of inquiry. Theory is therefore 'good' in terms of how it advances our understanding and how it is applied to the process of inquiry. What matters is not only how it is put to investigative use, but also how it acts in dialogue with the evidence that inquiry generates.

All three of the approaches outlined here have political agendas. Positivism sets out to produce robust predictions that can be used to regulate and control social life. By charting the multiple ways in which people make sense of their worlds, and by presenting unfamiliar ways of doing things non-judgementally, interpretive approaches aim to foster the mutual recognition and respect for difference that are essential to communal life in an increasingly divided world. By identifying the hidden springs of everyday action, critical realists hope to mobilise social knowledge in the interests of abolishing 'unwanted and oppressive' constraints on social and personal choices, and developing 'needed, wanted and empowering' rules for social life (Bhaskar 1989: 6).

We shall return to the politics of research in the final chapter, but as you read through the how-to-do-it chapters that follow, we would ask you to remember three major points. First, the three different approaches to social and cultural inquiry we have outlined in this chapter do not necessarily prohibit dialogue between them. There are definite incompatibilities. Neither interpretivism nor critical realism regards the idea of absolute certainty or unassailable authority as tenable, whereas these arguably constitute the basis of scientism and the positivist paradigm. But along with critical realism, interpretive approaches may recognise that broader formations and underlying structures condition everyday social action and the cultural frameworks which guide that action, as in attention paid to the influence of **tradition** in social and cultural life, for example. They may also point to the ways in which everyday cultural understandings are irredeemably linked to the past and to a history of those understandings recurring and changing over time, though perhaps without insisting as much as critical realism on the transformational quality of human activity. There is clearly overlap between the perspectives offered by these two approaches, even though they are relatively distinct. They are not hermetically sealed off from each other, and do not operate in ways which are absolutely incommensurate with each other. Regarding them in that light can lead to dogmatic adherences to certain positions or to mistaken assumptions. This caveat applies also to our third outlined approach, when all statistical procedures are seen as hopelessly tainted with a positivist epistemology. We hope to show that they are not. Where the potential exists, we want to encourage fertile interaction between, and mutual interrogation of, different theoretical positions and perspectives, for this also is a quality of being undisciplined in a disciplined manner.

Second, because cultural and communications media are so central in organising contemporary life, there is no single theoretical approach which can serve to govern and inform every line of research concerned with investigating them – it would be surprising if there were; but there are times when claims for supreme theoretical authority over other approaches have been made. It is best always to be on your guard against such claims, for they are usually evidence of intellectual hubris and little else. Clearly, exploring the sometimes complex interpretive uses made of such media as romance fiction or popular music requires approaches different to those appropriate to the investigation of patterns of conglomerate ownership or institutional chains of command in the media and cultural industries. This applies to both theory and method. Perhaps the most basic theoretical and methodological differences are found in approaches to media production and media consumption, for whereas with the former the focus may be on structures of power and control, with the latter we are more likely to attend to structures of experience and how media are consumed in ways which inform and are informed by them. It is always a question of horses for courses, but this does not mean that media production and consumption should necessarily be studied in analytical isolation from each other. This is a point we shall return to later in the book.

Third, as we have already insisted, no research project is politically innocent, least of all those that claim to have no politics. Because research is an intervention in the social world, it is always as much a matter of ethics as of techniques. It carries multiple responsibilities, to those who take part in our studies, to colleagues and professional peers, and to the wider society. What you choose to investigate, how you set about it and how you present your results can make a difference to the way we, collectively, talk and think about ourselves and our dilemmas. At its best, research offers us powerful tools for questioning received wisdoms, challenging the rhetoric of power, illuminating the blind spots on our social and cultural maps, helping us to puzzle out why things are as they are and how they might be changed, and finding ways to communicate our own gains in knowledge as widely as possible. These possibilities are, for us, what makes it worthwhile.

▶ chapter two

Dealing with Documentation

Taking advantage

When social scientists say they are 'doing' research, they usually mean that they are collecting new material for analysis, using questionnaires, interviews, group discussions or observation of people's daily routines. All these methods are central to researching contemporary communications, and in later chapters we will be looking in detail at how to use them. But we do not always have to do all the donkey work ourselves. We can take advantage of other people's efforts. We can examine their attempts to chronicle their personal thoughts, feelings and everyday lives. We can look at how organisations have documented their activities, strategies and decisions. We can consult the voluminous official records produced by state agencies, courts and legislative bodies. And we can return to the materials collected by other researchers.

Varieties of documentation

Most people think of documents as piles of paper, heaped up on desks, crammed into boxes on library shelves or filed away in metal cabinets. Written and printed materials are certainly very valuable sources, but they are not the only ones. As students of communications, we should be the first to insist that people's ideas, beliefs, hopes, fears and actions are recorded in and through a range of media. When dealing with documentary sources, then, we need to move beyond the page to consider all forms of representation.

Anyone working on popular culture in the Middle Ages, when most people were non-literate and books and documents were copied by hand, would need to look carefully at the material traces of everyday activity contained in the objects they used and the buildings and places they lived, worshipped and played in. Working on communications in periods before the arrival of print requires us to become archaeologists, painstakingly assembling a picture from the remains of cultures now mostly in fragments and ruins.

The spread and popularisation of printing added a whole series of new forms of recording and expression, from novels and newspapers to popular prints and advertisements, many of which have survived. However, research dealing with changes since the early twentieth century would also want to draw on the vast range of additional documentation provided by the development of lithography and other graphic techniques, by the ubiquity of photography, the growth of film and television, and the rise of technologies for recording and storing the human voice on disks and tapes. Similarly, work on the contemporary situation might want to add the proliferating forms of computer storage, particularly those such as messages posted on Internet bulletin boards, which do not exist in any other form.

Box 2.1 provides a basic checklist of the major sources of documentation that are relevant to communications research. We can think of these various sources as the cultural equivalent of rock strata, the sedimented remains of people's successive struggles to make sense of their world and to give these understandings public expression. Like additional geological deposits, new media of communication do not cancel out older forms of expression. Rather they add another layer, another possibility. Consequently, the closer our research approaches the present, the greater the range of sources.

Box 2.1 Major sources of documentation

- *Material artefacts* – physical objects; buildings; artificially created environments.
- *Written and printed sources* – books; journals; newspapers; magazines; comics; diaries; letters; minutes of meetings.
- *Statistical sources.*
- *Recorded sound* – radio programmes; records; tapes.
- *Visual media: single images* – paintings; engravings; posters; photographs.
- *Visual media: moving images* – films; television programmes; video; DVD.
- *Digital media* – Internet sites; email; blogs; CD-ROMs.

Primary and supplementary uses

We can use these various sources to *supplement* the materials we have collected ourselves (in which case they play a secondary or supporting role), or we can make them the *primary focus* of our research.

Supplementary uses

Here we are drawing on available sources to flesh out, cross-check or question the picture that emerges from the research materials we have produced ourselves. Suppose we were trying to find out how a large television station organises its news operation. As well as talking to journalists and executives working for the company, sitting in on editorial meetings and observing how reporters go about their work, we might learn a lot from taking a close look at internal documentation, from the minutes of board meetings and internal memos, to promotional materials and advertising campaigns. However, there are often problems in getting hold of sources originally produced for restricted circulation. Organisations do not welcome researchers probing behind their carefully constructed public relations front. But material intended for public consumption can also tell interesting stories. Our interviews with people working for an organisation may be the latest in a rather long line of attempts they have made to think out loud about their situation. Laying these alongside their published speeches, think pieces and past statements may well open up new lines of inquiry and analysis.

On its Internet site, Channel 4, one of Britain's major terrestrial television channels, hosts a newsroom **blog**, or **weblog** (at http://www.channel4.com/blogs/page/newsroom), where its presenters and journalists comment on their work and experiences on a day-to-day basis. In November 2006, Jon Snow, the principal presenter of the channel's evening news programme, attracted public criticism for refusing to wear a red poppy, the symbol commemorating the troops killed in the two World Wars traditionally worn in the week leading up to Remembrance Day. This sparked a lively debate among his colleagues. Lindsay Taylor, one of the other main presenters, took the opportunity to make a blog entry reaffirming his commitment to the core journalistic principle of impartiality:

> My grandfather was in the trenches. I have listened to tape recordings my parents made of him describing his experiences. I wish they had recorded more. However, I believe that when reporting or delivering news we have a professional duty to appear to be as objective and as neutral as possible. That, to me, means that I should avoid wearing anything that might betray my personal feelings on an issue. …the 'personal' part of me is something I try to leave behind when the camera goes on.
>
> (Taylor 2006)

An interview on the same issue might not have prompted such a direct answer.

In devising any piece of research, then, you should take full advantage of any available source that might supplement, back up or challenge the materials produced by your major methods of investigation. Not infrequently, however, available sources are not just useful additions to our own data; they are often the main or sometimes the only materials available. At this point they move from a supporting role to a central one.

Primary uses

There are four main situations where research may centre mainly or wholly around the analysis of available documentation:

1. In historical studies, where direct access to people and situations is no longer possible.
2. Where access to people or situations we wish to study is restricted or denied.
3. In secondary analysis, where a project is based on the re-analysis of material previously collected by other researchers.
4. When we are carrying out textual analysis where the organisation and meaning of the material itself is the major focus of research.

Historical research

The possibility of obtaining first-hand accounts of past communicative events and experiences, such as the arrival of regular radio and television broadcasts, has led to a flourishing branch of research known as oral history (see chapter 12). Memories and reminiscences are an invaluable source of insight into the successive waves of innovation in communication, and we will look more closely at what is involved in this kind of research later in the book. But the further back in time we go, the fewer witnesses survive. There is now almost no one still living who remembers the first public cinema shows in the 1890s, for example, and for earlier decades there is no one at all we can talk to. If we are interested in the readership of the popular press in the mid nineteenth century, for example, we have to rely entirely on the voices frozen in parliamentary inquiries, court proceedings, personal diaries and respectable commentary; on the images caught in paintings, engravings and early photographs; and on the statistical information contained in official and commercial sources.

Tracking power

Direct access is a particular problem when research focuses on key centres of control over communications. Media moguls like Rupert Murdoch are unlikely to allow a researcher to 'shadow' them as they move through the corridors of power. Participant observation of the kind described later in the book is simply not an option in these circumstances. In the absence of first-hand knowledge, researchers have to fall back on information and commentary available in the public domain. They can examine a company's annual reports to shareholders, parliamentary debates, official inquiries and court cases relating to the company's activities; they can check what journalists and other researchers have said; and they can read the accounts provided by business rivals, former employees and friends who were once on the inside.

Relying on secondary sources does not mean that we can say nothing useful about structures of media power, but we do need to be sensitive to the problems their use poses. These difficulties increase the further back we move through time.

Secondary analysis

A range of agencies regularly produces statistics and other materials that we can use in our research. We can, of course, simply cite their published results to illustrate a point or support an argument. But in some cases we can also go back to their 'raw' materials and re-analyse them in line with the aims of our particular project. This is known as *secondary analysis.*

There are three main sources of materials for secondary analysis:

1. The statistics produced by government departments and regulatory agencies, collectively known as *official statistics*, together with materials produced by intergovernmental agencies such as UNESCO.
2. The data produced by non-official agencies and industry bodies such as commercial market-research companies, professional bodies, trade unions and pressure groups.
3. The research materials generated in universities and independent research institutes.

Official and trade sources are particularly useful for answering certain kinds of research questions. Such studies are often conducted on a national or international scale that researchers working with more modest budgets cannot match. They are therefore very helpful for mapping general patterns, such as class and gender differences in media consumption. Furthermore, some research projects (like the television industry's audience measurements) are conducted on a daily basis. Others are undertaken annually, or at regular intervals. These running records, or *time-series*, help to identify changes and continuities over time.

Working on the web

In 1995, Bill Gates, the founder of Microsoft, the planet's dominant software company, pictured the **Internet** as an electronic highway, giving 'us all access to seemingly unlimited information, anytime and anyplace we care to use it' (Gates 1995: 184). Developments since then seem to have proved him right. The arrival of broadband connections has massively increased the amounts and types of material available, allowing users to download films and television programmes as well as written texts, music, sound recordings and statistics; while the increased popularity of laptop computers, the roll-out of wireless (Wi-Fi) connections and the integration of Internet access into mobile phones makes it possible to log on to the Internet on the move. Faced with this ever-expanding capacity and versatility, it is tempting to assume that all the sources and materials a researcher might need are now available at the click of a mouse, and that there is no need to visit a library or archive ever again. There are three major problems with this argument.

First, access to the full range of Internet resources remains both relatively expensive and geographically patchy. Although prices are falling, Wi-Fi-enabled laptop computers and broadband connectivity remain relatively expensive. There is great deal of useful material to be found within the public sector of the Internet known as the World Wide Web (indicated by the prefix 'www' in the site address), and a considerable amount of this is free at the point of use – but not all. Public bodies, under pressure from governments to become more market oriented, may charge for certain services. Added to which, a number of key resources essential to scholarly work are password protected and available only to subscribers. Students and staff working in universities are shielded from the full impact of these costs because their institutions subsidise their access and use. Computers are readily available for free use or loan. Unlike many public places, campuses are likely to offer Wi-Fi connectivity. And subscriptions to major software packages and to the electronic versions of major journals and databases are paid for collectively out of central budgets. In this book, we assume you are able to benefit from these various subsidies rather than working independently and having to bear the full costs yourself.

Second, although there are plans to digitalise most library and archive holdings, this process is far from complete at the time of writing (2007), and in some cases has not even begun. Consequently, there is a range of important sources of documentation, particularly moving-image archives, that can still be accessed only by physically going to the collection itself.

Third, even where an archive is available in digital form, it may not always be comprehensive or reliable. The electronic press archive offered by LexisNexis is a case in point. Because the keyword search facility makes it quick and easy to compile samples of stories on a particular topic or issue, it has become the archive of choice for many researchers wanting to analyse press content. But as we point out in chapter 6, relying solely on this single source is problematic. There are stories missing or duplicated, and the entries are text-only, making it impossible to analyse the use of photographs and visuals or to place the story in the context of the overall layout of the original printed page.

Even so, the Web, used critically, provides access to a huge range of resources relevant to research in culture and communications. Some, like the electronic versions of major scholarly journals, duplicate material that is available in other forms, but make access and use easier, quicker and more flexible. Others, like the Channel 4 newsroom blog mentioned earlier, or the growing number of e-journals ('e' for electronic), exist only on the Web. Finding what you want among this ever-expanding sea of disparate resources has given sites that sort and organise materials an increasingly important role. Two kinds of sorting mechanisms are particularly relevant to research: search engines and gateways.

Search engines

Search engines concentrate on collating material available on the public Internet and helping users to locate relevant items by using keywords to search for resources on a particular topic. The most widely used site at the time of writing (2007) is Google (http://www.google.com), which accounts for around half of all searches made. It covers websites, news, images and discussions on Internet message boards. The problem, which is shared by all current search engines, is that keywords are something of a blunt instrument. They throw up lots of material that is only tangentially relevant, and reading the list of 'hits' to locate the sources you actually want can be time-consuming. A search for 'books and children', for example, might well include entries on books about children and books written for children, as well as work on children's reading habits. In an attempt to tackle this problem, most search engines offer an 'advanced' version of the keyword system that allows you to limit the terms of your search in various ways. Google, for example, allows you to search for pages that contain only all the search terms you type in, or only an exact phrase, or only those pages that have been updated within a certain period of time. The next generation of search engines, employing a system known as the 'semantic web', will make searching more precise by enabling users to ask much more specific questions, but for the moment it is worth taking the time to learn how to use the 'advanced' search options to maximum effect.

Although Google is the dominant search engine, it is not always the best, and it is worth diversifying your searches by using one of the other major engines. We would recommend Ask (http://www.ask.com).

In addition to these general sites, there are a number of specialised engines. These are particularly useful for locating materials generated or posted by Internet users, such as searching for blogs relevant to your research topic (http://www.technorati.com).

To target your searches more effectively, you can compile your own database of websites relevant to your research using Google's Custom Search Engine facility (http://www.google.com/coop/cse/overview).

Gateways

Gateways (or portals, as they are often called) are the electronic equivalent of the gates set into the walls surrounding medieval cities. Entry is restricted, but once inside you have access to a range of sites and resources. Most of these are available by subscription only and access is restricted to password holders. Most university libraries will operate such a gateway, though the particular sites it covers will vary depending on budgetary priorities, so check what your library currently subscribes to. Group subscriptions cover all members of the institution, but you will need your own individual password. One of the most widely used systems is ATHENS, which allows you to log in remotely when you are away from the institution.

This chapter assumes that you are a member of an institution that gives you access to subscribed electronic databases as well as to the public Internet, and we will be indicating websites that offer useful resources from both sources. But bear in mind, these suggestions are intended to get you started. They do not provide a definitive list. New databases are constantly coming online and existing ones are disappearing or being discontinued. If you need help, ask your librarian and take full advantage of any training courses in searching and using electronic sources that your institution offers. But remember, becoming a competent researcher requires you not only to learn what resources are relevant to your research but, more importantly, how to use them critically.

Key questions

Whenever we work with any kind of documentary source, we are faced with two kinds of questions:

- questions of meaning;
- questions of evidence.

Questions of meaning

With any documentary source, we need to ask what the accounts we are working with mean. This seems straightforward enough. Surely we simply look at what they are about, the topics they deal with, who produced them and who is quoted or referred to? This is certainly useful, and as we shall see in chapter 6, *content analysis* allows us to produce systematic descriptions of what documentary sources contain. By counting how often particular topics, themes or actors are mentioned, how much space and prominence they command, and in what contexts they are presented, content analysis provides an overview of patterns of attention. It tells us what is highlighted and what is ignored.

Focusing on aspects of content that can be easily counted (the obvious or *manifest features*) tells us something of *what* a document is about, but it does not delve below the surface to explore implicit meanings; nor does it ask *how* the various levels of meaning are organised or conveyed. To tackle these issues, we have to turn to the techniques of *textual analysis* explored in chapters 7 to 10.

In everyday speech, the term 'text' is more or less synonymous with 'document', and both are identified with written or printed sources. In communications research, however, we use the term '**text**' in a much wider sense, to include any cultural product whose meaning we are trying to work out. Extending the metaphor a stage further, researchers often talk of their efforts to arrive at a convincing interpretation as 'reading' cultural texts.

In pursuit of this aim, the various approaches to textual analysis start where content analysis leaves off. They explore the ways that language is deployed, how images, sounds and statistics are organised and presented, and, where relevant, how these various elements are combined. Because techniques of textual analysis involve detailed, close-grained work, they are usually employed on small selections of material, and sometimes on single cases, rather than on the relatively large samples typically used in content-analysis studies. They aim to produce thick descriptions of how meaning is organised in particular documentary sources rather than statistical maps of their basic contents.

Both content analysis and textual analysis offer systematic ways of exploring the meanings of documents. Which method, or combination of methods, you use in any particular study will depend on the objectives of your research. Since these techniques are dealt with in detail in later chapters, we will concentrate here on the second set of questions we need to ask about documents – questions of evidence. But as we work through these, bear in mind that in using documents in research we always have to grapple with questions of meaning as well.

Questions of evidence

Questions of evidence involve asking how much weight we can give to the sources in front of us. What can we say about their authenticity, credibility and representativeness? How far are we justified in citing them as evidence? What caveats and cautionary notes do we need to add? We will return to these questions below, but it is worth noting that these problems are not confined to documentary sources. All research raises questions of **sampling** – how representative particular cases are (see chapter 3). Similarly, it would be very unwise to take what someone told us in an interview at face value, without asking how the social dynamics of the situation might have affected what they said and how they chose to present themselves (see chapters 4 and 12).

This chapter is concerned mainly with using documentary materials as a primary focus for research, but before we explore what is involved in this, we need to introduce briefly the main sources that can be used to support projects based on your own original research.

Documentary sources, both online and offline, can help with five basic aspects of communications research:

1. checking what research has already been done;
2. networking;
3. checking government, parliamentary and legal sources;
4. checking industry trends and facts and figures;
5. tracking contemporary events.

Checking what research has already been done

This is an essential first step in designing any research project. There is little point in duplicating work that has already been done. This does not mean that you cannot work on a topic that someone else has already looked at. You may want to take issue with their approach or arguments, or test their ideas against different cases or new data. But to make an effective contribution, you need to familiarise yourself with what is already available. This is one area where the rise of the Internet has made locating materials much easier.

One useful place to start is with the websites maintained by the major national libraries, such as the British Library in London (http://www.bl.uk). The Library's array of electronic catalogues allows you to search generally across the range of its extensive holdings of books and other materials, using the integrated catalogue (http://catalogue.bl.uk), and to undertake more targeted searches of journals (http://www.bl.uk/catalogues/serials.html) and academic theses written in the UK and the USA (http://www.bl.uk/services/document/theses.html). In addition, the site makes full use of the Internet's networking capacity to provide click-on links to a range of other major libraries around the world.

Two particularly useful gateway sites, providing directories of worldwide electronic library sites, are LibDex (http://www.libdex.com) and Cybrary, operated by the University of Queensland (http://www.library.uq.edu.au/ssah/jeast/).

If you find a book, journal article or academic thesis that looks relevant to your research, but which is not in your own institution's library or a library you can get to easily, it is often possible to obtain a copy through the inter-library loan system. Check whether your library is a member and whether the charges involved are paid by you or your institution.

Another useful source available on open access via the public Internet is the Scholar section of Google (http://scholar.google.com). This allows you to search for articles on topics you are interested in by keywords or phrases (appearing either in the title or the body of the text), or by author, publication or date. Entries provide full bibliographic details, together with links to related articles on the topic and other web entries for the author.

In addition to these general databases, there are sites devoted solely to scholarly work in media and communications. The most comprehensive is ComAbstracts (http://www.cios.org/www/abstract.htm), operated by the Communication Institute for Online Scholarship, which provides abstracts of articles from a wide range of communications journals, along with summaries of relevant books. Access, however, is open only to members of the Institute. If your institution does not have a subscription, you will need to become an associate member (at http://www.cios.org). This gives you access to the other useful services operated by the Institute, including indexes to journals, tables of current contents and the ComWeb MegaSearch engine, which covers web-based materials produced by university departments of communications.

Although much material can be read on the screen, it is a good idea to develop your own dedicated research library where you keep personal copies of the most important materials related to your topic. This allows you to add your own notes and annotations. For printed materials that have not yet been digitalised (which includes most books), photocopies remain the only option. Journal publishers, however, are increasingly moving towards electronic storage and making articles available in forms that can be downloaded directly to your computer hard drive or stored on a CD or memory stick. Two of the major publishers of journals in media communication, Sage (http://www.sagepub.com/) and

Blackwell (http://www.blackwell-synergy.com/), both offer this facility. As commercial companies, both charge for access, so downloads are available only to subscribers.

At the same time, increasing numbers of articles and conference papers are now being made available at no charge for educational use. A number of university libraries are developing dedicated databases that store electronic copies of research articles produced by staff. The Institutional Repository at the authors' institution, Loughborough University (http://magpie.lboro.ac.uk/dspace), is an example.

In addition, a number of leading writers and researchers in communications maintain personal websites on their institutions' servers, offering free access to their own writings. The site operated by the critical scholar Doug Kellner is a good example (http://www.gseis.ucla.edu/faculty/kellner/). If there are authors who are particularly important for your research, it is always worth entering their names in a general search engine to see whether they maintain their own sites or whether their institutions have an open repository. But be warned, these sites are often incomplete. Some people are more diligent than others in updating their websites or sending their latest publications to the institutional repository, and open access to some material is still limited by copyright agreements.

There is also a growing number of open-access electronic journals arriving online, many located in university departments of communication and maintained by enthusiastic volunteers. Current examples include *Participations: Journal of Audience and Reception Studies* (http://www.participations.org), *Studies in Language and Capitalism* (http://www.languageandcapitalism.info), *Transnational Broadcasting Studies* (http://www.tbsjournal.com/) and the *Global Media Journal* (http://lass.calumet.purdue.edu/cca/gmj/index.htm). You can find a developing online guide to free-access journals in the areas of media and communication by going to the 'Social Sciences' section of the website maintained by the Directory of Open Access Journals (http://www.doaj.org/).

When you first start a research project, it is well worth finding out which authors and articles are central to debates in your area. The most common indicators of intellectual centrality are the citation indexes, which record how many times an author or article has been referred to by other writers in the field. These indexes are not entirely comprehensive – not all journals are included – but they are a convenient place to start. The major indexes relevant to research on media and communications are the Social Sciences Citation Index (SSCI) and the Arts and Humanities Citation Index (A&HCI). Both can be searched by author or by topic, and both are available in the 'Web of Science' section of the ISI Web of Knowledge database (http://www.isiwebofknowledge.com). This is a subscription-only site, so you need to check that it is available through your library's gateway.

Networking

In addition to reading people's work, your research will benefit from live contacts with researchers working on the same topic – listening to them present papers, meeting them, corresponding with them, and debating their ideas and yours. There are two major international scholarly organisations in the field of media and communications: the International Communication Association (ICA) (http://www.icahdq.org/) and the

International Association for Media and Communication Research (IAMCR) (http://iamcr.org). Both offer details of upcoming conferences, publish newsletters and support specialist sections dealing with particular areas of interest, some of which maintain their own websites.

There is also a number of nationally based associations which organise annual conferences and publish newsletters. Some also publish scholarly journals and maintain message boards that members can use to make announcements or ask for help. Examples include the Australian and New Zealand Communication Association (http://www.anzca.net) and the Media, Communication and Cultural Studies Association (MeCCSA) in the UK (http://www.meccsa.org.uk/index.html). To gain access to the full range of facilities offered by these associations, however, you need to become a member.

Websites designed to encourage researchers working in particular sub-fields to pool information and debate issues are also growing. Examples include the Media Anthropology Network (http://www.media-anthropology.net) and the War and Media Network (http://www.warandmedia.org).

Participating in these various scholarly networks is an essential part of developing as a researcher. They help you to keep abreast of the latest research and thinking, connect you to others working in your topic area, provide advice and support, and offer a platform for testing out your own ideas in conference presentations and contributions to message boards and discussion groups.

Checking government, parliamentary and legal sources

There are four main sources of official materials that you might want to consult:

1. Reports and press releases from government departments and regulatory agencies with statutory powers.
2. The drafts and final forms of new legislation.
3. Debates in legislative assemblies and evidence given to official commissions of inquiry.
4. Records of court proceedings, where the practical applications of legislation relating to communications are deliberated and decided on.

Official statistics, legal decisions and policy statements are increasingly available online, often on websites that act as gateways to materials produced by a wide range of public agencies.

For US sources, the government website (http://www.usa.gov) offers a convenient and comprehensive first port of call for access to the statistics produced by federal and local agencies. Also useful is the Library of Congress site (http://www.loc.gov/index.html), whose THOMAS sub-domain (named after Thomas Jefferson) provides access to bills, laws and legislative proceedings.

The main gateway to official statistics in the UK is located at http://www.statistics.gov.uk. Those most immediately relevant to media and communications research can be found under 'Culture, leisure and social participation' within the 'Social and Welfare' theme, which deals with audiences and consumption, but there is much relevant material on other aspects of communications in the other thematic categories. UK parliamentary debates are also accessible electronically (http://www.publications.parliament.uk/pa/pahansard.htm).

The major gateway to material produced by the European Commission can be found at http://ec.europa.eu/index_en.htm, although you will also need to look at the websites maintained by the Commission's various Directorates, the agencies responsible for developing policy within particular areas (http://ec.europa.eu/dgs_en.htm). The directorate most centrally concerned with media and communications is 'Information Society and Media', but several other directorates (particularly 'Competition' and 'Education and Culture') also play key roles in shaping communications policies, so you need to search widely within the site. A useful source of statistics on the audio-visual industries in Europe is the website of the European Audiovisual Observatory (http://www.obs.coe.int/), which also tracks relevant legal and policy developments and provides links to official resources and regulatory agencies.

The regulatory agencies charged with overseeing the operations of the communications industries are a valuable source of information. Increasingly, governments have adopted variants of the long-standing model provided by the Federal Communications Commission in the USA (http://www.fcc.gov) and brought together previously separate agencies responsible for broadcasting and telecommunications to create a single comprehensive regulator. The Office of Communications (Ofcom) in the UK (http://www.ofcom.org.uk) is an example. In addition to detailing regulatory decisions, more and more of these sites offer free access to downloadable files of the research they have commissioned on various issues.

Checking industry trends and facts and figures

We can add to these official sources the regular digests of facts and figures published by a range of trade publications. The following are useful places to start:

- Advertising: the major US trade magazine *Advertising Age* (http://adage.com) and its British equivalent *Campaign* (http://www.brandrepublic.com/magazines/campaign/).

- Film and television: *Screendigest* (http://www.screendigest.com), *Variety*, the 'Bible' of the US entertainment industry (http://www.variety.com), and *Television Business International* (http://www.informamedia.com).

- The music industry: *Billboard*, the major US trade magazine (http://www.billboard.com).

Although some provide free tasters of the contents and services on offer, the full range of information and resources provided by these trade sources is open only to subscribers or members. As an alternative, albeit one with a distinct UK bias, the Media Guardian site operated by *The Guardian* newspaper in London (http://media.guardian.co.uk/) offers free access to up-to-date information on the media and cultural industries. You need to register as a user, but there is no charge. There are also a number of independent groups which track and comment on current trends and debates. The Centre for Media and Public Affairs (http://www.cmpa.com/) is particularly useful, although it is mainly concerned with developments in the USA. It offers news analysis and undertakes research studies. Some of these are available free; others require payment. Another valuable US site is Journalism.org (http://www.journalism.org), which offers a weekly content analysis of news coverage, as well as reports and commentaries on current issues in journalism.

Finally, it is well worth exploring the websites of the major communications companies and institutions. These are, first and foremost, public relations exercises, providing a shop window for the organisation's services and products, and designed to stimulate customer interest and loyalty, but they often contain useful research materials.

In order to sustain their claims to public funding, public communications organisations need to retain public support and trust. A state-of-the-art website is a key weapon in this battle for hearts and minds. This strategy has been pursued very effectively by the BBC, whose website (http://www.bbc.co.uk) has become a model for other organisations. It offers an ever-expanding range of resources, including a comprehensive online news service, opportunities to download recent radio and television broadcasts, and multiple message boards devoted to specific programmes and wider topics. It also provides a wealth of materials that allows researchers to track the Corporation's thinking on key issues. Press releases and public speeches made by senior managers can be downloaded (http://www.bbc.co.uk/pressoffice/), while research and analysis relevant to the Corporation's future (and, by extension, the future of public broadcasting more generally) in a digitalised, multi-channel environment can be accessed (http://www.bbc.co.uk/thefuture/).

Commercial media companies face the problem of retaining the interest not only of their audiences but also of advertisers and current and potential investors. To this end, their websites often contain links to their annual reports and accounts, and to financial analysis of their performance, as well as to the consumer products produced by their various divisions. The 'Investor & Financial' section of the website of Rupert Murdoch's News Corporation (http://www.newscorp.com/index2.html) is a good example.

Tracking contemporary events

Despite the many criticisms that can be levelled at the gaps and biases in their coverage, the copious materials produced by the world's major press and news organisations remain the most convenient place to begin a search for information and commentary on contemporary events, politics, corporate activity and social trends.

Keesing's Record of World Events, which scans a wide range of press and information sources to compile reports on major economic and political developments around the world, offers a useful starting point, but you will need to go further. Most major newspapers, and an increasing number of broadcasters, now offer electronic access to searchable databases of past news stories. These can be very useful, though full access is not always free.

Accessing archives: major holdings

The range of archives that may be relevant to your research can often be surprisingly wide. You may need to look at a variety of local collections or specialised holdings of personal papers. However, in many cases, much of what you need is likely to be held in one of the major national collections. There is space here to indicate only the basic *kinds* of resources that are available and to offer some illustrative examples. You will need to compile your own list for each research project you are involved in.

There are four main kinds of collections of relevant documentation:

1. National archives
2. National collections
3. Media holdings
4. Independent collections.

National archives

Most countries have national archives that house historical collections of materials dealing with the activities of government departments and collect the information required by legislation, such as census records. The UK's National Archives (http://www.nationalarchives.gov.uk/) provide a good example. The National Archives hold extensive materials relating to the history of the United Kingdom and any part of the world that the UK has been involved with since the eleventh century, together with records of the activities of all government departments. It also operates an image library, which includes collections of Victorian and Edwardian photographs and advertisements and World War II propaganda, and provides extensive links to other archives.

National collections

These are held by national libraries and major museums. Increasingly, they include images and sound recordings as well as printed matter. The most extensive collection in the United States is kept by the Library of Congress in Washington, DC (http://www.loc.gov/index.html). In addition to the collections of printed matter, it supports major archives of photographs and sound recordings, including radio broadcasts made over the NBC network between 1930 and the late 1960s.

The British Library is the equivalent institution in Britain. As well as its huge collection of books and printed materials (mentioned earlier), it operates two archives of particular interest to communications researchers:

- The British Newspaper Library (http://www.bl.uk/catalogues/newspapers/welcome.asp), located in north-west London, holds sets of the London editions of national daily and Sunday newspapers from the start of publication to the present, local newspapers and magazines published within the UK, plus a wide range of overseas newspapers.

- The National Sound Archive (http://www.bl.uk/collections/sound-archive/nsa.html), located in the British Library building, is the major repository of recorded sound of all kinds, though the collection mainly consists of recorded music and radio and television materials. It is particularly relevant if you are interested in popular music or in any form of broadcasting in which talk figures as a key element.

A number of countries now also have national archives of photography and film. In Britain, for example, there are two:

- The National Media Museum in Bradford (http://www.nationalmediamuseum.org.uk) holds a wide range of equipment, images and printed ephemera relating to photography, film and television, including the photograph archive of the *Daily Herald*, a major left-of-centre daily newspaper (now defunct), and material relating to Thames Television, which was one of the major independent television companies in Britain (with the weekday franchise for London) and is now the country's largest independent producer.

- The National Film and Television Archive (NFTA), administered by the British Film Institute (http://www.bfi.org.uk/nftva), holds stills, posters, designs and over 200,000 moving-image items. These include a wide range of feature films, shorts, newsreels and amateur films shown in the UK from the beginning of the film industry, together with a substantial collection of television programmes transmitted in Britain. Early programmes are available on film or broadcast-standard videotape. More recent examples have been recorded off air. Items in the collection cannot be borrowed, but research viewings can be arranged by appointment, for a fee.

Media organisations' holdings

Although media organisations keep extensive records and archives, these are mostly for internal use. Consequently, research access usually has to be negotiated on a case-by-case basis and is by no means guaranteed. The major exception in Britain is the BBC, which (as befits a publicly funded organisation) has an extensive archive that is open to public use.

The BBC Written Archives Centre at Caversham Park, near Reading (http://www.bbc.co.uk/heritage/more/wac.shtml), holds:

- correspondence, minutes and reports covering all areas of the corporation's non-current activities;

- papers of people closely associated with the BBC in some way;

- news bulletins and scripts of programmes as broadcast;

- collections of correspondence and other materials relating to the planning, production and reception of particular programmes;

- audience research materials;

- sets of BBC publications.

These materials are open to researchers. Indeed, the staff emphasise that 'they want the archives to be used' (Seldon and Pappworth 1983: 226). Because of the limited space and facilities at the archive's disposal, access is by appointment only.

Independent collections

Relevant archives are also held by a range of other institutions, such as universities, professional organisations and educational trusts. By way of illustration, we will mention three of these:

- The Television News Archive at Vanderbilt University in the USA (http://tvnews.vanderbilt.edu) is a comprehensive collection of American network evening news broadcasts from 1968 to the present, together with a range of documentary programmes and political campaign coverage. Tapes of entire broadcasts or compilations from the archive can be loaned for a fee.

- The History of Advertising Trust in Norwich, UK (http://www.hatads.org.uk) is an educational foundation established to encourage the study of all aspects of the development of advertising and is the major British source in this area. It holds over a million images and artefacts related to advertising in all media, dating back to the 1820s, together with material from major advertising agencies (including J. Walter Thompson and Ogilvy & Mather) and professional bodies. Membership is open to the public.

- The Data Archive, housed at the University of Essex, UK (http://www.data-archive.ac.uk), contains the raw data (both quantitative and qualitative) generated by all research projects funded by the ESRC (Economic and Social Research Council – the principal source of government support for British social science research) since the archive's launch, together with a range of materials from other sources. This is a major source of material for secondary analysis.

Using archives and collections: practical questions

Whenever you are thinking about consulting a particular archive or collection for your research, you should first run through the following checklist of questions:

1. Where is the material located? Will you need to go to the archive or is what you want available as a photocopy, videotape, disk or downloadable electronic file?

2. If you do have to travel to the archive to obtain material, make sure you check the opening times and whether it is open to everyone or only to registered members or users before you set off. If you need to register as a user, find out what is involved and whether there is a charge.

3. Most archives publish guides for users. Send off for these and read them before your first visit. This can save you a lot of time.

4. Always ask in advance if you need to make an appointment to visit the archive or to reserve facilities, and whether there are any charges for access.

5. Ask what forms the material is available in. Will you be able to work with the original sources or will you be working with copies? What formats are the copies in?

6. Are you allowed to use a laptop computer to take notes when you are working in the archive or will you have to take notes by hand? If laptops are allowed, can they be run

off a mains electricity supply or will you have to rely on the more limited time delivered by battery power?

7. Can you make or order copies of material to take away? What kinds of copies can you obtain and what are the charges?

Using documents: a closer look at questions of evidence

Having obtained the materials you want, you are now faced with assessing what you can and cannot say on the basis of your sources. This involves working through what we referred to earlier as questions of evidence.

There are three main issues that need to be addressed (see Scott 1990: ch. 2):

1. *Questions of representativeness:* How typical are the cases you are looking at? If they are not typical, in what ways might they be atypical?

2. *Questions of authenticity:* Is the evidence you have collected genuine? Is it what it claims to be?

3. *Questions of credibility:* How accurate is the material? Is it free from errors? Is it based on first-hand experience of what it describes? How knowledgeable is the author on the topic? Is there evidence of partisanship or special pleading?

Addressing these questions is particularly important when you are dealing with accounts of events.

Representativeness

Limited time and money almost always restrict the range of cases that can be included in any one research project. It would be prohibitively expensive, for example, to interview every adult in England about their media-consumption habits, or to examine the coverage of crime in every issue of every national newspaper printed over the last 20 years. Consequently, we have to make selections. The techniques for ensuring that these samples are representative are detailed in the next chapter, but research based on archival materials poses additional problems.

The first step is to draw up a list (or **sampling frame**) of all the cases that could be included in the study. Relevant lists, such as the register of electors (used for selecting a sample of individuals to interview) or the record of all newspapers published in the country (used for compiling samples for content analysis), are readily available for the present and the recent past. But the further back in time we go, the fewer comprehensive lists there are. Even if a list exists or can be reconstructed, there is no guarantee that it is accurate or comprehensive, or that we will be able to find all the items on it. Many records and artefacts are now lost, destroyed by fire, floods or bombs, or thrown away when a person died or an organisation closed or moved offices. Other records have perished over time or were never kept in the first place. Early films were shot on highly unstable nitrate stock, and many are now lost or damaged beyond repair. The first television programmes were broadcast 'live', and often no recording was made. Some were kept on film, but it was not until the late 1950s, when video recording became the professional norm, that keeping copies became standard practice (see Bryant 1989). Other materials that communications researchers are now interested in, such as comic books, were discarded because no one imagined that any serious scholar would want to study items so obviously designed to be disposable.

Although archivists and collectors have made enormous efforts to retrieve, restore and collate as much 'lost', damaged and ephemeral media material as possible, including amateur efforts (such as home movies, family snapshots and fanzines) as well as professional productions, we still lack comprehensive sampling frames in a number of areas. Nor do we always know exactly what has been lost. Whenever you undertake historical research, then, you must take into account these gaps and limitations, and make them clear when you present your results. You need to approach documentary sources as a detective, 'in the sense that everything is potentially suspect and anything may turn out to be the key piece of data' (Macdonald and Tipton 1993: 196).

In this spirit, the next step is to select a sample to work on. This involves decisions in four areas:

1. *When?* Deciding what time period to cover is not always as straightforward as it might appear. If we are interested in a particular event, such as news coverage of the Vietnam War, for example, we need to decide how much of the run-up and aftermath to include. Similarly, if we want to say something about 'modern' advertising, we have to decide when modernity began.

2. *Where?* When boiling down the wealth of national or international materials into manageable samples, you need to think carefully about social and cultural geography. Which areas or regions are representative of Europe, for example? Which cities, towns and rural areas typify a nation like Britain, the United States or Australia?

3. *Who?* This question poses particular problems for historical research. Much of what has survived in the archives was written or produced by those in positions of authority and privilege. If we are interested in popular culture in the mid nineteenth century, for example, we have plenty of accounts compiled by middle-class observers, who condemned popular media because they feared they would corrupt morals or foment unrest (see Murdock 1997a). But we have very few accounts from people who regularly went to the popular theatres or read the brash new Sunday newspapers or 'penny dreadfuls'. Faced with this massive imbalance, we have to work particularly hard to retrieve the voices and textures of popular experience by searching through sources such as court reports and evidence to official inquiries, which reproduce people's oral testimonies.

4. *What?* When choosing representative examples to examine, we also need to ask, 'Representative of what?' and 'According to whose criteria?' We have now celebrated 100 years of cinema, but which films, out of the thousands and thousands produced, would you choose to represent that history? Some writers would nominate titles that have stood the test of critical scrutiny and are now acknowledged by film critics as the 'best' examples of the art. Others would focus on the films that did the biggest business at the box office, arguing that these best capture the everyday experience of film. These choices would produce very different accounts, with little overlap.

Authenticity

Examples of material that has been deliberately faked are relatively rare, though the 'discovery' of Hitler's supposed personal diaries, which the London *Sunday Times* bought and serialised, shows that successful deceptions are still possible. Nor is authoritative opinion always a protection, since, like everyone else, experts may have strong reasons for wishing something to be true. It was partly the desire to believe that this crucial missing link in modern history had been found that prompted the distinguished historian Hugh Trevor-Roper to advise the paper that in his judgement the 'Hitler' manuscripts were genuine.

More common are misrepresentation, misattribution and mislabelling. In June 1998, for example, an award-winning British television documentary that featured a supposedly exclusive interview with the Cuban leader, Fidel Castro, was shown to have simply spliced in footage shot by Castro's personal cameraman. There was no original interview. Neglecting to mention this, the programme's maker claimed to have spent a 'nerve-shattering year' pursuing Castro (Gillard, Flynn and Flynn 1998: 5). The problem of 'faking' records has been thrown into sharp relief in recent years by the rapid transition to digital photography and the replacement of drawers of original negatives with databases of images that exist only as computer files. This shift in photographic technology makes it possible to alter and manipulate images in ways that are difficult to detect in the absence of an original negative for comparison, and poses major problems for the idea of photography as a historical record. This problem is not new. Suspicions that journalists may, on occasion, be 'economical with the truth' have a long history, and seemingly spontaneous news photographs have not infrequently turned out to be carefully posed or staged, but questions of attribution are also often raised about other materials that find their way into archives and collections. Who wrote some of the plays attributed to Shakespeare or produced some of the paintings credited to Rembrandt, for example, is still hotly disputed.

Problems also arise when material has been translated or copied (unless the copy is an exact facsimile). There are some 150 versions of Marco Polo's celebrated account of his travels in China, for example. Their contents vary widely, with frequent additions and alterations, and in the absence of a recognised 'original' copy, it is impossible to tell which is the closest to Polo's intentions (Wood 1995: ch. 6).

One way to address these problems is to follow the standard practice of art dealers and to trace the career (or provenance) of materials by finding out who produced them, who has owned them and where they have been kept.

Credibility

Judgements about the credibility of a source depend on the answers to three basic questions:

1. What information is the account based on?
2. How accurate, honest, frank and comprehensive is it?
3. Does it display clear signs of partiality and axe-grinding?

To answer the first question, we need to know how the information reported was obtained, by distinguishing between:

- *Primary accounts written or recorded at the time or immediately afterwards*, on the basis of direct involvement as either a participant or an observer. These would include diary entries, memos of meetings and eyewitness reports.

- *Primary accounts written or recorded some time after the event*. Examples include autobiographies and oral reminiscences.

- *Secondary accounts* produced by people who were not present at the time.

As a general rule, researchers are inclined to view primary accounts as being more credible than secondary sources, on the grounds that there is less likelihood of omissions, embellishments and statements added with the benefit of hindsight. However, this does not mean that they can be taken at face value. Some witnesses may be more familiar with the origins and organisation of the events they describe, and therefore less likely to misunderstand or misrepresent what is happening, and more able to notice important details that a naive observer might miss. We expect someone who has invested considerable time in getting to know a culture to produce better-informed accounts than a casual visitor. So you need to take into account differences in sources' relevant experience and expertise when assessing what weight to place on their evidence.

But a knowledgeable source is not necessarily an unbiased one, since the more involved people are in a situation or issue, the more likely they may be to have strong views on it. If your research is concerned with exploring differences of opinion and response (to, say, the rise of punk rock), partiality is not an issue. On the contrary, variations in experience and clashes of interpretation will be a central focus of the project. On the other hand, if you are trying to construct an accurate narrative of the early development of television services in the United States, or a comprehensive account of the organisation of Nazi propaganda during World War II, then the omissions and biases in the available accounts present major problems.

One way of addressing them is through *triangulation*. Just as a surveyor takes measurements from a number of vantage points to fix the 'true' position of a particular point on the ground, so researchers check the full range of available sources to build up the most accurate and comprehensive account possible. The idea is that the more sources you consult, the more likely it is that omissions will show up and that discrepancies in dates, times, places and the people involved can be resolved. If you are working on a project with other people, it is a good idea to ask someone else to look at the same materials (or a selection of them) to make sure that you have not missed important aspects.

You need to take particular care in using material retrieved from the Internet. A keyword search on a general search engine like Google will retrieve every relevant document in the database. These will range from papers written by major scholars to essays submitted by students and material from commercial companies. Always check the web address carefully. Where possible, run a search on the author or organisation.

Texts and contexts

A more fundamental way to tackle questions of evidence is to place the texts you are dealing with in their original context in order to gain a better grasp of their omissions, biases and peculiarities. Take official statistics, for example. At first sight, these appear comfortingly uncontentious. But their solidity is deceptive. In February 1996, in Utah, John Taylor, a criminal condemned to death, opted to have his sentence carried out by firing squad. Because he died an 'intentional death by another hand', which is how the state's legal system defines murder, his executioners are included in the criminal statistics as murderers. Nor are definitions always consistent over time. During the successive British governments headed by Mrs Thatcher, for example, the definition of who counted as 'unemployed' was altered over 20 times to reduce the size of the published figures for unemployment, which had become a major target for attack by opposition parties. So, always read the small print at the bottom of tables, or tucked away in appendices, before you use or quote any statistic that you have not generated yourself. We will be looking in detail in chapter 5 at the ways statistics can be used to misrepresent.

All the sources we might want to use in research have been produced in particular conditions, with certain aims in mind, and are indelibly shaped by the pressures, possibilities and temptations generated by the political and cultural contexts in which they are embedded (Hodder 1994: 394). 'Just as a researcher in 300 years' time would need to ask whether tabloid journalists truly believed in some of the stories they write', it is important to look carefully for inconsistencies, omissions and signs of insincerity or special pleading in all the documents we examine from the past (O'Connell Davidson and Layder 1994: 189), and to state all caveats and queries clearly in any presentation of our results.

From principles to practice

Having introduced the general issues you need to bear in mind when dealing with documentary sources, we now turn to some practical illustrations of how to set about working with them. We have chosen two of the major ways that documents can be used as primary sources for research: a historical case – the early years of the BBC; and a contemporary issue – patterns of ownership and control in the media industries.

Recovering history: the early years of the BBC

The BBC began transmissions on 14 November 1922. At that time it was the British Broadcasting Company, owned by a consortium of radio-set manufacturers. Following appraisals by two government-appointed committees (in 1923 and 1925), the company was relaunched on 1 January 1927 as the British Broadcasting Corporation, a publicly owned body financed by a compulsory annual licence fee on set ownership. Between then and the outbreak of World War II in 1939, the corporation established itself at the centre of national cultural life, with the number of licences issued more than quadrupling, from around 2 million to 9 million, though this figure considerably under-represents the organisation's audience.

This general pattern of development throws up a range of issues for research. Some focus on *institutional questions* to do with the corporation's internal organisation and its relations with major political and commercial actors. Others focus on the *cultural questions* raised by the emergence of radio programmes as novel cultural forms, and radio listening as a new communicative experience and domestic ritual. Some of the basic areas we could investigate are summarised in Box 2.2.

Box 2.2 The BBC's early years: major research areas

INSTITUTIONAL ASPECTS

Internal relations

1. The development of the corporation's internal organisation and structures of governance.

2. The development of the BBC's distinctive organisational ethos of 'public service'.

External relations

1. The evolution of official policy towards the BBC and the development of its relations to the state and to governments of the day.

2. The BBC's relations with suppliers of resources and talent for programme making and with potential competitors for audience time and attention, such as the national newspaper industry, the music industry, theatres and popular entertainments.

CULTURAL ASPECTS

Internal

The development of new production practices and new programme forms that explored the distinctive characteristics of radio as a communicative medium.

External

The rise of radio listening as a new dimension of everyday experience and domestic ritual, of radio personalities as a significant presence in people's imaginative lives, and of the radio set as an aspect of domestic decor.

The first step in any historical project is to read the basic narrative accounts compiled by previous researchers. These provide an essential context for more detailed work on particular areas and are useful in highlighting unanswered questions, under-explored themes and significant instances that would make good case studies. In the BBC's case, we have a solid basic narrative of development to draw on. This is provided first by Asa Briggs's (1961, 1965) monumental institutional and political history (which the corporation commissioned), and second, by Paddy Scannell and David Cardiff's (1991) pioneering cultural and social history of early BBC programming and its place in everyday life.

This situation is not entirely typical, however, for two reasons. First, because it enjoyed monopoly status as the only broadcasting organisation in Britain until the introduction of commercial television in the mid 1950s, external documentation on the BBC is relatively concentrated. We can therefore locate the pertinent parliamentary debates, government deliberations, official commissions of inquiry and public commentary relatively easily. However, if we are interested in broadcasting systems where there was always a mixture of commercial and public enterprise, and where activity was highly dispersed geographically, assembling relevant documentation presents much greater problems and it is easy to miss important sources. Researchers, therefore, are continually struggling to complete the picture. Bob McChesney's account (1993) of the fierce struggles around public broadcasting in the United States between 1928 and 1935 – a fight which previous authors had almost entirely neglected – is an excellent example of one important exercise in retrieval. Second, the BBC has maintained comprehensive and well-catalogued archives of its internal decisions and activities, and of many of its programmes, and has opened them to researchers. This is not always the case with media organisations, as Lesley Johnson found when she began exploring the early history of broadcasting in Australia (another mixed and highly dispersed system):

> Gathering material…was often difficult and disheartening. I knocked on countless doors and made many fruitless telephone calls attempting to find material about the broadcast stations of the 1920s and 1930s… I could find little that was still held by the commercial stations themselves, the production companies or the advertising firms, and often the archival material on the Australian Broadcasting Commission was sketchy and poor.

> (Johnson 1988: viii–ix)

In contrast, the availability of a reasonably comprehensive basic narrative of the early years of broadcasting in Britain has encouraged researchers to go on to look at particular themes and issues in more detail. As Paddy Scannell notes, 'historical work begins with narrative, but does not end there' (Scannell 1996: 1). This is a two-way process. General surveys suggest areas for further research, while more finely focused work often questions prevailing generalisations and prompts revisions.

As a national broadcasting organisation supported by taxation, the BBC has always been caught in the crossfire between its own conceptions of its public role and government definitions of the 'national interest'. Because they expose taken-for-granted understandings and forces that are normally held in reserve, case studies of moments of confrontation provide a particularly useful way of exploring this area. Michael Tracey's study of the BBC's response to the major incident of labour unrest in Britain in the interwar period, the General Strike of 1926, is a good example (Tracey 1978: ch. 8). It builds up a detailed analysis of this defining moment in BBC–government relations through a combination of internal materials drawn from the corporation's Written Archives and the diaries of key BBC figures (notably the managing director at the time, John Reith), and a range of external sources, from parliamentary debates and contemporary press reports, to the memoirs of key political actors.

The autobiographies and memoirs of senior BBC managers have also been combined with material on policy formation and programme decisions deposited in the Written Archives, and a range of contemporary external commentary, to explore the formation of key aspects of the BBC's corporate strategy. Cultural policy, particularly concerning the tangled relations between 'elite' and 'popular' culture, offers a particularly rich field of research. Examples include Simon Frith's (1983) study of entertainment programming and Philip Elliott and Geoff Matthews' (1987) work on music policy. Both projects are also highly relevant to the question of how the BBC's declared ideals of 'public service' were translated into practical scheduling decisions and expressed through new forms of programming which experimented with radio's distinctive qualities as a communicative form.

This last aspect is also central to the BBC's development of relations with its audiences. These are explored, at the level of organisational policy, in David Chaney's (1987) study of the emergence of audience research, and at the level of programming in Paddy Scannell's work on the pioneering audience participation show *Harry Hopeful* (Scannell 1996: ch. 2). Chaney draws on the familiar mix of documents from the corporation's Written Archives, combined with the memoirs and statements of key managerial personnel and outside commentators, while Scannell works with archive transcripts of the programmes as broadcast. In the absence of sound recordings to accompany his analysis, this is the closest we can get to the experience of listening, but as he points out, it requires 'some imaginative effort to "hear" and "see" the programmes I write about' (Scannell 1996: 3). As he also notes, however, the possibilities for multimedia presentations offered by CD-ROM technology and online systems should help future researchers to overcome print's inability to fully convey the experience of sound or of moving images.

Since there are a number of people still alive who remember the launch of radio and can recollect their first experiences of the medium, it is possible to investigate its entry into everyday life through oral-history techniques, as Shaun Moores (1988) does. (See also Tim O'Sullivan's (1991) study of reactions to the launch of television.) However, oral history does not make documentary sources redundant. As Lynn Spigel has shown in her (1992) study of television's arrival in post-war American life, we can learn a lot about the shared meanings that surround a new domestic medium by looking at how it is promoted and talked about in public, particularly in sources like women's magazines that are centrally concerned with the arrangement of family life. These do not tell us how people actually responded, but they do reveal the images and ways of talking that helped to form people's everyday understandings of the new medium. Simon Frith (1983) reproduces an early advertisement for radio sets and a cartoon of a radio family in his piece, but there is much more to do in combining the study of private lives and public representations. The image of a family unpacking their first television set, on the cover of this book, is another example.

Mapping networks of power: questions of media ownership and control

Modern democracies depend on a media system that delivers accurate information and informed analysis and gives space to the broadest possible range of voices, opinions and perspectives. Many commentators argue that this ideal requires diversity of ownership, since the less concentrated control over public communications is, the more likely it is that the media system will engage with the full range of interests in a society. Media concentration was already well established by the end of the nineteenth century, with the rise of a new breed of newspaper proprietors, the 'press barons', who owned chains of titles. Since these papers were their private property, what, critics wondered, was to stop them using them for their personal advantage rather than the promotion of the common good?

The rise of the present-day media moguls, whose interests extend to all the major communications sectors and across the globe, has given renewed impetus to this concern, and breathed new life into research on media ownership and media power.

As we noted earlier, it is difficult, and often impossible, for researchers to gain access to the corridors of corporate power. Nor would access necessarily solve the problem. Observing the sites where key decisions are debated and taken reveals only one dimension of power. A full account would also need to explain why some options for action are taken off the agenda before they even come up for discussion, and how some forms of power – such as the ability to influence the behaviour of competitors – derive not from specific actions but from a company's pivotal structural position in the marketplace (see Lukes 1974). To tackle this third dimension of power, we need to look at how the fields on which companies play out their strategies are organised, and at who is in a position to draw up the rules of the game (Bourdieu 1998: 40).

Step 1: Identifying the major players

The first step is to identify the major corporations operating in the communications field which interests you. This could be a particular country, a specific media sector – such as broadcasting or the music industry – or the emerging global media marketplace. 'Bigness' and centrality are measured in various ways. One solution, which the *Financial Times* uses in its regular audit of the major companies in various world markets, is to rank corporations by capitalisation (the number of shares issued multiplied by the share price). Other similar audits use company turnover as an index of size. Another solution which is arguably more relevant to media research, where questions of public access and consumption are central, is to rank companies by market share. This produces a *concentration ratio*, which measures the percentage of total sales or total audience accounted for by the top (usually five) companies in that sector. Lists using one or other of these measures can be found in the business press, media trade journals and the reports of regulatory agencies.

There are several useful websites that offer relevant basic information. The Who Owns What site, housed on the Columbia Journalism Review (http://www.cjr.org/tools/owners), provides a list of the top media companies, though with a noted US bias. Also useful is the information on media conglomerates, mergers and concentration of ownership on the Corporate Influence in the Media website (http://www.globalissues.org/HumanRights/media/Corporations/Owners.asp).

Step 2: Company reports and company profiles

Once you have drawn up a list of the companies you want to include in your research, the next step is to compile basic information on them. To do this, you need to obtain the latest editions of their *annual reports and accounts*. Publicly quoted companies will normally send you a copy if you write to the company secretary at the company's headquarters and ask for one. If your sample includes American companies, you should also apply to the Securities and Exchange Commission (SEC) (http://www.sec.gov) for the various supplements to the annual report, such as Form 13F, filed by institutional investment managers and showing the shares held by their account holders.

Since May 1996, public domestic companies in the USA have been required to file basic documents electronically with the SEC's EDGAR Database of Corporate Information, accessible online (http://www.sec.gov/edgar/searchedgar/webusers.htm). However, this is not as comprehensive as the written records. For example, companies are required to file Form 10-K, which contains much of the information in the annual report to shareholders, but not the actual report itself. Other documents are filed only on a voluntary basis.

Information on companies registered in Britain can be obtained from Companies House in London (http://www.companieshouse.gov.uk). There is an online search service and company reports can be downloaded, but, at the time of writing (2007), only for entries made from 1995 onwards.

Annual reports are primarily public relations documents, designed to reassure shareholders and attract new investors. However, they do contain the information that the company is legally obliged to disclose. In Britain, for example, they include three lists that are essential for research:

- The list of what the company owns and its major investments. These holdings fall into three basic categories. The first is *subsidiaries*, where the company has a controlling interest in another company, by virtue of owning over 50 per cent of the voting shares or otherwise controlling votes on the company's key executive body, the board of directors. If the company has 5 per cent or more of the voting shares, but lacks effective control, the holding is classified as an *associate*. And if a holding is purely for investment purposes, with no intention to exert control, it is a *trade investment*.

- The list of shareholders with a stake of more than 5 per cent.

- The list of members of the company's board of directors and senior managers.

Although these sources provide an essential starting point, you will need to supplement and check them before moving on to the next stages of the research.

Checking subsidiaries and investments

The first port of call here is *Who Owns Whom*, an annual directory published by Dunn and Bradstreet International. This lists all companies by name and indicates the parent company where relevant, providing a list of parent companies and logging their various holdings. Since all printed directories are out of date by virtue of the time lag between compilation and publication, it is important to check for recent changes in holdings and investments using online sources for tracking contemporary events (see the discussion earlier in this chapter).

Checking the major shareholders

Because companies are only required to name shareholders who have 5 per cent or more of the stock, the list provided in the annual report is incomplete. To develop a more comprehensive list, you will need to consult the current file of shareholders held by the relevant regulatory agency. For most research projects, concentrating on the largest 20 shareholders is usually adequate. Compiling this list is not always easy, however, for several reasons. First, although shareholders are listed individually, their holdings may be part of a wider grouping, belonging to a family for example, which can be mobilised as a single voting block. One way to address this is to check the kinship and marriage relations of major holders, using *Who's Who* and other biographical directories, though this can be very time-consuming. Second, not all shares are held in the name of the person or company who actually owns them (the *beneficial owners*). Often they are held on the beneficiary's behalf by *nominees*, such as banks. There are ways to address this problem (see Scott 1986: 39–45), but, again, they can be very time-consuming.

As with records of holdings and investments, time lags in corporate reporting make it essential to check online sources for any recent changes in shareholdings.

Step 3: Shares, deals and directors: mapping corporate networks

Once you have assembled up-to-date information on the main individual and corporate shareholders, the next step is to chart the patterns of connection between companies which emerge, paying special attention to the clusters or nodes of influence suggested by the central position that particular companies occupy in the network. These maps of links are usually represented graphically. Corporations in the network are depicted by boxes or circles containing the company name, and links are shown by connecting arrows indicating the direction of the investment (see, for example, Prestinari 1993: 188–9). However, the more complex the pattern of interlocks, the denser and more difficult these diagrams are to read. One solution is to describe network structures using statistical techniques (see Scott 1986: 210–20). These are not for the novice, but if you feel comfortable with statistics they are well worth exploring.

In addition to shareholdings, companies are linked through interlocking directorships. When the director of one company sits on the board of another concern, it opens up a channel of communication between them, whether or not they are also connected by investments or joint ventures. This in turn lays the ground for shared understandings and coordinated action. The standard UK source for tracking these interlocks is the *Directory of Directors*, which lists directors' other directorships. Once again, though, to offset time lags in publication, it is essential to check key names in the online databases dealing with developments in the corporate world and with contemporary events more generally.

The website at http://www.theyrule.com provides software that allows you to create and save simple maps of interlocking directorship for the top US companies. It is intended to be updated annually, but at the time of writing (2007) it was based on 2004 sources.

Constructing charts of interlocking directorship and laying them over the top of maps of interlocking shareholdings allows us to produce a thicker description of the nodes of control and information flows operating within the communications industries. To produce a comprehensive account, however, we also need to look at social networks.

Step 4: Clubs and kin: mapping social networks

Corporate contacts and communalities are also sustained and repaired through a complex network of social bonds. Some of these, like business round tables and trade associations, are expressly designed to facilitate business contacts and provide a basis for common action (in opposing unwanted government legislation, for example). But other social networks function to link businesspeople with key actors in the political system and other sources of strategic resources and power which have a bearing on corporate activity.

As William Domhoff (1975) has shown, the elite American social clubs, such as the Bohemian Grove in San Francisco and the Links Club in New York, play a central role in cementing ties between major corporations and key politicians and policy groups in the USA. The exclusive London clubs operate in a similar way in the UK. Also important are family ties, links through marriage, shared education and connections established through military service and occupational careers. These links can be investigated by looking up the relevant entries in the major bibliographical directories. *Who's Who*, in its various national editions, is the best known of these, but there are a number of other, more specialised sources that cover prominent figures in particular fields. These are selective, however, so it is worth checking relevant online sources for additional profiles and recent biographical details.

Summary: key points

- The documentary sources we can use in communications and media research are not confined to written or printed records. They include anything that can help to document the organisation of public culture and personal and social lives: material artefacts, statistical sources, sound recordings, single images, moving images, and digital files.

- These sources can be used either as secondary materials, to flesh out, cross-check or question the picture that emerges from the research materials we have produced ourselves, or as the primary focus for a research project.

- There are five main secondary uses of documentary sources: to check what research has already been done in the particular areas; to check government, parliamentary and legal decisions and debates; to check industry facts and figures; to track contemporary events; and to engage in networking.

- There are four main situations where research may centre around the analysis of documentary sources: where access to people or situations we wish to study is restricted or denied; in historical studies; in the re-analysis of material previously collected by other researchers; and in textual analysis, where research focuses on the organisation and meaning of the material itself.

- Relevant documentary materials are available from a wide range of sources, from state agencies and official collections, to commercial organisations and private and public institutions. Conditions of access vary considerably, however, and must always be checked carefully.

- Problems of access have been alleviated to some extent by the development of electronic systems of documentary storage and retrieval, but many sources have not yet been digitalised and can still be accessed only by personal visits to the relevant library or archive. So always check to see whether or not the information you need can be accessed remotely in digital form.

- Before you use or quote from any documentary source, always consider its representativeness, authenticity and credibility.

chapter three

Selecting and Sampling

Introduction: samples and populations

Sampling is a central part of everyday life. Dipping a toe in the water, flicking through a magazine, 'zapping' across television channels, sipping a cup of coffee, are all examples of the kinds of routine sampling activity we engage in constantly. We sample from our environment for a range of reasons: to save time, to anticipate events, to minimise discomfort, to decide on future actions, to expand our horizons, and so on.

Just as sampling is an integral element of social life, so it is at the heart of all 'scientific' activity, whether in the human or natural sciences. Although researchers sample for similar reasons to everybody else, issues concerning sample validity are inevitably more crucial, because of the more complex and challenging questions being investigated. For example, you do not need to drink a litre of milk to decide whether it has gone sour. One mouthful should be sufficient for you to pour the rest down the sink. But if you were trying to assess the presence of an infective agent in a nation's milk supply, testing one randomly selected milk carton would be useless. You would need to cast your net far more widely and systematically. To give you some idea of what might be required, a study of the presence of *Listeria monocytogenes* in milk in Denmark took samples from 1,132,958 cows from 36,199 herds over a 23-year period (Jensen et al. 1996).

In communication and cultural studies, sampling issues involve all kinds of areas, most commonly: *people*, *social groups*, *events*, *activities*, *institutions* and *texts*. In this chapter we ignore the last area, as textual sampling is dealt with in detail in later chapters (see chapters 6 to 10, 12 and 13). But it is worth noting in passing the parallels in the debates surrounding the sampling of texts and sampling issues in other areas. For instance, the rationales for theoretical sampling explained below resonate with the arguments used to support many forms of selective qualitative textual analysis. Similarly, the concerns and strategies for achieving representative samples of large numbers of people match those that arise when using quantitative content analysis to map the macro-dimensions of media discourse.

Samples, populations and types of sampling

Samples are taken from **populations**. In research, the term 'population' is used in a very general way. Populations are not necessarily made up of people; they can be aggregates of texts, institutions, or anything else being investigated. Furthermore, research populations are defined by specific research objectives and alter in direct relation to them. A population can be very small or very large – it depends on who or what you are investigating. For example, if a wine taster sampled a bottle of wine to deduce the quality of the vintage, his population would be every bottle produced by the vineyard in that year. However, if a forensic chemist was called to examine the contents of a half-finished bottle of wine discovered beside the poisoned corpse of a wine taster, her population would be the specific contents of the bottle.

Sampling techniques used in analysing people and institutions can be divided into two categories: **random sampling** (or 'probability sampling') and **non-random sampling** (or 'non-probability sampling'). The key distinctions between these approaches are set out in Table 3.1. These are the foundation for many other variations in sampling styles, which we review later in this chapter. However, there are three matters that concern all forms of sampling: *sample error*, *sample size* and *non-response*. We begin by considering these general issues.

Table 3.1 Distinctions between random and non-random sampling

	Random sampling	Non-random sampling
Selection of sample units	Units are selected by chance.	Researchers purposively select sample units.
Estimating chances of inclusion	The chance of each unit of a population being selected for a sample (the 'sample fraction') can be calculated.	Selection-chance is unknown.
Equality of selection	Every unit of a population has an equal chance of being selected.	It cannot be guaranteed that every unit of a population has an equal chance of being selected.

Sample error: random errors and constant errors

Sample error is where the values from a sample differ from the 'true' or actual values of a population. This issue is most evident with samples that attempt to assert claims to general representativeness, but it does hold implications for all forms of sampling to some degree. (NB: As we discuss in the next section, not every sampling technique has representational aspirations.)

It is accepted that some degree of sample error is unavoidable, and statisticians have developed statistical tests to estimate the impact this is likely to have had on the accuracy of sample results (see chapter 5). The assumption made in these tests is that these errors are **random errors** – in other words, that sample error is due to the random variation that occurs when you select a smaller number of cases to represent a larger population.

However, there is always the risk that samples may contain **constant errors**. By this, we mean biases in the composition of a sample that distort systematically its representative qualities. Constant errors have a consistent pattern that marginalises or over-represents sections of the population. For example, suppose a student wanted to estimate the average age of all journalists working in the national press, and she compiled her sample by noting down all journalist bylines that appeared in six national newspaper titles over six months, and then sent each journalist thus listed a brief questionnaire. The problem with this sampling method is that it would build an elite bias into her sample, because not every journalist gets her or his name listed on a story (a 'byline'). It is an honour that tends to be conferred on the better-paid, more experienced members of editorial teams, who also tend to be older than those who do not get their work attributed. For this reason, the average age of the sample would probably exceed the average age of her population, because it would marginalise the younger and far more numerous minions.

Detecting constant errors in sampling is not always an easy thing to do. It is a matter of scrutinising a study's sampling and research procedures for significant skews.

Sample size

What size do samples need to be to be credible? Common sense suggests that the larger a sample, the more confidence you can have in its representativeness. Although this intuitive logic applies, to a large degree, to all sampling, it does not apply as completely as you might suppose. For example, in chapter 5 we show how the size of a random sample has a direct impact on statistical estimations of its accuracy: the bigger the sample, the smaller the estimation of the standard error of the sample. However, a point is reached where substantial increases in sample size begin to have only small effects on the calculated precision of sample measures (Henry 1990: 118). Once this starts to happen, the benefits of increasing the statistical accuracy of sample measures by sampling more extensively may be seen to be outweighed by the cost and inconvenience of greatly increasing the sample size.

It is in qualitative research that the assumption that 'big is beautiful' is challenged most directly. This is because a lot of qualitative studies are less concerned with generating an *extensive* perspective (producing findings that can be generalised more widely) than with providing *intensive* insights into complex human and social phenomena in specific circumstances (Maykut and Morehouse 1994: 56). This means that qualitative research tends to use small samples which are generated more informally and organically than those typically used in quantitative research. Moreover, these 'emergent and sequential' samples (ibid.: 63) do not aim to build up large numbers of similar cases for the purposes of making broader inferences, but rather stop gathering information once the research reaches 'saturation point' (where the data collection stops revealing new things and the evidence starts to repeat itself). According to Lincoln and Guba (1985), this point can be reached quite quickly, even after as few as 12 interviews. Some qualitative researchers do not even seek this saturation point. For instance, in a study of the limits to audience power in decoding texts, Condit (1989) sampled just two students, selected on the basis of their strong and contrasting views on abortion (pro-choice and pro-life). Condit shows that despite the vehemence of their beliefs, both participants made very similar readings of the intended message of an episode of *Cagney and Lacey* that dealt with the abortion issue.

We do not want to overstate this distinction between qualitative and quantitative sampling. Although there are examples where qualitative researchers have no concerns about drawing wider inferences from their research, in many instances interpretive studies are interested in drawing wider conclusions, a process described by Carey (1975: 190) as 'gingerly reaching out to the full relations within a culture or a total way of life'. The key difference is that within the qualitative tradition, samples tend to be seen as *illustrative* of broader social and cultural processes, rather than strictly and generally *representative*.

If there is one thing that does unite qualitative and quantitative research on the issue of sample size, it is that there are no definitive guidelines. In most cases, the final decision will be a compromise between the minimal theoretical and empirical requirements of the study and other external considerations (such as the time and resources available to the researcher).

Non-response

Non-response is a term that covers a variety of scenarios. Sometimes it relates to the refusal of respondents to cooperate with research because of their hostility, suspicion, apathy or confusion. This non-cooperation can be either overt (e.g. refusing to participate) or covert (e.g. choosing a 'don't know' category to answer a question to avoid revealing their real views). The term can also apply to those occasions where a researcher has failed to record accurately responses for analysis.

Non-response is an area where the representative or illustrative value of a sample can be undermined. The concern is that respondents and non-respondents may differ from each other in some important respect, and introduce constant errors into the sample. Random sampling gives a statistical indication of the levels of response, as once a sample has been selected, the researcher has no choice but to stick with it and do their best to achieve a high response rate (e.g. through callbacks or re-mailings). In contrast, non-random sampling techniques permit researchers to look elsewhere if anyone in their original selection refuses to cooperate, which speeds things up and normally ensures an adequate quantity of response. However, this can present its own dangers, as there is no way of knowing whether those who refused to cooperate differed in some important respect from those who cooperated. At the very least, response rates can alert the researcher to potential deficiencies in the sample composition.

Because of the dangers of there being significant differences between respondents and non-respondents, it is essential to maximise response levels. Where non-response is due to researcher error, this can be controlled by taking time and care when recording, coding or entering findings, in order to minimise data loss. Where non-response relates to the omissions or recalcitrance of respondents, as we see in later chapters, there are several ways in which these absences can be limited by effective research design and administration. Even so, researchers are not in ultimate control of this matter, and consequently need to be honest when high levels of non-response threaten the validity of their sample.

Random sampling

There are several forms of random sampling, but all of them involve consideration of two issues: defining a population and identifying a sampling frame.

Defining a population

As we have noted, the population of a piece of research is never constant; it is defined by research objectives. Defining a population fulfils two important functions: it provides a basis for deciding on an adequate and appropriate sampling strategy and it signals how broadly the findings can be extrapolated. This last point is important in that it helps those reading the research to appraise the validity of research conclusions. Say an Australian market researcher interviewed a random sample of 1,000 adults about their newspaper readership, in which all respondents were taken from an affluent suburb of Melbourne. If the researcher defined his population as being 'the adult population of Australia' and drew inferences about national press readership on the basis of his results, the validity of his sample could be criticised on two grounds. First, Australia's federal political structure is mirrored in its regionalised press, which means the research would underestimate the readership of titles produced outside of the state of Victoria. Second, the targeting of one affluent, suburban region would lead to the under-representation of certain sections of the Australian population (e.g. working-class readerships and certain ethnic minority communities). This, in turn, would distort the patterns of readership for particular titles. However, if the researcher defined his research population more modestly, as being 'middle-class adults in Melbourne', the first criticism would disappear, and concerns regarding the second would be reduced.

Sampling frames

A sampling frame is a list that should contain all (or most) of the 'elements' of the population you wish to sample. The identification of a sampling frame is another area where constant errors can intrude into the sampling process and compromise the representativeness of the research. This is because there may be a discrepancy between the working population of a study (the sampling frame) and the general population (Smith 1975: 107). For example, it is accepted that telephone directories make unsatisfactory sampling frames for surveying adult populations, as not every household has a telephone, and not every household that does consents to be listed in the directory (see Traugott and Lavrakas 1996: 59–60). Consequently, the directories tend to under-represent people at the top and bottom ends of the socio-economic scale. Even electoral registers are known to contain significant areas of under-representation, particularly among younger age groups and certain ethnic minority communities (Electoral Commission 2003). Sometimes you have to accept that your sampling frame may not completely capture your research population, but you should always be alert to the implications of any major discrepancies.

You may have to construct your own sampling frame from a range of sources, whether because a suitable list for your population does not exist, or, if it does, because it may not be comprehensive. For example, in a survey investigating the information and communication needs of British charities and voluntary organisations, two of the authors collated and cross-referenced 18 separate directories and local authority grant lists of these organisations from the sampled regions (Deacon and Golding 1991), since the existing, purpose-specific directories of voluntary organisations tended to under-represent ethnic minority groups, informal community-based groups and recently established groups. When compiling a sampling frame in this way, it is vital to remove duplications in entries, as random sampling procedures assume that every element in the sampling frame has an equal chance of being selected.

Once you have identified or compiled an adequate and appropriate sampling frame, you are in a position to start selecting your sample from it. Let us now review these procedures.

Simple random sampling

Simple random sampling is where each sample element is selected on a random basis from the sampling frame. This involves assigning each element on the sampling frame a unique number and then randomly selecting numbers between the top and bottom values, until you have the requisite number of units for your sample. Tables of random numbers provided in most statistics textbooks are used to guarantee a random selection. Computer packages have also been developed to provide a randomised selection more quickly. However, despite these technological innovations and the general simplicity of the procedure, this method can prove time-consuming when selecting a large sample.

Systematic sampling

Systematic sampling provides a less laborious method for random selection of sample units. You start by numbering the elements in your sampling frame, and then decide how many elements you need for your sample. Next you divide your required sample number into the sampling frame total, which gives you a 'sampling interval'. A random number is then selected between 1 and this value, which provides the first element of your sample and the starting point for the selection of the rest. From this point, you select every *n*th entry on the sampling frame (using the sampling interval) until you have completed your selection. A worked example of this process is provided in Box 3.1.

Box 3.1 An example of systematic sampling

In a survey of young children's attitudes to children's programmes, a research team obtains the class registers from 25 junior schools. In total, these list the names of 2,500 children, from which the researchers want to draw a sample of 500.

Step 1: divide 500 into 2,500. This produces a sampling interval of 5.

Step 2: select a random number between 1 and 5 (e.g. 3).

Step 3: Take the 3rd entry on the sampling frame as the first unit of the sample, then select the 8th, 13th, 18th, 23rd, 28th, 33rd, and so on, until 500 individuals have been selected.

One point you need to ensure when applying this strategy is that your selection procedure does not inadvertently tie in with patterns in the sampling frame. To give a simple illustration: if a sampling frame alternately listed females and males, and the sampling interval was an even number, the resulting sample would be made up solely of either females or males.

Stratified random sampling

Stratified random sampling involves separating the research population into non-overlapping groups (or 'strata'), each containing subjects that share similar characteristics. Sample elements are then randomly selected from each stratum using systematic sampling techniques. The main advantage of this method, compared with simple random sampling and systematic sampling, is that it allows you to ensure that the sample composition is representative in relation to important variables related to the research. For example, if you were investigating gender differences in soap opera viewing, you would probably want to ensure an equal divide of female and male respondents for the purposes of comparison. If you employed either of the basic random sampling techniques, you might not achieve such parity, particularly if your sample was small.

Most stratified samples are organised in such a way that the proportion of sample elements in each stratum matches known distributions in the population as a whole (known as 'proportionate' stratified random sampling – see Box 3.2 for an example). But stratified samples may be deliberately disproportionate in their composition (i.e. the proportions of the strata do not directly match known distributions in the population). This occurs when a researcher has an interest in strata that would contain very few sample elements if proportionality were strictly observed. For example, if somebody conducted a sample survey of 1,000 UK adults to examine differences in leisure pursuits among people from different ethnic communities, the total number of participants not defined as 'White' would not exceed 79 if the sample was proportionate. This is because people from minority ethnic communities constitute only 7.9 per cent of the UK population. Such a low proportional presence of representatives from minority communities would undermine the objectives of the research, so the researcher would probably seek to boost the presence of these communities in the research sample. Of course, when a sample is deliberately distorted in this way, any projections made regarding the population as a whole require arithmetical corrections, with data being appropriately re-weighted in line with known population distributions.

Stratified random sampling is a popular sampling technique because of its cost-effectiveness and the controls it provides to the researcher. But it is not always possible to apply it. On some occasions, the information contained in the sampling frame is insufficiently detailed to permit the sorting of its contents into different strata. For instance, you may not be able to ascertain the gender of people listed on a sampling frame because only surname and initials are provided.

Box 3.2 Producing a proportionate stratified random sampling

A research student in the USA wants to investigate the media strategies and relations of locally elected public officials. As part of this study, she wants to send a questionnaire to a random sample of 500 officials, stratified by gender and type of government (county, municipal, town/township). To produce a proportionate stratified sample, she first needs to identify the known distribution of this population in relation to these variables:

Distribution of locally elected officials by gender and type of government

	County	Municipal	Town/Township
Male	15%	34%	27%
Female	4%	10%	10%

(Source: US Bureau of the Census (1997) Statistical Abstract for the US: p. 218. Notes: Percentages add up to 100. Total number of cases: 281,636.)

She now needs to distribute the 500 sample units in proportions that directly replicate these population distributions. For example, she needs to include 75 male county officials in her survey, which represents 15 per cent of a sample of 500.

	County	Municipal	Town/Township
Male	75 officials	170 officials	135 officials
Female	20 officials	50 officials	50 officials

Cluster sampling

One of the drawbacks of the random sampling strategies discussed so far is that they present difficulties when researchers are investigating geographically dispersed populations. Say a student wanted to conduct a personal interview survey with a random selection of national and local journalists in India. The first problem she would confront would be to produce a comprehensive nationwide sampling frame. No centralised register of these professionals exists, and according to official figures there are 60,413 registered newspapers in India (Registrar of Newspapers for India, http://rni.nic.in/ming). Even assuming she had the time and patience to compile an adequate sampling frame, she would face a considerable amount of travelling to complete all the interviews if she randomly selected her sample on a nationwide basis. She could reduce her workload by randomly selecting several regions of India and focusing her sampling on these areas. This strategy would reduce the logistics involved in creating a sampling frame, and would mean a lot less travelling. It is an example of what is known as **cluster sampling**.

Although the 'clusters' in cluster sampling are most typically institutions or other physical locations, 'time' is occasionally used as an additional form of clustering. For example, a sample of cinema-goers might be compiled by randomly selecting people attending a random selection of cinemas at randomly selected times. But it is important to emphasise that a principle of genuine randomness must be retained in sample selection. As Schofield (1996: 34) explains:

> For a genuine probability sample, both the time periods, or any other form of cluster, and the individuals surveyed should be chosen at random. Simply accepting all the individuals who turn up or pass by at some specified time or times until the required number has been obtained would not constitute cluster sampling which is a probability method.

Although the main advantages of cluster sampling are that it saves time and can be used when a sampling frame listing population elements is not available and would not be feasible to create, it has deficiencies. The main one is that it reduces the precision of the sampling and increases the calculated standard error of the sample. (For an explanation of how the calculation of sample error differs for cluster samples in comparison with other random samples, see Henry 1990: 107–9.) This is because elements within particular clusters tend to be alike, and consequently there is a greater risk that the sample may be less representative of the population as a whole. For this reason, the greater the clustering in a sample, the less confidence we can have in its general representativeness. To illustrate this point, let us imagine an international survey of trade unionists' attitudes towards the mainstream news media, based on a cluster sample of two unions, one from the USA and one from the UK. As Manning (1998) demonstrates, there are considerable national and international variations in the disposition of unions towards the media, ranging along a continuum from those who see journalists as class enemies to those who are optimistic about their union's chances of getting a good press. It is questionable whether sampling two clusters would capture this diversity of opinion adequately, even if the survey sent questionnaires to hundreds of members from each union. It is possible that the political environment and history of each union (which are the 'clusters' of the sample) would produce distinctive attitudinal cultures that are atypical of the union movement as a whole. A more reliable strategy would be to sample the same number of respondents, but from a wider range of trade unions. As Moser and Kalton explain, 'a large number of small clusters is better – other things being equal – than a small number of large clusters' (1971: 105).

This example also highlights how it can be useful to introduce formal stratification into your cluster sampling: considering at the outset how your clusters may vary and building these differences into the sample selection process. For example, Fenton, Bryman and Deacon's survey of social scientists about their media contact (1998: 93) was based on a combination of cluster and stratified sampling. The clusters in this sample were the specific organisational units within which social scientists are employed, which were stratified by *type of institution* (university department, independent research institute, government department); by *social science discipline* (sociology, psychology, economics, political science, business and management, social policy and other social science orientated subjects); and, for the university departments, by *externally accredited research performance* (high, medium, low). This complex stratification was deemed necessary to capture the varied contexts within which social scientists work in the UK, which may have significant implications for their media relations. This combination of a range of stratification variables is an example of what is known as **multi-stage cluster sampling**.

Non-random sampling

The one element that all non-random sampling methods share is that sample selection is not determined by chance. It is important to emphasise that 'non-randomness' in this context is not meant negatively (i.e. that the researcher tried but failed to achieve true randomness). For this reason, this type of sampling is sometimes referred to as 'judgemental' or 'purposive' sampling, terms that stress the intentions of those who apply the procedures.

Although non-random sampling is frequently a feature of qualitative research, it is also sometimes used in quantitative research. This occurs most commonly with 'quota sampling' methods.

Quota sampling

Quota sampling shares similarities with stratified random sampling and multi-stage random sampling, in that researchers need to define their population and gain detailed information about it. However, quota sampling does not require a sampling frame. Instead, the researcher decides on a range of criteria that is likely to be important to the study and then sets a series of 'quotas' in relation to this that are filled to produce a representative sample. As with proportionate stratified random sampling, the size of each quota should be weighted to match with known distributions in the population.

The more selection criteria that are identified, the greater the number of quotas will be (see the example given in Box 3.3). This increases the logistical problems of filling each one. However, the more sophisticated and multilayered the quota categories are, the greater confidence you can have in a sample's representativeness.

Quota samples are widely favoured in research where speed is essential, for example in opinion poll research about developing events and in market research. Apart from the fact that they do not require a sampling frame, quota samples do not require callbacks to locate people who were not contacted initially, and the samples are not compromised by low response (you keep going until your quotas are full). But this presents ways in which 'constant errors' can creep into the sample. The technique can produce bunching in quota categories rather than an even spread, because interviewers approach people who most evidently fit into them and neglect people at the margins (e.g. in looking for respondents between 21 and 30, the interviewers may produce a sample with a high proportion of people in their mid twenties, because they are the most readily identifiable as fitting into the category). Furthermore, the time and location at which the sampling takes place can affect the sample's representativeness. If you quota-sample in a city centre in the middle of the afternoon, you may marginalise people who work in certain professions or who are resident outside of the city.[1]

---

1   Quota sampling was identified as one of the reasons behind the failure of British opinion pollsters to predict the victory of the Conservative Party in the 1992 British general election. First, because most samples were collated during the day, when large numbers of people are at work, certain sorts of professional people were under-represented who had a greater propensity to support the Conservatives than Labour. Second, because quota sampling does not quantify non-responses, the pollsters' use of the method took little account of the high level of 'refusers' who would not divulge their political preferences. Consequently, the method obscured 'the disproportionate probability for Conservative voters to refuse interviews to pollsters' (Noble 1992: 18).

Many researchers who employ quota-sampling techniques also conduct the kinds of statistical tests and population estimates that, strictly speaking, should be the preserve of randomly selected samples (see chapter 5). Their rationale for doing so is that a well-designed quota sample will be as representative as a randomised sample, and it is therefore legitimate to use them for making statistical inferences. This pragmatic reasoning, which is most frequently advanced by market and opinion researchers who value the cost-effectiveness and ease of administration of the method, is not accepted by statistical purists. They argue that the non-randomness of the sample selection means it is inappropriate to make statistical projections that are based on theories of probability and chance. (For a discussion of the controversy, see Moser and Kalton 1971: 127–37.)

Despite these disagreements about the 'scientific' status of quota sampling, we can see that this method shares the motivations of all forms of random sampling: to produce a representative sample from which you can make broader inferences. Advocates of the method claim it is merely a different means to the same end, and reject the argument that the intervention of human subjectivity in the selection process compromises sample accuracy. The formal, representative concerns make quota sampling atypical of most non-random sampling. With most other judgemental sampling methods, the intentions of the researcher are transparent, unapologetic and of pivotal significance, which reflects the different theoretical and empirical concerns of the mainly qualitative studies that use them as their basis.

Box 3.3 Designing a quota sample

A quota sample of schoolchildren incorporates three variables:

- gender (female/male);
- age group (5–10 years, 11–15 years, 16+ years);
- parental occupation (professional/intermediate, skilled manual/non-manual, partly skilled/unskilled, unemployed).

This means the researchers would have to find respondents to fit into 24 quota categories:

Gender	Age		Parental profession
Female	5–10 years	1	Professional/intermediate
		2	Skilled manual/non-manual
		3	Partly skilled/unskilled
		4	Unemployed
	11–15 years	5	Professional/intermediate
		6	Skilled manual/non-manual
		7	Partly skilled/unskilled
		8	Unemployed

	16+ years	9	Professional/intermediate
		10	Skilled manual/non-manual
		11	Partly skilled/unskilled
		12	Unemployed
Male	5–10 years	13	Professional/intermediate
		14	Skilled manual/non-manual
		15	Partly skilled/unskilled
		16	Unemployed
	11–15 years	17	Professional/intermediate
		18	Skilled manual/non-manual
		19	Partly skilled/unskilled
		20	Unemployed
	16+ years	21	Professional/intermediate
		22	Skilled manual/non-manual
		23	Partly skilled/unskilled
		24	Unemployed

Theoretical sampling

Theoretical sampling is a method that abandons concerns about representativeness (Glaser and Strauss 1967). Instead, the researcher seeks out respondents who are most likely to aid theoretical development. Instead of looking for typical cases, the researcher seeks people who are most likely to extend and even confound emerging hypotheses. This search continues until nothing new emerges from the sampling, and respondents only start to reiterate issues that have already emerged ('the saturation point'). To give a hypothetical example, imagine you wanted to use theoretical sampling as the basis for an exploration of journalistic attitudes towards the British royal family. To do so would involve, first, theorising the main points of diversity across the British media and then compiling a sample that captures all elements of these differences (e.g. press/broadcast, highbrow/lowbrow, generalist correspondents/specialist correspondents, news gatherers/news processors, entertainment orientated/news orientated). These distinctions may be added to or elaborated as the research progresses and new issues emerge.

Snowball sampling

Snowball sampling is not completely distinct from theoretical sampling, as theoretical samples are often derived from snowball-sampling techniques. Nevertheless, there is a value in retaining this distinction as snowball sampling is often adopted for practical reasons rather than because of identified theoretical objectives.

Snowball sampling is mainly used where no list or institution exists that could be used as the basis for sampling. Like a snowball rolling down a hill, a snowball sample grows through momentum: initial contacts suggest further people for the researcher to approach, who in turn may provide further contacts. This method is widely used in research into either very closed or informal social groupings, where the social knowledge and personal recommendations of the initial contacts are invaluable in opening up and mapping tight social networks.

Typical-case sampling

With **typical-case sampling**, the researcher seeks to identify a case that exemplifies the key features of a phenomenon being investigated. Because of this, the method needs to be supported by other generalised sampling evidence to support the claims to typicality. For example, a researcher might want to contrast the media usage of a typical middle-class Swedish family with that of a typical middle-class Norwegian family. To do so in a credible way would involve consulting demographic data (e.g. details about average family size, ages, occupations, education, ethnicity), in order to establish what typicality might mean in each context.

Critical-case sampling

Lindlof describes *critical-case sampling* as 'a person, event, activity, setting, or (less often) time period that displays the credible, dramatic properties of a "test case"... [A] critical case should demonstrate a claim so strikingly that it will have implications for other, less unusual, cases' (1995: 130). Critical-case sampling is more widespread than you might suppose, although it is not always conceptualised as such. For example, several studies of relations between journalists and the state during military conflict could be described as 'critical-case samples', as they often use the overt tensions during these periods to identify nascent aspects of political and professional culture. Witness the concluding remarks from two studies of the media's role in international military conflicts:

> The Falklands crisis had one unique and beneficial side effect. Its limited time-scale and crowded succession of incidents made it an experience of great intensity. It briefly illuminated aspects of British society normally hidden from view. It *exposed* habitual abuses by the armed forces, Government, Whitehall and the media; it did not *create* them.

(Harris 1983: 152, original emphasis)

> The Gulf war case...reveals the clash between the mythologies of journalists and politicians in American culture, mythologies that establish norms and roles that are more or less carried out in practice.

(Paletz 1994: 291)

Convenience sampling

Despite the differences between the qualitative sampling procedures listed above, one aspect shared by them all is that selection of sample units is consciously shaped by the research agenda. **Convenience sampling** differs in that sample selection is less preconceived and directed, and more the product of expediency, chance and opportunity. It is useful to think of there being two types of convenience sampling: a weak version and a strong version. 'Weak' convenience sampling is the least desirable form and is where sample units or clusters are selected because they are nearest to hand. An example would be the university professor who uses her students as research subjects, or the undergraduate student who dragoons friends, neighbours and family into participating in his final-year project. The 'strong' version of convenience sampling is where sampling focuses around natural clusters of social groups and individuals, who seem to present unexpected but potentially interesting opportunities for research. For example, a researcher might find she can gain access to members of a religious sect who make extensive use of the Internet to promote their beliefs. On these occasions, it is the chance availability of these natural outcroppings of data that initiates the research process.

Although convenience sampling tends to be viewed negatively, an international study of the marketing and reception of *The Lord of the Rings* film trilogy embraced the approach unapologetically (Barker and Egan 2006). The main aspect of the audience component of the study was a web-based questionnaire that was translated into 14 languages, with responses invited from audiences in 19 countries. The research team recognised that their sampling method skewed the sample towards enthusiastic fans of the film with Internet access, and away from 'the reluctant, the critical and the hostile' (Barker 2006: 5). To rectify this partially, several thousand paper versions of the survey were also collected at screenings of the film, but these responses constituted only a small percentage of the final responses received (the final sample size came to nearly 25,000 responses). What is striking in this study is that the researchers were not seeking to generate a representative sample: for their purposes, it was 'massification' of the sample that mattered:

> We were looking to discover what range of 'viewing strategies' can be found among different kinds of viewers of *Lord of the Rings*; how (differently or alike) they work; what responses to and judgements of the film they connect with; and how they help to 'place' the film within people's lives… Given these interests, what would it mean to try to identify the scope and character of a 'population' from which we might have sought a 'sample' *in advance of* answering our questions about the nature and operation of different viewing strategies? I would now argue that a flaw in quite a number of arguments in favour of quantitative approaches is their adoption of a *distributional fallacy* – that the relevance and importance of a phenomenon should be determined from how widespread it is. There are without argument some questions for which this is appropriate. But it should not be in any sense a condition of the validity of a question or an approach. What our research hopes to be able to demonstrate – and will use quantitative as well as qualitative procedures in order to secure this demonstration – is *the nature of the processes involved in all these*. For this purpose, the size of the overall population we have managed to recruit does matter – because it allows more sophisticated and sure explorations to

discover patterns, relationships, distinctions and oppositions. But their *frequency as against some other population is just not the issue.*

(Barker 2006: 10–11, original emphasis)

Focus group sampling

Focus group research involves bringing small groups of people together to discuss issues identified by researchers. It may seem strange to include a section dedicated to focus group sampling in a general discussion of non-random sampling methods: first, because there is no consistency in sampling procedures used in focus group research; and second, because the various sampling methods used are often hybrids of existing sampling strategies. Nevertheless, a dedicated section is required for several reasons. In the first place, focus group research is becoming an ever more popular qualitative research method within communication and cultural studies (Morrison 1998; Barbour and Kitzinger 1999). Furthermore, examining specific sampling strategies used in focus group research demonstrates how qualitative sampling strategies are rarely straightforward matters involving well-established sampling protocols. Rather, they often depend on the creativity and resourcefulness of the researcher.

Although the use of focus groups in communication research has a long history (e.g. Merton 1956), it is since the early 1980s that they have become one of the most popular means of analysing media audiences. In particular, focus groups have become closely associated with the *reception analysis* paradigm, described by McQuail as 'effectively the audience research arm of cultural studies' (1997: 19). This body of work has sought to introduce an 'ethnography of reading' (Morley 1980) into audience research, that highlights the social context of media consumption, and the agency and discernment of audience members in the decoding process. Focus groups have proved popular in this area of research because they are seen to produce rich qualitative material, well suited to detailed interpretive analysis (transcripts of people discussing their views and actions in their own words and, to some degree, on their own terms). Furthermore, their group basis is claimed to provide insight into the interactive dynamics of small groups (May 1993: 95), and to mimic the way that everyday media interpretations tend to be 'collectively constructed' by people in social, familial and professional networks (Richardson and Corner 1986).[2]

How do you go about designing a focus group sample that is sufficiently varied to enable you to capture and compare the social and individual constructions of meaning? As we show in the examples below, this is not a straightforward matter, and there is no consensus in the methods adopted in the studies published over recent years.

The first question you need to deal with is: which groups should you select? In some

---

2 It should be noted in passing that neither of these claims made for focus group research is uncontested. Some have disputed whether the material generated through group discussions can claim to be truly 'ethnographic' (Nightingale 1989; Murdock 1997b; Morrison 2000), and others reject the assertion that individual-based interviews treat people as social atoms divorced from social context (Wren-Lewis 1983; Jordin and Brunt 1988). How group interviews relate to broader social relations and dynamics remains, empirically and theoretically, a complex issue. We should also note that not all reception analysis studies depend on focus groups to gather their data. For example, Ang's (1985) study of Dutch viewers of *Dallas* used letters sent to her by fans of the show.

research, the selection is directed by the research topic, and the researchers focus on groups that are assumed to have strong and contrasting interests on the issue. Let us offer a concrete example. If you were concerned with analysing the 'gendered' reception and evaluation of media texts, and if you wanted to focus on cases where the reception process is itself associated with a specific gender of consumer, then the focus groups convened are likely to involve either exclusively male or exclusively female members. This is because research has shown that men tend to dominate conversations, and have different conceptions of the public and private divide from women (see Kramarae 1981; Fishman 1990; Tannen 1990; Cameron 1995). However, mixed gender groups could be chosen if you wanted to explore the ways in which the actual co-presence of people of the opposite gender affects media reception and response.

On other occasions, the researcher may simply seek to select a widely stratified range of groups according to a variety of social, cultural and economic factors. In many instances, group selection combines both these considerations.

Selection criteria have proved controversial among some reception analysts because of concerns that the design of the selection process may shape the nature of the conclusions reached. According to Wren-Lewis (1983), this process involves prejudging what the pertinent variables are behind decoding, which puts the cart before the horse. In his view, a more appropriate strategy would be to deduce the salient social variables 'after the fact', once you have looked at how individuals have responded of their own volition. However, such a strategy effectively rules out the use of focus groups and requires a complete reliance on individualised interviewing.

Another sampling issue with focus groups is whether you should use social and professional groups that already exist (pre-constituted groups), or create your own for research purposes (researcher-constituted). The advantages of pre-constituted groups are that they are more natural and participants may be comfortable in each other's company (Philo 1990: 223). The main advantage of researcher-constituted groups is that they give greater control over the composition of the sample.

Size is another issue that often arises in relation to focus group research. First, how many groups should you include in your study? The answer normally depends on your ultimate aims in conducting the research. If you are interested in 'going "wider" in analysis, embracing a broader range of variables and attempting to engage with these as far as possible as they occur in the settings of "everyday life"' (Corner 1996: 299), you are likely to need quite a few. However, if you interested in focusing around a particular issue or social group, 'to engage quite tightly with the interface of signification and comprehension' (ibid.), then the number required would be less. Additionally, you need to consider how many participants there should be in each group. In most cases, you would want to keep the numbers down, particularly when the groups are researcher-constituted and you need to minimise nervousness. However, you also want a sufficient number of people there to stimulate exchanges and debate. To strike a balance between these factors, the most common number of participants per group is between five and ten.

In Table 3.2, we summarise the sample strategies and design used in three reception studies, to illustrate how these, and other issues related to sampling, have been tackled in focus group research. The first is Schlesinger et al.'s (1992) *Women Viewing Violence*, which examined women's reactions to the representation of violent acts against women in films and programmes. The second is Corner et al.'s (1990) *Nuclear Reactions*, which analysed the responses of people from different political and social interest groups to documentary, PR and campaign material concerning the issue of nuclear power. The final study is Philo and Berry's (2004) *Bad News from Israel*, which examined links between general public understanding of the Israeli–Palestinian conflict and its coverage in mainstream news.

Table 3.2 Comparison of sampling strategies in three focus group audience studies

Project	*Women Viewing Violence* (1992)	*Nuclear Reactions* (1990)[3]	*Bad News from Israel* (2004)
Authors	Schlesinger, P., Dobash, R.E., Dobash, R.P. and Weaver, C.	Corner, J., Richardson, K. and Fenton, N.	Philo, G. and Berry, M.
Research issue	'Many women live lives in which they are subjected to physical and sexual abuse by their male partners or face the risk of such abuse by strangers, and most women watch members of their sex being similarly abused, at times, on television. What do they think about this? And are those reactions different for women who have actually lived through the real experience of violence than for those who have not?' (p. 1)	'[T]o explore some of the ways in which television, and then viewers, "made sense" of the nuclear energy issue during a period when public awareness of the topic had dramatically increased' (p. 1)	'We have shown the patterns of exclusion which exist in news coverage and the manner in which some perspectives on the conflict are dominant. We will now explore the possible links between these structures in news content and the nature of audience belief. This will cover issues such as the role of visual imagery and how the inclusion or exclusion of different types of explanation may influence audience understanding' (p. 200)
Number of focus groups/ participants	• 14 groups • 91 participants (all women)	• 12 groups • 65 participants (gender mix)	• 14 groups • 100 participants (gender mix)
Average group size (figure rounded)	6	5	7

3 The figures presented in this column are estimates, based on the limited sampling details made available in the book.

Focus group origins	Researcher-constituted	8 pre-constituted/4 researcher-constituted	pre-constituted
Media texts focused on	• *Crimewatch UK* (BBC One documentary programme that includes dramatised reconstructions of actual crimes. The episode chosen included a section on the murder of a woman.) • *EastEnders* (BBC One soap opera. The episode chosen included scenes of a man being violent towards one of the central female characters.) • *Closing Ranks* (ITV police drama. A dramatised account of the covering up of domestic violence committed by a male police officer.) • *The Accused* (Hollywood film examining the group-rape of a woman, and the trial and prosecution of the men responsible.)	• *Uncertain Legacy* (BBC Two documentary exploring the health and waste disposal issues related to the nuclear industry.) • *From Our Own Correspondent* (Dramatisation in documentary form produced by antinuclear activists highlighting the consequences of a radiation leak in the UK.) • *Energy – the Nuclear Option* (Promotional video produced by the nuclear industry.) • *A Life or a Living?* (BBC documentary examining incidences of child leukaemia near nuclear power stations.)	• A phrase from BBC One news was presented to groups of participants ('the settlers who have made their homes in occupied territory' 1/2/01). They were then asked a series of questions designed to assess their understanding of whose territory is under occupation. • Group members were invited to write dummy news stories based on 16 images from TV news of the Israeli–Palestinian conflict.
Factors considered in the stratification of groups	• Experience of sexual/domestic violence (yes/no) • Geographic location (Scotland/England) • Ethnicity (White, Asian, Afro-Caribbean) • Class (middle class, working class)	• Party political orientation (Labour/Conservative/SLD) • Proximity to the nuclear power issue (through campaigning or employment) • Social class • Professional status • Gender	• Income/social class • Age • Gender
Nature of stratification	Highly structured. The organisation of the groups closely resembled the procedures used in designing quota-sample categories. However, sample recruitment	Relatively unstructured. The sample selection blends the identification of 'interest groups' likely to have very firm opinions about the nuclear industry (e.g. workers employed in	Relatively structured. The sampling did not target communities or groups with a special interest in the Israeli–Palestinian conflict. Rather, the aim was to assess knowledge

	difficulties in gaining access to a sufficient number of women who had experienced violence and from some ethnic communities meant that quota-sampling 'logic' could not be applied completely. (If it had been, the inclusion of the four stratification variables would have generated 32 groups.)	the industry and Friends of the Earth campaigners), with pre-constituted groups that broadly and collectively range across the stratification variables identified above (e.g. groups from the local Rotary club, a women's discussion group, unemployed people from a trade union resource centre).	and attitudes in a sample that covered a wide cross section of UK society. Although the research team focused on 'normally occurring' groups, their nature and number reveal that stratification matters featured prominently in the sample design.
Other issues	A market research company was used to recruit the groups of women who had not experienced violence. The groups of women who had experienced violence were recruited via the researchers' personal contacts with women's aid organisations.	The inclusion of four researcher-constituted groups was due to the screening of the programme *A Life or a Living?* as the research was under way. The team felt it was such an interesting example of the mediation of the nuclear energy issue that they extended their sampling of members of the public to explore people's responses to it.	National journalists who have reported on the conflict were invited to participate in several of the focus group discussions.

There are several things worth noting from this comparison. The first is the different ways in which the research agenda of each study affected the selection of groups. In *Women Viewing Violence* and *Nuclear Reactions*, the groups were selected, at least in part, because of their proximity to the topic being investigated (women who had direct experience of sexual or domestic violence, and people who had either worked for, or campaigned against, the nuclear industry). In contrast, the selection of focus groups in *Bad News from Israel* was independent of the research topic. Instead, the groups were selected to match broadly socio-economic variation across the UK. (Although social and economic stratification was present in the first two studies' samples, this factor coexisted with the research-driven selection criteria.)

We can also note the different ways each study built social stratification into its sampling, and how these draw on sample strategies previously discussed. The *Women Viewing Violence* study closely approximates the procedures involved in quota sampling (Schlesinger et al. 1992: 26), albeit not precisely. Not every variation that would occur when linking four sampling factors was covered,[4] and the number of participants in each group was not weighted to mirror actual distributions of these groups in the population. Significantly, this is also the only study that was more or less solely dependent on researcher-constituted discussion groups,[5] which allowed the researchers to balance the composition of their groups precisely. There are also aspects of the sampling strategy that closely approximate snowball-sampling procedures. This involved the gathering of the groups of women who had experienced sexual or domestic violence, who were all approached via women's aid groups.

In contrast, the *Nuclear Reactions* study stratified groups more informally, by sampling mainly pre-constituted 'interest groups', defined in relation to several factors (e.g. known involvement in the nuclear energy debate, party political stance, professional status). In this respect, the sample selection bears quite a resemblance to the strategies used in theoretical sampling, which, as we have seen, strive to maximise the variation of the participants or cases involved. Such a comparison is further supported by the fact that the research team tagged on four further groups at the end, to explore responses to a programme that was broadcast as the research was in progress.

Summary: key points

- The distinction between samples and populations was explained, and three issues were identified that apply to all forms of sampling: sample error, sample size and non-response.

- The differences between random sampling and non-random sampling were identified. The issues involved in defining a population and identifying a sampling frame were discussed.

- The main forms of random sampling were set out, with examples given for each: simple random sampling, systematic random sampling, stratified random sampling, cluster sampling and multi-stage cluster sampling.

- The main forms of non-random sampling were discussed, beginning with quota sampling. It was explained that this method was atypical of other forms of non-random sampling, in that it shared similar concerns to random sampling procedures regarding sample representativeness.

4　Among the groups representing 'women with experience of violence', no distinction was drawn in relation to social class. Social class distinctions were also not made for the ethnic minority groups selected to represent 'women with no experience of violence'. Finally, there were no 'Afro-Caribbean women' groups selected for Scotland. These omissions were due to the extreme, possibly insurmountable, logistical difficulties that would have been created in attempting to cover all 32 possible quota categories. As it was, '[e]fforts to form the fourteen viewing groups proved to be one of the most time-consuming and difficult aspects of the research' (Schlesinger et al. 1992: 25).

5　The main exception to this came with the group of Scottish Asian women who had no experience of sexual or domestic violence. These participants effectively became a pre-constituted group because they 'were only willing to participate alongside other members of their families, considering themselves safe if they were with other women with whom they felt familiar' (Schlesinger et al. 1992: 207).

- Examples of sampling strategies used in qualitative research were provided: theoretical sampling, snowball sampling, typical-case sampling, critical-case sampling and convenience sampling.

- The discussion of these other non-random sampling methods highlighted how sampling issues in more intensive, interpretive research tend to depart from formal concerns about sample representativeness, and are more concerned with the illustration of social processes and dynamics.

- Sampling issues involved in focus group research were examined.

chapter four

Asking Questions

Introduction

In the most general sense, all research asks questions. How many hours' television on average do children watch per week? What are the 'taken for granted' assumptions used by social actors when engaging in particular personal, social and professional interactions? Does newspaper readership have any impact on voting behaviour? Is Buffy the Vampire Slayer a subversive cultural revolutionary?

If all research is underwritten by questions, however, not all researchers seek answers by asking them directly. Much research involves seeking circumstantial evidence: drawing conclusions on the basis of what people say and do in other contexts, and for other reasons. Sometimes this is because circumstantial evidence is the only information obtainable. For obvious reasons, historians of nineteenth-century journalism cannot interrogate their research subjects directly. Unfortunately, neither can many researchers investigating contemporary matters, whether because of the sensitivity of their research topic or the inaccessibility of their research subjects. (For example, if you are ever interested in investigating the corporate priorities of News Corporation, you would be far better advised to head for a good library than to bother asking Rupert Murdoch for a personal interview.) On other occasions, circumstantial evidence is preferred because it is felt to be more revealing and reliable, perhaps because research subjects are not willing or able to provide clear, accurate or honest answers.

This chapter is concerned with research techniques that do involve asking people directly about their activities and their views – to extend the detective terminology, what could be labelled 'interrogation' strategies. However, although giving a straight answer to a straight question is considered a social virtue, asking and answering questions is rarely, if ever, a straightforward matter. No question is asked in a social vacuum. Sometimes people give answers they think the interrogator would like to hear, that they believe are socially acceptable or that they wish were the case. Other times they tell the truth (or at least their perception of it). For all these reasons, all answers need to be appraised carefully, and occasionally taken with a pinch of salt.

Furthermore, researchers frequently ask questions with hidden motives. For example, a journalist might be asked about what it was that made her see a specific story as being particularly newsworthy, in the hope that her answer will provide insights into the general news values that underwrite the news-selection processes of her organisation.

Once you start to read between the lines of people's answers – whether to test their integrity or to draw conclusions about other issues – the difference between 'circumstantial' and 'interrogative' evidence starts to decrease. Also, many researchers, like detectives, use them in tandem, both to evaluate truth claims ('you are lying and we can prove it') and to search for explanations and insights into observed phenomena ('why did you do it?').

Questioning styles

Approaches to questioning in social research range from highly structured and standardised to highly non-structured and non-standardised. With structured questioning, the aim is to limit the influence of human factors on the data-collection process, such as the subtle ways in which the rewording, reordering or elaboration of questions may affect people's responses. Where interviewers are involved, strict rules are set down about how questions are asked and in what order, in an attempt to standardise and neutralise the questioning process, and thereby increase the basis for aggregating and comparing people's answers. It is rather like the doctor who uses a sterilised syringe when taking a blood sample for testing. Apart from protecting the donor from infection, the sterilisation of the needle ensures the sample is not contaminated in the collection process.

In contrast, informal questioning techniques are intended to encourage interactive dialogue with interviewees that conforms to the normal conventions of conversation. This sort of questioning 'takes on the form and feel of talk between peers: loose, informal, coequal, interactive, committed, open ended, and empathic' (Lindlof 1995: 164). As we discuss below, these interactions can be directive or non-directive, but advocates of these informal methods argue that this organic and responsive approach is essential to generate deeper insights into subtle and complex perceptions and beliefs.

Question delivery

Questions in research are delivered in a number of ways, and the options have increased since the arrival of the Internet and email. These delivery methods interlink with the differences in questioning styles mentioned above (see Figure 4.1).

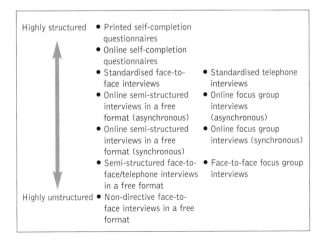

Figure 4.1 Methods for delivering questions

Printed self-completion questionnaires

As the name suggests, these are printed documents that people complete on their own. This method is the most structured form of questioning because no intermediary is involved in presenting the questions or recording answers.

Online self-completion questionnaires

Online self-completion questionnaires are delivered, completed and returned via email or the Internet (see Figure 4.2). These are administered in three main ways:

1. Respondents are invited to respond to questions written in the content of an email.
2. Respondents are invited to open an attached document, which they complete and return by reattaching it to the reply email.
3. Respondents access a website and complete the questionnaire at the web address. There is an increasing amount of software available for purchase online that guides you through designing and posting a web questionnaire.

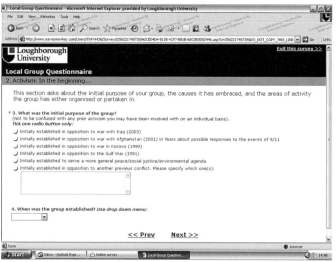

Figure 4.2 An example of an online self-completion survey (part of a survey of antiwar protest groups conducted by Ian Taylor, Department of Social Sciences, Loughborough University, January–May 2006)
Ian Taylor, Loughborough University. Screengrab provided by authors

According to Gunter et al., these new forms of questionnaire delivery should not be seen as directly equivalent to conventional, offline questionnaires. As they note:

> While electronic surveys require respondents to work through the questionnaire by themselves as with the standard self-completion paper instrument, the interactive element of the electronic survey meant that it also had something in common with face-to-face interviews in which respondents interact with the source of questions.

(Gunter et al. 2002: 234)

Standardised face-to-face interviews

Face-to-face **standardised interviews** are less structured than offline and online self-completion questionnaires because interviewers are involved in their implementation. This can bring additional benefits (see below), but it introduces greater uncertainty and variation into the questioning process. To control the impact of 'interviewer bias', strict protocols are developed to govern all aspects of the interview process. First, interviewers work with formal **interview schedules** that resemble the structure of a self-completion questionnaire. They are required to repeat question wording exactly and to observe the order in which the questions are listed. Second, where interviewers need to clarify an answer or push for further information, they are expected to do so in a standardised and neutralised way, using **prompts**.[1] Third, standardised protocols are set out for interviewer conduct in the pre-interview period, stating what should be said to people when asking for their assistance with the research.

Telephone interviews

Although telephone interviews can be structured or unstructured, they are more suited to standardised interviewing procedures, because of the pressures imposed by the mode of delivery. With telephone interviews you cannot gauge a person's reactions through visual clues, and it is often difficult to establish a relaxed rapport with a distant and disembodied voice.

A recent variation in the use of telephones and computers in asking questions is the 'touch-tone' survey. This is where respondents answer a set of pre-recorded questions by selecting options using the numbers on their telephone keypad.

Semi-structured face-to-face interviews in a free format

Face-to-face **semi-structured interviews** abandon concern with standardisation and control, and seek to promote an active, open-ended dialogue with interviewees. Although it bears some resemblance to an everyday conversation, the semi-structured interview does not conform to all the conventions of such a conversation: the interviewer retains control of the terms of the discussion, whereas in 'natural' conversation this would normally fluctuate between participants. The interviewer controls the discussion by referring to an **interview guide**, which sets out the issues to be covered during the exchange. This is why Lindlof (1995: 164) suggests that these sorts of interviews are better described as 'conversations *with a purpose*' (emphasis added).

Face-to-face focus groups/group interviews

As discussed in chapter 3, face-to-face focus groups and group interviews are interviews where questions are delivered on a group, rather than an individual, basis. The distinction between focus groups and group interviews is one of degree. In the former, discussions concentrate around a clear issue or object (e.g. a new product, a policy issue or a series of

---

1   For example, one strategy is to allow a pause to develop to indicate that more information is needed. Another is to use passive questions, such as, 'Could you explain in more detail what you mean by that?'

media texts); in the latter, discussions are still directive, but more wide-ranging. Interview groups in both categories can be either 'researcher-constituted' (i.e. brought together by the researcher) or 'pre-constituted' (a naturally occurring social group).

Apart from their collective nature, face-to-face focus groups and group interviews closely resemble semi-structured individual interviews in a free format. The interviewer works from a predetermined interview guide, but also encourages an open and creative dialogue with group participants.

Non-directive face-to-face interviewing in a free format

With non-directive face-to-face interviewing, it is the interviewee who dictates the form and direction of the exchange, essentially following the train of their thoughts. The interviewer plays the role of 'sympathetic observer or sounding board and "interprets" the material presented by the respondent' (Angold 2002: 32). This free-association interviewing is not widely employed in social research.

Semi-structured online interviews and group interviews in a free format (synchronous and asynchronous)

To date, the Internet and email have been used mainly for asking structured questions. However, interest is growing in using these forms of communication for qualitative questioning, both in one-to-one and group format interviews. We have grouped our discussion of individual and group online interviews (synchronous and asynchronous) here, and considered them out of sequence with that presented in the continuum in Figure 4.1, because these new modes of questioning share methodological features and implications.

Unstructured online questioning can be conducted in real time and is referred to as *synchronous* interviewing. This method requires conferencing software in which all participants are 'present' online simultaneously and interact through their typed exchanges. *Asynchronous* online interviewing involves the interviewer dispatching questions to individuals or group members and then experiencing a time lag before receiving their responses (email can be used for this type of interviewing). The time delay in these interactions, which permits participants to ponder and finesse their answers, means that they have a more structured quality than synchronous online questioning, which requires immediate thoughts and responses. (This explains why asynchronous online qualitative questioning is placed closer to the centre of the structured/unstructured continuum set out in Figure 4.1.)

Strengths and weaknesses of delivery methods

All these methods of asking questions have benefits and limitations. Rather than listing them method by method, which can make for very repetitive reading, we discuss them in relation to seven broad themes that concern all forms of research questioning.

Convenience

Non-face-to-face questioning is the most convenient and cost-effective means for questioning large and/or geographically dispersed populations. For example, if you selected a random sample of 2,000 adults in New Zealand for a newspaper readership survey, it would be far easier either to mail a questionnaire or phone people directly than to traipse backwards and forwards between North and South Islands.

Self-completion questionnaires have a greater potential reach than telephone interviews, as not everybody has access to a telephone. However, telephone interviews score highly in relation to speed of delivery, as they are not affected by the exigencies of the mail or travel networks, and provide a modicum of personal contact with the research subjects.

There has been considerable interest in the benefits and drawbacks of asking questions online, in comparison with more established modes of questioning (e.g. Hudson et al. 2004; Knapp and Kirk 2003; Huang 2004). Both structured and unstructured questioning via email and the Internet score well in convenience terms, as there are none of the costs involved in mailing questionnaires or conducting surveys by telephone. Furthermore, they offer benefits in data collection. Online survey software allows for the automated coding of survey results, thereby eliminating the need to process and enter data into computer software (Dominelli 2003), while in qualitative online questioning, interviewees' responses are already rendered as written text. However, there can be problems with 'abandonment' in Internet and email surveys, where respondents stop completing the questionnaire halfway. This is because completion of the research task has to be done online, and frequently at one sitting, which can prove inconvenient and tiresome for respondents (ibid.: 413). Abandonment can also be a problem with synchronous and asynchronous online qualitative questioning (Bryman 2004).

Standardised face-to-face interviews are more straightforward to conduct than free-format interviewing because the tight and controlled structure of the questioning and recording of answers means they tend to take less time and can be held in a wide range of contexts. In contrast, face-to-face free-format interviews work best when interviewees are placed in a comfortable (and comforting) environment, and are given adequate time to elaborate on their views. You should not try to conduct this sort of interview in the middle of a shopping precinct on a Saturday afternoon!

Face-to-face focus groups are perhaps the most demanding of all to arrange. Leaving aside the challenges involved in constructing a sample (see chapter 3), this method accentuates the challenges of individual, semi-structured interviewing. Instead of putting a single person at their ease, you have to allow a group of people to relax, and finding a convenient time and place for all participants often requires considerable planning. Online group interviews, by comparison, allow people to participate from the comfort of their own private or professional environments. Synchronous online interviews still require groups to be convened online at the same time, but asynchronous group interviews allow the participants some freedom to choose the timing and manner of their responses.

Comprehension

For obvious reasons, it is essential to ask questions in terms that people can understand. However, comprehensibility is not always easy to gauge at the outset. In this regard, less structured questioning techniques hold a significant advantage over other forms. They give the interviewer freedom to elaborate and rephrase questions to ensure they have been properly understood. In particular, less structured methods allow the interviewer to tailor the phrasing of questions to specific contexts, whereas with structured questioning the questions have to be 'all things to all people': as readily understood by the least educated and sophisticated respondent as by the most capable.

In a comparison of Internet and telephone survey responses, Fricker et al. (2005) found that web respondents were more likely to answer knowledge questions correctly than those questioned by telephone. They concluded: 'We suspect that the knowledge questions were generally easier when they were presented visually and when respondents could answer them at their own pace' (Fricker et al. 2005: 391). Furthermore, Internet-based questionnaires allow the introduction of 'skip logic' into the questioning process, directing respondents only to those questions that are relevant to them (Huang 2004: 337). This removes the need for routing instructions, which can improve the usability and comprehensibility of a questionnaire.

Because of the particular dangers surrounding comprehension that confront all pre-structured questioning, pre-testing (or **piloting**) your questionnaire or interview schedule is very important. This can help to identify (and allow you to rectify) any problems with terminology or design before deciding on a final version. Also, where qualitative interviewing is involved, piloting can help you develop your interviewing skills. Like the interview itself, **pilot interviews** should be recorded, and you should listen to them critically to see how you might be able to improve your questions or manner of questioning. You could also ask a friend or colleague to sit in on a pilot interview and offer feedback about what you ask and how you handle the interviewing situation. (See Mason 1996: 42–51 for more on planning qualitative interviewing.)

Rapport and response

All questioning in research depends on winning and maintaining consent. Although the questioner may have a degree of control in terms of the issues that are raised in the process, she or he is not the most powerful participant in the exchange. Unlike a prosecuting counsel in a court of law, researchers cannot compel people to answer the question and threaten them with dire consequences should they answer untruthfully. They have to persuade people to cooperate by convincing them of the value of their contribution and of the research as a whole. In other words, getting people to cooperate and respond depends on building rapport.

In this respect, self-completion questionnaires are disadvantaged. The absence of personal contact limits the opportunities to persuade people to participate (it is easier to ignore an envelope or an invitation to a web address than a person), and for this reason self-completion questionnaire surveys generally attract lower response rates than personal interview surveys. When using the offline version of this method, you need to think carefully of ways to maximise the chances of getting people to complete the questionnaire and return it. These range from observing the simple courtesy of arranging or paying for their return,[2] to providing a brief and courteous covering letter that explains the purpose

---

2   According to Moser and Kalton (1971: 265), putting stamps on a return envelope rather than reply-paid or FREEPOST labels can enhance response rates – on the one hand, because people are reluctant to throw them away, and on the other because they are uneasy about the ethics of using them for other purposes. Consequently, completing and returning the questionnaire is seen as the easiest option.

of the research, its origins and why the person's cooperation is needed.

With regard to online questioning of all kinds, several issues have been raised about the impact this type of questioning has on establishing rapport and maintaining response. The most obvious problem is that there is no universal access to computers and the Internet, which means that online research marginalises the older and less affluent sections of society who have least access to these technologies (Bryman 2004). But there are further rapport and response issues to consider in relation to this mode of questioning, which often result in lower response rates than those found for face-to-face questioning (Gunter et al. 2002: 233).

There can be difficulties in convincing respondents of the legitimacy and integrity of online research. Dominelli (2003: 414) points out that whereas traditional mail questionnaires can be supported by official letterheads and personal signatures to 'verify the legitimacy of the sponsors', the web equivalent cannot provide 'hard copy authentication'. One solution she suggests is to ensure that hyperlinks to the survey authors and sponsors are prominently displayed for the further reference of the respondents. There is a related problem that respondents may not take online surveys as seriously as their offline equivalents. Just as Internet content can be dismissed as 'cheap talk', so the ease of organising an Internet survey may make it seem more frivolous and trivial. This problem is particularly evident with surveys administered via email, which can be ignored as spam. Polite reminders and re-mailings to non-responders are essential for all types of structured questioning, but are particularly important for Internet surveys. Respondents may also have concerns about the confidentiality of any information they provide in digital format, and it is important to address these directly on the opening web page and to provide guarantees about confidentiality and anonymity.

With standardised face-to-face interviews, the personal persuasiveness of the interviewer can enhance the motivation of people to participate fully in the research (which tends to be reflected in response rates). However, there is always a risk that the artificially rigid and formal structure of these exchanges may undermine rapport during the interaction, because respondents have little opportunity to elaborate and challenge the terms of the interview schedule. For this reason, it is better to keep these sorts of interviews brief and businesslike, as the formality of the questioning soon becomes tedious and irritating for respondents.

With less structured face-to-face interviewing, the risk of alienating people by overdetermining the nature and form of their responses is reduced. But new threats to rapport can emerge as a consequence of the more informal structure. For example, by opening up the opportunities for people to develop the terms of their own response, less self-confident or loquacious interviewees may feel intimidated by the expectations that are placed on them. In a group interview context, this can lead to their marginalisation or silencing in the discussions. In a face-to-face interview, it may lead to the interviewee becoming hesitant and monosyllabic, which can make the interview increasingly awkward for both interviewer and interviewee.

Depth

The more structured and formalised questions are, the greater the need for clarity and concision. (A 55-page unsolicited questionnaire will generally be heading straight for the recycling bin.) However, the need for economy in the presentation of the questions and the recording of responses militates against detailed and deeper exploration of the issues raised by people's answers.

Free-format questioning generates richer data. Interviewees articulate their thoughts and opinions on their own terms rather than in relation to preordained response structures, which means they are better suited for exploring and understanding complex and sensitive social and personal issues. Of course, you may not always be interested in this deeper analysis. For example, you may just want to establish the number of final-year graduate students who watch low-budget Australian soap operas on a regular basis, rather than examine the ironic readings they may derive from these programmes.

In the previous section, we noted that online questioning seems to affect the *level* of response detrimentally. There is also evidence that it has an effect on the quality of responses, although the impact varies according to the mode of questioning adopted. In terms of structured online questioning, research suggests that people are more forthcoming in providing socially sensitive information via these means, leading to speculation that the impersonality of this type of questioning makes respondents feel less inhibited (e.g. Paperny et al. 1990; Kiesler and Sproull 1986; Moon 1998). It has also been claimed that Internet surveys may reduce the tendency for respondents to engage in 'socially desirable responding compared to interviewer administered surveys' (Gunter et al. 2002: 235). Gunter et al. note that online structured questionnaires tend to generate richer and more detailed responses to open-ended questions than their printed equivalents (i.e. questions where respondents are requested to provide an answer to a set question in their own words). This is because respondents have more opportunity to consider, edit and articulate their answers.

The situation with unstructured online questioning, however, is different. When the written word is the sole mode of response, as is the case in unstructured online interviewing, the depth and detail of people's responses can be affected detrimentally. Bryman (2004) identifies several reasons for this. The lack of direct personal contact between interviewer and interviewee makes establishing and maintaining rapport more difficult. The need for interviewees to type their responses places greater intellectual and time demands on them, and in doing so privileges the articulate, the literate and those with developed keyboard skills. (This is particularly the case with synchronous online interviewing, which demands real-time responses.) There is an unavoidable loss in the quantity and spontaneity of the qualitative data generated by these means, because people speak more freely and easily than they write, and speaking provides less opportunity for reflection, review and refinement.

Control and comparison

As we have noted, the key rationale behind all forms of structured questioning is that of control. It is argued that by standardising the phrasing and delivery of questions to respondents, you have a firmer basis for aggregating and comparing people's answers.

Different means of structured questioning provide different levels of control over question delivery. Because printed self-completion questionnaires cut out the middle man (or woman), a researcher can be more or less confident that their respondents have received identical questions. This removes the possibility that their responses are affected by question rephrasing or the social dynamics of the interview process. However, the absence of a person delivering the questions means the researcher has no control over the order in which questions are answered. Respondents can review the entirety of the document before answering any questions. Furthermore, where such questionnaires are filled in outside of a controlled research environment, there can be no guarantee that they are completed by the people they were sent to. This may compromise the accuracy of the sample selection. The latter problem also applies to online surveys, but there is more opportunity to control the ordering and flow of questions with web surveys, as you can specify that respondents are able to move on from a question only when they have provided a full response.

Face-to-face standardised interviewing does deliver greater control on question ordering and respondent participation, but threatens loss of control in other areas. The presence of an interviewer raises the spectre of **interviewer bias**. This can take several forms: from encouraging certain types of responses, to the inaccurate recording of answers, to the complete falsification of interview results. (This last issue is likely to be of concern only if you are getting other people to conduct interviews on your behalf.) Although the development and observance of strict protocols for the questioning process can help to control interviewer bias, they do not guarantee its absence.

As a general rule, the more non-standardised and informal the interviewing procedures, the greater the intervening presence of the interviewer. Moreover, the non-standardised nature of the delivery and responses intensifies questions about the validity of comparisons. Although some would argue that any attempt to neutralise the presence of the interviewer through rigid standardisation is doomed from the outset, formal interviews do provide a clearly thought-out foundation for cross-interview aggregation.

Elaboration and digression

Structured questioning formats deliver answers only to the questions you ask. They are not 'fishing' methods that allow you to trawl around for new issues. You need to be clear from the outset what you want to ask and why, as well as how best to phrase your requests for information. Informal questioning methods do not impose this restriction, although the more directive forms do require you to have a clear initial research agenda. Their informality makes them more responsive and flexible, and permits the researcher to adjust and develop their interview schedule to accommodate and explore any new issues that arise.

This sort of inductive process can be valuable, particularly when investigating complex and uncharted areas. However, there are dangers that too much elaboration of the initial research agenda can lead to a digression in the research aims. Interviewees might spend so much time talking about the things that interest and concern them that they never adequately address the issues that concern the researcher.

Demands on the researcher

Self-completion questionnaires make least demands on the personal and social skills of the researcher, as they do not depend on any active social interaction. With standardised interviews, social and personal pressures start to emerge, but the structure and purpose of the interview schedule mean these remain modest, as it is clear from the outset exactly what needs to be said, and when.

Less structured questioning makes the greatest demands of the interviewer. Effective face-to-face informal interviewing requires good listening skills, self-confidence, empathy and good humour. The interviewer needs to put people at their ease and to encourage them to air their opinions. But she or he needs to retain a sense of the purpose of the exchange, by applying the interview guide in a sensitive and creative way. This frequently involves dealing with issues as they arise in the course of the interview, rather than doggedly working through a checklist of things to discuss. People do not tend to answer in neat, linear ways: they often make conceptual leaps, return to issues already covered or digress from the matter at hand. When conducting these interviews, you need to be able to go with the flow, and not be disconcerted if your interviewee starts discussing an issue that you intended to address later on. The skill is to give people freedom to develop their thoughts, and in the order they want, while retaining a sense of the purpose and framework of the research. Bryman (2004) notes that these pressures are also evident in unstructured online questioning, particularly synchronous questioning.

Final comments on question delivery

Our reason for highlighting the various strengths and weaknesses of these different forms of questioning is not to advocate the use of one above others, but rather to show that no method can claim to be universally applicable and completely infallible. Your choice should be governed by the objectives of your research and by what is practicable. If you are interested in gaining a deeper understanding of a complex or sensitive social phenomenon, such as a person's sense of their sexual identity, a short self-completion questionnaire would probably be unsuitable. If, on the other hand, you are interested in establishing their favourite television programme, there is every chance that such a method would complete the task adequately.

It is also worthwhile thinking how formal and informal interviewing can be used in tandem, where the weaknesses of one method are traded off against the strengths of another. An interesting example of the combination of structured and unstructured methods is offered in Livingstone, Wober and Lunt's (1994) research into audience reception and audience participation in TV talk shows (e.g. *The Oprah Winfrey Show*, *Kilroy*, *The Phil Donahue Show*). In the first stage, a series of focus group interviews was conducted in conjunction with a textual analysis to explore the complex relations between 'reader, text and context' in this genre (ibid.: 376; Livingstone and Lunt 1994). These were followed up by a survey of a random, representative sample of 3,000 adults, who were asked to fill in a self-completion questionnaire that inquired about their viewing of, and views about, these TV talk shows.

Three points about this research are germane to our discussion here. First, the results of the focus discussions directly informed the design of the questionnaire: insights derived from unstructured questioning provided guidance for subsequent structured questioning. Second, the aim of the second, more extensive phase of the research was intended to test the general applicability and representativeness of the initial conclusions. This was because, in the authors' view, questions about the generalisability of findings from small-scale qualitative reception studies were a matter that had 'largely been avoided' in previous focus group-based studies (Livingstone, Wober and Lunt 1994: 376). Third, although these different methods produced many *complementary* insights into audience perspectives about TV talk shows, in some areas they generated unique perspectives. On the one hand, 'the focus group interviews identified more complex connections between text and reception, [and] identified contradictions within audience readings' (ibid.). On the other hand, the self-completion questionnaire survey 'highlighted what had been missed in the focus group analysis, namely, the importance of the viewers' age compared to, say, gender or social class' (ibid.).

Types of questions

Questions are used in research to gather information about a variety of different things. According to Dilman (1978), these can be grouped under four headings:

1. *Behaviour:* what people do (e.g. 'What newspaper do you read most regularly?').
2. *Beliefs:* what people believe to be the case (e.g. 'Do you detect any bias in the political coverage in the newspaper you read most regularly?').
3. *Attitudes:* what people would prefer to be the case (e.g. 'Would you support new legislation to regulate press reporting of matters involving people's private lives?').
4. *Attributes:* background information about the respondent's characteristics (e.g. 'What is your age?').

Questions about behaviour

You might assume that these questions are the most straightforward to ask as they concern the empirical reality of what people *do*, rather than the more intangible matter of what it is they *think*. To some extent this is a legitimate assumption, and it is widely accepted that these questions are less susceptible to influence by question phrasing and interviewer bias than other forms. But even these questions are affected by broader social dynamics: certain types of behaviour are deemed more socially desirable than others, and respondents may feel reluctant, consciously or unconsciously, to admit how far short they may fall of perceived social expectations (Sudman and Bradburn 1983). Take, for example, the apparently innocuous question, 'How many books do you read on average per month?' Because being 'widely read' is generally perceived to indicate a person's education, intelligence and discernment, some respondents may be tempted to overestimate the extent of their book reading. These sorts of aspirational impulses do not always correspond to widely accepted societal standards. They can often reflect values within subcultures and smaller social groups. For example, in a group interview context, 13-year-old boys might deliberately underestimate the extent of their reading to avoid seeming boring and bookish in front of their mates.

Another problem that can occur with behavioural questions is the matter of recall. People sometimes experience difficulties in recalling accurately aspects of their past behaviour, particularly routine or trivial forms of behaviour that happened quite a long time ago. For example, research has shown consistently that people are very poor at judging how much television they watch. Although this may partly reflect their wish not to be seen as couch-based TV addicts, it also reflects the fact that much television viewing is so habitualised that it is difficult to recall.

One final problematic area is in asking behavioural questions that respondents may find threatening. For example, if you asked a sample of adults, 'Have you ever failed to declare a source of income to the tax office?', your results might suggest impressive levels of fiscal probity, but there would be obvious questions about their accuracy. Income tax evasion is, after all, a serious matter, and tax inspectors, rightly or wrongly, are commonly seen as a devious bunch.

These factors mean that the behavioural questions most likely to produce accurate and 'honest' answers are those that deal with recent, non-threatening, non-trivial matters, and which offer no obvious incentive for the respondents to exaggerate or underplay their response.

Questions about beliefs and attitudes

Questions about beliefs and attitudes are also affected by the social factors outlined above (i.e. social desirability, periodicity and perceived threat). Additionally, these questions are the most sensitive to influence by the research process itself: question phrasing or interviewer prompting might encourage the adoption of certain stances by respondents. The mere act of asking a question may have an 'agenda-setting' effect. Not everybody has a developed opinion on everything, but if asked about issues in which they have little interest or knowledge, respondents may feel obliged to improvise viewpoints, whether because they feel they are expected to or because they do not wish to appear ignorant.

For these reasons, you need to be careful when asking these types of questions. In particular, you need to recognise that respondents are most suggestible when asked to comment on what agenda-setting researchers term 'high threshold issues' (Lang and Lang 1981) – matters that appear remote from respondents' immediate social, political or cultural concerns. With these kinds of issues, 'no opinion' or 'no attitudes' responses are legitimate and understandable, and people should not be made to feel uncomfortable about adopting them. That said, you do not want to make them too comfortable about sitting on the fence. High levels of noncommittal response can undermine the purpose of asking the question in the first place.

Another matter that needs consideration when asking these questions is how best to capture the complex, multifaceted and even subliminal dimensions of people's attitudes and beliefs. Single, blunt questions rarely succeed. Imagine you wanted to investigate racial prejudice among news professionals. A simple, straightforward question, such as 'Do you consider yourself to be a racist?' would probably produce a reassuringly large proportion of negative responses. However, if the same people were asked a suite of questions about their beliefs and attitudes on a range of issues pertaining to ethnicity (immigration levels, the size of indigenous ethnic minority communities, the legitimacy of equal opportunities and positive discrimination policies, etc.), their answers might suggest less sanguine conclusions about their antiracist credentials. This is because racism is not a simple 'yes/no' matter, but one of degree. Moreover, it is not always conscious: it often resides in people's taken-for-granted assumptions. Finally, few people will openly admit to being racist because, outside of fascist circles, it is not recognised as a socially desirable stance. This point is demonstrated by the number of times you hear people preface racist sentiments with statements like, 'I'm not racist, but…'

Questions about attributes

Questions about attributes (sometimes referred to as 'classification questions') are vital in that they allow the exploration of variations in responses across a sample. There is no standard list of attributes that is used; it depends on the concerns of each study. Nevertheless, there are several attributes that are routinely categorised when questioning people, such as 'age', 'gender', 'ethnicity' and 'occupation'.

It is important to be sensitive when asking for personal information. Although asking a person to identify their gender is unlikely to raise any objections, they may be more reluctant to tell you their exact age or their personal income. You should ask only for essential information: the longer the list of these questions, the more intrusive the exercise becomes. Also, do not request unnecessary detail. For example, if you want to place respondents in age categories for analytical purposes only, it is less intrusive to let the respondents indicate where they fall in the broad range of age categories, rather than asking them to provide their exact age.

It is also better to ask these questions at the end of the exchange. By this stage, people should be assured of the integrity of the research exercise and therefore more willing to provide the information. In contrast, a barrage of personal questions at the start of an exchange can appear threatening and invite suspicion, which can compromise the accuracy of the responses given and undermine the establishment of rapport. Where a sampling strategy demands that the exchange should begin with some attributional questions (i.e. quota sampling), these should be restricted solely to those needed to classify people in relation to the sample design. All other attributional questions should be left until the end.

Be careful not to give offence through the phrasing or direction of an attributional question (of course, this principle applies to all other forms of questions as well). Whereas 30 years ago an interviewer probably would have got away with asking a woman 'What is the occupation of the head of the household?', nowadays the same question is likely to invite considerable hostility, because of explicitly patronising (and implicitly patriarchal) assumptions. (See our discussion about the need to avoid racist and sexist language in chapter 15.)

Question ordering

Imagine you were at a social gathering and a complete stranger walked up to you and said 'Hello. Do you believe in God?' Unless you particularly enjoy talking to people with no social skills or small talk, your immediate reaction would be to start planning ways to terminate the conversation. However, had the person asked the same question after a relaxed, stimulating and wide-ranging conversation with you, it could seem perfectly acceptable. You might even be prepared to give an answer.

Although all forms of research questioning are artificial social interactions, they are not immune from the tacit conventions that guide everyday conversations and discussions. You should think very carefully about the ordering and presentation of questions, and wherever possible try to approximate the natural flow of conversation.

All questioning should be preceded by a brief and polite introduction, with the aim of reassuring respondents about the legitimacy of the research and their capability to deal with the questions you will ask. It is also a stage where you underline that their answers will be treated sensitively, discreetly and, where necessary, that their confidentiality will be respected. You should begin by asking questions that are general, unthreatening and easy for the respondents to answer. This will help to reassure them about the undemanding nature of the questioning, and allow them to relax into the interrogation. Always leave the more challenging, detailed or complex questions until later, as this is the period when respondents are most focused and committed to answering your questions, and when their recollections are likely to be at their most detailed and accurate. People do not conjure up all they know on a topic immediately; recollection occurs dynamically, and commonly depends on a process of association: remembering one thing stimulates the recall of others. When concluding your questioning, always thank people for their help and invite them to add any further comments they may feel are relevant.

Questions to avoid

From our discussion so far, we can see that there are certain strategies that can be adopted to maximise the amount and the accuracy of answers given to questions, as well as obvious pitfalls to avoid. In this section, we focus in more detail on the latter point, and provide a list of the sorts of obvious mistakes you should avoid when designing questions.

Ambiguous questions

Ambiguities can occur in questions as a result of several factors. A common problem is where the question is so generalised that it is difficult for people to know where to begin to answer it. Take, for example, a question that appears in a widely used questionnaire for classifying people's personality type: 'Generally, do you prefer reading to meeting people? – Yes/No'. As Heim observes, 'It is not just the intellectual who mutters into his beard "Depends on the book – depends on the people"' (quoted in Lodziak 1986: 17).

Ambiguity can also arise as a consequence of poor sentence structure, and the use of negatives and double negatives. Wherever possible, keep your questions crisp and short, and express them in a positive rather than a negative way (e.g. 'Do you purchase a newspaper at least three times a week?' is clearer than 'Do you not purchase a newspaper at least three times a week?').

Leading questions

In some respects, all questions are leading questions. They bring an issue to the attention of the respondent, and in that respect they are setting an agenda. However, some questions are more leading than others. By this we mean that the implicit assumptions in the phrasing of a question tend to encourage certain types of answers. For example, Karl Marx once designed a questionnaire to be sent to French socialists appraising their attitudes to their work and employers.[3] One of the questions he proposed was: 'Does your employer or his representative resort to trickery in order to defraud you of part of your earnings?' Clearly, the use of emotive and pejorative terms like 'trickery' and 'defraud' suggests a particular view of employee–employer relations, which would be likely to encourage certain sorts of responses.

Double questions

These are questions that ask two questions at the same time, and where more than one answer is possible. An obvious example would be: 'Do you watch the TV situation comedy *My Name Is Earl*, and how often?' This requires separating into two: 'Do you watch the TV sitcom *My Name Is Earl*?'; 'If yes, how often do you watch the programme?' Another, less readily identifiable example of a double question is: 'Have your parents gone to the cinema in the last month?' The answer to this could be 'yes' for Mum and 'no' for Dad.

Jargon and technical terms

In the rarefied atmosphere of academic life, it is easy to forget that a lot of concepts and terms that are freely bandied about in a tutorial group are anything but received knowledge in society as a whole. This is not to suggest that 'ordinary people' are unable to grasp the subtleties and complexities that they contain, but rather to point out that the specialist discourses of academia do not always have a wide social currency. You should therefore do people the courtesy of phrasing questions in terms that are meaningful to them. Do not inject 'thesis-talk' straight into your questions (e.g. 'How do you deconstruct *Desperate Housewives*?').

Emotive questions

Some issues are difficult to ask about on grounds of sensitivity or social desirability. Typically, the most sensitive things to ask people about are sexuality, personal relationships, money, conflict and illegal practices. When you are interested in these sorts of areas, you should avoid blunt, direct questioning (e.g. 'Which of the following illegal sexual practices have you engaged in?'), and think about how you might glean information on the matter through more indirect means (Barton 1958).

---

3   Thanks to Alan Bryman for this reference.

Hypothetical questions

'What if' is a game we all play on occasions, but it should not be a prominent strategy adopted when asking questions for research purposes. Hypothetical questions such as, 'What impact will the arrival of digital TV have on your viewing habits?', can glean only hypothetical answers. These are unreliable predictors of future behaviour or opinion, not because people lie, but because it is difficult for them to predict what their actions will be before an event occurs. As a general rule, you should stick to asking people about their current views and actions wherever possible.

Dealing with answers

People's answers to questions can be recorded through 'open' or 'closed' formats. Open formats are where the respondent articulates their answer in their own words. With closed-answer formats, the respondent is required to provide a response in terms of a predetermined set of possible answers. Some types of questioning rely entirely on open responses (e.g. informal interviews), and others solely utilise closed responses (this is a common feature of many self-completion questionnaires). However, many questionnaires and interview schedules incorporate both frames, to take advantage of the specific benefits of each and avoid their particular limitations.

Closed-response format

Advantages

There are several advantages to **closed-response formats**. These include:

- Closed responses do not discriminate against less articulate or communicative respondents.

- Closed responses are quicker to answer, which means more questions can be asked and there is less risk that people will be annoyed by excessive demands on their time and articulateness. (Too many open questions can prove particularly onerous with self-completion questionnaires, where answers have to be written down.)

- Closed responses are easier to code and analyse.

- Closed responses can enhance respondents' understanding of the purpose and meaning of a question by giving them some sense of what are acceptable types of response. Additionally, they can help to jog respondents' memories.

- In some instances, providing answers in a closed-response format can seem less threatening and intrusive to respondents.

Disadvantages

- Closed responses can disguise variations and qualifications in people's responses. Often important qualifications to answers are lost.

- Simplistic closed-response frameworks can irritate respondents and undermine rapport.
- Over-elaborate closed-response frameworks can prove confusing.
- Sometimes closed-response frameworks may prompt certain types of answers as a consequence of their structure.

These points do not necessarily apply to all closed questions on all occasions. For example, through careful piloting and design work, you can often avoid producing simplistic or unnecessarily complicated pre-coded response frameworks. Box 4.1 lists some of the more elaborate closed-response options that are used in social research.

Alongside these variations, there are three further points you must always bear in mind when using closed responses. First, when respondents are required to tick only one box, make sure that the categories do not overlap. Imagine you asked people to indicate their age according to the following categories: up to 20 years, 20–30, 30–40, 40–50, 50 years and above. This would create obvious confusion for all 20-, 30-, 40- and 50-year-old respondents, as they would all fit into two categories. Second, wherever appropriate, provide a 'don't know' response option. Although it may be disappointing to lose responses to this category, it is far better than forcing people into hazarding a guess or improvising an opinion. Third, wherever appropriate, provide an 'other' category. No matter how extensively you may have pre-tested your response options, there is always a chance that they omit some important alternatives. Fourth, when asking a series of questions about people's attitudes or beliefs, beware of 'yea-saying'. This is when all the questions have a similar direction, which, in turn, can encourage a uniform and undifferentiated response. For example, if you were using the semantic differential technique (see Box 4.1) and your 'polar adjectives' were organised in such a way that all the negative terms were on the left and the positive were on the right, a respondent might be tempted to score them in an identical way, without giving thought to the different issues they raise. To avoid this danger, it is a good idea to reverse the directions of the initial questions, so people need to answer them differently to retain a degree of consistency in their answers. This will encourage them to consider each question separately.

Box 4.1 Types of closed-response formats (adapted from de Vaus 1990; Moser and Kalton 1971)

Name	Description	Most commonly used to investigate
Rating scales (aka Likert scales)	These invite respondents to indicate the strength of their responses in relation to a scale. Typically, these are five-point scales (e.g. 'strongly agree', 'agree', 'neither agree nor disagree', 'disagree', 'strongly disagree').	• Attitudes • Beliefs

Responses can be analysed individually or in groups (the latter occurs when a researcher is using a variety of measures to assess some complex social or psychological issue).

Semantic differential formats	With this method, 'polar adjectives' are placed at opposite ends of a continuum, and respondents are asked to grade between the two extremes using a seven-point scale. (e.g. 'How would you describe political coverage in your newspaper?' Good 1 2 3 4 5 6 7 Bad False 1 2 3 4 5 6 7 True Balanced 1 2 3 4 5 6 7 Biased)	• Attitudes • Beliefs
Checklists	Lists of potentially relevant responses are provided and respondents are asked to indicate as many as are relevant. (e.g. 'Which of the following do you own?' Television/DVD/Personal computer)	• Behaviour • Attributes • Attitudes • Beliefs
Ranking formats	A set of items is presented to respondents, who are asked to rank them in order of importance. (e.g. 'What features of your newspaper do you value most?' Place 1 for 'most valued', 2 for 'second most valued', 3 for 'third most valued' [etc.])	• Attitudes • Beliefs
Choosing attitude statements	Here, a list of contrasting attitudes are ranged from very negative to very positive, and respondents are asked to indicate which attitude corresponds most closely to their views. (e.g. 'Which of these statements comes closest to your view of *The Sun* newspaper?' It's the worst national newspaper It's quite a bad newspaper, but no worse than some others It's quite a good newspaper, but not as good as some others It's the best national newspaper Don't know Other [please specify])	• Attitudes

Open-response questions

The strengths and weaknesses of asking questions in an **open-response format** are largely the reverse of those for closed questions.

Advantages

- By letting respondents articulate their answers in their own terms, there is no danger of undermining rapport by imposing inappropriately restricted response frameworks.
- The method removes the possibility that certain types of responses are being prompted by the response options on offer.
- When the qualitative detail is fully recorded, these answers can provide richer, more sensitive insights into the views and activities of respondents.
- Open answers can be used to develop category schemes post hoc. These induced categorisations may be more appropriate than any preordained scheme conceived at the start of the research.

Disadvantages

- Open questions place the greatest demands on respondents.
- They are less easy to summarise.
- The recording of open responses in a standardised interview format can often prove difficult. Writing down comments word for word slows down the interview and increases the pressure on the interviewer. Too many of these will also undermine an interviewer's morale and are an invitation for corner-cutting, which may in turn have a corrupting effect. One way to avoid this is for the interviewer to invite an open response, but then code the answer on a preordained set of response categories. However, this can introduce a new uncertainty into the research process, as there is no guarantee that the interviewer is categorising the answers accurately or appropriately.
- Inducing clear and distinct categorisations post hoc from responses given can sometimes prove difficult. In particular, there is a danger that the subjective interpretations of the researcher about what categories need to be used and where responses fit within them may produce dubious and inconsistent codings. This approach is also very time-consuming.

Summary: key points

- We examined *structured* and *unstructured* questioning styles.
- The main ways in which questions are delivered in research were identified. The main strengths and weaknesses of each in relation to several broad themes concerning question delivery were discussed (convenience, comprehension, rapport, response, depth, control, comparison, elaboration, digression and demands on the researcher).
- Four different types of questions were identified (behaviour, beliefs, attitudes and

attributes). We discussed the specific issues that need to be borne in mind when asking each type of question.

- The issue of question ordering was considered, and why it is important to pay attention to the social and psychological 'flow' of questions.

- The main pitfalls to avoid when asking questions were discussed (ambiguous questions, leading questions, double questions, jargon and technical terminology, blunt questions and hypothetical questions).

- Different ways of capturing people's answers through open- and closed-response formats were compared. The strengths and weaknesses of each were discussed in turn.

chapter five

Handling Numbers

Why you need to know about numbers

The use of statistics in the human sciences can evoke strong reactions. For some people, numbers inspire an anxiety that verges on phobia. Others object to quantification on principle, perceiving it as a denial of the quality and complexity of our collective and individual worlds. Still others disapprove politically, pointing to the cavalier use of numbers to support all manner of dubious reasoning and partisanship. Conversely, there are some who treat statistics with a deferential respect. Media reports often quote crime rates, opinion poll data, unemployment figures and a host of other statistics as if they were objective measures of our society, with no consideration given to important questions about their creation.

All these positive and negative responses to statistics are understandable to some extent. It is undeniable that some statistical concepts and procedures are complex. It is not difficult to find examples where statistical measures have been crudely and inappropriately applied to complex phenomena. The mainstream media are awash with politicians and interest groups partially and cynically quoting numbers to support their own interests. And yet there are also occasions when statistical evidence is so convincing that one tends to accept it at face value.

However, while all these responses may find justification in particular instances, none of them represents a tenable position from which to evaluate the use of statistics in social research in general. To imply that statisticians are inevitably predisposed to sampling by convenience (i.e. deliberately misrepresenting findings to support their personal prejudices) is obvious nonsense. Statistics may be abused, but not all statisticians are abusers. Most quantitative researchers are driven by the same spirit of exploration and inquiry that motivates qualitative researchers, and they share a genuine interest in, and uncertainty about, the relationships and patterns that may emerge from their research.

Additionally, while there are many social and psychological phenomena that are too complex and subtle to be counted, it does not follow that all behaviour and attributes are beyond reliable quantification. As we discussed in chapter 4, there are many demographic, behavioural, even attitudinal, factors that can be quantified and analysed readily.

Furthermore, although some statistical concepts and methods are challenging, most are based on a clear and discernible logic. Indeed, the best way to get to grips with statistics is to look beyond the complex equations that loom menacingly out of most research handbooks, and try instead to understand the function and rationale of each measure.

Finally, although the charge that *all* statistics are lies is unfair, we should not accept the opposite proposition that they represent objective and incontrovertible 'facts' about our world. Social statistics are *constructs*: the end product of an inevitably value-laden research process. Quantitative researchers, like all other researchers, have to make decisions at every stage of their research, whether it is selecting an issue to investigate, deciding on a sampling strategy, organising data-collection procedures or interpreting the resulting data. And where there are decisions, there are values.

In pointing to the constructed nature of statistical evidence, we are not suggesting that all quantitative data are inevitably corrupt. Rather, we are emphasising that statistics should always be treated with caution, at least until their credentials have been thoroughly scrutinised. Just as a good suit is distinguished by the weave of its cloth, the skill in its tailoring and, sometimes, the label on the inside pocket, so the validity of numerical evidence is determined by the competence of its conceptualisation, the meticulousness of its collation and the rigour of its interpretation. Statistics do not speak for themselves and should not be taken at face value. They need to be read critically.

One obvious reason why every student of communication and culture should have some grasp of statistical concepts is because quantitative evidence is so widely presented, both in academic literature and in the media more generally. This alone demands some knowledge in this area, as you cannot be expected to comment intelligently about something you do not understand. However, there is another reason why a knowledge of statistics is important, which relates to their rhetorical power.

When Todd Gitlin (1978) described quantitative audience research as 'the dominant paradigm' in its field, he was not just referring to the number of studies displaying this characteristic. He was also describing an intellectual hegemony. Why do politicians generally prefer to quote numerical evidence to support their arguments, rather than qualitative evidence? Why might research-funding agencies be more prepared to support quantitative, rather than qualitative, research work? Why do journalists attribute greater credibility to statistical data than to other evidence? Although these preferences may reflect practical considerations (e.g. statistics are more easily quoted in a brief sound bite or news item), they also reveal the social importance attributed to numerical evidence. Numbers are paraded because they are seen to have greater objectivity and scientific status than other kinds of evidence, and we should not blind ourselves to the pervasiveness of these beliefs, however much we might want to challenge them. As Gadamer (1975: 268) explains, statistics 'are such an excellent means of propaganda because they let the facts speak and hence simulate an objectivity that in reality depends on the legitimacy of the questions asked'.

It is because statistics have this rhetorical power that the critical analysts must have the ability to comment on them *on their own terms*. To dismiss all statistics as bunkum can too easily become an act of political abdication, disengaging the researcher from wider public debates. This is Angela McRobbie's point when she criticises the tendency within cultural studies to dismiss empiricism (along with ethnography and 'experience') as an 'artificially coherent narrative fiction'. In her view, such purism makes it difficult for researchers

> to participate in facts and figures oriented policy debates, or indeed in relation to the social problem whose roots seemed to lie in innovative cultural practices, for example, the rise of rave and dance

cultures and the consumption among young people of E's (i.e. Ecstasy). It has instead been left to sociologists like Jason Ditton in Glasgow to do the dirtier work of developing policies on youth cultures like rave, which necessitate having access to reliable facts, figures and even 'ethnographic accounts' to be able to argue with angry councillors, police and assorted moral guardians.

(McRobbie 1996: 337–8)

This chapter offers a basic introduction to social statistics and makes no assumptions of prior knowledge. Our main aim is to familiarise you with basic statistical concepts, but in many instances we also provide details on calculation procedures. This might seem unnecessary, as there are many computer software packages that can calculate statistics rapidly and accurately (see chapter 14). However, we have chosen to present this additional detail because we believe it can help to expose the underlying assumptions of the procedures, and in doing so help to demythologise them. For example, understanding that the chi-square test is used to test the likelihood that an apparent relationship between two variables has occurred by chance is, in itself, an important piece of knowledge. But, if you also understand the *process* by which that probability is calculated, and the logic on which it depends, you are in a far better position to analyse its use in a critical and discerning way.

Examples are provided to help explain the various procedures and concepts. Some are fictional, but wherever possible we have provided actual findings from research. Several of the more detailed examples are taken from two research projects undertaken at our host institution. The first is a survey of 655 British voluntary and charitable organisations which explored many facets of their communications activities (Deacon 1999). The second is a survey of 674 UK-based social scientists, which analysed their media contact and publicity strategies (Fenton, Bryman and Deacon 1998).

The chapter is divided into two general sections. The first examines **descriptive statistics**, and the second explores **inferential statistics**. However, before we present these areas, there is a fundamental statistical concept that needs to be explained: **levels of measurement**. The differences captured within this concept are crucial because, as we shall see, they determine the kinds of statistical tests and measures that are appropriate to use when analysing numbers.

Levels of measurement

There are four levels of measurement: the *nominal*, the *ordinal*, the *interval* and the *ratio*. The order in which they are listed reflects their hierarchical relationship.

The nominal level

This is the most basic level of measurement and covers those occasions when numbers are used simply to label a particular quality or feature. For example, in a survey of cinema-goers, numbers could be used to categorise the gender of respondents (1 = female, 2 = male). Numbers that attain the nominal level of measurement tell us only about equivalence. They cannot be ordered, added, subtracted, multiplied or divided. In the hypothetical cinema survey, for instance, it would be nonsense to calculate the 'average gender of respondents'.

The ordinal level

Statistics that attain the ordinal level of measurement differ from nominal numbers in that there is some relationship between the values. Apart from indicating equivalence, ordinal values can also be ranked, from lowest to highest. For example, in the survey of social scientists and their media use, respondents were asked to indicate their highest level of academic qualification, on a scale ranging from pre-undergraduate (coded as 1), through undergraduate (2) and postgraduate (3), to doctorate (4). Apart from providing *nominal* information (e.g. how many respondents had doctorates), these data permit the ranking of respondents according to educational attainment (i.e. the higher the value for this variable, the greater the educational status of the respondent).

Although ordinal measurements allow us to rank values, they are not sufficiently precise to allow more detailed analysis of their mathematical relationship. For instance, with the social scientist example, you could not suggest that a respondent who scored 4 in relation to their academic qualifications had twice the educational attainments as one who scored 2. These numbers permit us to say only that the first is more formally qualified than the second.

The interval level and the ratio level

We list the interval and ratio levels of measurement together because they are generally treated as one and the same in most social scientific statistical research (Bryman and Cramer 2005). Values attain the *interval* level when the differences between them are constant and precise, but do not relate to an absolute zero. The most obvious example of this level is the Celsius temperature scale. Because zero degrees Celsius on a thermometer is an arbitrary figure (absolute zero is actually minus 273°C), we cannot say that 20°C is twice as hot as 10°C. However, we can say that the temperature increase between 10°C and 20°C is the same as the increase between 20°C and 30°C. The *ratio* level is a higher level of measurement than the interval level because the numbers do correspond to an absolute zero (e.g. the age in years of a survey respondent, or the number of hours a person watches television in a week).

In many cases it is easy to identify the level of measurement of a particular statistic, but there are times when it is a matter of fine judgement. For instance, questionnaires often use scaled response categories to attitudinal questions (see chapter 4) that are designed to assess the strength of people's feelings to the issues raised (e.g. 5 = agree strongly, 4 = agree, 3 = neither agree nor disagree, 2 = disagree, 1 = disagree strongly). Most statisticians would agree that individual measures like this attain only the ordinal level of measurement. Yet in many studies these sorts of ranked responses are grouped to produce 'meta-scales' on particular issues. For example, a survey of journalists might seek to measure their authoritarian tendencies by asking a suite of attitude questions related to law and order, capital punishment, immigration, education and welfare support. If five questions were asked, each with a five-point response scale, the grouped responses would produce scores ranging from 5 to 25 for each respondent. Some researchers argue that this sort of multiple-item scale can be treated as though it attains the interval level of measurement (treating it as a 'pseudo-interval' measure), even though it is a composite of ordinal measures. Others, however, would see this as an unacceptable sleight of hand.

To help you to familiarise yourself with the different levels of measurement, we list a range of variables in Box 5.1. Your task is to decide which are at the nominal, ordinal, pseudo-interval or interval/ratio levels of measurement. (The answers are provided at the end of the chapter.)

Box 5.1 Guess the level of measurement

1. The age, in years, of respondents in a public opinion poll survey.

2. The age of respondents in an opinion poll survey using the categories: 'less than 18 years', '19–25 years', '26–35 years', '36–45 years', '46 years and over'.

3. Percentage marks given for answers to a film studies exam question concerning the adaptation of Joseph Conrad's *Heart of Darkness* in Francis Ford Coppola's *Apocalypse Now*.

4. Students' responses to an attitude statement: 'I have enjoyed this statistics course', using a five-point scale ('Agree strongly', 'agree', 'neither agree nor disagree', 'disagree', 'strongly disagree').

5. The ethnicity of respondents in a survey of personnel in the Singaporean advertising industry.

6. A composite measure of African journalists' attitudes to US foreign policy, created by collating their responses (on five-point scales) to eight attitude statements.

Descriptive statistics

Once a researcher has collected a set of data, she or he will have to find some way of summarising, or *describing*, the general pattern of those findings in a clear and concise way. In this section, we look at several descriptive statistical techniques and show how their use is determined by the levels of measurement particular variables attain.

Measures of central tendency

Measures of central tendency describe how values for a particular variable group around the centre. There are three of these measures: the mean, mode and median. The mean is the arithmetic average. It can be calculated only for measures that attain either the interval or ratio level of measurement, as it assumes that the amount of variation across values is consistent. (This is not the case with ordinal values.) The mode is the most frequently occurring score, and is the only measure of central tendency that can be used to summarise data at the nominal level of measurement. The median is the midpoint between the highest and lowest values of a particular variable. The procedures for calculating each of these are explained, alongside an example, in Box 5.2.

Box 5.2 Calculating the mean, mode and median

- A group of ten college students are asked to keep a record of the number of times they go to the cinema over a three-month period. This produces the following scores:

  1, 1, 2, 2, 2, 4, 4, 6, 8, 10.

- *To calculate the mean*: add all scores together (= 40), then divide them by the total number of scores (40 ÷ 10 = **4**).

- *To calculate the mode*: work out which is the most frequently occurring score (= **2**).

- *To calculate the median*: place the numbers in order and identify the midpoint between the highest and lowest values. As there are ten scores, this will be between the fifth (2) and sixth value (4). To calculate the median in this case, it is acceptable to average these two scores (2 + 4 ÷ 2 = **3**).

Measures of dispersion

Apart from describing how values group centrally, it is often useful to indicate statistically how these values spread around these central measures. There are several ways of **measuring dispersion**, and their use depends on the level of measurement a variable attains. With nominal data, the only non-graphical way to demonstrate dispersion is through a **frequency table**. Frequency tables list the proportion of values that fall under each of the values used to categorise the variable. The frequency table shown in Table 5.1 comes from the survey of voluntary organisations and shows that only a minority of voluntary organisations (29 per cent) had received national television coverage in the preceding two-year period.

Table 5.1 Frequency table of voluntary organisations and television contact

National TV coverage	29%
No national TV coverage	69%
Didn't know/Didn't respond	2%
(Total number)	(655)

With data that attain the ordinal level of measurement or above, other options are available to summarise the spread of values. The most basic measure of dispersion that can be used is the 'range'. This calculates the difference between the highest and lowest values in a data set. Although simple to calculate, the range has obvious limitations. In particular, it is vulnerable to distortion by outlying values. If a set of numbers has an extraordinarily high or low value that is atypical of the data as a whole, then the range would give a misleading impression of the dispersion of all the values. For this reason, a more sophisticated measure of dispersion is needed when dealing with data at the interval/ratio level, which can take account of the variation of *all* the numbers, rather than just the two extremes.

The 'standard deviation' is a measure that is widely used to describe the dispersion of values at the interval or ratio level of measurement. It measures the extent to which each value for a variable deviates from its overall mean, and produces an average figure for this dispersion (see Box 5.3 for an explanation of how it is calculated). The figure for the standard deviation, when placed alongside the mean, gives the reader an understanding of how the values generally vary from that central measure. Where the figure for the standard deviation is low, we know that most of the values in a distribution are grouped closely around the mean. Conversely, where the figure is higher, we know that the values are dispersed more widely.

Box 5.3 Calculating the standard deviation

In a test, eight journalists are required to identify from photographs the names of 30 prominent international politicians. This exercise produces the following scores: 18, 18, 19, 25, 25, 26, 26, 27.

To calculate the standard deviation for these figures, you should take the following steps:

- *Step 1*: calculate the arithmetic mean for all values (184 ÷ 8 = 23).

- *Step 2*: subtract the mean from *each* value individually, to see how much they vary from it (−5, −5, −4, 2, 2, 3, 3, 4).

- *Step 3*: square each of these values (i.e. multiply them by themselves) to get rid of all the negative values (25, 25, 16, 4, 4, 9, 9, 16). (NB When you multiply two negative values, they become a positive value.)

- *Step 4*: sum these values (= 108) and divide the total by the number of values (108 ÷ 8 = 13.5).

- *Step 5*: take the square root of this value, to counteract the effect of having squared all the values in step 3. This figure is the *standard deviation* ($\sqrt{13.5} = 3.67$).

Exploring relationships: associations and correlations

Measures of central tendency and dispersion are useful for summarising the characteristics of individual variables (so-called **univariate analysis**). But one of the most interesting and important elements of statistical analysis involves exploring how variables interact with each other. In this section, we look at the most widely employed procedures used to explore relationships between two variables (often referred to as **bivariate analysis**). As we review them, you should note how use of the procedures is decided by the levels of measurement attained by one or both of the variables being compared.

Exploring association: contingency tables

The main technique for analysing and presenting the interaction between variables that are only at the nominal level of measurement is the **contingency table** (also referred to as a **cross-tabulation**). Table 5.2 compares the professional status of social scientists in Britain with their recent media contact. The categories along the top differentiate between 'senior' and 'non-senior' social scientists (assessed by their professional title and responsibilities), and the categories down the side differentiate between those respondents who said they had had recent media contact and those who said they had not. Cross-tabulating these two variables produces a four-cell table. In each cell in Table 5.2 there are two figures. The first indicates the actual number of cases that fall into each cell, a figure known as the 'observed frequency'. The second figure is the 'column percentage', and is calculated by dividing the actual frequency in a cell with the column total and multiplying the result by 100. If we look at the cell in the first column and first row, we can see that 122 senior social scientists in the sample had had media contact, which represented 85 per cent of all senior social scientists who responded. In comparison, 321 non-senior social scientists had had media exposure, which represented 61 per cent of all respondents who fell into this category.

Table 5.2 Contingency table comparing professional seniority of social scientists with media contact

		Status Senior	Non-senior	(Row totals)
Media	Yes	(a) 122	(b) 321	(443)
contact		85%	61%	
	No	(c) 21	(d) 204	(225)
		15%	39%	
(Column totals)		**(143)**	**(525)**	

When we compare these column percentages, it appears as though there may be some **association** between 'professional seniority' and 'media contact', as a smaller proportion of non-senior social scientists had received media coverage than their senior colleagues. (This is assuming there are no constant errors in the sample.) But should we take any notice of this difference? Does it reveal something important about variation in media contact across the social sciences in general, or could these differences have occurred by chance? To answer this question, we need to calculate the **statistical significance** of the relationship, an issue we deal with in a later section of this chapter, on inferential statistics.

When exploring the relationship between two variables, by whatever means, it is often possible to identify one as the 'independent variable' (i.e. the factor that causes a difference to occur in the other variable), and the other as a 'dependent variable' (i.e. the factor that varies as a consequence of the impact of the other variable). For example, if you were comparing the link between magazine readership and age, it is clear that age is the independent variable – as reading preferences do not affect your age, but age may well have an impact on the type and amount of reading you do. With cross-tabulations, if you are able to identify an independent variable, it is a convention that this variable should be used to create the columns in the table. In the example shown in Table 5.2, the existence of an independent variable is less easy to deduce, as it could be the case that greater media exposure enhances the professional prospects of a social scientist (and, hence, their seniority), or that the more senior a source is, the more likely it is that the media will report their activity.

Measuring correlations: Pearson's *r* and Spearman's *r*ho

When dealing with ordinal, interval or ratio data, social scientists tend to talk about the 'correlation' between variables rather than their 'association'. This is because, as Weiss (1968: 198) explains, 'Correlation suggests two factors increasing or decreasing together, while association suggests two factors occurring together'. In this section, we focus on statistical measures of correlation, known as **correlation coefficients**. Later we discuss the different procedures that can be used for demonstrating visually the correlation between variables.

Correlation coefficients provide an indication of the nature and strength of a relation between two sets of values. Whatever procedure is used to calculate a correlation coefficient (and there are several), the resulting value will always be somewhere between +1 (plus one) and –1 (minus one). The strength of the correlation between the two variables is determined by how close the number is to either of these extremes. A correlation coefficient of 0.899 would tell us that there is a very strong, positive relationship between two variables (a 'positive' relationship is where the value of one variable increases in line with an increase in a second variable). By the same token, a correlation coefficient figure of –0.22 would tell us that there is a weak, negative correlation between two variables (a 'negative' relationship is where one variable decreases as the other increases). We are always concerned with the proximity of these figures to either +1 or –1, because in social scientific research, pure mathematical relationships (where the value of one variable increases in exact proportion to the increase in another) never occur. (A perfect positive relationship between two values would come out with a correlation coefficient of +1, and a perfect negative relationship would be –1.)

The most widely employed procedures for calculating correlation coefficients are *Spearman's rank order correlation coefficient* and *Pearson's product moment correlation coefficient*. Spearman's correlation coefficient (often indicated as r_{ho}) is used when one or both variables attain the ordinal level of measurement, and it works by comparing the ranking, or order, of the two sets of values (see Box 5.4). It is a measure that allows us to answer the question: 'To what extent is it true that the more you have of the one quality, the more you have of another?'(Weiss 1968: 206). Pearson's product moment correlation coefficient (often referred to as *r*) is used to measure the correlation between values that attain the interval or ratio level of measurement. It is a more sophisticated measure than Spearman's, in that it measures the extent to which the values of one variable vary consistently with values of the other (see Box 5.5). In other words, it assesses the extent to which an increase of a certain number of units in one variable is associated with 'an increase *of a related number of units* in the other' (ibid., original emphasis).

Box 5.4 Calculating Spearman's rank order correlation coefficient

A student has conducted a small-scale investigation of the link between the prominence of local politicians in their local press and their initiative in seeking media coverage. In a questionnaire survey, eight politicians indicated the amount of local press coverage they had received over the previous six months and the frequency with which they had been personally involved in producing a press release or organising a press conference over the same period. Both variables were measured on an identical eight-point, ordinal scale (i.e. 'none', '1–10 occasions', '11–20 occasions', '21–30 occasions', '31–40 occasions', '41–50 occasions', '51–60 occasions', '61 occasions and over'). The resulting ordinal data collected allowed each politician to be ranked according to their amount of media contact and the extent of media-related publicity activity:

Politician	Press coverage (Column 1)	Publicity activity (Column 2)
a	1	2
b	2	4
c	2	1
d	4	3
e	4	5
f	6	8
g	7	7
h	8	6

To calculate Spearman's correlation coefficient for this data, take the following steps:

- *Step 1*: work out the difference between each of the rankings in columns 1 and 2 (i.e. politician a: $1 - 2 = -1$; b: $2 - 4 = -2$; c: $2 - 1 = 1$; d: $4 - 3 = 1$; e: $4 - 5 = -1$; f: $6 - 8 = -2$; g: $7 - 7 = 0$; h: $8 - 6 = 2$).
- *Step 2*: square each of these values (= 1, 4, 1, 1, 1, 4, 0, 4).
- *Step 3*: add them together (= 16).
- *Step 4*: multiply this number by 6 ($6 \times 16 = 96$).
- *Step 5*: add 1 to the total number of politicians involved in the study (= 9). Subtract 1 from the total number of politicians (= 7). Multiply these numbers together ($9 \times 7 = 63$).
- *Step 6*: multiply this number by the total number of politicians ($63 \times 8 = 504$).
- *Step 7*: divide the number obtained in step 4 by the number obtained in step 6 ($96 \div 504 = 0.19$).
- *Step 8*: subtract the number obtained in step 7 from 1 ($1 - 0.19 = \mathbf{0.81}$).

This figure is Spearman's rank order correlation coefficient. The fact that it is very close to 1 (0.81) suggests that there is a very strong, positive correlation between the prominence in the press of these local politicians and the extent of their media-related activity.

Box 5.5 Calculating Pearson's *r*

In a more intensive follow-up study to the project described in Box 5.4, the same student conducts a content analysis of local press coverage that quantifies precisely the number of articles that referred to these eight local politicians during the previous year. She then negotiates access to all the politicians' administrative records, and quantifies the exact number of press releases and news conferences organised by each politician over the same period. These data-collection exercises produce the following ratio data:

Politician	Number of press items (Column 1)	Number of releases/conferences (Column 2)
a	63	58
b	45	48
c	39	67
d	36	52
e	34	32
f	23	17
g	20	18
h	20	26

To calculate Pearson's *r* for this data set, the following steps are involved:

- *Step 1*: work out the arithmetic mean for the numbers in column 1 (63 + 45 + 39 + 36 + 34 + 23 + 20 + 20 ÷ 8 = 280 ÷ 8 = **35**) and for the numbers in column 2 (58 + 48 + 67 + 52 + 32 + 17 + 18 + 26 = 318 ÷ 8 = **39.75**).
- *Step 2*: subtract each value in column 1 from the mean value for column 1 (politician a: 63 − 35 = 28; b: 45 − 35 = 10; c: 39 − 35 = 4; d: 36 − 35 = 1; e: 34 − 35 = −1; f: 23 − 35 = −12; g: 20 − 35 = −15; h: 20 − 35 = −15). **We will refer to these values by the letter *x*.**
- *Step 3*: square these *x* values and add them together (784 + 100 + 16 + 1 + 1 + 144 + 225 + 225 = **1,496**).
- *Step 4*: repeat step 2 for the values in column 2 (18.25, 8.25, 27.25, 12.25, −7.75, −22.75, −21.75, −13.75). **We will refer to these values by the letter *y*.**
- *Step 5*: square each of the *y* values and add them together (333.06 + 68.06 + 742.56 + 150.06 + 60.06 + 517.56 + 473.06 + 189.06 = **2,533.5**).
- *Step 6*: for each politician, multiply the values for *x* (see step 2) and *y* (see step 4) (28 × 18.25 = 511; 10 × 8.25 = 82.5; 4 × 27.25 = 109; 1 × 12.25 = 12.25; −1 × −7.75 = 7.75; −12 × −22.75 = 273; −15 × −21.75 = 326.25; −15 × −13.75 = 206.25).
- *Step 7*: add together all the values generated by step 6 (511 + 82.5 + 109 + 12.25 + 7.75 + 273 + 326.25 + 206.25 = 1,528).
- *Step 8*: multiply the total produced by step 3 with the total generated in step 5 (1,496 × 2,533.5 = 3,790,116).

- *Step 9*: take the square root of this number ($\sqrt{3,790,116} = 1,946.8$).
- *Step 10*: divide the total generated by step 7 by the total produced by step 9 ($1,528 \div 1,946.8 = 0.78$).

This final number is the value for Pearson's *r* for these two sets of data. The figure for this more sophisticated assessment of the link between publicity activity and media exposure is slightly lower than that found for the Spearman's coefficient outlined in Box 5.4. Nevertheless, the result is close to 1, thereby confirming the student's initial findings of there being a strong correlation between the activeness of these politicians in their media work and their visibility in their local press.

Visual presentation: using graphs

Quantitative data can often be presented and summarised very effectively using graphical techniques. In this section, we examine some of the main graphical techniques used to present data, and point out conventions that govern their use. Before we discuss these techniques, there is one important piece of terminological information you need to be clear about. Where a graph has a vertical axis, it is referred to as the *y* axis. Where it has a horizontal axis, it is referred to as the *x* axis.

Bar charts and histograms

Bar charts and *histograms* look very similar and are often confused. Figure 5.1 is a bar chart that compares the readership of the top ten daily newspapers in India. Figure 5.2 is a histogram presenting annual fluctuations in aggregate advertising expenditure in Japan between 1999 and 2005. The difference between these two types of graphs is that the bars which signify the numbers of cases that fall under each category are separated for the bar chart, but are adjacent in the histogram. The reason for this relates to the different level of measurement for the variables on the *x* axis. With Figure 5.1, the categories for newspaper titles attain only the nominal level of measurement: they are not connected in any way. When this is the case, the separate bars are used to symbolise the discrete nature of the categories. With Figure 5.2, the annual categories attain the ordinal level, and the touching bars of the histogram signify the connection between the values.

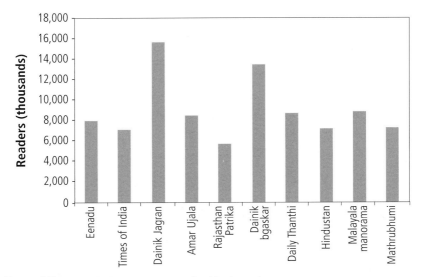

Figure 5.1 Indian daily newspaper readership (2004)
Source: Media Research Users Council

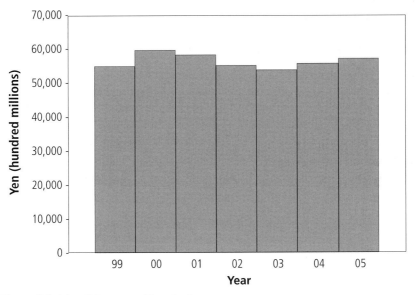

Figure 5.2 Advertising expenditure in Japan
Source: http://www.zakko.or.jp/eng/qa/01/index.html

When you are preparing a bar chart, the different bars should be placed in random order. You should not, for example, place the bars in order from highest to lowest, as this would give a misleading impression that the categories are continuous.

Bar charts can also be used to display two-way relationships. Figure 5.3 compares the percentage of households in the UK for 1998/99 and 2004/5 that had landline telephones, mobile phones, home computers and Internet access.

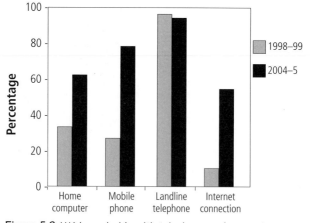

Figure 5.3 UK households with telephone and computer technology
Source: http://www.statistics.gov.uk/

Line graphs

Another widely used alternative to the histogram is the line graph (sometimes referred to as the frequency polygon). Line graphs should be used only with data that attains the ordinal level of measurement or above, because the continuous line implies a relationship between the values for each category. These graphs are suitable for variables that have a large number of values, which, if they were charted as a histogram, would produce a confusing mass of bars. They are also useful for comparing trends between two or more continuous variables. The example in Figure 5.4 compares fluctuations in US newspaper employment of people from minority ethnic communities between 1999 and 2006, and shows that the number of employees classified as 'Native American' has remained fairly constant over this period, but the numbers for other ethnic groups have increased.

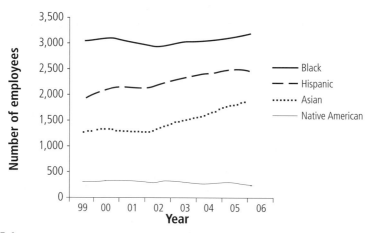

Figure 5.4 US newspaper employment of people from minority ethnic communities in professional newsroom jobs (1999–2006)
Source: American Society of Newspaper Editors, http://www.asne.org/index.cfm

Pie charts

Another widely used graphical technique is the pie chart. Unlike the graphs described above, pie charts do not have *x* and *y* axes. Instead, the grouping of data under each category is represented segmentally, as slices of a circle. The larger the segment, the more prominent that category is in the overall distribution of values. (The complete circle represents the total number of cases.) Figure 5.5 is a pie chart showing the linguistic orientation of weblogs in 2006. (A weblog, or blog, is a continually updated website, containing dated entries organised in reverse

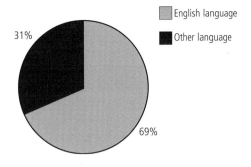

Total number of weblogs: 2,869,632

Figure 5.5 Global census of the linguistic orientation of weblogs
Source: The Nitle weblog census, http://weblogs.about.com/

chronological order.) Note that the size of each slice of the chart is calculated by relating the percentage value to the 360 degrees of the circle. For example, 1,970,366 of the weblogs identified in the global census were found to be written in English, which represents 69 per cent of the total of 2,869,632 weblogs analysed. Therefore, the slice should equal 69 per cent of the 360 degrees of the circle (248.4 degrees).

Pie charts are often useful as a visual variation on bar charts and histograms, but they can be confusing if poorly designed. Generally, pie charts work best when there are only a few categories to segment, as the more there are, the more difficult they are to label and interpret. Furthermore, because the segments are based on percentages, you need to be careful when comparing different pie charts with each other. For example, one pie chart may have been calculated on a far smaller number of sample cases than another, but by being presented at an identical size, the reader might be given the misleading impression that there is a sampling parity between the two sets of data. One way of avoiding this confusion is to draw pie charts that are based on fewer numbers on a smaller scale to those based on larger samples.

Scattergrams

A scattergram is a visual representation of a correlation. It has an *x* axis and a *y* axis and is used when you have two values for each sample unit. The two values are plotted separately on their respective axes, and a dot is placed at the place where these points would intersect if straight lines were drawn at 90 degrees from these two positions.

Once all the cases have been plotted in this way, the arrangement of dots reveals the strength and nature of the correlation between two variables. If there is a perfect correlation between variables, the points will form along a perfectly straight, non-horizontal line (see Figure 5.6), and if these values are calculated as a correlation coefficient, the resulting statistic would equal 1. Perfect correlations do not exist in the human sciences; therefore, the plotted points will be found to scatter to some degree around this perfectly straight line (known as *the line of best fit*). The more scattered the plotted points are from this hypothetical, straight, non-horizontal line, the weaker the relationship between the two variables. Correspondingly, the closer they conform to this straight line, the more powerful the correlation is between them. For example, if we compare Figures 5.7 and 5.8, we can see immediately that the relationship between the two variables in Figure 5.7 is stronger than the relationship between the variables in Figure 5.8, because the dots are far less dispersed, and all tend to cluster around the line of best fit.

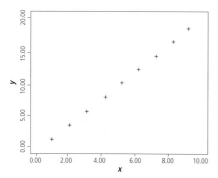

Figure 5.6 A perfect positive correlation

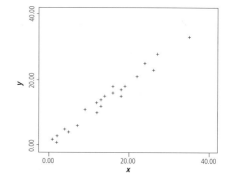

Figure 5.7 A strong positive correlation

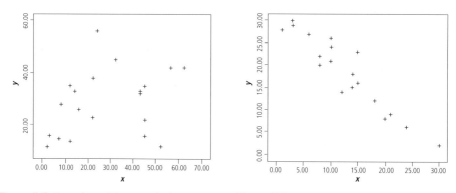

Figure 5.8 A weak positive correlation

Figure 5.9 A strong negative correlation

The second important point that a scattergram can reveal is the nature of the relationship between the variables. A positive relationship (where one variable increases as the other increases) is revealed when the dots tend to scatter from bottom right to top left. A negative relationship (where one variable decreases as the other increases) is revealed by a scattergram where the dots run down from the top left of the graph to the bottom right (see Figure 5.9). Once again, the closer the dots group around a line of best fit, the stronger the negative correlation between the two variables.

Inferential statistics: using numbers to ask wider questions

All the descriptive statistics outlined so far in this chapter represent ways of summarising *sample* characteristics. Although this is a vital part of any investigation, it does not represent an end in itself. The researcher also needs to consider how sample findings relate to the broader population to which they are assumed to apply. Do the sample findings reveal anything meaningful or 'significant' about the population from which they were drawn, or could the patterns and relationships suggested by the sample data have occurred inadvertently, as a by-product of sampling error and bias?

In many respects, judgements about the credibility of sample findings are critical, rather than statistical. As discussed earlier, the kind of credence we give to particular statistical findings has to be rooted initially in an evaluation of the research procedures and conceptualisations that underpin them. This is a qualitative and intellectual exercise. Beyond these judgements, there is a range of procedures that quantitative researchers can use to estimate the representativeness of their data and the hypotheses they develop on the basis of these. These techniques are referred to as *inferential statistics*, in that they allow researchers to 'infer' things about populations on the basis of evidence from samples. Specifically, inferential statistics are used for two purposes:

- to make population estimates on the basis of sample data;
- to estimate the likelihood that apparent relationships or associations revealed between variables in a sample are likely to exist in the population as a whole (known as hypothesis testing).

There are many types of inferential statistical techniques, and we can introduce you to only a few widely used procedures. Nevertheless, these examples do provide an insight into the theoretical assumptions that underpin all forms of statistical inference. Before we examine them, we must first discuss the pivotal concept on which all these tests rest: theories of *probability*.

Probability: 'long shots' and 'racing certainties'

Theories of statistical probability rest on the proposition that certain things are more likely to happen than others. In other words, when we talk of probability we are talking about chance. To take the example mentioned in most statistics textbooks, if you were to toss a coin, there would be a 1 in 2 chance that it would fall as heads. If you were to toss a coin twice, there would be a 1 in 4 chance of getting two heads in succession. This is because there are four possible outcomes (HH, TT, HT, TH). The odds of tossing three heads in a row increase to 1 in 8, due to the increased number of potential outcomes (HHH, HHT, HTT, TTT, TTH, THH, HTH, THT), and if we extend this logic, we can say there is only a 1 in 1,024 chance of tossing ten heads in a row. Not an *impossible* outcome, but certainly an *unlikely* one, and not the sort of bet you would want to stake your life savings on.

However, other outcomes are more likely to occur. For example, if you were to calculate the chances of getting five heads and five tails (in no particular order), you would find out that 252 of the 1,024 possible permutations produced by these tosses would contain an equal number of heads and tails. Therefore, the odds of getting this combination are just about 1 in 4 (i.e. 252 ÷ 1,024). All in all, a far more likely outcome.

A statement such as 'there is a 1 in 4 chance' is a probability statement. In statistical analysis it is conventional to express this information as a number between 1 and zero. In other words, instead of presenting probabilities as fractions (i.e. 1 in 4 = 1/4), they are presented as decimal figures (0.25). You will often see probability statements quoted in statistical reports alongside numbers or statistical tables, and it is important that you understand how to read them. Box 5.6 lists a few examples to help clarify how probability statements constitute statements about chance.

Box 5.6 Probability values and statements of chance

- $p < 0.05$ = there is less than a 5 in 100 (or 1 in 20) chance that this finding occurred accidentally.
- $p < 0.02$ = there is less than a 2 in 100 (or 1 in 50) chance.
- $p < 0.01$ = there is less than a 1 in 100 chance.
- $p < 0.001$ = there is less than a 1 in 1,000 chance.

The key point to remember is that *the lower the probability figure is, the less likely it is that the patterns suggested by the sample data occurred by chance, and therefore the more confidence you can have that it shows something 'significant' about the population as a whole.*

You may have come across research reports and articles that describe certain findings as being 'statistically significant'. The concept of statistical significance means there is an acceptably low chance that some feature or relationship displayed in a sample could have emerged accidentally. The most widely accepted 'confidence level' used to distinguish between statistically significant findings and statistically non-significant findings is a probability level of less than 0.05 ($p < 0.05$). In other words, there has to be less than a 5 per cent chance (or 1 in 20 chance) that a finding has emerged accidentally for it to be deemed 'statistically significant'. This confidence level has been established arbitrarily, but is generally seen to be sufficiently demanding to prevent what are known as 'Type I errors'. These errors are where non-representative sample findings are mistakenly treated as revealing something significant about a population. Some quantitative researchers feel that even this 5 per cent risk is too great, and therefore set their 'confidence levels' at an even more demanding level; for example, deeming a finding to be statistically significant only if there is less than a 1 in 100 chance that it could have occurred randomly (i.e. $p < 0.01$). Although setting this more exacting standard increases the confidence you can have in the findings, it does increase the risk that sample findings that do reveal broader insights about the population are neglected, because they do not quite attain this very demanding level of statistical significance (these are known as 'Type II errors').

It is not difficult to see how probabilities are worked out for coin tossing or dice throwing, but it is less obvious to understand how these principles apply to more complex data. To give you some insight into this area, in the following sections we work through four inferential statistical techniques. The first offers an example of how population values are estimated on the basis of sample values (**standard error of the mean**). The second and third show how the significance of associations between two variables is assessed (the *chi-square test* and the *t-test*). The fourth introduces basic procedures for exploring relationships between more than two variables at a time (**multivariate analysis**).

Before we examine these in more detail, there is one important point you need to be clear about. All the inferential statistics described draw on theories of probability or chance. *Therefore, they should be used only on samples that have been 'randomly sampled'.* As explained in chapter 3, when researchers talk of 'random' sampling, they do not mean that sample selection is disorganised. They are describing a method where the final selection of who or what is included in the sample is left to chance, and where each unit of a population has an equal chance of being selected. It is this initial randomness that permits the application of theories of chance to the sample data.

Estimating the standard error of the mean

The standard error of the mean is a technique used to estimate the likely parameters of a population mean on the basis of a sample mean. It is a way of accounting for the unavoidable effect that *random errors* in sampling will have had on the sample statistics.

As explained in chapter 3, no matter how carefully researchers seek to avoid *constant errors* in their sampling (i.e. structural biases in the sample selection), there is no way to avoid *random errors*. Random errors occur when a smaller sample is taken from a population. For example, imagine that two national surveys of newspaper readership are conducted at exactly the same time, using identical sampling procedures. Whereas the first survey finds that the average age of readers of a popular newspaper is 31, the second calculates the figure as 32 years. This slight discrepancy is most likely due to the random variation that occurs when smaller samples are taken from larger populations.

If thousands of these surveys were conducted at the same time, using identical sampling procedures, you would find that the distribution of the variation of these values conforms to a clear pattern. In isolated cases, the figure for average age would be very high or very low, but most values would tend to cluster around a set of middle values. If all the figures from these surveys were then plotted on a histogram, they would form a distribution pattern such as the one set out in Figure 5.10.

If this histogram is converted into a curved line graph, we would produce a distribution like the one set out in Figure 5.11. The pattern of this distribution is known as the *normal distribution curve*, and its

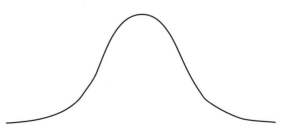

Number of cases

Years

Figure 5.10 Eventual distribution of average readership ages

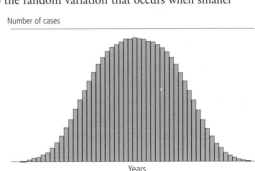

Figure 5.11 A normal distribution curve

application is very important to inferential statistical analysis. The use of the term 'normal' in this context does not mean 'usual', but rather 'standard'. It is a curve of distribution that approximates how things occur naturally in the real world. For example, if you were to measure the height of every two-year-old child in Britain, you would find a small proportion that are very small, an equally small proportion that are enormous, and a very large proportion of children who group around the centre. If this distribution were plotted, it would form a normal distribution curve.

Statisticians know a great deal about the mathematical properties of a **normal distribution**. First, the mean, mode and median are all the same. Second, the distribution is perfectly symmetrical and bell-shaped. Third, it is known that 68 per cent of all cases fall within plus or minus 1 standard deviation of the mean; 95 per cent of cases fall within plus or minus 1.96 standard deviations of the mean; and 99 per cent of cases fall within plus or minus 2.58 standard deviations of the mean.

The calculation of the standard error of the mean (SEM) works by linking the known mathematical properties of the normal distribution with the recognition that variation in sample means will be normally distributed, and that the true population value will be located at the centre of that distribution. This theoretical assumption is known as the *central limits theorem*. As already mentioned, the standard error of the mean is used to estimate where the 'true' values of a population lie, bearing in mind the probable impact that random errors will have had on the sample values. The actual procedure for calculating SEM is fairly straightforward and is explained in Box 5.7. It works by linking the value for the standard deviation of a sample variable with its sample size. Apart from understanding the technical calculation of this statistic, you should also appreciate two important points about its underlying rationale.

First, *the figure for the SEM is partly influenced by the size of the sample.* For example, if we were to calculate the SEM for identical mean and standard deviation figures in Box 5.7, but which were based on a far larger sample of 1,089 readers, the figure for SEM would be much lower than in the example given, decreasing from 0.5 years to 0.17 years.[1] Second, *the greater the standard deviation is for the sample data, the greater the figure for the SEM.* For example, if we were to change the figure for the standard deviation in Box 5.7 from 5.5 years to 11 years, the SEM would increase from 0.5 to 1 year.[2]

The first point rests on the obvious logic that the larger a sample is, the more confidence we can have in its representativeness. Where the total size of the sample is small, the figure for the SEM increases to take account of the greater uncertainty this inevitably creates. (That said, after a certain point, a law of diminishing returns starts to emerge, where even very substantial increases in the sample size produce only minor changes in the SEM statistic.) The second point rests on the connected logical proposition that if the sample data reveal a wide variance in values (as indicated by a high value for the standard deviation), then any projection of the figures must take this diversity into account. In other words, if the values of a sample do not obviously cluster tightly around one central value, then there are no grounds for assuming that this occurs in the general population.

1 $\sqrt{1,089} = 33$; $5.5 \div 33 = 0.17$.

2 $\sqrt{121} = 11$; $11 \div 11 = 1$.

Box 5.7 Calculating the standard error of the mean (SEₘ)

A readership survey, conducted on behalf of a new arts magazine, finds that the mean age of a randomly selected sample of readership is 32 years, with a standard deviation of 5.5 years. In all, 121 people were included in the sample. Calculating the standard error of the mean of this survey involves the following steps:

- *Step 1*: take the square root of the sample total ($\sqrt{121} = 11$).

- *Step 2*: divide this figure into the figure for the standard deviation ($5.5 \div 11 = 0.5$).

This figure is the standard error of the mean (SE_M). Therefore, taking this figure and applying the central limits theorem, the researchers can calculate that the mean of the population (i.e. the entire readership) has:

1. a 68 per cent chance ($p = 0.32$) of lying somewhere between 31.5 years and 32.5 years (i.e. plus or minus 1 SE_M from the sample mean);

2. a 95 per cent chance ($p = 0.05$) of being between 31.02 years and 32.98 years (plus or minus 1.96 SE_M from the sample mean);

3. a 99 per cent chance ($p = 0.01$) of being between 30.71 years and 33.29 years (plus or minus 2.58 SE_M from the mean).

Testing hypotheses (1): the chi-square test

The standard error of the mean is just one example of how 'true' population values are estimated on the basis of sample evidence. We now turn our attention to the second area in which inferential statistics are used: *hypothesis testing*.

Hypothesis testing sounds very impressive and scientific, but what does it mean? Hypothesis testing is about calculating the probability that distributions in sample data or differences and relationships occurred accidently, due to random sampling error, or whether this is so unlikely that we can be confident that they reveal 'real' patterns and relationships.

There are various procedures that can be used for testing hypotheses. We focus first on the **chi-square test** because it is widely employed and can be used on numbers that attain any level of measurement (nominal, ordinal, interval or ratio). As usual, we take you through the calculation on a step-by-step basis. Because of the length of this process, we have not placed the procedures in a separate box, but you should not let the length of this explanation discourage you. If you follow the steps carefully, this information will give you a clear insight into the logic that underpins this statistical test.

Calculating chi-square: an example

Our illustration of the chi-square test draws on data from the survey of voluntary organisations mentioned in the introduction to this chapter. The cross-tabulation (see Table 5.3) compares the relationship between the annual budget of organisations ('£1,000 or less p.a.', '£1,001–£10,000', '£10,001–£50,000', £50,001–£250,000', '£250,0001+') and whether they had received any television news coverage in the previous two years ('Yes', 'No').

Table 5.3 Cross-tabulation of voluntary agencies' annual budget and TV exposure

		Annual budget of organisations					
		<£1,000	£1,001–£10,000	£10,001–£50,000	£50,001–£250,000	£250,001+	
National or local TV coverage?	Yes	8 (7%)	22 (18%)	33 (26%)	43 (43%)	68 (57%)	174 (30%)
	No	103 (93%)	100 (82%)	95 (74%)	57 (57%)	52 (43%)	407 (70%)
		111	122	128	100	120	(581)

You will note that the total for all the sample cases in the survey at the bottom right of the table is quoted as 581, which is less than the total response of 655 organisations which participated in the survey. This is because of **missing values**. In quantitative research, this term is used in two ways. On the one hand, it is used to refer to incomplete data, where, for example, a small proportion of respondents in a survey has been unable or unwilling to respond to a particular question. On the other hand, it is used to refer to units of a sample that are logically excluded from a particular calculation. For example, a common technique used in questionnaires is to add subsidiary questions that are relevant only to respondents who answered a previous question in a particular way (e.g. 'answer this question only if you answered "yes" to the previous question'). Missing values in these instances would refer to those sample cases that would logically be excluded from the calculation because of their earlier response. With regard to Table 5.3, the missing values are of the first kind: there were 74 respondents who were either unable or unwilling to indicate their organisation's annual budget and/or whether their organisation had received any TV news coverage.

If we look at the column percentages in Table 5.3, there appears to be a relationship between television coverage of organisations and their annual income, as the proportion of organisations that received TV coverage increases the higher up the revenue scale they go. Only 7 per cent of groups with an annual budget of less than £1,000 had received any TV coverage, compared with 57 per cent of groups with an annual budget exceeding £250,000. Although this pattern may seem conclusive on its own terms, we cannot assume that it proves a relationship between television exposure and financial resources. It could be that the pattern can be explained by random error. The chi-square test calculates the likelihood that this is the case.

Step 1: conceptualising the null hypothesis

The *null hypothesis* is an abstract assumption that frames the way you interpret the chi-square significance test. It requires you to assume that there is *no* relationship between the variables being investigated, and that any differences are due to random sampling errors. In this example, the null hypothesis would be 'there is no relationship between the annual budget of voluntary organisations and their receipt of television coverage'. The chi-square test puts this hypothesis to the test. If the results suggest it is statistically improbable, then it is rejected and the converse proposition – that there is a significant relationship between the variables – is accepted.

Step 2: calculating expected frequencies

A cross-tabulation automatically provides 'observed frequencies' for each cell of the table (i.e. the actual numbers that fall into each cell). The next step in this test is to calculate the numbers you would expect to see in each cell if there were no relationship between the variables. These are called *expected frequencies*, and are calculated on a cell-by-cell basis, by multiplying the row total and column total for each cell and then dividing the result by the total sample number. Therefore, the expected frequencies for column 1, row 1 would be:

174 (the row total) multiplied by **111** (the column total), divided by **581** (the total size of the sample) = **33.2**.

Table 5.4 includes the expected frequencies for each cell under the observed frequencies. (NB The expected frequencies are in bold and rounded up to one decimal point.) Notice that if you add the observed and expected frequencies separately, they both add up to the column totals at the bottom.

Table 5.4 Cross-tabulation of voluntary agencies' annual budget and TV exposure (observed and expected frequencies)

		Annual budget of organisations					
		<£1,000	£1,001–£10,000	£10,001–£50,000	£50,001–£250,000	£250,001+	
National or local TV coverage?	Yes	8 **33.2**	22 **36.5**	33 **38.3**	43 **29.9**	68 **35.9**	174
	No	103 **77.8**	100 **85.5**	95 **89.7**	57 **70.1**	52 **84.1**	407
		111	122	128	100	120	(581)

Step 3: measuring the goodness of fit

Measuring the *goodness of fit* involves comparing the differences between the observed and expected frequencies. The reason for doing so is the key logical proposition on which the whole test depends: *the greater the cumulative difference between the observed and expected frequencies, the less likely it is that the relationship exposed could have occurred by chance.*

The values that measure the goodness of fit are calculated on a cell-by-cell basis, in the following way:

- subtract the expected frequency from the observed frequency (e.g. in column 1, row 1 this would be $8 - 33.2 = -25.2$);

- square this value (e.g. $-25.2^2 = 635.0$ rounded to 1 decimal point);

- divide this figure by the expected value (e.g. $635.0 \div 33.2 = 19.1$ (rounded to 1 decimal point)).

The residual values for each cell of the table are shown (in italics) in Table 5.5. Note that the largest residual values are in the first and last columns of the table. This signifies that these are the cells where there is the greatest disparity between what has been observed and what you would expect to see if no relationship existed.

Table 5.5 Cross-tabulation of voluntary agencies' annual budget and TV exposure (observed frequencies, expected frequencies and residual values)

		Annual budget of organisations					
		<£1,000	£1,001–£10,000	£10,001–£50,000	£50,001–£250,000	£250,001+	
National or local TV coverage?	Yes	8	22	33	43	68	174
		33.2	36.5	38.3	29.9	35.9	
		19.1	*5.8*	*0.7*	*5.7*	*8.6*	
	No	103	100	95	57	52	407
		77.8	85.5	89.7	70.1	84.1	
		8.2	*2.5*	*0.3*	*2.4*	*12.2*	
		111	122	128	100	120	(581)

Once all the residual values have been calculated for all the cells in the table, they are added to produce a final chi-square value. For our example, this figure would be:

$19.1 + 8.2 + 5.8 + 2.5 + 0.7 + 0.3 + 5.7 + 2.4 + 8.6 + 12.2 = 65.5.$

This total is the chi-square value for the table, which is signalled by the symbol χ^2.

Step 4: calculating the degrees of freedom

Following the reasoning explained in step 3, we can see that the higher the chi-square value (χ^2) is, the greater the likelihood that a real relationship exists between the two variables. This is because the chi-square value is based on the differences between the observed and expected frequencies in each cell. However, we cannot interpret this value in isolation, because it will also be affected by the size of the table from which it is calculated. The larger a table is, the greater the chi square value will tend to be, as there are more numbers that can be included in its calculation. (NB χ^2 is always zero or more.)

Therefore, before we can assess the statistical significance of the chi-square value, we must also compute the degrees of freedom of the table. This calculation allows us to take account of the size of the contingency table when interpreting the chi-square value. To calculate the degrees of freedom of a table, you subtract 1 from the number of rows in a table, subtract 1 from the number of columns, and then multiply the two results together. The degrees of freedom for our example equals: 2 rows − 1 = 1, multiplied by 5 columns − 1 = 4, or 4 degrees of freedom.

Step 5: relating the chi-square values and the degrees of freedom to a chi-square distribution

To work out the statistical significance of χ^2 values in conjunction with their degrees of freedom, you consult a chi-square distribution table, which can be found in most statistical textbooks. This table relates χ^2 values and degrees of freedom to probability levels (see Table 5.6). We do not have the space here to explain how probability levels are calculated on the basis of χ^2 values (for an explanation, see Weiss 1968: 257–8), but you should appreciate two basic points about the table:

- The more degrees of freedom a table has (i.e. the bigger it is), the larger the values for χ^2 have to be in order to be deemed 'statistically significant'. For example, a χ^2 value of 5.99 is significant at the 0.05 level for a table with 2 degrees of freedom, but it would have to be 7.84 to attain the same significance in a table with 3 degrees of freedom.

- The larger the χ^2 value is, the greater its statistical significance will be. For example, if we look at the values for tables with 3 degrees of freedom, if a χ^2 value were 7.81 or above, it would be deemed to be significant at the 0.05 level, but it would have to be 11.34 or above to be significant at the 0.01 level.

Table 5.6 The chi-square distribution table

Degrees of freedom	Level of significance 0.05	Level of significance 0.01
1	3.84	6.63
2	5.99	9.21
3	7.81	11.34
4	9.49	13.28
5	11.07	15.09
6	12.59	16.81
7	14.07	18.48
8	15.51	20.09
9	16.92	21.67
10	18.31	23.21
11	19.68	24.72
12	21.03	26.22
etc.		

In our worked example, there is a χ^2 value of 65.5 and 4 degrees of freedom. Reading across the row for 4 degrees of freedom, we can see that the χ^2 value needs to be more than 13.28 to be considered statistically significant at $p < 0.01$. Our χ^2 value comfortably exceeds this level, which means there is far less than a 1 in 100 chance ($p < 0.01$) that these differences between observed and expected frequencies occurred by chance. Therefore, we can reject the null hypothesis that there is no relationship between the annual budget of voluntary organisations and their television exposure, and accept the alternative interpretation that there is a statistically significant relationship between these variables.

There is one final point you need to be clear about regarding the chi-square test. All it tells us is the statistical significance of a relationship. It does not tell us anything about the strength of that relationship.

Testing hypotheses (2): the *t*-test

Another widely used statistical procedure for hypothesis testing is the *t*-test. This test is used to analyse continuous data that attain the interval or ratio levels of measurement, and is most commonly used to compare differences in means between two groups of data. There are, in fact, two types of *t*-test, which are calculated in different ways. The *t*-test for 'independent samples' is used to compare the means of groups that are independent of each other (e.g. comparing female and male participants in a survey). The *t*-test for 'dependent samples' (sometimes referred to as 'correlated samples') is used where the two sets of sample data are related (e.g. 'before' and 'after' testing of participants in an experimental study). The procedure we set out in Box 5.7 is for conducting a *t*-test for independent samples.

The *t*-test can be used on small samples, unlike the chi-square test, which requires a sample size to be of a certain volume before it can be conducted reliably.[3] However, the preconditions for using the *t*-test on small data sets are that:

- the data approximate a normal distribution curve;
- there is no great difference in the number of cases in the two categories being compared.

Box 5.8 Conducting a t-test for independent samples

A small-scale survey of students' Internet use identifies an age difference in the amount of time respondents spend per week using the Internet. Among respondents aged 20–29 years, weekly online activity averaged 16 hours, whereas for the 40–49 years age group, the average was 7.9 hours per week. The researcher conducts a *t*-test for independent samples, to see whether this difference is statistically significant.

20–29 years age group	40–49 years age group
6	2
12	4
12	4

---

3 It is generally accepted that each cell in a table must contain at least five observed frequencies for the chi-square test to be conducted reliably.

16	12
16	12
16	12
22	12
22	14
28	14
29	20

- *Step 1:* conceptualise the null hypothesis (i.e. 'There is no significant age difference in the amount of time spent using the Internet').
- *Step 2:* add together all the values for the 20–29 years respondents (179) and divide by the number of values (179 ÷ 10 = 17.9).
- *Step 3:* square each of the values for the 20–29 years respondents (36, 144, 144, 256, 256, 256, 484, 484, 784, 841) and add them together (Σ= 3,685).
- *Step 4:* square the sum of values for the 20–29 years respondents (179 × 179 = 32,041) and divide by the number of values (32,041 ÷ 10 = 3,204.1).
- *Step 5:* subtract the step 4 result from the step 3 result (3,685 − 3,204.1 = 480.9).
- *Step 6:* repeat all these steps for the 40–49 years age group. This produces a final value of 280.4.
- *Step 7:* add the step 5 and step 6 results (480.9 + 280.4 = 761.3).
- *Step 8:* divide this figure by the number of 20–29 years group values minus 1 (10 − 1 = 9), added to the number of 40–49 years group values minus 1 (10 − 1 = 9) (761.3 ÷ 18 = 42.29).
- *Step 9:* calculate the reciprocal of the number of 20–29 years group values (10) added to the number of 40–49 years group values minus 1 (10). (NB A reciprocal is a fraction. It is calculated by dividing values into 1 (i.e. 1 ÷ N).) The reciprocal values for the 20–29 years group would be 1 ÷ 10 = 0.1, and for the 40–49 years group, 1 ÷ 10 = 0.1. Added together, they produce a value of 0.2.
- *Step 10:* multiply the results of step 8 by the results of step 9 (42.29 × 0.2 = 8.458).
- *Step 11:* take the square root of this value ($\sqrt{8.458}$ = 2.91).
- *Step 12:* calculate the difference between the average scores for the two sets of data (see step 2) (20–29 years group = 17.9; 40–49 years group = 10.6, producing a difference of 7.3).
- *Step 13:* divide the result of step 12 by the result of step 11 (7.3 ÷ 2.91 = 2.51). **This result is *t*.**
- *Step 14:* Identify the degrees of freedom for your sample. To do this, add the number of values in the first column, minus 1, to the number of values in the second column, minus 1 ([10 − 1] + [10 − 1] = 18 degrees of freedom).
- *Step 15:* consult a statistical table that lists the values for the *t* distribution, which relates *t* values and degrees of freedom to probability levels (see Table 5.7).

Because our *t* value at 18 degrees of freedom (t = 2.51) *exceeds* the value listed for the

0.05 level of significance ($t = 2.101$), we can say that there is less than a 1 in 20 chance that the difference in the means of the two groups occurred by chance. If we have set our level of confidence at $p > 0.05$, then we can reject the null hypothesis and assert that there are statistically significant age differences in terms of the amount of time spent on Internet-based activities. However, if we have set our level of confidence at $p > 0.01$, we cannot reject the null hypothesis. This is because our t value is less than the value required for a finding to be deemed significant at this higher level (2.878).

Table 5.7 The t-distribution table (for two-tailed tests[4])

Degrees of freedom	Level of significance 0.05	Level of significance 0.01
1	12.706	63.657
2	4.303	9.925
3	3.182	5.841
4	2.776	4.604
5	2.571	4.032
6	2.447	3.707
7	2.365	3.500
8	2.306	3.355
9	2.262	3.250
10	2.228	3.169
11	2.201	3.106
12	2.179	3.054
13	2.160	3.012
14	2.145	2.977
15	2.132	2.947
16	2.120	2.921
17	2.110	2.898
18	2.101	2.878

4   Statistical tests are categorised as 'one-tailed' or 'two-tailed'. The 'tails' refer to the outlying values in a statistical distribution. A one-tailed test is used when (a) you have some reason for anticipating that there will be a significant difference between sample groups, and (b) you know the direction that difference will take (e.g. values attributed for group A will significantly exceed those found for group B). A two-tailed test is used where (a) you have no grounds for assuming that there are significant differences between sample groups, and (b) you have no way of knowing what direction any differences between groups might take. Two-tailed tests are the most frequently used, because there is no requirement of prior knowledge of the likelihood of a significant difference between sample groups and the direction of that difference.

Multivariate analysis

Thus far we have described methods for exploring two-way relationships between variables (e.g. cross-tabulations and correlations). Although *bivariate* analysis is a common aspect of statistical analysis, it has limitations. First, relationships between social and psychological factors often involve more than two elements, and we need to consider ways in which many multiple variables can be analysed. Also, bivariate analysis does not allow us to say how relationships between social and psychological phenomena may be reduced, mitigated or accentuated by the interaction of other variables. Second, we may erroneously identify one of the variables as an independent variable, when in fact both variables are dependent variables and their apparent relationship is the product of some other factor. One famous and absurd illustration of this point was the discovery that in the city of Copenhagen, for the decade following World War II, there was a consistent and strong correlation between annual increases in the country's birth rate and the annual number of storks nesting in the city. As recent advances in the paediatric sciences have categorically proven that these shy and inelegant birds have nothing whatsoever to do with the delivery of human babies, the correlation can be discounted as coincidental – a product of other factors.

There are many procedures that can be employed to explore multiple interactions between more than two variables. We only have the space here to cover one of the most basic procedures for multivariate analysis, using cross-tabulations and chi-square statistical testing.

Cross-tabulations and multivariate analysis

To demonstrate how cross-tabulations can be used to explore multiple relations between variables, we shall draw on the survey of social scientists and their media contact mentioned in the introduction. In this research, it emerged that media contact appeared to be linked to both gender and hierarchical factors. A higher proportion of men had more media contact than women (see Table 5.8), as had senior social scientists compared with their more junior colleagues (see Table 5.9). These differences were found to be statistically significant using the χ^2 test.

Table 5.8 Gender by media contact

	Male	Female
Had media contact	70%	60%
Had no media contact	30%	40%
Number[5]	421	249
p < 0.01		

---

5 The observant reader will note slight variations in the totals of numbers presented in Tables 5.8 to 5.11. This is due to the varying impact that missing values have on individual calculations.

Table 5.9 Seniority by media contact

	Senior	Junior
Had media contact	85%	61%
Had no media contact	15%	39%
Number	143	531
p < 0.00001		

These findings raised a number of questions. Do gender and seniority factors work separately and independently, influencing media contact and revealing a separate journalistic preference for men and for bosses? Conversely, might one of the relationships be spurious – a product of the other factor? For example, did senior staff have more media contact simply because journalists prefer to talk to men, and men are more likely to have senior positions? If one of the relationships is spurious, which one is it?

One way of trying to answer these questions is to run two 'three-way' tables (see Tables 5.10 and 5.11). To construct a three-way table, you first divide the sample according to a particular variable (e.g. in the case of Table 5.11, between *senior staff* and *junior staff*). Then, taking each of these parts separately, you examine the links between two other variables (e.g. *gender* and *media contact*). This is what statisticians mean when they talk of 'controlling' a particular factor. It means holding one variable in the analysis constant, while exploring relationships between other variables. The first table (Table 5.10) shows the relationship between *seniority* and *media contact*, while 'controlling' for *gender*. The second (Table 5.11), exposes the links between *gender* and *media contact*, while controlling for *seniority*.

Table 5.10 Seniority and media contact controlling for gender

	Male social scientists				Female social scientists	
	Senior	Junior			Senior	Junior
Had media contact	(a) 87%	(b) 64%		Had media contact	(e) 79%	(f) 58%
Had no media contact	(c) 13%	(d) 36%		Had no media contact	(g) 21%	(h) 42%
Number	114	307		Number	29	220
p < 0.00001				**p < 0.02**		

Table 5.11 Gender and media contact controlling for seniority

	Senior social scientists			Junior social scientists	
	Male	Female		Male	Female
Had media contact	(a)	(b)	Had media contact	(e)	(f)
	87%	79%		64%	58%
Had no media contact	(c)	(d)	Had no media contact	(g)	(h)
	13%	21%		36%	42%
Number	114	21	Number	307	220
p < 0.306 (not significant)			p < 0.15516 (not significant)		

At first, the clues displayed by these two tables may not be self-evident. Therefore, let us interpret each one in turn. Table 5.10 begins by separating the survey data into two parts (male and female social scientists). It then examines the link between *media contact* and *seniority* for each gender. The table shows that senior male social scientists appear more likely to have had media contact than junior male social scientists (87 per cent compared with 64 per cent – see cells a and b); just as senior female social scientists are more likely to have had media contact than junior female social scientists (79 per cent compared with 58 per cent – see cells e and f). As the two probability statements at the base of each part of the table show, these differences are statistically significant.

Table 5.11 cuts the cake in a different way. First, it divides the sample by *seniority*, separating senior social scientists from junior social scientists. Then it examines the link between *media contact* and *gender*. When the relationship between the three variables is examined in this way, a different picture emerges. As cells a and b demonstrate, senior male social scientists are only slightly more likely to have had media contact than senior female social scientists (87 per cent compared with 79 per cent), and junior male social scientists are only marginally more likely to have had media contact than their female equivalents (64 per cent compared with 58 per cent – see cells e and f). Although these tables suggest that a gender imbalance is retained when *seniority* is controlled, the probability statements at the base of this table show that these differences are *not* statistically significant (i.e. we cannot be confident that these differences did not occur by chance).

So what does this multivariate analysis suggest? Because gender does not remain a significant variable once seniority is controlled, it would appear that the relative marginalisation of female social scientists in media coverage is not a product of a deliberate media preference for men over women, but rather a side effect of media professionals' greater interest in the news and views of 'senior' social scientists than 'junior' social scientists. In other words, women are under-represented in the media not because of the inalienable fact of their gender but rather because of institutional inequalities which see far more men attain authoritative positions than women. Therefore, in this case, it would seem that the media are not so much creating a sexist agenda as reinforcing it.

Summary: key points

- We explained that every student in communication and cultural studies should have some understanding of basic statistical concepts, because of the ubiquity of statistics in the human sciences and their broader rhetorical power.

- The different levels of measurement that numbers can attain were outlined (the nominal, ordinal, interval, pseudo-interval and ratio).

- Various descriptive statistical measures used in univariate analysis (measures of central tendency, measures of dispersion) and bivariate analysis (correlation coefficients and cross-tabulations) were examined.

- Various ways of presenting research findings visually using graphs were discussed (bar charts, histograms, line graphs, pie charts and scattergrams). We explained the protocols that should be observed when using different graphs, and in particular the need to consider the level of measurement of data when selecting a type of graph.

- The difference between inferential statistics and descriptive statistics was explained. It was shown how inferential statistics are used (a) to make estimates of population values from sample data (using the standard error of the mean as an example), and (b) test hypotheses (using the chi-square test and *t*-test as examples).

- Multivariate analysis was introduced.

Answers to Box 5.1

1. Age measured in years attains the interval/ratio level of measurement. You can, for instance, say that a respondent who is 36 is half the age of a respondent aged 72.

2. Once the age of respondents is bracketed in this way, the level of measurement drops to the *ordinal* level. For example, you can no longer say that a respondent categorised in the second group is half the age of a person in the fourth group, because of the distribution and imprecision of the categories.

3. Although a percentage like this may seem to attain the interval/ratio level of measurement, it actually attains only the *ordinal* level. This is because of the nature of the topic being assessed and the nature of the assessment. The 'rightness' or 'wrongness' of this sort of answer is not a straightforward matter, and depends on the judgement and interpretation of the examiner. For these reasons, you could not say, in any strict mathematical sense, that an essay that was awarded 80 per cent was twice as good as an essay awarded 40 per cent.

4. This individual scale would normally be treated as an *ordinal* measure.

5. 'Ethnicity' is a *nominal* measure. You cannot rank, add, divide or multiply the values assigned for different categories.

6. Although a composite of ordinal measures, this multiple-item scale could be treated as a *pseudo-interval* variable.

chapter six

Counting Contents

This chapter is the first of three examining different approaches used in the analysis of written media texts (see also chapters 7 and 8). To reiterate a general theme, it is our belief that the choice of techniques for use in the analysis of such texts should be dictated by the task at hand and the research questions you are seeking to address. You may want to establish the frequency with which certain kinds of stories occur in the press, or the degree to which they are slanted towards a particular perspective within a high frequency of occurrence. This will mean taking an expansive, panoramic view of the phenomena you are studying, and in doing this it is appropriate to establish the incidence of such phenomena by some form of measurement. Alternatively, you may want to look closely at the structure of a particular newspaper story, to examine how the words, sentences and paragraphs it is composed of combine and interact to privilege a particular meaning for the event the story revolves around, or to reproduce a contradiction in the way the event and its associations are conventionally viewed. This will mean taking an intensive view of written communication, putting a text or part of it under the microscope, as it were, in order to reveal features which you may usually take for granted, without examining how they are effective, why you may accept them as unremarkable, or why you do not view them with a critical eye.

Whichever analytical method you adopt in the study of written media texts, you must try to avoid the trap of regarding your own approach as mutually incompatible with others. Different methods may be appropriate to the different stages and focuses of your research, while the use of more than one analytical method has the advantage that 'the weaknesses of any single method, qualitative or quantitative, are balanced by the strengths of other methods' (Williams, Rice and Rogers 1988: 47). Using a method of analysis should not be akin to supporting a football team, which you stick with through relegation battle after relegation battle. Never be afraid to try out new angles of investigation, or different tools of analysis. If one of these does not seem to work, you can always drop it or make adaptations.

The reason we begin this chapter with a reminder of the benefits of methodological eclecticism is that, too often, quantitative and qualitative approaches to the study of media texts have been regarded as mutually incompatible. At its worst, this has meant that advocates of qualitative forms of analysis have dismissed quantitative methods of content analysis as irremediably positivist, obsessed with frequency counts as indices of significance and unable to get past the manifest content of communications to where the crucial meanings lie, beneath the textual surface. This caricature is unhelpful. There is a good deal of substance in criticism of inflexible uses of quantification, but quantitative research techniques can too easily be rejected out of hand, and in this chapter we hope to point up the value of such methods when used in combination with others of an avowedly qualitative character.

The approaches on which we focus in these three chapters are chosen for two reasons: first, because they have been pervasive and influential in the development of media studies, though not of course with any close degree of parity, and second, because they seem to us to be of considerable value in facilitating and enhancing the analysis of texts within communication and cultural studies. Basically, the task of such analysis is to examine the relationships between the internal dynamics of (in this case) written texts and the social organisation in which such texts achieve circulation. In this chapter, we concentrate on quantitative textual analysis. In chapters 7 and 8, we look at qualitative analytical approaches.

Content analysis

The term **content analysis** is used inconsistently within the literature. On the one hand, it is used generically to cover any method that involves analysing content. On the other, it is used to describe a specific analytical approach. In this section, we use the term in this second, precise sense.

Berelson famously described content analysis as: 'A research technique for the objective, systematic and quantitative description of the manifest content of communication' (1952: 147). This definition is useful because it highlights key facets of the method's origins and concerns. In particular, the claim to 'objectivity' and the emphasis on 'manifest' (i.e. observable) evidence reveal the scientistic ambitions that prompted its development. Like other quantitative techniques developed in the early twentieth century, content analysis was originally designed to bring the rigour and authority of 'natural' scientific inquiry to the study of human and social phenomena. However, as we shall see, the claim that the method provides completely value-free insights to the study of content is dubious.

A second impetus for the method's development grew out of the widespread and coincidental concerns before World War II about the growth and influence of new mass media industries. At this time, it was widely supposed that mass audiences were highly susceptible to manipulation by media messages, and quantitative content analysis was developed in part to provide academics and politicians with the means to police the symbolic arenas of mass culture, and in particular to detect the presence and influence of propaganda (e.g. Lasswell 1936; Lasswell and Leites 1949; for a critical treatment of propaganda research in the early twentieth century, see Robins, Webster and Pickering 1987).

But it was not just positivists and politicians who saw value in developing a systematic and broad-ranging method for analysing trends in mass communications. In an address to the German Sociological Association in 1910, Max Weber – one of the most influential historical advocates of *interpretive* social research – proposed a new sociology of the press that would be founded on quantitative textual analysis:

You will ask now: where is the material to begin such studies? This material consists of the newspapers themselves, and we will now, to be specific, start quite narrowly with scissors and compasses to measure the quantitative changes of newspaper contents during the last generation, especially in the advertising section, in the *feuilleton* [feature and short story sections], between *feuilleton* and editorial, between editorial and news, between what is generally carried as news and what is not presented. Because conditions have changed significantly.

(quoted in Hardt 1979: 181–2)

Although content analysis is employed across the social and human sciences (Holsti 1969), its natural domain is communication, media and cultural studies. Historical examples of content analysis studies in this field are legion, and the method is still very popular.

The purpose of content analysis is to quantify salient and manifest features of a large number of texts, and the statistics are used to make broader inferences about the processes and politics of representation. Several stages are involved in the generation of these statistics and we outline these below. To help illustrate the kinds of decisions and procedures involved in each, we work through a hypothetical example of a content analysis of crime reporting.

Defining your concerns

To use quantitative content analysis effectively, you need to be clear from the beginning what it is that you are interested in investigating. Content analysis is a directive method; it gives answers to the questions you pose. In this regard, the method does not offer much opportunity to explore texts in order to develop ideas and insights. It can only support, qualify or refute your initial questions – which may or may not be pertinent. Furthermore, it is better at providing some answers than others. Therefore, when deciding whether to use the method in your research, you need to be clear about what it is and is not good at analysing.

Because content analysis is a method that aims to produce 'a big picture' (delineating trends, patterns and absences over large aggregates of texts), it is well suited to dealing with the 'massness' of the mass media (Gerbner 1969), which, as Winston argues, can provide essential political insights:

[C]ontent analysis remains the only available tool for establishing maps, however faulty, of television output… Without 'the map', no case can be sustained as to any kind of cultural skewedness except on the basis of one-off examples of misrepresentation or libel (which are not the norm). And if no case can be made, then there is none to answer.

(Winston 1990: 62)

However, this big picture comes at a cost. By looking at aggregated meaning-making *across* texts, the method tends to skate over complex and varied processes of meaning-making *within* texts; the latent rather than manifest levels of meanings that are always evident (Graber 1989). For these reasons, the method is not well suited to studying 'deep' questions about textual and discursive forms. It is not good at exposing aesthetic or rhetorical nuances within texts.

To illustrate these points, let us contrast two different types of research question that might fall under the general rubric of analysing media reporting of crime, one of which would be suited to a content analysis approach, and one that would be less so. Imagine you wanted to see whether there were any major disparities between the representation of criminal activity in the media and levels of crime in society. Although, as we shall see, quantifying criminality in the media is not as straightforward as you might assume, this sort of question almost demands a quantitative approach, being concerned essentially with comparisons of extent. However, imagine you wanted to explore how journalists' *perceptions* of criminality, as conveyed through their reports, can often contest strict legal *definitions*, whether in pressing for the criminalisation of certain types of activity that are deemed unacceptable or in calling for the decriminalisation of others. Given the complexity and controversy of these matters, you would expect a considerable diversity of opinions, invoking different evidence and rhetoric as justification. Furthermore, it would be difficult to predict what forms these arguments might take. For these reasons, this sort of research topic would be more productively analysed, at least in the first instance, by detailed, qualitative textual analysis rather than rigid statistical procedures.

Sampling

Being clear about your research agenda from the outset is also of great value when considering sampling issues. Although content analysis can be used to analyse large numbers of texts, studies rarely cover every single piece of content relevant to their objectives. Most require the development of a sampling strategy, which involves considering similar issues to those addressed in chapter 3 in our examination of representative sampling methods.

There are several stages involved in developing a sampling strategy. First, you need to define the total range of content you want to make inferences about (this is the 'population' of your research). Taking the example of an analysis of crime coverage in the media, would you want to look at fictional and actual coverage of criminal activity, or would you prefer to focus on one or the other? If you looked at fictional representations, would you be interested in drawing inferences about all fictional genres (films, soap operas, one-off dramatisations, cartoons, etc.) or would you prefer to be more selective? Alternatively, if you focused on factual coverage, would you want to examine crime coverage across all forms of actuality coverage (talks shows, current affairs, news, lifestyle programming, etc.) or would you prefer to restrict your analysis to specific forms (e.g. news and current affairs)? These sorts of issues need to be clarified from the beginning, as they should guide your sampling strategy and circumscribe the eventual inferences you draw. For instance, it would be rather dubious to start making inferences about *all* fictional representations of crime, if you had sampled only soap operas.

The second issue you need to decide on is what your sampling unit will be (an issue that is referred to as *unitisation*). When you sample people or institutions, the sampling unit is self-evident, but with texts, the 'unit of analysis' is not so readily identified. Some quantitative content analysis studies have a very precise focus, taking individual words as their sampling units to explore 'the lexical contents and/or syntactic structures of documents' (Beardsworth 1980: 375). Other studies provide a more generalised analysis of themes in texts:

Theme analysis…does not rely on the use of specific words as basic content elements, but relies upon the coder to recognise certain themes or ideas in the text, and then to allocate these to predetermined categories. While both such approaches are applicable to the study of press output, in practice the latter seems to have been used more frequently.

(ibid.)

In this discussion, we focus on theme analysis, because of its wider application in communication research. But what unit of analysis do you use when conducting this sort of analysis? This is a matter for the researcher to decide. For example, the sampling unit could be an entire programme or publication, or component parts of these texts (e.g. separate news items, headlines, music videos within a pop show). Once chosen, the sampling unit becomes the host to all textual elements that are subsequently quantified (see the next section on 'Deciding what to count').

Some sampling units are easier to operationalise than others. While it is not difficult to see where a programme or publication begins and ends, once you start using component parts of texts as your unit of analysis, you need to establish some clear rules. If you decided to use individual news items in TV news programmes as your basic sampling unit, how would you decide where one item ended and another one began? For example, how would you deal with the following sequence of items?

1. Introduction from newsreader based in studio (live).
2. Report from correspondent based on location (taped).
3. Return to newsreader, who then conducts an interview on the topic of the report with a selected news source (live).

Should you treat all three stages as one single unit, because they all address the same topic, or as three separate units? Or could you treat the three components as constituting two units, taking the return to the newsreader at stage 3 as a signal that a new item has begun, even though the interview is on the same topic? Similarly, how would you deal with the next sequence?

1. Introduction from newsreader based in studio (live).
2. Report from correspondent on location (taped).
3. Report from a second correspondent in a different location but addressing the same topic (taped).

Again, should you treat all three sections as three units, or as one single unit because they share the same subject? Or should you treat the studio introduction and the first report as one single item, and the change of location and correspondent at stage 3 as signalling the beginning of a second item?

There are no right and wrong answers to resolving these sorts of coding dilemmas (and it is not difficult to think of equivalent examples in press reporting), but you do need to make some firm and explicit decisions from the outset as to how you intend to resolve them, and then apply the rules systematically.

The third issue you need to consider in your sampling is how much of your population you need to analyse to construct a credible, representative sample. With quantitative content analysis sampling, you need to think about representativeness in two ways. The first is in relation to time: how far backwards or forwards should you extend your sampling period? Obviously, the more limited the time period is, the more susceptible it is to distortion by one-off, unforeseen events. Imagine you wanted to conduct a content analysis of science reporting, and during your three-week sample period it was announced that scientists had discovered evidence that primitive organisms had once existed on Mars. The obvious impact on your study of such a newsworthy discovery would be to produce a disproportionately large amount of coverage of astrophysics and astronomy during that period. One way of limiting the risk of this happening is to extend the sample across as wide a time period as possible, but here again there can be difficulties. When sampling retrospectively, your research is inevitably affected by the availability and comprehensiveness of archival sources. (The simple reason why there are far more retrospective content analysis studies of printed 'elite' media texts than either populist or broadcast media is because the former are more widely archived by libraries.) One solution is to sample prospectively: taping and collecting your sample materials as you go. However, because you are sampling in real time, building up a sufficiently comprehensive time period can be a lengthy process. Furthermore, such an approach prevents longitudinal, historical comparisons.

The second vector to be considered is how extensively you should sample across the elements of your population. For example, if you were interested in news reporting of crime, should you sample every single national newspaper title and broadcast news programme produced during your sample period? Or could you be more selective, perhaps sampling just the main daily news programme broadcast on each channel, or selecting newspaper titles that could be claimed to represent broadly the diversity of the press sector? The obvious benefit of selective, stratified sampling is that it reduces the logistics involved in the research. But there is a risk that if you pursue this strategy too extensively, you may compromise your sample's representativeness.

For all these reasons, there is no simple answer to the question: 'How big must my sample be?' As a general rule, the bigger a content sample is, the better – if you want to paint a broad picture, you need a big canvas. However, practical constraints need to be appreciated (time, costs, the availability of archives, etc.), and, as with most research, you will often have to trade off what is desirable with what is feasible. But where practical restrictions have seriously inhibited your empirical ambitions, you should be candid about your sample's limitations.

Deciding what to count

This is a stage that demands careful planning and some imagination, as, although some variables appear recurrently in different thematic content analysis studies (see Table 6.1), there is no standard list of things that should always be quantified. What you count should be determined by your research objectives. As we have mentioned, content analysis is not an exploratory method; it only gives answers to the questions you ask. So you must make sure you ask the right questions. Never count things simply for the sake of it: if you cannot provide a good reason for including a variable, get rid of it.

Table 6.1 Textual dimensions commonly coded in content analysis

Dimension	Definition	Coding issues
Who appears?	These are commonly referred to as the 'actors' in coverage: the people or organisations that are referred to manifestly in texts. Actors are often coded to compare the differential presence of social and political groups in media coverage.	If you simply quantify the proportion of sampling units within which an individual, group or institution is mentioned, you can only draw conclusions about the extent to which they have been the subject of coverage. But media presence is not the same as media access. For example, in 1995, the total number of articles referring to the IRA in the *Daily Telegraph* and *Sunday Telegraph* exceeded the total references to the Liberal Democrat Party, the third largest political party in Britain (674 articles versus 529 articles). Although this may tell you something about the respective newsworthiness of these two political groups during that period, it would be highly questionable to suggest, on the basis of these figures, that this illegal paramilitary group has greater opportunities for conveying its views via these papers than the Liberal Democrats. It is highly probable that a considerable amount of this IRA-related coverage involved other political sources talking about them (and no doubt in a predominantly negative manner).
		For this reason, you might want to be more discerning in deciding whether you code a person or institution as an 'actor'. For example, you may decide that it is not enough for somebody to get a name-check to be coded. Rather, they need to be active subjects in the content: either being quoted, pictured or described independently of other actors. A simple way to operationalise this would be to say that if a person or institution's name appeared only in the context of other people's comments (e.g. 'Liberal Democrats condemn "IRA intransigence"'), then they should not be counted as an actor in the item.
		Sometimes it is necessary to put a ceiling on the number of actors coded for each sampling unit. When this is the case, clear procedures are needed to decide which are the most prominent actors (position, proportional presence in piece, etc.).

How do they appear?	These measures quantify the nature of the presentation of actors (e.g. are they pictured, quoted, paraphrased?).	This type of variable can be used productively in conjunction with actor codings to differentiate between media presence and media access.
Evaluative features	These measures assess the partisanship or bias of a text towards particular value positions, individuals or groups.	Bias is an easy charge to make and a difficult one to prove. This is because people's perception of bias is often influenced by their own views and beliefs. When applying evaluative measures, you should avoid reading too deeply into the semantics of text. Your judgements about partisanship should be based on what is manifestly stated in the text, and not on any prior knowledge. Only open partisanship can be quantified with any degree of reliability, and even then this may often be a matter of fine judgement.
Interpretive dimensions	These measures focus on the 'themes' of coverage: what is an issue seen to be about? Are there any elements that are significantly absent?	The main difficulty in developing a set of themes is ensuring that the categories adequately capture all aspects of the issue that are likely to arise. This is not always easy to predict at the outset, as debates can develop in unpredictable ways, and some issues are inherently amorphous.

Another thing you need to bear in mind is how feasible it is to quantify a variable accurately and reliably, as some things are easier to count than others. For example, although it is not difficult to code whether a news item is on the front page or a lead story in a bulletin, you might find it more challenging to quantify quickly and consistently whether an item adopts an 'ironic' or 'romantic/melodramatic' narrative mode in its structure and manner of address (Roeh 1989). This is because such a categorisation would require fine judgement, based on detailed analysis of each text. As a general rule, content analysis does not work reliably when coders are required to 'read between the lines' to get at latent structures of meaning (Van Zoonen 1994: 69).

So, what sorts of things would be straightforward, but nonetheless significant, to quantify in an analysis of crime reporting? This is where you have to impose your own agenda by referring back to the broad aims of your research. For the sake of argument, imagine you wanted to examine what sorts of crimes, victims of crimes and offenders received most news coverage, because of your wider concerns that news coverage might:

- provide a distorted picture of the frequency of certain types of criminal activity;
- provide a distorted picture of the likelihood of certain social groups becoming victims of crimes;
- pay disproportionate attention to the criminality of certain ethnic groups, despite professional guidelines that warn against 'spurious referencing' to ethnicity in crime reporting.

If you decided that your unit of analysis would be the individual items and articles featured in a sample of newspapers and TV news programmes, you could address these broad research concerns by coding the following details for each 'crime item' included in your sample:

1. The medium in which the item appeared.
2. The place where the item was positioned in the programme/newspaper.
3. The size of the item (whether in centimetres squared or seconds).
4. The age of the offender(s) mentioned in the item.
5. The gender of the offender(s) mentioned in the item.
6. The ethnicity of the offender(s) mentioned in the item.
7. The age of the victim(s) mentioned in the item.
8. The gender of the victim(s) mentioned in the item.
9. The ethnicity of the victim(s) mentioned in the item.
10. The crime(s) mentioned in the item.

This list is by no means definitive, but it does at least illustrate how you might go about distilling your research objectives into a specific set of variables to be quantified.

Deciding on qualifying criteria

In deciding on a sampling strategy, you inevitably ring-fence the range and extent of your study. A further set of decisions is also required to identify systematically which units of your sample fall within the remit of your study. For example, if you were studying crime coverage, you would need a standardised procedure for differentiating crime items from non-crime items.

Some topics are easier to provide qualifying criteria for than others. In one of our past studies, which examined news reporting of a controversial policy initiative (the community charge, or poll tax), we adopted a keyword strategy, in which any item was included that made any reference to the policy by either of these names (Deacon and Golding 1994). However, with another study, investigating media reporting of the voluntary sector, deciding on qualifying criteria was less straightforward (Deacon 1999). This was because there is no absolute consensus as to what distinguishes the voluntary sector from other sectors of society. One way of defining it is to distinguish it from the state, civil society and the market (Svetlik 1992): that is, it covers all non-statutory, formalised and non-profit-making activity. But although these distinctions offered a useful starting point, they were insufficiently focused on their own for the purposes of our research. If the sector is defined in these residual terms, then political parties, trade unions and other professional interest groups also fall within the remit of the study. In a British context, such a conflation is inappropriate, as the voluntary sector is usually seen as distinct from these sectors. Consequently, we drew up a list of five qualifying criteria for identifying relevant items, which all had to be met. An item was treated as 'voluntary sector-related' if it mentioned any organisation that:

1. was non-profit-making;
2. was non-statutory;
3. was non-party political;
4. was not affiliated to a professional group;
5. had a formalised organisational structure.

By comparison, deciding on the terms of inclusion for a study of crime reporting is more straightforward, as you can use legal definitions of criminality to help decide whether an item should be included. But here again there may be difficult cases to deal with. Would you include news items that reported acts suspected of being criminal in nature, but which were not the subject of formal charges at the time the report was written? Or would you include reports where criminal acts were anticipated but had not yet occurred? Again, there are no right or wrong answers to these questions: you have to make some careful decisions from the outset, and stick to them firmly and consistently.

Once you have identified your basic qualifying criteria, there is nothing to stop you stipulating further terms for inclusion. For instance, in your crime study, you might also decide to include only items that refer to crimes that have occurred within your own country, because you want to draw comparisons between your figures and national crime statistics, and such a comparison could be undermined if your findings included international crime reports. Similarly, you might decide to code only items that had crime as their main focus, ignoring those items where crimes are reported incidentally.

Designing a coding frame

You are now nearing the stage when you can begin your analysis. Before you can do so, you need to produce a **coding frame**, comprising two research instruments. The first is a *coding schedule*, which is a pro-forma sheet on which you enter the values for each of your variables. (NB You generate one sheet per unit of analysis.) Table 6.2 is a mock-up coding schedule covering all the variables proposed in stage 3 for your study of crime reporting.

Note that boxes have been provided to code information on up to three victims (variables 15–23), three offenders (variables 6–14) and two crimes for each item (variables 24–25). This is because individual items often mention more than one victim, perpetrator or criminal act, and these additional variables would help to capture these multiple cases. Of course, some items may contain more than these numbers of crimes, victims and offenders, and in these instances the only recourse with this list would be to quantify the most prominent cases. This in turn would require establishing clear guidelines for assessing prominence (e.g. amount of news space given to each, their position in the item, reference to them in headlines).

Additional classification variables have also been included to indicate:

- on what sample day the item appeared (variable 2);
- whether the item focused mainly on reporting criminal actions, or featured them only in a subsidiary manner (variable 26);

Table 6.2 Coding schedule: crime news reporting

Variable number	Variable name		Variable number	Variable name	
1	Case number		15	Age of victim 1	
2	Date		16	Gender of victim 1	
3	Prog/Paper		17	Ethnicity of victim 1	
4	Size (cm²/seconds)		18	Age of victim 2	
5	Position		19	Gender of victim 2	
6	Age of offender 1		20	Ethnicity of victim 2	
7	Gender of offender 1		21	Age of victim 3	
8	Ethnicity of offender 1		22	Gender of victim 3	
9	Age of offender 2		23	Ethnicity of victim 3	
10	Gender of offender 2		24	Type of crime 1	
11	Ethnicity of offender 2		25	Type of crime 2	
12	Age of offender 3		26	Focus?	
13	Gender of offender 3		27	Type of item	
14	Ethnicity of offender 3				

- what type of item each coding sheet relates to (this is assuming your study would examine different types of items – such as editorials, studio-based interviews, readers' letters, diary entries – not just hard news items) (variable 27).

These variables have been added to increase your options for exploring variations in coverage between different media at the data analysis stage.

The second research instrument you need to develop is a *coding manual*. This contains the numbers for each of the variables listed on the coding sheet. Producing coding values often involves a lot of careful consideration, as some things are easier to categorise than others. It is not difficult to categorise the gender of offenders or victims (1 = 'female', 2 = 'male', 3 = 'unclear/not stated') or the 'focus?' variable (1 = 'item mainly focuses on crime', 2 = 'item mentions crime in a subsidiary context'). But categorising the type of crime(s) reported would be more problematic, as you would have to devise a list of values that covered the vast range of acts which are defined as 'criminal' in nature. One strategy you might use to ensure comprehensiveness would be to adopt official classifications of criminal activity, such as the Home Office Counting Rules for the counting and classifying of notifiable offences recorded by the police forces in England and Wales (see Table 6.3). However, there is no guarantee that you would find these official classifications acceptable. For example, if you look at the British list, you may have some reservations about the categorisations. Are the broad categories (a–i) consistent? Is it acceptable to treat all sexual offences separately from violent offences? Is it better to transfer some sexual offences to the 'Violence against the person' category and make it a subcategory, leaving 'Sexual offences' to cover non-violent acts? Why are 'Obscene publications, etc. and protected sexual material' (number 111) and 'Indecent exposure' (number 118) not listed as sexual offences?

Table 6.3 The Home Office Counting Rules for the counting and classifying of notifiable offences recorded by the police forces in England and Wales (2006)

Source: http://www.homeoffice.gov.uk/rds/countrules.html

(a) Violence against the person
1. Murder
2. Attempted murder
3. Threat or conspiracy to murder
4. Manslaughter
5. Infanticide
6. Child destruction
7. Causing death by dangerous driving
8. Causing or allowing death of a child or vulnerable person
9. Wounding or other act endangering life
10. Endangering a railway passenger
11. Endangering life at sea
12. Other wounding, etc.
13. Possession of weapons
14. Harassment
15. Racially or religiously aggravated other wounding
16. Racially or religiously aggravated harassment
17. Cruelty to and neglect of children
18. Abandoning child aged under two years
19. Child abduction
20. Procuring illegal abortion
21. Concealment of birth
22. Causing death by aggravated vehicle taking
23. Assault on a police constable
24. Common assault
25. Racially or religiously aggravated common assault

(b) Sexual offences
26. Sexual assault on a male aged 13 and over
27. Sexual assault on a male child under 13
28. Rape of a female aged 16 or over
29. Rape of a female child under 16

30. Rape of a female child under 13
31. Rape of a male aged 16 or over
32. Rape of a male child under 16
33. Rape of a male child under 13
34. Sexual assault on a female aged 13 and over
35. Sexual assault on a female child under 13
36. Sexual activity involving a child under 13
37. Unlawful sexual intercourse with a girl under 16
38. Causing sexual activity without consent
39. Sexual activity involving a child under 16
40. Familial sexual offences
41. Exploitation of prostitution
42. Bigamy
43. Soliciting of women by men
44. Sexual activity with a person with a mental disorder
45. Abuse of children through prostitution and pornography
46. Trafficking for sexual exploitation
47. Abuse of trust
48. Sexual grooming
49. Other miscellaneous sexual offences

(c) Burglary
50. Burglary in a dwelling
51. Aggravated burglary in a dwelling
52. Burglary in a building other than a dwelling
53. Aggravated burglary in a building other than a dwelling

(d) Robbery
54. Robbery of business property
55. Robbery of personal property

(e) Theft and handling stolen goods
56. Aggravated vehicle taking
57. Proceeds of crime
58. Theft from the person
59. Theft by an employee
60. Theft or unauthorised taking from the mail
61. Abstracting electricity
62. Theft or unauthorised taking of a pedal cycle
63. Theft from a vehicle
64. Theft from a shop
65. Theft from automatic machine or meter
66. Theft or unauthorised taking of motor vehicle
67. Other theft
68. Handling stolen goods
69. Vehicle interference and tampering

(f) Fraud and forgery
70. Fraud by a company director, etc.
71. False accounting
72. Cheque and credit card fraud
73. Other frauds
74. Bankruptcy and insolvency offences
75. Forgery, etc. of drug prescription
76. Fraud, forgery, etc. associated with vehicle or driver records
77. Other forgery, etc.

(g) Criminal damage
78. Arson
79. Criminal damage to a dwelling
80. Criminal damage to a building other than a dwelling
81. Criminal damage to a vehicle
82. Other criminal damage
83. Racially or religiously aggravated criminal damage to a dwelling
84. Racially or religiously aggravated criminal damage to a building other than a dwelling
85. Racially or religiously aggravated criminal damage to a vehicle
86. Racially or religiously aggravated other criminal damage
87. Threat or possession with intent to commit criminal damage

(h) Drug offences
88. Trafficking in controlled drugs
89. Other drug offences
90. Possession of controlled drugs excluding cannabis
91. Possession of controlled drugs (cannabis)

(i) Other offences
92. Going equipped for stealing, etc.
93. Blackmail
94. Kidnapping
95. High treason and other offences against Treason Acts
96. Rioting
97. Violent disorder
98. Other offences (against state and public order)
99. Perjury and false statements
100. Libel
101. Betting, gaming and lotteries
102. Aiding and abetting suicide
103. Immigration acts
104. Attempting to pervert the course of justice
105. Absconding from lawful custody
106. Firearms Act 1968 and other firearms acts
107. Offences against laws relating to Customs, Excise and Inland Revenue
108. Bail Act 1976
109. Trade Descriptions Act 1968 and similar offences
110. Health and safety at work offences
111. Obscene publications, etc. and protected sexual material
112. Protection from eviction
113. Adulteration of food
114. Other knives offences
115. Public health
116. Town and Country Planning Act 1990
117. Disclosure, obstruction, false or misleading statements, etc.
118. Indecent exposure
119. Dangerous driving

These specific categorisation issues are important because one of the objectives of your research is to contrast the content analysis results with data about 'real-world' crime levels, and to raise questions about the fit (or lack of it) between these patterns. It could be argued that the more you depart from official categorisations, the more you may compromise the basis for comparison. Despite this risk, you may still feel that some recategorisation is necessary to increase the internal coherence of the categories.

As a general point, you should appreciate that the design of coding schedules and manuals is not a linear process. As you design them, you should always try to 'road-test' them on selected content examples, to see how easy the variables and values are to operationalise, and to gain some sense of their comprehensiveness. (Piloting is also useful for testing how systematically you can apply your chosen qualifying criteria.) Any difficulties or insights produced by this testing should then feed back into the continuing design of the coding frame.

Collecting data

Having piloted your coding schedule and manual thoroughly, you can commence your content analysis. At the start, coding often seems laborious, but as your familiarity with the codes and schedule increases, things generally speed up.

One thing that may surprise you is how much interpretation can be involved in applying a schedule to a sample of content, even on apparently simple matters. For example, in your proposed crime study, you might assume there would be no problems in identifying where manifest references to the ethnicity of a victim or perpetrator of a crime occur. But would you judge that an overt reference to the ethnicity of a criminal had been made where a newspaper report mentioned nothing in the text, but carried a picture which gave a strong visual clue to the ethnicity of the person? Or would you decide that an overt reference had been made when the mention of a victim's name gave some indication of their ethnic origin?

Again, the key principle is to be as consistent and systematic as possible in applying the research instruments. Of course, even with well-piloted coding schedules and manuals, you may encounter certain examples that do not fit neatly within your pre-designed categories. On these occasions, once you have decided on a coding solution, you should note down the decision, and repeat it studiously for any similar cases that occur. You do not want to end up improvising inconsistent coding judgements as you go along. (As a general rule, if you spend a lot of time forcing your categories onto the content being analysed, or you find there is considerable overlap between available coding options, then there is a problem with the design of this aspect of your coding frame.)

The issue of consistency and 'repeatability' is particularly significant when more than one person is involved in the coding, as there is a danger that even if all the coders are applying the instruments systematically on their own terms, there may be inconsistencies *between* their interpretations. Various statistical procedures can be used to check the degree to which coders tally in their analyses.[1] These tests for **inter-coder reliability** work by getting participants to code identical pieces of content and then comparing the degree of fit in the

---

1   A variety of statistical tests can be used, for example the Kappa test, or Scott's pi.

values assigned. Although it is not unusual to find some differences, where the tests reveal high levels of variation the data have to be discarded as 'unreliable'. (For this reason, it is a good idea to conduct these tests early on in the data collection process, to highlight problematic areas and adjust coding procedures.) But even if you are the only person involved in implementing a coding frame, you need to think carefully about coding reliability. Can you be sure that you would always apply the coding frame in the same way at the start of an analysis as you would at the end? Could your interpretation of the categories have shifted throughout the data collection process?

Analysing the results

Once your sample has been completely analysed, you can begin to make sense of the numbers. The bigger the content sample is, the more daunting this task can seem. For this reason, it is a good idea to familiarise yourself with a computerised statistical package to help you explore and summarise the numerical information quickly and easily. As we show in chapter 14, these packages are very user-friendly, and investing some time in familiarising yourself with them will pay great dividends.

Some people refer irreverently to this stage as 'number crunching', which implies it is a mechanistic, self-evident process. This is a misconception. In data analysis you need to describe your findings and to interpret their significance. In our experience, students tend to be better at the first task than they are at the second, and many a promising research report has failed to achieve a top mark because it has not considered the broader implications of the results.

To avoid this situation, you should bear in mind the following points when analysing your data:

1. Remember that when you have collected all your data, you are still only halfway home. Give yourself enough time to mull over and digest the numbers you have generated. Interpreting statistics properly requires a period of reflection. The students who begin with the blithe assumption that numbers will somehow 'speak for themselves' tend to be the same students who express bewilderment when confronted with a mass of results and feel overwhelmed by the task of drawing conclusions on the basis of these.

2. Be directive in your analysis of the results at the start. Remind yourself of what your initial research questions were, and concentrate firstly on addressing them in a focused way. If you have placed your data in a computerised statistical package, avoid the temptation of indiscriminately trawling for numbers (e.g. by cross-tabulating everything by everything), as this is a recipe for confusion.

3. In some cases, your findings will conform to your initial expectations (e.g. '78 per cent of the crimes identified in the media sample were "violent crimes against the person". This contrasts with official statistics, which show that violent crimes account for no more than 5 per cent of all offences recorded by the police'). However, on other occasions, the results may confound your assumptions (e.g. 'The research found little evidence to support claims that journalists routinely make spurious references to the ethnicity of offenders when those criminals come from ethnic minority groups. Only 1.9

per cent of offenders had their ethnic origin signalled, and where this occurred the largest single ethnic group was "white" – 79 per cent of cases where ethnicity was stated'). Alternatively, the findings may simply be inconclusive (e.g. 'Although, where age was mentioned, 59 per cent of victims were 55 years or older, no mention was made of the age of 73 per cent of victims'). Be aware that it is not unusual to find tensions between the statistical evidence and your initial conceptual assumptions: indeed, these disjunctions are why we bother conducting such research in the first place. In many ways, contradictory or counter-intuitive findings offer the greatest opportunities for theoretical development, as they may indicate that things are more complex than you initially supposed. Taken in this light, they can be seen to present possibilities, rather than problems. Certainly, you should never suppress or ignore inconvenient evidence, unless you have a justified reason for doubting its reliability or validity (see point 4). To do so would undermine the integrity and purpose of your research.

4. Be cautious about overstating the case for your findings. Once you see your numbers presented in a computerised table, it is easy to forget the factors behind their creation. However, you must always be reflexive about your data and their production. Although inter-reliability tests are useful for exposing inconsistencies in the application of a coding frame, you should also trust your intuitive feelings about the validity and reliability of particular measures. Having implemented a coding frame, you will know which variables were easy to operationalise and which proved difficult. These insights should always be remembered when you are analysing results. They are particularly important whenever you encounter a particularly dramatic or counter-intuitive finding. Could the findings simply be an artefact of your research design, or your application of the coding frame?

5. Once you have addressed your initial research questions, spend time on less directed data analysis, looking for other potentially interesting relationships within the data. Statistical analysis can be a far more organic process than many textbooks seem to suggest, and many interesting additional issues can emerge from more informal exploration. But leave this activity until the end!

What price objectivity?

These, then, are the stages involved in a quantitative content analysis and the kinds of issues and rules that need to be borne in mind when applying the method. As noted, the aim of the method is to provide a systematic means for quantifying textual and thematic features across a large number of texts. This involves developing clear coding protocols, which are observed strictly throughout. But does this systematic process – even if it is achieved effectively – deliver a truly 'objective', value-free perspective, as some have claimed?

Once you think of all the decisions involved in the production of these numbers, it is clear that it does not. Arbitrary decisions intrude at all stages of the research process: what you count, how much you sample, how you categorise, and so on; and all these decisions are ultimately produced by the researcher's subjective judgement of what is significant. For this reason, you need to resist the temptation to treat your findings as though they offer incontrovertible facts about the material you have analysed. As we discussed in chapter 5, statistics are 'constructs' not 'facts', and when presenting them you must be open about the construction process. For content analysis, this involves being explicit about the range of your sampling, how you operationalised certain variables, the qualifying criteria you used, the way you selected your unit of analysis, and so on. Without this detail, readers are in no position to assess the merit of the evidence you present.

Digital news archives: 'push-button' content analysis?

All the comments so far have concerned manual procedures for content analysis. It is evidently a time-consuming and labour-intensive process, and the resulting statistics often fail to convey the weeks, even months, of effort that are invested in their creation. However, newspaper and (to a lesser extent) broadcast content is now routinely stored in various digital formats, and these archives can be searched using keywords to identify and quantify coverage on specific topics. This seems to offer tremendous labour-saving opportunities, and it is not surprising to see a growing number of content analysis studies that are based on searches of these digital sources (e.g. Altheide and Michalowski 1999; Soothill and Grover 1997; Esser, Reinemann and Fan 2001; Reid and Misener 2001; Kerr and Moy 2002; Cameron 2003; Freudenburg et al. 1996; Domke 2004).

In many cases, such studies use the databases for identifying and collating relevant news material on a chosen topic that is then subjected to further manual analysis. But there are other examples where search facilities have been used for more specifically analytical tasks. These include using the search engines to quantify the prevalence (or otherwise) of certain terms over time, and analysing the ways key words may co-locate in news content.

Despite the growing popularity of this new mode of analysis, there has been surprisingly little consideration of its methodological implications (Deacon 2007). These can be broadly differentiated as questions of research *validity* ('The integrity of conclusions derived from research', Bryman 2001: 30) and *reliability* ('the extent to which results are consistent over time and an accurate representation of the total population under study', Joppe quoted in Golafshani 2003: 597). It is important that these questions are appreciated before embarking on 'push-button content analysis' of any kind.

Validity

There are four major validity implications for research that depends exclusively on the analysis of the 'proxy data' obtained from digital news archives.

Things, not themes

As mentioned, content searches of this kind are based on the use of keywords. In most cases, more than one keyword can be used, as can the Boolean logical operators 'Or', 'And' and 'Not', to extend or restrict the range of the search. However, while keyword searching is well suited to identifying tangible 'things' (i.e. people, places, events, institutions), it is less effective for analysing more complex and multifaceted 'themes'. Imagine you wanted to conduct a content analysis of news reporting of celebrities and celebrity culture. Clearly defining the terms of inclusion for such a study would be essential (e.g. should politicians, sportspeople or notorious criminals be counted as celebrities?). Once these criteria were established, however, it would be a fairly straightforward process for manually identifying, coding and quantifying relevant coverage. But how might you approximate this exercise using keywords? One strategy could be to look at coverage of particular celebrities you have pre-selected, but any resulting analysis could be treated only as illustrative of celebrity reporting, rather than as genuinely representative. This is because you would have prejudged and predetermined the terms of the analysis. Another strategy could be to look for any item that contains the word 'celebrity'. But even after you have weeded out all the 'false positives' (i.e. items that contain the term but do not relate to celebrity culture in any direct way), you would still end up with a sample that is likely to be seriously skewed. This is because the more celebrated a public figure becomes, the less likely it is that their 'celebrity' status will need to be flagged overtly. Consequently, your sample would be overpopulated with C-list and D-list celebrities, whose impact on public consciousness is so tenuous that journalists feel it necessary to signal their status.

Linguistic, not visual

Most digital news archives store news content in textual form only, thereby excluding analysis of all visual aspects of news presentation. This is unfortunate, as linguistic and visual elements are closely linked, but are not identical. Summarising Kress and van Leeuwen (1996), Higgins (2003: 2) states:

> Visual structures and linguistic structures both realise meanings. These in part overlap between the two modes but are also different; some things can be said only visually, others only verbally. The way in which meanings are realised will be different: language choices are between, for instance, word classes, tenses, and semantic structures; visual choices are between, for example, colours, camera angles, and compositional structures.

Media analysis has long tended to privilege linguistic analysis over visual analysis, and a reliance on digital archives can only compound this tendency, inhibiting understanding of the ways that meanings in popular media texts are created through the interplay between language and image. This is particularly regrettable at a time when the visuality of news has gained in significance, for example through the more extensive use of photographs and illustrations, larger dramatic headlines and other creative compositional techniques (see chapters 9 and 10).

Texts, not contexts

Digital keyword searches identify lists of individual articles that contain any references to the phrases entered. This form of unitisation actually fits quite neatly with the kind of thematic content analysis discussed earlier in this chapter. But these texts do not exist in isolation. They are often positioned strategically, and the context of their placement and relationship with other texts can tell us significant things. An amusing example of this point is offered by a full-page apology published by the British *Daily Mirror* newspaper on 22 October 2002. This apology was made to an American businessman, who is the biological father of a celebrity's child and who had been attacked by the *Mirror* for allegedly neglecting his paternal duties. In an unusually forthright expression of contrition, the newspaper apologised for the 'mean spirited and inaccurate articles' it had published. It continued:

> Our readers should know that Mr XXX is not the ignominious character that has been depicted by some in the media. He is a philanthropist and humanitarian who has dedicated himself to helping causes impacting children… We at the *Mirror* wish to take responsibility for our inappropriate actions, and are pleased to have this opportunity to set the record straight.

(*Daily Mirror*, 22 October 2002, p. 9)

As apologies go, it could not have been more abject. However, its sincerity was compromised by an article placed on the facing page with the headline 'Why Americans Can't Understand Irony or Sarcasm' (*Daily Mirror*, 22 October 2002, p. 8).

Recent events, not the distant past

The impetus for the creation of digital newspaper archives came from revolutionary changes in news production practices themselves. From the mid 1980s, the computerisation of text inputting and advances in desktop publishing meant that full-text computer files of the newspaper material could be saved and marketed on a commercial basis as an information resource. One implication of this is that the historical reach of most digital news archives is somewhat limited.[2] This can be seen to reinforce what some have lamented as an ahistorical tendency in much contemporary media and cultural analysis (e.g. O'Malley 2002).

Reliability

Questions of research reliability are essential to any research. On the face of it, computerised textual searches would seem to deliver strongly in this respect; remorselessly identifying each and any reference to a specific term, no matter how peripherally located in a newspaper's pages or how deeply buried in the substance of an article. However, on closer analysis, this aura of infallibility becomes questionable. Human intervention is evident in the data entry phase, search engines may have varying levels of sophistication, and the comprehensiveness of the archives may be affected by complex issues associated with publishing rights and copyright.

Detailed comparative analysis undertaken by one of the authors into the performance of the UK version of LexisNexis – the most widely used digital newspaper archive in contemporary media analysis – identified a range of reliability concerns (see Deacon 2007).[3] These included:

1. Inconsistent results produced by identical keyword searches conducted in LexisNexis and another major digital news archive.

---

2   A notable exception to this is the Thompson-Gale *Times Digital Archive*. This contains digitalised facsimiles of every page 'as published' between 1785 and 1985. Aside from reproducing the visual dimensions of coverage, all text can be searched using keywords.

3   The assessment focused on the LexisNexis 'Professional' service offered to UK-based subscribers.

2. Some internally inconsistent results produced by searches conducted within LexisNexis.
3. Examples of duplicated content.
4. Examples of missing content.
5. Inconsistent unitisation (i.e. occasions where separate items were bundled together as one item).

Do these validity and reliability concerns mean that digital news archives should never be used for media analysis? In our view, the considerations listed above highlight the need for caution, but do not preclude the use of digital news archives completely. However, you should observe the following practices when conducting content analysis via these means:

1. Always check any resulting list of items for 'false positives' (Soothill and Grover 1997). These are occasions where a keyword may have several meanings and the resulting search identifies content that is not related to the focus of your research.
2. Recognise the dangers of being too precise in the keywords you use, as this can create a problem of 'false negatives' (Soothill and Grover 1997). This is a situation where much relevant material is inadvertently excluded from the search because the terms of the search are too constricted.
3. Always check item lists for duplicated material.
4. Scrutinise individual items to check for any inconsistencies in the unitisation of the content.
5. As a preliminary exercise, conduct keyword searches using very general terms for the titles and periods you are analysing. This is to check that there are no significant, structural omissions in the archive coverage for your sample period.

To summarise, you should never take a raw count generated by these searches at face value, and you should always appreciate that a price is paid when media analyses depend heavily, or exclusively, on text-only digital news archives. Some degree of sampling error seems inevitable, and you should always bear in mind that the evidence you are analysing is proxy data – a mediation of a mediation (Althaus 2003). A lot of important material is lost in translation. For these reasons, you should still aspire to analyse media content in its original form wherever possible, and where this is not practical, avoid casting necessity as a virtue.

Summary: key points

- We identified the value of considering how different approaches to textual analysis can be integrated in research.

- The historical origins and enduring popularity of quantitative content analysis were examined.

- The main strengths and drawbacks of the method were discussed.

- A case study of a content analysis of crime news reporting was presented. The detail of this worked example was used to highlight the main stages in the implementation of the method.

- We discussed why claims that quantitative content analysis represents a completely objective and value-free means for analysing texts are misguided.

- Methodological issues concerning the use of digital news archives for quantitative content analysis were discussed.

▶ chapter seven

Analysing Texts

Against academic apartheid

In the previous chapter, we dealt with a research method for the analysis of media content that has a long pedigree, particularly in North America, where quantitative content analysis has been a favoured technique in mass communications research. For example, shortly after the Soviet Revolution of 1917, analysis of the way *The New York Times* covered this hugely significant event was one of the first examples to show the value of quantitative content analysis (Lippmann and Merz 1920). By contrast, the three modes of textual analysis which we shall deal with in this chapter are more recent. One of them derives from a particular strand of US sociology, while the others were associated from the outset with European developments in philosophy and linguistics. Before we go on to consider them, it is important to emphasise the value of using them in combination with the more quantitative approach associated with content analysis.

All too often in the past, the value of such combinations has not been sufficiently recognised. These different approaches have been broadly (and not very helpfully) characterised as quantitative and qualitative, and advocates of both have either rejected or ignored each other. At times, this has resulted in mutual neglect and miscomprehension. For example, some quantitative analysts in the past have dismissed qualitative approaches of any kind as impossibly subjective, whereas quantitative content analysis has been considered to equate significance solely with frequency. If you look at what practitioners of both approaches actually do, both these charges are flawed.

We have already acknowledged that objectivity in any absolute form is an illusion. A totally disinterested vantage point is simply not available, and we need to be aware that drawing on the pejorative connotations of subjectivity sometimes bolsters the claim to objectivity. A degree of evaluation and interpretation applies to all forms of cultural research. For instance, the statistical data produced by media content analysis is very much dependent on the categories selected for coding the material in the first place. There is no infallible checklist for choosing and labelling these categories, and the questions you ask of your material will influence the answers you get and the conclusions you reach. Acknowledging this does not automatically entail dismissing content analysis – rather the contrary. If, for example, you want to establish patterns of **representation** in media content over a given period of time – several months, say, or even several years – content analysis provides you with a suitable method for doing so.

The great advantage of content analysis is that it is *methodical*. It stipulates that all material within a chosen sample must be submitted to the same set of categories, which has been explicitly identified. To this extent, it ensures a reasonable degree of reliability in the establishment of a pattern of media representation. It also provides a guard against temptations inherent in less rigorous approaches of selecting items that seem to fit the case you may want to prove, or allowing your impression of a developing pattern of representation to be guided by your pre-existing prejudices and assumptions. This does not mean that your own prejudices, assumptions and ideas will not have any bearing on what you do, and we do not suggest that you should pretend otherwise. If all you do is end up reinforcing them, though, you can hardly be said to have engaged critically in any form of analysis worthy of the name. Simply selecting out certain items of media content that support some working hypothesis might make good journalistic copy – and be entertaining to read if nicely worked up – but researching communications in the social sciences requires that we are more attentive to participant bias, and more systematic in how we go about investigating media discourse and representation.

This, again, is the value of content analysis. If you are dealing with media content across a longitudinal timeframe, you need a systematic procedure for establishing both what is relatively constant and what might change across that frame. Otherwise, what basis will you have for using words like 'often', 'many', 'recurrent', or 'seldom', 'few' and 'isolated' when you are discussing your sample content? What sampling procedure could you refer to that would give your use of these evaluative words any real credibility? How, for example, could you establish that there has been a definite trend in representing certain social groups in certain ways, or in maintaining a silence about them? Content analysis may not be very exciting – methodical, time-consuming procedures rarely are – but it does ensure a degree of rigour, precision and trustworthiness with respect to the resulting data. These are qualities that would be lacking if you simply pasted together certain selective quotations and sensational images in order to prove the point from which, tendentiously, you began.

In the past, claims about frequency, or the lack of it, have often been made in qualitative analyses of media content. Such claims emphasise the need for cooperation between quantitative and qualitative approaches. In what was once a frequently cited article, Olivier Burgelin hypothetically gave as an example the narrative significance of a single 'good' act by a gangster in a film as something which analysis based simply on frequency criteria would fail to identify (Burgelin 1968). This has always seemed to us an unsatisfactory argument against quantitative content analysis, not only because you would have to be dim-witted not to grasp the significance of that one 'good' act, but also because implicitly it relies on counting – one 'good' act in contradistinction to many 'bad' acts – and because assessing the structural relationship of this one good action to the gangster's vicious behaviour elsewhere in the film is not something that content analysis in itself would necessarily neglect. In other words, quantitative and qualitative approaches can and do perform similar tasks.

Semiotics – one of the three major forms of qualitative analysis dealt with in this chapter – has had a significant influence in shaping film studies (see, for example, Wollen 1972; Metz 1974a, 1974b; Silverman 1983; de Lauritis 1984; and, for a summary, Lapsley and Westlake 2006: ch 2). Its applicability to the study of film is obvious enough, while quantitative forms of content analysis involving sophisticated forms of statistical correlation may seem completely inappropriate to the analysis of film narratives. This is not necessarily the case. It would depend on the kind of analysis you are engaged in. For example, over 60 years ago, Dorothy Jones produced a study of feature-film content based on quantitative measurement. While aware of the limitations of her method, and advising caution in the interpretation of her figures, she was able to establish numerically that in her sample of 100 typical Hollywood films, there were twice as many male as female performers, they were predominantly middle or upper class (poor or destitute people comprised only 17 per cent of movie characters), they were mainly unmarried and the majority were American (82 per cent). She then went on to an analysis of the values, wants and desires of mid twentieth-century Hollywood characters, and found that three-quarters of all the major characters had their main desires (for love, fame or wealth, for example) fulfilled in greater or lesser degree by the end of the film. She was also able to show that in Hollywood films of this period, marriage was commonly idealised, but rarely portrayed (Jones 1942). Among other things, these findings demonstrated the male dominance of cultural production, at least in this highly lucrative sector. They say a great deal about the American dream at that time and its relationship to the Hollywood 'dream factory'. Of course, as Jones acknowledged, hers was only one approach, and for single narrative studies, particularly those concerned with specific film genres, a more qualitative treatment is obviously preferable, since a finer grain of analysis is required. Jones was dealing with a sample of 100 films, though, and in preference to an impressionistic appraisal of their content, she systematically examined them according to explicitly formulated units of analysis. This seems to us highly appropriate to her sample, and makes the analytical benefits of her enumeration self-evident.

Such benefits are given little credit in contemporary media studies, and this is because of a continuing bias against quantification. In the mid 1970s, James Curran characterised this bias as a form of academic apartheid. Its profile may now be lower, but it has hardly been dismantled. This is regrettable, for when quantitative and qualitative approaches are used methodologically in combination with each other, the resulting analysis is invariably stronger. Even in the 1970s, Curran was able to point to the degree of convergence and complementarity that had actually been achieved, belying 'any fundamental substantive differences between the two approaches' (Curran 1976: 12). A more recent study of television and press news also shows that they can be employed harmoniously alongside each other. Ron Scollon adopts a social interactional perspective on media communications, while methodologically he draws on ethnography and discourse analysis. In dealing with the attributions of reportage in print and broadcast news, and with quotations and actuality footage, however, he uses content analysis productively and presents his results in the form of statistical tables (Scollon 1998: 205, 219). This is a fairly minimal use of content analysis in conjunction with other approaches, and it could have been extended, but it does show that content analysis is certainly not incompatible with the kinds of qualitative analysis on which we concentrate in this chapter.

This is in line with our general position in this book. Barriers between different approaches are often self-defeating, and instead we argue for mixing methods judiciously in the interests of analytical enrichment and the triangulation of research findings. It is in light of this that we now go on to outline three specifically qualitative approaches to the study of written media content: semiotics, linguistic analysis and frame analysis.

Semiotic analysis

In the 1970s and early 1980s, semiotics was the most fashionable mode of qualitative textual analysis, claiming for itself a universal relevance and applicability. Since then, it has blended in with other critical approaches, and is now regarded more as one of a number of strands in the methodological repertory than as an all-encompassing 'science' of cultural forms. Nevertheless, its influence has been considerable, particularly in its alliance with structuralism and its theoretical successors. Its basic concepts have entered into the general currency of analytical language in media and cultural studies. Some of the theoretical considerations associated with semiotics are complex, and their practical relevance to immediate 'how-to-do' issues in textual analysis is fairly minimal, so you should try to avoid getting bogged down in them. The basic utility of semiotics for media studies students is in advancing certain concepts which can be applied to the analysis of media texts. Semiotics helps us to think analytically about how such texts work and the implications they have for the broader culture in which they are produced and disseminated. Therefore we shall concentrate on the key concepts of semiotics, and show how these provide you with some important critical tools.

Ferdinand de Saussure (1857–1913), in his posthumously edited and published *Course in General Linguistics*, was one of the first to identify semiotics as a general area of study, though he referred to it as 'semiology'. The term semiotics actually comes from the other founder of sign theory, Charles Sanders Peirce (1839–1914), an American philosopher who was working independently in the same direction at the same time as Saussure. Semiology is therefore the preferred French term, and semiotics the term originating on the other side of the Atlantic. (For the sake of convenience, we shall use 'semiotics' in general terms, since, of the two, this is the one more commonly employed.) Saussure did not develop his proposed semiology himself. His efforts as a scholar concentrated on the study of natural language; indeed, he is commonly regarded as the founder of modern linguistics, which superseded the evolutionist study of language known as philology. Saussure was not so much interested in how words and languages had evolved over the centuries, as in how words and languages actually work in any current utterance – how, for instance, a sound becomes a word and a word becomes a meaning. What he said was that the meaning of a word exists only within a language system, only in differentiated relations to other words in that system.

This is an important point in understanding semiotics, for it broke with the notion that there is a world existing independently of **signification**, a world antecedent to language such that language gathers meaning into itself by reference to this world. For Saussure, meaning derives only from the language system within which we speak, write and think. There is nothing anterior to that. In relation to this key point of his linguistic model, Saussure made a crucial distinction. The language system from which we choose our words he called **langue**, whereas the specific utterances we make he referred to as **parole**. The system itself provides rules for its use, for using words in relation to each other. Our actual performance is another matter, and obviously varies enormously, but at the same time it has to follow the rules of the system, just as when, in playing poker, you can play your hand in whatever way you want (parole), but you have to do so within the rules of the game (langue). It is in this sense that the term 'language games' is meant.

Semiotics is centred on this linguistic paradigm. Among other things, it entails that media texts are treated as if they are basically the same as, or similar to, natural language. In the study of media texts, or cultural practices as text-analogues, what counts are 'the rules of the game' rather than how the game is performed. It is the underlying structure of the text, and how this determines the functioning of the text, which is under scrutiny. What always have to be identified are the structural components of texts, and for semiotics the fundamental component, both of language and of written texts which are made up of language, is the **sign**. (The term semiotics derives from the Greek, *semeion*, meaning 'sign'.)

One of the fundamental characteristics of the sign is that it is **arbitrary**. For semiotics, there is no necessary relation between the sign and its referent – that which the sign denotes. All signs are arbitrary in the sense that they are conventional, even those which are most onomatopoeic. The word 'dog' refers to a physical creature – in the shape of numerous breeds varying in size, physique and colour – which walks on four legs and which has, for the most part, been domesticated by human societies in the course of their historical development. But 'dog' is arbitrary as a linguistic sign, since other languages use other (equally arbitrary) words, such as 'chien', 'hund', 'canis', 'perro', 'pies', 'kararehe', and so on, to refer to the same species of animal. In other words, the arbitrariness of the signifying term 'dog' has become conventional in the English language, and it has acquired its semantic value as a result of its structural differentiation from other signs (e.g. 'cat'). To take another example, Saussure cites signs of politeness which, as he says, acquire over time 'a certain natural expressivity' in any given society, but which 'are nonetheless determined by a rule'. It is this rule which leads us to use particular signs of politeness, and not their intrinsic value (Saussure 1974: 68).

Semiotics distinguishes analytically between the **signifier** and the **signified**. The first of these is that part of the sign which consists of the actual material aspect of an artefact, act or image which holds the potential of signifying. This potential is fulfilled when it connects with the signified, the mental concept associated with the signifier. For example, the signifier *star* is the sound-image of the word 'star' before it has acted as a word which denotes the signified of a media performer who is credited with huge public acclaim. The sign is then these two elements in active combination, with the signifier becoming equivalent to the signified. Of course, there are different types of signs, and we shall elaborate on this when we discuss the analysis of media images (see chapter 9). We do not, for instance, mistake a family tree for an actual tree, but treat it as a visual metaphor conventionally used in the representation of genealogical lineage. Similarly, a windsock at an airport acts as a signifier which is highly dependent on convention. It is the cultural convention, and not the signifier, which determines the meaning of the sign. It is because of the conventionality of the visual code employed that we know it signifies aeroplanes landing and taking off, as well as wind direction, and do not mistake the sign for a form of prayer-flag or an indication that somewhere in its vicinity we shall be able to purchase a packet of condoms. To take a windsock as a symbolic public health warning about sexually transmitted diseases would be sensible if the code associated with it permitted this, but within our culture it does not.

A further point is that the signified is also arbitrary, or rather conventional to particular cultures within particular periods of their history, as for instance with the windsock, since it is only since the invention of flying machines and the widespread construction of airports that this has become conventionally associated with air travel, and there is nothing logically prohibiting it from becoming associated with sexually transmitted diseases in the future. The arbitrary nature of the signified can be taken further, though, in ways which may seem to threaten the stability of meanings associated with linguistic or other signs. For instance, the French psychoanalyst and theorist Jacques Lacan spoke of 'the incessant sliding of the signified under the signifier' (Lacan 1977: 154). This is a more controversial semiotic claim, and it can be ascertained only in particular cases, but the idea that there is no natural or absolute meaning attached to signifiers, their signifieds or the relationships between them is in many ways quite salutary. It reminds us that in studying media texts, we should approach their processes of signification and representation as conventional to the cultural configurations and social order in which they operate. At the same time, we can add a further point which semiotics usually omits. This is that such conventionality is historical in nature and thus subject to change, however that might be brought about. Ultimately, behind any conventional relations of signifiers and signifieds are decisions, however ingrained and natural these may now appear, and these decisions can always be modified and reversed, or their quality of seeming natural be called into question, with possible consequences for the ways in which public communications communicate, or in which particular sections of society are represented. If signs can change, so can cultural relations and social institutions.

Signs operate at different levels of signification. For instance, when we read in a magazine story of a love affair between a man and woman, the two signs 'man' and 'woman' function within a *first* order of signification to refer to the specific man and woman in the story, who will be given individual names and characteristics. But this first order of signification also operates within the ambit of a *second* order of signification, where the signs 'man' and 'woman' connect with the ways society typically regards that which is signified, at least as certain gendered types. The two signs 'man' and 'woman' thus become entangled with certain meanings and values which lie beyond the mode and form of any specific sign-vehicle, and are associated with more general recognitions and expectations of the social identities, roles and relations of men and women. These more general recognitions and expectations as an institutionalised cluster habituate understanding, and so in turn exert normative pressure on the mode and form of signification involved. Second-order associations may then connect with a *third* order of signification, which is that of a social **consensus**, legitimating **tradition** or social **myth**. In the case of this hypothetical magazine story, 'man' and 'woman' are the signifiers of the (stereo)typical values of male/female sexuality, subjectivity and social action to which they are attached. These conventional values may be said to be ideological when they are shown to render gender inequalities as inevitable and natural, to misrepresent what it means subjectively to be female, to employ a severely delimited conception of female social experience, or to recharge the currency of certain exploitative expectations of female sexuality. Such values also connect with the other third-order terms or forms of their combination, as in a traditional consensus on women's needs and interests or their appropriate roles (suiting them best for domestic tasks, for instance), which historically served to mask and mystify a hierarchical power structure, disadvantaging women for as long as the traditional consensus retained its unifying and pervasive hold.

This leads to two further important concepts in semiotic analysis, those of **denotation** and **connotation**. Denotation refers to the *manifest* content of a sign or set of signs – that which can be said to be objectively there. For example, in a written text, the words in a sentence are the ones which are actually there on the page, rather than any number of possible other words. Connotation constitutes the *latent* content of what a written text may be said to signify, and works at a more subjective level of perception and experience, as for instance through the emotional charge or political import which a text is taken to carry. Connotation operates at the second order of signification, and through this connects with particular social myths, or what have become consensually established as the 'truths' of social and cultural life. This brings us back to the **codes** and **conventions** mentioned earlier. Signs always operate structurally according to particular codes and conventions. These are themselves structured around various distinctions, various alternative or opposed categories, that distil and transmit meaning. So, for instance, we understand that a certain gesture signifies politeness because it is conventionally differentiated from impolite modes of address, and this distinction is established within a system of relations which allows one kind of gesture rather than another to signify politeness. Conventions are rules of communication which, for the most part, are tacit and taken for granted, and which mould communication in relatively fixed ways. Whenever we use the word *practice* in connection with communication, we invoke the presence of conventions as the usual protocol underpinning particular ways of signifying within particular cultural forms. Conventions breed expectations. These expectations become widely accepted, and the conventions then acquire a compelling force. They induce a certain degree of conformity. Generally, we only become aware of conventions when they are broken, when the expectations they breed are disappointed (as for example in situations where the rules of etiquette are ignored). All media texts are constrained and, at the same time, made possible by conventions. Media studies helps to reveal the building blocks of conventions out of which such texts are built, and shows us how they are put together in a particular order.

Just as conventions inform practices, so practices inform codes. Codes are the more systemic framing procedures of communication, the means by which signs in conjunction with signs (messages), and with particular ways of seeing and saying (practices), become constructed into cultural texts or forms. Codes are drawn on in all facets of cultural life, and not just in written texts. Take bright-red lipstick. As a signifier, this relates unmistakably to the signified of Western femininity to produce the ideological sign of female sexuality. The signified links with the signifier when we use an a priori code to interpret what it is that bright-red lipstick connotes. In this case, it is clear that the signifier lipstick will connote in this way in the West, but not in Tibet, Waziristan, Iran or northern Ungava, since there what is absent is the requisite code which would set off the appropriate positive connotations. Instead, alternative codes may set off negative connotations and provoke hostility to Western decadence and shamelessness. Different connotations to bright-red lipstick also occur when it is worn by a man in drag, for this subverts the code of Western female sexuality and gives rise to an alternative set of meanings. Codes are therefore interpretive devices, systemised clusters of context-specific meaning, which enable communication to occur within particular cultures, and which impart to combinations of signs their cultural and ideological meanings within those cultures.

In actual practice, there is no clear line dividing conventions and codes, which is why they are often spoken of together. Sometimes this depends on the case in question. We can, for instance, speak of the legal code or of aesthetic codes. These obviously apply across a wide range of practices and usually involve some broad meta-level questions as well, such as those of ethics or **ideology**. We can speak of technical codes in photography or television, or non-verbal codes such as hand movements, facial expression and posture, and these cannot be dissociated from questions about their consequences in cultural life. For example, the codes which come into operation in female fashion photography indicate the ways in which images and representations of women are constructed, and these in turn inform the way men see women and the way women see themselves. This is true at least to the extent that fashion sells and is successful, but of course, not everyone is influenced by fashion to the same degree, and some are opposed and even actively hostile to the presumptions or apparent dictates of the fashion industry. In order for this to be possible, codes have to be resisted, and this means that alternative social and cultural codes have to be drawn on. Codes are always in operation in the construction and interpretation of media texts. We refer to the process in which certain codes and conventions are drawn on in the production of a media text as **encoding**, whereas **decoding** refers to the process in which readers, viewers or auditors draw on certain codes in their interpretation of a media text.

There is no necessary one-to-one equivalence between these processes. This immediately throws into doubt any assumptions we might have that media texts are unitary and stable in meaning. How the text looks and what it means always depends, to some extent at least, on where you stand in relation to it. You cannot know or understand a text exactly as the producer knows or understands it. There is rarely that degree of coherence between the two processes of meaning-production, encoding and decoding. The media text is certainly a point of connection between the encoder and the decoder, but it does not bring them into a position of symmetry. If that were the case, there would be no evaluative differentiation between lies and truth. Media texts therefore bring people together at the same time as they keep them apart. Moreover, such texts do not have fixed and absolute identities, for what a text means to you is not necessarily the same as what it means to someone from another social group; even your close friends may disagree with your interpretive reading of a particular media text, film or popular song, for example. Of course, you might try to impose your understanding of a text on someone you know, or try to influence their understanding of it, but that is a different matter. So we must acknowledge an encoder text and a decoder text – or rather decoder texts, in the plural, for there is a large number of people involved in decoding media texts, as opposed to the relatively small number involved in the production of such texts.

For these reasons, we often say that a media text is *polysemantic* or *polysemous*. This means that a media text is not a self-sufficient semantic unity; consequently, although one particular textual analysis may have greater authority and cogency than another, a media text is not itself amenable to an absolutely definitive interpretation. In a phrase which wittily echoes a celebrated comment by the French structuralist philosopher Louis Althusser, 'the lonely hour of the final reading never comes' (Easthope 1991: 33). Volosinov, an early twentieth-century Marxist writer, wrote in a similar vein about the multi-accented nature of the sign. A sign for him is intersected by differently oriented accents, thanks to which 'a sign maintains its vitality and dynamism and the capacity for further development'. This capacity is lost or in decline when a sign is made to appear eternally and universally relevant (i.e. unaccentual), but within a sign or set of signs there is always a conflict between the social value judgements which occur within it: 'Any current curse word can become a word of praise, any current truth must inevitably sound to many people as the greatest lie. This inner dialectic quality of the sign comes out fully in the open only in times of social crisis or revolutionary change' (Volosinov 1973: 23).

It is important to stress that the concept of **polysemy** does not entail the possibility of an absolutely unlimited number of readings. There are two points to be made about this. First, as we have said, media texts do have certain identities which are governed by the codes and conventions they are constructed in relation to. If we deny media texts any identity in themselves, we remain locked in a binary logic, because our denial requires for its effectiveness a mirror image of that old-fashioned paradigm of literary criticism the self-sufficient text, the text 'in itself'. Encoding and decoding intersect within media texts, and such texts outline the ground on which meanings are made out of them. Second, the meanings of media texts, particularly when they refer to common-sense values or socially sensitive issues, are often structured in ways which exert pressure on the process of decoding, channelling understanding one way rather than another, and setting the stage for 'legitimate' interpretation. The transmission of established cultural codes means that their arbitrary nature becomes taken for granted. Most of the time, while we think about the content of what we read, we draw on these codes unwittingly. If we come to media texts with already existing alternative codes, we may notice that which has permitted the media text to be constructed in the way it has. Critical reading of media texts aims to reveal this by examining the technical means and normative parameters of their construction of the social world. In this sense of its analytical purpose, a conceptual understanding of codes links up with paradigms and syntagms.

A **paradigm** is a vertical set of elements from which one selects, whereas a **syntagm** is a horizontal chain in which elements are linked with each other according to agreed codes and conventions. In written language, the letters of the alphabet constitute the basic vertical paradigms, and we select from these, combining them together horizontally into syntagms called words. Words themselves then come to form paradigms from which one has to select, assembling them into coherent syntagmatic units called sentences. Paradigmatically, words constitute the vocabulary of a language. We select from our available vocabulary and, according to the rules of grammar and syntax, along with conventions of appropriate tone and style, combine what we select into speech or written communication. Often this is done in sentences, but not invariably. In appropriate circumstances, minimal phrases might act as sentences, as for example when we say, 'Knock! Knock!' to begin a certain type of joke. In constructing sentences that make sense and function grammatically, we need to choose words according to one set of rules (e.g. 'shout' instead of 'exclaim'), and to combine them according to another set which produces a coherent linear form (e.g. 'He shouted at me to come quickly'). The paradigmatic elements of our newly formed sentence could be exchanged for others, of course, and still satisfy the rules according to which syntagmatic combinations are produced, but such elements are not interchangeable semantically. Similarly, the syntagmatic relations can be changed in our sentence, but not totally at will, since they coexist grammatically with the paradigmatic elements (e.g. we cannot place the pronoun 'me' after 'he' in the above example).

As with language, so with culture. Paradigms operate culturally in the sense that there always exist certain models or norms from which one selects in order (semiotically speaking) to fall into line. The paradigmatic cultural signs from which one selects may operate variously in the media genres of documentary or TV chat shows, but they are generally intended, with greater or lesser success, to combine together syntagmatically in order to create an effect appropriate to the genre – a **genre** being a type of media text which conforms more or less to certain ground rules of form, style and convention, as for example in sitcoms, romance fiction or punk rock, where any specific case is intertextually related to other cases of the same type. There are thus paradigmatic cultural registers just as there are linguistic ones, and these are generically coded. Syntagmatic relations are about combinatory possibilities, whereas paradigms exist in relations of opposition. These relations, in turn, are about identity and difference. Paradigms are selected because they are different; they have a specificity which defines their identity. Elements are combined syntagmatically because they are different (e.g. the different letters of the alphabet), but once combined they assume a combinatory identity – media producers cannot wilfully substitute the letter 'b' for 'c' when they use the word 'car', if they hope to be understood in talking about problems of transport; nor can a television soap actor replace a dress or jacket and trousers with a swimming costume and still hope to create the same dramatic effect when she enters a fancy downtown restaurant. These are obvious points in themselves and may seem trivial, but we make them in order to illustrate the underlying principles on which, like all cultural phenomena, they are based. This leads us to the final pair of semiotic terms we need to deal with.

Paradigms and syntagms also relate to metaphor and metonymy. A **metaphor** is a signifier (e.g. a word) applied to a signified (e.g. an object or process) to which it is not conventionally applicable or appropriate. For example, in a ballad by the English singer-songwriter Richard Thompson, he describes the woman around which the narrative revolves as being 'a rare thing, fine as a bee's wing'. Strictly speaking, this is a simile, but although comparison in simile is usually more explicit than in metaphor, its principle of operation is the same. Metaphorical speech or imagery transposes the characteristic of one object onto another. In this case, the transposition is made in order to enhance a sense of the consummate but delicate beauty of the woman whose story is being told. A **metonymy** is a figure of speech in which a part or attribute of one thing is applied to the whole thing. For example, when we say 'the land here belongs to the Crown', the word 'Crown' is used metonymically. Here are two examples in one: 'The pen is mightier than the sword.' In this maxim, 'pen' and 'sword' stand for those activities associated with them. When we speak of 'blue-collar workers', we are speaking metonymically, and of course the phrase also carries with it certain connotations which are distinct from those carried by the term 'white-collar workers'. Metaphor and metonymy often work simultaneously, as in this example: 'The sign of a mother pouring out a particular breakfast cereal for her children is a metonym of all her maternal activities of cooking, cleaning and clothing, but a metaphor for the love and security she provides' (Fiske and Hartley 1978: 50). Metaphor is thus paradigmatic, while metonymy is syntagmatic, for metaphor is dependent on oppositions while metonymy involves combinatory identities. In this example, the syntagmatic activities of the mother function simultaneously to encode the normative maternal paradigm, with its meanings of love and security. Both metaphors and metonyms are figures of 'equivalence'. They posit an 'equivalent' status or meaning for different entities. But metaphor presupposes equivalence between otherwise opposed elements, as in the remark that 'the learner's car kangarooed down the road'; whereas metonymy proposes a contiguous or sequential association between elements, as in the example, 'The White House said tonight...' Together, metaphor and metonymy constitute fundamental linguistic devices in any human culture (see Knowles and Moon 2005 for an accessible guide to the theory and applications of metaphor in textual analysis).

These, then, are the basic conceptual tools of semiotics, and we shall add to them when we come to discuss visual images. We have tried to give examples of their analytical value, but the application of semiotics to the study of media texts may not seem quite as straightforward as content analysis, which is much more recognisably a method of analysis as such. Semiotics is more a bunch of concepts, derived in the first place from Saussurian linguistics, which sets out to identify the structural principles by which communication and culture are possible. These concepts tend to have a rather generalised bearing on the actual process of analysis, informing critical readings in these terms rather than through any more precise or specific application. The structuralist (and poststructuralist) study of signs thus requires the creative application of a conceptual and theoretical corpus to particular texts; in other words, the corpus provides a general framework for interpretive work on the media text. So, for instance, for any textual item we can establish what is obtrusively manifest at the level of denotation in order to extract what is more latently there among the connotative levels of meaning; identify the operative principles of various signs and the different orders of signification; explore the implications of the codes and conventions which are drawn on in any text; and develop some form of ideological analysis of the role of the text in contemporary public culture.

Before you embark on your own work, utilising the concepts we have introduced, it may be useful to consider a sample semiotic analysis. Roland Barthes's analysis of the front cover of an edition of the magazine *Paris-Match* is one of the most celebrated and oft-cited cases of semiotics in action, and also illustrates what he means by myth. We reproduce a section of it in Box 7.1, along with the magazine's front cover. The extract is taken from Barthes's essay 'Myth Today' in his seminal collection *Mythologies* (1973).

LE NAUFRAGE
DE RIVA·BELLA

•

Les enquêteurs recherchent
les responsabilités et
revivent par la photo les
dix minutes d'horreur de

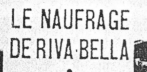

LA TRAGÉDIE
DU MANS

LES NUITS DE L'ARMÉE

Figure 7.1 Front cover of Paris-Match, no. 326, June 1955 (35 x 26.3 cm, original in colour)
Source: Photograph courtesy of *Paris-Match* IZIS

> I am at the barber's, and a copy of *Paris-Match* is offered to me. On the cover, a young Negro in a French uniform is saluting, with his eyes uplifted, probably fixed on a fold of the tricolour. All this is the *meaning* of the picture. But, whether naively or not, I see very well what it signifies for me: that France is a great Empire, that all her sons, without any colour discrimination, faithfully serve under her flag, and that there is no better answer to the detractors of an alleged colonialism than the zeal shown by this Negro in serving his so-called oppressors... It is this constant game of hide-and-seek between the meaning and the form which defines myth. The form of myth is not a symbol: the Negro who salutes is not the symbol of the French Empire: he has too much presence, he appears as a rich, fully experienced, spontaneous, innocent, *indisputable* image. But at the same time this presence is tamed, put at a distance, made almost transparent; it recedes a little, it becomes the accomplice of a concept which comes to it fully armed, French imperiality: once made use of, it becomes artificial... I can very well give to French imperiality many other signifiers besides a Negro's salute: a French general pins a decoration on a one-armed Senegalese, a nun hands a cup of tea to a bed-ridden Arab, a white school-master teaches attentive piccaninnies: the press undertakes every day to demonstrate that the store of mythical signifiers is inexhaustible.
>
> (Barthes 1973: 116)

Discourse analysis

Semiotics is not concerned solely with written media texts, as we shall see later. Nor is it concerned solely with the analysis of media representations: among other things, semiotics has been applied to the study of dance, food, fashion, architecture and sport. A good deal of the work that has utilised semiotics as its basic mode of analysis treats cultural phenomena generally as if they are structured in similar ways to language, or can be read in similar ways to texts. Linguistics was the major methodological influence on semiotics and structuralism, yet, somewhat paradoxically, close attention to the specifically linguistic structure of media texts was relatively uncommon in media studies during the 1970s, when semiotics was in the ascendancy. Since the 1980s, linguistic forms of discourse analysis have become more influential, at least partly because certain linguists themselves have shown a growing interest in media research. The most interesting linguistic analyses of media texts and representations have exposed the assumptions and values that are wrapped up in the construction of even relatively simple grammatical forms, such as headlines. They have also been helpful in illuminating different facets of the structures of media texts, and in attempting to trace the means by which language use in the media contributes to the ongoing production of social conceptions, values, identities and relations. While such attempts are not without their problems, for us the application of linguistics to the study of media texts has been most significant in helping to show the various ways in which media language use embodies relations of power and authority in society.

Examples of media linguistic analysis which have involved all these strands include the critical discourse analysis of Norman Fairclough; the work of British and Australian critical linguists such as Fowler, Hodge, Kress, Van Leeuwen and Trew; studies of news stories and bulletins by the New Zealand linguist Allan Bell; some of the analytical work on media discourse undertaken by Teun van Dijk; and work on the rhetoric and discourse of print news by John Richardson, which is grounded in material social realities (see Bibliography for details of the work of all these authors). As their work makes clear, there are various ways of embarking on a linguistic analysis of media texts. Although for the sake of convenience we shall refer to such work collectively as media linguistic analysis, we do not mean to play down these differences. Nor do we wish to create the sense that there are any fixed or settled ways of applying linguistic styles of analysis to the study of media texts, representations and discourses. Linguistic analysis is a field which is still in the process of development, and in light of this, we suggest that you adapt the ideas and techniques of these writers in ways which best suit your own specific analytical tasks and materials.

In the rest of this chapter, we want to sketch out some important characteristics of linguistic analysis. This should serve not only to introduce you to the general nature of work that has been done but also to acquaint you with some of the major terms and concepts that are used within the field. One of the most important terms is **discourse**. Despite their differences, all the writers mentioned above share several key concerns. The first of these is with the use of language in social life, and the second, following on from this, is with the relationship between language use and social structure. It is in the context of this relationship that the term discourse becomes important. Although it is used in different ways, most significantly it enables us to focus not only on the actual uses of language as a form of social interaction in particular situations and contexts but also on forms of representation in which different social categories, practices and relations are constructed from and in the interests of a particular point of view, a particular conception of social reality. It may be useful to take these two conceptual perspectives on discourse separately, even though they mutually inform each other.

First, attention to language as social interaction distinguishes media linguistic analysis from traditional approaches to the study of languages, which were preoccupied with the technical rules and principles of language structures, and which regarded language as an abstract system in isolation from its concrete social, cultural and historical contexts. These approaches are sociologically and historically sterile for media studies. Research into any aspect of the media is nothing if not social, so questions of context are of paramount importance. Second, the view of language as more generally constitutive of social reality is a characteristic of poststructuralism; and where the influence of the French philosopher Michel Foucault (1926–84) is felt, the emphasis is not so much on meaning-production in the uses of language, as on the relations of power and knowledge which certain formations of discourse allow and make possible. Very often, these relations are implied in the use of the term 'discourse' in contemporary forms of analysis.

Foucault's work has had a significant influence on the human sciences since the 1970s. The term 'discourse' figures more in his earlier work, where it was taken to refer to broad domains of language use which both condition and mobilise historically specific 'strategic possibilities' of meaning, understanding and practice. It is in this sense that he speaks of particular discourses of medicine or criminal punishment, operating during certain periods of history, in ways which were highly conventional and regularised. As such, they governed what could legitimately be said, for example, about mental illness and its treatment, in which appropriate contexts, and by which institutionally accredited personnel. Discourse in this sense – or what Foucault sometimes referred to as discursive formations – is at once singularly authoritative and deployed in the interests of existing structures of authority and power. It is also in this sense that it is closely related to ideology, as is evident in Fowler's definition of the term: '"Discourse" is speech or writing seen from the point of view of the beliefs, values and categories which it embodies; these beliefs (etc.) constitute a way of looking at the world, an organisation or representation of experience – "ideology" in the neutral, non-pejorative sense' (cited in Hawthorn 1992: 48). It is a matter of dispute whether a 'neutral, non-pejorative sense' of ideology can be isolated in this way, but the point to note is the connection with culturally ingrained and institutionally powerful ways of looking at, experiencing and understanding particular areas of social life. Discourses by way of this connection deeply permeate what is allowed as legitimate knowledge in particular domains of social life, and rigidly exclude other possibilities and other perspectives on those domains. This in turn begs various difficult questions concerning contestation and resistance to given discursive formations of knowledge and power, though the emphasis on the power–knowledge relation in authoritative discourses is crucial, and as such it has been productively taken up within the broad spectrum of social and cultural analysis.

As a term, then, discourse conjoins language use as text and practice. What we identify as 'discourse' and what we identify as 'social' are deeply intertwined. The discursive and the social mutually inform and act on each other, so that it is not as if discourse resides *here*, in our words or in the newspapers and magazines you read, while the social is *out there*, in some quite separate realm of living and thinking. All talk, all texts, are social in nature. Language is not some transparent medium through which we see the world, and nor is any cultural text. We build up our sense of the social world through the language we use, the talk we hear, the words we combine, while any sustained strips of social action and interaction would not be possible without the language we use, in specific cultural and historical contexts, as a means for engaging in them. This is where Norman Fairclough's definition of discourse analysis is relevant: 'Discourse analysis can be understood as an attempt to show systematic links between texts, discourse practices, and sociocultural practices' (1995a: 16–17, and see chapter 3).

The work of Fowler and his erstwhile associates (1979), for example, illustrates the concerns of critical linguistics with language use in concrete social situations, and with the language–society relationship. Among other things, they have been interested in the connections between the linguistic resources and styles on which people draw in speaking and writing, and the social groupings and relationships in which they participate in their everyday lives. This was a welcome break from earlier mainstream forms of linguistics, which perpetuated a dichotomous conception of the relations between linguistic structure and the social uses of language, and which, as a result, considered it possible to study grammar and syntax satisfactorily in isolation from social forces and institutions. The kind of linguistic analysis with which we are concerned is also dissociated from Chomskyian linguistics, with its conception of universal properties in language and its biological explanation of language acquisition. Critical media linguistics regards the linguistic patterning of texts and utterances as indelibly social in character, regardless of the ways in which particular texts and utterances are expressed. Expression, and styles of speaking and writing, cannot be hived off and treated separately from society's impress upon the production of meaning, or from the individual's communicative competence in a variety of social situations and contexts.

This is a crucial point. Any speaker puts together sentences and general combinatory units of words according to the rules of grammar, syntax and semantics, as they operate within any given language. These rules are learned in childhood as we enter into our cultural inheritance, and then learn to think and communicate within a particular **tradition**. It is only as we acquire a general competence in deploying them that we can begin to operate creatively within them. Yet competence in language use involves more than just linguistic competence per se. Such competence requires not only the syntactical mastery of sentence construction and combination but also mastery of the circumstances and settings in which particular forms of utterance and communication are appropriate. As Dell Hymes has put it, the speaker 'acquires competence as to when to speak, when not, and as to what to talk about with whom, when, where, in what manner' (1972: 277). So mastery of language is inseparable from mastery of the different contexts in which language is used.

There is obviously an affinity of critical media linguistics with sociolinguistics, which has focused a great deal on the dialectology of the modern city. For example, in a widely cited piece of research, William Labov (1972a, 1972b) examined patterns of pronunciation and other forms of speaking among a sample of the population of the Lower East Side in New York, and was able to show that these linguistic features correlated statistically with the social class of the speakers involved in the study. This illustrates a shared concern between sociolinguistics and critical media linguistics with the interrelationship of language and social structure. Questions concerning the analytical and theoretical import of these correlations between language and social structure are another matter, and it is here that different approaches to linguistic analysis may diverge. For example, among other problems, in the rewarding work of Labov, and in Trudgill's (1974) application of that work to a British context, there is an unexamined assumption of an a priori existence of the grammatical structure of language outside of social processes, which are influential only at the stage of language use. It is in light of this that sociolinguistics has sought to establish, through massive documentation, systemic correlations between particular linguistic forms and specified social variables. While it has sought in this way to contextualise language use, sociolinguistics does not move much beyond the richly detailed description of linguistic variation and the circumstances in which this occurs, and tends to operate with an empiricist conception of 'the bare correlational facts' (Fowler and Kress 1979: 191). These 'bare facts' include, among other things, the categories of social class, gender and ethnicity, and it is precisely such categories which are under-conceptualised in sociolinguistics. Sociolinguistics may focus axiomatically on the appropriateness of linguistic form to social context, but it has little to say about how, in any given case, this may contribute to the perpetuation of social divisions and inequalities. As a result, correlational sociolinguistics is weak in explanatory power.

Critical media linguistics differs from sociolinguistics in its approach to language use because it sees language itself as a social practice, and not something which can be correlated objectively with sociological factors because these are external to language. The concern is with the ways in which speaking and writing encode relations of power, authority and status, as is evident, for instance, in the type of speech act or modality of utterance deployed in particular contexts, or in the naturalisation of common-sense assumptions in media discourse. Media texts are not neutral in this respect, merely conveying information, say, or establishing the facts of a case. Media texts, more often than not, tend to mobilise or reinforce relations of control. An important point here is that linguistics constitutes a resource for the analysis of these relations as they are manifest in language structures: it looks at language with language. As a result of this, it has to be aware of its own critical assumptions and principles, for it is awareness of these which distinguishes it from everyday language use. People are not usually conscious of the assumptions and conventions on which they draw in their linguistic interactions, nor, generally speaking, is it appropriate that they should be, for in the context of everyday life this would lead to rigidly constrained, highly artificial forms of social intercourse. It is precisely because of this that a systematic understanding of how communication operates is necessary, and the value of critical work in the social sciences and humanities is that it provides opportunities to stand back and investigate, from alternative perspectives, the common-sense basis of the ways we communicate with each other and the ways the media communicate to their audiences. For us, the critical scope and potential of discourse analysis resides most of all in its examination of how relations and structures of power are embedded in the forms of everyday language use, and thus how language contributes to the legitimisation of existing social relations and hierarchies of authority and control.

The work of critical linguistics tended to do this mainly through analysis of the syntax of written communications. Taking their cue from the 'functionalist' linguistics of Halliday, Fowler et al. (1979) focused on the ways in which grammatical structures arrange, delete and assign a role and status to elements of texts and utterances. At a broad level, written texts may communicate about events and processes in the world, establish and reproduce social relations, or construct links with the situations in which they are used. In other words, the use of language may have what Halliday calls ideational, interpersonal and textual functions (see Halliday 1970, 1973). As Fairclough notes, this multifunctional conception of discourse 'harmonises with the constitutive view of discourse…providing a way of investigating the simultaneous constitution of systems of knowledge and belief (ideational function) and social relations and social identities (interpersonal function) in texts' (1995a: 58). So, in analysing media texts, we can try to identify which of these functions a particular text is seeking to fulfil, always bearing in mind that they are not mutually exclusive. We can then look at the intended purposes of texts, and their appropriateness to the situations in which they are encoded. From here, as we have noted, Fowler et al. tended to concentrate on the ways in which the generation of social meanings is conditioned by the syntactic choices which are made in the formulation of written (or spoken) communication.

Central to their method are what they call *transformations*: the restructuring of elements of language in both syntagmatic and paradigmatic dimensions of communication. Two in particular are singled out for the significance of their semantic effects. These are **nominalisation** and **passivisation**. Nominalisation transforms processes into objects, and does this linguistically by representing verbs as nouns. The effect is to attenuate the sense of activity, to depersonalise, to obscure agency, to blur questions of responsibility or culpability, as in the headline, 'Roof bolt fury after second pit collapses' (*Today* newspaper, 27 August 1993). Here the headline nominalised the verb 'to be furious', with the consequence that those who were reacting in this way to the pit collapse at Ellington Colliery in Northumberland were removed from the cause–effect relationship identified by the headline. In a linguistic analysis of a *Sydney Morning Herald* feature on the question of immigration, entitled 'Our Race Odyssey', Theo van Leeuwen (1995: 81–2) cites the following excerpt: 'Many Australians, the 1988 Fitzgerald Committee reported, were "bewildered" by the changing face of Australia today. They did not feel they understood or could influence this change. They felt "besieged" by immigration.' In contrast to the active sense of 'reporting' and feeling 'bewildered', where a specific body and category of people are mentioned, the process of immigration is nominalised as an abstract entity, with any sense of it involving specific individuals consequently being lost. They are an intangible facet of a generalised sense of change. 'Thus immigration itself remains an unexamined and unexaminable given, while the reactions to it are represented in all their specifics, as though they should be our main focus of attention' (ibid.).

The passive transformation – turning verbs into their passive form – also eliminates participants and prioritises certain themes. When agency is deleted in passivisation, the effect can serve 'to dissimulate the negative actions of elite or powerful groups' (van Dijk 1988a: 177). Linguistic transformations have a direct effect on the meaning likely to be construed from texts. Fowler and Kress (1979: 209–10) offered an example from *The Observer*: 'US coalminers are expected to return to work tomorrow.' This sentence conceals who it is who had this expectation. If those holding the expectation had been disclosed, then *they*, rather than the miners, would have become the subjects of the sentence, but the sentence is passivised and the agent (or agents) deleted. Our attention is thus apparently refocused, while the sequence in which we decode is directed in a particular way. Other writers use different terms for these linguistic transformations, or terms which relate to only small divergences from the same kinds of transformation. Theo van Leeuwen, for example, refers to nominalisation as 'objectivation', and passivisation as 'de-agentialisation', and these are pretty much synonymous with each other (van Leeuwen 1995: 93–8). Passivisation can be precipitously reversed, of course, as for instance in the ways in which social minorities are represented, being placed 'in a passive role (things are being decided or done, for or against them), unless they are agents of negative actions, such as illegal entry, crime, violence or drug abuse', in which case 'their responsible agency will be emphasised' (van Dijk 2000: 39–40). The general effect of such transformations and their sudden reversals is either to simplify or mystify, or both. Linguistic analysis can expose these effects by reconstructing the underlying structures from which the syntactical surfaces of texts have been derived.

Linguistic analysis involves examining the classificatory functions of language: the means by which language creates order out of the welter of phenomena in the world, brings social experience and what is made of it under control, and defines how social reality is to be understood. As Fairclough (2003: 143) has noted, uses of language generally 'reference complex sets and series of events which involve people doing things or things happening to people'. So with such language uses as nominalisation and passivisation, analysis needs to restore the sense of semantic complexity that has been lost. What gives linguistic analysis its critical edge is not only the reconstitution of the complexities that lie behind certain simplicities of meaning but also the attention that is given to agency or loss of agency – which agents have power and authority over others, and who *does* things as opposed to those who have things *done to them*. Where power, authority, responsibility and inequality are obfuscated by the uses of language in the media, critical media linguistics must set out to reveal how this works. The task also applies to questions of social and cultural identity. How individuals or groups are defined is crucial to their social and cultural identities; and the positive and negative connotations associated with the descriptive labels attached to people in social life are evidence of conflict over identity, position and the ascription of status and respect.

The discursive power of classification is revealed particularly in relexicalisation and over-lexicalisation. **Relexicalisation** involves relabelling ('Argies' instead of 'Argentinians', for example, in the context of the Falklands/Malvinas war) or coining new lexical items ('Sellafield', say, or 'substance abuse'). **Over-lexicalisation** is the heaping up of synonymous words and phrases to designate items of intense preoccupation in the experience of particular groups. By way of example, Fowler and Kress cite the alternative terms for 'loan' in an *Observer* article: 'credit deal', 'credit bargains', 'low-interest finance', 'low-interest-rate schemes', 'special credit scheme', 'overdraft', 'personal loan', 'credit alternatives', 'finance house loans', 'hire purchase' and 'bank loans' (Fowler and Kress 1979: 211; see also Teo 2002 on representations of Vietnamese people in Austrian media). Such over-lexicalisation is suggestive of the socio-economic status and position of many *Observer* readers, as well as being more generally indicative of the money-oriented and property-conscious values of the British middle classes.

It may seem that this is tantamount to jumping to conclusions. To claim that there is a definite link between such over-lexicalisation and a particular set of class values may strike you as an unwarranted assumption and generalisation, for even if it is true, it is not sufficiently demonstrated by any sociological evidence. In a later section we shall come back to such problems when we discuss the limits of linguistic and other forms of textual analysis. What should first be emphasised and applauded is the attempt to develop a social analysis of media language and discourse. Norman Fairclough's work exemplifies this (see, for example, 1989, 1995a, 1995b) by approaching textual analysis as the first stage in a threefold process of analysis.

This first stage concerns itself descriptively with the formal properties of a text. But a media text such as a newspaper article or the transcript of a TV news bulletin is not a definitively accomplished entity. It is rather the product of interaction between a process of production and processes of interpretation in which participants draw on the resources of knowledge, belief, ideas, values and assumptions which are available to them. Texts in this sense occur as the interplay between the 'traces' they bear of their production and the 'cues' they provide for their interpretation. The second stage of analysis is concerned with the relationship between the text and these processes of production and interpretation. We are moving, here, in a particularly fruitful way, from 'text' to 'discourse'. While we need to remember that media production involves processes of interpretation, and audience interpretations are themselves forms of meaning-production, the social conditions of the interactive processes of production and interpretation can be related to three 'levels' of social organisation: the immediate situation of interaction, the social institution in which that situation is placed, and the social order as a whole. Productional and interpretive processes are conditioned by the situational, institutional and societal contexts in which they take place, and the third stage of analysis focuses on the shaping influence of these contextual factors.

The operation and ordering of discourses are, for Fairclough, determined by the unequal power relations of social institutions and society more broadly. Although he acknowledges that these relations need to be understood with respect to various lines of social differentiation, such as gender and generation, he sees them primarily in terms of class structure: class relations have 'a more fundamental status than others' and set 'the broad parameters within which others are constrained to develop'. Language is then 'both a site of and a stake in class struggle' (Fairclough 1989: 34–5). From a feminist perspective, this may seem to exaggerate the pervasive scope of one particular type of power relation (see, for example, Barrett 1980: ch. 4). What is welcome in Fairclough, however, is the recognition that social analysis must be central to the development of the critical study of discourse, rather than something added after the fact. For Fairclough, discourse is determined by social structures, though those structures are also partly a product of discourse, and continue to be reproduced by discourse. There is therefore power in discourse, and power behind discourse.

Fairclough constructively adopts Gramsci's notion of common sense to show one way in which texts contribute to sustaining unequal power relations. Common sense in Gramsci's formulation of it refers to values, meanings and beliefs which are implicitly contained in everyday practical activity, rather than being systematically set forth and developed, as in a philosophical treatise or academic paradigm, for instance. Gramsci defines common sense as 'a chaotic aggregate of disparate conceptions' of the social world and how it is held to operate. As such, it is relatively self-contradictory and fragmentary in character. This does not mean that there are no 'truths' in common sense, but rather that it is ambiguous and multiform, a mishmash of assumptions, precepts and so on, some of which conflict with or negate each other, so 'to refer to common sense as a confirmation of truth is a nonsense' (Gramsci 1978: 422–3). It consists most of all in what is taken for granted and unexamined, and through this is generated much of its efficacy in informing what people think and do. Its political significance is directly connected with this. Common sense is held to serve the sustaining of unequal relations of power, and to do this smoothly because it works within what is assumed and tacitly accepted to be the case in any particular instance. In this sense, it is clearly related to the concept of ideology, which for Fairclough is 'most effective when its workings are least visible' (Fairclough 1989: 85). Common sense, therefore, amounts to a sort of popularisation of conceptions and values which, directly or indirectly, support existing divisions and asymmetries in the relations of power and authority in society, and which limit the thinking and action of subordinated groups and classes in a negative direction rather than stimulating the development of alternative conceptions and values critical of the social and ideological bases of their subordination (see Gramsci 1978: particularly 323–30, 419–25). In media representations, this involves 'the translation of official viewpoints into a public idiom' in such a way as to invest such viewpoints 'with popular force and resonance', bringing them commonsensically 'within the horizons of understandings of the various publics' (Hall et al. 1978: 61).

For Fairclough, the ideological work of texts has the effect of naturalising such relations. Naturalisation, he says, is 'the royal road to common sense' (1989: 92). Through the cues for interpretation which texts provide, readers are positioned in such a way that it seems entirely appropriate when they draw on the common-sense assumptions that view those relations as natural, inevitable and taken for granted. It is thus through naturalisation that particular types of discourse appear to lose their ideological character. 'The apparent emptying of the ideological content of discourses is, paradoxically, a fundamental ideological effect: ideology works through disguising its nature, pretending to be what it isn't' (ibid.). Common-sense assumptions are, by definition, common to many people, but that is not the same as saying that they are universally shared. Ideology is not monolithic either in content or in practice. The more particular ideologies prevail, the more effective they will be across society, but when different social groupings struggle over institutional power, alternative ideologies are generated or called on. Discourses are linked with these diverse ideologies, which may be simply alternative or more strongly oppositional to those which are dominant in society, as for example in the ways Thatcherism was the dominant political discourse of the 1980s in Britain (articulating the liberal discourse of the 'free market' with conservative discourses of 'tradition, family and nation, respectability, patriarchalism and order' (Hall 1988: 2, *passim*)). Where dominated discourses are oppositional, strong pressures are exerted in attempts to contain, marginalise, suppress or eliminate them, and these attempts are roughly proportionate to the struggle to naturalise the dominant discourse in any given instance, to make it appear as common sense rather than ideology. To emphasise its paradoxical nature, ideology is most effective when it erases itself.

Discourse analysis can show these processes at work in the realm of natural language by pointing to attempts to close meaning down, to fix it in relation to a given position, to make certain conventions self-evidently correct, to do creative repair work when something becomes problematic, and to make the subject positions of discourse transparently obvious, without any viable alternatives. Discourse analysis is at its best when it turns these ideological strategies inside out. It is important to bear in mind at least two points here. On the one hand, such strategies are not necessarily formulated in any deliberate and systematic fashion, and on the other, appearances to the contrary, ideologies are inherently unstable. They are fraught with their own internal contradictions: contradictions between what is claimed about the social world and the experience of the material realities of this world; contradictions between ideology as 'lived' and ideology as a specifically formulated philosophy of 'how the world is'; and contradictions between opposed ideologies and the different, antagonistic interests to which they stand in relation. Where questions of power are involved, conflict and struggle are key features of the discursive practices of ideology, continually re-establishing certain ideas, values, beliefs and assumptions, which sustain existing power relations in society in the face of efforts to question, challenge or subvert them.

This may seem to take us a long way from textual analysis itself, so let us now turn back to the ways in which Fairclough deals with the formal features of texts. Here, again, he presents a threefold structure of procedure. First, the content of a text may be examined for the traces and cues it provides of its value as social experience, and thus of the knowledge and beliefs which are meant to be attached to such experience. Second, textual features may have a relational dimension, enacting in discourse some aspect of social relations which the analysis should bring out. For instance, and most obviously, relational functions of discourse can be addressed by asking how pronouns such as 'I', 'you', 'we' and 'they' are constituted in media texts. Third, texts can be studied for the traces and cues they offer for expressing evaluation of the aspect of social reality the text relates to, and for acting on social identities through this expressive dimension. The experiential, relational and expressive values of textual features can then be addressed in relation to choice of vocabulary, syntactic form and any broader textual structures which are apparent in your sample text or texts. In these ways, then, the analysis of grammatical structure, lexical choice and the like can be absorbed into the broader framework developed by Fairclough, so integrating into the procedures of textual analysis the social dimensions of language and the linguistic dimensions of the social. Interpretation of the semiotic and linguistic codings of media texts needs to be informed by social analysis to show how, as a social practice, interpretation is constrained and enabled by social structures, which shape discourses and in turn are shaped by them, within an overall matrix of relations of social power, authority and control. The key question is always how you trace the complicated web that connects the minutiae of texts with this much broader matrix of relations. It is a question somewhat problematically raised by the third mode of analysis we want to discuss in this chapter.

Frame analysis

Frame analysis has become a prominent paradigm in media and communication research. Whereas semiotic, linguistic and discourse analysis have their roots in European philosophy and language theory, frame analysis has North American origins, emerging from the symbolic interactionist tradition, as exemplified by the work of George Herbert Mead, Herbert Blumer and the Chicago school of sociology (Blumer 1969). The term 'frame analysis' was first coined by Ernest Goffman in his 1974 study, *Frame Analysis: An Essay on the Organisation of Experience*. Goffman was not concerned principally with media analysis in this work, although it includes many media-related examples (Ytreberg 2002). Rather, his aim was:

> to try to isolate some of the basic frameworks of understanding available in our society for making sense out of events and to analyze the special vulnerabilities to which these frames of reference are subject... I assume that definitions of a situation are built up in accordance with principles of organisation which govern events – at least social ones – and our subjective involvement in them; frame is the word I use to refer to such of these basic elements as I am able to identify. That is my definition of frame. My phrase 'frame analysis' is a slogan to refer to the examination in these terms of the organisation of experience.

(Goffman 1974: 10–11)

Within Goffman's initial formulation, frames are defined as unconsciously manufactured and adopted, even though they structure 'which parts of reality become noticed' (Koenig 2004: 1). Whether anything can be unconsciously manufactured and adopted is a moot point, but of course the frames to which Goffman refers can be either implicit within the experience of an event and not explicitly acknowledged, or quite deliberately and knowingly manufactured, as for instance in those specific types of event known as invented traditions (see Hobsbawm and Ranger 1984; and Negus and Pickering 2004: 103–14, for a critique of the term). Goffman's stated aim in frame analysis is also worth considering in another respect, for it relates to a distinction which, if not carefully made and applied, can be the source of considerable confusion or inconsistency.

Goffman begins by using the term 'framework', which he regards as synonymous with the term 'frames of reference', but as he goes on to talk of principles of organisation which govern events and our subjective involvement in them, he uses the term 'frame' instead. If it is a frame which comprises the organising principles of an event and our experience of it, this is fine, but easy slippage between these different terms is where confusion and inconsistency can arise, gratuitously or otherwise. This needs clarifying, since it is often unclear if the term 'frame' is simply a metaphor or whether it means more than a metaphor, and, if so, how. It is also unclear whether it is an appropriate metaphor to use in media and cultural analysis. When we talk about the frame of a photograph or picture, this may set off what it contains, but it is the content of what is contained that is of paramount importance. When we apply this to a media text, it is what the text says and how it is said that are the key initiating questions. In other words, we attend primarily to the picture of reality offered by the text rather than to how the text is framed. Here, the other sense of frame – not as the four-sided surround of an image, but as a framework underlying a media image or text – is preferable. The sense is of a basic idea, outline or plan. In this quite different application, the reference is to the method of a text's construction, the order and structure of its narrative organisation. It is a more appropriate metaphorical sense for thinking about the relations between how a text is put together and what can be said of its social, cultural and ideological import, for it brings together the sense of a media text's discursive framework and the sense of media discourse framing what can be said and thought about a particular issue. When these two senses are understood as acting in concert with each other, frame connects with other tools in the methodological toolkit we are putting together in this book, such as *encoding* in semiotics, or the analytical concepts of *thematic structure* and *discourse schemas*, which we shall introduce in the next chapter. These are not synonymous with frames, but they relate closely to how frames operate and to what frames do within any particular media text or discourse. They are compatible with each other because of the way they help to provide a text or discourse with a central governing framework which conditions the meanings it produces. In this way, the concept of frame is clearly more than a simple metaphor, but how it is applied, and which senses of it are being preferred, is of critical importance. It is sensible for you to be aware of the distinctions between them and explicit about how you deploy them.

This is not always the case with some of the research using frame analysis that you may encounter. Since Goffman, the concept of frame has become widely adopted in media, communication and cultural research, but in this process, Goffman's original definition, which clearly preferred the sense of frame as framework, has been somewhat revised and extended. It is still the case that these studies retain an interest in how 'frames' structure our social reality. For example, according to the American sociologist Todd Gitlin (1980: 6): 'Frames are principles of selection, emphasis and presentation composed of little tacit theories about what exists, what happens, and what matters'. Later in the book, Gitlin tells us that the role of frames is 'to certify the limits within which all competing definitions of reality will contend' (ibid.: 254). It is worth looking more closely at these two statements because, again, they offer rather different formulations. In the first statement, the emphasis is on the organisational functioning of frames as they are informed by certain definitions of reality, whereas the second statement emphasises the power of frames to define the boundaries within which these definitions are able to contend with each other. The first points more to how texts are constructed in particular ways according to particular framing principles, while the second points more to how an ideological horizon governs the general orientation within which texts are framed. These two roles of frames are interrelated, of course, but are nevertheless distinct from each other: the first attends more to the internal principles of textual organisation; and the second to the broader sanctioned possibilities of meaning, external to specific media texts (which, as we have already seen, Foucault called discursive formations), the regulatory regimes of power and knowledge that are constitutive of what can be said about certain realms of social reality and the practical actions that can be taken in relation to them.

These two senses of frames in media and cultural analysis are not easily reconciled because they move between little tacit theories and large-scale definitions of reality, operating at quite different orders of discourse and meaning; but perhaps we can bring them together in a single conception that is somewhat more modest in scope, yet not confined to any specific textual realisation. In this conception a frame is a central organising or structuring device that gives definitional shape to a particular issue. It does this through what it selects and omits, highlights and elaborates. Alternatively, a frame can be understood as the consequence that follows from the application of this conception within a media text. A frame can therefore be seen as either sense-making, or the sense already made of an issue, or both, of course, since this is a classic chicken-and-egg situation. Whichever way we look at them, what remains distinctive about frames is the slant or weight they give to an issue. This is different to the actual content, the informational or factual detail contained within a text. It is instead concerned with the particular orientation taken by a text. The text in question is usually a news text, for framing theory is usually applied to news narrative and discourse, but it could also be a magazine or television advert, a documentary film or a party political broadcast. In moving from attending to how a text works in terms of the organisation of its various elements, to how it develops a definite angle or preferred line of interpretation, we are moving towards a consideration of the text's ideological force. This can be seen as a two-step methodological movement within any particular analysis, but it is also indicative of the way attention has shifted in the analysis of media framing generally.

From Goffman's interest in the tacit principles of organisation which govern social events and our subjective involvement in them, the focus of attention has moved to the active creation and promotion of frames in media discourses and how these may advance the political and material interests of social groups (sometimes referred to as 'frame sponsorship'). According to Robert Entman: 'To frame is *to select* some aspect of a perceived reality and make them more salient in a communicating text, in such a way as *to promote* a particular problem definition, causal interpretation, moral evaluation, and/or treatment for the item described' (1993: 53, emphasis added). Attending to the organisational devices of a text is still vital, of course – and Entman emphasises selection and salience as key among these devices – but the point of this is to identify how framing then promotes a particular way of seeing or thinking about a social issue or problem. In other words, we should move in a two-step process from Gitlin's first statement to his second. This is not to give analytical priority to how frames define the ideological horizon in which social reality or some aspect of it is set, since we can only begin to understand this through analysing the particular ways in which frames operate within specific media texts. Nevertheless, the move does mean a shift up from micro-levels of meaning in certain textual instances to the ways these draw on and connect with macro-levels of ideology and power. The aim of this analytical move is then to arrive at an understanding of how frames reveal 'the imprint of power' by registering 'the identity of actors or interests that compete to dominate the text' (ibid.). This is some distance from Goffman's original formulation, which saw framing as 'an innate property of all social processes, not only those most consciously manufactured' (Koenig 2004: 2). The distance involves an arrival at something more definite and less diffuse.

An example of research into the intentional manufacturing of frames is offered by a study of news framing of the debate concerning the link between genetics and mental illness (Conrad 2001). The study identifies a frame of 'genetic optimism' that has dominated news reporting of this issue from the mid 1980s onwards. This frame contains three propositions:

1. that mental illness is genetic in origin;
2. that the relevant gene will be identified;
3. that the effects of this discovery will be positive.

Despite successive scientific failures to prove the link, these 'disconfirmations' have not displaced the genetic optimism frame in media reporting, whose endurance is explained by the 'hype and hope' of the scientists, editors and journalists involved in reporting this topic (ibid.: 225; see also Paterson 2006).

We have talked so far about how frames help to structure a media narrative, and how you can begin to go about identifying the devices which enable frames to operate, but interest in the social and political origins of media frames means that frame analysis in media research is not restricted to the textual analysis of media content. D'Angelo identifies four empirical goals that framing studies pursue, to varying degrees:

(a) to identify thematic units called frames, (b) to investigate the antecedent conditions that produce frames, (c) to examine how news frames activate and interact with an individual's prior knowledge to affect interpretations, recall of information, decision making, and evaluations, and (d) to examine how news frames shape social-level processes such as public opinion and policy issue debates.

(D'Angelo 2002: 873)

This raises a number of questions. First, it forces us to ask whether frames are cognitive or discursive. It would seem that they actually involve the interaction of both cognitive and discursive structures, but this remains unclear and unresolved. Second, if much frame analysis is 'extra-textual', textual analysis surely has to remain central to the project, for without an identification of the frames in media texts and discourse, there would be no antecedent or consequent social processes to examine. Third, if we begin with analysis of particular media texts, how far do we then move beyond them in order to identify, assess and understand, as D'Angelo suggests we should, the origins of frames, the reception of frames and their consequences for memory, interpretation and judgement, and the way frames structure public knowledge, public opinion and public debates – perhaps even, as is implied, the formation of social and cultural policy? All this is a very tall order. It would involve huge extensions of the initiating focus of attention in the identification of particular thematic units. This is of quite a different order to Fairclough's attention to the articulation of broader social relations and structures within media texts, and to the cues in such texts for the ways they may be connected to more general formations of experience, knowledge and belief. D'Angelo's fourfold purpose for frame analysis also raises another question which we shall address in more detail later, and from another angle. The question is: how much weight of subsequent investigation, data and discussion can the initial analysis of a text or set of texts be made to bear? We could look at this another way and say that what is being proposed is a series of investigations, beginning with media texts and moving on not only to audience study but also to broader sociological forms of inquiry and to research in policy formation. This would be quite different, but we are still talking about research on a large scale, and it may be more sensible to stay within the scope of media texts and discourses themselves rather than claiming that framing theory needs to stake out a vast expanse of research territory. Showing a little analytical modesty is sometimes a wise step to take.

There are other problems, beginning with some practical ones. If you want to use frame analysis in a research project, how do you do this beyond the twofold analytical procedure we have suggested? This question raises another, which is the issue of frame identification: how, in the first place, do we identify and define these influential thematic units which are described as frames? Here we reach another point where the picture gets murky. The problem is not helped by the lack of any clear agreement within the literature as to what actually constitutes a frame. Carragee and Roefs identify a range of conceptual inconsistencies in the ways researchers define frames. For some, the concept of framing is simply employed in a loose, metaphoric sense, 'with little or no reference to its theoretical or substantive implications' (Carragee and Roefs 2004: 217). Others equate frames to story topics, issue positions or negative and positive characterisations of reported sources. In Carragee and Roefs' view, these are all lamentable simplifications:

The reduction of frames to story topics, attributes, or issue positions ignores the ways in which frames construct particular meanings and how they advance specific ways of seeing issues. This reduction also neglects how particular frames apply to multiple issues, and how a single issue position can be a product of more than one frame… By identifying frames as little more than story topics, attributes, or issue positions, some contemporary approaches to framing neglect the ideological nature and consequences of the framing process as well as the power relationships that influence that process. Framing research that ignores the ways in which frames construct meanings and the interests served by those meanings deprives the concept of its theoretical and substantive significance.

(ibid.: 217, 219)

We agree with this criticism. It means that only the first step in our two-step movement of analysis has been taken, and not the all-important second step. This does severely limit the potential of frame analysis. But if frames are more complex and ideological than some allow, and have such deeper and determining significance, how we go about identifying their character and existence is not so straightforward (Maher 2001). What does the second methodological step actually involve? This is another area of confusion, as many framing analysts often say little about the precise process by which frames are identified. It is clearly an interpretive activity that depends very greatly on the knowledge and skill of the analyst, but there is always the potential that a frame identified by a researcher may be a reified construct of the study rather than a meaningful categorisation of a pre-existing thematic cluster.

Another area of confusion relates to the methods used to analyse frames in media discourse. Several commentators have commented on the fractured nature of the frame analysis paradigm (Entman 1993; D'Angelo 2002), and this fragmentation is particularly evident in methodological terms. There is no single, definitive frame analysis method as such; rather, studies adapt and appropriate the qualitative and quantitative textual approaches we have already outlined. For example, d'Haenens and de Lange's study (2001) of the framing of asylum seekers in the Dutch regional press used quantitative content analysis procedures to compare the prominence of five frames in press discourse (conflict; human interest; economic consequences; morality; responsibility). Other examples of quantitative frame analysis include Park's investigation of US TV coverage of Japan and Korea (2003), and Noakes and Wilkins' analysis of US press coverage of the Palestinian movement (2002). In contrast, others have favoured more qualitative and micro-discursive approaches that draw directly on discourse analysis and critical linguistics (e.g. Johnston 1995; Skillington 1997; Durham 1998). Still others integrate qualitative and quantitative textual analysis methods (e.g. Downey and Koenig 2006; Pan and Kosicki 1993).

Viewed positively, this eclecticism could be seen as showing that frame analysis is a paradigm which successfully avoids the pitfalls of academic apartheid mentioned at the start of this chapter. Viewed negatively, it could be argued that the conceptual confusions surrounding frame analysis remove any possibility for methodological cohesion. We have tried to clear the air of at least some of these confusions, but it remains the case that the centrally informing term itself requires further elaboration and refinement. This would help advance frame analysis, as, in any particular case, would the explicit presentation and discussion of what analytical procedures have been followed. Compared with semiotic and linguistic analysis, framing analysis may at present (time of writing 2007) be less developed in terms of the clear methodological steps it provides the media analyst, but when used in combination with other analytical methods, it does possess considerable value. It is in this way that we suggest you should consider it.

Box 7.2 Framing terrorism

Defining and explaining 'terrorism' is one of the most fiercely contested areas of public debate. It is not difficult to see why. To label an action as 'terrorist' is to condemn it as illegitimate and to support the claims of the state against which it is aimed. This decision is always highly charged politically. When Nelson Mandela was convicted of 'terrorism' in 1964 by the white minority apartheid government of South Africa, he argued in court that since the regime had made legitimate political action impossible by banning the ANC party he helped to found, he had no choice but to resort to acts of sabotage. He was finally released in 1990, became the first president of a now fully democratic state, and was universally hailed as one of the most important political figures of the century.

Democratic states are characterised by their commitment to relative freedom of movement, political association and speech, but this openness creates its own problems. People expect to go about their daily business knowing that they are safe from violent attack and sudden death. By exposing the state's inability to guarantee this security, terrorist assaults on shopping areas, business offices and tourist sites undermine popular confidence in government. They also pose acute problems of response. Terrorism is a clandestine activity and its proponents go to considerable lengths not to draw attention to themselves. Identifying them requires extensive surveillance of the civilian population, compromising the civil liberties of citizens with no connection to terrorist groups. Second, democratic states are distinguished from authoritarian and dictatorial regimes by their adherence to the rule of law. This core principle requires suspected terrorists to be arrested, given a fair trial and, if convicted on the basis of the evidence, handed an appropriate sentence. Conventional court proceedings, however, give terrorists a public platform for their views and may be ineffective in securing a conviction. Faced with these dilemmas, democratic states may be tempted to suspend or tamper with due process to varying degrees. They may detain suspects without trial, replace civil courts with military tribunals and hold hearings behind closed doors. As a last resort, they may sanction police and security personnel to shoot suspected terrorists on sight. By employing some of the same tactics as their opponents, however, democratic governments undermine the claim to moral superiority on which their legitimacy rests.

Looking at the contemporary debate about 'terrorism', we can identify three main frameworks. Based around concepts of threats, rights and redress, they offer competing ways of thinking and talking about its origins and causes and how best to respond. These interpretive schemas, which are advanced by political actors and expert commentators, provide the raw discursive materials that media professionals draw on in constructing news stories, editorial comment and popular fictions. As Teun van Dijk, one of the leading researchers on media discourses, notes, 'The construction of news is most of all a reconstruction of available discourses' (van Dijk 1983: 28). Each discourse schema frames 'terrorism' in quite different ways.

The *threat* frame occupies the centre of contemporary debate. It has been vigorously promoted by the administrations of George W. Bush in the United States, in the wake of the 9/11 attacks on New York and Washington, and strongly supported by the governments of Tony Blair in Britain, particularly after the London Underground bombings in 2005. It identifies these events as marking a decisive shift in the nature of contemporary terrorism and the threats that it poses. Old-style 'terrorist' movements in the West, such as the IRA in Ireland and the Basque separatist movement ETA in Spain, had their roots in historic disputes over the legitimacy of national borders, and their supporters often pursued electoral politics alongside armed struggle. Their causes and solutions could therefore be placed within a political narrative. In contrast, the movements responsible for the attacks of the early twenty-first century are seen as engaged in a distinctively 'new' form of terrorism. They are identified with an extremist fringe within Islam, waging a holy war against 'modernity' and 'Western values', rather than as political actors pursuing a political cause. This definition of the situation received powerful support from George W. Bush's declaration of a 'crusade' against al-Qaida, which is led by Osama bin Laden, in retaliation for its destruction of the Twin Towers in New York.

The argument that the 'new' terrorism marks a decisive break with the past and is an unprecedented threat is continually bolstered by references to the number of casualties, the scale of destruction, the targeting of civilians (rather than military personnel or political figures), the total disregard for human life, the globalisation of 'terrorist' action, and the pervasive sense that attacks could occur anywhere at any time.

This sense of intensified and pervasive risk is then mobilised to support the introduction of new control measures. As Tony Blair told a press conference held in 2005, 'let no one be in any doubt, the rules of the game are changing' (10 Downing Street 2005). This definition of the situation has been used to sanction pre-emptive strikes against overseas regimes thought to be actively supporting al-Qaida, most notably the invasions of Afghanistan and Iraq. It has also been employed to license a de facto 'state of emergency' in both Britain and the United States, in which measures previously used only in wartime (and during the cold war) are reactivated – a move supported by the claim that Western democracies are engaged in a 'war against terrorism'. In Britain, for example, surveillance has been intensified and generalised, detention without trial has been introduced, evidence obtained under torture has been accepted, and new curbs on open debate have been forcefully argued for. By ignoring the political context in which insurgencies or armed attacks take place, Tony Blair's efforts to introduce a new offence of 'justifying or glorifying terrorism *anywhere*, not just in the United Kingdom' (emphasis added), makes open debate on the causes of terrorism more difficult.

The case for this and other new restrictions is strongly opposed within the *rights* frame, advanced by critical judges and lawyers, civil rights campaigners and sceptical expert commentators. They reject the core assumptions of the *threat* frame and offer an alternative interpretive schema. They point out that despite the influence of al-Qaida, the majority of terrorist attacks are still carried out by 'old-style' groups, like the Tamil Tigers in Sri Lanka, with clear political objectives. Even in the case of suicide bombings, seen by proponents of the *threat* frame as prima facie evidence of Islamist terrorism's irrationality and fanaticism, they argue that the root causes lie with politics rather than religious fundamentalism. As Robert Pape, author of the most extensive empirical study of suicide bombings, concludes: 'there is little connection between suicide terrorism and Islamic fundamentalism, or any one of the world's religions… what nearly all attacks have in common is a specific secular and strategic goal: to compel modern democracies to withdraw military forces from territory the terrorists consider to be their homeland' (Pape 2006: 3). If this proposition is correct, proponents of the *rights* frame argue, at least some of the motivations for present-day terrorism lie with the foreign policies pursued by the major Western powers, and the most effective solutions are likely to lie with political and diplomatic initiatives, rather than with an escalation of force.

Advocates of the *rights* frame are fiercely critical of the military and security responses to Islamist terrorism instituted by Western governments, arguing that the Iraq war was illegal under international law, and that by disregarding the Convention against Torture and the Geneva Convention, the emergency measures sanctioned by the 'war on terror' violate international agreements on human rights. They point particularly to the practice of 'extraordinary rendition', whereby suspected terrorists and their associates are flown clandestinely to be questioned in countries where torture is a routine interrogation practice; and to the labelling of suspects detained at the American base in Guantánamo Bay in Cuba as 'unlawful combatants', a definition that denies them both access to the regular legal system and the rights accorded to prisoners of war. In a speech in Australia in 2006, for example, the British Lord Chancellor, Lord Falconer, denounced the US Government's decision to 'deliberately put the detainees beyond the reach of law' as a 'shocking affront to the principles of democracy' (Fickling 2006), and insisted that: 'The rule of law must prevail just as much in times of terrorism as it does in times of peace. Every battle fought by a country that abides by the rule of law must be fought in accordance with rules and laws' (Dyer 2006: 5). To do otherwise is to undermine the moral case for democracy and to move a step closer to the exercise of state terror, designed to maintain order by keeping the civilian population in a state of constant fear.

The third main frame, the *redress* frame, is advanced by terrorist groups themselves, who argue that their actions are redressing real or imagined wrongs and injustices arising from invasion or occupation by 'foreign' powers, or rule by governments whose legitimacy they refuse to recognise. Osama bin Laden's original aim, for example, was to expel American troops from Saudi Arabia, the location of Islam's most holy sites, and to reduce Washington's power and influence in the region. Later, in a speech released in 2004, he claimed that the attacks on the Twin Towers were launched in retaliation for earlier American-sanctioned attacks on Islamic territories.

> We have been fighting you because we do not remain silent in the face of injustice. We want to restore our [Islamic] nation's freedom. Just as you violate our security, we violate yours... When [in 1982] the US permitted the Israelis to invade Lebanon...many were killed and wounded, while others were terrorised into fleeing. I still remember those moving scenes – blood, torn limbs, dead women and children everywhere, and high-rises being demolished on top of their residents... As I was looking at those destroyed towers in Lebanon, I was struck by the idea of punishing the oppressor in the same manner and destroying towers in the US...punishing the wicked with an eye for an eye – is that reprehensible terrorism?
>
> (Osama bin Laden quoted in MEMRI 2004: 1–2)

In divergent ways, these three distinctive frames inform media discourse on 'terrorism'. It is important to remember, however, that a simple one-to-one relation between particular media productions and particular frames is often the exception rather than the rule. As Schlesinger, Murdock and Elliott argued in their (1983) analysis of the coverage of the conflict in Northern Ireland, different frames may coexist or contend with each other within the same newspaper feature or television programme. Indeed, examining how open different media forms and genres are to competing frames, and how they organise the relations between them, is an important topic for research. Whereas news items are likely to be based primarily around official sources working within the *threat* frame, with critical commentary from recognised proponents of the *rights* frame given some right of reply, space for the elaboration of variants of the *redress* frame is generally offered only in some genres of popular fiction where terrorists feature as central characters.

Summary: key points

- In this chapter, three key approaches to the analysis of media texts were discussed: semiotics, media linguistics and frame analysis.

- The major concepts of semiotics were outlined and explained, with examples to show how they may be applied.

- The characteristic elements of linguistic and discourse analysis were sketched, and the main differentiating features of the work of various analysts of written media discourse were made clear.

- An outline of frame analysis was provided, some of the problems raised by this mode of analysis were discussed, and the relation of the concept of frame to other analytical concepts we deploy in the book was also made clear.

- Encouragement was given to the combination of these three approaches with quantitative content analysis, the procedures for which were outlined in chapter 6. Frame analysis already provides examples of how this can be achieved. Such combinations were urged in the interests of balancing the different strengths and weaknesses of qualitative and quantitative methods.

- As an example of frame analysis, media discourse on 'terrorism' was discussed in terms of the three frames which centrally inform it. These three framing schemas provide the major ways in which 'terrorist' activity is reported, discussed, interpreted and understood.

▶ chapter eight

Unpacking News

A sample linguistic analysis

In this chapter we shall undertake a linguistic analysis of a sample news story in order to show how the principles of such analysis can be applied to the particular use of language in popular journalism and the particular narrative and textual structure in news reporting. We shall highlight the kinds of detail of a media text's organisation and structure to which you should attend, and then go on to extrapolate from this analysis the methodological procedure involved in its actual accomplishment. The aim will be to provide you with a set of steps to take when you come to do a similar analysis yourself. We shall follow this up with a few notes on some of the limitations of this kind of textual analysis, and suggest that certain weaknesses can be overcome by developing this approach alongside others, in a more eclectic methodological combination.

Most media studies textbooks deal with recent news stories. We have deliberately taken as our sample text a story that is almost half a century old, and we have done so for three main reasons. First, in taking up an older example of news reporting, we can show that contemporary journalism has developed gradually over a considerable period of time. Its style and structure bear many similarities to the ways in which news was being constructed not only 10 or 20 years ago, but even 50 years ago. News reporting in the past is not as dated as it may seem at first glance. Second, because news reporting itself is almost solely focused on recent events and the circumstances attending them, media studies should counter the rather closed, present-centred viewpoint and understanding that can ensue, and develop instead a more long-term perspective on immediate events, for these frequently have deep-rooted connections with the past. In taking this position, we follow the famous dictum of the American novelist, William Faulkner, who wrote: 'The past is never dead. It's not even past.' The past may seem to be dead when, day after day, we pick up our copy of the morning paper and read through 'the latest news', which is always different to the last 'latest news', but such news does not belong in a historical vacuum, and awareness of immediate current affairs needs to be balanced with historical awareness, with a sense of the past-as-not-even-past. Our third reason for choosing one particular news story from the past follows on directly from this, for it illustrates exactly that sense, showing the deep-rooted nature of recent events and developments, and the ways these are depicted in forms of discourse like news journalism. In this way, the story carries various contemporary resonances – resonances of action and resonances of representation. These will be obvious enough and we do not need to labour them, but they could, clearly enough, be taken up and elaborated far more thoroughly, in any more avowedly historical form of study.

Our own focus here derives more from cultural analysis, and the text we shall analyse is taken from the front page of the *Daily Mail* newspaper, for Thursday 8 October 1959. The main story for this day was concerned with the general election and an apparent Tory lead, but the foreign news story we are concerned with was given more or less equal prominence. It concerned an assassination attempt on the Iraqi premier, General Abdul Karim Kassem.

As three distinct *vilayets*, or provinces, Iraq had long been part of the Ottoman Empire, but following World War I, Britain was given a mandate by the League of Nations to administer Iraq until it established its own independent government. As colonial secretary in 1921, Winston Churchill was central to the mistaken decisions involved in the creation of modern Iraq. These included the installation of a monarchical system of rule under the Hashemite dynasty, and the amalgamation of the three Ottoman *vilayets* that constitute contemporary Iraq. To these decisions, Churchill brought to bear a compound of arrogance, incompetence and ignorance (see Catherwood 2004). In 1958, the regime set in place by Churchill was overthrown in a military coup in which various members of the royal family and their close associates were killed. Kassem (or Qassim) became president of the new republic. He withdrew Iraq from the pro-Western Baghdad Pact and severed relations with Britain and the United States. His administration mixed the suppression of civilian organisation and free speech with an attempt to improve the conditions of life of ordinary people in Iraq. While he opposed British military intervention in the Middle East, he also opposed Iraq's entry into the United Arab Republic, led by President Nasser, and it was this which led to the bungled assassination attempt in 1959, led by pan-Arabists, among whom was a Ba'athist street-gang fighter, one Saddam Hussein. Apparently he lost his nerve and shot at Kassem prematurely. In the subsequent exchange of gunfire, Saddam was hit in the leg and forced to flee the country. The event, and his flight to Cairo, became key components of the Saddam legend in Iraq.

The prominence given to the *Daily Mail* story about this attempt on General Kassem's life is realised in three ways, which can be summarised under the categories of position, composition and intertextual relations.[1] The text of the story is derived, at least in part, from the newspaper's reporter in Baghdad, but this does not explain why, of all the stories available for this edition, an editorial decision and directive clearly led to this particular story being given front-page placement. Such choice of placement implies an assumed purpose to the story, both in itself and in relation to the functions of other stories, with their different discursive features. This applies also to its composition, for its centrality and layout in terms of the overall composition of the front page also contribute to its prominence. Its centrality is attained by its position in the top-right quadrant of the front page, its banner headline, its accompanying photograph, and its attribution to an on-the-spot reporter. It may seem that the stories published alongside each other in a newspaper are randomly associated and bear no cross-narrative relation, but against this impression it is important to emphasise that news stories do not exist in isolation from each other, in either a newspaper or a broadcast news bulletin. Rather, they relate intertextually in a number of

---

1   The story also attained prominence in four other national British newspapers on 8 October 1959: the *Daily Telegraph*, the *Daily Express*, *The Guardian* and the *Financial Times*. It featured on p. 3 of the *Daily Mirror* and p. 3 of the *Daily Sketch*, and because of its different compositional format, on p. 12 of *The Times*.

Figure 8.1 Front page of the Daily Mail late edition, 8 October 1959.

Box 8.1 Kassem hit by bullets in a Bagdad street

From Daily Mail reporter: Bagdad, Wednesday

A would-be assassin fired several shots at Iraq's strong-man Premier, General Kassem, as he drove through Bagdad tonight. Kassem escaped with three superficial wounds and later appeared on the balcony of the hospital where he was treated.

In the street below stood a vast crowd, cheering with relief at his escape and shouting "we love Kassem". In a voice breaking with emotion Kassem told them: "I am with you and you are with me and God is with us against traitors, imperialism and the greedy ones.

"Imperialism is still working to liquidate this republic" he cried as armoured cars patrolled the streets and troops took up positions at strategic centres throughout the capital.

Then the crowds hurriedly dispersed as an all-night curfew was declared in Bagdad and other key cities.

'Conspiracy'

The news of the 'foul conspiracy' to kill Kassem was given in an official communiqué issued by the military governor, General Ahmed Saleh el Abdi and broadcast over Bagdad Radio. It said:

'While our leader, Abdel Karim Kassem, was passing Rashid Ali-street (*a major thoroughfare*) in his car at about 6.30 tonight, a criminal hand fired at his car, wounding him very slightly in his shoulder.

His condition is very good and calls for absolutely no anxiety. We request members of the public to rest assured that our leader is in very good condition, and we urge them to remain calm and cool.

We communicate to the public that as soon as our leader saw crowds of people thronging the hospital to inquire after his health, he gave them his greetings and salutations.'

Later Kassem's recorded voice was heard over Bagdad Radio. He sounded strained, as though in pain. His words at one stage poured out in a jumble of repetitions as he grew more and more emotional.

No traitors, he declared, would be allowed to interfere in the internal affairs of Iraq. "We shall win a victory over a band of evil-doers, just as we shall win a victory over imperialism and destroy any force with an appetite for our country."

'Liberated'

He went on: "Thanks to God we have liberated this brave and manly people and the rule has passed into the hands of the people. "

After the broadcast the announcer said: "You have heard the voice of our leader, son of the brave people, Abdel Karim Kassem speaking to the good Iraqi people."

Telegrams of congratulation and support were then read. One of these was from the commander of the loyal Fifth Army division.

Geoffrey Wakeford writes: The references in Kassem's speech and in Bagdad Radio statements to "a band of evil-doers" and "a foul conspiracy" suggest that the assassination attempt was part of a plot and not the work of a single fanatic.

The key cities placed under curfew probably included Mosul and Kirkuk, where loyalists in recent months have quelled uprising and nationalists and Communists are engaged in a ceaseless underground struggle for power.

Warnings

In London the news was received with consternation. But Western diplomats generally have all been warning that serious trouble is on the way.

Whether last night's attack on Kassem was meant to start a counter-revolution to rid the country of pro-Communist influence is not clear. But Kassem himself unleashed dangerous forces a fortnight ago when he ordered the execution of 14 army officers and four civilians.

Reports to the West show that Bagdad has been seething with unrest ever since. The flames of revolt have been fanned from Cairo where in recent demonstrations – apparently not discouraged by President Nasser – the Iraqi Premier was denounced as the "Butcher of Bagdad".

different ways. The intertextual relations of this story to other stories are manifest most immediately in its juxtaposition to the other front-page items, such as those concerning the death of the popular singing star, Mario Lanza, and the rescue of holidaymakers from Southend Pier after it had caught fire. Even if these relations were not intended, the juxtaposition of different stories can nevertheless create linkages of meaning and association between them. They are an important, and sometimes overlooked, feature of newspapers, and we discuss them in further detail later on.

In analysing the text of this story, we need to begin by trying to identify its central meaning and main narrative thread. Here it is useful to draw on two interrelated linguistic concepts: **thematic structure** and **discourse schemas**. A thematic structure is a preoccupying conception or proposition which runs throughout a media text, usually around an initiating topic. It strategically ties together a number of more specific conceptions or statements on the basis of particular social forms of knowledge and social forms of perception and belief. A thematic structure helps to make a media text cohere – it orients a text around a central theme or strand of related themes running through a story. Without thematic structures, media texts would be fragmentary and narratively dissolute. Their function is to provide a sense of the overall organisation, hierarchy and relations between different aspects or properties of the text, and between different units of the text, such as sentences and paragraphs. Thematic structures are linked linguistically with discourse schemas. Schemas group information and circumstantial detail into sequentially and hierarchically ordered categories and units of meaning. In news discourse, data are structured in a functional order of narrative disclosure, which is specific to its particular mode of storytelling. Again, we should stress that this is nothing new; it is true of this story in the *Daily Mail* in 1959, as it is of today's newspapers. A news schema entails a patterned movement from the headline and lead paragraphs, through secondary events attendant on the main news event, or statements by witnesses and commentators, which are ranked in an implicit order of priority, to the further elaboration of detail and possible extrapolation and evaluation, often coming from key players, accredited sources or officially recognised experts. This characteristically takes the familiar pyramid structure of news narrative, or what van Dijk calls the instalment character of topic realisation or elaboration, whereby information is hierarchically sequenced, with each subsequent layer adding further details of specification to those preceding (1988a: 35). In this form of narrative, we are told the denouement right at the start of the report, with succeeding parts of the report providing amplification and support for this initiating statement, in what is a structural opposite of the narrative ordering of crime fiction, where the question of culpability is a matter of final revelation (see Figure 8.2).

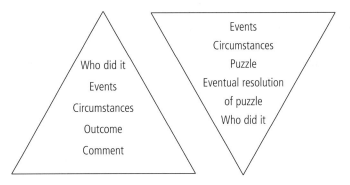

Figure 8.2 Narrative structures of news and crime fiction

Of course, the reverse analogy with crime fiction does not work literally, as in this case, where, although for the Iraqi president at the time a definite crime had been committed in an attempt on his life, it was not known to the reporter or the Iraqi authorities in October 1959 'who did it', that is, who had fired the shots or who was behind the assassination conspiracy. The analogy here is designed to show both the similarity in formative and constitutive features of the narratives in crime fiction and news stories, and their dissimilarity, because for each the other is turned upside down.

News schemas are conventionally influenced by the salience of particular news values in a particular type of story, as well as by journalists' rhetorical priorities of facticity and objectivity, rather than being determined by concern for chronological order. But even at a micro-level of description, a schema may also be related to particular knowledge and beliefs, to particular ideas about the world and how different societies are organised and governed. 'Thus, a simple *because* may betray a large set of assumptions about the social or political world the news describes' (van Dijk 1988a: 43–8, original emphasis; see also ibid.: 52–9, 117; van Dijk 1986: 155–85). Stereotypes are particular, highly crystallised versions of schemas, and the cues these provide are clearly quite prescriptive for potential readings (see Pickering 2001). It is in this sense that the notion of textual cueing – which was noted in sociolinguistics and dialectology before being taken up within critical linguistics and discourse analysis (see, for example, Hudson 1980: 22–3) – is connected with the concepts of thematic structures and discourse schemas. Generally, a schema operates tacitly as a frame for making sense of things (see chapter 7 on frame analysis), but whatever its mode of operation, it is inter-subjective as a model for seeing and thinking in certain discourse- and culture-specific ways. In many respects, the concept of a schema is close to the earlier media studies concept of inferential framework or interpretive structure, though the major difference is that this concept was applied mainly in relation to news encoding, whereas schemas have a rather broader reference and are held to be characteristic of, say, both encoder and decoder texts in media culture (see chapter 7).

We can readily apply these linguistic concepts to our sample story. Its schema is realised through its discursive sequencing and ordering of information and detail in a movement from its nucleus to its various satellite elements. The nucleus of the main headline, photo caption and lead paragraph, all printed in bold type or italics, provides the gist of the story, as well as the gist of the newspaper's suggested 'message to be taken' from it. The nucleus summarises or (either directly or indirectly) signals the underlying thematic structure of the text, and in fulfilling this function it enables readers to apprehend at the outset the basic thread that will run throughout the news article, without having to trace it for themselves through all the sentences and paragraphs of the text, as they would with a fictional crime narrative. The nucleus is thus a conventional category unit of news discourse, which acts strategically as the pre-eminent textual cue for interpretation, for the construction of the decoder text. It offers this cue through its provision of 'the intended highest macroproposition' of the news report (van Dijk 1986: 161). Together, the main headline, photo caption and lead paragraph combine as a unit to furnish readers with what are regarded as the key details of who, what, when, where and why. The introductory unit does not necessarily provide an answer to all these questions. Indeed, an attempt to do this would generally lead to semantic overloading, and usually the news angle is defined by the selection of two or three questions, with the rest of the story perhaps going on to answer the others. In the case of our sample story, we can see that certain key questions are immediately answered in the following way: who = 'Iraq's strong-man Premier, General Kassem'; what = 'assassination attempt'; when = 'tonight', or the evening before this edition of the paper appeared on the news-stands; 'where' = 'a Baghdad street'. The question of 'why' could be only tentatively addressed at the time the story was put together, but speculative reasons were nevertheless put forward as the report unfolded.

The various satellite elements of the text consist of subsequent backup in the form of factual data and quotations from 'interested parties' or those with relevant expertise. These elaborate the story in various ways, weaving the narrative around different sources and different 'voices'. Quotations from these sources are used strategically to provide supporting evidence by the paper in terms of the narrative schema. This is done in three ways:

1. *Through their sequencing.* First of all, in words characteristic of the populist rhetoric for which he was famous, Kassem is quoted as responding to the crowds who were 'cheering with relief at his escape': 'I am with you and you are with me and God is with us.' He

then refers vaguely to their enemies and presumably those behind the assassination attempt: 'traitors, imperialism, and the greedy ones.' While these can be identified historically – by the broad reference to imperialism, for instance, Kassem presumably meant, at least primarily, Britain and the United States – the vagueness underwrites the lack of knowledge at the time of who was responsible for the 'foul conspiracy'. Kassem's hospital balcony address is followed by an official communiqué from the military governor, designed to calm the populace and restore order, by reference to Kassem's recorded voice being heard over Baghdad Radio (with, again, only vague references to the culprits being imperialists and 'a band of evil-doers'), and a short, two-sentence paragraph mentioning telegrams of 'congratulation and support'.

2. *Through their balancing against each other.* The three main sources cited initially are all Iraqi military. This is true even of the brief mention of telegrams of support – only one is attributed and this comes from the commander of the loyal Fifth Army division. These three main sources are then balanced by three sources from outside Iraq. The first cited is Geoffrey Wakeford, the newspaper's diplomatic correspondent at the time, whose 'expert view' points to a careful plot rather than 'the work of a single fanatic'; second are unattributed diplomatic sources, who refer to 'dangerous forces' unleashed by Kassem a fortnight before, when he ordered the execution of 14 army officers and 4 civilians; and the third is even less clearly identified, merely described as 'reports to the West'. Paradoxically, although these are the vaguest sources mentioned in the report, they come closest to fingering the most likely origin of the 'foul conspiracy' in its connections with the United Arab Republic, a coded reference to which is made through reference to Cairo and Nasser, and pan-Arabist campaigners in Iraq.

3. *Through their framing.* This balancing of sources may seem equal – roughly three from within Iraq and three from without – and more than fair to Kassem in that his own and other military 'voices' are cited first. This impression is certainly created by the discourse schema, at least initially, but because this is closely linked to the thematic structure of the story, the impression is undercut by the main theme, which begins to emerge as the story unfolds, so that while suggesting fairness and neutrality to begin with, the discourse schema actually works in quite another way, which is to erode the legitimacy of Kassem's position and that of his military spokespeople, and begin to lay blame for the conspiracy at Kassem's own feet. The concluding section of the report claims that it has been brought about by Kassem's actions, by his dictatorial behaviour in ordering the executions and by his eschewal of any affiliation with the United Arab Republic. In terms of the discourse schema, then, the sources quoted are clearly distinguished in terms of origin, but also set up in such a way that those from outside Iraq progressively discredit those from within Iraq, or at least move firmly in this direction. The sequencing and balancing are integral to the framing of the sources. In this way, the schema used to organise the narrative supports and provides endorsement of the thematic structure of the report.

This involves a reversal of priority being given to the news sources as we move from the first sections of the report to the concluding section. It is worth looking a little more closely at the report to see how this is achieved, and how the thematic structure prevails and retains coherence throughout the story, for it is not only a matter of what is done with the main sources. The story as a whole is built around a progressive reversal of credibility given to these sources, and we can see how this occurs, even through the use of certain telltale linguistic signs. These may seem insignificant, but, as becomes apparent through our analysis of the news text, they are quite the opposite.

Altogether the report is divided into four sections, the first of which contains the nucleus of the story. The following three sections are introduced by a subhead in bold font, but it is only the last of these, in which sources from outside Iraq are cited, that is not in inverted commas. These small but commonly used devices are sometimes referred to as scare quotes, and their use is intended to show that those involved in the writing are not necessarily in agreement with the word or words the commas contain. Scare quotes cast doubt on the veracity of what is quoted. In the case of this story, the claim that a foul conspiracy has been perpetrated, and that Kassem and his fellow army officers have liberated the country, is made equivocal at best, and downright false at worst, by the use of inverted commas around the key words cited: 'conspiracy' and 'liberated'. The remaining lexical item used in the subheads is not in inverted commas, and this ensures, by contrast, that the warnings about 'serious trouble', 'dangerous forces' and 'seething unrest' thereby gain legitimacy. These 'warnings' are given credibility; their truth value is far higher than that claimed for political conspiracy and national liberation. In this way, the structured representation of the cases for and against a conspiracy, by 'traitors' and other reactionary forces implacably opposed to 'liberation', is embellished by the use or non-use of simple lexical markers. The presence or absence of these markers helps the work of rebuttal at key junctures in the news narrative and operates like the apparently simple word 'because' in van Dijk's observation. The presence or absence of scare quotes betrays certain underlying assumptions 'about the social and political world the news describes'. The structure and order of the news schema, in its movement from summary to main action and reaction, then provides an appropriate entry to centre stage for the reiteration of the 'warnings' that Iraq is – at least at that time – in a volatile and highly unstable state, and that the attribution of culpability for this belongs with a tyrannical leader.

News coverage in a political democracy with a press that is separate from the state has to distinguish itself as a form of discourse apart from any form of editorial commentary. It has to do this in order to offset potential criticism of biased reporting. This is achieved in time-honoured fashion by various strategically ritualised devices of news 'objectivity' (Tuchman 1972). These include the appearance of offering an even-handed presentation of both sides of the story – in this case, government officials in Iraq and political or diplomatic commentators outside Iraq. The narrative ordering and framing of selective quotation is part of the characteristic rhetoric of news journalism in that it deflects attention away from the persuasive function of the storytelling by creating the appearance of a factual account. This sample news report also attempts to enhance its truth-appearance through the provision of supportive circumstantial evidence, though this is unevenly weighted in such a way that the reader is textually cued to ask questions about which side of the story carries greatest weight. Cueing the reader in this way provides command and authority for the thematic structure of the story, which we now need to look at in closer focus.

As we have said already, the thematic structure is initiated by the lead paragraph of a news story and its attendant apparatus of headline, possible illustration and possible secondary headline. Iraq's premier at this time is identified as a 'strong-man' leader, a term which acts as a euphemism for tyrant or dictator. The accompanying photograph provides a sideways facial profile of this leader. He is smiling, but he has just been shot. The wounds may be superficial, but they symbolise 'dangerous forces', 'seething unrest', and the like. The caption tells the reader that this leader spoke from a balcony. It transpires that this is a balcony in the hospital where he is recovering from his wounds, but the implication is nevertheless clear enough from other characterising features: what kind of leader normally speaks from balconies? The Pope may do, but he is not a political leader. Political leaders who speak from balconies are political demagogues, fanatics, dictators. That is the conventional symbolic association, and in the immediate post-war period, images of Hitler and Stalin in similar locational positions, spouting passionate oratory from balconies high above the listening crowds, would still have been fresh in many readers' minds. Such association is further supported by the photograph and caption. This is an army general, and generals do not rule in political democracies such as Britain, only in less 'civilised' countries like Iraq. The man shown in army uniform is not a 'normal' political leader. He is the head of a military junta. And the report of his speaking talks of 'a voice breaking with emotion', and later as sounding strained, 'as though in pain'. 'His words at one stage', according to the report, 'poured out in a jumble of repetitions as he grew more and more emotional'. This is hardly descriptive of a rational man, the kind of rational man, for example, that you would expect in a position of high command in the British Army. These details simply reinforce the stereotypical impression of an irrational dictator or tyrant, driven by his emotions and unable to think or speak in an ordered, logical, reasonable fashion.

The verbal and visual cues to meanings directed by the thematic structure of this report are internal to it, but we spoke earlier of any news story being part of a more general assemblage, and for the need for you to be alert to possible relations being set up across and between otherwise separate stories. The front page of a newspaper is always carefully composed. It is never stitched together randomly like a patchwork quilt. In this case, the report about General Kassem is buttressed by two stories involving death and possible death. The first concerns the tenor singer Mario Lanza, who 'dies singing', softly crooning one of his hits, 'Come Prima'. The second concerns rescue from possible death by people trapped on a blazing pier in Southend, a popular seaside town in the county of Essex. Both stories contrast with the leading story about General Kassem. Lanza died singing, and, by implication, happily or at peace with himself, but if Kassem had died following the assassination attempt, this would hardly have been with a song on his lips. The fire on Southend Pier is what is conventionally called a 'natural disaster'. Again, there is a strong contrast with the Kassem story, for an attempted assassination is hardly a natural event, hardly an accident for which no one in particular is to blame. The event involving Kassem is instead an 'unnatural disaster' and the story about it is replete with questions of blame.

There is a further intertextual relation that is set up by the overall composition of the front page of this edition of the *Daily Mail*. The other lead story concerns the general election then in full spate and the 'record poll expected by some experts'. It forecasts 'a substantial Conservative victory'. Together, the two lead stories both concern political governance and rule, and again, an intensely sharp contrast is struck by their juxtaposition.

The main lead story concerns the political process of popular election in a democratic system, while the second concerns the denial of this process in a country run by military officers and subject to martial law, which is given added colour by reference to the all-night curfew imposed in Baghdad and other key cities in Iraq. The intertextual contrast supports the orientalist thematic structure of the Kassem story. Orientalism is a system of discourse and representation in which the Middle East and countries such as Iraq are characterised as the binary opposite of 'the West'. Among other things, this involves portraying the Middle East as reactionary, backward and barbarian, tendencies conducive to despotism and tyrannical rule. People of the Orient are driven by their passions and emotions; they are irrational and not to be trusted. The Orient is radically unlike the West and represents the converse of everything the West stands for, such as order, rationality, progress, civilisation.[2] In ways like these, the Orient is set up as the inferior Other of the West, including countries such as Britain, where the people decide who should form their government. As the editorial comment puts it on the front page of the *Daily Mail* for 8 October 1959, they vote freely for 'the kind of land this is to be'. This is contrary to a political system of authoritarian rule. Collectively, the British belong to 'the main stream of 20th century advance', unlike countries like Iraq, which is essentially stuck in the past and largely unchanging. It remains always potentially caught up in 'seething unrest' and subject to the unleashing of 'dangerous forces'. There is thus a direct binary opposition of East and West in the intertextual relation between the two lead stories on the *Mail*'s front page, one of which operates in terms of an orientalist system of representation. It is the sense of the Middle East as ontologically distinct from Britain and 'the West' that constitutes the 'macroproposition' of the two lead stories.

We are not suggesting that this overarching proposition was being made overtly or was likely to have been formally drawn out of any reader's consumption of the story about Kassem's sudden brush with death. News narrative is neither produced nor consumed in that way. It is regularised and routine. As a communicative event, the discourse practice of this particular story strategically uses various 'voices' derived from previous communicative events, and the discourse schema of the story arranges and orders these 'voices' in such a way as to legitimate those which provide a perspective on the situation from outside the country. That perspective routinely supports a regularised orientalist point of view. The process of mediation in the story involves a transformation of news material into a journalistic idiom deemed appropriate to the newspaper's readership, which in this case was predominantly lower middle class. It is through this idiom that news discourse purports to speak on behalf of its readership *in the name of common sense* (Fairclough 1988: 132–3). This connects us back to the question of populist values. Orientalism has always been identified as an instrument of Western imperialism, with the imperialist forces against which Kassem spoke in his hospital balcony address to the crowd in Baghdad. For him, in his populist identification with the Iraqi nation, what he said would have seemed another form of common sense. It was in the name of that common sense that he and fellow army officers

---

2   The most celebrated example of Orientalist critique remains Edward Said's (1985) landmark text on this form of representation and discourse, but the book has been subject to various criticisms. We do not have the scope to review these here, but it is important that you note what some regard as the weak or questionable aspects of his general argument (see, for example, Pickering 2001: ch. 6; Moore-Gilbert 1997: ch. 2; Young 1995: ch. 7; Sardar 1999: 65–76).

staged a *coup d'état* and committed the act of regicide. So it is only within the terms of any particular hegemonic form of cultural discourse that it is possible to speak of common sense. There is literally no such thing as common sense, because different social groups and categories in society do not share their sense of the social and political world, of existing social arrangements and priorities, or of international alliances and orders. Between different societies, even less sense is held in common, though recognising such cultural difference is not the same as claiming an inevitable 'clash of civilisations'.[3] Common sense is an ideological construction, produced and reproduced around certain ideas, beliefs and values, which are held to have the greatest populist appeal. Common sense runs against the interests of both social minorities and those constructed as a nation's inferior Other. It acts in support of existing social, national and international relations. Nothing is more ideological than common sense, precisely because it makes invisible its assumptions and values: common sense is unquestioned sense. It is for this reason that, in this particular case, it spoke in orientalist terms. The *Mail*'s news story articulated a form of orientalist common sense. The populism that is to the fore here is that of the newspaper, not that of the leader of Iraq. His discourse is anti-imperialist rhetoric. The *Mail*'s is orientalist populism. Both were forms of common sense, and yet, in being diametrically opposed, they show that common sense is impossible.

There is an important postscript to our account. Saddam Hussein had been sentenced to death *in absentia* for his role in the 1959 assassination attempt, but in 1963, another attempt on General Kassem's life was successful. This cleared the path for Saddam's return from exile. Those responsible for Kassem's murder were army officers and members of the Ba'ath Party. This change of rule and the subsequent ascendancy of the Ba'ath Party in Iraq eventually paved the way for Saddam Hussein's assumption of the position of president. The rest, as they say, is history.

Guide to our method of operation

We have given you a concrete example of the linguistic analysis of a news story. It is important to point out that this is only one approach to the linguistic analysis of media texts. Our intention has been simply to show for one particular case how such an analytical mode can be realised. Even for news reports – even, indeed, for the one report we have dissected – there are other ways in which linguistic and discourse analysis can be done, and when you move to the analysis of other media genres you will need to draw on other linguistic concepts and tools. With this caveat, it may be useful to summarise how we have actually gone about carrying out this analysis of a front-page story.

Stage 1

The first phase of our analysis involved an examination of the *position, composition* and immediate *intertextual relations* of the example of print journalism on which we focused. This phase can be described as the study of *the formal staging of a news text*. It is centrally concerned with the ways in which a text is assigned an identity and role within a broader

---

3   The reference here is to Samuel Huntington's (1998) highly contentious thesis of incompatibility between fixed and unchanging civilisational blocs, and the need to defend the West's 'superior' lineage in the face of 'inferior' Oriental cultures.

structure, within an overall assemblage and ordering of various types of text and story as these are manifest across the daily output of a written medium of public communication. While any one news report has its own constitutive features, it is not separate and independent from other texts and discourses, but is interrelated with that which surrounds it and that which assigns it a contributory function in a more general ensemble. Although we stress that you should examine such interrelations at this stage, having done so in this case, we decided to return to them later in the analysis, and give them greater elaboration once other things had come to light analytically.

Position

Before you begin a close study of the content and structure of a news story, look at where it is located in relation to other stories. Where is it placed within the newspaper as a whole, and where is it placed on the page on which it begins and ends? If it is not contained on one discrete page of the newspaper, where does it continue, how is it positioned on its page of continuation, and what, if any, are the implications of the point at which the text breaks? In the case of the story about the attempted killing of General Kassem, the story culminates at the bottom of the front page; but in the case of the story of Mario Lanza's death, it continues on page three, as is made clear by the short lead into it on the front page, the purpose of which is to flag up a longer version of the story on the inside pages of the newspaper, and so keep the reader reading. Further questions that should be asked at this stage are: What does the news story's initial and overall positioning tell you about the significance it has been accorded? What does such positioning suggest to you about the relative values of newsworthiness it has been felt to have as good journalistic copy? Can you infer from this any traces of the process of news production? And on what grounds can this inference be established?

Composition

Look next at its composition, its typographical arrangement and style. How is it laid out on the page? For a story which continues on a subsequent stage, look particularly at its initial compositional set-up. What, in descriptive terms, are the major defining features of its nucleus – that category unit of the news text which combines together the main headline, a possible secondary headline and the initial summary paragraph? How is this nucleus arranged and stylistically defined? How does any photo caption anchor its meaning in the main narrative thread running through the story, or what we have called the thematic structure? And how do these factors add to or complement what you have discerned from its position as a text within the newspaper and from its juxtaposition to any immediately surrounding texts?

Intertextual relations

Thinking about this last question will lead you to consider its **intertextuality**, the relations it has to other news stories and other discourse types within the newspaper (e.g. advertisements or editorial commentaries). Can you establish any links of topic or theme across the items on the same page, or to other items in the paper? What are the main features of these links? Once you have established one or more links, try to assess how they operate. What is it that allows them to function intertextually? Examining intertextual relations in this way may then involve you in looking at the ways news texts draw on and discursively adapt other texts which have been generated outside of any immediate journalistic activity, such as a government White Paper or a press release summarising the major findings of a social science research project. What is involved in the process of mediating these secondary sources? How do these other texts contribute to the constitution of the news text? How are these other texts represented, how are they distinguished from the news text itself and what transformations can be said to have occurred in their journalistic translation? Is it possible to infer any attitudes or values from these intertextual relations, and, if so, how are these stylistically rendered, for example in syntactical composition, idiom and tone? These are the sorts of questions you should begin to ask at this stage of the analysis, though you may want to return to them once you have undertaken the final stage, as this may lead you to additional questions or to a different angle on the questions you have already raised. This is exactly what happened when we started our analysis of the 1959 *Daily Mail* report. We could see straightaway that several of the front page stories were thematically linked by the topics of political rule and death or escape from death, but we thought that the full ideological import of these thematic relations as they were established across the stories would not become apparent until we had analysed the thematic structure and discourse schema at work in the narrative of this particular report. That was why we decided to consider again the question of the story's intertextual relations.

Stages 2 and 3

The second stage of analysis is the study of your sample news text's *thematic structure*. This involves you in a movement through the pyramidal structure of the news text and between its various constitutive stages of narrative instalment. In doing this, you should try to identify the key underlying conception or proposition which, although formally undefined, nevertheless informs the text as a whole and imparts to the text its relative coherence by interlinking its component parts. What makes the text hang together as a narrative with a beginning, middle and end, and with particular passages operating within these stages of the narrative as well as contributing to the sense of a sequenced development of the story as a whole? What assigns each part of the news text – the events described, the quotations used, the outcome forecast, and so on – its position within the hierarchically ordered progression of the narrative?

In attempting to arrive at answers to these sorts of questions, it is difficult, in practice, to dissociate your task from the third stage of the analysis, which is the examination of the working of the *discourse schema* running through the text and acting as its general organising mechanism. Textual schemas operate in a close inter-functional relationship with thematic structures, but can be distinguished most of all in terms of process and product. The former isolates for analysis the narrative conventions for combining, ordering and hierarchically assigning the different category units of the text into a structured whole, while the latter distinguishes the central interpretive thread that makes all the rest relevant and 'fixes' their value as evidence or comment.

In any concrete analysis, then, your discovery of the thematic structure will go hand in hand with your examination of the discourse schema. We have described them as separate stages of analysis only in order to emphasise the different properties of the news text with which they are concerned. With this in mind, your study of the textual schema of any particular news article should be concerned to identify the following three strategies of news discourse.

The sequencing structure

Here you will look at the overall arrangement and narrative contouring of the material out of which the news text is constructed. The material derived from a journalist's news sources is assembled in an implicit order of accreditation and importance. That which is highly accredited may come early or later in the sequencing structure, but what you need to attend to is how the order of accreditation in your sample news text is achieved. In considering this question, you should first identify the stance taken and the values advanced by each source, and then plot out the relative position each is given in the overall sequence as this is arranged in the explanatory order, from the 'who did it' initiating summary, downwards through the representation of the main events, circumstances, possible consequences and comments. Second, you should try to establish how this evaluative ranking of prioritised and relegated sources relates to the underlying thematic structure of the news report you are dealing with.

Source quantity and quality

Journalists often report events and developments without being direct witnesses; that is, without constituting the source of news themselves. Generally, their material is derived from other sources, other discourses, such as eyewitness reports, official statements, interviews, documents, government and diplomatic offices, press releases, press conferences, press agencies and other news media. The construction of news, therefore, is 'most of all a reconstruction of available discourses' (van Dijk 1983: 28). A news story will often appear to treat different sources and discourses in an even-handed way, but you will need to investigate the extent to which this is actually the case. It is quite likely that you will find a greater number of sources cited in favour of a particular outlook or line of interpretation and evaluation than against, or in support of a particular thematic structure as this emerges through the news narrative. We were also able to notice a *qualitative difference* in the sources cited by the *Daily Mail* journalists responsible for our sample story: emotive references to 'evil doers' and 'greedy ones' hardly compares with the measured, neutralist, discursive tones with which the report concludes. Try to do this for your own sample text. How do the attributed sources and discourses vary in terms of degree of certitude, qualification, authority and emphasis of phrasing and tone, and how are these qualities evident in register, vocabulary and figures of speech?

Framing procedures

The use of certain news sources to frame and contain other sources is a common device in the structuring of news narrative (see chapter 7 on frame analysis). Analytically, where you have been able to identify the division of 'voices' cited in your sample text into, say, oriental and occidental camps, you should now proceed to look at the ways they are deployed in relation to each other. How, for example, are certain sources used to undermine, discredit or disclaim what is advanced by others whose identified position is at variance with those which are given priority? And how does this deployment of sources support their evaluative scaling in relation to the dominant discourse of the text that you have discerned? Framing devices operate not only in terms of the overall discourse schema of news narrative but also through the ways in which certain sources are presented by their immediately surrounding textual features. For example, there is a considerable difference between the verbs 'said', 'claimed' and 'made out' when these are used to set up a particular reported comment, for each of these frames what is then reported in terms of its relative truthfulness, unreliability, duplicity, and so on (Fairclough 1995a: 83).

Stage 4

In analysing the *Daily Mail* lead story, our methodological procedure then led us to consider how lexical choice and lexical markers supported the thematic structure of the story, as for example by negatively constructing the impression of General Kassem as an irrational dictator, and positively underwriting the expertise or truth-value of certain sources and discourses at the expense of others. It is also worth emphasising here how the use of the words 'hit by bullets in a Bagdad [sic] street' in the headline of the story reinforces the thematic structure right from the start, for what kind of political leader is shot at by gunmen in the street? The question is rhetorical of course, for the use of these words in the headline falls smartly into step with the implied notion of Kassem and Iraq that will be built up in the story as a whole. The common-sense, taken-for-granted orientalist assumptions underlying the story make even the General's smile in the photograph seem suspect. The smile of a military ruler is a smile that could readily be treacherous, and the quality of treacherousness is itself one that is readily associated with orientalism, or at least with what one of us has previously discussed in terms of a distinction between benign and brutal forms of orientalist imagery and discourse (Pickering 2001: ch. 6). We should perhaps point out that the ideological implications of lexical choice have been examined not only in the linguistic work of Fowler and others but also in more mainstream sociology. There are, for instance, some revealing examples in the Glasgow University Media Group's study of the typical lexicalisation involved in news coverage of worker–management disputes in the 1970s (see, for example, Glasgow University Media Group 1980). Lexical choice is thus an important feature of news discourse in that it can suggest, at a relatively simple level of analysis, certain ideological beliefs and values underpinning particular stories, and in more immediate terms can provide further evidence of the ways in which various words in a news text support the overarching semantic structure of its narrative. The same is true of lexical markers. The credibility of a source can be called into question by the tiniest of punctuation marks, as in the case of the inverted commas used in scare quotes. What is small in size may sometimes be huge in terms of its significance.

Stage 5

As we stated at the outset of our discussion of critical linguistics, we do not wish to prescribe any rigid set of procedures or any fixed catalogue of analytical tools for use in your own approach to the study of the linguistic structure of media representations and discourses. Our intention in this section has been to provide you with an outline of the kinds of methodological steps which we find useful in conducting this particular mode of textual analysis. You should adapt it according to your own purposes and your own data, and apply other linguistic concepts where these seem appropriate and useful. This advice is consistent with our general approach to research methodology in media studies. However, we would also suggest that in relation to your own sample news texts you should return, finally, to review the ways in which the thematic macro-structures of the texts are mobilised in different ways at each instalment stage of the discourse schemas, beginning with the all-important initial formulation of the thematic core in the headlines and leads. In the case of our own *Daily Mail* front-page story, we did this in connection with Tuchman's work on objectivity as strategic ritual; through reference to the concept of orientalism and the body of theoretical work associated with it; and then, following Fairclough, by taking up and adapting Gramsci's conceptualisation of common sense, and in turn relating how this operates to how orientalism operates in popular daily journalism. This also enabled us to see more clearly how the text's thematic structure was given further point and purpose by the intertextual thematics of the front page more generally. The intertextual relations of the report and other news stories next to it made clear the broader ideological and discursive matrix of which it was a part. In your own work you may find other concepts – from political science, cultural anthropology or the sociology of media communications – more directly relevant to your analysis. This will depend on the news topic and its treatment, or the news genre and its style.

The limitations of textual analysis

It is always good research practice to take a critical view of the analytical methodology you have applied to your objects of study. With this in mind, we include some consideration of the weaknesses or drawbacks of the various research methods outlined in each of the chapters of this book, though in what is primarily a guide to the practice of undertaking media research, rather than a critique of research methodologies, we do not develop such considerations in a systematic or comprehensive manner. Nevertheless, we do want to emphasise the importance of methodological self-critique, because too often in media research a particular mode of analysis is set up and deployed in such a way as to exclude the introduction of other methods. Either implicitly or explicitly, the method used is the method advanced as an approach superior to all others. It is in light of this point that we now want to offer some critical observations on the limitations of textual/discourse analysis.

The expansion of applied linguistics into forms of discourse analysis marks the point where media studies began to develop an interest in linguistic concepts and approaches. This occurred during the 1980s, and it heralded new means of analysing media texts and representations. The move to discourse analysis enabled linguistics to tackle the structures of whole texts, rather than just the sentences, words and parts of words taken in isolation, which, to a great extent, it had concentrated on previously. This has proved fruitful, as we hope to have shown. However, how the text as a whole relates to its micro-components, and vice versa, is not as straightforward as it may appear at first. In the kind of critical linguistics with which we have been dealing, it is clear that there is a congruity of approach to the analysis of sentences and the whole ensemble of sentences and paragraphs which constitute a complete text – a parallelism in the study of component parts of a text, such as clauses and sentences, and the linguistic analysis of the text as a whole. This parallelism involves a way of reading the 'global' macro-structural features of the text which is analogous to the linguistic analysis of its micro-features of choice of vocabulary or localised syntactic composition. The analytical categories are differently labelled – episode, instalment, theme, and so on – but both macro- and micro-structural components of the text are taken as contributing to the structuring of the text in ways which are functionally complementary. If this means simply that a text as a whole has a structure which can be analysed in a similar manner to that of a sentence or clause, that is all well and good, but it is here that the problems begin. How you move from the single sentence, never mind the single lexical item or marker, to the text as a whole is not actually that straightforward. In some ways it is methodologically opaque.

Shifting back and forth between the syntactical analysis of particular sentences and analysis of the structure of the text as a whole, as we have seen, can be facilitated by the identification of a text's thematic core and its means of organising itself as discourse. But there is in itself no formal methodological procedure for doing this, despite the heuristically useful deployment of concepts relating to the 'grammar of the text', through which, in turn, we can examine the localised linguistic features which contribute to it. Clearly, applied linguistics is more open in its elaboration of concepts and methods than old-fashioned ex-literary critical approaches; it enables a more systematic approach to the close reading of written texts, and it does so without aesthetically privileging any particular kind of writing, such as that involved in the poetic use of language. Yet there are aspects of what it involves which seem to rely more on the analytical ingenuity of the individual researcher than on any explicit and non-random method. This should not be taken as a derogation of the value of an imaginative dimension in media and cultural studies. If its importance in cultural analysis is sometimes underestimated or misunderstood, this is all the more reason for emphasising how an imaginative engagement can often be what vitally imparts quality to the analysis. It is, for instance, what makes Barthes's essay on the spectacle of wrestling such a bravura piece of writing (Barthes 1973: 15–25); or, to take an example from outside Europe, what gives general impetus to Geertz's celebrated analysis of the Balinese cockfight (Geertz 1993: ch. 15). However, in media and cultural studies your imaginative engagement with a text needs to be combined with the explication and application of certain methodological principles. The development of such principles is readily apparent in linguistics, though to claim that linguistic criticism provides an 'objective description of texts' is dubious (Fowler 1986: 4), for, as our treatment of the *Daily Mail* example should have demonstrated, there are times when you need to make imaginative leaps in your analysis of textual signification and representation. The note of caution we are making here is simply this: look methodologically before you leap imaginatively. For if the textual analysis of media discourses is not anchored in any explicitly acknowledged and elaborated methods, it is always in danger of being blown hither and thither by the winds of conjecture and surmise.

Now, if this is one problem associated with forms of textual analysis generally, a more serious one for linguistically oriented forms of analysis is connected with the interpretive weight which is often put on the localised features of written texts. For this reason, it is doubtful how far the predominantly syntactical form of analysis in the critical linguistics of Fowler et al. (1979) can adequately explain the social relations of power which language incorporates and generates. This is a central point in John Thompson's criticism of their work. Thompson questions the extent to which meanings can be 'read off' from the grammar and vocabulary of language use, as Fowler et al. claim they are able to do (e.g. Fowler and Kress 1979: 197). In his book *Linguistic Criticism*, Fowler states that the 'linguistic activities which are visible in communication between individuals reproduce processes occurring at levels of broader social organisation' (1986: 39). This statement can be taken as axiomatic for critical linguistics, and while we would strongly endorse it, it is by no means always clear how the complex lines of connection between social reproduction and language use in everyday culture are to be explained, never mind demonstrated. It is because of this that Thompson points to the contrast between the conceptual sophistication of linguistic analysis and the conceptual vagueness of the social analysis often advanced by those who wield it, particularly in relation to questions concerning ideology and its 'effects' (Thompson 1990: 124–6). At its weakest, this is reliant on a sense of transparency between the structures of media texts and the social meanings made of them, and tends to reduce ideology to syntactical structures. The question of interpretive polysemy is not seriously engaged with, for there is no necessarily straightforward relay between linguistic mediations of ideology and an uncritical acquiescence in them by the readers or viewers of media texts. Furthermore, it is difficult, in practice, to sustain the presumption that every linguistic form has a specific ideological consequence which can be isolated and pinned down.

For example, in the previous chapter we cited an example offered by Fowler and Kress of an *Observer* headline: 'US coalminers are expected to return to work tomorrow.' The claim made about the syntactical ordering of this sentence was that in its passivisation, the deletion of the agent (or agents) involved in the act of expectation surreptitiously endorsed the expectation, deflecting attention away from the reasons why the workers themselves had taken strike action. The promotion of the miners to the front of the sentence made them the focus of attention, rather than those who expected – and presumably had a vested interest in expecting – their return to work. This is to identify the way in which a preferred reading is channelled by the syntactical composition, and is akin in its mode of operation to some of the textual cues we identified in our analysis of the *Daily Mail* story. But how do we know that this reading of the *Observer* headline was the one intended? And even if that question is dismissed as irrelevant for the ideological 'effect', how do we know that the particular structure of that sentence had such an effect, either in itself or in its relation to the article it headlined? In short, the link made between passivisation and ideological mystification is surmised rather than demonstrated. To push this a little further, in our analysis of the front page of the *Daily Mail* we identified certain intertextual linkages, which we said occurred around the themes of death or escape from death, and political rule and form of governance. We could have gone on from this to suggest that such linkages across texts on the same key page of the newspaper were neither accidental nor coincidental, but that they were editorially intended, and that they were so because they supported the political position of the newspaper. The question is: how would we know, and how could this be proved? It seemed to us that our analysis showed that the Kassem report operated according to an engrained orientalist viewpoint and perspective, and our warrant for this claim was provided by certain theoretical ideas which appeared to have a high explanatory value in relation to the news text we were analysing. While we would stand by this, a worry remains. Can we really ask one front page of a newspaper to bear all that interpretive tonnage and remain valid as a form of explanation?

This worry is perhaps compounded by the fact that the story was published a good while in the past, and it would be even more difficult to reconstruct what was involved in its production and consumption than it would be for a contemporary news story. That may well be the case, but it is not as if there is some definite or absolute meaning to this story. Analysing it is not much different from analysing other forms of historical documentation, in that, while attending to the constitutive features of the discourse of any historical documentation, we face an inevitable temporal distance between ourselves and our chosen text. As well as raising problems of historical interpretation more generally, this distance has both advantages and disadvantages, which are shared with historical inquiry and analysis more generally. Also shared with such inquiry and analysis are the same principles and standards of weighing the available evidence, and assessing its historical meaning and significance, but again, there is no fixed or absolute version of these, which is one reason that historical understanding changes. The pitfalls are similar, for if we over-egg the cake with speculation or unsubstantiated interpretation, we become less than convincing and leave ourselves open to criticism. The watchwords, then, should be caution, scepticism and modesty in our own validity claims. Again, though, we can approach this from the other direction and say that it is all very well following certain methods – and outlining how to do this is germane to the whole purpose of this book – but all methods have their limits. These can be compensated for by the mixed-method approach we advocate, but we have also acknowledged the indispensability of interpretation and its appropriate uses of the imagination. In the end, what counts is being as cogent in your analysis as you can possibly be.

It remains the case that textual analysis, however sophisticated in discerning patterns of meaning and linking a given text to the wider use of language and discourse in the social order, suffers from the same limitations as any other form of content analysis when applied in isolation. It cannot make safe assertions about the intentions of a text's producer, nor can it validly infer the impact of the text on readers, viewers or listeners. All such analysis can do is offer provocative and productive hypotheses about these processes. This may seem obvious, but it can often be forgotten. When conducting textual analysis, it is easy to swing into bold claims about what a text is 'really about', or how a number of detected associations in the text clearly reflect a given intention or an inevitable shaping of the readers' views. You should be careful to assess your own analysis to ensure you do not leap to premature conclusions or make grandiose assertions.

One example of this problem is provided in an acute analysis of a newspaper article in the *Daily Express* (3 May 1991) about a boy excluded from school because his parents could not afford a uniform. In this analysis, Gunther Kress claims that the clausal syntax surrounding the word 'afford', allied with potentially different meanings that can be attributed to the word itself, shows that 'the producer of the text' wished 'to provide a particular set of accounts of poverty, both as *caused* (by heartless bureaucrats and so on) and as *uncaused* (something which simply is, in which people *are*)', and that this facilitates different groups of readers (Kress 1994: 37). This is unwarranted supposition, for a number of reasons. First, that the story is about poverty as constructed in this way is no more convincing than an alternative reading that, in view of the newspaper in which it appeared, it is primarily about fusspot teachers and myopic educational bureaucrats. The point of saying this is not that such an alternative reading of the story is right and the original analyst's is wrong; it is that either is equally plausible and they cannot be arbitrated by applying the methods of critical linguistics. Second, Kress assumes that the journalists involved in the production of the story intentionally set forth these different readings through their construction of the report. We do not know what the political machinations were in the *Express* newsroom, though we can make an intelligent guess from the paper's political record. However, neither that record nor the journalistic practices, ideology and procedures which follow from it were the subject of this research. Nor were the responses of the newspaper's readers. This is our third point. From the ambivalence of the text, Kress builds up various groups of putative readers, each of them served by a particular discursive strategy which will satisfy their socio-political views. Each of these readership groups arises, genie-like, according to the way the verb 'afford' in the first sentence of the report is interpretively rubbed. This is textualism with a vengeance.

One of the more intriguing findings of research on newspaper readers during election campaigns is that a surprisingly high proportion seem not to recognise the partisanship of their regular newspaper, however explicitly, even stridently, it is voiced. This may be because they get so used to it that it becomes almost literally invisible. It may also be because what is undoubtedly partisan in one person's view may just seem common sense to someone who shares that viewpoint. Indeed, many would argue that it is in the creation of a 'common sense' of particular flavours that the media have their most powerful ideological significance. In this context, the point is that, without talking to the readers themselves, we do not know that this story finally functions to reassure. The claims that emerge from the linguistic analysis help us to know what questions to ask of readers, and can give powerful clues as to likely readings, but they can only be provisional and hypothetical without complementary research. So, for example, if you want to assess the degree to which any particular news report is conventional in its intertextual and inter-discursive relations, you can only begin to do this systematically in combination with the kind of content analysis we discussed earlier, for anything other than an impressionistic view of a news story's relative conventionality as a discourse type is dependent on – at the very least – some basic proof of frequency. It is important to insist on this point because, as we noted, frequency can be too easily assumed in news analysis.

To think about frequency is to begin thinking about relations of texts across time, for it is only in **diachronic** terms that the relative degree of textual conventionality in a report can be established initially. This is important because you need to establish this conventionality in some such way in order to stake out the empirical ground for analysing its 'common-sense' ideological significance. In linguistic and discourse analysis, the focus of your examination is on the structure of particular texts and the **synchronic** relations these may have to other texts within the overall ensemble of texts and discourses in a particular edition of a newspaper. Forms of linguistic and discourse analysis are characteristically intensive and micro-logical. This does not necessarily entail their confinement to an exclusively synchronic mode of attention, however, and with sufficient sampling, evidence of broad trends and configurations of news coverage of a particular social topic or issue could eventually be adduced. This would be extremely time-consuming, and for this reason, among others, it is more efficient to combine such analysis with the broader kinds of content analysis we have outlined. Though these can also be applied to single-story news texts, their characteristic strengths lie in their suitability to a longitudinal timeframe. This is a further instance of our general research principle that virtue lies in combining various distinct approaches, drawing on their relative strengths and attempting to make their different contributions analytically complementary. Nonetheless, what seems conventional takes time to become conventional. In taking a news text from the past, we have tried to demonstrate that textual conventionality is a product of time in its gradual development, acquiring certain longer-term characteristics that are part of a more general media history. Our aim has been to suggest how the textual codes and conventions of news reporting, and its modes of discursive organisation and operation, now and in the comparatively recent past, share many similarities, which are part of a developing tradition of journalism. In pursuing this aim with one particular news story about Iraq, we hope to have shown that the past is neither dead nor even past.

Summary: key points

- A sample analysis was offered of a historical lead story in a British newspaper.

- Each stage of our analysis was comprehensively set out, in a step-by-step guide.

- The first stage of analysis involved examining the position, composition and immediate intertextual relations of the story in what we call the formal staging of a news text.

- The second stage involved study of a text's thematic structure, and this was closely related to the third analytical stage of determining the discourse schema in operation throughout the text. In this connection, we identified three discursive strategies of tabloid news journalism: sequencing structure, source quantity and quality, and framing procedures.

- The fourth stage entailed examination of lexical choice and lexical markers. The fifth involved considering a text in light of broader ideological concepts, which we found illuminated by returning to certain intertextual features of the front page of the newspaper in question.

- Finally, we discussed the analytical limitations of text-centred modes of analysis, whether connected with historical or contemporary cultural analysis, as a further illustration of the need for reflexive methodological eclecticism and auto-critical assessment.

chapter nine

Viewing the Image

From texts to images and back again

The last three chapters have introduced the main methods you can use to analyse how modern media forms mobilise written language. In two later chapters (12 and 13) we take this exploration a stage further, looking at ways of approaching speech and talk. In both these areas we can draw on a range of well-established approaches, produced by the rich traditions of work in linguistics and discourse analysis. When we turn to images, however, we have much less to go on, since work on the visual dimension of media communication remains relatively underdeveloped. This is not to say, of course, that new visual technologies are totally ignored – there are some recent studies that do attend to them, as is the case with Ron Burnett's (2004) exploration of new spaces of visualised intelligence, for example – but the point generally holds. This presents major problems because many of the central forms of mass communication, from photography and film, through television, magazines, popular newspapers and advertising, to changing landscapes and ecologies of the image in video games, Internet websites and alternate reality gaming, are saturated with images. Such images, in their various different forms, open up for us a broad range of experiences. They mediate the interaction between people, cultures, histories and environments. In digital form, images are now central to most existing media (solely audio media such as radio and phonography are obvious exceptions), and we move among them or through them continually in our everyday lives.

In response, some researchers, particularly in film studies, focus almost exclusively on the organisation of imagery, conveniently forgetting that since the introduction of 'talkies' at the end of the 1920s, films have also had dialogue, soundtracks including music, and possibly voice-over commentaries. Conversely, much linguistically inspired work on television proceeds as though news stories and other forms of programmes were simply segments of talk, and has little or nothing to say about the images that appear on the screen. The tunnel vision involved in both these cases ignores the ways that meanings in popular media are created through the *interplay* between language and image – news photos appear under headlines, advertising images have captions, the talking head of the television newsreader is seen in front of a graphic distilling the key theme or subject of the story.

Consequently, you should read this chapter alongside the chapters on analysing texts and talk. The two case studies we introduce later demonstrate in detail how meaning is organised through the interaction of language and imagery, and provide practical examples of how to set about exploring these relations. But let us take one step at a time. We cannot integrate image analysis into a more general project of textual analysis unless we have first developed an analytical vocabulary and approach that allows us to investigate the specific ways that still and moving images are organised in the popular media.

The camera: an unerring eye?

Photography was launched in the late 1830s when, within months of each other, Frenchman Louis-Jacques-Mandé Daguerre and Englishman Henry Fox Talbot announced rival processes for creating a permanent record of whatever was in front of the camera lens. Daguerre attracted the most attention initially, since his images (daguerreotypes) were more detailed, but it was Fox Talbot's process of reproducing positive impressions from negatives that won out, since it had the major advantage of generating multiple prints, as against the single impression offered by Daguerre.

In July 1839, when the Chamber of Deputies debated whether or not to buy the patent to Daguerre's process for the French nation, supporters were quick to present the camera as the latest in a long line of valuable scientific instruments (Winston 1995: 127). They saw it as an entirely 'objective' extension of human vision, like the microscope and the telescope. Since the camera was a mechanical device, they reasoned that the images it produced would be free from the omissions, selections and personal biases that characterised written accounts. The cameraman's point of view might be subjective, but the camera's was not. As Daguerre put it when he first announced his process to the public, 'the daguerreotype is not merely an instrument which serves to draw Nature; on the contrary it is a chemical and physical process which gives her the power to reproduce herself' (cited in Trachtenberg 1980: 13).

This strong belief in the camera as an automatic recording device, with an unjaundiced eye and an unerring capacity to tell the 'truth', provided a potent metaphor for the new philosophy of objectivity that gained ground in both journalism and the positivist social sciences from the 1840s onwards. Reporters and researchers wanting to break away from subjective forms of commentary aspired to become human cameras, producing comprehensive and non-partisan captures of the contemporary world. To this end, they drew a sharp distinction between facts and values. They saw their job as assembling 'objective' evidence, not drawing political lessons or passing moral judgements. Reporting was clearly demarcated from editorialising or personal commentary in the 'serious' press, while positivist sociologists bolstered their claims to scientific status by trading in the statistical 'social facts' produced by the proliferating range of official and academic investigations into contemporary life.

The characterisation of photography as a machine for producing 'objective' evidence, uncontaminated by personal bias, was later taken up by promoters of the new medium of film. Indeed, some commentators argued that moving images were even more 'truthful', since they were less easy to doctor. As Boleslaw Matuszewski argued in 1898, just three years after the Lumière brothers had mounted the first public cinema show:

> Perhaps the cinematograph does not give the whole story, but at least what it gives is unquestionable and of absolute truth. Ordinary photography allows retouching which can go as far as transformation, but try retouching in an identical way each shape on the thousands of

microscopic plates! One can say that animated photography…is the true eyewitness and is infallible.

(Matuszewski cited in Macdonald and Cousins 1996: 13–14)

Belief in the camera's ability to produce a 'warts-and-all' capture of social action also underpins another very influential notion in contemporary media practice: the idea of 'realism'. We shall unpack this central concept in more detail later in the chapter, but for the moment we need to introduce another important term into the discussion: the iconic sign. It is because photographs are iconic signs par excellence that they can be mobilised so easily to support the claims to objectivity expressed in the familiar adage 'the camera cannot lie'.

Icon, index and symbol

In chapter 7 we outlined various semiotic terms and concepts relevant to the analysis of written and spoken texts. These can also be applied to the study of visual images, but the term which we now want to add is particularly relevant to the visual dimension of media communications. It derives from a threefold distinction between basic types of sign made by C.S. Peirce, the American philosopher who, quite independently of Saussure – but, coincidentally, at around the same time – developed a theory of semiotics. Peirce distinguished between iconic, indexical and symbolic signs.

With an *index*, the relation between the signifier and the signified is causal and linear: the sign is directly the effect of the object. So, for instance, smoke is an index of fire; a weathercock is an index of the direction of the wind; and a knock is an index of someone's presence outside the door. Differentiating this particular kind of sign from others entails a qualification of the general point about the arbitrariness of the sign in Barthian semiotics. Clearly we would not get very far in life if we took smoke to be an index of water, or pain as an index of a highly pleasurable sensation. Of course, the designation of that billowy grey stuff that rises upwards as 'smoke' is still arbitrary as a linguistic sign, even if it is causally an index of the presence of fire.

A *symbol*, by contrast, *is* arbitrarily connected to its object by association or habituation. The meanings attached to it are dependent on a cultural system. Consequently, it accords more closely to Barthes's concept of the sign in its general sense. In conventional English usage, for example, the word 'casket' is a symbol of the small, often richly ornamented box used in the past for storing things of value, such as jewels or sentimental letters. In the United States, however, the word 'casket' became conventionally used from the second half of the nineteenth century to refer to a coffin, in what was actually an extension of an older English use of the word as a synonym for a reliquary.

The term 'symbol' is employed in everyday speech, of course, where it is used to refer to something that represents something other than itself, though, again, this is always through a conventional relation, as, for example, with a skull and crossbones representing piracy and death, or a red cross on a white background acting as a visual metaphor for medical assistance.

This brings us to the **iconic sign**. With an icon, the relationship between signifier and signified is based on the quality of being like. For a sign to be iconic it must seem to match the physical characteristics of its object, as for instance in representational paintings or statues. Peirce's threefold differentiation of signs, then, suggests that they may be arbitrary to a greater or lesser degree. For example, a Rolls-Royce is 'certainly an index of wealth in that one must be wealthy to own one, but social convention has made it a symbol of wealth...an object which signifies wealth more imperiously than other objects equally expensive' (Culler 1976: 15). An iconic sign, by contrast, is based not on a system of interpretive cultural conventions but on close physical resemblance. It can thus stand on its own, as it were, and be its own interpreter of what it means.

The photographic image

It is in this sense that the photo image is the iconic sign par excellence. The photograph is more literal than any other sign. A photograph of a Rolls-Royce signifies the manufactured commodity in an apparently direct and indisputable way. It is as if the sign and the object are one and the same. Roland Barthes put this nicely in saying that the photo image transmits 'the scene itself, the literal reality'. Here the process of signification does not involve a transformation from one thing to another, as with the symbolic sign. Rather, it is 'a message without a code' (Barthes 1977: 17). The strong signifying power of the iconic sign is that it seems to be there, to exist in a real, palpable sense beyond the idiosyncrasies of the viewer's interpretive processes. In a material sense, the analogue photographic image has also been an index of the effect of light on photographic emulsion, but its real force lies in its iconic signification. This force becomes even stronger when the iconic moves into the realm of the symbolic. Because iconic signs transfer into symbolic modes of signification without losing their sense of the tangible, social myths rooted in iconic/symbolic combinations are that much harder to contest than myths based entirely within the realm of the symbolic.

The photographic image is, nevertheless, inherently ambiguous. It is both 'objective', seeming to transmit 'the scene itself, the literal reality', and connotative, an inflected view or version of reality. For example, we may take as acutely accurate documentary evidence those stark visual portraits of the effects of economic depression taken by the highly talented photographers (people like Walker Evans, Dorothea Lange and Ben Shahn) who worked for the Farm Security Administration project in 1930s America. But it can also be shown that these images were carefully constructed to evoke the suffering caused by poverty, hardship and ecological disaster. It goes without saying that the conditions they documented actually existed, and in one sense this is what they caught in the select frozen moments that now survive in the historical record. But the photographers also had certain aesthetic standards about the depiction of poverty which they wished to see met in their pictures. This trafficking of art and truth applies to a great deal of pictorial representation, but photographic images are distinguished by their mechanically attested reductiveness, their aggressive insistence that *this is how it is*.

With photographs, the denotative properties or qualities are foregrounded and connotation is repressed. An iconic sign stridently acclaims its 'thereness', but is remarkably silent about its 'howness'. Because it offers an apparently palpable, objective reality, it is capable both of invisibly reinforcing the symbolic, the mythic, and of rendering the symbolic or mythic invisible.

This peculiarly powerful signifying force of the iconic sign does not apply only to the still photo, of course. It is also present in film and television. A great deal of what these media do is based on the claim that what is represented are things as they are, scenes and events in the real world of which they are a reflection. In realist cinema, in social reportage, in current affairs programmes, in news and documentaries, the 'real' world is always there, as either background or foreground, in its indisputable 'thereness'. The iconic nature of electronic visual communication seems to give it a privileged status of objective representation, much more than in theatrical performance or fictional narration, for example, which appear more obviously tied to particular stylistic conventions or generic characteristics, and which are often seen as fantasy or make-believe.

It is against this background that visual media analysis has to be conducted. The peculiar and sophisticated power of contemporary iconicity is not the only reason why critical communications research is imperative, but it is certainly an important one.

Cameraworks: images and experiences

The meaning of any particular photographic image is made up of a combination of the connotations that have attached themselves to the people, places and objects it depicts, and the associations that have grown up around the particular formal and technical conventions used to organise and light the space in front of the lens. Writers on photography have developed a distinctive vocabulary to describe these techniques. They talk about the type of shot used, its composition, the way it is lit, and whether it uses colour or black-and-white film. Commentators on movies describe particular shots within a film in the same way, but because they are dealing with moving images they are also interested in how directors structure the passage of time by moving from one shot to another. We shall introduce the basic terms in this vocabulary of mobility later in the chapter, but for now we want to continue looking at ways of describing single images.

Introductory books often simply define key terms to produce a bald set of basic technical descriptions (e.g. Dick 1990: 31–3), though some writers are a little more adventurous. In his well-known text on media analysis techniques, for example, Arthur Berger borrows terms from semiotics to classify the meaning of particular shots. He argues, for instance, that an elevated shot, looking down from a height, signifies power and authority, whereas a shot from below, looking up, suggests smallness and weakness (Berger 1991: 26–7). As with all connotations, these associations are based on social agreements about what a sign means. But where have these conventions come from? It is particularly important to answer this question when we are dealing with photography and film because, as we have argued, these media consistently disguise the processes involved in their construction, producing images that appear to offer an entirely 'natural' way of looking. Challenging this assumption by uncovering the social processes at work beneath the appearance of 'business as usual' is essential to any research project that aims to offer a critical perspective. One way to do this is to examine photography and film-making as kinds of work, looking closely at how the professionals involved set about doing their job, as Barbara Rosenblum does in her 'sociology of photographic styles' (Rosenblum 1978). For this you would need to draw on the methods of interviewing and observation detailed in chapters 4, 11 and 12.

The technical and aesthetic choices that photographers make also have social and cultural histories. They activate conventions with strong roots in people's shared experience of the contemporary city and of modern visual media. Professional photography works on these experiences, refining them and offering new points of reference. The results appear entirely 'natural' precisely because they resonate with ways of looking which are now so securely woven into the textures of everyday life that we take them for granted. By way of illustration, let us look more closely at four core aspects of the way still images are organised: type of shot, composition, colour and lighting.

Shots: spaces and angles

Shots vary depending on how far away the camera is from the subject, and, in the case of pictures of people, whether or not the subject is looking directly into the lens.

For the first 50 years of photography, taking pictures was the preserve of professional photographers and well-off amateurs. Cameras were expensive and cumbersome, and the process of making prints was difficult and time-consuming. If people wanted a photograph of themselves or their children, they either went to a photographer's studio or asked a photographer to come to them. Most of the resulting pictures were *full shots*, carefully posed and showing the whole of the subject's body. Family portraits, wedding photos and group portraits of social clubs or school classes would be typical examples. This sense that photos of important occasions deserved to be posed and taken with care carried over into the age of popular photography, which began in 1888 with the arrival of the first easy-to-use Kodak cameras. Consequently, generations of amateurs have been exhorted to take care lining up their shots, to make sure that everyone in the picture is looking at the camera, and not to chop off anyone's head or feet.

Full shots, then, often connote a certain distance between the camera and the subject. With domestic snaps, it is the physical distance appropriate to the sense of formality called for by important moments in personal or family life, such as weddings, birthdays, anniversaries or graduation day. With professionally taken pictures, it is prevailing definitions of the 'proper' social distance between professionals and their clients.

Many photos, however, are *medium shots* or *mid-shots*, showing people from the waist up or simply the head and shoulders. These imply stronger, more intimate relationships. In amateur photographs they suggest that people know each other well enough not to 'keep their distance', and that whoever is holding the camera has been invited to come close enough to touch. With professional studio shots, the key relationship evoked is between the subject and the viewer rather than the subject and the photographer. Most of the mid-shot portraits that people commission are intended to be given to loved ones or displayed in the home, while publicity portraits of stars and celebrities play a key role in cementing the sense of intimacy on which the star system depends.

As we will see in chapter 10, mid-shots of journalists reporting from the scene of a story, and of newsreaders back in the studio, play a key role in news programmes. They suggest both authority and familiarity. The standard shot of a newsreader seated behind a desk, facing an open laptop, conjures up memories of going to see the doctor or meetings with bank managers, while the reporter on the spot, standing a handshake away, is reminiscent of a chance meeting with a trusted acquaintance. This sense of trust is further reinforced by the fact that both newsreaders and reporters always look directly at the camera and sustain eye contact with the viewer on the other side of the screen. In contrast, many of the other people featured or interviewed in the programme are likely to be shot from the side, with only part of their face visible.

Evocations of trust and intimacy are taken a stage further in *close-up shots* that focus solely on the face. These often carry strong erotic and sexual connotations, since this is the view that someone about to hug or kiss the person would see. However, not all intimacy is welcome. Close-ups can also activate strong negative connotations. Following the furore over news photographers' pursuit of Princess Diana, unauthorised pictures of celebrities taken by paparazzi are now widely seen as intrusive. Mugshots of criminals reproduced from police files also carry strong negative connotations. When they appear in press reports or television news bulletins reporting on a police inquiry, they remind audiences both of the pervasiveness of official surveillance and of the presence of potent threats to public safety.

Positive and negative connotations are conveyed even more forcefully by *extreme close-ups*, which focus on a particular part of the face or body. These may be used to convey the intensity of sexual passion, as lovers explore each other's bodies. On the other hand, as feminist media analysts have argued, images solely of breasts or other erogenous zones may objectify women by reducing them to the body parts that male spectators are most interested in, and, at the same time, dehumanise men by placing them in the role of voyeurs. This is most obvious in the case of pornographic images, but many critics see the same basic dynamics at work in advertising imagery. Extreme close-ups are also widely used to heighten the impact of scenes of violence. Shots of the killer's wild eyes and the victim's face distorted in a scream are part of the stock-in-trade of popular cinema.

At the other end of photography's scale of distance is the *long shot*. This either shows a broad sweep of landscape or cityscape, with or without human figures, or places people in particular geographical and social contexts. The opening sequences of the major British television soap operas are a good example. These programmes are defined generically by their focus on the lives of people residing in a particular neighbourhood – a characteristic signified, first, by naming the programme after the place (*Brookside, Coronation Street, Emmerdale*) and, second, by the *establishing shots* that accompany the opening titles. The popular soap *EastEnders*, for example, opens with an *aerial shot* of the Thames, east of the Tower of London, placing the action firmly in the working-class area of the city known as the East End.

Particular localities may also play an important role in the plots of feature films, as in they do in *West Side Story*. Here, again, we have an establishing sequence that begins with an aerial shot, this time of the familiar topography of Manhattan. The camera then travels slowly to the left, across the screen, moving westwards over poorer and poorer neighbourhoods until it closes in on a group of youths in a run-down street. This sequence does two things very economically. It locates the action firmly in a particular place and, through a continuous shot of the tangle of buildings, streets and railway tracks that lie between this neighbourhood and the glamour of central Manhattan, suggests the strength of the barriers to upward mobility. Before a word of dialogue has been spoken, viewers have been given a strong impression that the boys who live here are stuck, with no way out. This sense of enclosure plays a key role in preparing audiences for the inevitability of the tragedy that then unfolds, using a variant of the *Romeo and Juliet* story.

In the age of package holidays and cheap air travel, when more and more people have seen landscapes and cities from the window of an aircraft, aerial shots taken from helicopters or light aircraft have become increasingly consonant with everyday experience. Aerial photography has also helped us to interpret the past in a radically different way. Starting with balloonists and biplanes and progressing to radar and hi-tech digital equipment, aerial photography has revealed to us extraordinary archaeological features that would not otherwise have become apparent. One of the first examples of this was the famous view of the prehistoric ruins at Stonehenge, taken in 1906 by Lieutenant Philip Sharpe of the Royal Engineers. It quickly became apparent how heatwave conditions showed up hidden details best of all. Grass and crops of various kinds wilted more quickly over buried walls, and remained green over old wells and rubbish tips. Sometimes evening shadows did the trick. The overall organisation of ancient forts, palaces and settlements, farming systems and old town developments, became apparent, often for the first time. The person who firmly established aerial photography in archaeology during the 1930s, Osbert Guy Crawford, described it as a research tool as valuable for the study of the past as the telescope is for the study of the stars. Georg Gerster is among those who have vividly demonstrated this in their photographic practice, giving us an almost godlike perspective on the huge, wheel-like conception of the seventh-century Median capital at Hamadan in Iran, the immense scale and complexity of the fortified royal residence atop the 170 metre-high rocky massif of Sigiriya in Sri Lanka, and the amazing precision and sophistication of layout in the grass labyrinth at Saffron Waldon in Essex (Gerster 2003). But our second-hand views of the world do not remain there. We are now also readily familiar with camera shots taken from even further away. Through television weather forecasts that reproduce satellite photos, we are used to seeing images taken from space. By extending our sense of scale and indicating planet-wide forces, such as the El Niño weather system or Hurricane Katrina, these techniques suggest both our own relative insignificance as individuals and our interdependence.

Most aerial shots, of course, are taken from more modest heights and carry somewhat different connotations. The experience of looking down on a landscape or a city was already a popular entertainment in the early nineteenth century, with the rise of panorama shows. However, it was the erection of taller and taller buildings that made bird's-eye views a regular part of most people's everyday experience of the city. The Flatiron Building, which is generally thought to be the first skyscraper built in New York, was finished in 1903. It was 226 feet high. Ten years later, the Woolworth Building reached 791 feet, still some way short of Gustave Eiffel's tower in Paris at 993 feet. But even this was comprehensively eclipsed in 1931 when the Empire State Building opened, at a height of 1,250 feet, a record for the world's tallest building that remained unchallenged until 1972. By bringing aerial perspectives, which had previously been available only to balloonists and pioneering aviators, within the reach of significant numbers of people, these new elevations opened up potent new angles of vision. Film-makers even borrowed from the vocabulary of building construction, naming shots taken from the special metal gantries that were used to raise camera operators above the action *crane shots*.

Looking down on life on the ground became associated with the power derived from the observer's ability to see more and further than people at street level, and to notice how particular incidents were influenced by wider patterns and flows. This ability to grasp the 'big picture' and to make connections was strongly identified with knowledge and control. Even relatively modest elevations would do. In 1859, for example, the Victorian journalist George Augustus Sala boasted of 'unroofing London' 'from the top of an omnibus' perched 'above…taking notes' on the 'busy, restless, chameleon life' of the streets. Interestingly, in Paris at the same time, women were forbidden to ride on the tops of buses (cited in Wilson 1992: 96). The position of the elevated observer was seen as a male privilege. Many feminists would argue that it still is, though the barriers are less blatant now.

If *shots from above* suggest the observer's power over the people and objects shown, *shots from below* evoke their subordination and dependence. They invite the spectator to 'look up to' whoever or whatever is featured in the shot, to accept their authority. This perspective is rooted in a wide range of everyday experiences, from saluting the flag to looking up at a priest in a pulpit, a judge on a raised dais or a performer on stage or screen. It also activates potent childhood memories of feeling vulnerable when looking up at adults, particularly strangers, towering above.

To sum up, the distance between camera and subject combines with camera angle to activate a range of connotations. Prevailing social and visual conventions in middle-class North Atlantic cultures have taken full shots and mid-shots as the norm, with the subject looking directly at a camera held by an adult and meeting the viewer's eye, suggesting both respect for personal space and an equality of status based on a consensual relationship. Deviations from this norm are then employed to suggest greater intimacy, unequal power and authority, threat or vulnerability.

Composition: verticals, horizontals and diagonals

Images made up wholly or mainly of straight lines, either vertical or horizontal, appear static and self-contained. The picture frame seems to draw a boundary around the moment, fencing it off from what happened before and after the shutter was clicked. Such compositions are common in posed photographs, such as portraits of the royal family, where the time taken out of everyday life has been orchestrated carefully to produce a formal historical record and convey a sense of solidity.

In the case of news photographs, however, where the camera is trying to find a defining moment in a clutter of activity, this appearance of stability carries negative connotations. Consequently, news photographers and newspaper editors tend to look for images that are bisected by strong diagonal lines that appear to continue beyond the picture frame, reminding the viewer that the shot has been abstracted from a continuous flow of action.

These compositions convey a strong sense of dynamism and suggest that the expected order of things produced by careful planning has broken down. Since interruptions to normality, in the form of crimes, disasters and acts of exceptional heroism, are at the heart of our prevailing definitions of news, it is not surprising that many of the best-known news photographs of the century are organised around strong diagonals. They include Murray Becker's celebrated shot of the *Hindenburg* crashing to the ground in flames at the airfield in Lakehurst, New Jersey, in 1937, showing the giant airship dividing the frame at 45 degrees; and Joe Rosenthal's 1945 shot of American troops raising the Stars and Stripes on Iwo Jima during the Pacific War, where, once again, the flag on its pole bisects the picture at 45 degrees. (For more examples, see Faber 1978.)

In addition to conveying movement and dynamism in a still image, diagonals are also used in film and television to suggest disruption, uncertainty or spontaneity, a sense that normal boundaries are being broken. These shots, where the camera is *tilted* (or *canted*) to one side (sometimes called *dutch angles*), became particularly popular from the 1990s in television programming aimed at teenagers and young adults, where they are used to signify a break with convention.

Colour: glamour and grit

Colour did not become the norm in either photography or film until the 1940s, when Kodacolor film was launched and Technicolor's Monopack system was first used for feature films. Similarly, it was some time after television became a household fixture that transmissions finally moved from black and white to colour. As a result, monochrome images carry strong connotations of nostalgia, reminders of an age now passed. But they also have a complex relation to our dominant definitions of visual truth. 'We equate black-and-white photographs with "realism" and the authentic. Colour remains suspect' (Clarke 1997: 23). Even now, when it is relatively easy to reproduce colour images in newspapers, most news photos are still printed in black and white. At first sight, this seems distinctly odd, since the human eye sees the world in full colour. Once again, the explanation lies in the social history of visual experience in the modern city.

The closing decades of the nineteenth century witnessed an explosion of coloured imagery, as improvements in lithographic printing combined with the development of new synthetic dyes to transform street advertising into a vibrant field of vivid colour. The posters that the French artist Henri Toulouse-Lautrec produced for Parisian cabarets and nightclubs are perhaps the best-known examples, and reproductions can still be bought as domestic decorations. When posters like these first appeared, plastered onto every available surface in the city, they had an enormous impact. But the fact that they were almost all advertisements for branded goods or commercial entertainments also generated strong associations with the new commodity culture and with persuasive communication. Colour became associated with the promotion of glamour, with fabricated dreamworlds of luxury and leisure rather than the mundane world of everyday life. Since news promised the unvarnished truth, these associations were seen as inappropriate for images of distress, poverty and disaster.

There are exceptions, however. Most amateurs now take photographs, or shoot film or video footage, using colour film. Consequently, if they happen to record a significant event that becomes news, the fact that the images are in colour acts as a guarantee of their veracity. The best example of this is the dramatic film of President John Kennedy being hit by an assassin's bullets as his open-topped car moves along a street in Dallas, Texas. This footage was taken by an amateur cameraman, standing on the pavement directly facing Kennedy's car. Since none of the professional news crews was in a position to capture this decisive moment, this is the only visual record there is of one of the key events in modern political history. We will see the same dynamic at work in the front-page news photo that we analyse later on, when we put the concepts being outlined here to practical use.

Lighting: illuminations and shadows

Whether images are produced in a studio under artificial light or outside in natural light, the way illumination is organised is an integral part of the complex of meanings the shot offers the viewer. To understand how the present connotations around lighting have developed, we have once again to recover the relevant social history.

The development of mass photography and popular film coincided with electricity's displacement of gas as the dominant source of public and domestic lighting. For the first time it was possible to flood both streets and interiors with illumination bright enough to banish dark corners and unwanted shadows. At the same time, electricity also offered the chance to construct more intimate interior lighting effects, using standard lamps, wall lights and table lamps, and to guarantee their safety.

Photographers and film-makers entered this new world of illumination in two ways. They used specialised electrical equipment to illuminate studios, film sets and locations, and in choosing how to light particular shots they traded on people's experience of the new visual environment.

In a standard film studio set-up there are three principal sources of light: the main source, known as the *key light*; a side *fill light* to soften shadows; and *backlighting* to demarcate the foreground from the background. All these devices are out of shot, hidden from the viewer. But illumination may also come from a *source light*, such as a computer screen or table lamp that is visible within the shot. These separate illumination points can be used in varying combinations to evoke different moods. Where strong fill lights are used to eradicate more or less all shadows, the image appears uniformly bright. This 'look' is characteristic of American television soap operas like *Dynasty*, where all the elements of the action, including the deceits and deceptions, take place in full view of the audience. Love scenes in standard Hollywood productions are also typically suffused with light, although the textures here are more intimate, 'using reflectors to soften shadows…special lenses to imitate candlelight or lamplight, and carefully judged backlight to add highlights to the hair' (McDonnell 1998: 126). A number of these modern lighting techniques were pioneered by the lavish shop-window displays in the new department stores that developed alongside cinemas in the major cities, and were later taken up in television commercials, particularly those for shampoos, body-care products and domestic utilities. As a consequence, they have come to be widely associated with a fabricated and 'unrealistically' glamorous view of contemporary life.

Alternatively, assigning a dominant role to the key light produces dark areas and deep shadows within the shot, suggesting risk and danger. This mood is characteristic of interiors and street scenes in thrillers, or scenes where characters enter unfamiliar situations. Instead of glamour, it evokes the uncertainty and grit of urban and industrial landscapes that have seen better days. Consequently, it appears 'truer' to the harsh edges of everyday experience.

Images and words

So far in this chapter we have concentrated on introducing a basic vocabulary for describing key aspects of the way single images are organised. However, as mentioned earlier, images seldom appear by themselves in contemporary media. They are almost always accompanied by speech or written commentary. Consequently, while we need to pay close attention to the particular ways that images structure meaning, in conducting textual analysis we also have to look carefully at how they relate to or play against the language that surrounds them. These relations move in two directions.

First, language is widely used in news stories and advertising to **anchor** the meaning of an image. Captions and slogans attempt to reduce the connotations the image carries and encourage readers to activate the particular associations producers had in mind. These efforts are not always successful, for images are notoriously open to more than one interpretation. Street graffiti are a particularly fertile site of struggles over meaning. For example, an advertising hoarding showing a pack of cigarettes with the slogan 'Make a note of it' (suggesting that the product is special enough to be particularly notable) may find itself carrying the unlooked-for spray-can addition, 'Yes, a suicide note' (linking smoking to life-threatening diseases).

Conversely, particularly resonant images may be used to fix the meaning of events that have been widely reported and commented on. The study (which one of the authors worked on) of the press reporting of a mass street demonstration in London in the autumn of 1968, against the war in Vietnam, provides an excellent example (see Halloran, Elliott and Murdock 1970; Murdock 1973). The demonstration followed in the wake of a series of violent clashes between police and radical students, most notably in Paris and the United States, and the pre-reporting had built up an expectation that the London march would also see running street battles. On the day, the vast majority of marchers proceeded peacefully to a rally in Hyde Park. However, a small group broke away to demonstrate outside the American Embassy, where there were tussles with police. The photo that dominated the front pages the following day was taken at this fringe event. It showed a bearded young man (looking very like the celebrated Argentine-Cuban revolutionary, Che Guevara) apparently holding a policeman from behind while another man, standing sideways-on at the edge of the image, with his face partly concealed, kicks the policeman in the face. This incident was highly atypical of the day's events, but because it fitted perfectly with press predictions of what was likely to happen, it came to represent the entire occasion, and has subsequently been endlessly reproduced in popular analyses of the radical 1960s. It has been deposited in the archive of images that can be called on to make sense of new events by linking them with familiar cases. The photograph is not only highly graphic, but also strongly composed, with the kicker's leg tracing a strong diagonal line from the left-hand edge to the policeman's face in the centre of the image. Its composition and graphic impact are, at least in part, why it has entered into popular memory and become so resonant of the times to which it relates.

Being realistic

From time to time during the discussion so far we have touched on the question of realism. It is now appropriate for us to examine this issue more carefully, before moving on to deal substantively with the moving image.

The importance of realism cannot be underestimated. Though attempts are occasionally made to subvert it, it remains *the* dominant form of representation in contemporary visual media. In both factual and fictional genres, as these are conventionally designated, most television and film seeks to present itself as realistic. And being realistic is, at its simplest, what realism entails. But what is it in the presentation that makes a text 'realistic'? There is no easy or straightforward answer to this, and it is worth exploring why.

New developments in image and sound reproduction have, at least for a time, enhanced the illusion of reality for their audiences. In each case, the apparent realism seems to have been guaranteed by the technology, and the illusion involved is always that of seeing, or, in the cases of television and film from the advent of the talkies onwards, seeing and hearing. This, in turn, has affected our criteria for evaluating modern visual media, where we extol a film for being 'realistic' or condemn a television play because its effort to recreate the 'real' has seemed to us inadequate or contrived. What such judgements depend on, of course, are our conceptions of social and historical reality outside of film or television, regardless of how much these may have been influenced over time by our media consumption. We experience the illusion of realism by forgetting the illusion. So long as its force as illusion prevails, we allow ourselves to be absorbed into it, and it is only subsequently that we step back and consider its technical or artistic qualities precisely as illusion, as artefact.

This takes us on to an important point. The social reality which film or television may appear to reveal is never innocent of the procedures that have produced it. With a documentary television programme, for instance, the aspects of social reality it portrays do not exist in some original, given state which causally determines the record that is made of them. All documentary accounts are selective and sequenced ensembles of evidence generated by particular choices. The phenomena they deal with are therefore simultaneously both uncovered and constructed in the act of representing them. This returns us to the peculiar force of iconic representations, where the 'what' that is represented achieves its salience by suppressing the 'how' of representation.

Let us approach this from another angle. A good deal of documentary television achieves its generic identity through the sense it creates of presenting facts objectively, without editorialising or inserting 'fictional' matter or methods. What is strongly underwritten here is the idea of a dispassionate recording of real events and people. Yet documentary programming may also work with the idea that what has been produced is a 'human document' – something which is sensitive to subjective viewpoints, and which may involve questions of sensibility and the quality of 'lived' experience. In this sense it is the generation of or engagement with feeling about a particular issue or topic which is foregrounded. If we approach documentary in this way, we have to admit either the presence of subjective feeling in the text, or the arousal of feeling in the viewer, as integral to its accounts and what they set out to achieve. We then have to say that documentaries can never be just simply the dispassionate, coolly objective accounts that are represented in the first definition. And, most of all, we have to say that the project of documentary film or television rests most importantly on its potential for enabling us to 'see and feel', more clearly than before, the conditions of other people's lives and the texture of other people's experience. This perspective on the production and consumption of 'realistic' film or television leads to a rather difficult analytical question. In such cases, we need to ask whether our 'seeing and feeling' relates more to the experiences being represented or to what is imposed on them from outside, through the central framing devices mobilised by the programme producers, according to their particular professional standards and aesthetics.

If we add to this that filmic and televisual mediation necessarily entails a transformation and generalisation of specific materials, we get close to two further strategies of 'being realistic'. The first of these is the use of a particular instance as emblematic of general conditions. Not all the facts about marital problems, terrorism, MRSA, obesity, contemporary fiction, a popular music genre like the blues, or whatever our topic is, can be covered by a half-hour or hour-long television programme. Under the variable constraints in which television is produced, selectivity is inevitable, and the major criterion for choosing what to include is often its typicality. Here, the instance selected is taken to be representative of a broader pattern of reality. For documentary film, John Grierson captured this strategy well in saying that 'The quintessence will be more important than the aggregate'.

In talking about the process of transformation involved in filmic or televisual mediation, we are referring to the ways that the production team brings particular aesthetic and critical standards to bear in creating 'realistic' portrayals of social life. In this sense, 'being realistic' involves the criteria by which this quality is judged. A television programme, for example, may be evaluated according to how the aspect of social reality at issue has been 'brought to life', dramatised or creatively treated in such a way that we feel a sense of recognition, connection or participation. In this case, the subject material of the programme has involved a transformation so that its dramatic potential is realised and its power to engage us is maximised.

Why are these sorts of consideration important for the analysis of visual images in contemporary media? The short answer is that they should enable us to avoid the superficial assessment of such images which their iconic nature encourages. In pointing to their rhetorical construction, we are suggesting that iconic images require exactly the kind of analysis which their carefully constructed sense of 'being realistic' struggles to circumvent. This does not mean that photography, film and television are unable to say anything significant about social reality or convey some sense of the texture of everyday social experience. But the more we become analytically aware of the techniques and conventions by which media images and representations are produced, the less we shall be swayed by the rhetorical force of their quality of being, or rather seeming, realistic. As we noted earlier, critical media analysis involves us in attending historically to the emergence of certain codes and conventions, such as the reliance on monochrome images (colour film being thought to beautify or glamorise, and thus to undermine the type of account intended as documentary), on apparently haphazard mobile framing (the hand-held camera), and on the participants' direct gaze at the camera, which is, by contrast, rare in television drama or feature films. In addition, we could note that voice-over commentary, when it has functioned successfully as a meta-discourse of documentary, has done so because it has taken its sense of authority from the visual images whose meanings it has simultaneously structured and attempted to tie down.

However, things do not end there. The quality of seeming to be realistic has recently been further complicated by a major technological revolution in photography and moving imagery.

Altered images, digital deceptions

Since 1839, when Fox Talbot announced his pioneering process, most photographs have been positive impressions taken from a negative. This establishes a direct link between *what* is represented and the *way* it is recorded and stored. Suppose we hold up to the light the negative of a family snapshot taken at the seaside. We can clearly make out the faces and bodies of two adults and a child, sitting on a towel on the beach, with the pier behind them. The new technology of digital imaging severs this link. It translates visual information into the universal digital language of computing and stores it as an array of 0s and 1s. There is no negative of the image we can 'read'. There is simply a file, which can only be deciphered by a computer.

In this new system, images are made up of a fine grid of very small cells or pixels (short for 'picture elements'), which contain the basic information on the light, colour and composition of that part of the image. These cells are infinitely manipulable. Images can be altered pixel by pixel. Light and colour can be doctored at will. The composition can be changed, moving figures or objects closer to each other or further away, to reinforce an appearance of greater intimacy or separation. One part of a picture can be reproduced, or 'cloned', and used elsewhere in the image, to increase the size of the crowd shown cheering the royal coach, for example. Elements from another picture can be imported and invisibly stitched into the image. 'A graphic designer, for example, can produce new images for a brochure by taking a single photograph of a car and digitally placing it into a photographic scene of snow-capped mountains, a quiet beach, or a busy metropolis' (Ritchin 1990: 29). Alternatively, unwanted elements can be banished, without the telltale signs of excision left in conventional analogue photographs, such as the famous image of Russian revolutionary leaders after Stalin had ordered the removal of Trotsky following their falling-out. Similarly, putting another face onto a body, to change someone's appearance or to make them look younger, is no longer as obvious as it was when images had to be physically cut and pasted together. Since there is no original negative to refer to, these changes become more and more difficult to detect and prove.

Digitalisation is also becoming increasingly important in film. It has already produced spectacular special effects using computer-generated figures and vantage points that could not be physically reproduced in the studio. We are now readily familiar with computer-generated animations, but digitalisation also affects realist film and TV. The next step is to body-map actors so that their computerised clones will be able to stand in for them in stunt scenes, or indeed, substitute for them throughout the entire film.

Techniques of digital manipulation are already being widely used both in fictional feature films and in fashion and advertising photography. Since these areas of image-making have long been associated with fantasy, or with an overly glamorised and 'unrealistic' picture of the world, we might argue that they do not really matter that much. But what about photographs and film footage that claim to capture actual events: a politician addressing a crowd; prisoners of war in Bosnia behind barbed wire; a celebrity coming out of a nightclub drunk? If news is, as many commentators have claimed, a first draft of history, then the veracity of visual documents matters very much. Right-wing groups have long claimed that Hitler's mass murder of Jews in the concentration camps in World War II never really happened, and that the documentary footage produced by the Allies after the Liberation was staged as a propaganda exercise to discredit the Nazis. We can refute this claim by referring to the thousands of photos taken across the range of camps and to the testimonies of the many surviving eyewitnesses. But what if there is only one witness and one photograph and that image has been produced digitally?

Digital technology comprehensively undermines the basis of photography's traditional claim to truthfulness, or at the very least raises a permanent question mark against it. As we have seen in this chapter, 'For a century and a half, photographic evidence has seemed unassailably probative… The emergence of digital imaging has irrevocably subverted these certainties, forcing us all to adopt a far more wary and vigilant interpretive stance' (Mitchell 1994: 49). The critical image analysis we are advocating will be at the forefront of this necessary scepticism and continual questioning.

Moving images: from frames to flows

Photography is centrally concerned with the organisation of space and illumination (the term deriving from the Greek words for 'light' and 'writing'). These are also issues in film, television and video production, but because these media deal with moving images, they also have to grapple with the problem of how to organise time.

Early film cameras were cumbersome and relatively immobile, so scenes were taken from a fixed position offering a long shot of the area in front of the lens. Like the theatre, where spectators looked through a proscenium arch, action was confined within a static frame. Workers streamed out of the gates of a factory; a train arrived in a station; actors performed as though they were on a stage. As cameras became more mobile and new lenses developed, new ways of looking opened up. The camera moved into and around the action. Faces appeared in close-up. The early experience of frames gave way to a dynamic experience of flows. Contemporaries' sense of excitement at this new fluidity of vision was perfectly caught by the German cultural commentator Walter Benjamin, writing in 1936:

> Our taverns and our metropolitan streets, our offices and furnished rooms, our railroad stations and our factories appeared to have locked us up hopelessly. Then came the film and burst this prison-world asunder by the dynamite of the tenth of a second, so that now, in the midst of its far-flung ruins and debris, we calmly and adventurously go traveling.

(Benjamin 1970: 238)

By intervening with all 'the resources of its lowerings and liftings, its interruptions and isolations, its extensions and accelerations, its enlargements and reductions', Benjamin argues, the film camera disrupts our habitual ways of looking and forces us to see the familiar world in a different light (ibid.: 239).

There are five main aspects of film and television's organisation of movement, each with a descriptive vocabulary.

Movement within a shot

The smallest unit we can use in analysis is the single *shot*, where the camera records a particular scene from a fixed position; but of course, movement can occur within shots. It can do this in one of two ways. First, objects or people may move into and out of the frame, as when a security camera fixed to the wall records a robber walking into a bank or shop, forcing the cashier to empty the till, and walking out again. Second, like a person standing in the street, the camera's attention may shift from one aspect of the scene to another. This can be done either by altering the focal length of the lens or by swinging the camera sideways or up and down.

The standard focal length of lenses used in film-making is between 35 and 55 mm. If a longer lens (such as a *telephoto lens*) is used, the background will be blurred. Conversely, with a shorter lens (such as a *wide-angle lens*), both background and foreground will be more or less equally sharp, which is why this technique is often called *deep-focus*. Some critics argue that this produces a richer, more democratic image, since viewers are free to focus on whatever they find interesting, rather than having to follow the director's choice of what is significant. This technique was pioneered to great acclaim in Orson Welles's film *Citizen Kane* (1941), which many film critics still regard as the best movie ever made. At that time, it was necessary to use different lenses to secure different effects, but since the 1960s, *zoom lenses* (which combine a series of focal lengths) have made shifting focus much easier. Such shifts are frequently used either by following a person or object moving towards or away from the camera while keeping them in sharp focus (*follow focus*), or by diverting the viewer's attention from the foreground to some key feature in the background (*rack focusing*).

Shifts in focus may or may not be combined with movement created by swinging the camera, either from side to side along a horizontal axis (known as a *pan shot*), in the same way that someone standing in a street might scan the crowd for someone they are waiting for, or up and down along a vertical axis (known as a *tilt shot*), as a person might look up at a window or down at the pavement.

Moving the camera

The next option is to move the position of the camera. Sometimes this is done by the camera operator physically walking or running with the camera to produce *hand-held shots*. These are very common in amateur video footage where people do not have any equipment apart from the camera, but they also appear in professional productions. The fact that the resulting footage looks like an amateur video, with the same jerky, unstable quality, may be used to reinforce a sense of immediacy and veracity in television documentary or current affairs programmes, by appealing to the idea that the shot was taken on the run, right 'there', and is unedited.

Since the 1970s, the *Steadicam* (which uses a gyroscope to keep the camera stable as it moves) has allowed directors to capitalise on the immediacy and impact of hand-held images while complying with professional definitions of a 'good' shot. Stanley Kubrick's film *The Shining* (1980) provides a particularly good example, as a homicidal father, played by Jack Nicholson, chases his young son through a maze in the snow, at night. Having the camera at knee-height allows Kubrick to underline the sense of threat by shooting the scene, literally, from the child's viewpoint.

Even with this advance, cameras are still normally moved using some kind of mechanical device. We have already mentioned *crane shots* and *aerial shots*. The other main way to move a camera is to mount it on tracks. Once again, the visual effect of such shots was already familiar to audiences in the modern city before they were used in the cinema. As the name suggests, *tracking shots* reproduced the experience of looking out of the window of a moving railway carriage or trolleybus, watching the passing parade of objects and people or seeing people moving alongside, running down the platform or the street. Similarly, a passenger looking out of the rear window of a bus or the observation car at the back of a train would see stationary people and objects falling away into the distance, or mobile figures or objects (such as a speeding car) moving towards them, an experience reproduced in the *reverse tracking shot*.

Tracking shots are also called *dolly shots*, after the platform with wheels (the dolly) that carries the camera along the tracks. In a television studio, the dolly is simply wheeled around the studio floor.

Moving from one shot to another

Movements from one shot to another act in the same way as punctuation marks and paragraphs in a written text, to indicate a shift of speaker, topic or viewpoint. They are usually done by a simple *cut*, in which one shot is immediately followed by another, but this transition can also be achieved rather less abruptly by *fades*, *dissolves* or *wipes*.

With a *fade-in*, the screen is initially black and an image gradually appears until it brightens to full strength. *Fade-outs* reverse this process by moving from full illumination to black. Fades indicate the end of a sequence, and act as paragraph changes or even chapter endings. In contrast, *dissolves*, where one shot gradually replaces another, are often used to move the action along within the same sequence. *Wipes*, which imitate someone cleaning a dirty window by introducing a new image which appears to wipe away the preceding one, serve the same function, though they are used now much less than they used to be. The end of a scene, or more often the end of the film, may also be marked by stopping the action and showing a still image (a *freeze-frame*), which acts as the visual equivalent of the final full stop in an article or novel.

In scenes where there are two or more people, cuts are often used to move attention from one to another. In the standard interview in a television studio, for example, the camera regularly cuts between speakers or shows the responses of listeners. These *reaction shots* are often called *noddies*, because they typically show the listener nodding attentively. If the interview is recorded rather than live, the noddy shots will usually be taken after it is over, and then spliced in at whatever points the director feels are appropriate, which may or may not coincide with the responses displayed during the interview itself.

Often the camera will assume the position of an observer, showing the interview area in mid-shot or long shot, and using close-ups to underline the emotions of speakers and listeners at key points. It may also shoot over the shoulder of one or both of the participants. This produces a *subjective* or *point-of-view shot*. We are no longer watching the proceedings as detached observers. We are seeing events unfold through the participants' eyes – or rather, *seeming* to see events unfold in this way.

Regulating speed

A film consists of a series of separate exposures taken in quick succession so that the gaps between them are not visible to the viewer. Consequently, as well as developing various techniques for moving the camera, film-makers also had to find reliable ways of moving the film past the lens. Since 1927, when this speed was standardised, film has moved through a film camera at 24 frames per second (though European television films are shot at 25 frames a second). When a film is projected at this same speed, the action on the screen appears to be taking place in normal time. By keeping to the standard projection speed, but altering the number of exposures per second, it is possible to speed up the action or to slow it down.

For example, a sequence filmed at the rate of 6 exposures per second, rather than the standard 24, would appear to move four times as fast as 'normal' when projected. This effect is often used in comedies such as *The Benny Hill Show*, one of British television's most successful overseas exports, where the sexist Benny is frequently shown chasing women, or being chased, in a *speeded-up* sequence.

Conversely, if the camera shoots, say, 240 frames a second instead of the standard 24, when projected each frame will be on screen for ten seconds, so that the scene will appear in *slow motion*. One of the best-known uses of this device is the denouement of Arthur Penn's film *Bonnie and Clyde* (1967), where the two central characters are finally cornered and shot to death in a car. This scene, and subsequent portrayals of violence using the same technique, have prompted heated debate on the grounds that their balletic quality invites viewers to revel in a highly stylised portrayal of violence which glamorises a sordid 'reality'.

Assembling time: shots, sequences and stories

In film and television, shots are combined to form *scenes* showing action taking place in the same location. These, in turn, are assembled to produce *sequences*, which form a self-contained segment, like a chapter in a book. Finally, sequences are put together to tell an overall *story*.

Joining shots together into larger units is known as *editing*, because, like the editing of the first draft of a novel or the first edition of a daily newspaper, the art is in looking at all the footage that has been shot and deciding what to keep, what to emphasise, what to throw away and how best to move between shots and from one scene to another. The overall speed and rhythm of a film or television programme play a key role in establishing its look and feel. Rock and pop videos, for example, tend to use brief shots and frequent rapid cuts, whereas soap operas typically have relatively long scenes and fewer cuts, and hold individual shots for longer. The first style conveys the dynamism and rapid turnover of rock culture, while the second supports the illusion of a fictional world that appears to move at more or less the same pace as everyday life.

Editing is also known as *cutting*, because traditional film stock has to be physically cut and joined together during editing. Editing is most often used to establish an unfolding sequence of events or argument, a technique known as *continuity editing*. A story (or, more usually, a particular episode within a story) may also be presented through *parallel editing*, where two separate but related sequences are intercut. This was common in early cinema series, such as *Perils of Pauline*, where shots of the heroine tied to a railway track, with the train getting closer and closer, would alternate with shots of the hero riding to the rescue. One variant of this idea is to use a *split screen*, where the two sides of the screen follow separate sequences of action taking place at the same time. In the documentary film of the celebrated rock festival, *Woodstock* (1967), for example, shots of performers on stage are matched with shots of the audience.

Juxtaposing images has a long history in art designed to make a political point. Take, for example, the etching entitled *At Five O'clock in the Morning* by George Grosz, an interwar German artist with strong socialist convictions. The top quarter shows labourers trudging to work across a bleak industrial landscape, while the rest of the frame is filled with fat businessmen in a room, drinking champagne, smoking cigars and fondling half-naked women. Making political points through juxtapositions was promoted most forcefully in film by the Soviet director Sergei Eisenstein, in his technique of *montage*. Whereas the continuity editing developed in mainstream Hollywood films strives to conceal the process of selection involved by making cuts as unobtrusive as possible, Eisenstein deliberately drew attention to them by presenting stark contrasts and abrupt shifts of viewpoint. The central scene in his most famous film, *Battleship Potemkin* (1925), shows unarmed demonstrators on a flight of steps, caught between soldiers advancing on them from the top and mounted Cossacks whipping and trampling them as they reach the bottom. At one point, a woman with a pram is hit near the top of the steps. The pram careers down the steps, passing dead and injured bodies, until it hits the bottom and overturns. The baby's arbitrary fate underlines the general sense of terror and helplessness that Eisenstein has already built up with rapid cutting and close-ups of screaming faces. It also reinforces the message that the authorities' reaction was indiscriminate and totally out of proportion to the threat posed. Often Eisenstein would underline his political points by presenting obvious comparisons, a practice many writers have criticised for its heavy-handedness. As one commentator noted, if a man 'is figuratively a horse's ass, pair him with a real one. If the purpose of a scene is to show people being killed like animals, cut from workers being massacred to an ox being slaughtered… This is the kind of montage that Eisenstein practiced' (Dick 1990: 67). These negative reactions have not stopped Eisenstein's techniques being widely adopted in contemporary advertising for household products, as well as for political parties and causes.

For example, ads for shampoo, a product that is almost entirely synthetic, may strive for associations of freshness and 'naturalness' by dissolving a shot of a girl's newly washed long hair into a shot of a waterfall in an idyllic setting.

Images and sounds

As we noted earlier, moving images almost never appear by themselves in the modern media. In the silent era, films were accompanied by music and the scenes were separated by brief explanatory captions (inter-titles) explaining the action or what was being said. Sometimes someone (known as a lecturer) would stand beside the screen offering a running commentary. With the arrival of the talkies at the end of the 1920s, commentary was integrated into the film's soundtrack, along with a musical score, sound effects and dialogue. Writing also frequently appears on both the cinema and television screens, in the form of the opening titles and the closing credits, the captions announcing the identity of speakers in documentary and current affairs programmes, and, in the case of foreign-language films which have not been dubbed, subtitles translating the gist of the dialogue.

It is the spoken word that most consistently links the moving image with the world of language. Speech is used in two main ways. First, someone who remains unseen by the viewer may talk over the images, explaining them or pointing to particular aspects. These *voice-overs* may either reproduce the role of the lecturer in the silent cinema, offering a voice-of-God commentary that seeks to direct the audience's look, or offer a more personalised testimony. The first presents itself as the voice of the disinterested and 'objective' observer of events and is typical of classical documentary forms. The second, which is avowedly 'subjective', offers a commentary closer to a diary than to an expert analysis.

These forms of commentary may or may not be combined with people in shot speaking directly to camera or to each other. Their speech may either be recorded at the same time as the footage was shot (*synchronised sound*) or dubbed in afterwards in a studio. Items using synchronised sound (*syncs*) are one of the main ways that television news bolsters its claims to immediacy and authenticity, since they suggest that the reporter is indeed there, 'on the spot', speaking directly to the viewer (or the anchorperson back in the studio) in their own, unedited words.

Summary: key points

- In this chapter we have introduced various terms and concepts used in the analysis of visual images.

- Those primarily concerned with the still photographic image were dealt with, concentrating initially on its iconicity, and then moving on to different kinds of shots, composition, colour and lighting. The relationship between images and words was also addressed.

- The quality of seeming to be realistic in visual media was examined. How digitalisation affects this quality was also discussed.

- Terms relating primarily to moving images were outlined, including those designating different kinds of shot, editing techniques, and the relationship between images and sounds.

- The origins of key technical conventions were traced to the new social experiences and ways of looking forged in the modern city. It was argued that recovering this history is a necessary step in developing a critical approach to image analysis that can unpack photography and film's claims to offer an unvarnished capture of 'reality'.

chapter ten

Interpreting Images

In chapter 9 we worked through a range of terms and concepts relevant to the study of both photo and moving images to provide you with a full repertoire of tools for analysing the use of visual images in modern communications media. We also encouraged you to be sceptical about any sweeping claims for the realism of such images, and sensitive to the ways in which visual media images create an illusion of veracity.

We now want to show how you can put some of these analytical tools into practice by way of two case studies. The first deals with one particular still photo image and its journalistic use in a British tabloid newspaper. A parallel analysis focuses on the use of moving images in a television news bulletin.

It is important that we point out two things about this chapter. The first is that our choice of news is deliberate: we want to offer two samples of image analysis that operate within the same overall field of media production. Second, we will not draw on all the concepts outlined in the previous chapter, but only on those relevant to the task at hand. All media analysis involves choosing which conceptual tools are the right ones to deploy.

Case study 1: everybody look what's going down

Before we begin our first case study, we should emphasise that the field of possible meanings that can be constructed for visual images, at the points of both production and reception, will be defined, at least loosely, by the particular genre, narrative and discourse in which they are deployed. These influences will lay down certain limits, channel certain images into certain functional applications and, initially at least, direct the viewer in a way immediately relevant to their specific properties. When the visual image is photographic, its iconic power often upholds the verbal meanings that are attached to it, in a news story or advert. It seems to provide an incontrovertible corroboration of their claims to truth. We shall have more to say about this when we come to apply the concept of *anchorage* to our case study.

It is also important to stress that the variable, yet relatively distinct fields of meaning in which photo images are used are also influenced by the social, economic, political and cultural contexts in which they are situated, contexts which are not fixed or permanent across time, but change and are modified by historical processes. In some ways, it is easier to recognise aesthetic conventions and technical devices in the cultural products and forms of previous periods – in a documentary film of World War II, for example, or in the photojournalism of early twentieth-century popular newspapers and magazines. Textual features constraining the past uses and meanings of visual images become clearer precisely because they have changed and are not as familiar and taken for granted as they were initially. Somewhat paradoxically, it can be harder for us now, in our changed circumstances and from our altered historical perspectives, to interpret visual images as they may have been understood in the past. While the formal or technical features of their construction may be more apparent to us, the contextual forces shaping that construction, the complex transactions occurring between social dynamics and media products, have now to be reconstructed by us in our changed conditions of cultural life.

In our first case study, we have chosen a tabloid news story that was published nearly 40 years ago, in 1970 (time of writing, 2007). This may suggest to you that it would be quite different to the form taken by tabloid news today. You could perhaps anticipate its narrative conventions, and use of a photo image to consolidate its central thematic message and meaning, showing up in the way we have suggested is often the case with news stories from earlier historical periods. Perhaps if we had gone further back this would be the case more obviously, but 40 years is a considerable span of time and we might well expect this particular distantiating effect of the passage of time to apply. We have chosen this particular story precisely because it does not apply. Instead, the overall contemporary quality is quite remarkable, while the strategic risk taken in the coupling of image and text appears to have a recent feel rather than seeming dated or outmoded. The news event, of course, is clearly of the time in which it occurred, as you will see, but its journalistic treatment seems closer to the present. So the use of this particular example for our case study emphasises a certain pattern of continuity across time, which for us is worth highlighting, especially when changes in news media conventions and approaches have in other respects been very considerable, across the same time span. With this in mind, we turn to our particular example, which is the photographic image used on the front page of a British tabloid newspaper, the *Daily Mirror*, on 5 May 1970.

We can begin our analysis with reference to the technical and compositional features we outlined in the previous chapter. First of all, the type of camera shot involved is, or appears to be, a mid-shot taken close to the action it depicts. It shows a man lying face down on a pathway and a woman kneeling in front of him. Other participants are clearly involved, but we only see their legs, or in the case of the figure on the right-hand side of the photo, legs and midriff. The two main participants are placed centrally within the composition. The shot places us as witnesses fairly close to the action, as if we were approaching it and looking across at what is happening from only a yard or so away from the two figures. This helps to draw us in to the photograph, for there is no intervening distance between us and the action in the image. Our observational space is immediate to the action; we are not removed from it or in a position where we can stand outside of what is happening, in a more detached or elevated position from what is taking place. Our position is instead equivalent to someone entering directly into the small local ambit of the scene. This is reinforced by the camera angle, which is neither at exactly the same level as the woman nor, presumably, the figures in the background. It is as if the photographer is beginning to crouch down as the photo is taken, so coming halfway between the two levels of view that would have been involved in the scene from the participants' positions within it. Photo composition and camera angle combine to impart a sense of intense concern and on-the-spot involvement that appear to guarantee the veracity of the image.

The photo image is spread horizontally across the whole of the middle of the front page. This further increases its heightened quality of immediacy and drama, an effect that would have been considerably foreshortened if it had been reduced in size or given less centrality on the page. This is indeed what happened with its use in other newspapers, such as *The Times* and the *Daily Express*. As we move from the visual evidence to the meaning given to this evidence, our sense of involvement in the action is consolidated by the enormous tragedy of the event. Three words in the three headlines of the news story confirm this: the two nouns 'tragedy' and 'death', and the passive verb 'killed', combine to make the meaning of the image starkly apparent. The figure lying prone on the pathway is not drunk, or playing the fool. He's not an actor in some street theatre production. He is dead; a young man cut down in his prime. This is the primary meaning given to the image, though the condition of giving meaning is entirely obscured by its reality effect, for the meaning seems to lie entirely in the tragic image itself. The meaning seems to be inherent in the dead body lying on the ground. It is as if the words in the headline are merely reinforcing the stark obviousness of the image's primary meaning – a killing has occurred, a dead body lies horizontally across the middle of the page. As with any killing, we immediately seek an explanation. We need to know the cause.

This leads us further into the news text. The dead body is that of a student, one of four who were killed by National Guardsmen at Kent State University in Ohio in May 1970. The headline at the bottom of the page tells us that he was one of four students 'killed in new demo on Cambodia'. While the reason for this political demonstration would have been readily apparent to a *Daily Mirror* reader at the time, now it needs to be put into its broader historical context. At this time, the USA was involved in a full-scale war in Vietnam. The war was being fought in support of the corrupt regime of South Vietnam and against communist North Vietnam and the Vietcong in the south of the country. This was the most significant manifestation of America's world mission against communism, and it was full of brutal consequences, including atrocities committed against unarmed civilians. Dissent against the war was voiced across Europe, with the largest political demonstrations of the 1960s in Britain being staged in opposition to US policy. In 1968, tens of thousands of students had marched through London to the US Embassy in Grosvenor Square to demand an immediate end to the war.[1] The war divided opinion in the USA, with the antiwar movement there being broadly supported. There had been many previous demonstrations against the war (and not only on university and college campuses), but when President Nixon announced a military incursion into Cambodia, this created a new and even bigger wave of student protest. The National Guard was called out in 16 states; students at 350 colleges went on strike; and two black students were shot at the African-American Jackson State College in Mississippi. The demonstration which took place at Kent State University on 4 May 1970 resulted in the deaths of the four white students

---

1   The media coverage of this demonstration was the object of an extended study in which one of us was centrally involved (see Halloran, Elliott and Murdock 1970; also Murdock 1973; Caute 1988). As mentioned in chapter 9, the overwhelmingly peaceful nature of the demonstration was ignored in favour of extravagant concentration on a tiny violent minority. Such concentration conformed to the pre-event coverage anticipating considerable violence on the part of those involved in the march. This remains a classic instance of self-fulfilling prophecy, with the media reporting not what happened but what they expected would happen.

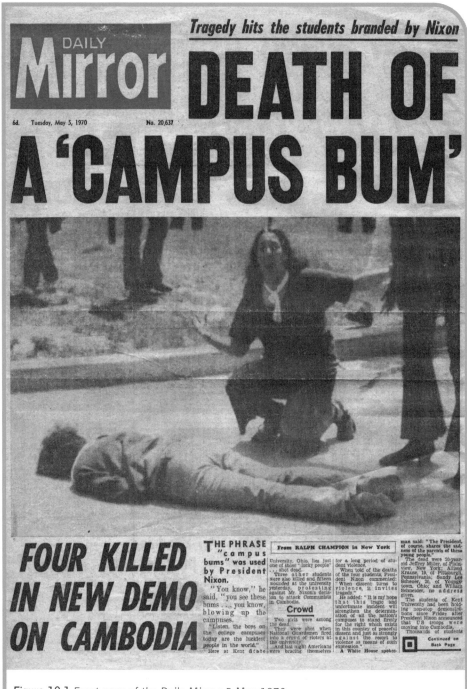

Figure 10.1 Front page of the Daily Mirror, 5 May 1970

Box 10.1

Death of a 'campus bum'

Four killed in new demo on Cambodia

From Ralph Champion in New York

The phrase "campus bums" was used by President Richard Nixon.
"You know", he said, "you see these bums ... blowing up the campuses.
"Listen, the boys on the college campuses today are the luckiest people in the world."
Here at Kent State University, Ohio, lies just one of those "lucky people" ... shot dead.
Three other students were also killed and fifteen wounded at the university yesterday, protesting against Mr. Nixon's decision to attack Communists in Cambodia.

Crowd
Two girls were among the dead.
They were shot when National Guardsmen shot into a crowd of rioters at the university.
And last night Americans were bracing themselves for a long period of student violence.
When told of the deaths of the four students, President Nixon commented: "When dissent turns to violence, it invites tragedy."
He added: "It is my hope that this tragic and unfortunate incident will strengthen the determination of all the nation's campuses to stand firmly for the right which exists in this country of peaceful dissent and just as strongly against the resort to violence as means of such expression."
A White House spokesman said: "The President, of course, shares the sadness of the parents of these young people."
The dead were 20-year-old Jeffrey Miller, of Plainview, New York; Allison Krause, 19, of Pittsburgh, Pennsylvania; Sandy Lee Sheuer, 20, of Youngstown, Ohio; and William Schneider, no address given.
The students of Kent University had been holding non-stop demonstrations since Friday after President Nixon announced that US troops were moving into Cambodia.
Thousands of students went on the rampage, burning down an officers' training centre.
National Guardsmen – America's Territorials – were called in to help police control them.
Three thousand students, defying a curfew and a ban on meetings, stormed on to the college football ground, and started to shout insults at the armed guardsmen.
At first the troopers and police retaliated by hurling teargas bombs. The students were driven backbut soon gathered again and hurled bottles and stones.
It was then that the firing started.

A senior officer claimed that the guardsmen opened fire after they were shot at by the snipers.

Wounded

Two National Guardsmen were wounded in the riot.

But a student said: "The guards just turned around and started firing into the crowd."

After the shooting, Mayor Leroy Satrom declared the emergency in Kent.

All phone and telegraph communications were cut off and cars were stopped from entering.

Frantic parents were unable to make telephone calls to get news of their sons and daughters.

The Kent violence is so far the worst of a series of student protests throughout America.

And last night, the National Student Association called for a shutdown of all universities in protest against American action in Cambodia.

In San Francisco, about 1,500 anti-war demonstrators stormed into the city hall and urged the city government to demand the impeachment of President Nixon for his war policy.

They were later removed from the hall by riot police.

already mentioned, and the wounding of nine others.[2] The war, then, was the broader tragedy in which the less grand-scale but still appalling tragedy of these student deaths was set.

The appalling nature of what has happened, leading to the death of Jeremy Miller, the unarmed student in the photograph, would be apparent enough if the image contained only his supine body on the ground, never to rise again of its own volition. But its awful meaning is hugely enhanced by the kneeling figure of the young woman, Mary Ann Vecchio, who is proclaiming her sense of outrage at what has happened. Her posture of supplication before his corpse almost seems to carry religious connotations, as if she were kneeling down in grief-stricken homage at the death of a holy martyr. It is this quality of the image that makes it so compelling, reinforcing that sense of drawing us in as witnesses to the event which we spoke of earlier. Her arms are outspread in a gesture of anguish. Compositionally, this imparts a sense of symmetry and completeness to the image. Her arms run in parallel with the line of the student's body, and this makes her gesture of unbelieving protestation at his death appear to complement the tragedy of the death itself, and so increase our own sense of absorption in the scene. The image is undoubtedly intense and powerful in its effects, and it seems we cannot help but become so absorbed, sharing in her sense of anguish and outrage. It is hardly surprising that the photograph became one of the most resonant and widely circulated images of the anti-Vietnam War movement. There are two different, but related problems with this.

---

2   For fuller accounts of the Kent State killings than we are able to provide here, see Bills 1988; Caputo 2005; Gordon 1995.

The first is that the image that was used on the front page of the *Mirror* was not the photograph as it was taken. A photography student at the university, John Filo, had borrowed a camera to take the photograph, which he shot from a distance of 30 feet. The sense of closeness was artificially created by the zoom lens he had attached to the camera. Our absorption in the image is at least partly dependent on this sense of closeness, but this sense is an illusion; the photograph was not taken from just a yard or so away. Following this is the motivation for the shot; we may think that the reason for taking the photograph was to record the death of the student, but as Filo said later: 'I didn't react visually. This girl came up and knelt over the body and let out a God-awful scream. That made me click the camera.' So the catalyst for the photograph was not the body lying on the ground but the unanticipated reaction of the woman as she knelt before it. That is not all, for the image as reproduced by the *Mirror* was severely cropped. In the picture taken by Filo, the full length of the student standing next to her on the right was included, as were the figures of a number of other students at different distances from them in the background. The picture was cropped on three sides. The legs of those nearest to the prostrate and kneeling figures remain somewhat untidily in the cropped version of the image. These could have been airbrushed out, but their partial inclusion arguably retains some sense of the confused melee accompanying the incident, and so enhances the quality of the photo image as documentary evidence. In a brief discussion of the cropping of this image, which went on to win a Pulitzer Prize, Harold Evans compared the different cropping that occurred in other newspapers' use of the photograph. *The Times*, as he put it, 'cropped too much for documentation and undersized for drama', whereas *The Express* 'scored on sizing but failed in headline words to create a single picture-headline unit' (Evans 1978: 231–2). The headline in *The Express* was 'Girls Shot Dead in Riot'. While this was true, the headline did not tally with the image, since the body lying flat on the ground is that of a male student. The comparisons made by Evans lead us to the second problem with the image.

This is the commonplace contrast between documentation and drama. As Evans notes, for evidence of what had happened the full frame of the image would be needed, whereas the cropped version located centre-page by the *Mirror* carries much greater emotive force. Its dramatic quality is considerably heightened by being cropped in the particular way preferred by the newspaper at the time. So which image is historically true? There is no easy answer to this question, because how the image works historically depends very much on how its past meanings are now approached. Those meanings do not reside in any single, permanent or fixed place.

It is certainly the case that a fuller sense of the surrounding context of this particular student's killing by the National Guard is given by the photograph as it was actually taken, though this in itself captured just one moment out of the many in all the action on campus that day. But how readers of the *Daily Mirror* would have responded to the highly effective picture-headline unit on the front page was heavily directed by the use of the cropped image. Its power as an image-text amalgam was dependent on this use, so its historical meaning in this respect may be said to lie in that use and the impact it had, and not in the full frame of the original photograph. We cannot know for certain what force this impact had, or the kind of response by contemporary readers as they picked up the paper from their doormat or lifted a copy of it from a shelf in a local newsagent's. We could try to interview *Mirror* readers of the period, of course, but such a method of retrospective questioning would be subject to at least some of the vicissitudes, fallibilities and foibles of human memory at an individual level, and the difficulties of combining them into anything approaching a consensus view on a collective level. There can be tremendous value in interviewing people about their media consumption in the past, as we hope to show in chapter 12, but trying to pinpoint the nature of impact for one particular image-text amalgam across a 40-year time span would be to work with a hugely inflated sense of investigative optimism.

Despite these difficulties, it would be hard to deny that the impact of the image-text combination would have been considerable, even to the relatively casual reader. Its impact remains powerful today, still creating that sense of drawing us in close to the tragedy of the event. In the contemporary context of the Vietnam War, and amidst other tales and images of the suffering and misery it caused, its impact is likely to have been even more powerful. After all, it was during this time that the story of the massacre of at least 20 civilians at My Lai in South Vietnam was emerging through the trial of Lieutenant William Calley. The details this revealed related to one of the most horrific experiences endured by the ordinary Vietnamese people caught up in the war. If the more dramatic quality of the cropped image in the *Mirror*'s front-page story helped to bring home to readers the full scale of what the war involved, in the West as well as in Vietnam and Cambodia, this surely reinforces the case for historical meaning and significance being said to lie in that version rather than the full-frame documentation of the original photograph. Yet it remains a question of historical approach and perspective, for when you are focusing primarily, or in any given instance, on campus protest in the 1960s and early 1970s, you may want to use the full-frame photograph as historical evidence; and when you are focusing primarily, or in any given instance, on coverage of such protest by the contemporary press and its influence on antiwar feeling, you would surely have to consider the cropped version of the image, as we have been doing here.

So these alternative approaches are not mutually incompatible. They relate to different parts of the same story. Historical evidence can have symbolic as well as more directly factual meanings, but without either set of meanings being necessarily more significant than the other. They are actually interdependent, with symbolic meanings enhancing the condition of factual details, and factual details enhancing the symbolic force of specific events or a whole chain of events, as in the case of a long war. To illustrate this, we can quote the historian Arthur Marwick, who wrote:

> The events of 4 May 1970 at Kent State stand out as the most horrific and the most appallingly wasteful of promising young life in all the sixties' turmoil in the United States, and as a terrible indictment of the evils of American society against which students and radicals had been continuously protesting.

> (Marwick 1998: 750–1)

When the symbolic meaning of a news image helps to make that sense of horror and waste stand out, and emphasises the indictment of those evils, its historical meaning and significance resides there just as much as in the factual details that were set on record in, say, the court martial of Lieutenant William Calley.

It is this historical sense and indictment, which Marwick's judgement supports, that leads us on to consider the secondary meaning of the *Mirror*'s lead story for 5 May 1970. We describe this meaning as secondary only because of the more direct impact of the news image and the symbolic force it carries, now and in different ways in the past, when it was encountered initially. The two main narrative threads of tragedy and irony in the news story are nevertheless closely interrelated, and the one to which we now turn becomes just as primary when the news text is read, following the more immediate apprehension of the image. Where the first thread is entirely visual in nature, the second is entirely word-based, but its importance for the whole is flagged up in the banner headline, 'Death of a "campus bum"'. The death is immediately confirmed by the visual image and the expression of horrified protest on the part of the female student, but how this death is to be interpreted, now it has been confirmed, is signalled in the second part of the headline, in the words 'campus bum'. Both narrative threads are echoed in the headline prop, sometimes known as a shoulder or kicker, which runs across the top of the page. The word 'tragedy' relates to and provides an immediate verdict on 'death' in the main headline, while the verb 'branded' relates to and provides an immediate verdict on President Nixon. This is taken up right at the start of the news text, in the lead paragraph that is printed in bold font. Nixon's glib dismissal of student protesters as 'bums', who should remember that they are 'the luckiest people in the world', is treated to withering irony in the news narrative, which is attributed to the newspaper's New York correspondent, Ralph Champion. For one of those 'lucky people' lies 'shot dead' on the ground in the centre-page image. This makes the newspaper's own response to the events at Kent State, and to Nixon's comments, abundantly clear.

The rhetorical use of irony in the main text then explains why, in the banner headline, the words 'campus bum' were placed in inverted commas. We have already dwelt at length on the enormous significance that can be attached to such small textual features as inverted commas (see chapter 8). Here, their use in the headline is vital for the newspaper's treatment of Nixon's insensitive, self-serving remarks. They set this treatment in narrative motion and convey a different sense of outrage at what is conveyed by the visual image. The news text which follows the subhead 'Crowd' simply adds further detail to both threads of the story, the stark factual details of the students killed contrasting with the mealy-mouthed expressions of regret from Nixon and the White House. The story continues on the back page of the newspaper, adding more information about what happened in the student protests and how the National Guardsmen retaliated by firing into the crowd that had gathered on the college football ground. The story concludes by adding news of a call by the National Student Association for a shutdown of all universities in protest against American action in Cambodia, and the occupation of the city hall in San Francisco by 1,500 antiwar demonstrators calling for Nixon's impeachment. These further contextual items of information help to create a sense of a bigger picture, but do not alter significantly the twofold thematic structure of the story, which is set up on the front page and, to all intents and purposes, fully played out there rather than in the continuing paragraphs on the back page.

The front-page section of the news story uses the rhetoric of the photo image to bolster the narrative twist that is given to it through the use of irony. The use of the word 'bum' renders the death of the student inconsequential for the President, for the negative sense of pejorative inferiority that had become attached in North America to such figures as hoboes and railroad bums in the economic depression of the 1930s was still strongly attached to the word at the time of this news story. The sense of social unimportance would have been readily understood in Britain as well – everyone knew that a 'bum' was equivalent to a no-good nonentity. That is why Nixon's use of the word was taken by the *Mirror* to be tantamount to a dismissal of the students' deaths as of no consequence, despite any formal assurances subsequently issued from the White House. This is the source of the irony about 'being lucky', and within that irony is entwined the connection between the President and the National Guard. It is this connection which is made in Neil Young's song 'Ohio':

> Tin soldiers and Nixon coming,
> We're finally on our own.
> This summer I hear the drumming
> Four dead in Ohio.

Of course, Nixon was not directly to blame for the students' deaths at either Jackson State College or Kent State University, but for many people he was just as implicated in these events as he was in the atrocities and massacres taking place in Vietnam. The *Mirror*'s lead story calls his credibility and sense of perspective (if not his veracity and honour) into serious doubt, and is clearly an indictment of the way student protests against the war were being handled. In addition, it would seem that the deployment and cropping of John Filo's photograph was intended to engage readers in feelings of sympathy for the students' deaths and thoughts of concern for the US curtailment of freedom of expression, which includes the right to engage in peaceful public demonstrations. Here we should remember that newspaper readers at the time would only have realised that the central picture had been cropped if they had bought other newspapers on the same day and compared their versions of the image with that in the *Daily Mirror*. It is true that this kind of comparison might have been made by looking at different newspapers in a local newsagent's, but given the intense pressures of time on most people's weekday mornings, such an exercise would have been unlikely. The sense that would have struck most readers would not have been of a manipulated and therefore potentially suspect image, but of a camera having captured the truth of a tragic event. It is this sense that remains fundamental to the ideology of the mechanically recorded visual image in modern culture.

Without the headline and its two auxiliaries, followed up by the initiating paragraphs in the story, the meaning to be attributed to the image would not be known. Without them, a large range of possible meanings could be inferred, yet there would be no way of knowing which should be preferred or singled out as the historically exact attribution. This is the importance of the concept of anchorage. Anchorage involves attempting to tie down the meaning of the image verbally, through headlines, captions and accompanying news text, so that the news image seems to belong naturally to the news text while simultaneously confirming it. The iconicity of the photographic sign (as we defined it in the preceding chapter) seems not to need this interpretive work, since it relies for its meaning on the sense that it is what it is – the image is the reality it shows – whereas, of course, the opposite is the case. The image has to be interpreted, its meaning made definite and apparently fixed, by the circumambient language and discourse of the news text. This is, we might add, another source of irony in this particular news story, but it is germane to most journalistic uses of images in print and broadcast news. It is through the way words anchor the meaning of images in this way that drama and documentation are brought together. The apparent split between them disappears in the mutually consolidating force of photo images and the discourse schema of any particular news story.

What we have tried to do in this analysis is to show how the news image works as a form of rhetoric. What seems to us particularly interesting in the case study we have chosen is the relationship set up between the iconic nature of the photo image and the thematic structure of the news text. The thematic structure depends on a single, but bitter narrative twist: those whom President Nixon regarded as inconsequential campus bums were exercising their legitimate right to protest against the war in Vietnam and Cambodia, as a result of which four of them are dead, another is paralysed and eight are wounded. The rhetorical effect of this twist, which is signalled in the two small punctuation marks around 'campus bum', relies directly on the harrowing expression on the face of the woman in the photograph. It would have nothing like the same effect without the iconic 'proof' of this image. The image, in turn, gains in rhetorical force as a consequence of the words – along with their composition and sequence – used at the start of the story. The authenticating 'rawness' of the semi-amateur photographic evidence seems to permit the licence of the textual irony, which generates various political meanings without undermining the status of the photograph as an apparently indisputable record of the event. There was a strategic risk in this. The crucial relationship set up between image and text may not have worked; what Harold Evans called its single picture-headline unit would not have existed as a unit, but would have fallen apart into its different component elements. If, for example, the irony of the text's thematic structure did not work or did not appear to be warranted, we would be left simply with an image without meaning, or with a potentially infinite number of meanings. Yet because the strategic risk in the discursive rhetoric of the story plays off, the irony involved seems to be directly supported by the stark, dramatic, incontrovertible evidence inherent in the iconic character of the photo image. The sense is the familiar one – pictures do not lie, whereas politicians do little else.

Our analysis reveals the way that manipulating the image and using the small linguistic device of inverted commas generates a huge imagined sense of excesses beyond the photo frame. It is through the relation between these excesses and the irony in the bold banner headline that the interpretive frame of the news story is established and the stage set for this tragic tale. Iconic visual sign and ironic thematic interpretation act together in rhetorical harmony.

Seeming to see

Words and images operate with a different relationship in television news bulletins and in newspapers, primarily because the visual images used on television are constantly shifting, sequentially ordered and narratively continuous. Their more 'lifelike' quality considerably enhances their iconic character and naturalistic appearance – the ways in which they appear to be unmediated depictions of reality. Generically, the manner in which news programmes are produced and visual images are woven into them operates with this 'seeming-to-be' effect. It is an effect at the forefront of television news production values. Because of this, spoken discourse in television news *seems* always to turn to the visual images for verification of what is said by the newsreader or news correspondent 'there at the scene'. For what images of particular events and situations seem to offer is the actual witnessing of reality. They seem to substantiate an objective record of what actually happened – or, on occasion, of what might actually *be* happening in live reporting from a designated news site. This, at least, is the productional aspiration. In many cases, what actually happened is in the past, and the reporting is, of necessity, having to catch up with the event, or rather the event as it has become a news event; but then the visualisation involved usually works to create a sense of the energy, alertness and urgency of the reporting process itself, 'allowing the personalised investment of a trust in the visible processes of inquiry, of the search for truth' (Corner 1995: 61). Visual images are used in these various ways to obliterate evidence of choice and selection, decision and motivation, in their production for television, regardless of whether these production factors are relatively long-term or spur-of-the-moment. The premium is always on the use of visual images to create the semblance of direct perception, on-the-spot witnessing, drawing the viewer in as apparent participant in the 'seeing' of 'what is going on'.

The task of image analysis is to turn this appearance of seeing inside out. In place of an emphasis on the iconicity and naturalism of the news image, analysis investigates the various ways in which visual images in television news are built up and formed into a constructed generic package. In view of this, it is important that you attend to the anchorage of the apparently self-evident meaning of visual news images in spoken commentary or text. The images are rarely sufficient in themselves, either in primary terms of what specifically they depict, or in secondary terms of conveying some abstract notion or explanation. What visual images mean as evidence, or points of reference and/or association, is generally not apparent until words have been used to interpret and evaluate them. Speech remains the main carrier of information in television news discourse, though, of course, it does not so much carry the information as produce it, in its actual utterance. What is seen on the screen is often a visualised version of this information or a visual backdrop to it. Nonetheless, the visual continues to have a general verificatory function in relation to the spoken discourse, even if its power to give primary definition to a particular event, situation or historical moment is less common. Visual images can certainly help to shape perception and meaning of what they depict, as through the various signifying effects we presented in the previous chapter, for example.

In order to see how this operates, we can adopt several different approaches within the same analytical framework. For the sake of convenience and concision, we want to introduce three such approaches here. While others could be outlined, and integrated into the framework of analysis, these seem to us the most immediately useful approaches in the analysis of visual images in television news, which is our concern in this and the following section.

We suggest that you begin with an examination of the technical codes involved in the construction of visual images. These were outlined in chapter 9. We put these forward as a starting point because they are closest to the process of news production itself, and to the intentions that motivate it, however routinised they may have become in practice. In this way, they are integral to the activity of broadcast journalism in that they are built into the habitual practices of news production. In particular, these techniques of camerawork and subsequent newsroom editing act to determine focus, angle, framing, composition, camera distance and movement, perspective and point of view, and the articulation of these visual framings into the news discourse as a whole. You need to see how these codes are manifest in any given sequence of images, as they are used in relation to the spoken news commentary that accompanies them. Following this initial, rather formal examination, you need to consider the ways they may (together) affect the meanings made for the viewer out of what is 'seen' in the visual images on display, there on the screen. Whether these meanings are actually taken up by viewers, in what manner and to what extent, is of course another matter. It is not as if this is unimportant, but rather that image analysis in this mode is concerned primarily with the construction of meaning in visual terms, and it would require a switch of analytic mode to begin addressing other aspects of the broader communication process involved in their transmission and reception.

Second, image analysis should proceed from technical codes to more substantive questions of signification, to an examination of how visual images work as signs or sign-vehicles. The particular signifying practices, and the orders or levels of signification, are what is in the analytic frame. This shifts our attention from denotation to connotation, from first to second and third orders of signification and representation, as these are inscribed in image formation, narrative and setting in verbal/visual news discourse, in ways that should be familiar to you from your work on specifically written forms of media communication (see chapters 6, 7 and 8). The technical codes inscribed in the composition and sequencing of visual footage, and the semiotic encoding of this footage as instances of media representation, are part and parcel of the same television product, and analysis needs in various ways to move between them, rather than dealing with one and then the other as if crossing between two entirely separate areas of consideration. The kinds of shots taken, or the editing of shots into continuity sequences, will inform the denotative and connotative production of meanings in the overall visual/verbal assemblage of TV news discourse.

Analytically moving between different orders of signification involves a progression of attention from the micrological elements of media 'texts' – in this case, the 'grammar' of certain visual news footage – to the macro-structural level to which the overall assemblage 'speaks' – in other words, the system of representation governing the social discourse in which any news topic is made to signify and make sense. So, in an often cited example, camera position in footage of scenes of industrial conflict can both articulate and reinforce the thematic structure organising the overall representational pull of the news coverage of such conflict. Specifically, placing the camera behind police lines in such conflict may make the camera operator feel more secure, but it is not going to help convey the perspective from the picket line. Analysis involves moving back and forth between the syntagmatic minutiae and the paradigmatic structures informing media discourse in any given case. It is a movement of attention from, as it were, the particular fibre, threads and stitching of a text in its various parts, to the complete canvas of the discourse of which its smaller elements are seen as constitutive. The concepts of cultural **code** and **intertextuality**, among others, are useful in enabling this alternation of analytical attention between textual elements and text, and between text and discourse.

A further way in which the construction of television news images has to be considered is in relation to the value of these images as items of commodity. Such value is not that of commodities in general, of course: the commodity value of a visual image is not the same as that of a bag of oven-ready chips or a packet of cotton buds. News footage, nevertheless, has commodity value in the sense that it is bought and sometimes resold, and is assessed, at least in part, for its ability to contribute to the maintenance and increase of audience ratings. What is visually woven into news bulletins, therefore, needs to be seen in the context of the struggle between television channels for the audience share that will justify their financial backing or continue to attract appropriate revenue from advertisers and sponsors. For this reason, an image or set of images that has high dramatic impact is likely to be preferred to those which adopt a more sensitive or nuanced perspective, for it is the former which is adjudged to best 'hook' an audience (who may be inherited by other programmes, later in the evening, on the same channel). The political economy of the image is just as significant as its iconographic resonances or its semiotic codes and conventions. It is significant because, among other reasons, it runs against the conception of news as producing or enhancing knowledge about the world. The commodity value of visual images in news production introduces a reverse emphasis to news as information, and yet it is news as information which is held up professionally as a quality indicative of the social responsibility of journalists and broadcasters. What this social responsibility is, or what it should consist of, in a political democracy is a source of considerable commentary and debate, but it is generally accepted that it has been eroded by the commodification of information and knowledge. The general ascendancy of market criteria in this sense has direct consequences for the production of news, leading to greater importance being placed on visually sensational or shocking images (as the saying cynically has it, 'if it bleeds it leads'), for example, or at the very least to a greater emphasis on the inclusion of images that appear stunning in terms of their sheer visuality, rather than in view of any specific informational content they may possess. Impact is not automatically synonymous with significance or nodal status, and so the contribution which news discourse may make in informing public citizens is thereby diminished. The value of news as entertainment is a threat to its value as information.

The extent to which this is broadly true should not be turned into facile denunciations or sweeping statements. We have to attend to its specific manifestations and effects, not only in themselves, but also in the degree to which they are stable and capable of being reiterated, in the character of a pattern. From there, we can attain a better assessment of the ways in which the market values and relations underpinning media production actually drive and direct news content and form, in what seem to be increasingly pervasive ways. The commodification of news as information has to be investigated empirically. It cannot be taken as an absolute yardstick of critical evaluation. The assumption that market share is the only accurate or abiding index of cultural or political significance can only lead to ham-fisted forms of analysis.

Case study 2: watching the news

In trawling for material that we could potentially use in our second case study in this chapter, we recorded half a dozen stories taken from rolling news on the British TV news service, BBC News 24. These recordings were made on a random basis on three adjacent dates. We then decided to take one particular story for two main reasons: firstly, because it involved a murder and so matched the topic of our analysis in the first case study; and secondly because, as the lead story in the 9 p.m. bulletin on Friday 16 June 2006, it was given prominence above all of the other stories featured. Flagged up before the lead story were trailers for stories dealing with Japan's campaign to bring back whaling and an alleged plot to hijack and crash a British Airways plane, followed by others featuring the Microsoft billionaire Bill Gates, the British tennis player Andy Murray, and the match between Argentina and Serbia in the 2006 World Cup. Two of these stories had clear implications for international politics. Trailing them obviously assigned them significance at the outset of the bulletin, but not as much as with the lead story. This concerned the killing of a gay man in a frenzied attack on Clapham Common. The two attackers were reported as receiving jail sentences of at least 29 years for the murder.

Aside from these factors, our choice was fairly arbitrary, and this seems to us appropriate given that our analysis is intended only as a sampler, a piece serving to indicate the kind of work involved if conducted on a larger scale. We could have conducted a similar analysis of any broadcast news story. In producing it we shall concentrate on the broadcast's visual track, since the images on the screen are our central concern in this chapter. In view of this, though, it is important to emphasise two points.

The first is a reminder that visual images in television always work in conjunction with other elements, in particular those of the audio tracks involving natural sound, music and spoken discourse. In TV news, for example, the spoken discourse is centred on the newsreader. In our sample news bulletin, two newsreaders are apparent in the studio, but the story involved begins and ends with only the male newsreader, Chris Lowe. The change to a female newsreader at the end of the story signifies progression to another story, in what is a staple device in the grammar of news language on television – a televisual equivalent, if you like, of section headings or chapter titles in written texts – whereas the movement between different shots and scenes within a story is the equivalent of paragraphs in written texts. Within a TV news story, the spoken discourse switches between the newsreaders, who provide the establishing factual details, and further contextual information and evaluative appraisal by reporters on location, chosen witnesses and those regarded as having expertise appropriate to the story, who may be interviewed in the studio or on screen from some other studio-based location. In the sample material we shall consider, the switches in spoken discourse are between Chris Lowe as the opening newsreader and 'on-the-spot' commentary by a BBC correspondent, which, in turn, lead to switches between voice-over commentary and spoken commentaries from other people involved in the event around which the story is built. In all these cases, as we shall see, the visual is drafted into the service of the spoken discourse.

The second point to note is that because our analysis is partial by design, given our circumscribed concern with the visual, you should always remember that in any more extensive project on television news, an analytical focus on visual images will need to be combined with attention to the other elements of communication in play, and techniques for dealing with these can be drawn from other chapters in this book (see, in particular, chapters 7, 8, 12 and 13). Even within our relatively confined examination of the use of visual images in a sample news text, we do not intend to consider them in isolation from other elements in news discourse, simply because in practice they do not operate in that way, separated from the anchorage of their preferred meanings in the words and forms of language chosen for assemblage in broadcast news. This is true of any element of a news text, whether we seek to understand the text as a whole through an investigation of its component parts or the value of those parts through the constructed unity of the text. To examine any part of a news text analytically is also simultaneously to develop an interpretation of it as a whole.

Bearing this in mind, we start with a breakdown of the news story we chose, dividing up attention in the way we shall suggest in chapter 13 also. In that chapter, our concern will be chiefly with political rhetoric in its *spoken* delivery, while here we reverse that concern by giving analytical priority to the *visual*, even though the mode of breaking down the television text into its constituent parts remains identical. We thus proceed from (1) identifying shot, which is mainly useful for reference purposes; to (2) a consideration of framing, which is concerned here mainly with the technical codes of television camerawork; to (3) attending to what substantively is in the scene, its visual composition as opposed (at least analytically) to the form given to it by the technical framing of the camerawork; and finally to (4) transcribing what is said by the source indicated by the person identified in the scene. This will be the first stage of your own analysis, where you need to note down the main details relevant to each category. It is on the basis of this that you will then elaborate your analysis by looking at how the details in each category interrelate, and there you should grasp a basic analytical point: interrelation, as a key focus of the analysis of anything, always denotes 'more ways than one'.

Guide to abbreviations:
BLC   bottom-left corner
BRC   bottom-right corner
CU   close-up
ECU   extra close-up
ELS   extra long shot
LH   left-hand
LS   long shot
MS   mid-shot
RH   right-hand

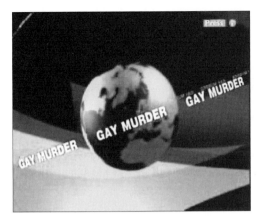

Shot 1. Fig 10.2

Framing Computer animation of BBC News 24 logo. **Scene** Black-and-red image of turning globe with 'gay murder' repeated strapline circling around it. **Soundtrack** BBC News signature tune.

Shot 2. Fig 10.3

Framing Computerised logo fades into LS of male newsreader, Chris Lowe. **Scene** Male newsreader Chris Lowe at desk, looking sideways across at standing female newsreader. Two images of murdered man in background. Male newsreader turns to face second camera frontally. **Soundtrack** Intro music fades.

Shot 3. Fig 10.4

Framing Cut to MS of male newsreader at desk. **Scene** Newsreader Chris Lowe in suit and tie sitting at desk, with two laptops open in front of him. Blown-up image of murdered man on screen behind him. Animated BBC News sign in BLC. Red box sign for BBC News 24 with 24-hour digital clock in BLC. This remains in all remaining shots. **Soundtrack** Hello, good evening to you. Two men who murdered a gay man in a homophobic assault have been told they will spend at least 28 years in jail. Thomas Pickford and Scott Walker kicked and punched **** to death on Clapham Common in South London in October last year. His family described the attacks as an outrage and an act of terrorism. Our correspondent Andy Tighe is at Clapham Common.

231

Shot 4. Fig 10.5

Framing Cut to CU of correspondent Andy Tighe shot from waist up. **Scene** Andy Tighe in suit and tie standing on Clapham Common during daylight hours. Written script appears, informing viewers that Andy Tighe is Home Affairs Correspondent. **Soundtrack** When **** was found by these two men they showed him no mercy. It was late at night; it was a completely unprovoked attack. The judge at the Old Bailey described it as an act of homophobic thuggery. But, because of a recent change in the law, it was thought that for the first time he was able to pass a stiffer sentence.

Shot 5. Fig 10.6

Framing Cut to video images shot from surveillance camera overhead. **Scene** street scene, looking down on figures walking on pavement. Young man with rucksack and suitcase on wheels on left, Thomas Pickford and Scott Walker walking on right side of pavement. **Soundtrack** Fired up and looking for trouble. On the right, Thomas Pickford and Scott Walker caught on CCTV. Within minutes they will find a young gay man they've never met before, and murder him.

Shot 6. Fig 10.7

Framing Cut to CS of photo of ****, moving to ECU of his face. **Scene** Scene of ****'s murder, with photo in memory of him leaning against tree surrounded by floral tributes. **Soundtrack** This was their victim, 24-year-old ****, a barman described by his friends as lovable and gentle. By the time his attackers had finished with him…

Shot 7. Fig 10.8

Framing Cut to scene of murder with photo removed, MS. **Scene** Bouquets lying on ground, BRC of screen, police tent covering murder spot in trees LH side of screen in middle distance. **Soundtrack** ...in a remote spot here on London's Clapham Common, he had 33 different injuries...

Shot 8. Fig 10.9

Framing Cut to MS of men walking across shot. **Scene** Murder scene marked off by blue-and-white police tape, with forensic experts walking behind tape. **Soundtrack** ...and his head was so badly disfigured his own family couldn't recognise him. Today they paid tribute to him.

Shot 9. Fig 10.10

Framing CU of mother. **Scene** Scene outside Old Bailey with **** surrounded by family and friends as she reads from prepared script. **Soundtrack** An intelligent, funny, hardworking and beautiful man, whose life was brutal... [slight hesitation] ...brutally and mercilessly punched and kicked from him, who fought for some hours to stay with us, and whose big, dancing feet left behind such gentle footprints on this earth.

Shot 10. Fig 10.11

Framing Cut to MS of Clapham Common. **Scene** View of trees and police crime tape, policeman walks behind tape to RH side of screen, woman walks from RH side to middle of screen, disappears behind tree. Pavement light and litter bin LH side of screen. **Soundtrack** The killing happened in a popular gay cruising area, close to the hostel where Pickford and Walker lived.

Shot 11. Fig 10.12

Framing Cut to one corner of crime scene. **Scene** Another view of crime scene, again marked by tape, policeman immediately in front of camera, another in middle distance walking towards him. **Soundtrack** After a night's drinking, they set out to find a gay man to attack.

Shot 12. Fig 10.13

Framing Cut to MS of two police tents. **Scene** Two policemen between two white-and-yellow tents, one sits down in chair. **Soundtrack** They screamed antigay insults…

Shot 13. Fig 10.14

Framing Cut to ELS of crime scene. **Scene** Scene looking down a path, police tents in far distance. **Soundtrack** ...as they beat **** to death.

Shot 14. Fig 10.15

Framing Cut to CU of still image of ****'s face, zoom in to ECU. **Scene** Black-and-white still image of ****'s face. **Soundtrack** One witness said they were kicking and jumping on him as if they were trying to kill an animal.

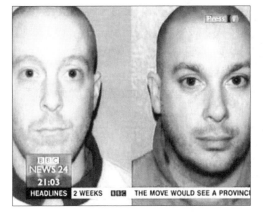

Shot 15. Fig 10.16

Framing Cut to CU of two murderers, zoom in to ECU. **Scene** Colour mugshot images of Pickford and Walker set side by side. **Soundtrack** Unemployed Pickford, who is 25, and Walker, a 33-year-old decorator, showed no emotion as they were jailed for life after admitting murder. They'll serve at least 28 years.

Shot 16. Fig 10.17

Framing Cut to MS outside Old Bailey. **Scene** Friends of **** milling about outside Old Bailey. **Soundtrack** At the Old Bailey today, ****'s friends heard that this minimal sentence was longer because it was a homophobic attack.

Shot 17. Fig 10.18

Framing Cut to CU of mother again. **Scene** **** surrounded by friends and family. **Soundtrack** **** wasn't the first man to be killed, or terrorised, or beaten, or humiliated, for being homosexual, or for being perceived to be homosexual. Tragically, he won't be the last man to suffer the consequences of the blight of homophobia which is endemic in this society.

Shot 18. Fig 10.19

Framing Cut to MS of two gay men. **Scene** Two gay men in T shirts and jeans, with arms around each other. Still shot taken from rear. Banner headline appears out of crowd in front of the two men: GAY HATE CRIME. Below appear in succession boxes with gay hate crime figures for 2003–4 and 2004–5. **Soundtrack** Gay hate crime appears to be rising. In the first year for which the Crown Prosecution Service has figures, there were 103 cases identified in England and Wales, with 73 convictions. From 2004 to 2005, there were 317 cases, resulting in 224 convictions.

Shot 19. Fig 10.20

Framing Cut to CU of man. **Scene** Ben Summerskill, spokesperson from Stonewall, in blue shirt and tie, inside TV studio. **Soundtrack** It's hardly surprising that this sort of thing takes place when in the wider public domain expressing homophobia, expressing prejudice against gay people, is still acceptable.

Shot 20. Fig 10.21

Framing Cut to MS of police on Clapham Common. **Scene** Police walking towards and left of camera, police caravan on left in middle distance. **Soundtrack** Since the killing the police have increased their patrols around the area…

Shot 21. Fig 10.22

Framing CU of floral tributes. **Scene** Image of flowers and teddy bear at scene of murder, along with card from two friends reading '****, we love you'.**Soundtrack** …and they want this case to show that antigay crimes will be investigated…

Shot 22. Fig 10.23

Framing Cut to MS of police. **Scene** Policemen walking away from crime scene. **Soundtrack** …rigorously, and prosecuted robustly.

Shot 23. Fig 10.24

Framing Cut to CU of Andy Tighe again. **Scene** Correspondent on location shot again from waist up. **Soundtrack** Of course homophobic violent crime isn't restricted just to London, but it's hard to know just how much of it there is, hard to quantify really because the police are not obliged to keep these kinds of figures. However, most people agree that it's most probably seriously under-reported, and that is something which the police and the Crown Prosecution Service hope they can reverse with today's successful prosecution.

Shot 24. Fig 10.25

Framing Cut to CU of female newsreader back in studio. **Scene** Black-and-white switch to female newsreader signals shift to another news story. **Soundtrack** Andy Tighe reporting there…

Opening steps

As this breakdown makes clear, the news story we have chosen begins with three shots that settle the viewer into a fresh round of rolling news and initiate the lead story. Whatever story has been given priority in this way has not attained this position by any natural process – it has been selected deliberately as a matter of editorial choice. There may be any number of specific reasons for this choice, but there is one general rule which runs through them all, and this is that the top story has been adjudged to carry sufficient significance to warrant that position. This is often made clear not only by the subsequent sequence, but also through the short trailers of main news items that are going to be covered, which are generally offered at the outset and at times given added emphasis by being announced against the attention-grabbing sound of the opening music that has been used to introduce the bulletin.

The selectivity and sequencing that is involved is only tacitly realised, of course, for any formal announcement of order, or the criteria by which this has been decided, would detract from the immediacy and vibrancy which television news producers and newsreaders strive to impart to their viewers, and might call into question the seeming-to-be effect of TV news and the naturalisation of its imaging. The immediate consequences of this are twofold: on the one hand, we have to infer what lay behind the choice from the topics or the salience of the stories themselves, but on the other, their dramatic presentation may work to conceal the fact of choice in the first place, since the rhetorical effect of this style of presentation is to direct attention away from such selection and towards the resounding impact of the stories as a quality substantively intrinsic to them. In the present case, the dramatic presentation of this opening story is achieved at the outset in three ways:

- Through being preceded by the pulse-quickening tempo of the programme's signature tune, which operates alongside the computer graphics in shot 1 to announce the imminence of a delivery of accounts dealing with affairs of national and international importance, or, more precisely, with affairs which are intended to be taken as having such import. This is signified by the visual sign of a turning globe.

- Through the repeated strapline circling the globe with the words 'gay murder' written on it. This directly links the words used to signify the topic of the lead story with the visual sign that connotes its vast, if not universal importance.

- Through the double images of the murdered man in the story presented in the background behind the two newsreaders. We do not need to be told the identity of the man. This can be readily inferred from the strapline in shot 2, leading into shot 3, where the image of ****'s face is given this dual presentation. Showing anything twice is clearly meant to emphasise its importance, and by instantly recognising this importance, the link between the man's image and the 'gay murder' of the news topic is clearly established. The sideways position of the newsreader Chris Lowe in shot 2 also stresses the link by inviting the eye to move from one background picture to the next, since this is the direction of his own crosswise view in this shot.

In turning to a full-frontal position at the start of shot 3, Chris Lowe visually announces his intention to address us, the viewers. This is confirmed immediately by his opening words of greeting. These are kept short in order not to detract from the importance of the lead story, as this has already been established. Indeed, he launches into the gist of the story without further ado. He speaks with the enlarged image of **** in the background just behind him. The scene in the whole of this shot is the BBC news studio, with Chris Lowe in mid-shot sitting behind his desk, a position that visually denotes the authority of what he is saying throughout the shot. The verbal dimension of this shot is interesting primarily for the way it establishes the temporal structure of the subsequent news narrative. This is based on a continual movement between past and present, between the time of the murder, in October 2005, and the time of the sentencing of the two murderers, in June 2006. The spoken discourse in shot 3 shifts back and forth between these two different, but obviously directly linked events of past and present, and certain intervening or forwardly projected points in time. These shifts are achieved by the varying tenses of individual verbs occurring in the following order: 'murdered' (past); 'have been told' (more recent past); 'will spend' (future); 'kicked and punched' (past); 'described' (more recent past); 'is' (present). This final opening shot thus achieves in compressed form the temporal framing of the story and signals this ahead of the subsequent narrative elaboration.

More implicitly, the final opening step of the news story prefigures the spatial movement that subsequently occurs between the scene of the murder, which is Clapham Common in south London, and the scene of the sentencing, the Old Bailey in north London. The immediate event that has led to the story is the sentencing, but because of the intervening period of time, this has to be connected to the murder itself. The moves made within the discourse schema of this television news story, between these two sites north and south of the Thames, present the immediate event within its broader context, which, as we have said, is as much temporal as spatial. Indeed, the story's temporal and spatial coordinates are continually inter-coded throughout the bulletin.

Dancing feet, gentle footprints

Shot 4 takes us from a descriptive studio account to direct, 'on-the-spot' reporting from a BBC reporter, whose journalistic expertise is dedicated to news events of this nature: a subhead bottom-screen announces Andy Tighe as the Home Affairs Correspondent. The scene is that of the murder, Clapham Common. It is important to begin here, for this is where 24-year-old **** died. And right from the start, the brutality of the attack on him and the motivation behind it are made clear. It was 'completely unprovoked' and 'they showed him no mercy', in what the Old Bailey judge described as 'an act of homophobic thuggery'. The 'recent change in the law' which is referred to in the soundtrack in shot 4 is Section 146 of the Criminal Justice Act 2003, which empowers courts to impose tougher sentences for offences motivated or aggravated by the victim's sexual orientation. But there is more than descriptive detail here. The move from shot 3 to shot 4 involves a step forwards in the evaluative weighting given to the representation of the murder, so bringing the discourse of the news into close alignment with the discourse of the law. Both openly acknowledge the murder as a social disgrace and clearly condemn it.

The relationship between the homophobia of Thomas Pickford and Scott Walker and the criminal act to which it led is reinforced in shot 5. This shows the somewhat blurry images of the two murderers taken by an overhead surveillance camera. Such images have become a conventional visual code for crime, for they are often used to provide what is taken as irrefutable evidence of wrongdoing of one kind or another, whether this is shoplifting, street vandalism or violent assault. The coded reference in these images is stridently emphasised by the words that open the shot: 'fired up and looking for trouble'. These emotively charged words separate Pickford and Walker from the innocent traveller who is also caught in the image sequence, with his rucksack and suitcase on wheels. He will go his own way almost immediately after the time these pictures were recorded. Pickford and Walker, however, will pick on 'a young gay man they've never met before, and murder him'. The contrast is stark, and is meant to be; the words chosen are unmistakable in their meaning, emphatic in their expression.

The cut to shot 6 takes us not only to the scene of the homophobic attack, which occurred 'within minutes' of the previous CCTV images shown in shot 5, but also, more poignantly, to the photo and flowers that have been laid there in remembrance of the murdered man. The camera emphasises the poignancy by focusing on the photograph and moving from close-up to extra close-up; as we are told by the voice-over commentary that this was the victim of the attack, we move closer to the image of his face in the photograph. The bouquets of flowers mourning his passing are visually concordant with the words 'lovable and gentle' that are used to describe his personality and disposition. Semiotically, this is an interesting shot because it involves an image within an image. The televisual image is fairly static, using only a slow zoom to give emphasis to the double visual articulation of the on-the-spot shot and the photo-image shot, taken on some occasion in the past, that has captured the face of **** and enabled it to be brought forward into this changed, commemorative present. The double articulation of the visual signs in shot 6 throws into stark relief the changed temporalities that are involved, for they bring together the hitherto separate periods of being alive and passing away, and they do so within the spatial location of the attack that led to ****'s time of dying. In these ways, the visual track supports the spoken discourse, for a sentence that begins in shot 6 starts with a temporal reference, and is broken with the cut to shot 7, which begins with a spatial reference – 'in a remote spot here on Clapham Common'. The image contained within this shot is a police tent covering the actual spot where **** was attacked by Pickford and Walker. The next reference in the soundtrack is to '33 different injuries', so that the visual and spoken tracks again act in concert with each other.

The final shot in this particular sequence from Clapham Common gives added stress to the horrific nature of ****'s injuries: 'his head was so badly disfigured his own family couldn't recognise him' (he was identified by his fingerprints). What is going on visually in the scene and its framing simply reinforces the seriousness of the crime before the voice-over commentary announces a move from this south London location to one north of the river, as we cut to the close-up shot 9. The mother's tribute is a statement of defiant love. It gives further emphasis to his gentleness and beauty, details supported at the time of his murder by *The Times*, which spoke of his sense of humour, love of singing and dancing, hatred of any confrontation and enjoyment of working in the buzz of a busy bar or club (*The Times*,

22 October 2005). Tellingly, this shot is left to act on its own behalf. There is no voice-over substitution for it, and it is contained within one single shot outside the Old Bailey, with **** supported by family and friends. Unlike the preceding and succeeding sequences, this shot is isolated as a stand-alone image, with its self-chosen words: an island of maternal devotion amid the turbulent waters of detail concerning her son's murder. It is to these that we return immediately in shots 10 to 13, as the story switches back to the spatial location of Clapham Common and the temporal occurrence of the attack. Both these references are supported by the images of the crime scene in mid- or extra long shot, which were recycled from the original reporting of the murder in October 2005.

Shots 14 and 15 are clearly paired. They both involve close-up images, with the camera moving into an extra close-up framing. They both involve images of faces. The first is that of ****, which we see as we are told that his attackers were seen by a witness 'kicking and jumping on him as if they were trying to kill an animal'. Shot 15 jumps to mugshots of the two murderers, who, we are told, 'showed no emotion as they were jailed for life'. This reference to their prison sentence enables the next shot to segue into a mid-shot of people milling about outside the law court where the sentence was passed, and this in turn provides the broader context for shot 17, which shows a mid-shot of ****'s mother again and enables her to make a more general statement about the homophobia that remains endemic in Britain. This move from the specific to the general is reinforced by the voice-over commentary in shot 18, for this supports what **** has said by referring to the rising incidence of gay hate crime and providing statistical figures from the Crown Prosecution Service to demonstrate this.

Following establishment of the thematic conception of the story, and the provision of supporting detail and evaluative comment from those with direct involvement in the event being reported, in this case ****, we then reach the stage in the familiar discourse schemas of news narrative where a statement is sought from an outside commentator, or from someone with appropriate expertise. In this case, it is a spokesperson from Stonewall, a campaign group founded in 1989 with the objective of opposing Section 28 of the Local Government Act, which was designed to prevent the apparent promotion of homosexuality in schools. Along with other successes that have secured greater equality of rights for lesbians and gay men, it has not only achieved the repeal of Section 28, but also continues to tackle homophobia and homophobic bullying in schools and places of work. Shot 19 provides a Stonewall representative with the right of final appraisal, so setting out the broader significance of ****'s brutal murder. Neatly attired, the chief executive of Stonewall, Ben Summerskill, adds further emphasis to the points made in shots 17 and 18, saying that what happened to **** on 14 October 2005 was a direct consequence of the continuing public acceptability of homophobic expression. The shot was taken inside the television studio, as is apparent from the background detail. This, on top of the previous two shots in which **** provides a mother's response to the killing and the sentences received by the two men involved, is an important departure from the reportorial norm of balance and objectivity. Its importance is such that we shall discuss it further in the next section.

Before we do this, it is useful to note how the story winds down during shots 20 to 24. We are taken back to Clapham Common and shown again the floral tributes, as the voice-over commentary informs us that the police have stepped up their patrols in the area and that the lesson of this case will not be ignored. The inclusion of a teddy bear among the flowers acts as a coded reference to ****'s gentleness and we can read the expression of love from two friends on one of the cards. The pathos involved in the visual track is countered by the information provided in the spoken track, of the intention to 'rigorously investigate' and 'robustly prosecute' any further incidence of antigay crime. These words are a summary of the post-sentencing response from Detective Chief Inspector Nick Scola, who led the investigation into the murder. If this is not confirmation enough that this item of broadcast news is not returning full circle, in shot 23 we switch back to the BBC correspondent, Andy Tighe, in which he says that despite the serious under-reporting of homophobic violent crime, there is a promise of this being reversed as a result of this successful prosecution. Before the shift back to the studio and the beginning of another item in the endless round of news stories, the BBC's treatment of the event ends on a note of cautious aspiration. In light of ****'s murder, anything beyond this would have been inappropriate; nevertheless, the ending is not unreservedly negative. It is reservedly optimistic.

Texts and pretexts

It may seem that the value of our two case studies is merely technical. We certainly hope to have shown that through the application of particular concepts, and the adoption of particular procedures for organising the data at hand, you can arrive at a better understanding of how visual images are deployed in the assemblage and structuring of news narrative. But you may well ask if arriving at such understanding constitutes the whole point and purpose of news analysis.

News analysis of any kind is rarely conducted entirely for its own sake. It is more commonly motivated by broader political concerns, such as how the generic features and particular constructions of news in the reporting of significant issues may shape public understandings, or whether media representations privilege the definitions, and hence interests, of specific individuals, institutions or social groups. These can be defined as 'so what?' questions, in which consideration is given to the broader political implications of the representative practices identified through textual analysis. To demonstrate what we mean, let us consider some 'so what?' questions presented by our two case studies.

Although opinions differ as to the degree of autonomy media professionals have in their work, much news analysis has identified a tendency for Western news discourse to replicate the definitions of the most powerful political and economic interests in society. Some identify a clear and direct link between media content and the structures of media ownership and the external influence of powerful elites (e.g. Edwards and Cromwell 2004; Klaehn 2005). Others see the hegemonic processes involved as more complex and unstable, although they too identify clear conservative ideological orientations in news content (e.g. Hall 1996: 20). The general view emerging from analytical work on news texts and news production since the mid 1970s is that, within mainstream print and broadcast journalism, there is little scope for taking or developing a more subversive or progressive position on any particular social or political issue.

In both the case studies presented in this chapter, there are details that seem to challenge, even confound, this general view. We can illustrate this with reference to how particular voices or positions are integrated in the two stories. Roland Barthes (1973: 150) once remarked that the appearance of social activists, trade unionists, peace demonstrators, representatives of social movements and other 'non-official' spokespeople in mainstream news discourse, represented nothing more than a 'small inoculation of acknowledged evil', the longer-term consequence of this being the maintenance of the existing social body. Just as the controlled dose of a disease in an inoculation strengthens the physical body against the disease, so the controlled dose of oppositional content in news strengthens the resistance of the 'dominant ideology' (Fiske 1987: 39, 290–1). In both case studies, 'non-official' sources are neither stigmatised nor marginalised. In no way are they regarded as an 'acknowledged evil' or subject to attempts to relegate them to this degraded status. In the *Daily Mirror* report, it is the antiwar demonstrators who are portrayed as the victims of illegitimate state violence, and although President Nixon is the main accessed voice in the report, his prominent quotation is patently intended to expose his cynicism and callousness. In the BBC News 24 report, a representative of the gay rights pressure group Stonewall is invited into the news room and his statement is assigned 'official' status. No sources are quoted to balance or rebut his opinions. This is significant because it shows how his role discursively conforms to what Bauman has identified as the 'legislator' function. This involves 'making authoritative statements which arbitrate in controversies of opinions and which select those opinions which, having been selected, become correct and binding' (Bauman 1987: 4). A further notable aspect of the BBC news item is the amount of broader information that is provided about levels of homophobic violence in society and the adequacy of police and government action. In our view, the journalist in this piece does a commendable job in identifying the broader issues and implications behind this particular personal tragedy.

We can only speculate as to why these two news items display these features. There are just as many dangers in drawing hard-and-fast conclusions about production practices from textual analysis as there are in extrapolating the specific dynamics of media reception. Nevertheless, a range of likely possibilities present themselves. In the first case, it is important to appreciate the particular editorial politics of the *Daily Mirror* and the broader politics of the Vietnam conflict at the time the shootings occurred. After World War II, the *Daily Mirror* repositioned itself politically as a left-of-centre newspaper, and through the 1950s, 1960s and 1970s became the dominant newspaper in the UK, selling 6 million copies a day at its peak (Horrie 2003). During this 'golden era', it gained considerable renown for its editorial quality and independence (e.g. the *Mirror* was one of the few national newspapers in Britain to oppose the British and French invasion of Suez in 1956). In this context, it is not surprising that the paper should criticise a Republican US President so trenchantly, particularly in connection with a foreign war that the paper opposed. More generally, it needs to be remembered that the British Government refused to participate in the Vietnam War; and although the British Prime Minister avoided public criticism of US foreign policy, this created a political climate that was more receptive to antiwar sentiments, and at an earlier stage in the conflict. By 1970, the antiwar movement in the UK was well organised, diverse and included a wide range of political and socially influential figures. All these factors combined to broaden the field of discourse in this paper, on this topic, at this time, so confirming Philip Schlesinger's observation that 'the relative openness and closure of media systems is strongly dependent upon divisions within the political classes' (1989: 302).

In relation to the second case study, the authority granted to the views of the Stonewall campaigner reveals the broader 'sphere of consensus' (Hallin 1986) that now exists about the evil of open, malevolent homophobia. (Of course, this is not to suggest that legal, official and social discrimination against gay and lesbian people does not exist in the UK. We are solely referring to acts of violence and open bigotry.) Coupled with the fact that the item was presented by a prestigious public broadcast organisation with a public service remit, the conditions were highly conducive for allowing a 'non-official' source to dominate the discourse.

Three points follow from these observations. First, we need to be mindful of the specific political, temporal and cultural contexts from which news texts emerge, and to be wary of being totalising and deterministic when describing the ideological and political proclivities of 'the media'. Second, we must always maintain perspective when doing so, as, on their own, these two case studies do not prove that most British news coverage was consistently critical of US foreign policy in Vietnam or that gay and lesbian issues are now always dealt with sensitively and respectfully. How representative these case studies are of broader trends in news reporting can only be established on the basis of longitudinal content analysis. Third, these examples show that taking a critical perspective on news reporting does not necessarily demand a negative appraisal of media performance. A critical approach to news analysis should be just as able to acknowledge examples of journalistic responsibility and perceptivity as it is in identifying areas of reportorial deficiency. There are occasions when news construction should be celebrated.

A summary of our analytical steps

We began our analysis of this item of broadcast news by breaking it down into its constituent parts, dividing details of the encoding process according to the familiar categories of shot and sequence, framing, scene and soundtrack. Even before this, though, we made some brief notes on the content and ranking of the news items announced at the head of the bulletin. We did this in order to gauge the relative importance attached to each item, and to gain some sense of the weight of significance being accorded to the news of the sentencing of gay victims' killers. Our rough working notes for the first half of the programme were as follows:

- Opening sequence: five stories flagged up (not including the lead story).

- 1st main story: Japan's bid to resume large-scale whaling.

- 2nd main story: plot to hijack BA plane.

- 3rd main story: less weighty story about Bill Gates taking more of a back seat at Microsoft.

- 4th and 5th stories: sports (tennis and football).

This then led into the computer animation of the BBC News 24 logo and the dramatic BBC News 24 signature tune as cues for the start of the lead story about ****.

From this broad mapping exercise, we then embarked on the identification of each shot in its sequential place in the news narrative. This was the first substantive stage of our analysis, and it was generally concerned with descriptively recording the major details involved in the visual and verbal composition of each shot. In the second stage of our analysis, we began to examine how the component elements in each separate category of the breakdown worked in combination with each other in the overall assemblage of the shot. This led on to the third stage of our analysis, where we explored the discursive interweaving of the different strands of the story in its general organisation. We considered how each shot succeeded its predecessor, building on what had come before and coming together in an overall combination, a cumulative narrative with a clearly recognisable start, middle section and end. Overall, our concern was with the story as an interlocking assemblage of discrete parts and as a completed whole.

In these ways, we moved from consideration of specific instances of signification and representation to consideration of their interrelated ordering. As we suggested earlier, this involves a shift from an initial examination of the small-scale grammar and syntax of the news as it has been constructed at the level of camera shot and spoken utterance, to a subsequent exploration of large-scale questions concerning, among other things, the voices heard and the degree of accreditation given to them. Most significantly, we were struck by the way in which this particular news story may be seen as contributing to a changing public discourse in which response to violent crime against people on the basis of their sexuality is articulated and represented. In view of the specific exercise at hand in the chapter, this question does not figure much in our discussion. In any broader attention to crime and the media to which our analysis might contribute, it would have to be given considerably greater scope.

Narratives involve movement between different times and places. In our analysis, we also attended to these and the movement between them. The temporal structure of the narrative in our example shifted between the time of the bulletin, as viewers were being addressed by the newsreader, journalist or accredited spokesperson; the time of ****'s murder, in October 2005; and the time of the sentencing of the two murderers, earlier in the day on which the story was broadcast. We looked at how these shifts across time were accomplished, in both the verbal and visual dimensions of the broadcast, and at how they were central to the construction of the narrative as a whole. There were similar, interlinked shifts across space, as for instance, between the news studio, the location of the journalist fronting the story, the scene of the murder, and the scene outside the court where the sentencing took place. We also attended to the way these spatial movements were inter-coded with different temporal references in the bulletin.

This leads us to one final point we would like to make in concluding this chapter. Everyone knows that the news is remarkably perishable. It arises each day in its usual dramatic fashion, full of emphatic insistence on the importance of its main stories, all eager, imperative and declarative of their up-to-the-moment, seemingly self-evident significance. Just as rapidly, news recedes from view, many of its items quickly forgotten, as each day brings a fresh tide of stories, erasing those that had previously clamoured for our attention. It is not always like this – certain stories are retained in individual memory, for myriad reasons, and a few also attain a high profile in public memory because of their lasting impact and implications – but perishable presence is usually the case. The second of our two case studies in this chapter brings together two major events from different points of time and relates them to a broader set of data built up over time, even as it emphasises the difficulty of giving quantitatively verifiable figures for information about antigay crime. This can be seen as a faint glimpse of something different, a pointer towards an alternative form of news discourse that would contribute to a more historically informed understanding of social process and change. For us, it shows how the general here-today gone-tomorrow pattern of news could be productively disturbed if news stories attempted to elaborate and refine their temporal structures, building up references across and between times to reveal longer-term links and continuities, changes and breaks. In this way, they would begin to challenge their own discourse of eternal evanescence.

Summary: key points

- This chapter has presented two case studies: the first dealt with the still photo image in tabloid journalism, and the second with the use of moving images in a television news bulletin.

- The two case studies draw on some of the terms and concepts introduced in chapter 9, and exemplify their use in practical media analysis.

- The analysis of news images and texts always involves 'so what?' questions, and in discussing these, we made the point that news studies need to attend to value questions as well as ideological questions.

- A step-by-step summary of how we went about the second case study was offered.

chapter eleven

Being an Observer

When we think of the mass media, we tend to think of artefacts: television programmes, newspapers, films or books. But these cultural products are made by people, and their significance lies in what people do with them. Newspapers are made by thousands of journalists interviewing people, covering stories, working in newsrooms and, even these days, having the occasional drink in the local wine bar. Television is not just flickering pictures on a screen, but a part of people's lives, commanding a great deal of their domestic leisure, small talk and family life. The production and consumption of mass media products are major concerns of communications research, and we have evolved a number of ways of investigating these processes. In this and the following two chapters, we shall be looking at the ways researchers gather material about such questions. We begin with the apparently simple matter of observation.

Why observation?

Research into the 'effects' of the mass media usually conjures up images of social surveys about people's attitudes to violence on television or the political views of different newspapers, for example. But many researchers argue that such surveys do not get to grips with the complexity of such attitudes. Indeed, they suggest that the very notion of 'attitudes' oversimplifies the contradictory, differentiated and variegated views of the world which lie beneath such seemingly simple questions. For that reason, they seek to use other methods to uncover these views. In particular, they have turned to qualitative methods, including observation.

Studying the production of mass communications also requires a variety of methodologies. Suppose we want to find out how a newspaper arrives at a policy view on education, and how that influences its choice and treatment of stories. We could do some kind of content analysis of the paper's education coverage. That would tell us about the character of its coverage, but not why or how it is produced in that form. Like all content analysis, it is circumstantial evidence. We could do a small-scale social survey of the newspaper's staff, with questions such as: 'Should all university students spend a year in the army?' But most of the staff probably have nothing to do with education news. In any case, how would we know how these views have an impact on coverage? And is it worth doing a survey of a few dozen people? Studies of media production almost inevitably rely on some form of observation of the production process, and because of the practical difficulties this entails, it is no surprise that the literature of such studies is the smallest of any branch of media research.

We have suggested above that observation is a form of qualitative research, different from quantitative research such as a survey. But, as discussed earlier in the book (see chapter 1), this distinction is not a rigid one, and it can be misleading. What is the difference between saying '33.7 per cent of *Daily Bugle* journalists thought hanging was too good for left-wing university lecturers', and saying 'the prevailing culture in the *Daily Bugle* newsroom encouraged a highly sceptical view of the political credentials of academics'? Is the first statement more precise than the second? Is it more reliable? As Hammersley (1992a: ch. 9) points out, qualitative studies are often full of terms like 'more', 'less', 'majority', 'sufficient', which are quantitative, but not numerical. In looking at observational methods, we shall be keeping this distinction, or its inadequacy, firmly in mind. We shall look in a moment in more detail at the types of observation research methods, and at the advantages and disadvantages of observation. Mason (1996: 61–3) usefully sets out, in general terms, why researchers turn to observational methods. The reasons include an ontological belief that interactions and behaviours, and the way people interpret them, are central to social life. The researcher may also have an epistemological concern that only natural or 'real-life' settings can reveal social reality, and that it has to be experienced and shared by the researcher for research accounts to have any validity and adequacy. The researcher may also believe that only observation can provide adequate complexity and richness of data, or even that it is more ethical to enter into the lives of those researched rather than remain aloof and distant from them.

Audience research, for example, has often been criticised for supplying only one-dimensional accounts of the relation of people to mass media. It may tell us how many sets are switched on, but not what people are doing while watching television, or even if they are watching at all. And if they are watching, are they attending to the programme seriously, or thinking about something else, eating dinner, making love (or perhaps all three)? Morley (1992: 175–7) notes that television audience research measures not viewing but something else: the presence of a switched-on set and a person in the same room. It assumes motivation to watch, and that the decision to do so is an individual one. It leaves unquestioned the context in which that choice has been made (who has access to the set, what else there is to do, where else there is to go in the house, and so on). As a consequence of these problems, he argues that

> the kind of research we need to do involves identifying and investigating all the differences behind the catch-all category of 'watching television'… we do need to focus on the complex ways in which television viewing is inextricably embedded in a whole range of everyday practices… We need to investigate television viewing…in its 'natural' setting.
>
> (ibid.: 177)

His own research has mainly involved interviews with families, and he is very sensitive to the need to remain aware of other, non-observational methods which put the viewing experience in social context.

The important thing is to be sure that the method you have chosen is adequate to the task; it may be one of several methods used complementarily. Most important is to recognise that observation is not an easy alternative to more quantitative, and apparently rigorously structured, forms of inquiry. Observation has its own rigour, and may not always be the best method for the problem at hand.

Observation, then, includes a range of research methods which allow direct access to the social behaviour being analysed. It may or may not offer advantages over other approaches, but it has been an important part of the armoury of communications research, and in this chapter we shall review what is involved in observational research. We shall look at the advantages and disadvantages, and also suggest some practical approaches to actually carrying out observational research.

Types of observational methods

The term observation actually disguises a number of different research approaches, which we can classify loosely as three broad types: simple observation, participant observation and ethnography.

Simple observation is being a 'fly on the wall'. The observer has no relationship with the processes or people being observed, who remain unaware of the researcher's activities. Certainly such studies are perfectly possible in communications. For example, you might be interested in cinema audiences – how they appear to choose which film to see in a multiplex, or how much time they pass in the foyer, spending money on drinks and confectionery. You could ask them questions about these things, or you could spend a few nights just hanging around and watching what people do (having obtained permission from the manager, of course). Or you might be interested in how people select books in a bookshop. Do they come in knowing what they want, or is there a large amount of browsing, or of impulse buying based on displays? Such behaviour can be observed inconspicuously, and can reveal patterns of activity which tell us a good deal about the everyday encounters of people with cultural institutions.

You will notice that both these examples are set in relatively public places; anybody could be 'hanging around' in such a place. One of the requirements for simple observation is that such free access is available to the research location, which is a 'natural' or real-life one. Experimental research involving, for example, the observation of controlled behaviour of children viewing television, perhaps in a social psychology laboratory, also fits the definition of 'simple observation' being discussed here, as we illustrate below.

The second form of observation is *participant observation*. This means that the researcher is taking part, to some degree, in the activities of the people being observed. The term participant observation is often used quite loosely to describe observation in which little participation actually takes place. Brief or occasional interaction with the people observed is not really participation. The term is more properly reserved for research in which the participation is necessary, and is intended to generate more information and data than would be possible without participation. It is clearly more likely that participant observation will be used in the study of consumption rather than production of mass communications. Apart from problems of access, few researchers have the skills or training to become a working member of a news team or production crew, though there are many less skilled occupations where participation is easily engineered. It would not take too much training to equip someone to become a popcorn salesperson or a bookshop cashier, to take the two examples given above.

Many participant observation studies of journalism have involved researchers actually playing a role related to their professional competence. In a study of an American metropolitan newspaper, the organisational sociologist Chris Argyris was concerned not just to produce a sociological account of how the newspaper worked but also to assist the newspaper in handling organisational change. Much of his account reads like that of a management consultant, undoubtedly a role which legitimated his presence and activities in the study, which took place over three years, afforded him an office in the newspaper's premises, permission to attend any meeting he felt necessary, and endless opportunity for unstructured observation (Argyris 1974). Few researchers receive such hospitality and cooperation, but few offer as much in return. At a lower level, there are a number of ways in which the researcher can offer some token of reciprocity to justify their intrusion into the life of the observed. In a study of crime reporting in Canadian newspapers, one of the research team was of Chinese origin and was on occasion called on to act as a Chinese–English interpreter, while the team as a whole was invited to offer its criminological expertise as a resource for the journalists being studied (Ericson, Bararnek and Chan 1987: 90–1).

Some observation studies have been conducted by researchers who have professional credentials in the fields they are studying. Former journalists who have undertaken academic research can use their familiarity with people, jargon and practices to sell both themselves and the credibility of the research task. Marjorie Ferguson, a Canadian media sociologist who was for many years a magazine journalist, conducted a study of women's magazines in the UK in the 1970s. She notes that 'my previous participation in their [the magazines] production…conferred advantages as well as applied restraints. It facilitated access to informants at all levels of hierarchy…while familiarity with women's magazine language, legend, and history, added to understanding, analysis, and interpretation' (Ferguson 1983: 217). The distinguished British journalist Alastair Hetherington, who edited *The Guardian* for nearly 20 years and was also a controller of BBC Scotland, later conducted a study of national news media. The detailed, blow-by-blow account he is able to construct of news production in the major television and newspaper newsrooms undoubtedly results from the quite exceptional access he was able to obtain as a senior and respected professional (Hetherington 1985). We will return below to some of the trade-offs between participation and observation that need to be considered in this kind of research.

The third form of observation is *ethnography*. This is a term that has lost much of the precision it may once have had. It is often used as a diffuse description of any qualitative research involving extended observation, or indeed interviewing, over a period of time. Ethnography has been defined as a 'research process in which the anthropologist closely observes, records, and engages in the daily life of another culture' (Marcus and Fischer 1986: 18). It is probably rare that mass communications research matches this definition entirely, not least because not much of such research is conducted by anthropologists (more's the pity). As Nightingale has noted, the term is probably used more often as a badge of allegiance to a particular style of analysis. It 'possesses connotations which include cultural, community-based, empirical, and phenomenal', which afford a legitimisation to the research (Nightingale 1989: 55–6).

Nonetheless, the claim to ethnographic status does remind us of the deep roots in anthropology which nourish observational methods. First and foremost, these come from classic anthropology. The Polish-born researcher, Bronislaw Malinowski, planted many of the seeds which flourished as the great bloom of British anthropology in the first half of the twentieth century. For him, the new science was the study of 'exotic peoples and outlandish cultures', a description perhaps readily transported to many a newsroom or television studio, if not to the average viewer's living room (Malinowski 1944: 15). Just as importantly, Malinowski, who was trained in mathematics and the physical sciences, stressed the methodological rigour and attention to detail at the heart of the anthropologist's work; and, like Max Weber in sociology, he emphasised the need for interpretation of first-hand experience shared with the peoples studied, allowing ethnology, as he termed it, 'a new vision of savage humanity' (Malinowski 1922: xv). We shall see later in this chapter how often Malinowski's strictures on methods find ready echoes in the practicalities of observational communications research.

The second and more immediate root for observational studies lies in the soil of Chicago sociology in the interwar years. Robert Park, one of the founding fathers of American sociology, had himself been a newspaper reporter in the last decades of the nineteenth century, before embarking on an academic career. His own work, and that of many others in the 'Chicago school', stressed an interpretive understanding of urban life, obtained by what Park referred to as 'nosing around', a task he felt was best undertaken by those who had mastered the 'art of looking' (Lindner 1996: 81). Park would often just walk around the city with his students, getting them to observe urban life and 'get the feel' for what was going on. The art, of course, and no less the science, is knowing what to do with these observations once obtained.

Without dwelling on the precise definition of ethnography, this chapter describes participant and non-participant forms of observation as a tool in researching communications.

Structured experimental observation

Most of the observation methods described in this chapter take place in natural settings – the people observed are doing whatever they would be doing anyway. But one tradition of observation, with a major role in the development of communications research, derives from experimental psychology and involves the highly structured observation of behaviour in controlled 'laboratory' settings. These 'experimental' methods seek to achieve the tight discipline over 'variables' which obtains in experimental methods in the natural sciences, and thus to arrive at reliable and valid measures of the relationship between communication sources and effects on behaviour.

Laboratory studies of this kind have been especially significant in the study of the social effects of television violence. Many of the broader and vaguer generalisations about arousal, desensitisation, imitation, and so on, associated with this literature derive from laboratory experiments, often with children. A classic example is work by the social learning theorist Albert Bandura. In one of his studies he showed three groups of children a film of an adult pummelling and punching an inflatable 'bobo doll'. One group (the 'control group') just saw the film; a second group saw the adult being rewarded for his actions by a second adult; and a third group saw the offender being chastised by a second adult for his unwarranted aggression. The children were then observed, individually, in a playroom which contained a number of toys, among them a bobo doll and a mallet. The third group showed far less aggression to the doll than the other two (Bandura 1965).

From this work, and other studies like it, lessons are drawn about the impact of violent media material on children. The difficulties of such deductions are obvious. First, the situation observed is a highly unnatural one, unlikely to be reflected in the 'real world'. Second, the behaviour observed is immediate. There are few opportunities for discovering the more diverse and gradual or incremental consequences in which we might be interested. Third, often unwarranted extrapolations are made from the observed and controlled behaviour (bashing the bobo doll) to other, more familiar behaviour (mugging old ladies in the street). All these difficulties render such studies liable to heavy criticism, and their 'positivism', 'behaviourism' and 'empiricism' have all increasingly marginalised their impact in mainstream communications research in recent years (see chapter 1).

Nonetheless, it is important to recognise that such controlled observation will be an essential tool for the communication researcher if properly used and interpreted (and, not least, if conducted ethically – see chapter 15). It is the very artificiality and control which are, for the experimental observer, the virtues of this method. As Bandura argued: 'the impact of television can be isolated and measured precisely only when parental influences are removed and the children are given the instruments they need to reproduce behaviour they have seen on television. These are the conditions we achieved in the laboratory' (Bandura and Walters 1963: 49).

For example, suppose we wanted to study how gender differences affect the way teenagers use computer games. We could ask a sample about their use. But would their answers be reliable? And could they tell the researcher about what they are doing when their attention is, by definition, applied to playing the game, not to observing their own behaviour? We could select a sample and observe them, one by one, playing at home in 'natural' settings. This would be extremely laborious, however, and could we be sure we were examining the same processes in each case? How would we 'control' for other influences – distractions, parental intrusion, bedroom topology, the researcher's presence? We could, however, set up a computer in a psychology laboratory and observe a sample of teenagers (whose precise ages, computer experience, other leisure interests, etc. we could document with brief questionnaires) to time their attention span, observe their body language, and so on, so that we could see very precisely how variations in use might correlate with variations in other characteristics. Of course, the laboratory is not the bedroom (except for the occasional work-obsessed psychologist), but the data would be far from meaningless.

The feminist critique

We have noted that one of the presumed advantages of observation is that it overcomes the limitations of quantitative methodologies. Some writers from within the feminist tradition have emphasised the particular benefits this creates for researchers who feel those methodologies have an inherent patriarchal bias. This, of course, is an argument developed within social research more generally, but it can have particular applicability to the production and consumption of cultural forms and expression.

One argument in this context is that social research methodologies lend themselves to making the masculine view of social life appear natural, as though it is the view of everybody, male and female alike. Since social research has been devised and developed largely by men, it is suggested, its primary concerns and methods are those of men, their gendered nature concealed in the presumption that no alternative exists. By contrast, feminist researchers stress the importance of everyday experience. They emphasise that those who are researched are themselves subjects, not merely objects of research, and they pay particular attention to their subjectivity.

That assertion, of course, chimes with the objectives of much observational research, and indeed with the axioms developed many decades ago by Malinowski and others like him. But such classic anthropology stressed what Malinowski (1922) called the enormous distance between the 'brute material of information' (i.e. the observations and statements in the 'kaleidoscope of tribal life') and the 'final authoritative presentation of the results'. Feminist researchers are, by contrast, insisting on the extent to which researchers and researched inhabit the same universe of discourse and are in a relationship which is a fact of the research. 'Taking the standpoint of women means recognising that as inquirers we are thereby brought into determinate relations with those whose experiences we intend to express' (Smith 1987: 111). They are also drawing attention to the framework within which observed worlds are understood. For example, many such writers note that in examining workplace situations, sociologists have adopted a definition of work which excludes much of the work done by women, notably in the home. 'Expanding the concept of work for our purposes requires its remaking in more ample and generous form' (ibid.: 165). Thus a study of television production which sought to understand the motives and concerns of the producers would need to look beyond the studio, to the continuity of the communicators' lives outside the workplace defined by paid employment. A study of television viewing would need to look into how family dynamics played a part in decisions about what and when to watch, and how and by whom those decisions were exercised.

It might, of course, be argued that such sensitivity to motive and meaning, and indeed to the wider context of production and consumption of culture, does not require a feminist rewriting of the canons of social research – a counter-argument developed by Hammersley (1992b). There is, in any case, as Williams points out, no single feminist position on ethnography, though the emphasis on the shared experience of researcher and researched tends to be a common theme (Williams 1993). However, there can be no doubt that the feminist critique has played its part in underlining that sensitivity, and in promoting a greater attention to the potential of ethnographic and observational studies in communications research, as in other fields of inquiry.

Advantages of observational methods

What, then, can observation offer as a research technique that makes it a valuable addition to the communication researcher's toolbox? In listing these advantages we shall also assess any inherent dangers.

Subjective understanding

In observing behaviour, we can assess what the people observed understand by what they are doing. Rather than just knowing how many times the television was on in a given week, we can see who is watching and how they respond to the programmes they view. Similarly, if we want to find out about the motives and ideas that propel a news team to cover a story in a particular way, we can get a lot more from watching them at work, and eavesdropping on their discussions, than we could from asking them retrospectively to describe their work, or even from content analysis of the outcome.

The sociologist Philip Schlesinger points out that one of the benefits of this direct access to the understanding of those involved in media production is that it might dispel any undue resort to 'conspiracy theories' in describing news production. In reviewing his own studies of the BBC in a period when coverage of Northern Ireland was much debated, he recalls that some commentators felt the corporation's output could be explained by the presence of an 'Ulster mafia' in the Northern Ireland newsroom. His own observations produced an account far more rooted in newsroom routines and corporate culture than in any such intentional manipulation (Schlesinger 1980: 363–4).

On the other hand, as we shall discuss below, if we become too drawn into the view of the world constructed by those we are studying, it may be that we lose distance and analytical detachment. It becomes impossible to arrive at any explanation of the experiences and motives of those we observe other than those they express themselves. Some would argue that this is a good thing, since it allows the 'subjects to speak', rather than the researcher speaking on their behalf. However, it is also seen by many as a problem which restricts the analytical capacity of the researcher and produces descriptions rather than explanations. We shall return to this difficulty in looking at the disadvantages of observation below. Schlesinger describes this process as 'captivation' and the escape from it as 'disengagement', and in Box 11.1 you will find a brief account by him of the risks this entails.

Box 11.1

The process whereby I got under the BBC's skin was also one whereby it got under mine. There was a time when it was exceedingly difficult to detach oneself from the persuasiveness of corporate ideology. The process whereby I arrived at this point may usefully be labelled 'captivation'; the gradual retreat I call 'disengagement'. This experience is typical in ethnographic research.

In many respects a high degree of personal involvement in the field being observed is desirable. It enables one to penetrate a given culture more thoroughly. I shared the excitements of bulletin production, the gossip about promotion and private lives, the overall sense of being in a charismatic organisation exposed to the political winds. There came a time when people on the desk would make 'serious' jokes about my being there for so long that I knew the job better than they did. To 'work' through the newsday shifts, eat, drink, and talk with the newsmen brought me quite close to some in personal sympathies. While I was not a participant in the process of making the news, nor was I eventually just an observer.

The research style adopted meshed so well with the way in which corporate identity was expressed on an individual level that eventually I had the somewhat vertiginous realisation that my own commitments and convictions were in the process of becoming thoroughly submerged. In essence, I became partially socialised, and this explains why at one point it became so difficult to generate problems for investigation. While the kind of rapport established was essential for an effective analysis, it went beyond necessary good relations and began to exact a certain sociological price. [...] When the fieldwork first began the BBC had just been assailed by the British Government for screening 'The Question of Ulster', and a debate was under way concerning the censorship of news from Northern Ireland. I realised that this was of importance, but certainly had no strategy for investigating the BBC's handling of Northern Ireland coverage, other than wishing to talk to people about it. Eventually, in 1975–76, I began to see more clearly how Northern Ireland was a crucial illustration of the BBC's complex relationship to the State. In 1972, I simply saw it as a potential talking point.

In fact, it proved to be no real talking point at all. I did touch on it in a number of interviews, and even collected some field material germane to the question of censorship – reporters' opinions, the ground rules for Northern Ireland coverage. But quite rapidly it ceased to be a matter for investigation.

[...]

When I came to write my thesis...Northern Ireland was discussed in a dozen or so pages at the end of a general chapter on impartiality. I certainly raised the issue of censorship but my views were very equivocal, and I showed no full appreciation of the way in which constraints actually operated. Captivation, therefore, produced a kind of suppression effect, a self-censorship *malgré soi.*

[...]

Disengagement from the field material only really began after completion of the second draft of the thesis. Integral to this process was the gradual reassertion of the primacy of sociological concerns. The main effort of simply decoding a journalistic setting was in the past; it was now possible to address the material I had gathered more theoretically. My own sociological interests had shifted from the micro to the macro level, and from more phenomenological to more structural concerns. Having a job in a sociology department was in sharp contrast with the intellectual isolation of writing a PhD. The rapid growth of academic work on news also forced my attention in new directions and reminded me of older concerns which had become more peripheral while in the field.

(Schlesinger 1980: 353–5)

Being there: seeing the unseen

Malinowski pointed out that 'there is a series of phenomena of great importance which cannot possibly be recorded by questioning or computing documents, but have to be observed in their full actuality' (Malinowski 1922: 18). He called such phenomena 'the imponderabilia of everyday life'. It is these 'imponderabilia' to which observation pays particular attention. If we ask someone what television programmes they always watch, or how much time they spend reading the newspaper, they may give us a thoughtful and honest response. But most people do not reflect on these activities very much, and are unlikely to know in precise detail about their media-consumption behaviour. Of course, it may be that their impressions, even if not literally accurate, are more important than a behavioural account in constructing a full analytical explanation. But the advantage of direct observation is that it gives us an opportunity to produce an independent assessment of these claims, informed by the rigour and discipline the researcher brings to the observation process.

Another aspect of this advantage is that, unlike audience research, for example, we can have access to the meanings deployed by people in consuming broadcasting, since we observe them in 'natural settings'. Of course, observational studies need not necessarily take place in such settings; as we have seen, experimental studies using psychology laboratories are expressly designed to be 'unnatural' so that as many 'variables' as possible can be controlled. But the observational styles we are discussing here observe communications behaviour in the places and with the people we would 'normally' expect. As Ang argues, 'ethnographic knowledge can provide us with much more profound "feedback", because it can uncover the plural and contradictory meanings hidden behind the catch-all measure of "what the audience wants"' (Ang 1991: 169).

An example is a study by Bausinger of family television viewing. The author describes a family he observed in which television viewing on some occasions involves the husband coming home in a temper and switching on the set in sullen silence to convey not a desire to watch television but a wish just to 'switch off' from all contact. At other times the mother joins her son to watch sport, not because she is interested in the programme but as a gesture of fondness and maternal involvement (Bausinger 1984). Quite obviously, these complex meanings would not be accessible to any other form of research than observation. It could be claimed, of course, that the presence of the observer might mute, or even inhibit entirely, such behaviour. Equally, an interview study might claim that people are perfectly capable of explaining such variety of meaning to a researcher, and their mature reflections may be more useful than the possibly unrepresentative instances accidentally witnessed by the researcher. As always, no advantage of a given research method is without its complementary disadvantage.

Immediacy

The strongest claim made by observation studies is about being there – actually witnessing the events or processes being researched, rather than being dependent on second-hand indicators such as a survey questionnaire, a recording or the frailties of memory. There is no time lag between the event happening and the researcher's access to it. So, instead of saying to a film director, 'How do you usually deal with child actors?' we can witness, as it happens, the unholy mix of cajoling, bullying and controlled manipulation which produces prodigious performances.

It is sometimes suggested that this is especially important in researching the production of communications, since this is a creative process in which the spurs and actions which lead to the finished product are often fleeting and unrepeatable. Of course, what the researcher is trying to discern is precisely the routine and pattern that lies behind this apparently ephemeral and protean activity. Nonetheless, given the particularity of cultural production, being there has undoubted advantages. Similarly, cultural consumption, say of music in a disco, will have a somewhat different impact on the researcher after several hours' sweaty fieldwork in the dark than if solely uncovered from reflections on events in the cold light of morning. The complete researcher, of course, will employ both sorts of data collection.

A further advantage of immediacy is that the experience is observed in the round. In a study of television viewing among Venezuelan families, Barrios notes that the researcher was able to 'observe family members' behaviour not only around the television set but in other moments of family life'. Being there meant that verbal and non-verbal behaviour ('body position, togetherness, interruptions, parallel activities') could all be observed as they happened (Barrios 1988: 57). For example, we can see how television viewing becomes part of what Lull refers to as 'rituals' which extend the usual rules and practices of family life (Lull 1988: 238). In the Venezuelan study, the watching of telenovelas (Latin American soap operas) became the focus of a 'sacred time' which ordered the day's domestic schedule.

Grounded research

Observational studies allow a flexibility of approach which permits researchers to modify their assumptions as they go along. More formally, this means that hypotheses can flow from the research, perhaps to be tested by complementary methods, or that hypotheses arising from the research can be tested while continuing the research, by reformulating the research plan as it progresses. It would be impossible to rewrite a questionnaire in the midst of conducting a survey because the first 200 interviews had revealed a couple of irrelevant questions; that is what pilot studies are for. But observation produces a continuous stream of data which is at one and the same time a body of findings and a renewed set of hypotheses.

An example of this arose in a study of journalism in Nigerian television (Golding and Elliott 1979). At first, the researchers focused on the powerful influences of instructions issued from the then military headquarters of the government, which were, not surprisingly, accorded considerable attention in the state-run broadcasting station. The researchers' attention was on the press releases received and their broad impact on news selection and construction. But it soon became apparent that in a number of ingenious and only semi-deliberate ways, even these forceful external interventions were being incorporated into news production routines like any other news sources. The focus turned to the editorial process, and to its similarities with, rather than differences from, news production in the broadcasting organisations of liberal democracies in Western Europe.

Two further advantages are suggested for the flexible, dialectic or grounded character of observation. First, the unusual can be understood in the context of the routine. By considering how observed practices fit into a range of like and unlike activities, the researcher can obtain some perspective on the more uncharacteristic examples. In a study of a Midwestern television newsroom in the USA, Berkowitz (1992) describes what he calls the 'what-a-story' syndrome. During a six-week observation spell in the newsroom, he took particular interest in a story about a jet which crashed into the lobby of a hotel near the local airport. He remarks that his extended stay 'allowed me to put the what-a-story into the context of the station's everyday routine. It also helped highlight the transition back to everyday news-work, a transition guided by newsworkers' negotiations over a period of several days' (ibid.: 85).

Second, the flexibility and dialectic character of observational research allow it to make a more forceful intervention into policy debate. Ang suggests that there is a continuing conversation about public expectations and requirements of communications institutions. 'Ethnographic understanding of the social world of actual audiences can enrich that conversation because it foregrounds a discourse on quality that takes into account the situational practices and experiences of those who must make do with the television provision served them by the institutions' (Ang 1991: 167–8).

In other words, rather than just measuring audiences and claiming that tells us something about good and bad television, or what people want, we can exploit the flexibility of observational research to provide a more complete account of audience responses, and thus of audience demands and requirements.

Willis, who has conducted a number of studies of how young people make sense of their lives in relation to popular culture, has made extensive use of ethnographic methods. He stresses that one of their many advantages is a capacity to surprise, to generate 'knowledge not prefigured in one's starting paradigm' (Willis 1980: 90). Of course, it is unrealistic to expect the researcher to wholly abandon or overturn the world view with which they enter the situation. But reflecting on much of his own work with young people (e.g. Willis 1978), he stresses that 'a qualitative methodology be confronted with the maximum flow of relevant data. Here resides the power of the evidence to "surprise", to contradict, specific developing theories' (Willis 1980: 90–1).

Richness and colour

Probably the most attractive feature of observation studies for many researchers is the expectation that they put flesh on the bones of quantitative methods, producing a depth and fullness of texture, or what the anthropologist Clifford Geertz famously explained as 'thick description', which is more satisfying as well as more accurate than less intense procedures.

Given a choice of generating reams of SPSS printout (see chapter 14) or a pile of coding schedules, on the one hand, or diving into the seductive world of cultural consumption and production on the other, it is not altogether surprising that many researchers would prefer to 'go qualitative', especially in the form of observational studies. This may often be the right choice, and indeed it need not always be a choice at all. It is important, however, to be clear about the possible weaknesses in claims to validity and representativeness that may be inherent in observational studies.

Certainly, in researching the production of communications, there is no substitute for the rich encounters to be found in witnessing the messy business of cultural manufacture. In a classic study of the BBC, for example, the organisational and industrial sociologist, Tom Burns, used a lengthy programme of interviews as his main source of data. But as the study proceeded, he detected what he describes as 'the cultural ambience of the Corporation' arising increasingly from his observation in the 'private world' he found in the BBC (Burns 1977: xiii). This added a density of colour and three-dimensional realism to what might otherwise have remained a formal analysis of structures and organisation.

In a study of the long-running BBC science fiction series *Doctor Who*, Tulloch and Alvarado were able to learn a lot about the ideas and conceptions which fed into the programme by close analysis of its production. As they narrate the decisions, anxieties and exchanges of the production crew, they build up a complex profile of the roles of its members, and how they mediate ideas about production that would have been invisible to a purely interview-led methodology. Illustrating the relation of producer to director to actor, we are told of an incident in which the producer 'forcefully pointed out to the director, and through her to the actor, that…the acting must be very restrained in order to avoid the character seeming to be "in drag"' (Tulloch and Alvarado 1983: 258). Such observations build up a more general account of the attempt to avoid a 'self-referencing excess' in the programme, which in turn feeds into a larger-scale portrayal of the culture of the programme and its links to wider constructions of drama, melodrama, realism, science fiction – the cultural codes of television.

Disadvantages of observational methods

Participation hinders observation

Malinowski notes the importance of 'plunges into the life of the natives' (1922: 21), but also warns that this can hold its dangers. It is important to note things before they become so familiar that the observer takes them for granted, not least because they are taken for granted by the observed. Being able to take part in the work or activities in the research situation can not only give the researcher fresh insight into the meanings of those activities, but also increase access to situations and further the credibility of the researcher and cooperation with her. But close involvement with the observed situation carries with it the danger of what, borrowing from its anthropological forebears, observational research calls 'going native'.

This involves acquiring such a strong familiarity with the people observed that their view of the world becomes natural and taken for granted, to the point where it simply becomes invisible. This is a common risk where the researcher and the researched have a lot in common. In a study of American television news at the major networks, carried out in the 1970s, the sociologist Herbert Gans worried about the fact that he held political views somewhat to the left of the journalists he was studying. He tried to avoid actively discussing such views, but decided, in the end, that these differences were probably an advantage. 'The hardest task in fieldwork is to study people who are politically or culturally akin to the fieldworker and who take the same things for granted' (Gans 1979: 77).

In Box 11.2, Philip Elliott reflects on the difficulties that arose in his study of the making of a British commercial television series, in which the production team were people much like himself, with a common educational background and shared social and political views.

Box 11.2

Researcher and researched in this study came from much the same social level (though clearly at different stages of individual careers) as evidenced, for example, by the fact that three of the production team and the researcher had all been to Oxford University. There was no initial problem of socio-cultural distance such as faces the social anthropologist in a tribal society or the sociologist in a slum community. This obviated the need for a lengthy run-up period to sensitize the researcher to a new way of life. The organizational and occupational cultures which were the subject of study were all part of the same socio-cultural system to which research and the researcher belonged. It has been argued that distance is necessary to objectify the situation researched. But while distance may encourage a feeling of objectivity, it is anything but a guarantee that the researcher has completely understood the dynamics of the social experience. Distance may also help at a later stage in the making of broad generalizations, but this seems to be more an argument for a comparative approach than for distance *per se*.

Nevertheless, there were a number of problems in fitting into the television production situation. With so few people involved in the core production team there seemed to be a real danger that the intrusion of another would drastically alter the situation. For this reason I adopted the role which Strauss and his colleagues have identified as that of 'passive observer with minimal clarifying interaction'. Possible observer roles vary, according to the range and type of participation in the situation they involve. Each of these has various advantages and disadvantages.

One of the disadvantages of the passive observer role is that it takes some time to win acceptance for it. Once it has won acceptance it provides a secure basis from which to widen the range and scope of interaction. Getting accepted, however, involves personal difficulties for the researcher as well as for the group. In this case, unwilling to trust my memory, I took notes constantly as the production team was working. Not unnaturally members of the team were continually puzzled and occasionally suspicious about what I was noting. Note-taking was also important personally as it gave me something to do. There are problems in justifying an observer role to oneself, especially in an occupational milieu like that of television with its emphasis on the projection of personal charisma. One such problem was whether to get involved in general discussions within the team, especially during the early planning and researching stages. I tried to avoid this, initially adopting a rule of not speaking until spoken to and then saying as little as possible consistent with not appearing rude or completely vacant. Again, however, it was not surprising to find some people suspicious of an apparently silent presence (although I did use words to explain what I was doing!). Acceptance is only a matter of time, however, helped by sharing common experiences.

Once in the field the practical problems of following what was going on, deciding what to record when and managing my own interaction in the situation became so engrossing that initial theory appeared to have little relevance. Then came the stage, known in the literature as 'going native', in which I began to recognize beliefs and actions so clearly that it was hard to imagine how they could be different. The data acquired a shape based in a descriptive sense on the way the process appeared. The initial write-up of this study ran to well over 200 000 words and played a crucial part in the analysis process. I felt I had to put as much as possible on paper, both to justify the data to myself and to others, and because I could not distance myself from it while it was only partially analysed but all interrelated in my mind. Working from the initial write-up focused the process which had been going on throughout the research, of formulating ideas and then checking them against the data. The second version and the third (this book) became progressively less descriptive, sharpening up the analysis and cutting down the length. I am very conscious of the twin dangers, however, of allowing the analysis to take leave of the data and of not presenting the full evidence in a digestible form. The important test to apply to the analysis of participant observation data seems to me not to be simply how many other cases is this likely to be true for – a question which cannot be answered within the terms of the method; but how plausible is the posited relationship between belief, behaviour and situation in the light of possible alternative explanations?

(Elliott 1971: 171–2)

A practical difficulty that arises from participation is that it interferes with, or even prevents, getting on with the business of data collection and recording. Participant observation can often be fun, whether in mundane or glamorous locales. A balance has to be struck between remembering the practical necessities of getting notes written and recording observations, while at the same time responding positively to requests to help or take part in observed events.

Observation hinders participation

Participation is a means to an end. If joining in the activities being observed aids access to those activities, or fosters a deeper and more complete understanding of them, then it is a research tool. But the primary purpose is observation, and it may be that this prevents or impedes the participation required to increase trust or access. After all, perching on the edge of someone's desk, asking awkward and intrusive questions about what they are doing, or simply looming around, can be a somewhat disorienting addition to workplace or home, however much people have agreed in principle to the research.

Equally, the routine business of organising observation, which we shall discuss later in the chapter, may make it difficult to participate naturally in the research setting. If you have decided you need to spend a certain amount of time with each department in an advertising agency, for example, you may just be settling into one section when you realise that you need to transfer your attentions elsewhere. Not only must new relationships be established, but you may generate suspicions as an interloper from another, possibly rival section, from whom confidences must be withheld.

The balance between observation and participation is a matter of fine judgement, and no textbook can offer 'rules of engagement' to define how that balance is achieved. It will depend on the particular setting, and on changing relationships as the research proceeds. The important thing is to ensure that a research plan is in place so that you know what you are trying to discover, and what is required to achieve your research ends. At different times in the research, this will dictate how far you can compromise the needs of participation to facilitate observation, and vice versa.

It's not what you know, it's who you know: sponsorship and representativeness

Observation studies are not surveys; they are not intended to be. For that reason, they are not designed to ensure that you gather data from a representative sample of the people in the setting or organisation you are studying. Nonetheless, you are likely to arrive at generalisations about that setting derived from the observations. This poses two kinds of problem. The first is based on the problem of entry and what is called 'sponsorship': that is, the status and role of the key 'gatekeepers' who allow your entry into the situation. The second is the more general problem of representativeness: ensuring that your data is not skewed by being drawn from an unrepresentative fraction of the population you are studying. These two problems can be seen as a fundamental disadvantage of observation studies used in isolation.

As we will discuss below, many observation studies in natural settings require permission and some degree of control from the people being observed. Often one key member of the groups being observed will take responsibility for the observer, or may, indeed, be their guarantor, reassuring her colleagues that this person is 'OK' and will not be a nuisance or undertake unacceptable activities. This obviously demands a reciprocal debt from the observer; you may spend an undue amount of time with the 'sponsor' or simply see the observed world through her eyes in all sorts of inconspicuous ways.

For this and other reasons, the data you obtain from an observation study may be 'unrepresentative'. That is to say, the people you speak to and the events you observe cannot be tightly controlled in the way they would be in a survey or experimental study. You might spend so much time with the camera crew that you come to the sound empirical conclusion that, but for the inane and ignorant interventions of a philistine director, the documentary you are studying would have won endless awards. Possibly, a redistribution of your observation efforts would have prompted a different conclusion.

Of course, such criticisms make disputable assumptions about the degree of 'representativeness' delivered by other methodologies, but the peculiar difficulties associated with observation are real enough, and should be built into the design and planning of such studies.

Making an impact: the effects of observation

In one of the classic studies in industrial sociology, a group of researchers studied the production workers at the Western Electrical Company's Hawthorne works in Chicago (Roethlisberger and Dickson 1939). They examined the effects on productivity of different degrees of illumination in the workplace. Their failure to find a direct relationship between improved illumination and the very significant increases in productivity they observed left them puzzled. In the end, they realised it was the increased attention given to the workers, as a side effect of the study itself, which produced the better human relations that, in turn, increased productivity. Since then, the 'Hawthorne effect' has been used as shorthand to describe the unintended consequences of observational research in changing the behaviour of the observed.

This disadvantage is possible only where the observer is observed, of course. In settings where the observer simply 'merges into the background', this is not a problem. If you propose to study a cinema audience, you are unlikely to provoke much in the way of uncharacteristic behaviour. However, in typical study situations, such as a small workplace or a home, it is difficult to disappear, and the dangers of distortion are significant.

There are two possible ways of dealing with this problem. Either you can reduce the effect or you can calibrate it into your analysis. One way of reducing the effect is to prolong the period of observation, so that people become familiar with the observer, and even begin to take her for granted. Some studies involve many months, or even years, in the field. Both Argyris and Gans, in the studies mentioned earlier, spent many months in the workplaces they were studying. However, this is a luxury not always available. Another way of reducing the effect is simply to work hard at being as inconspicuous as possible. This is not too easy in a very small setting, such as a family living room, but a degree of sensitivity and adaptability can reduce the more obvious reminders to people being studied that they are under the microscope. Whipping out your notebook at the first sign of significant dialogue or incessantly asking for explanations of the everyday decisions of an advertising creative director are not best designed to elicit useful data or facilitate a lengthy and welcome stay.

The second mechanism is to accept that the observer effect is unavoidable, but to build it into your method. People may well respond to your presence by 'playing to the gallery', but what do they choose to play up? Which aspects of their work or play do they seem to believe to be worth promoting? If your presence is bound to have an impact, perhaps this can be utilised as a research device. It is not uncommon for researchers to be drawn into participation levels inappropriate to their role or expertise. In a newsroom study carried out by one of the authors, the journalists, very short-staffed and under the illusion that the researcher had advanced journalistic skills, insisted that he help out with the rewriting of press releases as a deadline approached. In turning a moment of cowardice into what was subsequently rationalised as shrewd research flexibility, the researcher used the opportunity to produce deliberately differing approaches to the task to see what response they provoked, thus generating a good deal of data on journalists' attitudes and expectations.

What you see is what you get: the limits to immediacy

One of the presumed advantages of observation is its immediate access to social process. The corollary disadvantage, however, is that the observer only sees what is in front of her nose. She cannot be in several places at once, and cannot easily control for the accidents of witnessing atypical occurrences.

One way of dealing with this problem is to have numerous observers. Lang and Lang call this 'multiple observation', and have used it to good effect in several classic studies. It is most useful where one is fortunate enough to be able to call on a well-motivated, or at least dutifully cooperative, body of collaborators, like the teams of graduate students used by the Langs. In one study, they observed the public welcome home to Chicago, in 1951, of General Douglas MacArthur, hero of the Korean War. The authors used 31 observers, scattered along the parade route, who recorded detailed data on the crowds and their behaviour. The contrast between the excitement and acclaim apparent in media coverage of the event, and the relatively low-key occasion observed 'on the ground', generated valuable insights into 'unwitting bias' and the role of 'inferential structures' in shaping news reports (Lang and Lang 1953).

The Langs contrast their method with the famous 'mass observation' studies used by Madge and Harrisson in the UK in the 1930s and later (see Calder and Sheridan 1984). These employed volunteer observers, who kept quasi-anthropological notebooks on the everyday lives of the British working class, to create an invaluable archive of descriptive material. But although these studies were pioneering, and contained a great deal of original description, they involved very little further analysis. By contrast, the Langs' studies provide the observers with predetermined categories against which to check their observations. They term this 'enumeration'.

How perceptive are you?

A final problem with observation is its dependence on the perspicacity of the individual researcher. A survey or content analysis coding can, in principle, be conducted by any trained researcher given clear instructions by the research designer. Indeed, it would be seen as a validation of the 'research instrument' that a change of researcher would make no difference. There is not much use in a survey questionnaire which requires the architect of the study to go round with the interviewers, whispering, 'No, what I really meant was…' Observation, on the other hand, as we have seen, requires a number of personal skills, from tact and flexibility to good memory and intuition, in order to be effective. Does this mean that only a few highly skilled and personally exceptional people can ever carry out observation studies?

Well, yes and no. Undoubtedly, a good level of interpersonal skills is valuable for the observational researcher. But it would be misleading to assume that this is unique to this style of research. No research method is so foolproof that it can be implemented mechanistically by the proverbial monkeys on a keyboard, though many published studies suggest otherwise. Equally, and probably more importantly, observation research requires the same attention to detail and rigour in planning and execution as any other method. While this does not make the method foolproof, it does transfer the guarantee of reliability from the personal to the methodological. It is also important to recognise the role of insight and creative thinking in other, apparently more rigorous, or at least quantitative, methods. All research involves such capacities, and we should not be blinded to thinking that they are unique to observation.

Doing observational studies

We now turn to the practicalities of conducting observation studies. As in so many other methods discussed in this book, there are no hard-and-fast rules which must be followed unthinkingly. However, observation studies, above all other methods, need to be conducted carefully to reflect the rigour and structure they entail. They do not just involve 'hanging around', waiting for light bulbs to illuminate over the researcher's head. Most important is to recognise the various stages in the observation process:

- Stage 1: entry;
- Stage 2: sponsorship/gatekeeping;
- Stage 3: planning;
- Stage 4: data collection;
- Stage 5: data analysis.

Stage 1: Entry

The first task for any observation research is to ensure you have access to the situations and people you need to observe. Often, this may turn out to be the most difficult, and lengthy, part of the research process. Yet much hinges on it. Essentially, there are two types of research location, open and closed. A *closed location* is one to which access is conditional. Private homes, for example, are closed. If you want to undertake observation of children's responses to advertising in domestic settings, you cannot just invite yourself round for the evening to a couple of dozen local family homes. Media organisations are also closed, at least in their main organisational base. You may, perhaps, observe a camera crew on location, though rarely with ease or at close quarters. You cannot wander into a television studio and just hang around, hoping not be noticed. These days you would not get past the glossy, high-tech reception.

Open locations are public. The reading room in the library, a bookshop, cinema foyer and video shop are all open locations. Notice, however, how few such locations there are. Paradoxically, given their public character, both production and consumption of mass communications are largely private activities, and cultural consumption has become increasingly a domestic matter. Thus most locations for observation studies are closed. Some are conditionally open. For example, a cinema or disco is in principle open to anyone subject to payment, though some media researchers (probably increasing numbers) might have problems disappearing in the crowd at a teenage disco.

The second distinction we must make is in the role the observer adopts, which can be overt or covert. If you wish to play an *overt role*, you ensure that the observed are aware of your research and enter the situation as a researcher. Alternatively, you can play a *covert role*: your activity as a researcher is not disclosed and your real reason for being there is not revealed. Again, there is a halfway point: you may let your purpose be known to some people in the observed location, who agree to collude with you in keeping the fact hidden. Equally, you may let it be known that you are undertaking research, but not reveal exactly what you are investigating. This is a common technique in experimental research, and can also be used in observation studies as a way of ensuring entry without provoking inappropriate behaviour change.

If we think about these two distinctions, we can arrive schematically at four possible research situations (Figure 11.1).

ROLE \ LOCATION	Open	Closed
Overt	Public arena	Negotiated entry: conditional access
Covert	Ethics of data collection and use	Ethics of research task; risk

Figure 11.1 Possible research situations in observation studies

Overt research in open locations clearly poses no problems of entry. It is, as we have noted, relatively little used in media research, since few of the activities researchers are interested in take place in open locations. Moreover, there is little point announcing your research intentions to an indifferent world for no purpose. Overt research in a closed location is probably the most common form of observation research, and will certainly be a frequent feature of projects undertaken by students. The crux to successful work in this situation is negotiated entry. If you plan to conduct research in a local newspaper, for example, or in schools, you must contact the relevant authority and explain clearly the purpose of your research, what access you require and what disturbance your research may cause. Ensure that you have the backing and accreditation required, for example from your department if you are a student, or from a funding body if conducting paid-for research. Any risk of rejection or obstacles and conditions raised at this stage will be less serious than the difficulties that would arise if your true purpose and requirements only became clear after the research had started. Negotiated entry is often a matter of chance contact or acquaintance. 'My thesis supervisor at the LSE, knowing of my interest in the media, mentioned that the husband of one of his colleagues worked for the BBC as an announcer. This person kindly broached the question of my gaining access to the Editor, Radio News' (Schlesinger 1980: 343).

We cannot all have well-connected supervisors or sponsors or fortunately placed relatives, but considering the possibilities of the contacts we do have is a start. For much research into consumption, the problem is access not to closely guarded elite institutions, but to the privacy of domesticity. The principles remain the same. Negotiated entry requires an honesty and openness with the objects of research which is not only ethical but strategically productive.

Covert entry to research locations poses a number of ethical issues to which we shall give further attention in chapter 15. Such a role in open locations is quite common in social research, not least because declaration of the research role is often neither required nor even possible. Much qualitative urban sociology, for example, involves the kind of 'hanging around' in public locales that might arouse the suspicion of the police, whose appreciation of the methodological advantages of 'purposive lurking' may not be well refined; but it is perfectly legal. It may well be that there is insufficient use of such methods in mass communication. A lot may be learned from observing the behaviour and activities, for example, of people in cinema queues, libraries, bookshops, video shops or newsagent's (though the owners' involvement would probably be necessary in some of these cases). Covert research in closed settings requires, almost by definition, a degree of deception, not to mention risk, which cannot be condoned. While sometimes necessary for the more heroic forms of investigative reporting, it is not appropriate for serious research (see chapter 15).

Stage 2: Sponsorship/gatekeeping

Once you have set up your research location, your activities while 'in the field' may well depend on the manner of your entry. Gatekeeping (who let you in) and sponsorship (who takes responsibility for you while you are researching) may have crucial consequences for your freedom of action and for data collection.

The key to this problem is the paradox that sponsorship is probably necessary for entry, but may prejudice or interfere with your research process. For example, you may be studying a local radio station, having persuaded the station manager of the value of the study or of your unique personal tact and diligence. However, staff may perceive you as a management tool or spy, and be very wary of what they say, knowing you have what may be better access to senior staff than they do. There is no simple solution to this problem or rule for coping with it. As with much else in observation research, it is a difficulty to be negotiated as you go along. Planning will indicate where the problems will arise, and sensitivity and common sense will see you through in most situations.

The second difficulty arises from the exchange relationship which is set up by negotiated entry. The gatekeeper or sponsor may seek status enhancement through association with a visiting researcher, or may implicitly demand from the researcher information, evaluation or assistance of various kinds which will be of use in the job being performed. Anthropologists offering medical expertise face this difficulty – hard to refuse, but hardly leaving the research scene untouched. In a domestic setting a visitor may be used, in time-honoured fashion, as a vehicle for conflict resolution – an uncomfortable role as well as a methodologically problematic one.

A degree of distance from sponsor or gatekeeper is necessary wherever possible. The sponsor should be used as little as possible to maximise both entry and access to research locations and material. The temptation to return to a familiar and friendly base will often be great, but should constantly be checked against the needs of data collection.

Stage 3: Planning

In observation studies, the key to good research is rigorous but flexible planning. No observation study is possible without careful planning. However open and flexible your research process, without a well-constructed plan, the research will drift from flexibility into confusion. It is imperative that you decide what you wish to find out, what information you need, who you need to talk to, what you must observe and what questions you must address. These will all change and evolve during the research, but must be set out clearly when you start and kept under review throughout the fieldwork period. The questions will be based on a clear theoretical understanding of the issues raised by your research. You are not merely going to see 'what it's like in x', but to try to answer a finite range of questions arising from your reading and planning. Of course, this does not mean you must construct a tightly formulated empiricist document, complete with hypothesis and list of variables to be measured. It does mean, however, that you set out on the fieldwork having thought about the questions that arise from your reading of relevant research, and with a realisable set of targets for data collection.

Let us suppose you had persuaded your local radio station to let you study how their newsroom deals with crime news. There is a considerable literature on crime news in the national media (see, for example, Schlesinger and Tumber 1994), but less research on local broadcasting, and you want to study if the relationships between police and reporters in local radio are similar to the newsroom–news source relationships investigated by Schlesinger and Tumber. Some prior discussion reveals that the local radio station does not have specialist crime reporters, so you know you will need to study the work of several reporters. You will also want to have access to editorial meetings. You have just a week in the building, so a time budget plan is essential. You plan to attend each day's news planning conference. Two days will be spent in the newsroom, following the editing process and observing decision-making within the organisation. Two days will be spent out with reporters covering stories. If you are lucky, one day will involve a good crime story, or a period in court covering a trial.

Such planning must be flexible. That is why there is a day spare in the above example, to allow for unforeseen contingencies. You may only work out late in the week that, actually, one of the reporters you have hardly met is the one who has the best informal contacts with the police. You make sure that he invites you to the liquid lunch he sets up on Friday with his contacts from the local police HQ.

Keep a careful list of all the questions you set for yourself in the research, and alongside them write out the kinds of data you will need to collect. (For example, you will want to find out about use of incoming news agency material as one of several sources of relevant news. Ensure you check people's use of the agency material: what they use, what they think of it, how they use it.) Review this list every day to see which data you have been ignoring or have simply overlooked, and rejig the plan to make good the missing data.

Stage 4: Data collection

There are two questions to address here: data recording and data organisation. Data recording is a practical problem as much as anything. In principle, the rule has to be 'record everything', but in practice this can be impossible. Taking notes may be so obtrusive as to become a major inhibition to natural behaviour. On the other hand, in a busy newsroom, as in many other likely research settings, the sight of people scribbling away in notebooks is commonplace and unlikely to excite much attention. Try to record significant speech verbatim. Not only will this add to the veracity and interest of your final report, but such 'situated lexicons' will provide more accurate and telling data than any synopsis you construct.

Simple fatigue is a predictable problem in recording. There is only so much you can write down. If writing down speech or events as you observe them is difficult, periodic retreat from the research scene is necessary. You will not be the first researcher whose regular disappearances provoke curiosity about the state of your intestinal health – 'researcher's bladder' is an occupational hazard of observational research! The alternative is to tape-record, or even video, the events being observed. This should only be done with the consent of the subjects, and care needs to be taken to ensure that it is not another inhibition. In a local newsroom, many others will have portable tape recorders slung over their shoulders. In a family lounge, on the other hand, the whirring of a tape on the table can all but paralyse natural behaviour and speech. Of course, familiarity breeds naturalness, and over time this problem may diminish, especially if you have an efficient, inaudible and inconspicuous machine. However, despite the apparent advantages of tape-recorded sessions, the subsequent analysis may actually take a lot longer than from notes, and no audio tape recorder, however sophisticated, has the researcher's eye for body language, or the sensitivity to switch attention to the key speakers in what may, on tape, turn out to be very confused and multilayered conversations. The temptation to rely on the tape recorder may also lower the attention of the researcher, in the mistaken belief that all the data is being safely held for later digestion at leisure. Many have lived to curse this expectation!

You will need to be aware that these practical difficulties will compound the inevitable reticence and concerns that your research subjects may have. In Box 11.3, Ericson and his colleagues outline their own practices in a study of Canadian crime journalism.

Box 11.3 Fieldwork techniques and process

The ethnographic fieldwork in news organizations was conducted in 1982 and 1983. It entailed more than 200 researcher days in the field, and a total of about 2500 hours including the preparation of research notes. We spent 101 days with *Globe and Mail* journalists over a nine-month period, and 86 days with CBLT journalists over a seven-month period. We spent additional days with radio, television, and newspaper reporters from other news organizations, observing their activities and interviewing personnel at various levels. All three authors conducted research in both the *Globe and Mail* and CBLT, as well as with reporters from a number of other news organizations. This system provided three perspectives on each news organization. It allowed the strengths of each researcher to be used to obtain information and insights from journalists which the other two researchers could not glean. On some dimensions it also allowed us to check the accounts of one another.

Detailed fieldnotes were written at the conclusion of each day in the field. More than 2000 pages of fieldnotes were indexed by topic for qualitative analysis. The data pertaining to the assignment of stories were systematized and quantified. Also available for subsequent scrutiny and analysis were copies of internal memoranda; draft or filed stories of journalists whom we were observing; assignment outlooks or lineups; television news scripts; and sources' news releases, documents, official reports, or any other material in connection with a story being studied; journalists' notes and research files connected with a story being studied; and, copies of published newspaper stories studied and videotapes of broadcast television stories studied.

[…]

Without regressing to a full account of the cultural- and social-organization processes by which our research was produced, it is instructive to consider some of the pitfalls and significant gains we experienced in the research process. As Geertz (1983: 56) states, referring to Malinowski's *A Diary in the Strict Sense of the Term*, the fieldworker is not a chameleon 'perfectly self-tuned to his exotic surroundings, a walking miracle of empathy, tact, patience and cosmopolitanism'. We sometimes found it difficult to tune in to what journalists were up to, to empathize with their approach, to tread carefully enough so as not to offend, to wait until we had a better appreciation or a full story, and to be as *au courant* with the myriad of organized life as they were. It is therefore instructive to discuss some of the journalists' general concerns about our research; their efforts to limit, control, or deny access; their instrumental use of researchers; the practical constraints we faced leading to self-imposed limitations; and, the level of co-operation that was ultimately accomplished.

Journalists expressed concern to us about our interference with the process by which their work gets done. Reporters complained that our presence made it more awkward to work generally. For example, it was difficult for reporters to be constantly giving details of a telephone conversation just completed when we were able to listen only to the reporter's end. It was also difficult for journalists to repeatedly give reasons for their decisions as they were taking them; this was found to be disruptive to their thinking processes. Many found our presence interfered with source interviews or their ongoing relations with sources, and we were sometimes excluded on these grounds.

[…]

Journalists expressed concerns about how our findings would be used. In this connection, several wanted extra assurance that confidentiality would be maintained and that they would not be identifiable in research reports. Some journalists said they were concerned that their work habits might be communicated to management with the effect that controls would be instituted that would cramp their style. This concern pertained to how they spent their time and paced their work, as well as to questionable practices. On three occasions reporters' sensitivity seemed to reach a peak, as they grabbed the fieldworkers' notes to ascertain what had been written about them.

> We also faced practical constraints of time and space which affected the research process. If we had to leave early for personal reasons, we would choose a story to follow, or other research activity, accordingly. On some stories it was quite impractical to follow everything that was being done because there were several reporters involved, covering different angles and conducting different source interviews pertaining to each particular angle. Sometimes it was simply difficult to hear conversation between reporters and sources, for example, when wide shots were being taken for television-news items. Sometimes we expected journalists to change their routines for our research purposes but they had difficulty remembering to do so because of the routines they were used to. For example, we asked the wire editors of one news organization to save all wire copy they perused, but they sometimes continued to throw it in the garbage as was their usual practice.
>
> The degree and nature of co-operation varied greatly among journalists, and we came to rely upon the more co-operative as key informants. We had a number of such informants in important organizational positions at several levels, thus providing for a range and depth of such data. Over time, some journalists began to appreciate that we had knowledge of their organization which they themselves did not possess, and they took this as a sign of the extent to which we had been accepted by their peers at different levels.
>
> (Ericson, Bararnek and Chan 1987: 86–90)

What, then, do you do with all this 'data'? The organisation of your material is crucial to the success of your observation study and should be a continuing process. Many researchers like to keep a fieldwork diary, a practice rooted in traditional anthropological fieldwork. Random notes, thoughts as they occur to you, significant incidents and your own responses to the fieldwork experience are all worth recording for later consideration. Another technique which many find helpful is to reorder their notes as they go along, perhaps on a daily basis. One good system is to reallocate your notes to a card index, using the larger size of index cards. These could be split into three categories, for example, one for people, one for locations, one for topics. In our newsroom study, you might keep notes on the practices, quotes and activities of individuals. At the same time, you would have cards with topics on them; these will develop as patterns become clear. Thus 'informal links with police' might be one card heading, 'legal constraints' another (meaning all allusions to or employment of them, not a formal documentation of relevant legislation). Places might include 'the news editorial meeting', 'the precinct canteen', 'the Rover's Return', the local bar.

As your work proceeds, you are likely to derive more and more analytical categories rather than descriptive ones. Thus one card might be headed 'informal organisation', as the identities of those wielding real power and influence become clear. Your disorganised notes, recorded simply in sequence as you watch and listen, can be coded by allocating them to categories before transferring them to cards. For example, having decided that the role of the police press office is significant, you might have evolved a draft set of categories, such as:

A   Role of police press office (ppo)
- A1   use of press releases
- A2   phone calls newsroom to ppo
- A3   phone calls ppo to newsroom
- A4   police requests for restraint
- A5   tension between journalists and ppo

and so on. It will be obvious that this somewhat traditional procedure lends itself to computerisation. Writing your notes into a relational database will afford a much neater, quicker and more elaborate version of the card-index approach. In chapter 14, we outline the use of some appropriate packages for this kind of analysis. However, even the most computer-literate researcher is often to be found fondly riffling through shoeboxes full of cards, as described here, and the pencil-and-card method should not be jettisoned too quickly.

Stage 5: Data analysis

What do you do with it all? You will certainly have a lot of material. Even in production studies, having gained access, you are likely to find people both communicative and reflective. As Gitlin found, 'the television business is a talker's business... So getting people to talk was not the problem I had anticipated: the problem was to evaluate millions of words' (Gitlin 1983: 14). In a study of specialist journalists, Tunstall notes that, using both interviews and observation, he 'produced approximately one million words of typed notes' (Tunstall 1971: 295). Not altogether surprisingly, these are the very last words in his book!

As we have noted above, data analysis and data collection are inextricably linked in observation studies. If you have been ordering your data as you go along, then analysis will already be well under way when the fieldwork is completed. The indexing and categorisation which have been employed in organising the data will, in itself, have imposed order, and that order is the preliminary phase of analysis. The key themes and patterns will have emerged as you go along, and a careful rereading of your data will throw up exemplary instances and illustrations of the patterns you detect. Of course, the temptation to see what you expect to see is great. Having decided that the crux of radio crime reporting is the powerful influence of the newly established police press office, you will undoubtedly be able to dig up examples to bear out your theory. There is no magic formula to avoid this very human process. Judgement and discretion are inherent to all research procedures; but they can seem more prominent in qualitative, and especially observation methods, where the researcher and the research are so intimately identified.

Boiling your data down in this way will make it manageable in both quantity and quality. That is, you will become increasingly selective about what is 'significant'. You will also move from what are termed 'first-order concepts', that is, the concepts and constructs used by the people you have observed and studied, to 'second-order concepts', namely the concepts you conceive in order to make sense of, and explain, the settings you have observed.

Observing online

Increasingly – though with significant exceptions and social patterning – people have access to the Internet and use it for receiving communications or for communicating. They may use the Internet as a supplement or substitute for traditional media, especially as an alternative to traditional news media, or for focusing on special interests within general news. They may also use it to communicate, either by email or by posting **blogs**. Researchers have increasingly been interested in investigating such behaviour, as well as using the new communication facilities as a means of obtaining access to respondents for research purposes. For example, we might be interested in how young people use the Internet or mobile phones for communications in ways that are novel and distinct (see, for example, Livingstone 2006). In Box 11.4, we discuss how the world of online gaming can offer a number of research opportunities. We have also discussed (see chapter 4) how the Internet might be used for collecting survey data. This can have many advantages, but is also fraught with methodological difficulties and limitations, as we have explained (see Lotz and Ross 2004 for a feminist critique of such methods). In addition, we can analyse online materials themselves, as we discuss in chapters 2 and 6.

Box 11.4 Massive multiple-player online role-playing games: an Internet research challenge

A new type of computer gaming has gained global popularity in recent years: 'massive multiple-player online role-playing games' (MMORPGs) connect players via the Internet to a three-dimensional gaming environment, run through a central computer server or array of servers. These environments offer synthetic worlds in which players create their own characters ('avatars') to perform tasks, acquire skills and money and, crucially, meet, interact and trade with other gamers from across the world. There are two main types of MMORPGs. Some replicate versions of offline landscapes and settings. *Habbo Hotel*, for example, provides its mainly teenage users with a variety of locations for socialising, from nightclubs to pizza bars and swimming pools. *Second Life*, which is targeted primarily at adults, offers a correspondingly wider range of locations. Others, such as *World of Warcraft*, *Legends of Mir*, *Everquest2*, *Eve Online* or *Rune-scape*, provide fully realised fantasy worlds. Extensive online communities have developed around all the leading games, both within the games themselves and in external chat rooms in which players swap advice, socialise and pour over the minutiae of these alternative realities. By the second half of 2006, *Habbo Hotel* was attracting 7 million unique users a month, spread across 29 countries; *World of Warcraft* had more than 7 million subscribers; and *Second Life* had almost three quarters of a million fully paid up 'residents' and was growing by 20 per cent a month.

How might you develop and conduct a research project to investigate this new communicative and interactive phenomenon? In our view, there is a range of research approaches you could take. These options are not exhaustive, nor should they be seen as mutually exclusive. Indeed, it would be productive to consider their combination (Miller 2006: 8).

Figure 11.2 Second Life

Approach 1: a political economic analysis

This approach would examine the commercial organisation and operation of these games. Many require players to make monthly subscriptions, and their revenue yields are already considerable. In 2006, the owners of *Second Life* were earning $1 million a month from renting virtual land, amounting to an area bigger than Boston, to players paying an average of $20 an acre (*The Economist*, 30 September 2006), while *World of Warcraft* was generating more than $1 billion in annual revenues (*Sunday Times*, 17 September 2006).

At the time, *Second Life* was controlled by the independent company that originated it, Linden Labs, but *World of Warcraft* was operated by Blizzard entertainment, a subsidiary of Vivendi, a major communications conglomerate. Unsurprisingly, other major players within the communications industries, like AT&T, are seeking to claim a share of this 'rapidly growing business segment' (AT&T podcast, http://att.sbc.com/, accessed 2 October 2006). Monitoring the corporate mergers, partnerships and acquisitions that develop as these games increase in popularity, offers one very fruitful avenue for research.

A political economic analysis would also take account of the extensive promotional activities related to these games. Corporate brands have started to purchase a presence in many of the online virtual worlds as part of their marketing strategies. Games have also become major arenas for music industry promotions. In May 2006, the BBC bought a tropical island in *Second Life*, where it stages online music festivals and celebrity parties (BBC Online, 12 May 2006), while the EMI subsidiary, Innocent, used *Habbo Hotel* to launch its new boy band, 365, recruiting a 'virtual street team' of players to spread the word and drum up interest. But promotion goes well beyond the youth market. In *Second Life*, product placement abounds, with virtual versions of Adidas, Nike and other branded goods all available for purchase using the virtual currency. In October 2006, Toyota became the first car maker to sell virtual versions of its new models in the game. There is also a lucrative business marketing clothes, games, magazines and other spin-offs. In 2006, 600 million Coke cans were emblazoned with characters from *World of Warcraft*. This synergetic commercial activity is likely to develop rapidly.

A political economic analysis would also need to investigate the trading economies that have developed around the characters, resources and products employed within these games. *Second Life* supports a thriving internal economy in which entrepreneurial participants sell the virtual objects they have created, often fashion clothes and hairstyles, or lease virtual islands and buildings. By mid 2006, the game's richest avatar, Anshe Chung, had built up a property empire on the site worth US$250,000 (*The Guardian*, 7 October 2006, p. 28). Some virtual goods are traded within the games, but others can be purchased on eBay and other Internet auction sites, at prices determined by the published exchange rates linking the games' fictional currencies to the US dollar and other major real-world currencies. In 2004, IGE, a virtual item trading website, calculated that the secondary market in virtual goods was worth approximately $880 million per annum and was increasing rapidly (*New Scientist*, 20 May 2006, p. 41). Many of these transactions are buying time. In fantasy games, players acquire status through greater strength, skill, weapons and martial proficiency. By 2004, the specialist sales sites, like Mysupersales.com, were offering a variety of resources for sale, from spider venom for use in *Everquest* for US$699, to a magician capable of operating at level 74 in the game *Final Fantasy XI* for US$1,299 (Meek 2004). The monetary value of these virtual resources has produced a new form of sweatshop labour, as entrepreneurs in China and other low-income economies pay local people to play the games for hours, in order to develop highly skilled avatars that can be sold to affluent gamers who lack the time and inclination to undertake the labour involved in building up these resources themselves. This practice, known as 'gold farming' (after the fictional currency 'gold' used in *World of Warcraft*), has prompted heated debate within the gaming community, since many players see buying rather than earning advantage as cheating. It has led Blizzard Entertainment to ban the resale of virtual resources and to delete the accounts of anyone engaged in the practice. Money also flows in the opposite direction, from the games to the 'real' world. In 2005, for example, Kermitt Quirk sold the offline rights to distribute *Tringo*, the popular board and card game he had developed within *Second*

Life, to Donnerwood Media for a five-figure sum (Malaby 2006).

The principal method you would use to investigate these developments would be documentary analysis (see chapter 2).

Approach 2: analysing the form and content of the games

This research approach, in which you would deconstruct the form and content of the games, would draw on a variety of methods of textual analysis. By 'form', we are referring to the architectural structure of the games, and how players' interact with and navigate through their virtual environments. Within gaming theory, this is sometimes referred to as 'ludology', which focuses on 'the nature of the interactive system, the rules and the game process' (Cascio 2005). Some games offer players freedom of movement and interaction within a highly structured environment, guiding their activities through a series of incentives, restrictions and tasks. Other MMORPGs are more open-ended, providing players with extended opportunities for creative and imaginative play. *Second Life* allows players to create their own characters from scratch, which can result in some spectacularly anarchic outcomes. As one player explained to a bemused British journalist: 'My avatar is a big yellow triceratops… I spend most of my time in the furry bath houses – I was actually born a homosexual dragon' (*The Guardian*, 7 October 2006, p. 27). Elsewhere in the same world, a US psychiatrist simulated schizophrenic hallucinations to demonstrate the visual and auditory experiences of people living with this condition to his students (ibid.). The rise of these kinds of 'user-generated contents' blurs the conventional distinction between the producers of the games and their consumers in interesting ways (Pearce 2006).

The environments and forms of interaction promoted or enabled by a game's protocols are underpinned, in turn, by manifest and latent values – what we refer to as the 'content' of the games. In gaming theory, this approach is sometimes referred to as 'narratology', which proposes 'that games can best be understood by the stories they describe' (Cascio 2005: 2). According to Myers (2006: 47), 'The study of games involves the study of representations. Games, like literature, use conventional signs and symbols in unconventional ways'. Approaching these representations from the perspective of ideological analysis would lead us to focus on those that support unequal relations of power. As we have already seen, the online world of *Second Life* replicates many of the core characteristics of contemporary American capitalism, including the fetishisation of consumerism, property speculation, the power of money and the acceptance of class inequalities as inevitable. Others have expressed concerns about the gender and racial stereotyping evident in many of these fantasy words (Leonard 2006). An alternative approach, informed by postmodernist and poststructuralist perspectives, might focus on the reflexive, playful and intertextual qualities of these games, and the ironic way they relate to, and challenge, corporeal realities.[1]

---

1   For an example on intertextuality, see the affectionate parody of *World of Warcraft* in an episode of the cartoon series *South Park* ('Make Love not Warcraft', episode 1008, first broadcast 6 October 2006).

A variety of visual and linguistic analysis techniques could be used in this kind of study (see chapters 6 to 10). However, to appreciate their form and content fully, you would also need to play the games extensively, using a variant of participant-observation research (see chapter 11; Boellstorff 2006).

Approach 3: analysing media coverage of the games

The negative effects these games may be having on those who spend their lives playing them has attracted an increasing amount of news attention. In 2005, a man stabbed a friend to death for selling a virtual sword he owned, and a couple were charged with child neglect when their five-month-old child died in its cot while they played an online game in a nearby Internet café. These stories can be seen as part of a wider **moral panic** about the risks and dangers of new communications technologies that spreads across the whole range of recent innovations, from concerns about paedophiles grooming children in Internet chat rooms, to worries about the potential brain damage from prolonged use of mobile phones. Exploring the construction of public debate around games in the news media, and teasing out the deeper fears that underpin it, offers a rich topic for textual analysis.

In this area, however, limiting research to major press and television outlets would miss some of the most interesting and innovative aspects of the emerging situation. In November 2006, Axel Springer, the publisher of Germany's best-selling daily paper, *Bild*, declared his intention of launching a weekly English-language tabloid, *SL News*, for citizens of *Second Life*, to be distributed to subscribers through their virtual mailboxes. His aim was to produce 'a colourful tabloid, with snippets about show business and human interest tales from the avatar world', based on material filed by a team of roving avatar reporters operating under a full-time editor-in-chief (*The Guardian*, 8 November 2006, p. 20). A month earlier, the major news agency, Reuters, established its own editorial office within the game, from which their full-time correspondent, Adam Pasik, operating under the name 'Adam Reuters', set out to file stories about developments within the virtual world, concentrating on economic and business affairs (*The Guardian*, 16 October 2006, p. 1). Detailing the stories generated by participants in the game, whether players or observers, and comparing them with mainstream, offline coverage, offers a novel and potentially very interesting area of news analysis.

Approach 4: playing the games

While we would caution against employing a crude 'stimulus-response' model of effects in any research you might develop, it would be legitimate to develop an audience-based analysis within an 'effects' framework. In seeking to establish what these games 'do' to people, you could employ a range of experimental, survey, interview and observational methods. However, it would be important to start with a broad conception of effects (behavioural, attitudinal and cognitive), and to avoid presupposing that all impacts are likely to be detrimental (Williams 2006). Children experiencing difficulty in negotiating social situations, for example, may be able to use the anonymity of the gaming environment to develop their social skills.

Another approach would be to address what gamers 'do' with the games: the meanings and pleasures they derive from their play and 'the ways that experience is constituted between player agency and textual determination' (Krzywinska 2006: 121). This fits within a reception analysis/ethnographic framework that highlights the agency and creativity of media consumers. One aspect of this could be to observe the online activities of game players and the nature of their interactions. In many cases, complex protocols have evolved to govern inter-player communication, cooperation and competition, and it would be interesting to examine how these rules are applied and enforced. Tracking talk and debate within the numerous Internet chat rooms that have developed around these games could also be fruitful sources of insight into the ways participants define their meanings and purposes. A second, related exercise could be to question gamers directly about their motivations and experiences, and the pleasures they derive from their immersion in virtual worlds. This could be conducted through online or offline questionnaires and interviews (see chapters 4, 12 and 13).

In this chapter, we have been concerned with ways of observing communications behaviour. One form of such behaviour is online communication, and we need to consider how the researcher can observe this. As with other forms of observation, this can be done as a participant in the behaviour or not. Non-participant observation of online communications has many of the advantages and disadvantages of its non-digital equivalent, as well as many of the same ethical dilemmas. Observing the communications of others while refraining from taking part can have its dubious aspects, and the term **lurking** has long been applied to such activity in news groups and the like. The connotation is plainly derogatory, suggesting a certain indelicate voyeurism, though this could be a charge levelled at many forms of observation research. Participant observation online is not uncommon in the world of online gaming, when researchers can find themselves locked in exhausting and time-consuming involvement in the world of multi-player online games (see Box 11.4), which they heroically endure in order to generate research data. Protests about the personal and financial costs of such research are seldom convincing, but you may be attracted to such research opportunities, despite the sceptical responses of less committed colleagues or supervisors.

A very important example of online observation is research into weblogs, or **blogs**. Sometimes produced by professional journalists, these online narratives are more often and typically produced by ordinary citizens who wish their everyday observations and accounts to be widely available and read. They can thus be taken as a ready-made sample of popular accounts, whether of the mundane, uneventful lives of a sample of people, or as an otherwise inaccessible set of data providing insight into events or places about which only official or otherwise restricted material is available. Like many Internet phenomena that start as somewhat anarchic or alternative activities, blogs have increasingly been 'mainstreamed'. One national UK newspaper (*The Guardian*) even introduced an annual 'best of British bloggers' award in 2002. The Iraq war was probably a major watershed in propelling the world of blogging from an enthusiastic resource for technophiliacs into a vast alternative source of news production and consumption. For journalists, blogs can offer the freedom to express views that would be unacceptable or impracticable in their more formal public outputs (see chapter 2).

The attractions for the researcher are obvious. The advantages of such sources of data are:

- They are readily available if you have access to the Internet.

- They provide a quick and easily editable volume of material.

- They are explicitly designed to be public and thus pose no problems of confidentiality.

- Unlike journalists' accounts, they are 'news in the raw' – unmediated accounts by people who, for major events, may well be participants or direct observers. At the very least, they present themselves as undiluted eyewitness accounts.

- They supplement, and are often intended to be alternative to, other forms of media output. For some consumers, they may even be regarded as sufficient to supplant such material.

- Their very subjectivity is an attractive expansion of other forms of data, adding the 'colour' which observational studies are often held to provide.

However, such forms of data are not without their disadvantages, of which you should be acutely aware before assuming that this bottomless goldmine of data is too good to ignore:

- The material is self-selecting, posing familiar problems of representativeness.

- There is no means of validating observations.

- There is seldom associated demographic data to correlate with the observations, and even if there is, there is no way of being certain of its validity – what we know about the author is no more than we can deduce from or are told in the posting itself.

- The researcher is dependent on using 'what's there'; the researcher is not in control of when, what or by whom postings are made.

- What is analysed is usually indirect evidence – it represents the output of behaviour, but not directly the behaviour itself.

It is important to recognise that using blogs and observing blogging pose exactly the same kind of advantages and difficulties as with other communications activities. Much related research confirms that you will need to face up to the same problems as for the kinds of research mentioned earlier in this chapter. For example, Singer, in studying blogs produced by national and regional journalists in the USA, deployed a relatively conventional content analysis in order to investigate how these professional communicators were using this new form: she found that in many ways they were, as she terms it, 'normalising' blogs, by imposing the same kinds of conventions and standards they would adopt in their day jobs (Singer 2005). Of course, this may tell us more about the inflexibility of professional journalistic codes than about the limits of online observation. But studies of online communities more generally tend to use surveys (e.g. of news groups) to find out about the users (see, for example, Parks 1996). Beaulieu (2004) has usefully reviewed some of the pitfalls and possibilities of observation using the Internet. She suggests that the Internet raises many, largely familiar, dilemmas for ethnographic work.

In order to undertake observation of blogging, for example, you will first have to address exactly the same questions as for any other form of observational research. Which material will you analyse? Questions of sampling over time arise and are very familiar.

If you wish to investigate the bloggers themselves rather than the topic (the Iraq war, life in Midwest America, the problems of domestic life for women, etc.), how will you select or sample them, and can you deduce much about them without resorting to more direct methods – in other words, turning your observation into an online survey? Ethically, the researcher is faced with the problem of needing access to material that is, after all, in the public domain, but then not declaring her or his presence and remaining passive – *lurking*, in other words. This actually poses no different questions to other forms of non-participant observation, and its ethical dimensions are mentioned earlier in this chapter and again in chapter 15.

The role of observation

Observation is rarely sufficient in itself as a method. It lends itself to use alongside other methodologies, both qualitative and quantitative. It is, however, a rich and rewarding component of the research tools available to the researcher in communications. As Elliott points out:

> One of the strengths of observation as a technique of research is that it implicitly includes within itself other methods such as interviewing, examination of documentary records, and output. Missing a single incident is much less important than failing to get an answer to a question in a questionnaire survey. Observation covers the total process of which any incident is only a part.

> (Elliott 1971: 109)

This is important, because many recent discussions of 'ethnography', as well as making exaggerated claims for the technique, have also left a daunting sense that the complexities and demands of observation set standards few can meet. These debates, which have focused on the business of writing observation and ethnographic studies, are so acutely conscious of the burden of authorship and the obligations of reflexivity incumbent on the researcher, that methodological paralysis has set in. As Morley and Silverstone note:

> If the traditional anthropological attitude to these questions ('Don't think about ethnography, just do it') is the problem, then equally, to fall into a paralysing (if vertiginously thrilling) trance of

epistemological navel-gazing ('Don't do ethnography, just think about it') is no kind of answer to anyone with a commitment to empirical research.

(Morley and Silverstone 1991: 162)

We have moved on since the pioneering work of Malinowski and his colleagues. But the simple task of observation remains, as he wished it to be, 'the love of tasting of the variety of human modes of life' (Malinowski 1922: 517). In concert with the many other methods explained in this book, observation will continue to be central in the work of communications researchers.

Summary: key points

- This chapter first introduced various types of observational methods:
  1. simple – 'fly on the wall';
  2. participant – but term used loosely;
  3. ethnography – roots in anthropology and urban sociology;
  4. experimental – controlled conditions but problem of inference and generalisation.

- We then considered the main features of the feminist critique:
  1. quantification aids male bias;
  2. researchers and researched inhabit same culture.

- The advantages of observation were discussed:
  1. subjective understanding;
  2. seeing the unseen;
  3. immediacy;
  4. grounded, flexible;
  5. richness and colour.

- This was balanced by discussion of the disadvantages of observation:
  1. participation hinders observation;
  2. observation hinders participation;
  3. is data representative?
  4. the 'Hawthorne effect' – observation provokes 'unnatural' behaviour;
  5. you observe only what is immediately accessible;
  6. depends on perspicacity of researcher.

- Observation can make use of online resources, not least in investigating news weblogs, but the methodological problems and approaches do not change.

- The five stages of doing observational studies were set out:
    1. Stage 1: entry;
    2. Stage 2: sponsorship/gatekeeping;
    3. Stage 3: planning;
    4. Stage 4: data collection;
    5. Stage 5: data analysis.

chapter twelve

Attending to Talk

The conditions and practices of media production and consumption are divergent in a number of significant ways, and one of the achievements of media studies has been to make these clear and provide detailed evidence of them. Any achievement casts a shadow, though, and in this case the shadow cast has been a tendency to consider media production and consumption more or less in analytical isolation from each other. While their divergent nature always has to be taken into account – involving a professional, and relatively composite, elite in media production, and, by contrast, a highly differentiated and heterogeneous range of audiences in media consumption – this is an unfortunate tendency because cultural production and consumption are not separable processes (Deacon 2003). They are interdependent in various ways, and they have direct and indirect implications for each other. For example, cultural production in the media is in part informed by a conception of media texts, images and genres as variable units of consumption, among differentiated target audiences and readerships, and cultural consumption is likewise informed by the resultant media products which, of necessity, provide the initiating points of use, reception and interpretation.

Throughout this book, we approach media communication as a long, complex, yet always interlinked circuit of different forms of communicative practices and events. This involves moving away from a separatist approach, which examines media production in one part of the syllabus and the audience consumption of media products in a later and unrelated block of teaching. Counter to this, we argue for the need to situate media production and consumption within the broader social processes and conditions which both shape and inform them.

In this and the following chapter, the category of talk provides us with another way of bringing media production and consumption into some sort of intellectual relationship. We shall begin by looking at some of the sites and styles of media talk, concentrating on how talk occurs in the different programming genres of radio and television, for these two media, above all, provide the primary media sites of social talk. We shall go on to consider forms of talk which occur outside the institutions and discourses of these media, but which have direct reference to them, in processes of aesthetic response, recollection and evaluation following or attendant on the experiences of media consumption.

This leads us to another shortcoming in contemporary media studies: its tendency to be present-centred, to lack a historical dimension of any significance. This is not as marked, perhaps, as it was in the 1990s, and, in general terms, attempts to build up that dimension have been stronger in the USA than in Britain or Western Europe, but historical myopia and a relentless focus on the present remain characteristic of much of the work done in media and communications. In a textbook such as this, we can only make a modest contribution towards facilitating and contributing to a change of approach that would make historical reference in media and cultural analysis as commonplace as contemporary reference. It is confined to three practical steps. The first of these we have already advised you to take, in using historical sound archives as a basic resource for communications research (see chapter 2). The second involves the textual analysis on historical news stories we have taken you through in chapters 8 and 10. The third step is covered in this chapter. It involves you in a small oral history project, manageable as a coursework assignment, the methodology of which is based very much on talk. The focus of this project is on media consumption in the past, and its generational configurations, though in the ensuing analysis, questions of media production should be carefully linked to the uses, meanings and values made of the media products consumed. We shall preface our outline of this project with a summary of the techniques of qualitative interviewing in media research, along with a discussion of some of their particular features and the issues they raise.

It will not be possible for us to touch on all forms of broadcast talk, less still on all forms of talk about them, but we hope that in your own media analysis you will be able to apply our discussion of talk in the media and talk about the media across the board, in whatever specific area of spoken media discourse and interaction you choose to work. The various methods we outline for generating, organising and analysing data about media talk among practitioners and audiences are likewise by no means exhaustive, but they should provide you with a number of approaches and a useful set of tools. If you are studying some particular genre of broadcast talk, then obviously your material will be taken from off-air or online recording. On the other hand, you may need to focus on the assimilation of media communications into the informal social discourse of everyday life. In doing this, you will become involved in some kind of interviewing. Interviewing is the main way in which talk is *generated* as a form of data in social science research, and following our general guidelines to interviewing methods and protocol, you will have an opportunity to start putting what you have learnt into practice.

Once again, though, we want to stress the importance of considering media products and the broad practice of media consumption in conjunction with each other. Talk as a general category facilitates this in that, whichever dimension you focus on initially, at some stage you will need to move backwards or forwards to other dimensions in the sequence, if you are to comprehend the inter-contextual relations which all contemporary media entail. From the generation of your material, you will then go on to deal with its analysis. The main way in which talk is *analysed* in the social sciences is through approaches derived from linguistic and interactional models of communication, and here, as well as semiotics, discourse analysis and conversation analysis figure prominently. Following an outline of what such forms of analysis involve, in chapter 13 we shall also set up another small research project, in which you can try out some of the concepts and the methods associated with them. The logic of progression, then, in both this and the succeeding chapter, is from the general to the concrete, from broad methodological and conceptual considerations to the practical application of social science methodology in media research.

Sites and styles of media talk

Talk has many forms, but these are usually tied in some way to particular sites and settings. You would not expect to be interrogated in the manner of a police interview while you were standing waiting for a train, just as you would not expect simply to pass the time of day if you were asked by the police to speak as a witness to a crime. *Where* talk takes place, and with *whom*, can influence considerably *what* it accomplishes, and *how*. The site and setting create certain expectations which participants usually find difficult to resist, at least in any sustained and thoroughgoing manner. In the broadcast media, such expectations are taken over and reproduced to the extent that programmes attempt to deliver realist representations of social life, in the kinds of setting or simulacra of the kinds of setting with which we are familiar. Talk in the media is also conditioned by the genres and types of programming in which it occurs: broad dialect, for example, would be acceptable in a documentary, but not in a national news bulletin. Even within the same general type of programming, though, the differential gradations can be quite steep.

In the now common populist TV discussion programme, a panel of interested participants interact with a live audience and an anchorperson, who mediates between panel and audience (including the audience at home) in a debate about topically sensitive or topic-provocative issues. Such programmes are characterised by their intense vocal contests, often leading to the open expression of vitriol and abuse. The result is a tabloidisation of discussion, the public sphere as a sort of spectacular circus show in which the anticipated conflict between different viewpoints, manifest in unrestrained forms of talk, is the premium entertainment value. This is at a considerable remove from the elitist TV discussion programme, in which such figures as university dons, writers and politicians explore differences of view about a given topic in a generally sedate and sequentially ordered fashion, and in a manner of mutual absorption in ideas raised. The result of this kind of discussion format is the televisualisation of academic talk, the public sphere as a professor's living-room forum on air, in which the anticipated conflict between different viewpoints, manifest in restrained forms of talk, is the premium intellectual value. The differential gradations between these two sorts of discussion programme can be said to correspond – in some ways quite obviously, in others not – to stratifications of social class, status and educational background. Social divisions are not only displayed in televised talk, whether populist or antipopulist, but are also intricately enacted and confronted. In his book *Confrontation Talk* (1996), Ian Hutchby investigates the verbal encounters of the radio talk show. His fine-grained empirical analysis shows, for one specific broadcast genre, the various ways in which power relations are given form, reproduced and resisted. Although these relations have to be understood sociologically, in terms of broadly theorised divisions, asymmetries and inequities, Hutchby reveals very clearly how, at a micro-level, power is instantiated in what is said and argued between participants in institutional settings.

Broadly speaking, we can distinguish between talk which is monologic, where one person is speaking to many listeners, as in a lecture or speech, and talk which is dialogic, a process of interaction occurring in spoken language between two or more people, whether in the hubbub of a pub before a football match, in the quiet intimacy of the bedroom or in the peculiarly faceless form of communication conducted over the telephone. Monologic talk tends to be more formalised, even where what is said and heard has a familiar structure, whereas dialogic talk can be informal and familiar, or formal and unfamiliar, as well as variants on these, depending on those involved and the context in which it takes place. The common-or-garden conception of talk is generally of spoken dialogue that takes place within a small focused gathering, situated in an everyday setting. Here, the roles of addresser and addressee characteristically alternate among the individuals involved; they change and are generally reversible, even when one person may tend to take up most of the speaking. So, for example, when someone who has been asked a question as an addressee directs an answer to the person who asked it, she or he then becomes the addressee of the reply, and the person who was first the addressee may then underline the role-switch by in turn addressing another question to the initial questioner, and so on. These sorts of role do remain distinct for certain moments, stages or sequences of a conversation, and in certain forms of talk the role of one participant may remain relatively fixed and stable throughout the duration of the talk, as for example when a barrister interrogates a defendant in a court of law. In fact, it is not only different social roles which constrain participation in talk, but also certain rules and conventions for how, in any everyday setting, talk should proceed. We do not normally regard it as reasonable or acceptable for one person to dominate all the talk in an entire conversation, or for the talk to jump about, willy-nilly, among myriad entirely discrete topics.

The interview is another common example of role-rule discourse, and it will be of major interest to us in this chapter. The reason for this is that while it can occur in a range of different modes which may affect the relative stability of the different roles, it is a form of talk that, in general terms, is common to both media discourse and communications research. As we made clear at the outset, this is why we have chosen to bring them together under the same umbrella category of *talk*. So, for instance, in a broadcast news programme, the newsreader or anchorperson remains the interviewer, the person who asks questions which others answer – although it is not quite as straightforward as that, of course. For example, up until the late 1950s in Britain, BBC interviewers were largely deferential in their questioning of politicians, with the result that politicians either prearranged the interview or used it, largely unimpeded, to fashion their own agenda. Since then, broadcast interviewing has not only eschewed any form of rehearsal, but has also become much tighter in its control of the politicians interviewed, with those involved pushing hard for an answer to the question asked and refusing to let interviewees take over the talk for the sake of addressing their own, usually variant concerns. Nonetheless, despite interviewers' shift in British media to a more adversarial approach and less tolerant attitude to politicians bending talk-in-interaction to their own ends, we are all familiar with the ways in which politicians attempt to sneak away from questions, shift the topic to another with which they feel more at ease, turn their answers into self-defensive assaults on other parties, or otherwise manipulate the talk. Several researchers have studied these attempts at resistance and evasion, agenda-shifting and topic-management by politicians in interviews. While some ducking-and-weaving tactics appear more acceptable than others, politicians have to weigh up the possible advantages to be gained by this type of behaviour against the counter-productive effects that may follow from their negative appraisal by viewers or listeners (Greatbatch 1986; Harris 1991; Clayman and Heritage 2002: ch. 7). As Steven Clayman and John Heritage have concluded: 'Resistant and evasive responses, while frequent, are done cautiously and are managed with an elaborate array of remedial practices that work to ameliorate the breach of conduct' (Clayman and Heritage 2002: 297).

While there are always recognisable structures within talk, the most fascinating feature of talk is its immense variation within historical periods and within social sites. We must always remember this, even as we try to think about what characterises talk as a basic medium of communication. In media research interviews, the researcher is the one whose primary fieldwork role is that of soliciting information from a number of informants. To the extent that this role is defined by asking questions, there is an obvious resemblance to that of the broadcast interviewer. This obviousness is beguiling precisely because the modes and forms of interviewing cover a broad range, and in view of this we always need to attend to the particularities of the interactive processes that are involved. How this interaction is accomplished, and the degree to which its setting is institutional and thus differentiated from ordinary talk, has implications for the meanings generated by talk and the relations between the participants. It is here that any comparison reaches its limit, for beyond that limit the concrete divergences between how the media talk to us and how we talk to each other necessarily take precedence, on the ascending steps of analysis, over more abstractly general features of communication.

As we have noted, the most general settings for social talk are those of our everyday lives, and broadcast talk is obviously different to this. When we talk to a friend or colleague about, say, a television discussion programme heard the evening before, this occurs in the familiar, routine context of our daily lives, but the talk we refer to is not synonymous with our talk about it, which is, by contrast, directly reciprocal, involving point and response in a single, immediate context. Media talk may often simulate ordinary talk, and use such talk as a basic template, 'the prototype of the exchange of utterances involved in talk' (Giddens 1990a: 126). Yet, because of its institutional and public character, how it operates and the values it evinces are, at the same time, at variance with ordinary talk in certain ways. For example, it often has devices within it which exhibit the need to think of the spatially absent and distant viewer or listener, as in the media interviewer's use of what Heritage calls 'formulations' – techniques of summarising what an interviewee has said, stressing certain aspects of what has been said over others, exploring their implications in order to keep the audience in the picture, or declining to act as the primary recipients of interviewee responses (Heritage 1985; Clayman and Heritage 2002: 120–4). Another technique involves manoeuvres in what Goffman referred to as shifts in the speaker's interactional 'footing', where statements or points of view are attributed to a third party (Clayman and Heritage 2002: 152–62; and see Goffman 1981: ch. 3). These devices can be used to establish 'points of identification' with viewers 'in ways which help to secure consent for the views expressed in the programme' (Brunt 1990: 65). As these examples of general features of media talk demonstrate, if you were to adopt similar 'formulations' in everyday conversation with your own peer group, the result would usually appear highly contrived. Talk is always contextually defined, and media talk clearly involves different discursive relations in different forms of context.

As television viewers, we often attend to interpersonal communication in a range of different kinds of programming, from soap operas to talk shows and news interviews. What is said and how it is said are, to all intents and purposes, framed by the generic and institutional features of the programme in question. In television drama, for example, we are listening to simulated interpersonal forms of talk, though in some cases we may identify with these precisely because they are similar to forms of talk which occur, regularly or irregularly, in the settings of our everyday lives. 'Broadcasting reproduces the world as ordinary,' writes Paddy Scannell, 'but that seeming obviousness is an effect, the outcome of a multiplicity of small techniques and discursive practices that combine to produce that deeply taken-for-granted sense of familiarity with what is seen and heard' (Scannell 1991: 8). While this is so, we need to remember that the form of our seeing and listening is, at the same time, always divergent, for we listen as media audiences, not as co-participants in an immediately realised conversation, where the alternation between the roles of addresser and addressee is, in contrast, generally abundant. The kinds of interaction which occur through mass communication are quite different to those associated with situations of co-presence. Those involved in media production operate in another time and place to those occupied by media consumers; and, by comparison with the kinds of social interaction facilitated by talk in the mundane settings of our day-to-day lives, media talk and media discourse do not generally involve direct feedback from audience members, or any of the immediate, huddled reciprocity that goes on in the talk that takes place in small groups.

It is vital that we keep these two scans of attention – towards the media and away from the media – in continual interplay. In this spirit, let us turn back for a minute to points of engagement with the media. These involve identification not only with the effective obviousness of 'the world as ordinary', but also with the affective tangibility of what is both the same and different. A good while before media studies became an established field in the human sciences curriculum, two researchers, Donald Horton and Richard Wohl, referred to this new kind of social relationship with media personnel or media characters as 'para-social interaction' (see Horton and Wohl 1956). They were particularly interested in the kind of vicarious or simulated relationships which members of the media audience establish with individual stars or personalities in the media, whether with a pop singer, a newsreader or a protagonist in a soap opera. What characterises such relationships is 'intimacy at a distance'. This actually gives rise to some difficult analytical problems we cannot discuss here – they are not only psychological, but also hermeneutical, sociological and historical in nature – but we should resist the still prevalent tendency to see para-social relationships as automatically deficient. For many people, the kind of regular interaction they provide makes the media companions of their everyday lives into a 'screen community' that operates as 'an extended kin grouping, whereby the viewer comes into contact with the wider society beyond his [sic] immediate family' (Noble 1975: 64). The interaction involved can only be a quasi-interaction because of the predominantly one-way flow of media communications, but we should remember that the meanings made of it are not only those generated through the practices of media production. Media audiences participate, and not only ritually, in meaning-construction. This means that the interpretive range of media talk is always potentially greater than it is in small groups, where talk can have highly normative effects.

We should also emphasise, perhaps, that predominantly one-way flows of communication are not confined to mass communication. This is something which university lecturers are consciously (and at times, self-consciously) aware of when they come to deliver that largely monologic form of communication known as the lecture. In addition, we should note that the vocal and visual communicative channels of radio and television permit a much closer approximation of everyday conversation or talk than do previous media, for electronic media, and especially television, make communicating individuals into '*personalities* with a voice, a face, a character and a history, personalities with whom recipients can sympathise or empathise, whom they can like or dislike, detest or revere' (Thompson 1990: 228, original emphasis). At the same time, the relationships with such personalities, and the valorisations associated with them, are structured by precisely the time–space distantiation which is intrinsic to media communications and which makes them possible.

These are, first of all, questions of technological production and diffusion. The communications media have changed and contributed to change in many areas of cultural life, and their ability to mechanically record and reproduce sounds of any kind has been central to such change and influence. It is only since the turn of the nineteenth to the twentieth century that this ability has become technologically possible, and thus only over this period that we have become able to record audio (and subsequently, visual) data and to access such data as a sociological and historical resource. This is a resource of inestimable benefit, and its fruits should neither be easily forgotten nor lightly dismissed. Yet there is a quite common assumption that academic research should concentrate on the generation of its own primary data, and this is commonly manifest as an evaluative yardstick in assessing the 'originality' of any piece of research. The degree to which you go about compiling your own first-hand material should depend, instead, on the stated need or desirability for doing so in relation to your research topic. Where there are already existing resources, in collections and archives, it would be silly to ignore them when they are relevant to your research. As we pointed out in chapter 2, some of the basic donkey work of collection may already have been done, and where this is the case you should make use of whatever resources are available. Your research may have been inspired in the first place by the existence of a particular batch of material in a local or national repository. The fact that you may then be engaging in secondary analysis, as, for example, you would almost certainly be in using the sound recordings of an oral history collection, does not matter in itself. Rather, it is the ideas you bring to such material, how you bring it into confrontation with other material, and what you do in your analysis generally, which count for far more.

Recording talk

In studying any aspect of talk in or about the media you have three basic alternatives:

- utilising existing resources in sound archives;
- recording samples of talk from particular kinds of radio and television programming;
- recording talk yourself as a newly generated resource in interviews or group discussions.

As we have said, your choice between these alternatives should depend on whether or not the resources you need are already available, and whether or not any existing resources require, for quantitative or qualitative reasons, any new material to supplement and complement them. The first of these alternatives has already been addressed in chapter 2. To what we said there, we want to add just three further points that you should bear in mind.

First, how talk has been recorded and stored will depend largely on when the recording was made. Even though the technological facilities for mechanical recording have existed since the late nineteenth century, following the inventions in sound transmission and reproduction of Thomas Edison and Emile Berliner, you will find that most recordings of media talk are from the 1930s onwards. Such recordings have been made on disc (shellac and vinyl) and, since the 1950s, on audio tape (reel-to-reel and cassette). More recently, they have been made in digital format. Further sources for recorded talk, though at one remove as it were, are the scripts and transcripts of broadcast programmes. With early broadcasting versions of these, it is helpful to know that what was scripted was usually and quite literally what was broadcast, as there was less institutional licence for spontaneous talk than in contemporary broadcasting. In Britain, a major national resource for these scripts and other production material is the BBC's Written Archives at Caversham, near Reading. Where recordings of particular programmes were never made or no longer exist, this written material is obviously extremely valuable, as one of us found in researching a BBC variety programme of the 1930s and 1940s (Pickering 1996, 2007: ch. 8).

Second, wherever you decide to work on any archival resource, you need to remember the laws of copyright. These are very likely to apply to the material of recorded talk, and you need to be careful to ensure that in any use of it, published or otherwise, you do not contravene their requirements (see Robertson and Nicol 1992: ch. 5; Welsh, Greenwood and Banks 2005: ch. 28). We shall say a little more later on about recording media talk, which can come either off-air from broadcast transmissions or from interviews with selected informants. In the former case, though, you should remember that principles of copyright will also apply, and you should be careful to adhere to them.

Third, it is crucial that you make an audio or video recording where you are not using secondary materials from the sound archives. Mechanical recordings will obviously be much more accurate than any notes you would otherwise make after the event. Such accuracy is vital, regardless of whether you are working primarily on the content or primarily on the form of what is said. In mechanically recording talk in an interview or group discussion, you are also free of the burden of having to make hasty decisions about the relative value and worth of what is said. You will be able to decide this afterwards, when working over your recording. This is an advantage if only because the significance of what is said (or how it is said) is sometimes only realised after careful scrutiny and consideration. Further, using a tape recorder is the least obtrusive way of recording talk. Most people today do not feel seriously inhibited in the presence of such an audio recorder, particularly where the value of using it is clearly spelt out, and where assurances are given about the confidentiality of what you collect and its strictly limited research use. Though digital cameras are a little more obtrusive, especially if camera movement is involved, they are nowadays small and unlikely to intimidate most people, particularly when similar assurances are given. The need for such recording devices is commonly accepted. Most people will not be anxious about their use, and will generally ignore cameras and recorders once an interview has got into its swing.

It is important that you become technically proficient in your use of recording equipment. Obviously you want to avoid having to repeat an interview due to failure to record or to poor-quality recording, but in the interests of making your interviews as smooth and relaxed as possible, you should resist the conversational gaps and stiltedness of interaction associated with note-taking. Skill in using recording equipment is also important because in qualitative interviewing you are interested in your informant's manner of expression, their ways of interpreting experience and producing narrative. More than anything else, the interview is always recorded because it ensures that the talk generated by the interview will be in the informant's own words, their own style and structure of speaking. This is crucial for the nature of the evidence generated by the interview. As Trevor Lummis has pointed out in respect of oral history interviews, the form of qualitative interviewing on which we focus in this chapter, the conversation involved acquires a 'different epistemological status' when it is not recorded: 'it becomes hearsay evidence' (Lummis 1987: 24).

In chapter 4, we distinguished between communications research interviews in terms of their degree of standardisation, moving from the highly regulated interview schedule, through semi-structured interviews, to focus group discussions. In recording talk about historical topics and remembered experience, interviews adopt a relatively free format. To a greater or lesser degree, they resemble everyday conversation, and in this sense can be described as naturalistic. 'The ideal in the naturalistic or unstructured interview is to approximate the "feeling" of the unforced conversations of everyday life' (Wilson 1996: 95). But as we made clear in chapter 4, the similarity to everyday conversation remains exactly that, for behind its guise of resemblance there exists the ulterior purpose and practice of research. The talk generated is, or will become, an object of academic study. This means that however naturalistic the interview may appear to be, it is at the same time managed by the investigator in the interests of a particular research agenda and according to certain methodological principles of operation. Naturalistic interviews ape everyday conversation, and yet simultaneously guide informants towards certain topics, encourage them to express their attitudes, beliefs and feelings, and discourage them from wandering too far from the chosen research track.

Generally, informants as well as investigators are aware of this double articulation of interview talk and accommodate themselves to it, though obviously with varying degrees of ease and sophistication. This is not especially difficult for most people in that it entails more or less usual conformity with the normative structures of everyday conversation outside of interview situations, such as turn-taking, the use of relevant transition points between turns, and coeval participation. The extent to which this conformity occurs will greatly affect the procedure of the interview and the relative diminution of any likelihood of informants reacting to being questioned in such a way that they speak or behave artificially (that is, at variance with their usual participation in everyday social interaction). In order to encourage this conformity, an important interviewing skill clearly lies in allowing the questions and answers to flow, to develop a movement and momentum that emulates the to-and-fro pattern of everyday talk. The trick is in eliciting information in terms of informants' own interpretations, their own frames of seeing, speaking and understanding, and the more the interview is similar to everyday talk, the more this sort of information will be forthcoming. Think also of the setting, for this can definitely influence the course of the interview. In the view of Beatrice Webb, a pioneer of the sociological interview, 'the less formal the conditions of the interview the better' (Webb 1950: 363).

One of the benefits of non-standardised interviews is that the researcher is able to follow up initial questions and responses, to encourage the interviewee to explore a topic or issue in its various ramifications. In this way, the research generates a fuller response than is possible in highly structured interviews. This kind of follow-up guidance and encouragement on the part of the researcher is usually referred to as **probing**. Probing may involve both encouraging the interviewee to develop a response, and following up a response by seeking clarification or amplification of what has been said. Again, the technique is similar to the ways in which, in everyday conversation, we seek to dispel ambiguity or ask for the elaboration of a particular point; yet, at the same time, it is distinct from such conversation not only by being more formalised and developed as a practical skill, but also, as a matter of methodological principle, by being disinclined to influence respondents unduly or force words into their mouths. Probing must be executed sensitively, especially because it can be of considerable benefit in helping to build up a fuller picture. Its use is generally greater in the informal kinds of interviewing on which we are concentrating here.

In conventional, one-to-one market survey research, the interviewer has relatively little latitude for probing, which is usually done in predetermined ways or through what are called (somewhat fancifully) 'neutral probes'. In non-standardised interviews, by contrast, there is much greater flexibility in prompting, procuring and cultivating, through the interplay of talk, the kinds of qualitative data required. Indeed, because probing in this way involves greater interaction between the participating parties than in highly standardised interview formats, it is cognate with the emphasis on 'sharing' experience which some feminist researchers have preferred to the 'masculine' emphasis on disengagement and control over exchange, and the sharp role-differentiation of researcher and researched, which in their view is artificial, undesirable and not conducive to the establishment of a necessary rapport within the exchange (see Oakley 1981; Finch 1984; for a general review of feminist interview research, Reinharz 1992: ch. 2). In any event, the relative 'open-endedness' of such interviews allows greater opportunities for clarification, expansion, comparison and the examination of what appears ambiguous or is left tacit in an informant's initial formulation. It is this that makes such interviews effective strategies for sociological exploration.

There are dangers in this, of course, for example in asking leading or overly directive questions, or in introducing distortion through what is rather simplistically referred to as interviewer bias. Certainly interviewers must be on their guard not to push their informants towards a desired statement or shared evaluation. That is why we have used the phrase 'sociological exploration' advisedly, for sociologically the emphasis must be on the exploration, and the imposition of the interviewer's own views or ideas on the informant inhibits this process.

Remember that in the unstructured or quasi-structured interview, a premium is placed on informants providing talk about the research topic in their own terms, their own vocabulary and frame of reference. This is one of its chief benefits and points of interest, for what it should facilitate is a fuller representation of particular issues and concerns from social 'insiders', and thus, potentially, a richer understanding of the values and viewpoints integral to the integument of 'insider' experience. Such interviews can be used in this way to recover certain forms of experience, the nature of which may previously have been heavily skewed in externally produced accounts. This will be effectively achieved, however, only when the researcher remains an attentive and sensitive listener, willing to adapt to the movement of the interview and be flexible in the way aspects of the topic are dealt with and discussed.

A non-directive interview resembles positive conversation in leading to inter-subjective understanding, but, again, it is distinct in seeking to avoid the imposition of the interviewer's views on the interviewee. This is not the same as the injunction to be 'neutral' or 'disengaged' in the interests of the collection of 'objective' data; rather, it could just as well be a recognition of the practical difficulties and tensions involved in qualitative interviewing, which always requires the establishment of trust, mutual respect and interactive rapport if it is to be successful. Clearly, these qualities cannot be established by anyone concentrating only on a specious detachment from the cooperative enterprise of the research interview, just as, and at the same time, the interviewer cannot allow exchange with an informant to ramble hopelessly or lose all sense of direction. The research interview has always to be a 'guided conversation', a 'conversation with a purpose' (Lofland 1971: 84; Burgess 1984: 102).

Oral history and the media

Having considered certain key aspects of recording talk and qualitative interviewing, we shall now concentrate directly on the specific form and mode of the oral history interview. This should show you, in much greater detail, how to utilise the interviewing method of generating data. It will also enable you to begin developing your interviewing skills in relation to a particular research project which you can conduct for yourself. First, though, it is important to set the stage for this small-scale project by outlining what is involved in oral history, and what makes it relatively distinct both methodologically and epistemologically.

It is only since the 1970s that oral sources have come back into vogue as a means of generating historical material. Representing the past through talk, through orally transmitted sketches and narratives, is nothing new, of course. Human societies have been doing precisely that for thousands of years (see Thompson 1978: ch. 2; Dunaway and Baum 1984: pt 1). Developing from the nineteenth century and becoming the preserve of a professionally trained elite, academic history tended to ignore these older forms of social remembering and historical representation. Formal written history has shown a strong bias towards print documentation, as for example with the documents deposited in archives, libraries and record offices. Such documents have comprised the bulk of the material on which historians have drawn in writing history, and intrinsically they have been considered more accurate and reliable than oral sources. Until comparatively recently, many historians assumed, or indeed firmly believed, that documentary sources were the only valid sources of evidence about the past. Such sources are not infallible, of course. They have their own biases, distortions and gaps. They are (at least partly) as they are because of the knowledge, beliefs and values of those who produced them; these elements are, in some way, always inscribed in the document at hand, and were, in some way, always instrumental in shaping them into the particular piece of the past which they represent.

For certain areas of historical inquiry, documentary sources also have little evidence to offer, even when we read them against the grain of what they contain. The power relations in family and other domestic settings, vernacular expressive practices in the workplace, courting and childbirth rituals, or the informal minutiae of symbolic exchange in everyday life are ready examples of where documentary sources and official archives have been deficient. More generally, it is the felt texture of people's lives in the past, especially for those at the social margins, which is often missing, and when this is so, no amount of painstaking grubbing around in the record offices and depositories will help to overcome the lack. We have to go elsewhere for these qualitative details, and when we do find them, in whatever traces of them we can recuperate, they can work to shed new light on what is actually available through documentary sources, allowing us to see their more formal evidence afresh, or suggesting ways in which we can call their underlying values or assumptions into question. This does not mean that other sources, such as those presented by oral testimony, simply redress the balance in each and every empirical case, providing truth in place of bias and distortion. But they do help to complete the picture, partial though it will always be; they do render more problematic its constituent elements, in form and in content; and they do encourage our questioning of all forms of evidence. To that extent, at least, they contribute to the production of better history.

A further point that should be made about documentary sources concerns their provenance. You do not have to go far back into the past to find many people in Britain unable to write much, or certainly not with any fluency. In any case, they were not disposed to write about their experiences or views. Many ordinary working people were not in a position to produce the kind of documentation which now provides the material for writing history. In countless cases, their experience has thus been swept away and lost to history. At best, it has been recorded from the point of view of those who were literate; and, in some cases, these people have been in positions of structural superiority, and have looked down on those who were without the skills of literacy or the benefits of an extended formal education. It is not only the case that many people did not leave documents, or that any documents they did leave have tended not to survive. It is also that, again, until fairly recently, 'ordinary' men and women – 'the common people', as they used to be known – were not in the business of writing history, or history as professionally legitimated. It was predominantly middle- and upper-class men who engaged in the activity of producing history books. This did not mean that ordinary people had no sense of history, or that they did not pass on stories about life in the past, whether their own or that of their forebears, but generally these stories were not written down, and so were always more vulnerable to becoming lost from view. During the course of the past century, in particular, this situation has been changing. More and more men and women have been putting pen to paper and recording the events and experiences of their own lives and those around them, in their immediate neighbourhoods and communities, and this has considerably expanded the scope and reach of social history and histories of everyday life. Even so, most people do not leave records in any ordered narrative fashion, and the need to preserve in some form their experiences of the past remains as insistent as ever.

History will always be full of gaps, but once certain gaps have been spotted, oral history has the obvious merit of being able to come in and set about the task of gathering the appropriate material needed to plug them, and so recreate more comprehensively the broken terrain of the past. Oral history does this in ways which are methodologically different to the use of documentary sources, not least because it involves generating new historical evidence rather than locating it in a filed storage box in the archive. It is true, of course, that this evidence is always going to be primarily about the recent past, a past which has been personally lived through and is now recalled by particular individuals, but it is, nevertheless, evidence which is not usually available in the customary sources. Because of this, oral history 'is useful for getting information about *people* less likely to be engaged in creating written records and for creating historical accounts of *phenomena* less likely to have produced archival material' (Reinharz 1992: 131, original emphasis). Oral history is also epistemologically distinct from documentary sources in that, as evidence, it has directly involved the work of the interviewer. The interviewer has asked certain questions, guided the informant in various ways, and asked for clarification and amplification. It is for this reason, among others, that the oral history interviewer always needs to be well prepared, and certainly a good deal more so than anyone involved in a standardised market survey. There is no point going into an interview with no preconception about the aspects of a person's experience on which the interview is to concentrate; nor is there any point in not having prepared beforehand a series of questions for which you require answers. We shall return to this matter later.

Though some of the research associated with the pioneering work in sociology at the University of Chicago during the second quarter of the twentieth century is now considered an important forerunner, oral history has only recently come into its own. Even in this short span of time, some very significant contributions have been made by oral history to our knowledge of ordinary people's lives in the past – a past which, for reasons already acknowledged, has generally been confined to the later nineteenth and twentieth centuries. It is important to note another particular feature of oral history, though. It is a methodology for mining certain sources of information, and is not a substantive field of history in the same way as urban, political, gender or cultural history. Methodologically, its benefit is that it can generate new material in these substantive fields of historical writing, and can do so in ways which illuminate aspects not available to the historian through other sources and methodologies. We should add a further qualification, perhaps, for despite the impression we have given, oral history is not confined methodologically to the study of the pasts of so-called ordinary people. It can be used just as well in the study of social elites and eminent figures who have attained a high public profile. Generally, its use in connection with such individuals and groups has been minimal, and raises particular problems concerning the status and quality of the evidence which is produced (see Seldon and Pappworth 1983 on elite oral history). The best use of oral history has been in providing fresh material about 'ordinary' people's everyday experience in the past, ranging in topic from the parental or institutional treatment of children and forms of childhood recreation, through the sexual activities of men and women in different social strata and the difficulties under which working-class women struggled in their efforts to keep 'house and home' together, to the activities of London's criminal underworld or the politicisation of workers through their experience of industrial exploitation and the abuse of management power. Though oral history has exhibited certain complacently populist tendencies, it has proved highly successful in widening the horizons of historical research (Passerini 1979: 84). The material generated is extremely diverse, and is only limited by certain factors which may prevent or inhibit people from recounting aspects of their past lives and those of their families, neighbours and fellow workers.

Yet one area is largely missing from this diverse range of material. The new mass media of the twentieth century have received remarkably little attention from oral historians, despite the fact that we have only a sketchy picture of the day-to-day detail of people's media consumption during the course of the century. There are very few exceptions (see Clayre 1973; Moores 1988; O'Sullivan 1991; Simpson, P.A. 1996). It is true that popular leisure has been covered much more, but where it has, use of the media has not figured very prominently. How people use various media as vehicles of personal and social memory, and how cultural technologies of recording, preservation and playback mediate the past in various ways, represents an even larger area of neglect (but see Keightley and Pickering 2006). This is why we suggest that, in attending to talk as a serious source and form of evidence, you embark on a practical research project focusing on the oral historical investigation of media consumption among earlier generations. This involves three basic tasks: first, the gathering of qualitative data concerning the first-hand experience of one or, at most, two individuals; second, the analysis of this data in relation to other, secondary historical sources; and third, the evaluation of the method used in relation to other methods for acquiring material and engaging in the work of historical representation and interpretation. In setting out this project here, we intend to provide you with a small-scale, eminently 'do-able' piece of research that will provide you with invaluable practice in interviewing, as well as enabling you to produce some fascinating material for analysis and interpretation. Basically, what you are attending to is media consumption and popular leisure activities in the experience of a particular member (or members) of a previous **generation** during his or her youth. How they recall and express their memories of such experience will also be a matter of concern. We shall now take you through the basic steps which are involved in undertaking an oral history project of this kind, beginning with your preparation for the interview.

Preparing for the interview

Any full-scale oral-historical project concerned with media consumption and popular leisure in the past would have to follow appropriate procedures of sampling, though the usual mode of sampling in this kind of research is purposive rather than random. This is not invariably the case, one example being the use of a quota sample by Paul Thompson and Thea Vigne in their oral-historical research into British society at the beginning of the twentieth century (Thompson 1975: 5–8; and see chapter 3 of this book for quota sampling). In most cases, however, the selection of sample informants for oral history is directed by the defining topic of the investigation. Generally, this involves lengthy interviews with a fair number of people, the actual number depending on the intended reach of the project. In your own, more limited investigation, you will interview no more than one or two individuals. (It is important, nevertheless, that you think later about the representativeness of your evidence, and you can do this by reference to other historical materials. We shall come to this when we deal with your analysis.)

The first thing to do is to select your informant(s). Choose either one or two people you would like to interview. Your decision as to whether to do one or two interviews may be determined, for example, by the question of contrast. You may be interested in divergent points of engagement and pleasure in the use and experience of the media by men and women, or members of different ethnic groups, but you should try to work with only one major contrasting variable (such as gender or generation); otherwise you would lose the sharp sense of differentiation you are aiming for, amidst a host of varying factors. You will then have to conduct two separate interviews in order to generate material that will provide you with clear data on the divergent experience involved. We do say 'separate' because there is always a danger that one person may dominate the interview if you interview a man and woman together (and, in our experience, it is usually the woman who is sidelined). On the other hand, you may be concerned primarily with female media use and consumption, and this would mean that, for the purposes of this project, you can concentrate on just one interview. Whatever you decide, once you have selected the person(s) you want to interview, you must ask their consent. Provided they agree to be interviewed, you can go on to arrange a date and a venue for the interview. Do not try to do it straightaway: not only would this be potentially discourteous, but you are also less likely to get good results if you do not give your informant(s) any preparation time. Once they know an interview is to take place, they will start to think back, going over memories of their earlier lives and sifting them for their significance and value. The importance of this will be enhanced if you have given them a clear outline of what you are interested in, and a thorough briefing about the areas of their life experience you hope to cover.

Before you approach your informant(s), you should design your questionnaire. There are various steps in doing this.

- You will need to decide whether to cover all media of communication and all aspects of popular leisure which were significant in the early lives of your informants, or to concentrate on just a few (e.g. radio and popular music), or indeed to focus on only one medium and/or activity (e.g. gramophone records and/or popular dance). If you confine your focus of attention, you will have to be sure a sufficiency of material, in range and depth, is likely to be generated by the interview. Whatever you decide, you should find out as much as you can beforehand about the topic, or topics, of the interview. This will require some prior research and some background reading, which will have a further pay-off when you come to write up the project. In Beatrice Webb's estimation, as set out in her classic guide to interviewing: 'The first condition of the successful use of the interview as an instrument of research is preparedness of the mind of the operator' (Webb 1950: 361).

- You can certainly draft out an initial version of your questions before you begin this reading, but your background reading should enable you to elaborate and enhance your first-draft questions. Your background reading may also make you aware of certain gaps which need to be filled, or certain deficiencies which need to be remedied. You may come to realise that existing evidence and explanation is rather thin, and in need of considerable supplementation, or that it provides only a partial picture. Alternatively, it is possible that existing sources you have consulted are misinformed or distorted, and the evidence you acquire through the interview can then be used to critique or offer evidence contrary to these sources. You may be able to add new angles on controversial topics or debated lines of interpretation. Remember: historical knowledge is contestable.

- The questions you ask should have a certain order and sequence to them. You are only going to confuse your informant if you switch erratically from one topic to another, while making the transitions logically and smoothly will not only give your informant the opportunity to explore each topic with a reasonable degree of thoroughness, but will also enable you to ask for amplification where required, or, if necessary, to guide the informant gently back to the topic at hand if he or she begins to stray into other areas. So make sure there is order, continuity and flow in your questions. If you can, try to go beyond this and think of other desiderata. For example, Jennifer Mason has suggested that, for qualitative interviewing of any kind, researchers should ask themselves questions about substance, style and scope, as well as sequence (Mason 1996: 43–5).

- In an oral history interview, you do not work from a set script. A list of category headings distilled from a longer series of notes should be used for the actual interview as an aide-memoire. This makes it all the more important for you to prepare the substance, style, sequence and scope of your questioning. For example, do not ask vague, imprecise or complicated questions. Be specific. Concentrate on particular things. If, for example, you are focusing on radio listening, ask about particular programmes, and then follow through with more detailed questions about each of these programmes or types of programme. Your first question should be along the lines of: 'What kinds of radio programme do you listen to?' rather than: 'Do you listen to the radio?' Then you can move into further areas of questioning, dealing with frequency, occasion, motivation, gratification, and so on. But you should always avoid asking loaded questions, or questions which invite a particular answer, and you should steer clear of as much technical or conceptual vocabulary as you can. Keep your questions concise and to the point, and speak to the informant on his or her level. (You may find it helpful to refer back to chapter 4 for more information on the errors involved in asking questions.)

- While it is important that you seek to cover the required ground, it is equally important that the informant feels relaxed and at ease: the need (so far as it is possible) to emulate the ebb and flow of an everyday conversation, cannot be overestimated. If your informant wants to sidetrack a little or elaborate on a particular issue, by all means allow him or her the scope to do this. It is a question of balance. If your informant is straying in other directions too much, gently guide him or her back to the route you wish to pursue. Almost inevitably, you will also find that, during the course of the interview, certain subsidiary questions crop up, as, for instance, in relation to a point of clarification, to a particular broadcaster or musician whose name or career is unfamiliar to you, or to an aspect of the topic which you find of particular interest. You should bend the interview to such requirements, and be prepared to follow certain things through on the spur of the moment, though, again, you should be careful that anything of this nature does not distract too much from the main lines of questioning. Remember what we said about the value of 'probing', for this is something you cannot do interactively with documentary historical sources. For this reason, oral historians have argued that oral recordings are more rather than less objective than written documents: 'the personal frame of oral expression is explicit, so, unlike the arguably equal subjectivity of written records, can be directly taken into account' (Finnegan 1996: 48).

- Finally, you will need to find out from your informants certain basic factors concerning their identity and life history. These should be noted carefully. In standardised interviews they are usually filled in on what is called a 'facesheet'. The following are suggestions, but you may well want to add to them.

1. Surname and given name
2. Date and place of birth
3. Gender
4. Ethnicity
5. Religious affiliation (where relevant)
6. Occupation of parent(s)/carer(s)
7. Details of family in which informant grew up
8. Details of house, neighbourhood and schools attended
9. Own subsequent occupation(s), etc.
10. Date and place of interview.

Further to these details, it is important that you establish the particular period of time which the various memories of your informant refer to. It is also important that you develop a clear sense of the social and geographical location of the experience of which your informant is speaking in her or his recollections. These are not additional extras of information; they are vital details of context. Without them, your transcript will lose a good deal of its intrinsic worth, precisely because of the difficulty of placing the information and experience it contains in a particular period, place and milieu.

Doing your oral history interview

The growth and development of oral history has been explicitly connected to the availability of, and improvements in, audio-recording technology. We have already stressed that your oral history interview must be recorded. The importance of mechanical recording is now commonly recognised (for more on this, see Ives 1980). You will only be able to properly establish your evidence as that provided in the informant's own words by recording them in this way. As a result of recording, you will also be able to transcribe your interview(s) directly, and so note any significant analytic features of the talk of your informant. Here it is preferable to record digitally, as you will then be able to transfer the recorded material directly to your PC, and so ease the process of transcription. It is a fairly straightforward process to transfer analogue recordings to your PC, however, by connecting the audio input on your PC to the headphones connection on your tape recorder (see Box 12.1 for more information on transcribing taped conversations). There are other important considerations, as mentioned earlier in the chapter. Mechanical recording means you will be much freer to concentrate on the interview and how it is unfolding. This is vital in qualitative interviewing, which is generally a more intensive form of interviewing than that involved in social surveys, requiring an ability to think on your feet, to maintain sharp attention to the structure and flow of the interview, and to adapt flexibly to what is being said with prompts and probes, and the like. Electronic recording is eminently preferable to note-taking because it enables you to follow Lofland's injunction to give your full attention to the interviewee (Lofland 1971: 89). In the end, though, the documentary significance of recording is that 'a recording establishes beyond doubt whatever was said by whom and with what expression' (Lummis 1987: 24). It also enables someone else to check its authenticity, if for some reason this should become necessary. (For more on equipment, see Perks 1995: 14–17.)

As for the interview itself, Stephen Humphries (1984) usefully notes some dos and don'ts. Not all of these are relevant to this project, and others have already been covered; those which are relevant and which remain to be dealt with can be summarised as follows:

- *Be friendly and reassuring.* If your informant is a little self-conscious about speaking in the presence of a recorder, mention casually that it is just a machine that will help you to preserve what they have to say, and stress the importance of their information and experience. Spend a bit of time before the interview in casual conversation – it could be about anything, the topic is not important – so as to put your informant at their ease. Another way of providing reassurance is to stress the seriousness of your research motivations, and to offer confidentiality and the possibility of switching the tape recorder off at certain times if your informant wishes to say something 'off the record'.

- *Show an active interest.* Maintain eye contact and respond to what is said in an appropriate way (e.g. by nodding your head, smiling or lifting your eyebrows). Show interested body language.

- *Be a good listener.* Do not interrupt the flow of speech or fire a constant hail of approving noises at your informant. As just suggested, you should seek to show approval or some other appropriate response through facial expression and gesture. Be prepared to sit out a digression, then gently guide the informant back by such means as: 'Yes, that's fascinating, and perhaps we could come back to it later, but earlier on you were saying that…'

- *Do not impose your views.* The purpose of qualitative interviewing is not to make conversions to your way of thinking, but rather to elicit information on the informant's terms. You should avoid creating a situation where an informant is speaking in order to please you, saying what he or she thinks you want to hear rather than what they actually think. However, 'if your interviewee is a member of a minority or victimised group, then it is essential to express some sympathy with their viewpoint in order to encourage them to talk honestly about their experiences (even though you may have an opposite opinion to theirs)' (Humphries 1984: 21–2). It is perhaps worth adding to this the importance of recognising the potential for control that can lie in the hands of the interviewer. As Gunther Kress and Roger Fowler have pointed out: 'In the hands of an experienced practitioner, the devices for control granted to the interviewer by the format and situation of the interview itself constitute a formidable armoury' (Kress and Fowler 1979: 63–4). This is the case with all kinds of interviewing, but with oral history interviewing, which depends on the establishment of a certain mutual respect between the parties involved, the interviewer should be particularly sensitive to the need not to abuse or misuse this armoury.

- *Do not contradict or argue.* During the interview, you should try as much as possible to take an interested but unobtrusive stance. This is not the kind of interview setting where you might try to emulate Jeremy Paxman or John Humphrys interrogating some beleaguered politician. In fact, in this and in many other ways, the media interview and the oral history interview are sharply divergent. In the case of the latter, the confidence and trust of your informant are at a premium, and you should not risk betraying these by getting into an argument or expressing incredulity, indifference or scorn at what she or he has said. This is something Beatrice Webb counselled against in social science interviewing more than three-quarters of a century ago, and her strictures have certainly stood the test of time (Webb 1950: 362, originally published 1926).

- *Finally, be sure to thank your informant.* Do this orally once the interview has finished, and also with a short letter of thanks a few days after the interview has taken place.

In developing the substantive topic of your interview on media consumption and associated leisure activities among previous generations, you should remember that little work has been done on this in media studies and, at least in relation to media usage and all that entails, not much more in cultural history. The central media in question span the successive waves of media development since at least the mid twentieth century, so you should include public and personal uses of photography, attendance at the cinema in all its chronological and idiomatic variations, attending to radio and early television, listening to popular music of all sorts (both live and recorded, in different formats), reading magazines, comics and newspapers, and so on. Associated forms of popular leisure cover a range of even greater diversity. Potentially, forms of popular leisure among earlier generations include activities unconnected to the media, such as joining CND marches or a motorcycling club, playing card games or collecting foreign stamps. For this reason, you should concentrate as much as possible on areas of popular leisure which are media related. Examples of these would be dancing, partying, playing jukeboxes and having celebrity pin-ups on the walls of the bedroom or workplace. The emphasis throughout your interview should be on those activities which were centred around media use or were in some sense adjuncts of media use.

You will need to explore with your informants such things as why certain media were used, what directed them to these media, what particular aspects of these media were consumed most and for what reasons, whether the consumption occurred alone or in groups (and, if the latter, which groups were involved), how often certain media were used, what pleasures and rewards your informants drew from their media use, how these related to the rest of their lives, how they now assess the media with which they were most involved, and so on. Again, the particular questions you ask will be oriented to the way you decide to focus the interview, but the above should provide you with a rough guide to the aspects of media consumption and use you should attempt to uncover.

Box 12.1 Transcribing taped conversation using computers

Once you have taped and conducted your interview, you have to transcribe the content into text to proceed with the analysis. The amount of detail you provide in your transcript will be governed by your research approach. For example, conversation analysis requires very detailed transcription of the speech act, noting all changes in intonation, timings and hesitations. To do so, sophisticated notation systems have been developed, such as Transcript Notation (Jefferson 1984), Discourse Transcription (Du Bois et al. 1993) and CHAT (Codes for the Human Analysis of Conversation) (MacWhinney 1995). (For a review of the performance of these systems, see O'Connell and Kowal 1999.) Other types of qualitative linguistic analysis are more concerned with the content than with the form of the discourse, and do not require the notation of these paralinguistic features.

Whatever type of analysis you are conducting, the task of turning recorded words into written text is a time-consuming process. Until recently, this work involved playing, replaying, pausing and rewinding tapes, which was laborious and imprecise, due to the difficulties in cueing tapes exactly (transcription machines, with foot-activated controls, alleviated this problem to some extent). Such work was also haunted by the possibility that tapes can break as a result of winding and rewinding. However, recent developments in computer software mean it is possible to copy your interview material on to your computer hard drive as an audio file. Moreover, several of these programmes are available as open source software and can be downloaded for free from the Internet. One type of software that has been used extensively by ourselves and colleagues is Audacity, which is available from http://audacity.sourceforge.net/ (see Figure 12.1).

Software like this assists with transcription in many valuable ways. You can slow down or speed up recorded speech, which can assist both in achieving greater accuracy of transcription and allowing you to review the audio content more rapidly. It is also possible to edit the sound quality, to reduce tape hiss and ambient noise. You can edit the audio file, using the visual editor, to clip out relevant or irrelevant material, and the audio visualisation makes it much easier to review and replay sections of discourse. One thing that software like Audacity cannot do is transcribe oral talk into written text automatically.

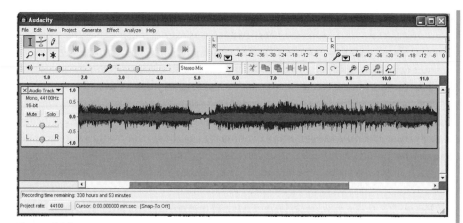

Figure 12.1 Taped speech recorded using Audacity software

Although voice recognition systems are available, they are unsuitable for transcribing interview material. This is because, as things currently stand, they have to be customised to recognise the diction and dialect of individual users, require that the user speaks clearly and ponderously, and need constant visual monitoring to ensure the accuracy of their transcription.

Assessing your evidence

As well as presenting your evidence and locating it socially and culturally in relation to its time, you should attempt to assess its value and worth in historiographical terms. This involves thinking about what, as evidence, it provides and shows, and what it does not. Here, the primary question should be: what useful qualitative information, and then what modality of insight into the past, has your interview generated which is not available through other historical sources of both a primary and secondary nature? In answering this, you need to compare and contrast the historical evidence generated by your interview with other available evidence on media audiences and popular leisure in the historical period, or, more precisely, in the generational segment of historical period to which your informant has centrally referred in his or her narrative account.

You should then go on to tackle a few further, subsidiary questions. What specifically do other historical sources provide which cannot be gleaned from an oral history of media consumption? What other historical material do you need to draw on in order to arrive at a fuller picture of media consumption in the past? What would that fuller picture consist of which is not generally amenable to recovery through oral-historical methods? If oral history fills gaps, what are the gaps in its own methodological provision and procedure? Altogether, then, what you should try to arrive at is some sense of both the strengths and weaknesses of oral history as a method for finding out about media consumption in time past.

These are just some of the ways in which you may find it significant to present and interrogate the material you will generate through your oral history interview(s). One of the many values of doing historical research is the relativisation of your own experience. This project will perhaps only provide the first steps towards this, and, of course, such steps lead to some difficult methodological and epistemological problems. But if you do take these first steps and then begin to think reflexively about the historically specific nature of your own acquaintance with the media, and the manifold ways in which you have put the media to use yourself, we think it will have proved worthwhile. This can be enhanced by a further set of considerations that you may bring to bear on your evidence. Although there are no clear-cut distinctions with the analytical questions already posed, there are also certain theoretical implications raised by the kind of discourse involved. We cannot elaborate extensively on these here, but it might be useful, particularly in light of the evaluative questions raised earlier, to say a little about one or two problematic issues connected with oral historical data.

Oral history is based on memory, and the fallibility of human memory may lead to omissions, compressions, elisions and idealisations in the experiential record provided by the interview. We have already pointed out that written accounts and records are not to be considered, in contrast, as necessarily preferable or superior; they have their own sources of fallibility as well. But in assessing your orally derived data, you should definitely consider the ways in which the complementary processes of recollection and reconstruction have operated in the interview you have recorded. Oral history is also based on trust, and while you may well feel that this is validated by what is said in the interview, and maybe by the manner in which it is said, it is vitally important that, so far as this is possible, you check your informant's narrative account with other primary or secondary sources for comparability and accuracy. Following from this, and in more general terms, you should ask yourself what you can infer about the relationship between past and present in your informant's narrative. Does the way this relationship seems to be regarded configure the narrative in any significant way? Does it, for example, lead from or to any evaluative process about life then and life now, and what bearing does this have on the narrative construction? These are questions concerning the evidential status and character of your material, and we could obviously pose others, but they necessarily lead on to considerations about the aesthetic and symbolic form of this material, rather than the empirical accuracy or representativeness of its content.

There are some thorny epistemological problems involved in this contrast between form and content in cultural representations, and while there can be no easy resolution of them, it does seem to us unfortunate that the contrast is so often abruptly polarised, as for instance in the now orthodox assumption that there is a clear and implacable theoretical opposition between realist and constructionist positions. We would hold instead that, as a crucial starting point, it is beneficial to regard oral forms of evidence as an important mode of bearing witness to the past, of providing testimony to events and experiences that have been lived through historically, and of attempting 'to give social history a human face' (Tosh 1989: 176). What this produces has to be evaluated and interpreted critically, of course, and it goes without saying that to see such forms of evidence as simply offering a relay of past realities would constitute a highly crude form of realism. This is precisely the significance of our general category of talk and of our thematic distinction between situated and mediated voices.

One of the distinctive methodological features of oral history is that, as a form of inquiry, it is dependent on talk, generating its primary material through talk with those who have in some way experienced the history. This means that, as a form and field of history, it is constituted, at least in part, by the talk it generates, so that what it is and how it is produced share a common basis: dialogue between historical researcher and historical witness. This active dialogue between past and present lends an agile methodological strength to oral history, by enabling you, as researcher, to participate judiciously in shaping the account, through your questions and through such ancillary procedures as discretionary probing. As we have stressed, though, oral history requires a hermeneutics of trust that turns axiomatically on the empirical value of those situated voices whose witness to the past it solicits. In this way, though always problematically, it taps into the referentiality of what is past. While deliberate and calculated 'misinformation about the past is very rare' in oral history (Perks 1995: 13), you should always remember that in presenting and analysing any evidence which has direct reference to generational experience in the past, you, with your voice, are also mediating that evidence. The relatively situated voices of your informants are always, to some extent and in some way, mediated by your own voice as historian.

By way of conclusion, then, we would like to suggest that you need to recognise three aspects of your evidence in particular. The first of these is that in providing it, your informants have inevitably been involved in the process of self-presentation, and you need to think about how this qualifies the nature of what has been provided. It is important that you consider oral narrative in its character as a discursive performance, doing work within the present for the person who has provided it in a particular social setting. The second is that the epistemological character and status of your evidence are directly and indirectly influenced by your own participation, through your involvement as an interviewer in generating evidence and through your historical presentation and assessment of that evidence. Perhaps rather more than for other forms of history, this requires your attention to questions of methodological and analytical reflexivity, in which you consider carefully what goes on in the process of translation between the situated 'voice' of the story-laden evidence and the mediated 'voice' of the ensuing history. The third aspect we would ask you to consider is that, as a form of narrative expression, your material has particular linguistic features *as talk*, as a way of using language.

In asking how we should listen to interviews without immediately leaping to interpretations suggested by prevailing theories, Kathryn Anderson and Dana Jack have proposed that we should look, first, at an informant's *moral language* – the relationship between self-concept and cultural norms, and the values embodied in the discourse of the interview; second, at the subject's *meta-statements* – observations on what has been said, or evidence of awareness of a discrepancy within the self between what is expected and what has been said; and third, at the *logic of the narrative* – 'the internal consistency or contradictions in the person's statements about recurring themes and the way these themes relate to each other' (Anderson and Jack 1991: 19–22). These are useful and suggestive steps, not only in themselves, but also in pointing to others. Focusing academically on any kind of talk demands an artistry of listening, an adeptness at tuning in to the plurality of its manifestations and connections. The particular ways of listening suggested by Anderson and

Jack are directed to the structure and performance of the discourse of the interview, and they can be extended to include many of the rules and conventions of spoken communication to which discourse analysis and conversation analysis attend. Focusing on such features of social talk does not necessarily imply that there is 'nothing beyond' the talk, or that 'interviews are interesting only for the way in which people use language to produce accounts' (May 1993: 107). But it is certainly of great importance to analyse any socially produced form of talk in terms of its features as interaction and as discourse, and this is where conversation analysis and discourse analysis have proved of great value. In the next chapter, we shall look at what these analytical approaches involve, for they have now attained centrality in the academic study of talk.

Summary: key points

- Sites and forms of talk in and about the broadcast media were addressed in the interests of studying media production and consumption in analytical relationship to each other.

- Focused interviews as a key way of generating talk about the media were considered as purposive forms of talk in themselves.

- Oral history was introduced as a method of generating evidence, through talk, of uses of the media among previous generations, and a small-scale project in oral history was set up as a way of bringing cultural production and consumption into mutual consideration.

- The constitutive features of oral history, both as talking about the past and the past as talk, were outlined, and cues for thinking about oral history, methodologically and epistemologically, were suggested.

- A practical guide to undertaking oral history interviews, and transcribing, presenting and assessing the data was outlined.

- The need to keep simultaneously in the analytical frame the situated and mediated character of the voices in talk was emphasised.

chapter thirteen

Taking Talk Apart

Talk as interaction

In any discussion of talk, we move from a methodological focus on *langue*, as an underlying matrix of linguistic structures, to *parole*, specific utterances and series of utterances occurring within particular settings. Such settings have their own contextual features and situational dynamics, which always need to be taken into account, but in this shift of focus the central emphasis is on forms of talk viewed as an intrinsically social activity. The interest is now in language in its complex mundane usages, not only as a means of enabling social interaction between people, but also as constitutive of that interaction, so that talk is understood as action, as ways of *doing*. Talk is seen as performing an act, or rather a whole series of acts, whether these be accepting an apology, making a promise, uttering a threat, refusing advice, and so on. Looking at language in everyday use in this way marks out the area in linguistics known as pragmatics. In its Anglo-American version, one of the key developments of pragmatics has been speech-act theory, associated particularly with the work of Austin and Searle. This has emphasised the performative functions of acts of speaking, such as those just noted – promising, threatening, and so on. In broad terms, this is also the general approach to language taken by discourse and conversation analysis.

In the following sections, we shall outline conversation analysis and its associated field of study, ethnomethodology, and then go on to make a few remarks about discourse analysis (a summary term relating to a broader and more diverse ensemble of approaches and positions). Before we begin to consider the distinctive and divergent features of these variant forms of talk analysis, we should perhaps make the point that there are no rigid boundaries between them or the other areas of study we shall mention. Analysts often move between them and borrow different elements of them in their actual analytical practice; and some ways of taking talk apart have drawn on semiotics and ideological analysis, which developed during the 1970s out of the structuralist and poststructuralist tradition. We encourage you to be similarly eclectic, tailoring your methodology to your topic and purpose of inquiry, while at the same time taking into account the theoretical implications that are attendant on what you study and why.

Conversation analysis

Conversation analysis was pioneered in the 1960s in the work of Harvey Sacks and his colleagues, and is closely aligned with the microsociological form of analysis known as ethnomethodology (see, for example, Garfinkel 1967; also Turner 1974). It is in view of this alignment that conversation analysis can be said most generally to be concerned with meaningful conduct in routine social settings. More specifically, its focus is on how talk operates to enable interaction between people. It applies this focus by a meticulous attention to the sequential and consequential structures of spoken discourse in specific contexts, which are usually, though by no means exclusively, situations in which individuals are co-present. Conversation analysis treats language in actual use in terms of the rules and structures which make such use possible, which indicate specifically how participation in talk should proceed and provide the means for realising social intercourse and relations as an inter-subjective accomplishment. Such analysis can be seen as taking its bearings from Wittgenstein when he advised us to 'let the use of words teach you their meaning' (Wittgenstein 1967: 220). Lexical meaning does not reside only in the pages of a dictionary. The meanings of words are realised in their everyday forms of assemblage and usage, in the regularised practices of mundane talk. Characteristically, conversation analysis attends to such features of talk as turn-taking, topic maintenance, establishing transition from one topic to another, offering appropriate forms of initiating and terminating talk, and so on. In developing this approach to talk, it regards everything that occurs interactionally through talk as having relevance to it. In communicational terms, nothing in talk is redundant, including gaps and 'ums' and 'ahs'; even intakes or exhalations of breath are regarded as significant where these are demonstrably observable features of the interaction for participants, as, for example, in the performative distinction between a gasp and a sigh.

Equally, as a basic principle of the analysis, this approach to talk restricts itself to what occurs in the conversational interactions it studies, in other words, to what is available to the participants at the time, and only at the time, when the interaction occurs. In this sense, conversation analysis can be described as a 'chronically synchronic' methodological approach. It contrasts markedly with the diachronically sensitive methodological focus of oral history, despite the theoretical naivety sometimes displayed by its practitioners. This distinguishing feature of it as a social science method also indicates its further characteristic of agnosticism about research purposes and questions beyond those associated with the general concern to study talk in interaction, or talk *as* interaction. Its focus is directed to what is specifically relevant to the interaction that goes on in linguistic and paralinguistic ways in social encounters; and relevance within this focus is defined in terms of those involved in the interaction rather than being filtered through the interests, preoccupations or motivations of the researcher who is studying the interaction. In this rather idealistic way, conversation analysis attempts to develop an empirical, naturalistic form of research into social action and intercourse. Most of all, it is interested in making explicit, and explaining, the usually tacit standards and procedures which are deployed in particular social situations and contexts as the intricate ground rules of communication. For communication to be possible, these rules must be shared to a great extent, though this will vary according to the formality and informality of the occasions in which communicative acts occur. Conversation analysis assumes that, in concrete terms, these rules are realised in temporally sequenced yet always finite and locally manifest forms of interaction. For this reason, it is sensitive to the dangers of imposing on data an a priori template consisting of leading ideas, issues or assumptions associated with the researcher rather than the researched.

Ethnomethodology has provided the most appropriate basis for the development of this approach because of its general concern with how people routinely operate in social ways – how they conduct their everyday participation in the social world, make accounts of it and account for themselves within it. The overall emphasis is on how people appropriately and justifiably enact their participation in particular forms of social life. An interesting application of this is the tendency, when we are talking to others about our local social worlds, to assume the existence of a common reality which can be accessed inter-subjectively. This is fundamental to what Melvin Pollner (1987) calls mundane reason, a particular kind of reasoning or 'method' for understanding our everyday world and maintaining that understanding, often in the face of threats to it, such as conflicting reports of an event or someone's behaviour. Conversation analysis applies this approach specifically to the interaction occurring through, and constituted by, different forms of talk. It extends key ethnomethodological principles of understanding in taking speech, occasioned by its specific uses, purposes and settings, as integral to our ongoing monitoring of self and others, and of social reality and its potential disjunctures. In the main, its focus falls on how units of words and utterance are relationally combined and sequenced, and how talk operates as a skilled accomplishment of action in interaction. It differs from certain branches of linguistics, such as semantics, in that it does not view language simply as a vehicle for the conveyance of meaning, but sees it instead as forms of social action that contribute to the organisation and ordering of everyday life. It is for this reason that conversation analysts talk of *doing* talk, rather than just talking. Talk is a socially constitutive activity, and to think of talk as 'just talking' may encourage us to understand it transparently as the individualistic realisation of an intention to speak and make meaning out of our experience.

Before we go on to consider how conversation analysis can be applied in media studies, it is important to be a bit bolder about some of its limitations. The first of these relates to what we have called its 'chronically synchronic' project. Looking only at what happens in naturally occurring talk, and examining only those features of the interaction involved in the talk which are immediately there for the participants, gives to conversation analysis a particularly sharp focus of attention. This generally leads to finely grained qualitative analysis specifically centred on, and directly relevant to, the phenomena that are being studied. In this sense, it is radically inductive, proceeding only from the data resulting from the recorded talk and refusing to take into analytical consideration what it would regard as extraneous information, such as the biographical trajectories or categories of social membership of participants in the talk, except where these become an explicit or implicit topic of the talk. It is worth noting here, perhaps, that although conversation analysis contrasts itself with positivism, ironically it displays many of the epistemological features that can be identified with positivism and what C. Wright Mills (1970: ch. 3) memorably referred to as 'abstracted empiricism'. In line with this, conversation analysis is wary of attempts to interpret the meanings of what people say from any other perspectives than those which can be said, on the basis of the analysis, to be the participants' own. While this begs the question of how these perspectives can be known and clearly distinguished from the everyday understandings of researchers, a more important issue is whether this confinement of attention to what is empirically immediate may render conversation analysis too restricted in its approach for the kinds of social and cultural analysis with which communication and media studies is concerned. Obviously, there are at times certain heuristic virtues or benefits attached to the procedural 'bracketing off' of certain factors or issues, in that this will permit a more concerted take on what is, for any immediate purpose, the focus of social scientific analysis. The question that always follows from this, though, is whether the bracketing should be temporary or permanent.

For social and historical studies of communications media, conversation analysis leaves too much out of consideration, on what would seem to be a permanent basis. There are various aspects to this, but let us return first of all to questions of meaning, interpretation and understanding. As we have noted, conversation analysis exhibits a high level of reluctance to impute meanings to utterances from outside the specimens of talk with which it is dealing in any particular case. It tries to develop an exclusivity of focus on conversation or talk alone. This can obviously be to its advantage in warding off alien interpretive or explanatory factors which are not present in the talk studied, but its contextual purism is revealed by the fact of research itself, for research practice is not a defining feature of everyday talk. Conversation analysis claims to study talk in its own terms, without theoretical imposition from outside the talk, but its own specialist language and concerns are not those of the participants in the conversations studied. The terms of the talk are different to the terms in which the talk is studied, regardless of the degree to which they are explicitly theorised. Moreover, in studying talk, conversation analysts 'disattend' to the topics of the conversation and the significance these may have for the participants in everyday discourse. Ironically, they veer away from the life-embedded meanings these may have for the participants (Billig 1999: 547). Talk in its own terms will never be synonymous with the study of talk, not only because the practice of research occurs in another space and time to that of the talk, but also because, in various ways, research derives from a different set of concerns and preoccupations, purposes and objectives to that of any example of 'ordinary' discourse. To regard these as amenable to a permanent bracketing off is tantamount to proposing that they can be mentally blanked out in the activity of social analysis. This is an idealist proposition.

We could say that the point of analysis in the social sciences is to explore other ways of understanding certain phenomena, which are not available in the frames of reference intrinsic to the phenomena in question, but the more specific point we are raising is that in the subject–subject relation between researcher and researched, various means of negotiating this relation have of necessity to be considered, at least in the long term. Conversation analysis has not moved into these longer-term considerations, even in respect of other approaches, such as hermeneutics, which are sensitive to the relationship between researchers and those they research, to the constitutive structures of everyday life and to what people actually say and do as they seek to utilise and actively operate within these structures. (Thompson 1990: ch. 6; Pickering 1997: chs 4 and 5.) Yet even without bringing the difficult issues raised by hermeneutics into the analytical frame, for media and cultural studies any form of talk needs to be placed in a broader context than that of its immediate locale or setting. Talk itself is not, in any case, impermeable in its specificities, but is part of longer-term social processes which may condition what participants bring to talk in terms of assumptions, beliefs, knowledge, and so on. As Pertti Alasuutari (1995: 105) has put it: 'Conversations are only one type of social interaction and relations. There are other sites and ways of constructing realities and establishing relations between groups of people, and these types also have a bearing on the sites of conversation'.

The more recent attention paid by conversation analysis to 'institutional talk' may be seen as an attempt to acknowledge and address these points, but this requires 'that one takes distance from the strictly inductive CA research programme' (ibid.: 106). It also requires that one takes into account the structuring properties of social relations and institutions which have a broader reference than the structures of conversations in specific instances. Surely one of the great insights of ethnomethodology is that social structures are not formations which are simply abstract, grand-scale and external, 'out there in the world', into which people somehow fit, but that they have to be seen as being produced and reproduced in the most mundane forms of social interaction between people. When attention is restricted to this level, however, we soon arrive at a limited and limiting formalism that cannot move beyond the talk and what is 'given' by participants. We are then hampered in our attempts to understand how the micro-structures of achieved interaction in conversations relate to the broader processes and formations in which they participate. As Norman Fairclough puts it, conversation analysis is 'resistant to linking properties of talk with higher-level features of society and culture – relations of power, ideologies, cultural values' (1995a: 23).

This is actually part of a larger problem with phenomenological and ethnomethodological approaches more generally, for although concerned with the understanding and knowledge which are held, shared and produced by individuals in their day-to-day interactions, they rarely exceed this level of analysis: 'what should be treated as an indispensable aspect of inquiry becomes the whole of the inquiry, and other aspects are either neglected or dismissed' (Thompson 1990: 280). Obviously, in attending to processes of communication, it is important to examine the indexical, reflexive relations of an utterance and the sequence of communication into which it is placed. Making meaning and making sense are always occasioned, but are not processes entirely dependent on any one, specific occasion, since occasions themselves interrelate and are woven into a broader social fabric. Their interrelations contribute to social process. In chronically focusing on 'what is there', ethnomethodology and conversation analysis rightly ask us not to take the significance of attitudes, beliefs, motives, and so on, for granted, and not to wheel into play 'the "big" sociological variables' of 'age, social class or cultural background', uninspected for their relevance to the events, occasions and settings of interaction and talk (Potter 1996: 67). Yet to make such a sweeping virtue of these injunctions can lead too easily to the dismissal or playing down of such variables in the course of the analysis itself. Being cautious about 'big' variables does not mean that we should always go 'little'. It is not simply fatuous to remind ourselves that any such variable may have a crushing, or at least severely delimiting, effect on lives as they are actually lived. To say of these pejoratively labelled 'big' factors of social existence that 'they should be shown to be consequential for the interaction' (ibid.) presupposes that their consequential effects can be known for the interaction, and where they cannot this may lead to a sociologically and historically foreshortened view of both the interaction and its contextual determinants.

Discourse analysis

The common unit of linguistic analysis used to be the sentence, parts of the sentence or parts of words, outside of any social context of their actual occurrence. It is hardly surprising that such a confined, avowedly technicist orientation to language was felt to have little bearing on, or relevance for, communications research. Conversation analysis moves a good way beyond this limited orientation, and not only because it is concerned with broad slabs of talk in given social settings. As we have suggested, its parameters of concern are still rather too restricted for the kinds of research questions and issues which arise from attempts to amalgamate – or at least bring into productive tension – studies of media production and consumption. Conversation analysis nevertheless offers considerable potential for communication and media studies. Its benefits are perhaps most felt in the approach it offers to communication analysis which is alternative to the semiotic model. This model, as we have seen, is based on Saussurian linguistics, with its langue/parole dichotomy. Semiotics developed out of ideas generated through the study of the structures of language, and while this was fruitful in itself, it entailed the dismissal of parole, that volatile dimension of communication as spoken discourse, operating in the hurly-burly of its actual social use. For this reason, semiotics offers little to the study of talk. Indeed, despite its concentration on the 'message', the encoding/decoding model was in some ways remarkably similar to the sender/receiver 'transmission' paradigm in communication studies, which is perhaps why 'aberrant' readings were first defined as such rather than as alternative (or heteroglossic). There was an emphasis on the multi-accentedness of the sign, but how this related to the messy interactivity of talk in everyday life or in various broadcast genres was rarely taken up. That is why conversation and discourse analysis offer a salutary counter to the structuralist/semiotic model of communication.

Discourse analysis represents a more diverse grouping of approaches to the analysis of talk than conversation analysis, and not only because it is concerned to examine written as well as spoken forms of communication. Indeed, though it has hardly been applied in this way at all, it could also prove a particularly valuable adjunct to media reception analysis. Discourse analysis overlaps with conversation analysis to a considerable degree, but is broader in scope and more varied in coverage, so that it can be applied to media texts of various kinds as well as to media talk, as exemplified in the generically contrasting types of a deliberately sequenced news broadcast or a DJ's rambling patter. It is perhaps worth noting that both approaches are image-blind, displaying a curious awkwardness in the face of the sheer visuality of many forms of modern public communication. This does not mean that visual images cannot be seen in terms of discourse, but rather that discourse analysis as so far developed has been largely insensitive to the specific properties of visual codings and representations. Discourse analysis is fundamentally language-oriented. This is yet another reason why we emphasise so much that a critically oriented eclecticism of methodological and analytical approach is vital to the health of media and communication studies.

We have already dealt quite substantially with discourse analysis in chapters 7 and 8, where we considered its uses in the study of written forms of signification and representation. Many of the points made there are relevant also to its application in the study of talk. For this reason, we want to concentrate here on what is a particularly useful and suggestive term in its conceptual repertory. Discourse analysis is generally concerned with extended samples of talk or text, with the structural, stylistic and rhetorical features of these samples, and with the form of dialogue or communicative interaction that occurs through talk and texts, as for example between participants in a telephone conversation, between a newsreader and her television audience, or between magazine writers and their readership. Clearly, the kinds of communicative interaction involved in these examples are dissimilar, for a magazine reader cannot make an immediate response to the writer of a magazine article in the same way as participants in a telephone conversation respond to the content and manner of their interactive talk. Indeed, we cannot focus analytically on talk as interaction occurring in a conversation in the same way as we do on a television newsreader using talk as a means of conveying information about recent national and international events. Talk as utterance is in these ways defined by the form and context in which it is produced. A relevant linguistic concept for examining how context in place and time both conditions talk-production and is produced by the talk is **deixis**.

Deixis is the Greek word for 'pointing', and in linguistics and discourse analysis it is used to identify the 'pointing' functions of spoken or written language. It refers to the time, place and participants involved in discourse. So, for instance, when a television news correspondent such as Rageh Omah ends his report by citing his name, the news programme for which he is working and where he is located at the time of delivering his report, this conventional termination operates deictically to specify his temporally located place and identity as addresser to the camera, to the anchorperson in the studio and to the audiences watching the news in their home, bar or common room. Similarly, the title of BBC Radio Four's *Six O'Clock News* or BBC Radio Five Live's *Midday News* deictically specifies the time at which these news bulletins are broadcast. If, while we are listening to, say, the *Midday News*, a friend phones and we say that we are listening to the *Midday News* and that a news item of mutual interest has cropped up, then explicitly and implicitly deixis – the time, place and identity of 'us' as addressees of the programme – has been established by the statement. Deixis therefore consists of indexical devices which can be identified temporally, with words like 'now', 'then' and 'tomorrow'; spatially, with words like 'here', 'there' and 'this'; and interpersonally, with words like 'I', 'you', 'we' or 'together' (Fowler 1993: 63–4; and see Fowler 1986: 57–9, 90–6). In actual usage, these devices are not always straightforward, particularly in media discourse, with its characteristic time–space distantiations and producer–consumer disjunctions. For example, since media audiences are socially and culturally heterogeneous, who 'we' are when addressed as 'we' by a broadcaster or a politician on TV is never a simple form of designation. The pronoun 'we' is open to varying interpretations, which may specify 'us' in a number of possible ways, and either include or exclude 'us' according to whom the category 'we' may apply.

In his book *Banal Nationalism*, Michael Billig has used the concept of deixis to demonstrate how the devices associated with it are used rhetorically in nationalist constructions. He cites as examples ex-Prime Minister John Major's claim that '*this* is still the best country in the world', and former US President Bill Clinton's reference to '*this*, the greatest country in human history'. In both cases, 'this' points to and routinely evokes the nation as an imagined community, distinguishing 'us' from 'them' in other places or other times. These forms of deixis do not only 'point' – whether they do so obtrusively or (more commonly) unobtrusively; they are also constitutive of the spatio-temporal context and participants in the communication involved, helping 'to make the homeland homely' and 'we' the nation 'as some sort of family'. They act as a means by which 'to shut the national door on the outside world' (Billig 1995: 107–9, and see also 114–19, 144–5).

We have taken you on what might appear to be a slight diversion in order to show you the sort of thing that discourse analysis does in bringing out the implied meanings and tacit codings in language use. This approach is recommended as a general way of developing your acquaintance with discourse analysis. It is important to understand the key ideas which generally underpin discourse analysis. These include, for example, the proposition that discourse is constitutive of the objects and categories it represents, rather than the other way round, and that talk itself, in particular situations and particular settings, will condition what people say, so that what people say is not necessarily consistent across contexts, but is occasioned, to a much greater extent, by such contexts and the functions of talk within them. Now comes the practical question, for beyond such propositions, what steps should you follow in doing discourse analysis?

Talking heads: the political speech and television

Rather than answering this question in terms of a number of abstract formulations, in the remaining part of this chapter we want to take a particular form of mediated communication, the televised political speech, and provide you with a set of guidelines for analysing it. As with the oral history project, we shall deliberately limit the scope of what is involved so that you can accomplish it as a set piece of coursework. In light of this, you should concentrate on just one broadcast speech for the purposes of close analysis, though you should recognise that in any substantial research into this form of communicative discourse, you would have to sample a broad range of particular examples in order to identify common characteristics and general features. In setting out our guidelines for this project, we are drawing on research previously conducted by discourse analysts, and we shall refer to them in what follows. When we have done this kind of work with students at Loughborough University, they have generally taken the speech given either by the prime minister or by the leader of the opposition at the relevant party's annual conference, and we suggest, for the purposes of this exercise, that you do likewise.

This is a further way of delimiting the analytic scope of the project, for in general terms such speeches are intended to be, and are publicly taken as, highly significant addresses and important rallying points, not only for conference delegates and the party faithful, but also – it is hoped – for 'the nation' as a whole. They are always widely reported and discussed in the press and broadcasting media, and, at least in Britain, are televised live as a culminating or nodal point of the television coverage of party conference proceedings. To the extent that certain general expectations are applicable in the planning, production and reception of these keynote speeches, they will exert a shaping influence on the planning of media coverage, as well as on certain criteria of evaluation once they have been given. So there are a number of ways in which they are directly comparable. At the same time, though, how they are planned and anticipated will vary according to the specific circumstances in which they are made and the particular needs they must address: restoring a party's image and reputation, mollifying disaffection or dissent within a party, attacking political opponents or reviving the leader's own credibility being just a few examples from recent Conservative and Labour administrations in Britain (1992–2006).

At the same time, there is one cardinal purpose underlying the art of political speechmaking. This is to prevent audiences from falling asleep. Obviously a speaker can seek to arouse an audience with words that stir their passion, but there are limits to how much this can be done. There are only so many times a politician can rise to a rhetorical crescendo without the trick becoming tired and predictable. Speechmakers have to use other devices to keep the attention of their listeners. Listening to speeches is different to participating in ordinary conversation, as there is no 'flow' pattern of interaction and turn-taking involved. In terms of our earlier distinction, a political speech is monological. For the most part, you have to sit and listen to one person talking and you only have a few highly routinised ways of articulating your response – by clapping or booing, for example. We say 'your' response, but normally you do not make an individual response as such; rather, you make it as part of a collective social ensemble. The only exception to this seems to be heckling. By and large, as an audience member, you are confined to a very small repertoire of responses, and normally must act in concert with the rest of the audience (the case of the TV audience at home is obviously another matter). It is important, therefore, that the audience hearing the speech 'live' should be able collectively to recognise the appropriate times for a response. This recognition seems to be prompted by a variety of cues from the speechmaker. You should try to spot what distinguishes these discursive features and how audiences are alerted to them.

Throughout a political speech, you need to listen carefully and maintain a high and stable level of concentration if you are to follow everything that the speaker has to say. If the effort is not likely to be amply repaid, the temptation to drift off into your own thoughts can be quite strong, and when you are faced with what seems to be an interminable speech, delivered in a flat monotone, it is difficult to resist the balm of a brief snooze. That is true of British politicians, at least, in both the lower and upper houses of parliament. Clearly, then, in speeches at annual conferences, leading politicians must make every effort to engage their audiences and win frequent shows of affiliation and approval. Content is obviously important, but so also is the way in which that content is structured as political rhetoric, the vocal manner in which it is presented to the audience and the accompanying gestural movements of hands and face (known as paralinguistic forms of communication). Politicians must employ certain proven and established devices to enhance the style of what they are saying and the mode in which it is transmitted to the audience if they are to maintain audience attention and gain their plaudits.

First step: data

What you need to examine in this project are the rhetorical techniques of one sample of contemporary political speechmaking (as a form of talk) and the associated visual grammar and syntax of television's coverage of the event (as a form of mediation of talk). The overall focus is on the interaction of spoken language and visual semiosis. The first step you need to take is to create a descriptive account of your sample, or at least those aspects of it on which you decide to concentrate. This means transposing what is communicated in spoken and visual terms into written notation according to specified conventions of transcription. What follows is intended as a set of guidelines for how to go about this.

Begin your transcription with the spoken dimension. Given the length of the speech, you will have to choose particular aspects of it on which to focus in detail. We suggest six criteria for the selection of passages.

1. Following Max Atkinson, we can look at those passages already discussed which are intended to cue applause: 'displays of affiliation' or 'affiliative responses' are the terms he uses for audience expressions of approbation. You will find numerous instances of such cues and of the ways in which they are structured as political rhetoric in Atkinson (1984a, 1984b). Heritage and Greatbatch (1986) neatly identify seven major categories of political message associated with audience applause:

   - external attacks;
   - approval of own party;
   - combinations of external attacks and approval of own party;
   - internal attacks;
   - advocacy of policy positions;
   - combinations of internal attacks and advocacy of policy positions;
   - commendations of particular individuals or collectivities.

2. Added to this, you should examine any passages which lead to a negative response of some kind, such as heckling, booing, barracking, or failure to clap. Although less frequently than on the hustings, instances of this do occur at national party conferences, and the extent of their occurrence at such gatherings of the party faithful is always one measure of the degree to which a political party is united or divided at any particular time or on any particular issue. This is perhaps especially so with respect to the speech of a party leader, who, of all the holders of high office within a party, conventionally expects the greatest respect from delegates and members. Because of this, instances of audience disapprobation are likely to be fewer, but for that reason all the more significant. Ask yourself what inferences can be drawn from any specific instances of audible negative response. It may be, of course, that you find no examples of audience discontent in your chosen speech, in which case what you need to assess is whether this can be taken as an indication either of the success of the speech or of the degree of containment of dissent by party managers – or rather, perhaps, of the delicate balance between the two. The absence of vocal dissent does not necessarily mean that dissent does not exist. There are even times when dissent is deliberately staged in order to manipulate kudos for the unruffled or witty way in which the speaker handles it, and you should be on your guard for any instance of such duplicity.

3. Following from the above, but not necessarily connected with any audible negative response, are those passages which involve what Norman Fairclough calls 'cruces' or 'moments of crisis' (see Fairclough 1989: 165). In general terms, these can be identified as those moments in the discourse where 'repair work' of some kind is going on, or where a politically difficult or sensitive topic is reached and the difficulties of the speaker in handling it leave their traces in the spoken discourse. Two obvious examples involving Tony Blair are the issue of Clause 4 in the Labour Party constitution and the Iraq war, but you should note that not all examples of 'cruces' will be as obvious as these. How, then, do you go about identifying them? Repair work and signs of the awkward handling of a troublesome topic are evident in a variety of ways in the talk and in its delivery, as for example in nervous correction, modification, hesitancy, repetition, precipitous shifts in direction of argument or style of speech, excessive accommodation of certain points of view, contrived efforts to balance different positions in relation to each other, tactics of evasiveness, symptomatic features of body language, and so on. In discussing the discourse of Thatcherism (ibid.: ch. 7; and see Fairclough 1995a: ch. 9), Norman Fairclough gives an extended treatment of such creative work around those points in the discourse when something is amiss. As Fairclough puts it, 'Such moments of crisis make visible aspects of practices which might normally be naturalised, and therefore difficult to notice; but they also show change in process, the actual ways in which people deal with the problematisation of practices' (Fairclough 1992: 230).

4. A further tactic of selection would be to examine what you regard as significant points in the discourse where social values and beliefs, social relations and identities are either implicitly referred to or explicitly addressed. More broadly, you should think of the constraints in the speaker's discourse on content, relations and subjects: how do these frame and delimit what is said? Fairclough suggests that we can think of these constraints as exerting 'power in discourse' in a relatively immediate and concrete way, or as exhibiting and reinforcing the 'power behind discourse' that is a pivotal component of longer-term structures of knowledge and beliefs, social relationships and identities (Fairclough 1989: 74). There are a number of analytical questions you will have to ask about these structural effects of the discourse, but one of them will always be whether they are socially reproductive or transformative.

5. As specific instances of the ways in which beliefs, relations and identities are flagged in the discourse of political speechmaking, you should identify some of the ways in which your sample speech operates deictically, in the specification of place, time and the categories associated with them. To take an example of deixis in operation, following the declaration that his 'three main priorities for government' were 'education, education and education', in his speech to the 1996 Labour Party conference, Tony Blair cited the statistical placing of Britain as 'thirty-fifth in the world league of education standards today', a ranking which he emphasised by repetition and intonational stress. He then went on:

They say *give* me the boy at 7 (2.0) and I'll give you the man at 17 (1.0) WELL [nodding vigorously] GIVE ME the education system that's thirty-fifth in the world today, and I will give you the economy that's thirty-fifth in the world tomorrow!

Aside from its narrow functionalist conception of education as the motor of the economy, what this extract illustrates is the deictic use of 'today' and 'tomorrow' as indexical terms for the incremental advantages of investing in contemporary education in light of future economic performance as this is measured by a global league table. These terms are mapped analogously on to the development, through time, of an individual moving from childhood to late adolescence, though of course the comparison is intentionally ironic. The extract also operates implicitly with a spatial linking of these temporal pointers to Britain's economic 'place' *in the world*, now and in the future, while the 'you' who are specified are those who are expected to identify themselves with the geopolitical configuration that is 'the British nation'. 'You', the imagined community of the nation, is then 'placed' in a competitive hierarchical pecking order within a nationalistic conception of economic development. In this way, 'you', representative of the national homeland addressed 'as some sort of family', operates once again as a means by which 'to shut the national door on the outside world', as Labour 'comes home' and, in his summation, Blair envisions a potential unleashing of 'our people' as Britain 'comes *alive*' with its 'new *energy*', 'new *ideas*' and 'new *leadership*': 'Britain', he triumphantly announced, '*can* take on the world and win'. In his book on the language of New Labour, Fairclough (2000) offers various telling uses by Blair of the deictic categories of 'we', 'our', 'us', with easy slippages of meaning and reference between the government ('we are committed to one-nation politics'), Britain and the British people ('we must be the best'), even everyone in the world. In such cases, you need to ask if the 'we' is used inclusively or exclusively, or ambivalently somewhere in between.

6. A final reason for selecting certain passages in the speech moves us more specifically into the area of ideological analysis. In identifying any such passages for selection you are already operating beyond any purely descriptive level of work. It is therefore all the more important that you make clear the definition of ideology that you are working with, and follow through any conceptual implications your definitional approach may have, so that this approach governs your selection and is then consistent with the specifically analytical treatment you will provide. There is clearly a large degree of overlap between this and the previous criterion of selection, but here you are looking more specifically at the dimensions of the speech which advance, as 'common sense', or as commonly and universally applicable, certain conceptions and assumptions supportive of existing patterns of social power, authority and privilege. Of course, formulating the criterion in this way already implies a certain definitional approach to ideology. It is up to you to decide how and where you stand in relation to it.

In summary, then, you could select passages because they are:

- instances of audience approval or disapproval;

- instances of attempts to forestall disapproval, to engage in some form of remedial activity or damage limitation, or to stitch together disparate values, conflicting views or contrary tendencies;

- instances of the consequences of what is said for the ways in which social knowledge, beliefs and relations are thought about, institutionalised and lived;

- instances of deictic language use in 'pointing to' place, time and particular relations as social and historical constructs of 'us' and 'them';

- instances of discourse which sustain a particular view of the world, and a particular set of interests in relation to it, as natural, inevitable and absolute.

Transcription: the spoken dimension

Once you have selected your passages, you should begin to transcribe them. In doing this, you should adopt certain conventions of notation, generally including the following:

( )	if empty, this indicates an indecipherable utterance; otherwise, a best guess at what was said
(…)	omission
[ ]	verbal description of non-verbal behaviour, or additional comment (e.g. about body language or change in accent)
(2.0)	intervals between or within utterances, in seconds
–	brief, untimed pause within an utterance
word–	word is cut off abruptly
(.)	slightly longer untimed pause within or between utterances
=	latching together separate parts of a continuous utterance or indicating that B's utterance follows A's with no gap or overlap
[	point at which overlap occurs between speakers
word	stress added to a word or a syllable
WORD	extreme stress
co::lons	stretching of a vowel or consonant sound
ɬ	terminal falling intonation
_	rising intonation
/	intonation rises somewhat, not as much as with _ intonation
,	brief pause at a syntactically relevant point in an utterance
.hh	audible inhalation
hh	audible exhalation
heh	laugh token
"	utterances marked lexically or prosodically as quotes
!	excited intonation

We are sometimes asked by students if these conventions always need to be used in their entirety in the study of any sample of discourse, and it may be worth adding a brief note on this. These conventions are extremely useful as a means of indicating aspects of speech as *performance*, as showing how speech is dramatised in its vocal and paralinguistic delivery. They are vital in identifying the ways in which talk occurs as a form of social interaction, or, putting it more strongly, as constitutive of how language and discourse operate *as* social interaction. They are also vital in showing facets of spoken discourse which would not be noted if only the words themselves were transcribed. For example, it has been claimed that 'most purists would argue…that the hesitations, self-corrections, inflections and other nuances of speech are far more revealing than can be conveyed in any written account' (Weerasinghe 1989: vii). This is certainly true, though one does not have to be a purist either to make such an argument or to agree with it. For these reasons, the inclusion of the above conventions in any transcription from spoken to written discourse is descriptively of considerable importance, both in itself and in ways which have a direct bearing on the analysis.

In our view, though, the actual degree to which you use them should depend on the purpose and limits of your analysis in any specific case. In conversation analysis, for example, there will always be a large premium placed on their use, but such high incidence of use need not be taken as a yardstick for all forms of social, historical and cultural analysis. Oral history transcription provides a convenient example where this applies, though requiring immediate qualification. For us, the greater deployment of these notational symbols and their take-up in historical presentation and analysis could at times considerably add to and enhance much of the work done in oral history. Even so, their benefit can only be realised where they are relevant to the analysis, and even in conversation and discourse analysis they sometimes seem to be included in the transcription *only for the sake of it*. In other words, quite often you find that their presence as descriptors of the discourse sample has no equivalence in the analysis of the sample – that is to say, they are only partially drawn on when the sample is analysed more directly. As a general rule of thumb, we suggest that, in media and cultural analysis, these conventions of transcription be used only (or at least primarily) where there is some sort of tangible analytical pay-off, for otherwise they are in danger of becoming little more than presentational clutter, so hampering your reader's engagement with your sample and what, analytically, you make of it.

In addition to these conventions for signifying the performative features of spoken discourse, you should add the following, which are more specifically relevant to the discourse of political speechmaking and its immediate reception:

xxx	soft clapping
XXX	loud clapping
xxxXXXXxxx	soft clapping leading to a crescendo of applause followed by its diminution
-x-	isolated clap
-x-x-x-x-x	hesitant or spasmodic clapping
[	point at which one activity (e.g. clapping) stands in relation to another (e.g. speaker talking)

Finally, for any extract you have chosen from the speech as a whole, you should measure the length of any affiliative or disaffiliative audience responses in seconds, and note this in a line above the xxxXXXXxxx signs, as follows: – [2.0] –. (If you require further transcriptional detail, we suggest that you look at the section on transcription notation in Atkinson and Heritage 1984.)

Transcription: the visual dimension

Having transcribed selected passages of the spoken dimension of the speech, you will now need to develop a breakdown of the camera action going on during and immediately after those passages. This is important because the camera is not neutral in the media transmission of a political speech (or any other item of communication): it actively influences how we see what we see, as viewers in a domestic or other context. It is in a sense itself a narrator, constructing a position from which we are encouraged to read the visual dimension of the action taking place before the camera. Examine, for example, how the camera action occurs (e.g. pans, cuts, tracks) and then what kind of shot/focus is involved. (You may want to refer back to chapter 9 here for a reminder of the various distinct modes of camera action.) Following this, you should compile a shot breakdown. There are various ways of doing this and you may want to add your own variations, but the set of categories we used in chapter 10 can be readily adapted for dealing with the televisual mediation of political speeches:

SHOT   FRAMING   SCENE   SOUNDTRACK

You should fill in each *shot* numerically if you are starting from the beginning of a narrative sequence; in this case, you will be dealing with selected passages, but these still need to be numbered for ready identification. There are numerous conventions for denoting the kind of televisual framing which is involved in any one shot or sequence of shots. The following should suffice for this exercise:

CU   close-up
ELS   extra long shot
LS   long shot
MS   mid-shot

To these indications of camera focus, add camera movement occurring in any one shot (e.g. pan left, zoom out and up, tracking shot, slight pan to right, short zoom). If there is no camera movement, say 'no camera movement'. Then note also under *framing* how transitions between shots are achieved (e.g. dissolve, cut, fade to black). For the category of *scene*, you should briefly describe the scene (i.e. conference rostrum, background details), whether this is shot at eye-line, from above or below, and how it might compare to previous shots (e.g. reverse of shot 2). *Soundtrack* in this case will consist of your written transcription of your chosen extracts from the speech you are dealing with, but it should also include any voice-over commentary if this occurs. Where it does, you should be sure that presentationally you make it quite distinct from the discourse of the politician giving the speech, and we suggest that you use three dots […] if you need to signify a shift from one shot to another. There are other kinds of camera action not covered here, of course, but given the above guidelines it should be clear how you can notate these.

You will now have completed the transcription for both the spoken and visual dimensions of your selected passages, and you can go on to the second step in the exercise, which is given over to the analysis of your extracts and their relation to the speech as a whole. Before you do, we just want to add that the relative simplicity of the camera movement in the televising of political speeches by party leaders is another reason we have chosen this form of media(ted) talk for this particular project. In other forms of television and for most kinds of film, you will find the language of the camera considerably more complex. One reason for this is that in the televising of such speeches a premium is put on the semantic content of the speech, though evaluation by pundits and other politicians may also include mention of its stylistic delivery, of the speech as a staged performance. In film, or television drama, however, the aesthetic and dramatic contribution to the narrative is generally of much greater importance, and for this reason camerawork tends to be much more intricately developed. The intention here is simply to provide you with a grounding in the analysis of visual language which you may go on to develop in other ways for relatively more sophisticated forms of visual media.

Second step: analysis

It should be apparent to you by now that distinctions between descriptive and analytical levels of work can by no means be regarded as hard and fast. In selecting your data, for instance, you will already have begun the process of interpretation and explanation, in that your selection will have been guided explicitly by certain conceptions of the significance of each sample. Such choice can never be simply random or cleanly separate from interpretive activity. So the best way to proceed with this second step is to return to your criteria of selection and to explore their ramifications for the specific samples of speech/camerawork you have selected.

1. The first kind of sample dealt with cues for audience applause, with 'claptraps'. Note the particular sequential position at which applause occurs. Then ask the following type of questions: What is the content of the speech immediately preceding the occurrence of audible audience affiliation? What is the structure of the talk immediately preceding such moments of affiliation? How has the speaker appealed to the audience in what s/he has had to say and the way in which s/he has said it? How has s/he indicated the onset and development of an applaudable message, and how has s/he signalled the point at which applause is appropriate? Are these indications linguistic or paralinguistic in nature? (NB It is important to specify these clearly, for example in stating whether they involve particular words or names, stresses, hand gestures, arm movements or emphatic movements of the body, and so on.) Has the speaker shown an effective sense of timing? How long has the affiliative response been occurring before the speaker reaches a completion point? Such questions should enable you to begin teasing out analytically the various ways in which speakers attempt to milk the audience of their approbation. In doing this, you might also want to say something about the implications of speech/applause overlap.

    Another way into your analysis of the rhetorical elicitation of applause would be to isolate any use of three-part lists in the speech you are tackling. Triadic clusters range from fairly elaborated examples, through specific points, to the use of descriptive adjectives or adverbs, and include any rhetorical play on the rule of three ('education, education, education'). They exist in such a range because they are more memorable than single cases (which may have the effect of reducing the significance of what is said) or the piling up of many examples on top of each other like cartoon plates (which may have the effect of distracting the audience, not to say collapsing the whole stack of what is said into a confused heap of words). Where lists of three occur, you should explore their relative effectiveness in terms of linguistic structure, stylistic features, rhythmic variation, volume, intonational quality, and so on (see Atkinson 1984a: 57–62). You might then go on to ask whether there are other types of parallelism in the speech worthy of comment. Are there any other formulaic features in evidence, for example naming, listing, contrasting, offering self-directed/opponent-directed statements or comments? If so, what are their major features as language, as verbal constructions? For an example of such features, you could take contrastive pairs and evaluate their rhetorical effectiveness as claptraps in the same terms as three-part lists (see ibid.: 73–82). By way of summary, here is the list provided by Heritage and Greatbatch (1986) of seven categories of rhetorical device associated with applause:

- contrasts;
- three-part lists;
- puzzle solutions;
- punchlines;
- combinations of the above;
- position-taking;
- explicit pursuit of applause, as for example by the repetition of a previous point or by underlining its importance.

2. The second kind of sample dealt with the opposite of claptraps: instances of audience disapprobation. In such cases, you should ask how the speaker deals with the sudden unplanned eruption of violent antipathy to what s/he is saying. Is s/he successful (e.g. does s/he 'get the best' of a heckler?), and if so, how? What inferences can be drawn from any evidence of audience disapproval of what is said? For obvious reasons, you should try to place these in an appropriate context. And you should also ask how such instances of disaffiliation compare with instances of affiliation. Would it be accurate to describe them as spontaneous? How would you then describe applause?

3. Typical questions you might ask here are: What do any 'moments of crisis' you have identified signify to you? How are they recognisable? What is the repair work or damage limitation associated with them? Is it effective? Do these moments occur with respect to experiential, relational and/or expressive values? What are the specific inconsistencies or other problematic features involved? What do these moments of crisis suggest about aspects of the discourse which appear unproblematic with respect to experiential, relational and expressive values? Are these moments in the speech related to traces of struggle between the speaker and his or her opponents, both inside and outside the party? What you are looking for here is anything that might have caused the speaker some difficulty or discomfort – some issue that had the potential to ruffle feathers or raise hackles – and what you are examining is threefold: how the speaker handles them, with what degree of success, and with what consequences for any resolution of the difficulty or ironing out of the ideological wrinkles in the political fabric of either party or state.

4. The fourth section dealing with key points of analysis basically involves the question: What are the societal dimensions of the discourse? (As a sample treatment of this question, see Fairclough 1989: 194–6.) The focus here is on the functions of political discourse in constructing social identities or subject positions, social relationships between people, and social knowledge and beliefs. How are these identity, relational and ideational functions of language accomplished in the speech? Is the accomplishment of these functions reproductive of the existing social organisation or in some way transformative, seeking and advocating change or realignment of some kind, as for example in relations between workers and management, between different ethnic groups, between teachers and students, between parents and children, between the UK

and the rest of Europe, and so on? These functions of the content of the speech will perhaps be most obvious in relation to issues of social or cultural policy, but they are by no means confined to them. Relational functions, for example, can also be addressed by asking how pronouns such as 'I', 'you' and 'we' are constituted in what is said. It is in asking questions of an interpretive nature like these that you are investigating the social dimension of discursive texts, seeing discursive practices as a part of social practices, and considering the outcomes and effects of discourse on social identities and relations, social structures and conflicts.

5. As a fifth criterion of selection of parts of the speech to deal with in depth, we suggested that you focus on examples of deixis. Let us (if only for the sake of consistency) take another example from Tony Blair's speech to the Labour Party conference in Blackpool in October 1996. As part of his peroration, Blair made the statement, 'I don't *care* (1.0) where you're coming from, it's where your country's going that matters.' The first thing to note about this is that Blair emphasised the word 'care' with a semi-chop movement of his arm, as well as an intonational stress and a slight pause. More importantly, the rhetorical effect of this utterance depends on the oppositional structure of its two parts, and it is in respect of this that the emphasis on 'care' is important, for implicitly it invites the question: 'If he doesn't care about that, what does he care about?' – and it is this question, of course, which is answered in the second part of the sentence.

This can be broken down a little more. We can point to the contrastive use of the participles 'coming' and 'going', for instance, where the positively accented 'going' gains in allure by being set against the relative worthlessness of the negatively evaluated 'coming'. This rhetorical strategy is aided by the reference to and recycling of a clichéd phrase. Just as the phrase 'where you're coming from' is well worn, so the past(s) to which it refers is worn out. The strategy is further enabled and supported by the deictic parts of the sentence which refer to past and future in relation to contemporary society, 'the world today', in which Blair was speaking. The subjects of the sentence are 'I' and 'you', but deictically the subject 'you' is transformed as the sentence unfolds. 'You' in the first part of the sentence are particular individuals, with their different backgrounds, different formative influences, different experiences, and so on; taken together, these make for diversity and so might also make for social divisiveness. Collectively, these different cases of 'you' are associated with the past, which is *pointed to* by the deictic term 'from'. The contrastive elements of the utterance are then developed in that the potential divisiveness of an individual 'you' (in the abbreviated 'you're') is cancelled by the potential *unity* of the rhymed 'your' in the phrase 'your country', where 'I' and 'you' come together plurally as a tacit 'we' or 'us'. The potential unity of this collective 'us' is implied in the ideological phrase 'your country' (which is challenged by such common-or-garden deictic questions as 'whose country is this anyway?'). The appeal is to what is regarded as held in common, 'our' nationhood, 'our' collective sense of direction and purpose as a nation, 'our' national future or destiny – 'where your country's going'. Interestingly, the deictic term 'to' is omitted in the second part of the sentence; its presence or use is rendered implicit by force of the contrast around which the whole statement is built.

This is just one example, involving what is superficially a simple sentence, and if you take a longer extract of a political speech you will easily find a number of cases of words, phrases and sentences which are doing deictic work. It is, though, the social and ideological implications of any deictic reference or construction, rather than simply their discursive features, which you need to unravel and deal with in greatest detail. So, for example, the implications of this statement by Blair need to be examined in relation to New Labour, to the process of 'modernisation' in the party, to the conflict between divergent political values within the party, to the presence of alternative conceptions of Labour Party values and beliefs, to the tensions attendant on maintaining the party's political success at the polls, and so on. This connects with the final part of your analysis, where you should go on to tackle the issue of ideology more directly.

6. In talking briefly about the question of ideological dimensions of the speech, we emphasised a 'common-sense' approach to understanding ideologies. The element of 'naturalisation' – that aspect of discourse which turns it into 'common sense' or uses it to speak in the name of such (always hypothetical) sense – is an important feature of how ideologies operate, but, contrary to the appearances which are thereby created, ideologies are not set rigidly in place for all time and thus forever stable. Ideological power may consist in 'making a meaning stick' (Thompson 1984: 132), but ideologies themselves are fraught with their own internal contradictions: with the contradictions between what is claimed about the social world and people's diverse experience of the material realities of this world; with the contradictions between ideology as 'lived' and ideology as a specifically formulated philosophy of 'how the world is'; and with contradictions between opposed ideologies and the different, antagonistic interests to which they stand in relation. In view of these always particularised features of ideology, you should not lose sight of processes of ideological struggle, of the fact that such struggle is an important feature of many kinds of discursive practice, and is especially so in political speechmaking. Such struggle is precisely that of establishing or re-establishing certain ideas, values, beliefs, assumptions, and so on, which sustain or restructure power relations in society. In respect of such relations, you should ask questions of your material which address issues of power, for example by looking at how consent for existing relations of power is assumed or argued for; how strategic alliances across different social groups, institutions and domains are forged; how divisions between 'them' and 'us' are (re)constructed; and how alternative currents of thought and formations of discourse are undermined or junked.

The overlap between (4), (5) and (6) is, as mentioned above, obviously considerable, and this is so for at least two reasons. First, in so far as it is legitimate to make such distinctions, these three sections involve a movement from the intra-discursive, with which (1) to (3) are concerned, to the inter-discursive and extra-discursive, in relation to which (4) and (5) are pivotally transitional. Second, these three sections involve questions of power structures and relations at the societal level, and are concerned with how these are supported through particular effects of the discourse and through the specifically ideological work of the text in question. In moving from section (1) to section (6), therefore, there is a strategic logic in operation, for you are moving from text to context, from an examination of textual features and properties, through 'interpersonal' and 'intertextual' questions and the conflicts or critical moments associated with them, to a consideration of how they contribute to, and are embedded in, wider social practices, processes and structures which produce and reproduce existing orders and relations of social power.

You will now have reached the final part of your analysis. Here you need to extrapolate on your shot breakdown in order to see how the visual grammar of television language – its syntax of sequential images – relates to the substantive communication which is the object of the broadcast. How has the television production responded to the politician's cues as to a developing claptrap, for instance? Alternatively, how has it responded to any signs of audience disapprobation? Look for camera switches, camera movement, types of shot, and so on, and ask about the significance of any camera action in terms of what it encodes, what it signifies as a visual code or what visual effect it has in relation to the person on whom the camera is focused. You might also want to discuss the visual design of the setting which constitutes the background to the speech, and the visual appearance of the speaker, others on the podium, delegates in the main body of the hall, and so on, in terms of what semiotically such features of the event may be said to connote.

A further feature of contemporary political speechmaking which you need to consider is the 'sincerity machine'. This is a device which enables speakers to read their speeches from transparent, Perspex screens placed either side of the lectern. The words of a speech are projected upwards on to the screen from below the speaker's platform, and are visible only to the speaker. To the members of the audience it may seem that the politician is speaking spontaneously, as well as addressing them directly. The impression is enhanced as the speaker moves his or her head from side to side in following the script on both screens, though somewhat betrayed by the way their gaze is directed at a fixed point on either side. This item of technology has been called the 'sincerity machine' because it is held to increase the feeling of sincerity imparted by a speech, but as an obviously intended oxymoron, the term is also meant to be read rather more cynically. It was first widely used by the Conservative Prime Minister in the 1980s, Margaret Thatcher, and has since become commonly used by cabinet members and politicians in other parties. If it is in evidence during the speech you are working on, how do you feel it 'frees up' the speaker? What are the effects it is designed to simulate? Does it make the speaker more telegenic, and if so, how? And do you think it is a 'legitimate' aid in political speechmaking?

One last point of consideration. If the broadcast contains any voice-over commentary, what discursive work is this doing for the putative viewer? What are its main characteristic features, and does it add to or detract from the speech as it is mediated by television?

Towards a conclusion

The primary preoccupation of this second project on talk has been the development of a detailed account of the verbal and visual dimensions of a single keynote political speech. In order to enrich your presentation and analysis, you could attempt, at least in summary form, to interpret and evaluate the effectiveness of the speech in relation to the rhetorical and performative aspects of political speechmaking more generally. We would also suggest that you give some consideration to the chain of communication which on the one hand precedes and anticipates the speech and on the other follows and assesses it, as for example in press and broadcast news coverage, periodical editorialising, or current affairs and specialist television programmes, bearing in mind the often predictable, routinised transformations which these various links in the chain bring about. This would enable your analysis to be, at least tentatively, more conclusive. It would also correct a sort of empiricist tendency in some forms of discourse analysis to assume that any chosen section of discourse is sufficient unto itself. Cultural texts always entail various other texts, just as any texts entail various social and historical contexts. This necessary consequence implies certain necessary conditions as well.

These corrective points link us back to our earlier criticisms of conversation and discourse analysis. Any sample of media discourse needs to be understood in its location within a wider social, cultural and historical canvas. It does not hold that canvas entirely within itself, in miniature, as it were, and it is only when we see any particular sample against its broader canvas that we can gain any perspective on it which is not directed in the first place by the discourse that is in the analytical frame. Although, characteristically, forms of linguistic and discourse analysis are intensive and micrological, and many of their strengths derive from this tight-in focus on what is studied, such an approach needs to be complemented by others which operate in different ways and so offer alternative takes on the same object. Further to this, the social world as represented by the media does not exist only in the discourse of those representations. Terry Eagleton has neatly expressed the problem posed by the tendency to believe otherwise: 'The thesis that objects are entirely internal to the discourses which constitute them raises the thorny problem of how we could ever judge that a discourse had constructed its object validly' (Eagleton 1991: 205). The danger of an approach to the study of media talk through a discourse-analytic perspective is the danger of self-referentiality.

There is also a danger of assuming that such a perspective is methodologically sufficient of itself. This is nowhere the case in the human sciences. The sheer diversity of what is studied, and the range of problems raised by the material studied, demand that no one methodological approach can satisfactorily monopolise the whole general field of inquiry. Any movement towards that eventually leads to an inward-looking tendency to try to filter everything through a single intellectual mesh. The question as to whether it is appropriate to do this rarely arises, and any approach which starts to operate in this way gradually becomes isolated from other approaches as it settles complacently into the ever-finer grading of its sub-disciplinary patch. This is simply to point up some of the problems we identified earlier in the chapter. We do not believe they are either inevitable or unavoidable, but we do think that you should be aware of them and try to find ways round them. In view of this, you could ask what other methods might be utilised in studying televised political speechmaking, and how they would enhance the kind of approach outlined in this chapter. Would they be compatible with this approach, and would they have any theoretical implications that might clash with those of conversation and discourse analysis? If so, what would they be, and could they be resolved?

These are, together, the kinds of general issues which we think you should take into consideration in any study of media talk or talk about the media. We began our discussion of this distinction by advocating that media production and media consumption should be brought into open relation alongside each other, and we can only conclude by observing that the question of whether it is possible to arrive at any long-term integration of the study of media production and consumption remains, at least in more general terms, unresolved. Nevertheless, the future of communication and media studies will depend in part on the ways in which these over-separated branches of study manage to keep each other in active view.

Another point in tentative conclusion is that, as you will have seen, the two approaches we have chosen, in this and the previous chapter, have quite different strengths, and at the same time almost opposite forms of weakness: in particular, a tendency to an analytically complacent resurrectionism in the case of oral history, and a tendency to an analytically complacent chronocentrism in the case of conversation analysis and some forms of discourse analysis. These are the kinds of theoretical implications we have mentioned. What we would finally ask you to remember is that we have only skimmed the surface of what it is possible to do in the analysis of forms of media talk, whether this is talk produced by the broadcast media or talk produced by the consumers of those media when they come to recollect and discuss what they have consumed. Political speeches and their rhetorical techniques are only one form of broadcast spoken communication which it is possible to treat, and when you come to other forms of media talk – in sitcoms, stand-up comedy, soap operas, chat shows, late-night studio discussions, current affairs interviews, documentaries, reality TV, and so on – you will need to vary your approach and think through the specific issues and problems raised by each particular genre and form that produces talk. The field is wide open, and there are both difficult obstacles and appealing vistas on every pathway across it.

Summary: key points

- In this chapter, two key approaches to the analysis of talk were discussed: conversation analysis and discourse analysis.

- Deixis was considered as an example of the tools of linguistic/discourse analysis.

- A practical project involving the analysis of a televised political speech was set up.

- The selection of material for your analysis was discussed, and methods for transcribing and notating the verbal and visual elements of the speech were introduced.

- A step-by-step approach to your analysis of political rhetoric was outlined.

chapter fourteen

Using Computers

Anything is possible... Things like a computer that can fit in a single room and hold millions of pieces of information.

(Tom Hanks, playing Jim Lovell, in *Apollo 13*)

When we wrote the first edition of this book, our discussion of the role of computers in research was restricted to a single, discrete chapter. This is no longer appropriate as computers are integral to research activity, rather than an adjunct to it. As the graphs in Figure 14.1 show, dramatic increases in the hardware specifications of personal computers (i.e. their physical processing and storage capabilities) have come at a significantly reduced cost to the consumer. Moreover, these data reveal nothing about the vast and coincidental advances in networking opportunities (via the Internet) and software design (the computer packages that allow people to marshal this computing power in ever more flexible and user-friendly ways).

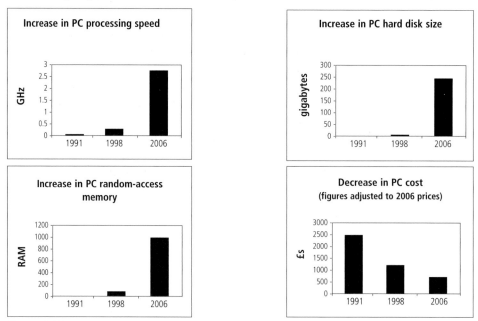

Figure 14.1 Changes in the performance specifications and cost of personal computers, 1991–2006

(Note: the figures here represent the median deals advertised in the UK national press in July of each year.)

For these reasons, in this revised edition of our book, we have already dedicated a considerable amount of space to examining the role of computers in communication, media and cultural research. In chapters 2 and 11, we addressed the expansion of the Internet and its dual function, as an information resource and as the subject for research in its own right. Elsewhere, we discussed how computer technology offers new opportunities for questionnaire design and delivery (chapters 3 and 4), for conducting media analysis (chapter 6), and for storing and transcribing interview material (chapter 12). The reason why we have retained a dedicated chapter on the role of computers is that these preceding discussions have focused mainly on the role of computers in gathering data and seeking and retrieving information. Little has been said about the role that computer technology plays in *data analysis*.

The discussion in this chapter introduces you to computer-aided data analysis and makes no assumptions of prior knowledge. It is important that you develop a familiarity with computers, as blinkered technophobia can not only restrict your methodological options, but also, as a consequence, your academic horizons. Would you ever countenance conducting a large-scale questionnaire survey or media content analysis, if you knew you would have to tally up all the figures manually? And even if you were prepared to undertake such an exercise, would you have the time, patience and expertise to do anything other than basic frequency counts and some perfunctory bivariate analysis? We would doubt it, which would mean you could hardly do justice to your data's permutations.

In the first section, we examine statistical data analysis using the Statistical Package for the Social Sciences (SPSS) for Microsoft Windows® (Version 14). The second section examines computer-aided analysis of qualitative data using Nvivo (Version 7). There are many other packages that can analyse qualitative and quantitative data equally as effectively and efficiently, and our neglect of these alternatives here should not be construed as a negative comment on their suitability.

We can only offer a preliminary introduction to the operation of these two software packages. Nevertheless, the first step is often the hardest to take, and if you follow each section through, you will have sufficient basic knowledge of each package to use as a springboard for further exploration of their more sophisticated features.

Knocking around numbers – SPSS for Microsoft Windows®

To explain how SPSS works, we conduct an analysis of an actual set of numbers. We begin by providing some background information about this data set.

The data set

The data are based on a comparative study of general election campaign reporting in the UK (Deacon et al. 2005). Each line of data represents statistical measures of individual campaign-related news items that appeared on the BBC1 main evening news in the 2001 and 2005 UK general elections. As the data set is so small, we have selected the data to produce results that correspond closely to distributions found in the full-scale study. (NB

More than 400 news items were coded for the BBC1 news in the two campaigns.)

There are four variables in the data set. The first indicates which campaign the item appeared in (2001 or 2005). The second quantifies the length in seconds of the news item. The third variable provides an average in seconds of the total speaking time of each quoted political source in that item. The fourth variable indicates the position of the item in the news bulletin (1 = 'lead item', 2 = 'other item headlined at the start of the programme', 3 = 'non-headlined item').

The reason for our interest in such basic measures links to a broader debate about the rise of a 'sound-bite culture' in British politics, in which it is claimed that the amount of political reporting in television news is reducing and political sources are required to articulate their views in ever more compressed and potentially simplistic statements.

Table 14.1 The SPSS data set: BBC 1 news coverage of the 2001 and 2005 general elections

Election	Position of item in programme	Length of item (seconds)	Average speaking time of quoted source (seconds)
2001	1	209	20
2001	3	120	30
2001	1	268	32
2001	2	240	36
2001	3	172	19
2001	3	92	12
2001	3	159	28
2001	3	219	38
2001	2	208	40
2001	3	119	18
2001	1	227	36
2001	3	68	9
2001	3	189	22
2001	3	204	36
2001	3	126	16
2005	2	226	28
2005	3	112	34
2005	3	243	45
2005	2	196	29
2005	3	116	28
2005	3	155	16
2005	2	278	28
2005	3	46	12
2005	3	153	35
2005	3	196	32
2005	1	183	26
2005	3	32	2

2005	3	118	38
2005	1	196	29
2005	3	168	39

Getting started

To analyse these data using SPSS for Microsoft Windows®, you need to open the program, either by clicking on the SPSS icon on the desktop or by selecting the program from the Start menu. On entering the program, a dialog box will appear, asking, 'What would you like to do?' When starting a new project, select the *Type in Data* option and then *OK*. This will bring up the screen shown in Figure 14.2.

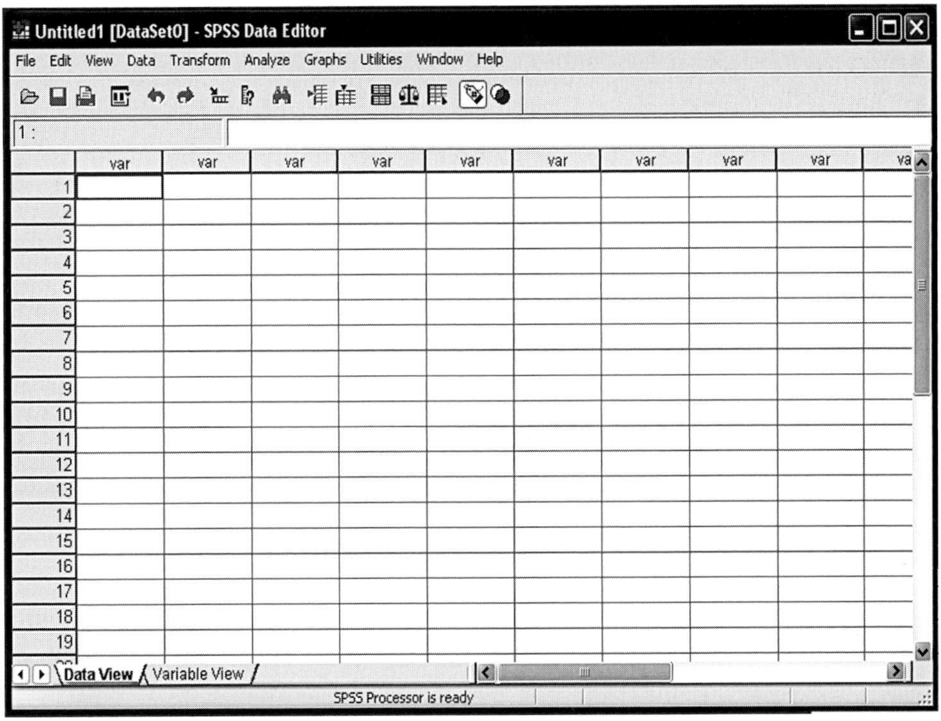

Figure 14.2 The SPSS Data View screen

This is the *Data View* screen, the place where you enter your data. The columns represent the variables of your analysis, and the rows, the individual cases. Before you enter the data, you must first define your variables and assign values to the data (where that is appropriate). When we talk of 'variables', we are referring to something that has been counted (e.g. 'the position of election news items in their bulletin'); when we talk of 'values', we are referring to the actual numbers that are collected in connection with these variables (1 = 'lead item', 2 = 'other item headlined at the start of the programme', 3 = 'non-headlined item').

Defining variables and values

You will notice that in the bottom left-hand part of the *Data View* screen there is a grey tab titled *Variable View*. This is the part of the package that allows you to define your variables and values. When you select it, the screen shown in Figure 14.3 appears. In this screen, each row is used to define details of individual variables. In the first column, *Name*, you must assign a brief name to the variable. To continue with the example of the variable that indicates the position of each item in a programme, we shall use the name 'Position'.

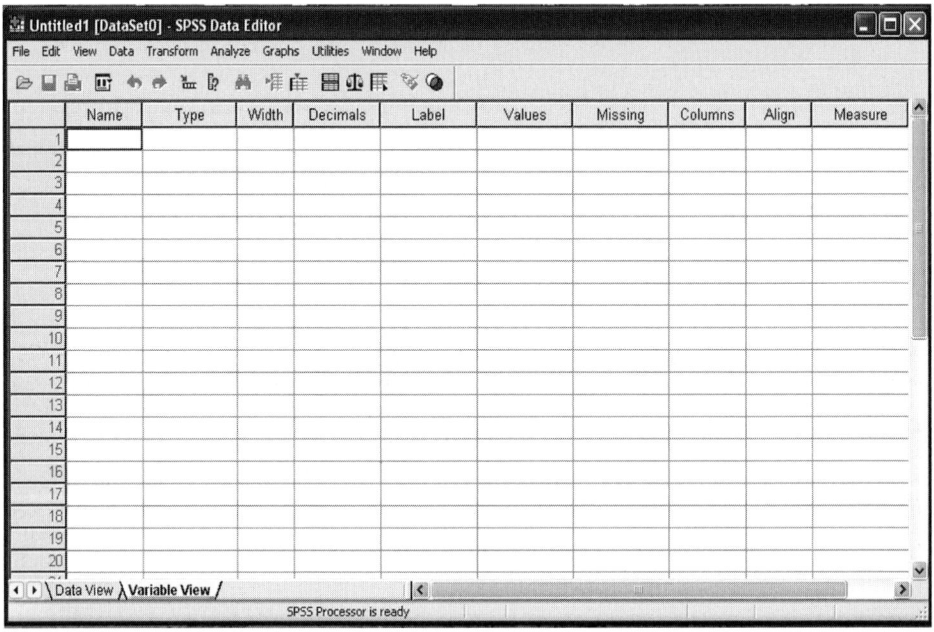

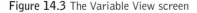

Figure 14.3 The Variable View screen

Once you enter a name, a range of default settings appear in the remaining columns. In SPSS you can enter words as well as numbers. The *Type* column indicates whether the variable is numerical or textual. (NB Text data is referred to as 'String' data in the package.) It also allows you to define the exact numerical form of your data ('numeric', 'comma', 'dot', 'scientific notation', etc.). In this case, the default setting of 'Numeric' is the appropriate option, so there is no need to adjust this setting. The next two columns relate, respectively, to the width of each column on screen (i.e. a setting of 8 means that no more than eight numbers will be displayed on screen) and the number of decimal places that will be presented. As the numbers we will use to indicate the position of items in a bulletin are simple categories, you might wish to change the number in the *Decimals* column to zero.

The *Label* column allows you to enter a more elaborate title for your variable. This is an option, not a requirement, but as the name 'Position' is rather gnomic, we will enter the fuller title 'Position of item in BBC One news'. The *Values* column is where you define what the numbers actually represent. Where these numbers have an actual arithmetical meaning (e.g. 243 = 243 seconds), it is not necessary to provide labels. With the 'Position' variable, however, the numbers are used to categorise different qualities of the text, and it is useful to indicate what the different values mean. To do so, you click the cursor into the 'Values' cell and a grey button will appear in the right of the cell. When you select this button, a *Value Labels* dialog box appears. Enter the first value into the *Value* box, and the text label into the *Label* box. Then click *Add*, and the value and its label will appear in the larger white box below. When you have entered all the value labels (see Figure 14.4), select *OK* and you will return to the *Variable View*.

The *Missing Values* column allows you to define those occasions when individual cases do not have values entered for this variable. As was explained in chapter 5, this may be because they would be logically excluded from being coded,[1] or because the data has accidentally not been recorded for this variable. To define any missing values, you select the variable cell and click on the grey button that appears on the right. This allows you to specify up to three missing values or a range of values and one discrete missing value. The *Column* column replicates the function of the *Width* column, allowing you to adjust the number of values that can be displayed; and the *Align* column allows you to specify whether the data should be right, left or centrally positioned.

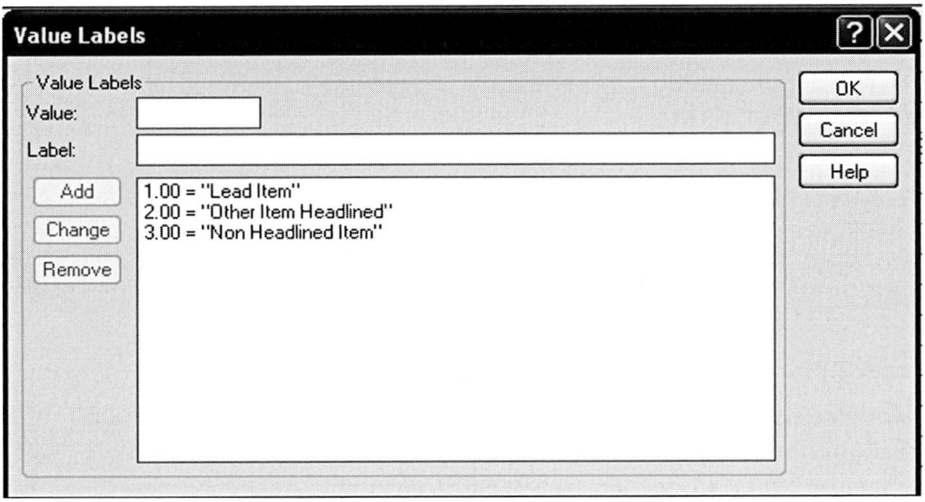

Figure 14.4 The Value Labels box

The *Measure* column requires you to indicate the level of measurement of the variable data (see the discussion at the start of chapter 5) and three options are offered: 'Nominal', 'Ordinal' and 'Scale'. (Note that the 'Scale' category combines the 'interval' and 'ratio' levels of measurement.) It is valuable to address this matter at this stage because, as explained in Chapter 5, the level of measurement of a variable determines what type of statistical procedures you can apply in its analysis. In the case of the 'Position' variable, the data can be

---

1   For example, if a respondent in a survey had indicated in a previous question that he never watched football on television, no entry would be required for a question that measured the frequency of his televisual football viewing.

seen to achieve the *ordinal* level of measurement. This is because a value of '1' indicates that an item had more prominence in the news bulletin than those assigned with a '2', just as those assigned a '2' indicates greater prominence than those with a '3'.

Figure 14.5 shows the completed Variable View screen for our worked example. You will notice that all the other variables have been defined as *Scale* variables. This is because they can all be treated as mathematical numbers (i.e. you can average them, sum them, subtract them, etc.). Once you have completed this stage to your satisfaction, click the *Data View* tab at the bottom left-hand side of the window. (NB It is possible to adjust variable details retrospectively should you need to.) You are now ready to enter your data.

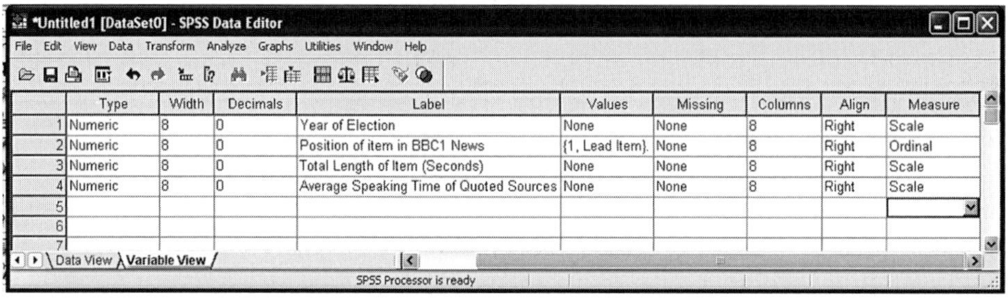

	Type	Width	Decimals	Label	Values	Missing	Columns	Align	Measure
1	Numeric	8	0	Year of Election	None	None	8	Right	Scale
2	Numeric	8	0	Position of item in BBC1 News	{1, Lead Item}.	None	8	Right	Ordinal
3	Numeric	8	0	Total Length of Item (Seconds)	None	None	8	Right	Scale
4	Numeric	8	0	Average Speaking Time of Quoted Sources	None	None	8	Right	Scale
5									
6									
7									

Figure 14.5 Completed Variable View screen

Entering your data

Figure 14.6 shows the first 16 lines of data from our case study entered under their appropriate columns. Data are entered just as in a spreadsheet: you place the cursor into each cell, type the appropriate number and press the 'Return' button. It is also possible to cut and paste numbers in from other software packages, provided they are stored in a tabular format that corresponds exactly to the set-up in the Data View window.

Saving your file

When all numbers have been entered accurately, you should save your data and their definitions. To do so, select the *File* command from the main menu at the top of the window, then *Save As*. In the *Save Data As* screen, give the file a name and select an appropriate location for it to be saved (e.g. in a directory on your hard disk). Note that *Data* files (the files with the numbers in) always end with '.sav', which is automatically added when you give the file a name. *Viewer* files, which contain the results of your analysis (see below), end with '.spo'. This difference is important to remember when reopening files, which you start by selecting the *Open* option on the *File* command. Initially, the *Open File* screen will only show saved data files (i.e. those ending in '.sav'). If you want to open a saved *Viewer* file, you must first select the '.spo' option from the 'Files of type' listed at the bottom of the window.

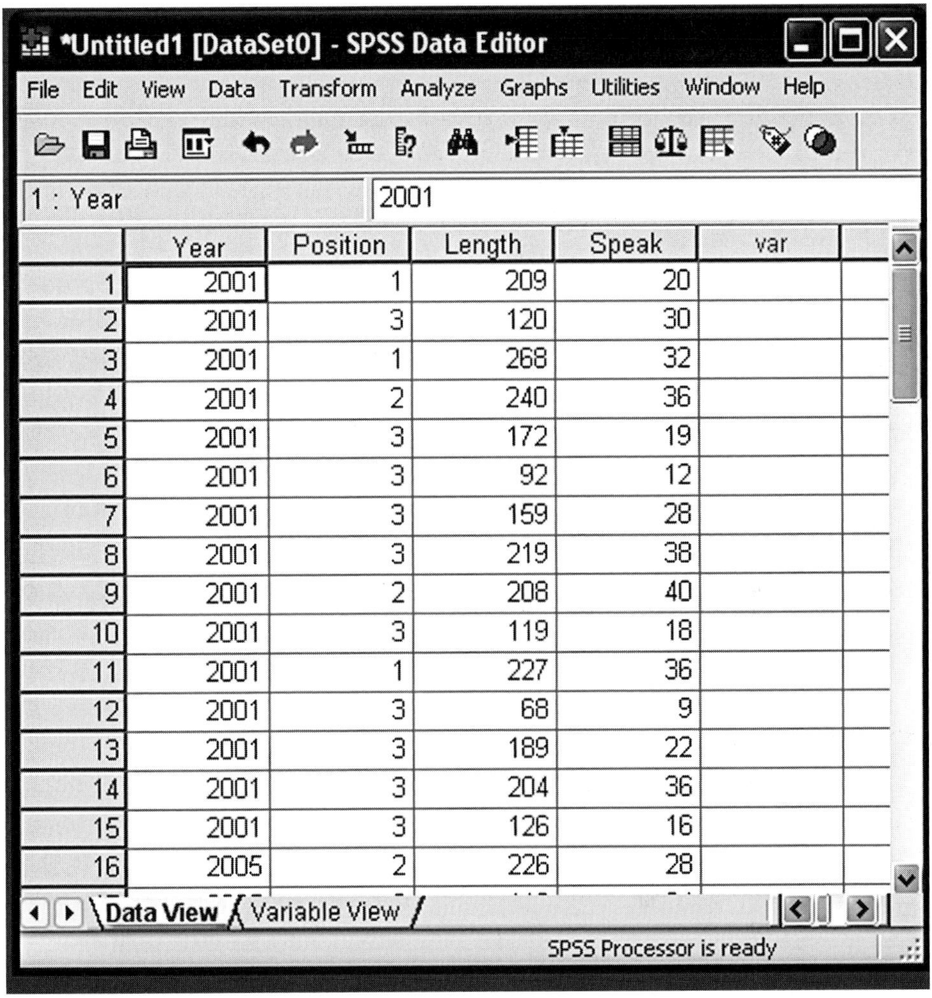

Figure 14.6 The Data View screen with variables and values defined and data entered

Data analysis

You can now commence analysing the data. SPSS for Microsoft Windows® can conduct a vast range of sophisticated statistical tests and procedures, but here we focus on its most basic uses: generating frequency tables, cross-tabulations and providing descriptive statistical measures.

Frequency tables

To generate frequency tables, click your cursor on the *Analyze* command from the top menu bar. From the menu that drops down, select *Descriptive Statistics*, which will reveal another set of options. Click on *Frequencies…* and the dialog box in Figure 14.7 will appear.

As you will see, the four variables from our case study are listed in the box on the left.

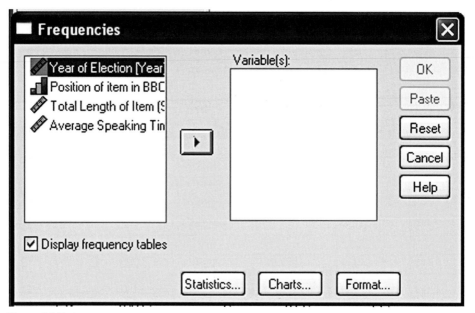

Figure 14.7 The Frequencies command

To analyse a variable, you transfer it to the box on the right (*Variable(s)*) by highlighting the one you want, then clicking on the black arrow between the boxes. The variable will then appear in the right-hand box. Once you have placed all the variables you want to analyse in this box, click on *OK* and the analysis will begin.

As this process is initiated you move into the SPSS Viewer screen, which presents the results. Before we look at these numbers, we need to explain how this screen is organised.

You will see that the Viewer screen divides into two parts. The right-hand section is where your results emerge. When a Frequencies command is run, this section will show an initial *Statistics* table as well as the tables requested. The statistics table lists the number of cases that have been included in the count, which can be useful for reference purposes. The frequency tables appear immediately below it.

Each frequency table contains five columns. The first lists either the value labels entered for a variable or the range of values entered into the variable. The second column (*Frequency*) provides the raw count of numbers that corresponds to each of the values. The third column (*Percent*) lists the overall percentage distribution for each of these categories. The fourth (*Valid percent*) provides adjusted percentages which exclude missing values. The final column (*Cumulative percent*) provides the cumulative percentages across the different values (i.e. the percentage for the first category, then the percentage for the first and second categories added, and so on).

The information on the left-hand side of the screen provides a log of all the SPSS output contained within the output file, and is a useful reference source when you have a large output file containing many results. To move to a table in the right-hand screen, select the relevant section on this left-hand list with your cursor. You can also use this section to delete results and information you do not need. For example, if you want to get rid of the initial Statistics table, highlight its reference in the left-hand section with your cursor and press the delete key. (NB If you want to conduct further data analysis, you do not need to return to the *Data Entry* screen. The *Command* menu at the top remains the same, whatever screen you are in.)

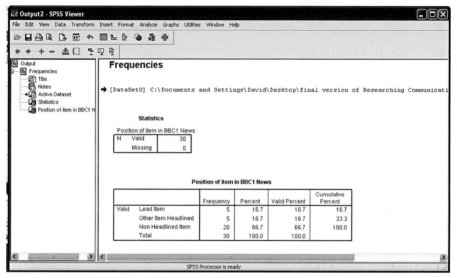

Figure 14.8 Frequency tables and the SPSS Viewer Screen

The frequency table in Figure 14.8 shows that 5 of the 30 items in the data set were lead items in their bulletins, and 5 other items were mentioned in the bulletin headlines (each representing 16.7 per cent of the total sample). The *Percent* and *Valid percent* figures are identical because there are no missing values in this worked example.

Cross-tabulations

To cross-tabulate one variable with another you select *Analyze> Descriptive Statistics> Crosstabs…* from the main menu at the top. This will produce a *Crosstabs* dialog box (see Figure 14.9) that lists all the variables in the left-hand column and three boxes on the right-hand side.

The left-hand box lists all the variables in your data, and the right-hand boxes allow you to specify the variables you want to cross-tabulate, and the manner in which you want to present the comparison. If you are interested only in bivariate analysis (i.e. looking at the relationship between two variables), you only need to bother with the top two boxes. If you want to do a multivariate analysis, in which three or more variables are involved, then you place the 'controlling' variables in the boxes below. As with frequency tables, you navigate the variables into (and out of) the relevant boxes by highlighting the variable names with your cursor and then clicking on the appropriate black arrow.

When you have decided on the variables you want to cross-tabulate and in what way (i.e. which you want to be the columns in the table and which you want to appear as rows),

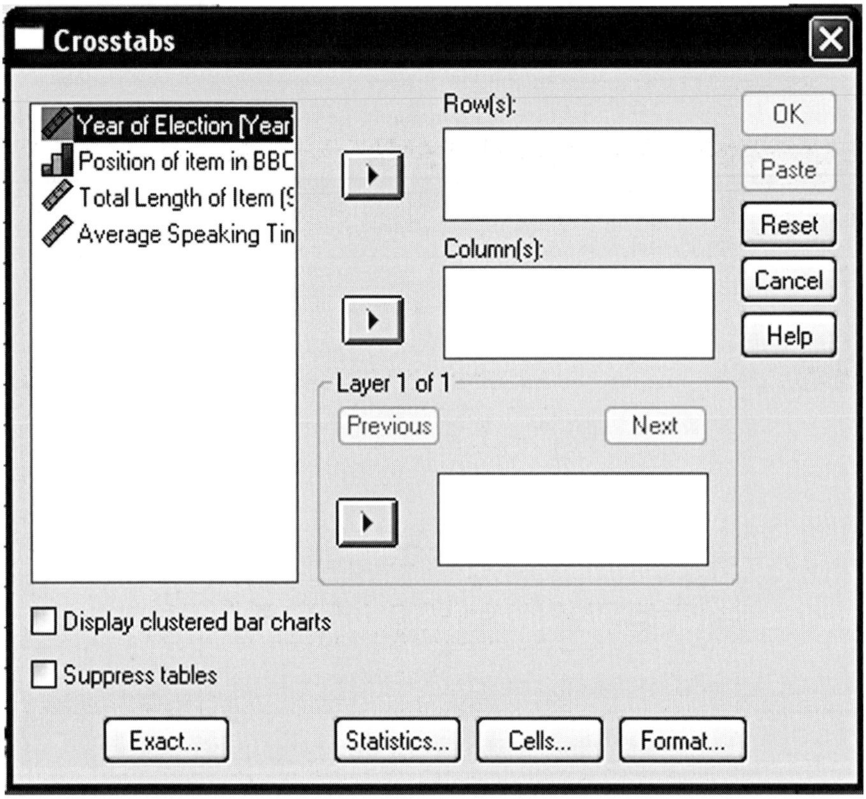

Figure 14.9 The Crosstabs dialog box

you click on the *Cells* button. This brings up a new window that allows you to specify what information you want to appear in each cell. In the *Counts* box, you will see that the *Observed* option is automatically selected. As explained in chapter 5, 'observed frequencies' are the actual number of cases that fall into each cell. Because cross-tabulations are most commonly used to explore differences within data sets, the column and row per cent are the other options you are most likely to want to request. To select either or both of these options, click on the white box next to each and a tick will appear in each one to denote that these have been selected. Once you have selected all the options you require, click on the *Continue* button to return to the main Crosstabs screen.

You can also request statistical tests to conduct in relation to cross-tabulated data. To do so, select the *Statistics* button at the bottom left-hand side of the window. This produces a menu of test options, including the chi-square option. Select the test of your choice and then press the *Continue* button.

Once you have selected all the information you require for your cross-tabulation, press the *OK* button and wait for the table to appear in the SPSS Viewer screen. Before you get to the results, a *Case Processing Summary* is provided, which gives you reference details about the number of cases included in the calculation. Figure 14.10 compares the positioning of BBC One election news items in the 2001 and 2005 general election campaigns. Each cell contains an observed frequency and column percentage, and shows a higher proportion of lead items in BBC One news coverage in the 2001 campaign compared with 2005 (20 per cent compared with 13.3 per cent).

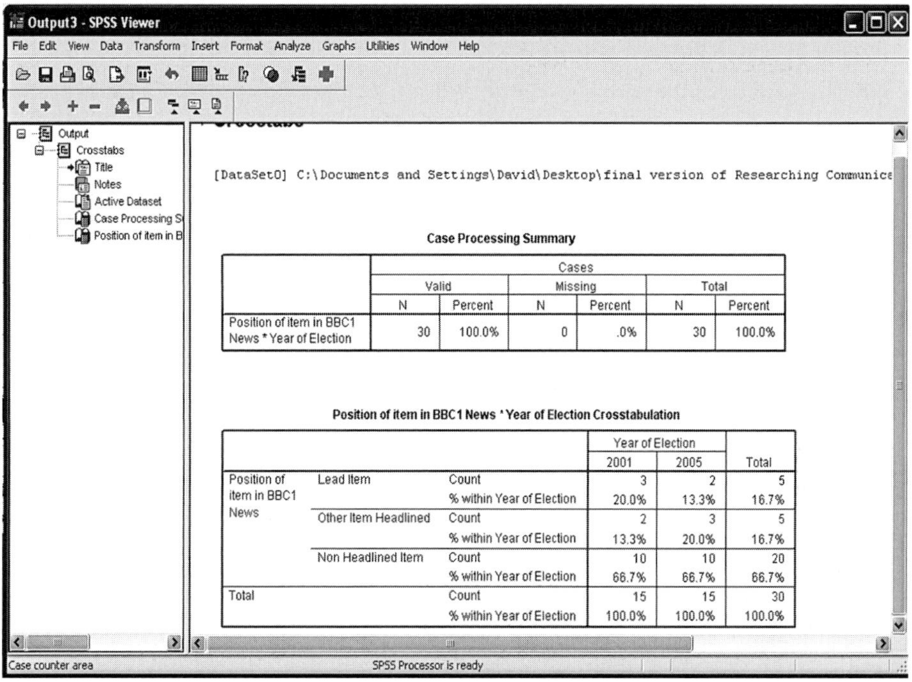

Case Processing Summary

	Cases					
	Valid		Missing		Total	
	N	Percent	N	Percent	N	Percent
Position of item in BBC1 News * Year of Election	30	100.0%	0	.0%	30	100.0%

Position of item in BBC1 News * Year of Election Crosstabulation

			Year of Election		Total
			2001	2005	
Position of item in BBC1 News	Lead Item	Count	3	2	5
		% within Year of Election	20.0%	13.3%	16.7%
	Other Item Headlined	Count	2	3	5
		% within Year of Election	13.3%	20.0%	16.7%
	Non Headlined Item	Count	10	10	20
		% within Year of Election	66.7%	66.7%	66.7%
Total		Count	15	15	30
		% within Year of Election	100.0%	100.0%	100.0%

Figure 14.10 Cross-tabulation tables and the SPSS Viewer screen

Descriptive measures of central tendency and dispersion

Frequency tables and cross-tabulations are valuable in analysing numbers that attain the nominal level of measurement. SPSS for Microsoft Windows® can also conduct statistical analyses that are appropriate for data that attain higher levels of measurement (i.e. the ordinal, interval or ratio levels).

All variables in our case study, apart from the 'Position' variable, attain the ratio level of measurement. They have an 'absolute zero' and can be added, subtracted, multiplied and divided. In this section, we show how to generate summaries and comparisons of central tendency and dispersion for these sorts of variables.

To generate these descriptive measures, click on the *Analyze* command on the menu bar, followed by *Descriptive Statistics* and *Descriptives....* As with the *Frequencies* and *Crosstabs* dialog boxes, you select the variables you want to analyse by highlighting them with your cursor and transferring them into the right-hand box by clicking on the black, central arrow. You then need to specify which descriptive statistical measures you want. This involves clicking on the *Options* button at the bottom left of the window, which brings up the *Descriptives: Options* window (see Figure 14.11).

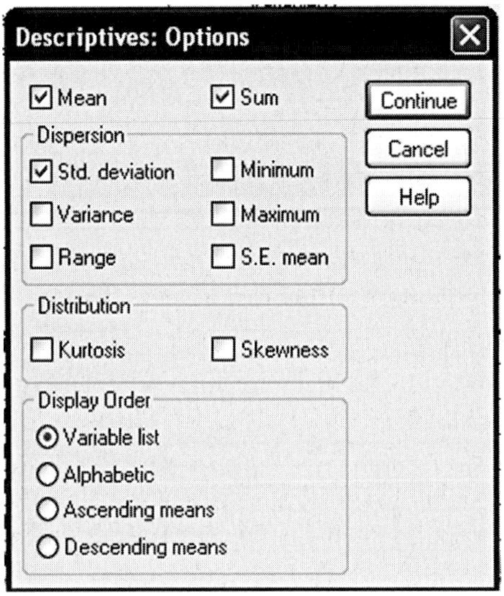

Figure 14.11 Descriptives: Options window

Here again, you have a range of choices available, which you can select by clicking on the appropriate boxes. For the purposes of this example, we shall request the mean, standard deviation and sum for the variables 'Total length of item' and 'Average speaking time of quoted source'.

When you have chosen your options, select the *Continue* button to return to the *Descriptives* window. Press the *OK* button and the results will appear in the SPSS *Viewer* screen. Figure 14.12 shows the output you would get from the case study data. The variables are listed in rows in the first column. The second column (N) indicates the number of cases included in the analysis (all 30). The third indicates the sum of all the values for each variable. The fourth column shows the average (mean) value for each variable. The final column gives standard deviation of the values.

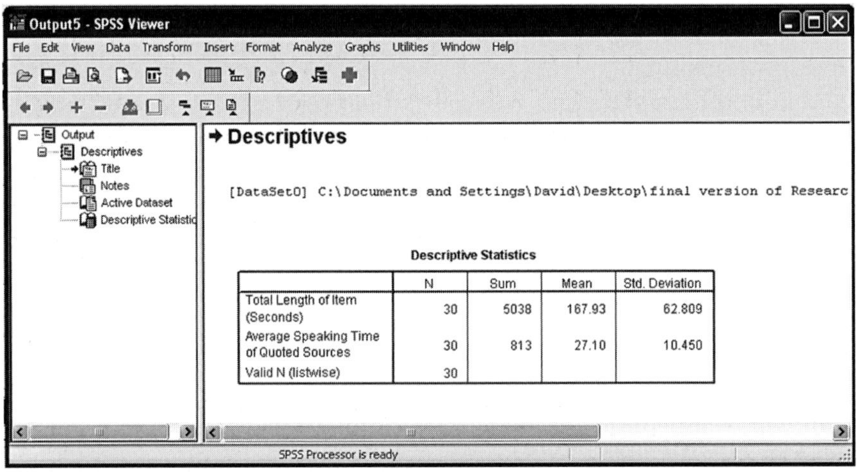

Figure 14.12 Descriptives measures and the SPSS Viewer screen

From this table we can see that the total length of all items in the sample was 5,038 seconds (see the *Sum* column), which works out an average item length of 167.93 seconds (see the *Mean* column). The standard deviation of this measure was 62.809 seconds (see the *Std deviation* column). In comparison, the sum of the averages for the speaking time of quoted sources in the coverage was 813 seconds, with an average of 27.10 seconds and a standard deviation of 10.45 seconds.

Comparing means

Taken on their own, these general measures of dispersion and central tendency do not tell us very much. A next step would be to assess the extent to which these figures differed in the two election campaigns analysed. To break down the descriptive information contained in Figure 14.12 into the two separate campaigns, you first select *Analyze* from the main menu bar, followed by *Compare Means> Means...* This will bring up the *Means* dialog box, which closely resembles the *Crosstabs* box (see Figure 14.9) Initially, all the variables are listed in the white box on the left-hand side. On the right-hand side are two boxes labelled *Dependent List* and *Independent List*. As we are interested in examining any differences in BBC1 coverage of the elections, 'Year of election' should be placed in the *Independent List* box and 'Length of item' and 'Average speaking time of quoted sources' placed in the *Dependent List* box.

As with the *Mean* box, there is an option button that allows you to select a range of descriptive measures for comparison purposes (mean, sum, range, etc.). For this example, we shall solely request a comparison of the *means* for our two selected dependent variables.

After you request the analysis by hitting the *OK* button, two tables will appear in the SPSS Viewer screen. The first is the *Case Processing* summary, which lists the numbers of cases included or excluded from the analysis. The second table, *Report* (see Figure 14.13), contains the statistical comparison.

You will note that there are two rows that separate the averages for the 2001 and 2005 election campaigns. The results show that the average length of BBC1 news items *reduced* from 174.67 seconds in 2001 to 161.20 seconds in 2005, and that the average amount of speaking time allocated to quoted sources *increased* slightly from 26.13 seconds to 28.07 seconds.

Computer Aided Qualitative Data Analysis (CAQDAS)

In our experience, some students prefer to conduct qualitative rather than quantitative research, not for any clearly thought-out theoretical or epistemological reasons, but because qualitative research is seen as something of a 'soft option': there are no nasty numbers to deal with; all you have to do is switch on a tape recorder, transcribe what people say, select a few quotes and you are home and dry.

This is an entirely misguided view. In particular, it underestimates the scale of the demands and responsibilities involved in analysing qualitative data. Qualitative analysis should be as thorough and systematic as any statistical analysis. Skimming through transcripts to gain a loose impression of the salient issues and to cherry-pick juicy quotes for

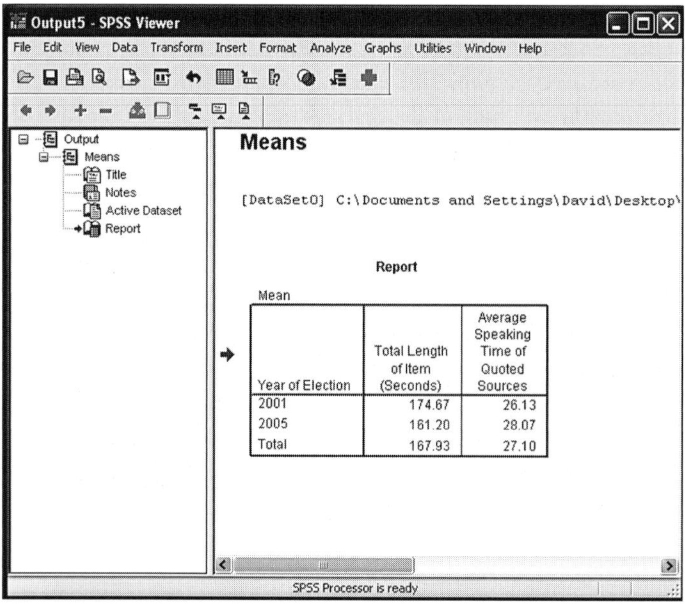

Figure 14.13 Compare means and the SPSS Viewer screen

the final report does not constitute an adequate qualitative analysis. You need to immerse yourself in the detail available, to look for the kind of subtle insights and qualifications that tend to escape most quantitative perspectives. Moreover, when people refer to qualitative research as 'small-scale' they are generally referring to sample size rather than the amount of material that is produced for analysis. For example, even a relatively small number of semi-structured interviews of moderate duration can generate a considerable amount of research material when turned into a fully transcribed text. Simply mapping the emergence and re-emergence of different themes in the texts can prove a complex and time-consuming task.

In recent years, interest has grown in utilising computer software to assist in qualitative data analysis, and a range of computer-assisted qualitative data analysis software (**CAQDAS**) is now available.[2] In this section, we review the NVivo 7 package. As with the SPSS section, we introduce the basic features of the package by using data from actual research. In this case, they are transcripts from interviews with British journalists about their views of, and relations with, voluntary organisations and charities (Deacon 1999).

Getting started

To enter the package, double-click on the QSR NVivo 7 icon on your desktop. As you enter, a screen will appear, welcoming you to the package and offering three options ('Run a tutorial', 'Start a new project' or 'Open an existing project').

At this stage, you should select the *New Project* button.[3] You will then need to enter a

2 For a review of different CAQDAS software packages see Koenig (2004).

3 When you are returning to a project, you select the 'Open an existing project' option. NVivo 7 will then list all the projects it has saved, from which you select the project you want.

name for your file in the *Title* field. Because this worked example is looking at journalists' views of the voluntary sector, we have called this project 'Voluntary'. You can also add more information about the project in the *Description* field. By default, all projects are stored in the *My Documents* folder on your desktop. The location can be changed, should you wish, by clicking the *Browse* button. You then click on the *OK* button and the screen in Figure 14.14 will appear.

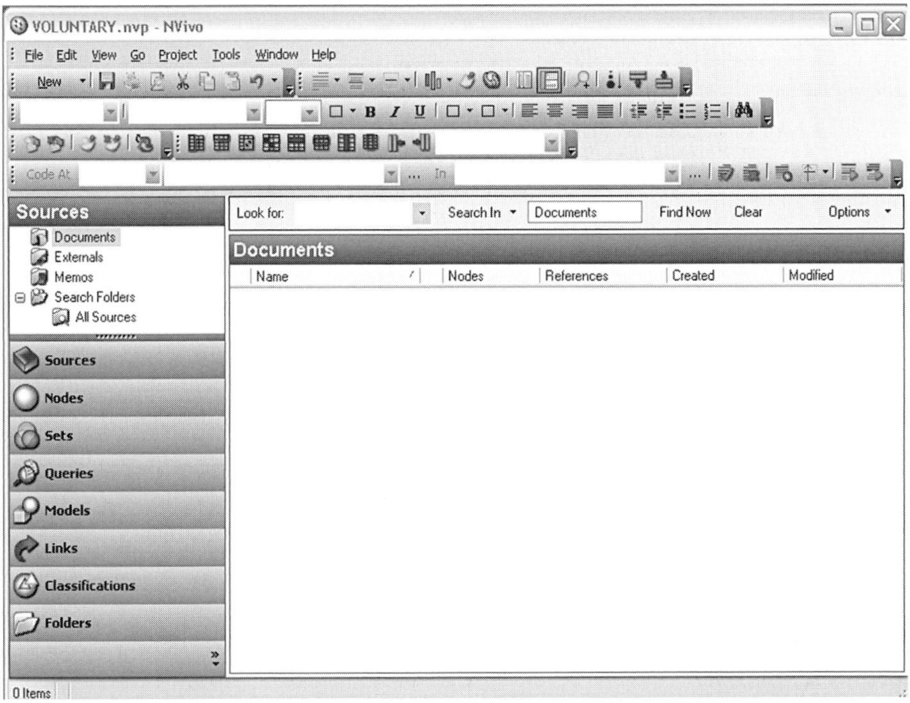

Figure 14.14 The NVivo 7 entry screen

Note that the screen comprises three elements. Along the top you have a list of commands (*File, Edit, Project*, etc.) and an associated main toolbar that is operated in a similar manner to other Microsoft Windows® based software (i.e. you click on different commands with your cursor to pull down menus from which you select different options, or you select appropriate icons). Underneath this is a window listing *Sources*, and under this another window listing a range of options, each of which, when clicked, changes the details appearing in the window above. These two windows are collectively referred to as the 'navigation view'.

Gathering source material

The default navigation view that appears is the *Sources* window (see Figure 14.14). In NVivo 7, 'sources' is a collective term used to refer to any materials used for analysis. These can be digital text, audio and video files, photographs or digital copies of physical documents. The procedures for importing sources are slightly different depending on their type. Digital text documents saved in text (.txt), rich text (.rtf) or Microsoft® Word (.doc) format can be imported straight into the package. Other types of digital research material (photos, audio clips, etc.) cannot be imported directly and require the creation of 'externals' that link to this material. In this chapter, we restrict our discussion to the importation of digital text.

To import a text document you click on the *Documents* folder. On the *Project* menu, select *Import Documents*. This displays the *Import Documents* dialogue box. You then click the *Browse* button in the *Import from* field and locate the document you want to import. (You can import multiple items using the CTRL key, or use the SHIFT key to select several at once.) You then click the *Open* button and you will see the selected files in the *Import from* field. At this stage, a dialog box will appear, offering you four options you can select.[4] At this stage, you only need to click *OK* and the imported document will appear in the 'list view' part of the operating environment (see Figure 14.15). In this example, the imported document is an interview conducted with a national TV social affairs editor.

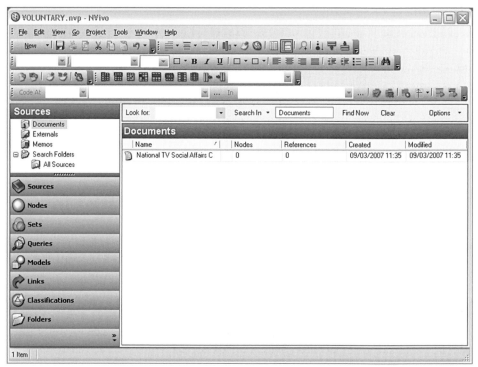

Figure 14.15 Imported documents in the 'list view' screen

---

4   'Update text file' standardises the text style to that set in *Project Properties* (located under the *File* command at the top of the screen). 'Create descriptions' allows you to write a new first paragraph to describe the contents of the document. These can be reviewed via the *Document Properties* option on the *Project* menu. 'Code sources as cases' automatically creates a case for each document. This allows you to code background information about the file (e.g. the age, profession and gender of an interviewee), which can be useful when subsequently collating and comparing the contents of the text files. It is not necessary to create a case at this stage, as this can be done retrospectively (see our later discussion of *attributes* and *cases*, which explains their function in full). 'Create as read only' gives you the option of protecting the integrity of the original textual version, while still allowing you to add new codes or annotations.

This process is repeated for all text files to be used in an analysis. However, it is not necessary to introduce all the files in one go, or to complete this stage before embarking on the analysis. You can introduce new texts whenever you want, and allow this work to coincide with the analytical tasks described below.

Creating attributes and cases

It is often helpful to code background information about your imported text material. For example, when importing personal interview material, you might want to indicate the age and gender of the interviewee. This information could then be used to collate responses from particular types of interviewees, or to make comparisons between them. To do this, you need to define which background variables ('attributes') you want to use to code each imported document ('cases').

Assigning attributes

To assign attributes, you must first select the *Classifications* button from the bottom part of the navigation view window. You then click on the *Attributes* folder and select *New> Attribute in this Folder*. This will display a *New Attribute* dialog box and you will need to provide a name for this attribute (see Figure 14.16). You then click the *Values* tab, followed by the *Add* button. You enter all the relevant value names in the *Value* cell and click *OK*. One of the attributes we might want to code for our journalist study is the type of news media each interviewee is employed by. These values would be:

1. national TV;
2. national press;
3. national radio;
4. local/regional TV;
5. local/regional press;
6. local/regional radio.

Assigning cases

'Case nodes' refers to the part of the programme that stores classification information about individual documents. Whenever you introduce new sources to NVivo 7, you are offered the option of automatically creating a case node for the document, but you do not have to do so at this stage if it is not convenient.

To define cases, you first click the *Node* button in the navigation view window and then select the *Cases* folder. At the main toolbar, select *New> Case in this Folder*. This will open the *New Case* dialog box, where you enter a name into the *Name* field, and, if required, a description in the *Description* field. You then click the *Attribute Values* tab to assign values to the case. (NB This is why you need to define your attributes before assigning cases to them.) The example in Figure 14.17 permits two attributes to be assigned to each individual interview; these indicate the gender of each interviewee and the news organisation they work

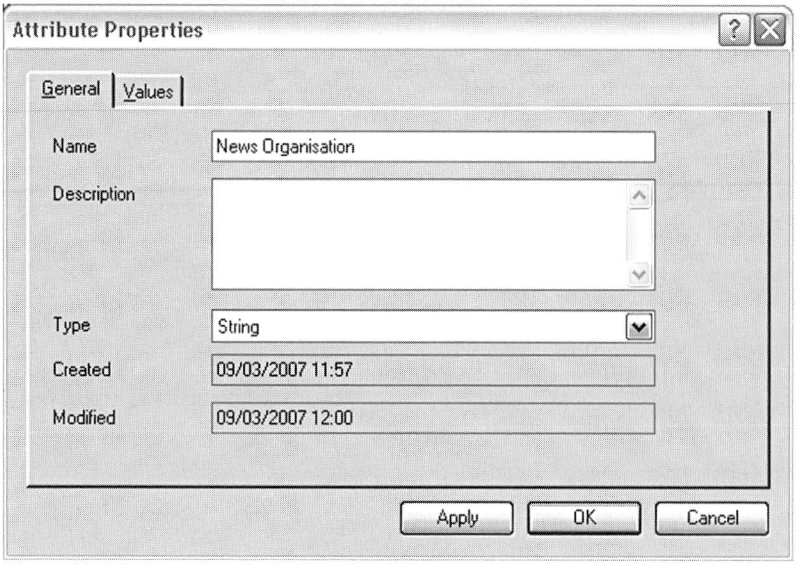

Figure 14.16 The Attribute Properties dialog box

for. To select the appropriate category, click on the blue down-arrows on the right of each *Value* cell, and the options will present themselves.

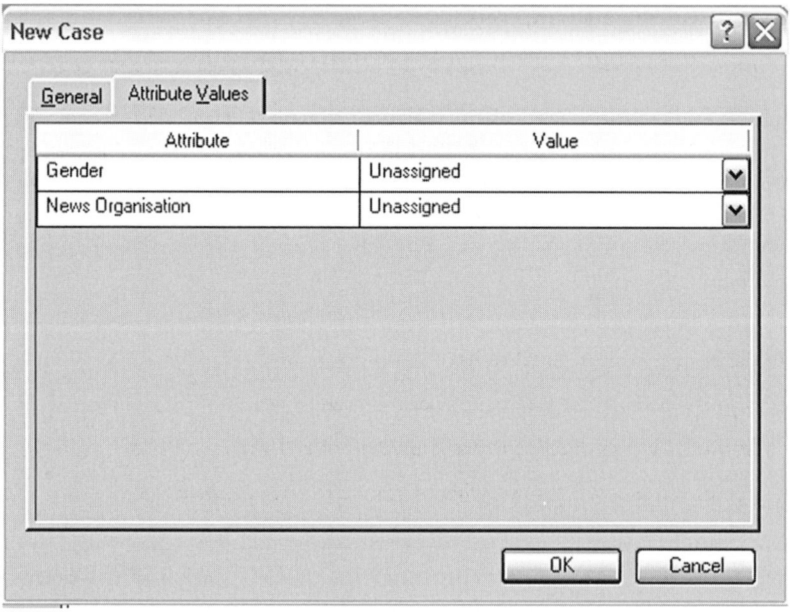

Figure 14.17 The New Case dialog box

Analysing texts

We are now at a stage where we can begin to analyse the details of the texts imported into the package. To do so, you need to define coding categories that will organise the analysis of the imported qualitative text. Coding frameworks in NVivo 7 can be planned in advance, altered during the course of the analysis, or induced from direct analysis of the qualitative data. This analysis can be structured (by creating *Tree Nodes*) or unstructured (by using *Free Nodes*), or it can combine the two. Nodes are the containers for ideas, themes or information about your data. They are used to categorise the different issues and themes that emerge from a detailed reading of the text. In many respects, they resemble the variables and values you develop when conducting a content analysis, although their design can be developed and adjusted in a more flexible way as you proceed with your analysis. Let us begin by looking at the more structured form of textual coding: creating Tree Nodes.

Creating Tree Nodes

Tree Nodes are hierarchically arranged categories that are whimsically described as existing in 'parent–child' relationships. That is, you start off with wide-ranging categories (the 'parents') that produce generations of offspring that narrow and refine these macro themes (the 'children'). To help explain what we mean, let us consider how we might organise analysis of one aspect of the interviews with journalists about their views of voluntary organisations and charities.

Let us assume we are interested in assessing journalists' comments in relation to three themes:

- their perceptions of the *news value* of voluntary organisations and charities;
- their perceptions of these organisations' authoritativeness and *credibility*;
- their perceptions of the *efficiency* of these organisations in their publicity and media work.

These three broad areas cover a wide range of variation in responses. For example, journalists will see some voluntary sector organisations and activities as more newsworthy than others, just as they will invest some organisations with far greater credibility and authority. We can add a range of subcategories that follow on from these initial categories, to capture these differences:

1. News value:
   - organisations/activities deemed to have a high news value;
   - organisations/activities deemed to have a low news value;
   - organisations/activities deemed to have uncertain news value;
   - other themes related to the news value of voluntary organisations/activities.

2. Credibility:
   - organisations/activities deemed to have high credibility/authoritativeness;
   - organisations/activities deemed to have low credibility/authoritativeness;
   - organisations/activities deemed to have uncertain credibility/authoritativeness;
   - other themes related to credibility/authoritativeness.

3. Efficiency:

- organisations commended for their publicity/news making;
- organisations criticised for their publicity/news making;
- ambivalence about organisations' publicity/news making;
- other themes related to publicity/news making efficiency.

This is a simple example of a Tree Node structure. To introduce it into your NVivo 7 project, the first step involves introducing the 'parent' nodes. In this example, there would be three parent nodes ('news value', 'credibility' and 'efficiency'), and they are entered in the following way:

1. Click on the *Nodes* button on the bottom left-hand side of the window. (NB This area of the screen is called the navigation view.)
2. Click on the *Tree Nodes* folder that appears in the window above.
3. Click the *New* button on the main toolbar at the top of the screen and select the *Tree Node in this Folder*.
4. A *New Tree Node* dialog box appears. You need to enter the node name here (e.g. News value). Should you wish to do so, you can enter a more detailed description of the Node in the *Description* field.
5. After clicking *OK*, you will see the node appear in the list view window.
6. Repeat for all parent nodes.

The next step involves adding the subcategories (or 'children') to these parent nodes:

1. Click on the parent node.
2. Select the *New* button from the main toolbar.
3. Select the *Tree Node* in the *Folder* option, which will bring up the *New Tree Node* box.
4. Enter the name and description of the 'child' node and click *OK*.

Figure 14.18 shows the completed tree for the categorisation of journalists' perceptions of the news value, credibility and efficiency of voluntary agencies. You will see that details are provided for each category that show when the node was created and when it was modified. There are also two other columns ('Sources' and 'References'), which indicate, respectively, the number of imported texts that have some content coded in relation to each node, and the number of individual codings made in relation to them. All these figures read as zero as no coding has been undertaken with our example at this stage.

Creating Free Nodes

Not every node you create needs to be located within an index tree. You can also develop *Free Nodes*. These are categories that can be used to store particular ideas or themes that do not fit within an established index system, but which raise interesting issues to which you will want to return. To create them, you click on the *Nodes* button in the navigation view, then select the *Free Nodes* folder. On the main toolbar at the top, click the *New* button,

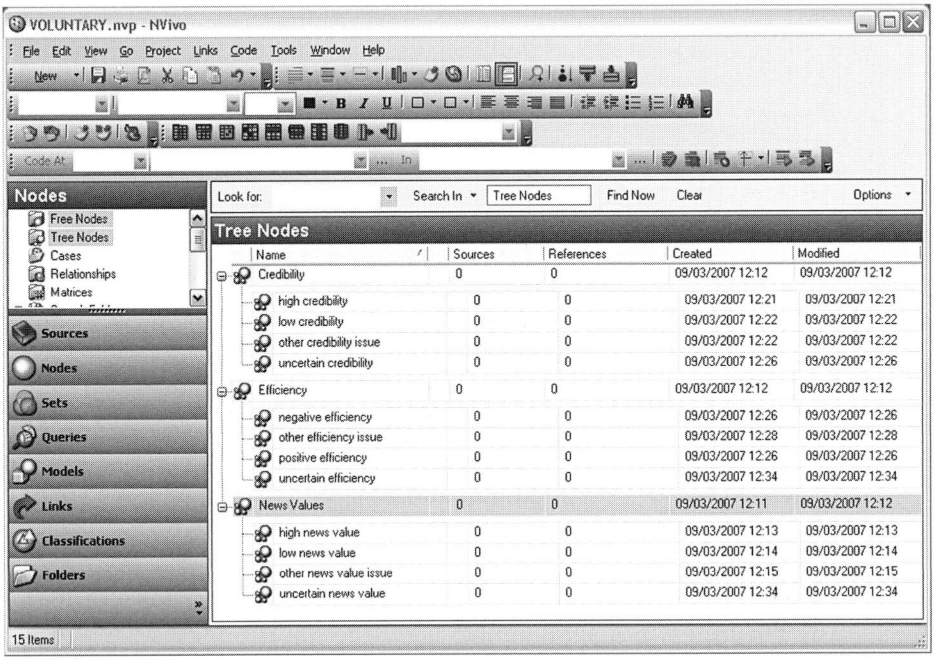

Figure 14.18 Tree Nodes in the list view window

followed by the *Free Node in this folder* option. As with Tree Nodes, you then fill in the nominal and descriptive details.

Coding texts

To code text files, you browse through them to find parts that correspond to the nodes you have defined in your Tree Nodes or that you have designated as Free Nodes. To start coding text, you select *Sources* in the navigation view and double-click on the imported text document you want to analyse, which appears in the list view opposite. This will open up a third part of the screen, which is known as the 'detail view', and allows you to scroll through the text contained in the file.

It is generally easier to code with the Tree Nodes and Free Nodes displayed to the left of the screen and the text to the right. To rearrange the view in this way, go to the *View* option on the main toolbar, deselect *Navigation View* and click on *Detail View> Right*.

If you read through the text in the detail view window in Figure 14.19, you will see that the journalist is making some rather acerbic comments about the limited news value of a lot of voluntary organisations and their activities. In our view, the comments made in all but the last two sentences should be assigned to the 'low news value' child of the 'news value' parent node. As you will recall, this covers all comments concerning the limited news value of voluntary agencies and activities.

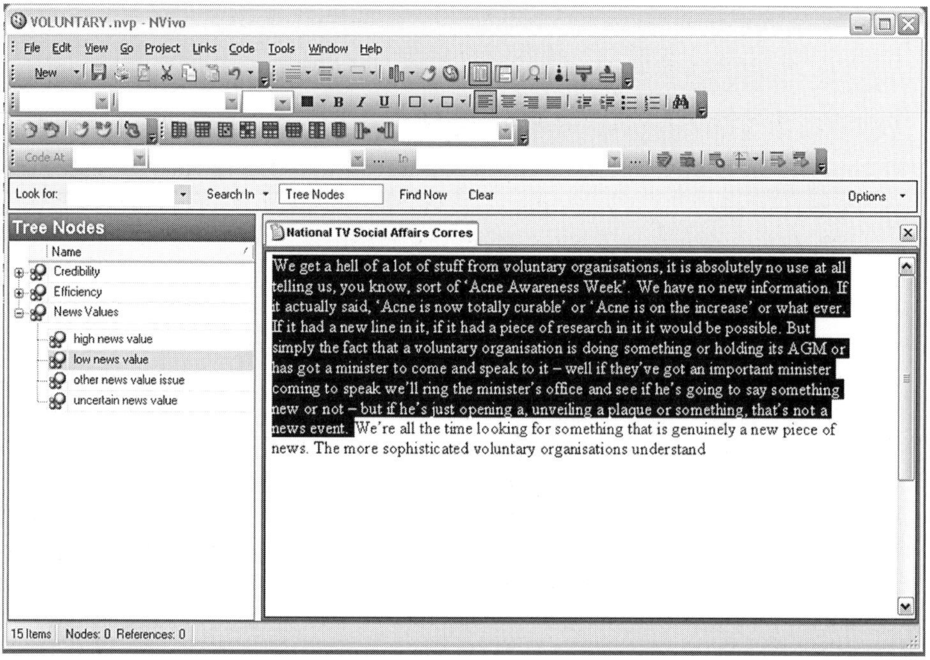

Figure 14.19 Coding text in the detail view window

The coding itself is a simple process of drag and drop – that is, selecting the relevant text in the detail view and moving it across to the appropriate node in the navigation view. You repeat this process as you work through the text, assigning text to relevant nodes in your Tree Nodes and Free Nodes. As you do so, you may find that additional issues arise which are not covered adequately within your tree system. For example, in these journalist interviews, we might encounter a considerable amount of comments that do not relate to the *efficiency* of voluntary agencies in the media and publicity work, but rather concern the *ethics* of these bodies using public donations and charitable resources to promote their concerns and activities in a slick and professional manner. Although these comments could be placed at the 'other efficiency node' (which covers all 'other issues related to the PR efficiency of these agencies in this area') you might want to create a new series of sub-nodes that deal specifically with these ethical questions.

To introduce new nodes to cover new themes, you can either create a Free Node, as explained previously, or highlight the relevant text and on the *Coding* part of the toolbar at the top of the screen, select the *Name* option from the *Code At* dropdown list, enter a name and select its location in the existing *Node* structure.

This flexibility demonstrates that although this part of the package depends on a degree of a priori categorisation (in deciding on your preliminary coding categories), it has sufficient flexibility to allow you to alter these conceptual frameworks as you develop your analysis. In this respect, the coding process is more inductive and flexible than the kind of coding you do when implementing a pre-designed coding frame (such as those used in quantitative content analysis). NVivo 7 also allows you to adjust and delete your coding as you go along, should you feel that is necessary.

Analysing qualitative data using NVivo 7

Once you have coded some text units, you can commence with the analysis. It is not always necessary to wait until you have imported and coded every document. You can always do some informal analysis, alongside the coding and importing, to help develop some preliminary ideas and insights about the themes and patterns that are emerging.

The most basic analytical task that this kind of software can do is to retrieve all text that relates to a particular theme or concept. This can help speed up your research work considerably, particularly when you are dealing with a large number of lengthy documents. Moreover, it ensures that you get a comprehensive record of all that was written or said on that particular theme or issue, rather than just the most memorable comments or points that have stuck in your mind. In this alone, the package reduces the danger of you producing a superficial and impressionistic summary of your qualitative data.

To retrieve text coded at a particular node, you first select the *Queries* option from the navigation window. You then select *New>Coding Query* from the toolbar at the top left of the screen. A *Coding Query* dialog box will appear, and you indicate the node you want to analyse by clicking the *Select* button. This opens a screen with folders that contain your Tree Nodes and Free Nodes. You browse through the files until you identify the node location

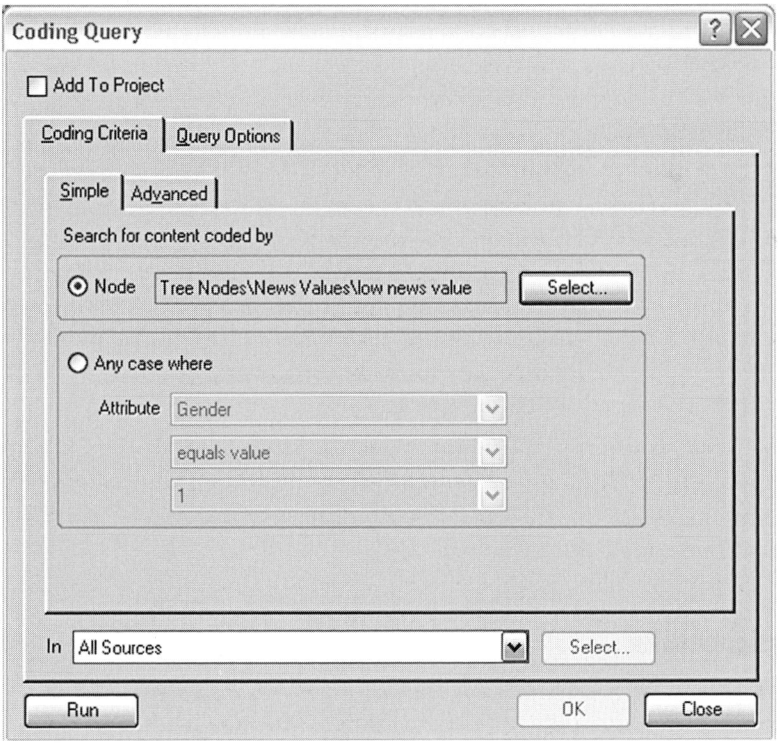

Figure 14.20 The Coding Query dialog box

you require and click *OK*. The appropriate node address will appear in the dialog box. In the example set out in Figure 14.20, we are searching for all content coded at the '\news value\low news value' node. You will also notice that another range of options is offered at this stage of the analysis. Of particular relevance is the *Query Options* tab. If you select this, you are offered a range of options as to the amount of coded text you want to retrieve. As a default, NVivo 7 will present only the specific text you have assigned to a node. However, if your coding has been very precise (e.g. coding individual sentences or parts of sentences), the material that appears in the final report may be difficult to interpret because the text lacks meaningful context. For example, a coded segment of text might refer to 'they', but contain no indication as to who 'they' might be. To help avoid this problem, you can request that the text retrieved is 'spread' to include surrounding material. The spread can be limited to surrounding words and paragraphs, or extended to include the entire content of the source documents which contain material coded in relation to this node.

Once you have selected your node and are satisfied with the spread of the search, click on the *Run* button. Figure 14.21 shows the results of our search of the '\news value\low news value' node. As well as the text coded under this heading, the detail view also indicates how frequently this reference was coded for each interview (one reference only for each interview), and what proportion these words represent in terms of the total text of the interview.

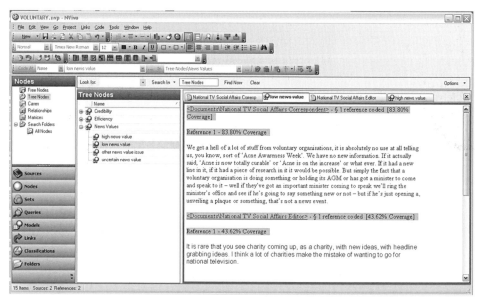

Figure 14.21 Search results in the detail view window

Other analytical tasks

Apart from this basic but very valuable collating exercise, the NVivo 7 package can also be used to conduct a range of further analytical tasks. We do not have the space here to review them in detail, but some of the additional analytical functions available include:

- Filtering sources on selected criteria (e.g. selecting all interviewees who work for local or regional news media).

- Full text searches of all documents to find the location and frequency of appearance of individual words or strings of words in imported documents. For example, with our journalist interviewees, we might want to find the proportion who use the phrases 'corruption' or 'incompetence' when talking about the voluntary sector.

- Full text searches for lists of related words in the text. This involves specifying a list of words that are related to a particular concept you are interested in (e.g. corruption) and running an 'alternation' search that locates their presence and regularity of appearance.

- The importing of 'base data' about research participants (e.g. age, gender, occupation) which can be cross-referenced with textual codings to connect comments formally to their sources.

- The conduct of 'intersect' searches to see how different codings relate to each other, both in their appearance and their proximity.

- The production of statistical summaries and tables that enable you to identify coding patterns and thematic clusters.

CAQDAS – some methodological questions

The development of computer-assisted qualitative data analysis software like NVivo 7 has generated considerable excitement in social research. However, in the rush to embrace computer technology in the analysis of qualitative data, there has been little consideration of the methodological and theoretical implications of conducting qualitative analysis through these means. MacMillan and Koenig (2004), in a valuable review of precisely these issues, highlight how these packages are not methodologically neutral, and, indeed, privilege certain types of qualitative analysis over others. In particular, the software has an implicit orientation to *grounded theory* and *ethnography*. The former is an ambiguous methodology that 'treats theory as derived from a process of comparisons, from, for example, interview data, conversations, observations and even surveys... Although there are no initial hypotheses, the researcher is engaged in a continuous search for evidence to disprove the research findings and to support the final conclusions' (Macmillan and Koenig 2004: 183). Not all qualitative approaches agree with this inductive process of coding, conceptualisation and categorisation. For example, as Koenig (2004) explains elsewhere:

> Much of Discourse Analysis requires a 'holistic' exegesis of data that does **not** lend itself to coding, which, effectively, is a first step towards the quantification of data. The structure of a text or an entire communication might, for example, tell you important things that cannot be revealed by any parts of that text.

Therefore, a key matter to bear in mind when considering using software such as NVivo 7 is whether it is suited to the epistemological framework of your research. As Macmillan and Koenig (2004: 184) conclude: 'This reasserts the role of theory in research, in which research questions are defined not by the software tool but by the problems to be examined.'

Summary: key points

- The chapter began with a discussion of why it is important to understand how computers can assist in both quantitative and qualitative data analysis.

- This chapter provided an introduction to SPSS for Microsoft Windows® (Version 14), using a detailed case study to show how it can analyse statistical data.

- This was followed by an introduction to NVivo 7, which is used in the analysis of qualitative data.

- The chapter concluded with a discussion of the implicit theoretical and methodological orientations of qualitative software programs.

chapter fifteen

Beyond Methodology: The What, How and Why of Researching Communications

This book is a guide on how to research communications, especially the production, contents and impact of the mass media. But the tools we have introduced, and the details of how to use and apply them, do not exhaust the questions we must ask as researchers. Social research is never just a matter of technique. Questions of ethics and politics will always lurk behind the many decisions that have to be made about research in practice. Sometimes these questions will be explicit ('What size of sample do I need to get a good mark?'), sometimes less so ('Will anyone notice if I don't tell the school it's really a study of kids' exposure to teenage porn?'). But questions about the conduct and character of research must always be addressed in thinking seriously about researching communications.

Three types of questions concern us in this final chapter. First, questions about *what* to research. Choosing a topic is often quite difficult, for example when deciding on a project in the final year of a degree. Practical questions about what is manageable and practicable must be balanced against what will be interesting, worthwhile, attractive and, not least perhaps, impressive to readers. Such issues weigh just as heavily for the professional researcher, though perhaps in different form. Second, there are questions of *why* to undertake research: motives and purposes can affect how research is conceived and designed, no less than when planning a dinner menu or a party invite list. Third, there are questions about *how* to conduct research, a range of ethical issues which must be posed and considered, even though it is often difficult, or even impossible, to be as virtuous and meticulous as the textbooks would wish us to be.

What to research

Some researchers choose their topics; others have topics thrust upon them. The professional researcher, as we shall see in the next section, often has to juggle ideals about what needs investigating with pragmatic judgements about what it is possible to study given constraints of funding and peer review. Students choosing projects are often in a much freer situation, with the sheer boundlessness of available subjects sometimes giving rise to indecision and even panic. By the time people are choosing topics for doctoral research, it is often a matter of obsession with a particular question – though this may be of equal significance to no more than a handful of other people in the field. Indeed, without that level of commitment and engagement – whether propelled by intellectual curiosity, or even shrewd calculation and ambition – it is unlikely that a task as single-minded and demanding as a doctoral thesis could be completed.

Most research choices are less pressured. The first question to ask yourself is: 'What interests me?' The topic must matter to you, and be about things that you have some enthusiasm for. As a student, you might think that a study of the cultural legacy of Mick Jagger will appeal to your ageing rocker of a supervisor, but if you are more into hip hop yourself, and remember little and care less about the pop icons of yesteryear, it is unlikely you will get much pleasure from the study, or even do it well. Try to select a topic that relates to something you have real concern for, whether intellectually, politically, culturally, or just because you have always wanted to find out more about it.

Second, try to select a topic that has broader implications. Very often you will see a piece of research described as a 'case study'. This suggests it is an instance of some broader phenomenon. The best way to arrive at a researchable topic is to start by deciding what general area interests you, then gradually to focus in on some aspect of it that you will study. You might be broadly interested in how the media portray crime. But this is a very wide subject and has been investigated many times. What do you think is missing from existing studies? Is there some particular area of crime you are interested in, or some part of media output you think has been insufficiently studied in this context (crime in comedy programmes, perhaps, or the image of lawyers on radio)? Of course, any study will relate to some wider issues or concerns, but you should be aware of those, and be able to see the links to make sense of and provide context for your own study.

Third, and related to the previous point, you should be able to define a theoretical context for your research. This does not just mean a ritual or token 'review of the literature' prefacing the research report. It means that the data you present, or the observations you offer, are articulated to a wider set of ideas about how communications or culture works. If you conduct a study of how teenagers use mobile telephones, the research will be related to some general understanding of youth culture, or gendered relations to technology, or family dynamics – some broader way of understanding or explaining the social process or institutions you are examining.

Finally, in choosing a topic for research you have to be pragmatic. Is what you want to do achievable? This has two facets. First, is the project manageable by you, given constraints of time, resources and access? You may feel that a national survey of all women journalists in television is the best or only way to explore your chosen topic, but a moment's reflection will suggest that even a well-financed professional study might have difficulties reaching such a sample, while even the best and most energetically conducted student project might do better tilting at a less ambitious target. Second, is the research doable at all? A content analysis of the entire run of a parish magazine might be quite an intriguing pathway into local cultural history, but if the only archives mildewed quietly away in a church vault some years ago, this bright idea will have to be rethought.

Sometimes it can be very discouraging to be told that restraints on access or scope make a proposed study impossible. However, a little imagination can often produce a feasible project with the same focus and broad concerns. National media – broadcasting organisations and networks, major newspapers – are understandably cautious about approaches from researchers. In the business of publicity and information themselves, they feel vulnerable to potentially critical or intrusive examination by people they consider ill-informed or even hostile. Local media, however, may be less sensitive or mistrustful, and a well-prepared and considerate approach can produce dividends.

Why to research

There are many reasons for carrying out research, and most users of this book will probably be in no position to question them. Having to do a project to complete a degree programme, or providing research assistance on a commissioned investigation, leaves little time to interrogate the larger question, 'Why?' The history of communication research is replete with accusations imputing undignified motives to various well-known research projects, in which academic and noble ideals are seen to be sullied by questionable aims or sponsorship.

Of course, personal motives can, and perhaps should, propel research as much as institutional ones. You may be keen to develop a project because you feel it will further your career, or make a mark in a currently fashionable field. Or you may believe the research opens politically potent issues, and might even contribute directly to the liberation of the oppressed or the vindication of the innocent. The importance of the research, its social resonance and impact, are distinct from questions about its methodological validity, though the two are often difficult to disentangle. Undertaking research at all is both an ethical and a political decision. As Kimmel (1988: 35) suggests, 'ethical problems can arise from the decision to conduct research and the decision not to conduct the research'.

Social research has always been awkwardly involved with charges of social engineering, particularly where research is sponsored or defined by government. An infamous example of this was Project Camelot, a research programme funded by the US Defense Department in the 1960s, addressed to discovering and anticipating the causes of revolutionary activity in Latin American countries. While the topic was clearly a significant and appropriate one for political science, the project's inception (shortly after US marines went into the Dominican Republic) was seen as just too close to US foreign policy aims and too intimately involved in US Army planning and operations. After international protests, the research was curtailed and a US State Department review of all federally funded research was established (Horowitz 1967).

Of course, research applied to policy issues, or funded by government to assist in policy formulation or implementation, is not inevitably tainted or unethical. Indeed, many would argue that if research has no such potential application it is indulgent and irrelevant – it is better to have policy informed by valid and sound research than by whim or prejudice. Others would suggest that there is no research without roots in some assumptions about policy or politics, that the very construction of a research question is ideologically drenched. In any case, the idea that research offers some kind of neutral expertise, which can be deployed by technocrats with no axe to grind (a favoured notion of the Fabians, who were influential social reformers in Britain in the late nineteenth and early twentieth centuries), is a myth. All research carries with it tacit assumptions about the way the world works, or should work. However, some researchers argue that the more research is articulated to immediate policy objectives, the more it loses its capacity for critical and independent inquiry.

In this debate there are two distinct threads, both of which have been important in communications research. The first follows the funding and genesis of research, and questions whether the close links between policy or pragmatism and research unduly curtail the questions that research poses. The volume of audience research, in all its guises, undertaken by both academic and commercial researchers, massively dwarfs the scale of production research, even though it is generally more expensive to undertake. It is not unlikely that this is because media industries, frequently both the sponsors and the objects of research, would rather find out about their readers, viewers and listeners than the social dynamics of their own production systems or workplaces. The second thread follows the methods that are employed in research, and asks whether they are themselves a reflection of practical needs defined by funding or policy application. Some critics of survey research, for example, suggest that it is popular because surveys provide credible, readily understood and clear-cut answers to overly simple questions, where more complex investigations of audience response and reception, with their elaborate and multilayered portrayal of how people respond to the media, are seen as less acceptable and less immediately comprehensible to a lay audience. Equally, much experimental research is seen as having an appeal, unjustified methodologically, because of its capacity to provide apparently neat and tidy answers to complex questions about media 'effects'.

Certainly, the history of communications research, especially mass-media research, cannot be understood apart from its links to its parentage in both industry and government. Research in the USA, whose approaches and output have dominated much of this history, finds most of its roots in the radio industry in the 1940s and 1950s. One observer suggests that many studies now considered classic cases, 'with their rather pedestrian findings and asides of liberal concern, were helpful...in disarming more sweeping criticisms, while exhibiting responsible concern' (Tunstall 1977: 205). His target here is the broadcasting network CBS, in particular, the source of much early communications research funding. One of the key summary textbooks towards the end of this early period, itself the fruit of a CBS grant (and written by a subsequent director of research at CBS), produces a typically reassuring conclusion, after assessing the available research, that the media reinforce rather than change attitudes (Klapper 1960). The enthusiasm for surveys of listeners, developed particularly by Paul Lazarsfeld at the Bureau of Applied Social Research at Columbia University, made them a pre-eminent form of research and produced work of formative methodological importance. Some of the classic studies of the media and voting behaviour were funded by press companies. One concern was to warn the public of the dangers of propaganda (which is, of course, what *other* people and nations produce). Thus, the Institute of Propaganda Analysis, financed by a wealthy Boston store owner, produced a number of studies to warn of the dangers of media manipulation.

Equally important to this commercial genesis, however, was the relationship with government. Cold war concerns in the USA about political change overseas, in areas potentially subject to Soviet interest, were often the prompt for both research questions and funding. Research was at pains to demonstrate the naturalness and desirability of the American way of life and government, and the disastrous effects of any departure from that road. One such classic is Lerner's United States Information Agency-funded survey series in the Middle East, which attempts to demonstrate the necessary link between levels of media growth and 'development' in proper democratic form (Lerner 1958). In many ways, the cold war was the soil from which communications research grew, with funding from the CIA and the US Defense Department. Cmiel suggests this amply explains the tone and themes of the work the many new institutes produced, with their acclamation for the 'free flow of information' and the 'free press', and their comforting dismissal of undue concern about media power (Cmiel 1996). The Rockefeller Foundation also funded a good deal of research (and the journal *Public Opinion Quarterly*), to demonstrate the potential of 'genuinely democratic propaganda' aimed at helping the war effort (Gary 1996). Scholars involved in this work spent a lot of time debating the proper place for their expertise in an explicit programme of social engineering. By the end of the 1940s, American media research, for long the core of much international scholarship in the field, was firmly in the embrace of either the media industry or the state.

In recent years, questions about the role of funding or political intent have continued to stalk much research conducted in independent institutes and universities. In the 1980s, the British Government changed the title of the major body providing state funds for social research from the Social Science Research Council to the Economic and Social Research Council, in an explicit signal that the priorities of the academic research community should be addressed to the economic needs of the nation as defined by government (which dismissed the notion of 'social science' as an oxymoron). This view was reaffirmed in the 1990s, when the Council adopted a mission statement defining its aim as to support research 'that will contribute to economic competitiveness, the quality of life and the effectiveness of public services and policy', while in the twenty-first century its role is 'providing high-quality research on issues of importance to business, the public sector and government'.

Such accounts of the funding of research make assumptions (not always confirmed) about the political or ideological intentions of the final outcome, suggesting that the research findings and analysis reflect the aspirations of the project's begetters. This can also relate to the personal ideologies of researchers. A famous example is the public accusation against the distinguished German researcher Elisabeth Noelle-Neumann that her political views coloured her influential work on public opinion. Noelle-Neumann (1984) developed the concept of the spiral of silence, which suggests that people with views they perceive to be in a minority are less likely to voice those views, which thus have limited currency and, in turn, less chance of becoming more widely shared. Since the media are a reference point for people's judgements of others' views, the views held by the media themselves become a central force in the 'spiral'. Noelle-Neumann worked as a polling and political strategy adviser for the right-wing Christian Democratic Party, and made no secret of her political views and not least her dislike of what she perceives to be the unacceptably left-wing views of many German journalists. In a fierce public critique Christopher Simpson draws attention to her former apparent associations with the German Nazi party, and finds in her work not merely a 'willingness to scapegoat an ostensibly liberal mass media for a broad range of social ills' but also a continuing racist approach to social issues, and, crucially, 'exploitation of research designs that produce politically useful results', so that her 'resulting argument is better described as a political statement than as a scientific theory' (C. Simpson 1996: 151, 163).

In a spirited defence, Kepplinger disputes some of Simpson's biographical evidence, though not its main thrust. More centrally for our concerns here, however, he argues that, in effect, Simpson is inappropriately concerned with the singer, rather than the song. In the critique, Kepplinger complains, 'It is no longer the scientific work that counts, but rather the presumed mentality of the scientist' (Kepplinger 1997: 116). The epistemology behind this riposte is a complex one, which we cannot explore here. How far it is possible to construct a scientific approach to communication, or any other research, which is quite distinct and independent from the theoretical suppositions or world view of the investigators, is impossible to examine without disappearing down the complex byways of the philosophy of science. The lesson for present purposes, however, is that the informed and aware reader of communication research will at least consider the genesis and motivation of the research she is reading, or the broader programme of work of which it may form a part.

It is common in reconstructing the history of media research to draw attention to this issue by distinguishing 'critical' from 'administrative' research. The former depends for its formulation on theoretically generated ideas designed to take nothing for granted and to question given dispositions of power and structure. The latter is propelled by its sponsors' immediate and practical need for information. One can only to a limited extent expect the media themselves to sponsor, or even promote, inquiry independent of or even potentially damaging to their primary concerns. As a former director general of the BBC points out, 'I doubt if we should feel free to contribute towards [long-term social] research in any substantial way…unless we were reasonably satisfied of a "return" directly applicable to our responsibilities as broadcasters' (Curran 1971: 49). Not surprisingly, exponents of critical research are often scathing about the limitations and improper malleability of administrative researchers. But as university researchers have seen their own world increasingly circumscribed by pressures of funding and accountability, so too researchers in the world of commerce and marketing have often been in the forefront of methodological innovation and exploration. One should not take this paradox too far, however. It remains the case that critical and unbounded research into communications requires an independent institutional and funding base, an argument we cannot develop here, but which deserves at least a momentary mention, even in a methodology text.

The distinction between critical and administrative research was originally drawn by one of the key figures in the history of communications research, Paul Lazarsfeld (1941). Later writers, like Rogers (1982), critical of the critical school, preferred to see the distinction as between empirical (i.e. as he saw it, well founded on research) and critical (politically driven, but careless of evidence), but such a distinction has become less and less meaningful – if indeed it ever was. Summarising debate between various exponents of each school, the late George Gerbner suggests that professional integrity among researchers requires that they are 'not just hired hands, but women and men prepared and free to scrutinise the ends as well as the means of any project. That I believe is the essence of the critical versus the administrative stance' (Gerbner 1983: 356). Thus the crux of critical research becomes not just its funding or organisational setting, but its broader conception of the social and cultural complex within which its project of inquiry is understood and conceptualised.

Why research is done will always have an impact on how it is designed and prepared. When developing your own research, you will need to be conscious of any such impact and consider whether it is leading to research methods or data analysis other than those you really intend or need in order to answer the question with which you started. Pleasing an external examiner, getting publicity, promotion, wealth or acclaim, becoming a best-selling academic megastar, or making the world a wiser and better place are all perfectly acceptable reasons for doing research; if all were eschewed, little research would get done. But the aims of the research should not distort or taint the methods employed to the point where the research loses validity and credibility.

The 'how' of research

The conduct of research itself requires careful consideration if it is to meet not merely technical standards of accuracy, reliability and validity, but also ethical standards. Some of these standards are set by professional bodies, such as the sociological or psychological associations in various countries. Others, for example on the use of facilities like computers or libraries, are established by institutions such as universities. You may be required to confirm that your research has met the requirements of such codes, whether you are engaged in undergraduate or doctoral research, or conducting a commissioned project.

We can think of these standards as relating to four relationships the research must consider: with the subjects of the research; with the data; with the audience; and with the research community.

Relationships with research subjects

Social research of any kind is unique, in that the object of study is, like the researcher, human, with relationships, feelings, rights and a biography originating before and continuing after the research. Even content analysis is dealing with the product of human activity, but the issue is particularly acute when people are directly involved in the research process. The very vocabulary we use reflects the uncertainties within the research world produced by this relationship. The people we study are 'subjects', 'respondents', 'informants', 'members', 'actors', depending on the style or intellectual background of the study. Each has problems avoiding pejorative or patronising overtones, and none is entirely satisfactory. There is no instant answer to that particular problem other than to be sensitive to it.

As we saw in chapter 11, participant observation throws up especially sharp difficulties in the relationship between researcher and researched. One dimension to this is the question of whether the research is overt or covert. Some researchers argue that there is never any justification for covert observation. It is both wrong and unnecessary. Erikson argues that 'the practice of using masks in social research compromises both the people who wear them and the people for whom they are worn' (Erikson 1967: 367). The practice may injure those being studied in ways that are unpredictable and which they have no way of anticipating and evaluating. But writers like Erikson claim that it is also bad research. It is probably not really possible to disguise fully the researcher's true identity, and the data thus collected may be less reliable than that collected by a declared observer. Dingwall argues angrily that the researcher using covert methods 'prefers to skulk in corners than to take up the challenge of educating suspicious informants – and all informants are initially suspicious. Underlying this is the sort of morality which can mock the sacraments of the group being studied in an hypocritical participation' (Dingwall 1980: 888).

There are two kinds of deception that must be considered. The first is to disguise, or simply not declare, the very fact that research is taking place at all. Covert observation is necessarily deceptive in this way. In practice, it might be that to announce that a study is under way would be more intrusive than not to do so. In public settings – for example, a cinema foyer in which an observer is studying the mood and demeanour of audiences leaving different types of film – it might seem preposterous for the researcher to display a banner saying 'researcher at work', or to hand out leaflets explaining the study. It is, after all, a public space. On the other hand, why should the objects of the research not be aware of the study? They would be pretty annoyed if the cinema had secret cameras watching them.

The second form of deception, common in experimental studies, is to mislead the people being studied about the purpose of the research. How far this kind of deception is necessary or acceptable in any form of research has been a major concern for social science professional bodies. While totally ruling out any form of deception would be straightforward and defensible, it would also disqualify a great deal of social research. As the British Psychological Society (BPS) (2006) points out in commenting on its own code, 'there are very many psychological processes that are modifiable by individuals if they are aware that they are being studied'. If those being studied were informed of the hypothesis or purpose of the study, it might render the data gathered totally invalid. For example, if an experimental study was investigating tolerance among different social groups to bad language or nudity in television programmes, to tell the subjects the purpose of the study could well make them unnaturally sensitive or responsive to material they might otherwise view only casually or indifferently. The solution proposed by the BPS to this conundrum is to distinguish 'withholding some of the details of the hypothesis under test and deliberately falsely informing the participants of the purpose of the research, especially if the information given implied a more benign topic of study than was in fact the case' (ibid.).

One principle commonly advanced by many bodies to guide researchers on these issues is that of **informed consent**. This suggests that people being researched should both know about the research and be willing to take part in it, having been fully informed about its purpose and consequences in so far as these are predictable. It may be that this informed consent is only obtained after the event, so that subjects have a right of veto over data analysis and publication, but not over data collection. This is obviously a weaker interpretation of the principle. It might even be argued that this is 'misinformed consent', and poses even more ethical problems than it is designed to solve. The principle of informed consent, on closer inspection, turns out to be a rather complicated one. How much and what kind of information is sufficient to make subjects 'informed'? Do people being surveyed on their newspaper reading habits need to be sent a number of background papers on theories of reception or the political economy of the press to make sure they are informed about the researchers' intentions? This may seem absurd, but where does the line need to be drawn? What counts as consent? Is a grudging general acceptance of the researchers' probity and good faith sufficient, or do we need formal contracts? And what of coercion? How many studies of students conducted by their teachers and mentors have employed just a little subtle (or not so subtle) pressure to ensure cooperation?

One consequence of informing respondents, whether in experimental studies or in surveys, is to affect response rates. Told that a survey is designed to improve local public library facilities, people might well be willing to answer questions on their book-buying and reading habits. Told that it is part of a marketing campaign by a new local bookshop, they might be far less willing to participate. By and large, studies of response rates have found that they are not reduced by informed consent, as feeling better informed about a research project might make respondents feel reassured and confident, even if they are not wholly in sympathy with the purpose of the study. In any case, as Kimmel suggests, 'omitting the purpose of the study from the informed consent procedure will not present an ethical problem provided that participants are informed of all possible risks that can be reasonably anticipated by the investigators' (1988: 74). Like all attempts to unravel these complex principles, this involves formulations which would keep lawyers mischievously busy for decades. What can be 'reasonably anticipated' and when does a little careful packaging of the study become 'omitting the purpose'? Ultimately, there is no clear-cut rule which can be simply and mechanically applied to a research design other than to assess with all possible care how best to meet ethical requirements when constructing the research. An extract from the BPS code on these matters is given in Box 15.1.

Box 15.1 Extract from BPS Code – sections on consent and deception

3. Consent

1. Whenever possible, the investigator should inform all participants of the objectives of the investigation. The investigator should inform the participants of all aspects of the research or intervention that might reasonably be expected to influence willingness to participate. The investigator should, normally, explain all other aspects of the research or intervention about which the participants enquire. Failure to make full disclosure prior to obtaining informed consent requires additional safeguards to protect the welfare and dignity of the participants (see Section 4).

2. Research with children or with participants who have impairments that will limit understanding and/or communication such that they are unable to give their real consent requires special safe-guarding procedures.

3. Where possible, the real consent of children and of adults with impairments in understanding or communication should be obtained. In addition, where research involves any persons under 16 years of age, consent should be obtained from parents or from those in loco parentis. If the nature of the research precludes consent being obtained from parents or permission being obtained from teachers, before proceeding with the research, the investigator must obtain approval from an Ethics Committee.

4. Where real consent cannot be obtained from adults with impairments in understanding or communication, wherever possible the investigator should consult a person well-placed to appreciate the participant's reaction, such as a member of the person's family, and must obtain the disinterested approval of the research from independent advisors.

5. When research is being conducted with detained persons, particular care should be taken over informed consent, paying attention to the special circumstances which may affect the person's ability to give free informed consent.

6. Investigators should realise that they are often in a position of authority or influence over participants who may be their students, employees or clients. This relationship must not be allowed to pressurise the participants to take part in, or remain in, an investigation.

7. The payment of participants must not be used to induce them to risk harm beyond that which they risk without payment in their normal lifestyle.

8. If harm, unusual discomfort, or other negative consequences for the individual's future life might occur, the investigator must obtain the disinterested approval of independent advisors, inform the participants, and obtain informed, real consent from each of them.

9. In longitudinal research, consent may need to be obtained on more than one occasion.

4. Deception

1. The withholding of information or the misleading of participants is unacceptable if the participants are typically likely to object or show unease once debriefed. Where this is in any doubt, appropriate consultation must precede the investigation. Consultation is best carried out with individuals who share the social and cultural background of the participants in the research, but the advice of ethics committees or experienced and disinterested colleagues may be sufficient.

2. Intentional deception of the participants over the purpose and general nature of the investigation should be avoided whenever possible. Participants should never be deliberately misled without extremely strong scientific or medical justification. Even then there should be strict controls and the disinterested approval of independent advisors.

3. It may be impossible to study some psychological processes without withholding information about the true object of the study or deliberately misleading the participants. Before conducting such a study, the investigator has a special responsibility to

    (a) determine that alternative procedures avoiding concealment or deception are not available;

    (b) ensure that the participants are provided with sufficient information at the earliest stage; and

    (c) consult appropriately upon the way that the withholding of information or deliberate deception will be received.

Source: British Psychological Society, *Ethical Principles for Conducting Research with Human Participants*, revised 2006 and available at http://www.bps.org.uk/the-society/ethics-rules-charter-code-of-conduct/code-of-conduct/ethical-principles-for-conducting-research-with-human-participants.cfm#introduction

This extract is part of the British Psychological Society's Code of Conduct, and is reproduced with their kind permission.

Consent for research may also sometimes be required formally from bodies with authority over the research situation. This is as much a legal and practical question as an ethical one. For example, if you want to undertake research with schoolchildren, you must certainly obtain the consent of the head teacher or principal. You should take their advice as to whether consent from the children's parents is also required. A safe rule is to err on the cautious side. In many situations, you may also require formal approval for the research from some higher authority, perhaps the school board or local government body with statutory authority over the school.

In many countries, social surveys are not permissible without some reference to local police or government authorities. If you propose to undertake quota sample surveys by interviewing people in a shopping centre, check that you are permitted to do so. You may need formal approval by the appropriate authority. If you use interviewers, they should carry identity cards and some kind of authorisation. It is impossible to spell out all the possible variations on regulatory requirements, but be aware that research is a social activity which presumes on people's privacy and rights, and checking on what is formally required is not only practical research design, but may also be a legal necessity.

Relationships with data

When we undertake research into people's communication activities, we find out more about them than we knew previously. What gives us the right to collect such information, and how can we use it? The question of confidentiality is a central issue for research. Two aspects of this arise: collecting data and using it. We begin with data collection. Suppose you are undertaking a newsroom production study. You have been given permission to spend time in the newsroom, to 'hang around' and observe, even to sit in on editorial meetings.

367

But where does this licence end? It is late in the day, most people have gone to a bar, and strolling through the newsroom you notice a file marked 'Confidential: Newsroom Guidelines Review'. This is research gold dust, a treasure trove of journalistic ideology and organisational thinking which would immeasurably enrich your insight into how the newspaper sees its problems and plans to solve them. You knew the document existed, but had already been told it was not available to you. Do you read it? After all, not to do so might make your account of news work uninformed and inadequate. On the other hand, to read it might break the implicit (and possibly explicit) contract between you and the organisation facilitating your research. You could, of course, read it, put it back and never admit to having done so (perhaps eventually persuading yourself that you had not really discovered anything from the file that you did not discover by other means). Alternatively, you could reopen the question of its availability with whoever has authority to release it, offering your integrity in having spurned the opportunity to read it covertly as encouragement to trust you. Or you could just stick to the agreed procedure, pass it by and regret the loss of valuable data, but feel virtuous and professional in your conduct. What would you do?

Most professional codes for research recognise that investigation inevitably intrudes on the privacy of those researched, and may generate data that was intended to remain confidential. The codes thus focus on the informed consent of participants as much as on the collection of the data. The British Sociological Association (2003), for example, says that

> Research participants should understand how far they will be afforded anonymity and confidentiality and should be able to reject the use of data gathering devices such as tape-recorders and video cameras. Sociologists should be careful, on the one hand, not to give unrealistic guarantees of confidentiality, and, on the other, not to permit communication of research films or records to audiences other than those to which research participants have agreed.

This touches on the consequences of publication, which we discuss below.

In much research, the confidentiality of the data becomes a methodological problem if the data (never intended to be published prior to analysis) becomes available to those being researched, with consequences for their behaviour. One example of the unintended consequences of research performance is described in Box 15.2.

Box 15.2 The unfortunate case of Dr X

Dr X was a distinguished media researcher, undertaking a study of newsroom practice in a leading newspaper. She had obtained full permission from the senior management of the newspaper, and had been welcomed and generally accepted by the journalists. This included attendance at the morning news conferences and access to informal settings like the canteen and after-work socialising. Gradually a valuable and detailed picture was evolving of relationships between news staff, informal hierarchies, and the values, tastes, concerns and foibles of the staff. As an assiduous and diligent observational researcher,

Dr X kept detailed notes of everything and interpolated her own provisional judgements about situations and people.

Being a thoroughly modern researcher, Dr X realised that mountains of pencilled notes would soon become unwieldy. So when a helpful journalist suggested she use the desktop PC of a journalist on long-term leave, the offer was accepted gratefully, and soon, significant quantities of the notes were entered carefully into the machine. Dr X was nonplussed the following morning to find a distinctly frosty atmosphere when she turned up as usual for the morning editorial conference. Several previously friendly and cooperative journalists cut her dead, while others were decidedly cool. It was only when a sympathetic journalist took Dr X on one side and explained that all the office PCs were networked, and curious colleagues had spent considerable time poring over her notes, intrigued and bewildered, that she realised the source of the antagonism. The journalist described in her notes as 'a bit old-fashioned and unpopular, seems not to understand modern practice', and another, annotated as 'social isolate, rather discredited professionally by colleagues', not altogether surprisingly, had rapidly developed a vehement antipathy to social research in general and this social researcher in particular. A good deal of fence-mending and sheepish apologies, together with considerable assurances about the purpose and confidentiality of the notes, largely rescued a potentially disastrous situation.

Moral: judgements are not data; watch where you keep your notes; and if possible use your own laptop.

Confidentiality of data need not apply when the data is in the public domain anyway. Thus, television programme schedules, economic data in media company reports, published personnel lists or audience research data need not be treated with confidentiality if already publicly available. Data that is made available knowingly by those researched should still be treated as confidential if it was intended to be used anonymously. Box 15.3 outlines some of the guidelines on these matters prepared by the American Sociological Association.

Box 15.3 Extract from ethical guidelines of ASA (sections 11.02 to 11.08)

11.02 Limits of Confidentiality

(a) Sociologists inform themselves fully about all laws and rules which may limit or alter guarantees of confidentiality. They determine their ability to guarantee absolute confidentiality and, as appropriate, inform research participants, students, employees, clients, or others of any limitations to this guarantee at the outset consistent with ethical standards set forth in 11.02(b).

(b) Sociologists may confront unanticipated circumstances where they become aware of information that is clearly health- or life-threatening to research participants, students, employees, clients, or others. In these cases, sociologists balance the importance of guarantees of confidentiality with other principles in this Code of Ethics, standards of conduct, and applicable law.

(c) Confidentiality is not required with respect to observations in public places, activities conducted in public, or other settings where no rules of privacy are provided by law or custom. Similarly, confidentiality is not required in the case of information available from public records.

[...]

11.04 Anticipation of Possible Uses of Information

(a) When research requires maintaining personal identifiers in databases or systems of records, sociologists delete such identifiers before the information is made publicly available.

(b) When confidential information concerning research participants, clients, or other recipients of service is entered into databases or systems of records available to persons without the prior consent of the relevant parties, sociologists protect anonymity by not including personal identifiers or by employing other techniques that mask or control disclosure of individual identities.

(c) When deletion of personal identifiers is not feasible, sociologists take reasonable steps to determine the appropriate consent of personally-identifiable individuals has been obtained before they transfer such data to others or review such data collected by others.

[...]

11.06 Anonymity of Sources

(a) Sociologists do not disclose in their writings, lectures, or other public media confidential, personally identifiable information concerning their research participants, students, individual or organisational clients, or other recipients of their service which is obtained during the course of their work, unless consent from individuals or their legal representatives has been obtained.

(b) When confidential information is used in scientific and professional presentations, sociologists disguise the identity of research participants, students, individual or organisational clients, or other recipients of their service.

11.07 Minimising Intrusions on Privacy

(a) To minimise intrusions on privacy, sociologists include in written and oral reports, consultations, and public communications only information germane to the purpose for which the communication is made.

(b) Sociologists discuss confidential information or evaluative data concerning research participants, students, supervisors, employees, and individual or organisational clients only for appropriate scientific or professional purposes and only with persons clearly concerned with such matters.

11.08 Preservation of Confidential Information

(a) Sociologists take reasonable steps to ensure that records, data, or information are preserved in a confidential manner consistent with the requirements of this Code of Ethics, recognising that ownership of records, data, or information may also be governed by law or institutional principles.

(b) Sociologists plan so that confidentiality of records, data, or information is protected in the event of the sociologist's death, incapacity, or withdrawal from the position or practice.

(c) When sociologists transfer confidential records, data, or information to other persons or organisations, they obtain assurances that the recipients of the records, data, or information will employ measures to protect confidentiality at least equal to those originally pledged.

Reproduced with kind permission of the American Sociological Association.

Source: http://www.asanet.org/page.ww?section = Ethics&name= Code+of+Ethics+Standards#11 (accessed 2nd April 2007)

Relationships with the research audience

Some of the most acute ethical questions in social research have arisen in considering what and whether to publish. The researcher owes a commitment of honesty to her audience, but may have to balance this against the potential consequences of publication for the people involved in the research. This does not only apply to research that appears in books and journals. Even student work read only by teachers or examiners is 'published' and must be evaluated against ethical criteria.

It used to be traditional in social research to invent anodyne pseudonyms for places or people, so that monographs were replete with names like 'Mr Gates', 'Coaltown', 'Greenville' or the *Daily Bugle*. This does not wholly solve the problem since, while a wider readership may not be able to penetrate such disguises, anyone with knowledge of the research situation will very often be able to identify people and places from even the most sketchy or modified descriptions. This can sometimes be disastrous, for example in researching illegal or dangerous activities. Even everyday activities can be embarrassing to their practitioners if reported in social research. The problem is that the more data is disguised or distorted to protect the anonymity of sources or people studied, the more one is 'cheating' the readers of the research.

Johnson suggests that research manuscripts should be subjected to an 'ethical proofreading'. This would 'assume that both the identities of the location studied and the identities of individuals will be discovered. What would the consequences of this discovery be to the community?' (Johnson 1982: 87). That helps with one side of the equation (though only by sensitising us to the issue), but it does not address the need to meet the commitment to one's readers. That can be achieved only by honesty and clarity about what is direct reporting and what is disguised for the protection of the people studied.

When you write up research, the audience for the study must be quite clear about what is original and what is derived from past work or other researchers. This raises the issue of **plagiarism**. It has been flippantly suggested that using one person's work and presenting it as your own is plagiarism, while using two or more sources becomes library research. All research draws on past work. Indeed, any good research project examines the existing body of knowledge to see what new knowledge is needed, or where, in the author's judgement, there is need for reinterpretation or rethinking. The necessity is to acknowledge all such sources. Explain and give references for all the ideas and information you import into your work, so that it is quite clear what is yours and what is a summary of or commentary on past work.

One way in which the concerns of the reader might properly be taken into account is in the language used in writing up research. Offending or patronising one's readers does nothing to assist comprehension or persuasiveness. In particular, the use of racist or sexist language is avoidable and unethical. There will always be an imprecise area where avoiding such language can become a precious and somewhat token exercise in political correctness. Nonetheless, it is probably better to be cautious and considerate than unduly cavalier. Often, non-sexist language is more precise than sexist. Using 'man' when you mean people in general will simply be misleading in many contexts and inaccurate in others. Communications researchers should be especially sensitive to the power of language to construct meaning, and also to the dynamic nature of terminology and concepts. What is offensive and inappropriate in one time or place may not be so in another. Increasingly, social researchers are also sensitive to language used to describe the disabled – indeed, that very term as a collective noun is found by many to be unacceptable and offensive, reference to 'disabled people' or to 'people with disabilities' being preferred. In all such areas, due sensitivity to the issues and a recognition that writing that offends is neither persuasive nor impressive should be to the forefront. Box 15.4 includes extracts from the guidelines on language issued by the British Sociological Association (2003).

Box 15.4 Extracts from British Sociological Association guidelines on racist/sexist/disablist language

The following are extracts from the guidelines. You should read the full documents, available at http://www.britsoc.co.uk/equality

1. Anti-racist language

African, Caribbean and/or African-Caribbean

African-Caribbean has replaced the term Afro-Caribbean to refer to Caribbean peoples and those of Caribbean origin who are of African descent. There is now a view that the term should not be hyphenated and that indeed, the differences between such groups mean the people of African and Caribbean origins should be referred to separately.

Black

Black is a term that embraces people who experience structural and institutional discrimination because of their skin colour and is often used politically to refer to people of African, Caribbean and South Asian origin to imply solidarity against racism.

Developing Nations/Less Developed Countries

These terms are used to refer to less-industrialised, non-western or Southern parts of the world. They are questionable where an implicit hierarchy with developed countries is placed at the top.

Diaspora(s)

(diasporic- adj.) In its contemporary use it refers to colonial and now post-colonial peoples who have been dislocated and scattered to other lands from their countries of origin through the process of voluntary and involuntary migration. Now settled for many generations in other countries, people of the (black) diaspora bring with them their own history and cultural experiences from which new (hybrid) group and individual subjectivities emerge.

It must also be remembered that the migratory process can occur more than once in the same person's lifetime, and that there needs to be a concept of multiple migratory processes and diasporisations.

Ethnic

Refers to cultural groups of various kinds. Although it is often erroneously used to refer to Black communities only, all people have ethnicity so that white people are also part of particular ethnic groups. To avoid this confusion, it is best to spell out the relevant ethnic groups explicitly, where this is appropriate depends upon the context.

Race/'Race'

Originally associated with social Darwinism, eugenics and in these cases, highly pejorative. In a biological sense the word is unhelpful since it does not describe the variety of ethnic groups which sociologists would normally wish to identify. Some have felt that it is necessary to put the word into inverted commas ('race') in order to make it clear that these are social distinctions being referred to rather than biological ones and in order to distance themselves from the original meaning of the term.

Racism

An ideology, structure and process in which inequalities inherent in the wider social structure are related in a deterministic way to biological and cultural factors attributed to those who are seen as a different 'race' or ethnic group.

Third World

This has been a term used to refer to countries outside Europe and the 'new world' (USA, Australia, etc.). It usually simply means poor nations. However, some feel that it is outdated, and groups too many diverse nations and cultures unproblematically. North/South may be a better alternative.

West Indian

This term is used to refer to people from the West Indian territories, a region that is highly culturally diverse. 'African Caribbean' has generally replaced it when referring to people of African descent. However, caution must be applied in using this term as it also homogenises distinct groups of Black people.

2. Anti-sexist language

'He/Man' Language

Do not use 'man' to mean humanity in general. There are alternatives: **Sexist** – man/mankind, mankind; **Non-sexist** – person, people, human beings, men & women, humanity, humankind.

When reference to both sexes is intended, a large number of phrases use the word man or other masculine equivalents (e.g. 'father') and a large number of nouns use the suffix 'man', thereby excluding women from the picture we present of the world. These should be replaced by more precise non-sexist alternatives as listed below:

SEXIST	NON-SEXIST
man in the street	people in general, people
layman	lay person, non-expert
man-made	synthetic, artificial, manufactured
the rights of man	peoples'/citizens' rights; the rights of the individual
chairman	chair
foreman	supervisor
manpower	workforce staff, labour force,
craftsman/men	employees, craftsperson/people
manning	staffing, working, running
to a man	everyone, unanimously, without exception
manhours	workhours

the working man	worker, working people
models of man	models of the person
one man show	one person show
policeman/fireman	police officer/fire-fighter
forefathers	ancestors
founding fathers	founders
old masters	classic art/artists
masterful	domineering; very skilful
master copy	top copy/original
Dear Sirs	Dear Sir/Madam
Disseminate	broadcast, inform, publicise
Seminal	classical, formative

The 'generic' 'man' is often accompanied by the 'generic' 'he'. The 'generic he' should be avoided. Both feminine and masculine pronouns can be used where appropriate: he/she, s/he, his/her, etc. Alternative strategies include the use of the plural, and the omission of third person pronouns entirely:

(A) SEXIST: Each respondent was asked whether he wished to participate in the survey.
NON-SEXIST: Respondents were asked whether they wished to participate in the survey.
(B) SEXIST: The child should be given ample time to familiarise himself with the test material.
NON-SEXIST: Ample time should be allowed for the child to become familiar with the test material.

When by 'he', 'men', etc. you do actually mean only men, it is advisable to make this explicit. 'Male managers' or 'men executives' is less ambiguous than 'businessmen' which is either used 'generically' or with the implicit assumption that all business personnel are male. Such careful, non-sexist use of language helps in avoiding the mistake of referring to, e.g., 'managers and their wives'. Women managers do not have wives!

Non-disablist language

- Avoid using medical labels as this may promote a view of disabled people as patients. It also implies the medical label is the over-riding characteristic; this is inappropriate.
- If it is necessary to refer to a condition, it is better to say, for example, 'a person with epilepsy' **not** an epileptic, or 's/he has cerebral palsy' **not** a spastic.
- Avoid mental retardation/mentally retarded.
- Avoid acronyms when referring to people e.g. 'the SEN child'.
- It may be necessary to place apostrophes around terms when referring to historical (and some contemporary) terms.
- The word disabled should not be used as a collective noun (for example as in 'the disabled').

More specifically, the following are recommended:

DISABLIST	NON-DISABLIST
Handicap	Disability
Invalid	Disabled person
The disabled/The handicapped	Disabled people or people with disabilities
Special needs	Additional needs or needs
Patient	Person
Abnormal	Different or disabled
Victim of	Person who has/person with
Crippled by	Person who has/person with
Suffering from	Person who has/person with
Afflicted by	Person who has/person with
Wheelchair bound	Wheelchair user
The blind	Blind and partially sighted people or visually impaired people
The deaf	Deaf or hard of hearing people
Cripple or crippled	Disabled or mobility impaired person
The mentally handicapped	People/person with a learning difficulty or learning disability
Retarded/backward	Person with a learning disability
Mute or dumb	Person with (a) speech impairment
Mentally ill or mental patient	Mental health service user
Able bodied person	Non-disabled person

British Sociological Association: Language and the BSA, www.britsoc.co.uk/equality

Relations with other researchers

Where you tread others may follow. The researcher has an obligation to peers in the research community, not merely in some vainglorious way to recognise that they are carrying the flag for research, but that in a far more mundane way they are affecting the likelihood of future research being permitted or successful. This is most obviously true in closed institutions where the researcher is normally supplicant, seeking admission to non-public worlds via gatekeepers usually unconvinced of the value or relevance of research. This is most acutely true in media organisations, whose paradoxical sensitivity (and even occasional paranoia about external scrutiny), despite their own claims to act as society's surveillance and investigation troops, has been a frequent cause of complaint by researchers.

The BBC is a large and highly unusual broadcasting body, with a long and sometimes turbulent history. It has rarely opened its doors to social research, and when it has, the experience has increased its resistance. Burns's classic study of the 'private world' within the public corporation was published some 14 years after the initial fieldwork, because of a veto over publication exercised by the BBC (Burns 1977: xiv). The corporation has rarely been penetrated by social researchers since. Studies by the Glasgow University Media Group, which were severely critical of the corporation's news coverage of industrial relations in the 1970s, made it especially reluctant to open its doors, as Schlesinger found in 1974, when his own requests for access followed shortly after a research visit by a researcher from the

Glasgow Group. 'The researcher's conduct was, according to several journalists' accounts, not especially endearing. This had tended to cancel out my own credit, and would have made it necessary for me to work very hard to re-establish relations of trust' (Schlesinger 1980: 349). The next major such study was not undertaken for a further 20 years and published in 2004 (Born 2004). Georgina Born was trained as an anthropologist and undertook research mainly in the drama, news and current affairs of the BBC. Her study is replete with field notes and personal musings, and occasionally becomes 'a fictional document based loosely on a real original' (ibid.: 20). The author suggests she became, at times 'a kind of psychoanalyst of the institution' (ibid.: 17), acting as a lightning conductor or recipient for the anxieties and neuroses of staff at a time when the BBC was, in the author's view, under severe stress.

Of course, this does not mean that research must be obsequious in conduct and anodyne in conclusion simply to ensure entry to sensitive situations for future researchers. It does mean that the researcher must be aware that what they do is understood by people being researched to indicate the general nature of research. But does that mean criticism must be muted? Clearly not. As long as judgements are well founded on robust evidence, there is no reason to inhibit firm conclusions which are unflattering to the organisations or people researched.

One problem that arises from past research is that of diminishing returns. Some places and situations become over-researched in ways that make it almost counter-productive to investigate them further. Schools and communities on the doorsteps of universities are especially prone to this. When children start telling you the socio-economic status and ideological leaning of their parents the minute you appear at the classroom door, you know that this is a school suffering from research overload. Try to avoid digging into research situations well mined by others. Equally, when undertaking research, remember you may not be the last researcher to venture into the situation. Two reasonable maxims to work by would be: 'Do as you would be done by' and 'Leave things as you find them'. In other words, undertake research as you would be willing to tolerate it if you were yourself the object of research, and do not use your research activity as a means to change the situation you are in unless that is part of the 'contract' with the people being researched.

Finally, part of the obligation to peers is to make your research as widely available as possible. The American Sociological Association guidelines say that researchers 'anticipate data sharing as an integral part of a research plan whenever data sharing is feasible'. This seems perhaps just a little pious in today's competitive world in academia, but is not a bad yardstick in general. The aim of research remains the enlargement of knowledge, and that will not be fulfilled by research kept secret. We can all learn from others' mistakes, and publication in some shape or form should be the aim of any serious research.

Researching communications for what? A final thought

Many of the ethical concerns outlined in this chapter invite the view that bending the rules is justified by the outcome. If good research is the result, then does it really matter if we are a little casual about rules and codes that can often seem removed from the messy practicalities and harsh realities of real research? After all, codes produced by academic bodies are often accused of being more to do with public relations and spurious professionalisation than the serious policing and adjudication of research practice. So why not ignore them if by doing so you can get good research? In other words, do the ends not justify the means? (As the philosopher Bertrand Russell once pointed out, what else could?)

This question provokes a utilitarian calculus beyond the range of this volume. Suppose a piece of research on television and racism involved a little innocent deception, the occasional minor intrusion into producers' privacy or a relatively minuscule 'management' of the data. Might this not be justified by the significant reduction in racist broadcasting that resulted from publication of the research? If publishing a highly critical and revealing study of exploitation and manipulation of journalists by a leading media magnate meant doors were suddenly and tightly closed to other researchers seeking cooperation from organs within the same empire, would this not be justified by the gain in public knowledge and the progressive legislation that possibly resulted?

Social research of any kind, including researching communications, is a social act. It may result in glory or wealth for the researcher, though neither is on offer very often. But it is safer to presume it has less dramatic ends, namely the widening of our common understanding and knowledge of the social processes and institutions which frame our lives. Whether curiosity or a burning ambition to make the world a better place is at the root of the researcher's concerns, without a framework of ethics to govern that research it will not command the respect and credence that any form of research requires to play its part in society's debate with itself.

Summary: key points

There is more to research than techniques. Three key areas are:

- *What to research*:
  1. Find something that interests you.
  2. Make sure the broader context is apparent.
  3. Relate your topic to wider theory.

- *Why research?*
  1. Much communications research has been government- or industry-led.
  2. Consider the distinction between administrative and critical research.

- *How to research: four relationships*:
  1. With subjects: the principle of informed consent and dangers of deception.
  2. With data: ensure confidentiality and privacy.
  3. With audiences for research: use ethical proofreading; avoid plagiarism; use non-sexist and non-racist language.
  4. With other researchers: consider the needs of future researchers; make research outputs widely available.

Glossary

anchorage: quite often, the meaning of a visual image is relatively indeterminate; anchorage refers to the attempt to fix or delimit the meaning to be derived from the image by the viewer or reader. This is usually done through a written caption set above or below the image, but it can also be accomplished by the surrounding discourse of the text, regardless of whether this is written or spoken.

arbitrary: the linguistic nature of the **sign** in its relationship to that which it represents by rule or convention, as with the English word 'rose', which signifies both denotatively and connotatively. The term is contentious in its philosophical sense concerning the relations between language and forms of communication and **representation** more broadly, on the one hand, and reality or the material world, on the other.

association: see **cross-tabulations**.

bivariate analysis: involves comparing the interaction between two variables. **Cross-tabulations** and correlations are the most common forms of bivariate analysis used in social research.

blog: abbreviation for weblog. These are websites taking the form of written accounts, very much like diaries, of everyday life or special events, which people post to the Internet in the expectation and hope that they will be read. They commonly have links to related sites and appear in reverse chronological order, with the most recent entries uppermost. Emerging in the mid 1990s, their appearance accelerated with the ready availability of tools making their construction and posting to the net very much simpler. Though counts exist, they are inevitably rough estimates, which become dated before they are published. However, there are almost certainly several million blogs produced throughout the world. Indeed, one search engine specifically designed to track blogs had no fewer than 55 million listed by the end of 2006. Many are ephemeral, and large numbers are doubtless never seen by any but their proud authors. Sometimes celebrated as a major democratisation of communications, they are more probably composed of largely unnoticed individual impulses and indulgencies. However, on notable occasions of constrained flows in traditional news media, for example during the Iraq war, or from restricted populations, such as in China and elsewhere, they can come into their own as important sources of popular views and experiences. The verb 'to blog' has become increasingly common among users and enthusiasts, as has the term 'blogosphere' to describe the world of 'blogging' and the blogs collectively.

CAQDAS: this unwieldy acronym stands for computer-aided qualitative data analysis software and is used to categorise computer software used in the analysis and organisation of qualitative data, particularly textual data. Although not often acknowledged, this software is most suited for particular types of qualitative research, in particular ethnography and grounded theory.

chi-square test: an inferential statistical test that is used for hypothesis testing. It compares observed frequencies in a sample with expected frequencies (i.e. the frequencies you would expect to find if there were no unusual variation in sample values). The greater the disparity between these values, the greater the likelihood is that the findings are statistically significant and that the null hypothesis can be rejected.

closed-response formats: provide people with a predetermined set of options for answering questions. They can greatly speed up the recording and analysis of people's answers, and for this reason are commonly used in standardised interviews and self-completion questionnaires. The types of closed-response formats used vary in their sophistication, and several have been designed to try to capture more varied and subtle details in people's answers (e.g. Likert scales, semantic differential formats, checklists, ranking formats).

cluster sampling: a sampling method that involves randomly selecting a range of 'clusters' (e.g. geographic areas or institutions), and then sampling all units in these clusters or selecting units randomly from these clusters (the latter option is sometimes referred to as 'staged' cluster sampling). Cluster sampling is widely used where the research population is widely dispersed and it would be impractical to generate a comprehensive sampling frame and gain access to all units randomly selected from it.

code: a systemic device or procedure which operates to organise and frame material in particular forms of communication. Codes operate hand in hand with conventions, and in order to interpret any item or unit of communication, we need to understand its constitutive codes and conventions, for without these we shall either be baffled or make culturally inappropriate guesses at what is meant.

coding frame: see **content analysis** and **inter-coder reliability**.

connotation: see **denotation/connotation**.

consensus: involves a collectively approved set of notions, values or beliefs among a wide number of people or, putatively at least, a society as a whole, and as such carries the assumption of unity among those individuals collectively adhering to them. The problem with the term is that it is often invoked for ideological purposes, that is, in the interests of particular groups who claim universal applicability for their own ideas, principles, social objectives, and so on. Consensus can then obscure or occlude the existence of real conflicts between meaning and value systems and the different groups generating them. Accordingly, the term consensus has profound sociological implications, and as a result we need to attend closely to particular media texts, representations and discourses for their varying propensity to promote social and political consensus, rather than regarding consensus as referring to some unassailable or 'natural' conception of social order. Consensus is always a social construct.

constant errors: although all sampling is likely to have some degree of sampling error (see **random errors**), some samples can be seriously compromised by structural biases that systematically distort their representativeness. Constant errors can be caused by a range of factors, such as high levels of non-response, poor sample design, poor question wording, poor interviewing, and so on.

content analysis: a term mainly used to describe the *quantitative* analysis of content. Quantitative content analysis mainly focuses on manifest features of texts, and requires the development of a coding frame that identifies which aspects should be quantified and in what way. This method is useful in generating an extensive perspective of trends across large numbers of texts.

contingency tables: see **cross-tabulations**.

convenience sampling: the least formalised of all non-random sampling methods. With convenience sampling, the selection of units is essentially opportunistic. The researcher either exploits a chance research opportunity or selects sample units simply because they are conveniently to hand.

convention: this term refers to the manner in which a practice is structured and the way in which it has become habitual and routinely accepted. Conventions are the rules or regulative structures underpinning both forms of communication and ways of social life.

correlation coefficients: a descriptive statistic that measures the strength of a relationship between two variables. The closer the statistic is to either plus or minus 1, the stronger the positive or negative relationship between two values. Pearson's r is a correlation coefficient used in analysing the strength of a relationship between values that both attain the interval or ratio **levels of measurement**. It examines the degree to which the values of each variable vary consistently with each other. Spearman's r_{ho} is used to calculate the strength of a correlation between numbers that attain the ordinal level of measurement. It works by comparing the degree of consistency in the rank order of values across two variables. Correlation coefficients only tell us about the strength in the association between values. They do not reveal anything about causation (i.e. which is the independent variable and which is the dependent variable).

critical realism: a realist approach to social inquiry which accepts that the social and cultural world has a 'reality' that is independent of people's ability to describe and understand it. Unlike **positivist** approaches, it sees this 'reality' as created not by unchanging patterns of forces (as in the natural world), but by historical formations that are continually reproduced and transformed through human action. Most people, however, are unaware of these formations or how they work to organise the choices available in daily life. The researcher's task is to identify these concealed structures and demonstrate their impact on everyday action. Critical realism is 'critical' in the sense that it seeks to identify the constraints imposed by existing systems and to argue for transformations that could promote greater choice, equity and social justice.

cross-tabulations: sometimes alternatively referred to as contingency tables, this method of **bivariate analysis** involves intersecting two **frequency tables** (one along the top and one along the side) to explore the association between variables. The proportional distribution of observed frequencies across the resulting cells can be used to highlight important variations *within* samples.

decoding: see **encoding/decoding**.

deixis: a linguistic category for terms designating some aspect of spatial or temporal context. For example, 'here and now' is a classic deictic phrase.

denotation/connotation: these two related concepts refer to the production and communication of meaning at different expressive levels. Denotation refers to the primary, initial or manifest meaning of any given **sign**, whereas connotation refers to extra meanings that have become further associated with it. So, for instance, the term 'red' denotes a primary colour, and this is its initial or manifest meaning, but it also connotes danger or provides a warning, indicates social embarrassment, or stands – as in its opportunist deployment in **moral panics** – for radical or 'subversive' ideas or activities associated with left-wing politics.

descriptive statistics: numbers that are used to describe or summarise the properties of a sample. On their own they should not be generalised to the population from which they are drawn, as we cannot assume their accuracy or representativeness in this wider context. This sort of statistical projection is normally the preserve of **inferential statistics**.

diachronic: an analytical category associated with change and development over time, and with the historical dimension of any cultural product or process. It is usually referred to as the binary opposite of synchronic, which is associated with a particular moment of time, and with the contemporary or present dimension.

digitalisation: up until the late twentieth century, the modern media of communication were based on analogue technologies of recording, storing and transmission, where there is a direct relationship between what is being represented and how it is represented. The negative/positive process in photography, where the negative displays recognisable images of what was in front of the camera lens when the shutter was clicked, is an obvious example. Since each medium used its own distinct analogue technology, they developed as separate industries. We have now entered the digital era, where emerging technologies allow all forms of information – text, images, statistics, sound – to be translated into the universal digital language of computing and expressed as a series of 0s and 1s. Digitalisation is the process of moving from analogue to digital media. Digitalisation allows the full range of media materials to be stored and used together, as in a CD-ROM. Because information stored in digital form takes up far less space, the new digital media can carry far more material or compress many more channels into the space now used by analogue systems, as in digital television systems. The digital merging of media materials also paves the way for a convergence of the media industries, since they now share common technologies.

discourse: a term generally used to refer to talk and texts as component parts of social practice, though the French philosopher Michel Foucault used it in a rather different sense, to designate large-scale, institutionalised domains of language which circumscribe and regularise what is possible within them, as for example in the discourse of medicine. In each such domain there is a crucial interdependence of discourse, knowledge and power. This more specialised use apart, some implication of values and beliefs, relations and identities, usually informs social discourses of any kind.

discourse schemas: see **thematic structure and discourse schemas**.

encoding/decoding: the paired processes by which a media text or other form of communication is put together according to certain **codes** and **conventions**, and by which media consumers or general recipients of communication appropriately draw on codes and conventions in their interpretation of what has been or is being communicated. There is no absolute 'fit' between these processes, and so what is decoded may well differ from what has been encoded. Nonetheless, a certain degree of correspondence between the two is generally required if, for instance, what passes between speaker and listener is not to end up as a mess of mangled meaning.

focus group research: a methodology using unstructured interviewing of small focus groups, commonly between five and ten people, in which topics introduced and prompted by the researcher as facilitator are freely discussed by the group to provide qualitative data on their views and attitudes. The method is essentially exploratory, providing insight into the character, range and components of views of a given set of issues on which the group's attention is focused (sometimes using stimuli such as film or photographs). A number of groups are usually used, either internally mixed or each fairly homogeneous, to collectively provide a range from, though not necessarily a rigorous demographic reflection of, the wider population. The method has become very popular, not least among political parties, and is sometimes mistakenly seen as an alternative to survey research, or even as a preferable method, offering more detailed and qualitative data. In fact, it has been used for many years, especially in market research, as a method of exploring, in a preliminary way, dimensions of people's values and beliefs which can subsequently be explored more intensively.

frequency table: a table that is used to display the distribution of values across a single variable. A commonly used form of **univariate analysis**.

generation: as a non-biological concept, the concept of generation is specifically modern, dating from the early nineteenth century, when it was first used by writers such as Comte and J.S. Mill. The late nineteenth-century German philosopher, Wilhelm Dilthey, further developed the concept as a threefold term of reference, indicating at once a temporal duration, an interiorised conception of social and cultural identity, and a historically specific relation of individuals and groups to each other. For its later connections with Raymond Williams's concept of structure of feeling, which was widely influential in cultural analysis and theory in the second half of the twentieth century, see Pickering 1997: ch. 2.

genre: a term deriving from the Latin *genus*, meaning 'family', and used to refer to a typological category of media texts or cultural products in which characteristics of form and style, code and convention are shared, to a greater or lesser degree. This allows such texts or products to be grouped together and leads to intertextual relations between them. It ensures that we do not mistake romance fiction for sadomasochistic porn, or criticise an example of talking blues because the singer does not sound like Frank Sinatra. Genres set up expectations and involve cultural and other values, which are said to produce genre communities – sociologically a problematic notion at best, and one to be regarded with scepticism and caution (see Negus and Pickering 2004: 70–8).

iconic sign: an icon is a **sign** (e.g. a representational painting or statue) based on its apparently exact resemblance to its object or referent. The relationship between signifier and signified is here based on the quality of being like (or at least very closely similar).

ideology: a set of ideas, values, assumptions and beliefs, and the ways these govern our choices, tastes, actions and commitments. Ideology is a form of cultural power, since it is characteristic of and operates in the interests of social groups who are ranked in terms of their relative social power. Ideology entails the naturalisation of interested knowledge, beliefs

and values, presenting these as generally applicable, absolute or eternally relevant to all groups in any given society.

inferential statistics: allow researchers to 'infer' things about research populations on the basis of sample data. They are used in two ways in statistical research: first, to make 'population estimates' on the basis of sample evidence, by estimating the effect that sample error may have on the accuracy of the data; second, in hypothesis testing – estimating the likelihood that patterns or relations uncovered in a sample are likely to be replicated more generally in the research population. Because these statistics draw on theories of probability and chance, they should normally only be applied to data obtained by **random sampling**. However, they are also controversially used with some **non-random sampling** methods, in particular **quota sampling**.

informed consent: the principle of ensuring that those being researched are fully aware of that fact, and of the purposes and consequences of the research. Informed consent was originally developed in the medical and scientific world, but has increasingly been adopted and adapted by professional social science bodies. Although it seems a clear guideline, in practice (as discussed in chapter 15) it is difficult to define precisely and is open to many qualifications and reservations.

inter-coder reliability: an issue that relates to any formal quantitative analysis that requires using different people to numerically code research material (e.g. in quantitative content analysis, or in coding observed behaviour). You need to ensure that everybody involved interprets the coding instruments in as consistent a manner as possible, as coder variation can seriously compromise the reliability and validity of the resulting data. Various statistical tests can be used to check the degree of consistency among coders.

Internet: a worldwide network of linked computer networks, arising originally from military developments in the USA, and later evolved mainly in North American higher education. Subsequent development has been exponential, and any estimate of the Internet's scale will be out of date the minute it is consigned to paper. Increasing commercialisation has raised the prospect that the initially anarchic and libertarian philosophy inherent in the system will become more oriented to marketing, dominated by large corporations, and controlling access to information and services by price. The Internet is easily and cheaply accessible to academic users in most countries, and makes available much useful online information and communication, though rarely as much or as easily as enthusiasts often suggest.

interpretive research: sets out to explore the ways in which people make sense of their world and to communicate these understandings through a variety of expressive forms and everyday practices. In contrast to **positivist** approaches, it does not accept that there is a social 'reality' that exists independently of the ways people imagine and define it. It belongs to the *idealist* tradition within philosophy, which regards the world as the product of ideas. The researcher's task is to show how cultural forms are organised, how they produce meanings, and what they mean to the people involved. To this end, interpretive scholars collect mainly *qualitative* materials – talk, texts, material objects, observations of interaction – that embody the complexity of meaning. The process of interpreting these materials is radically different from the procedures used in the natural sciences, and marks a deep division between them. Interpretive scholars see themselves as engaged in a continuous conversation with their subjects, and it is this dialogue that produces the accounts they offer. Rather than setting out to develop general laws of social life, interpretive studies aim to foster the recognition and respect for human creativity and difference that is essential to communal life in a world fractured by multiple divisions.

intertextuality: the relations between media texts which affect the ways in which any one of the texts in question is understood. Intertextuality operates through the linkages provided by cultural codes, helping to sustain the various networks of meaning and value which make up particular forms of social life. Intertextuality is a critical feature of the permutation of meaning occurring across and between the boundaries of particular texts, which are variable and unstable because the cultural codes mediating them are not singularly applicable to particular texts.

interview guide: see **semi-structured interviews**.

interview schedules: see **standardised interviews**.

interviewer bias: the concern that interviewees may be encouraged to provide certain types of answers by the phrasing and delivery of the interviewer. Standardised interviewing methods attempt to control, if not eradicate, the impact of interviewer bias by imposing strict protocols for the conduct of the exchange. Some would argue that this is a vain ambition, rooted in discredited positivistic aims to create completely value-free social and psychological research.

langue: the system and structure of a language as it exists at a particular time in history, providing an integrated set of rules and conventions to which language in its actual use, in speech or in writing, must apply. Such applications are generally routine and unselfconsciously generated in language as we employ it to communicate with each other in everyday social life. Langue is conceptually paired with the term **parole**, which refers to language use in concrete utterances or texts. The term langue derives from Ferdinand de Saussure and has subsequently been widely adopted in a number of disciplines in the social sciences and humanities.

levels of measurement: numbers do not always attain the same levels of measurement. Some numbers are solely used to 'nominate' or categorise particular qualities or features of a sample unit. This is the *nominal* level of measurement, and when we compare different values all we can consider is their equivalence or difference. The *ordinal* level of measurement is higher in that numbers signify differences in order or ranking, but these numbers are not sufficiently precise to conduct any more detailed mathematical analysis. The *interval* level of measurement relates to those statistics that do have a more precise numerical relationship, but which have no absolute zero. The *ratio* level is the highest level of measurement and covers values that have a precise mathematical relationship (i.e. they can be added, subtracted, divided and multiplied). In social research, interval and ratio levels of measurement are generally treated as one and the same. It is vital to ascertain the levels of measurement attained by variables in an analysis, as this dictates which descriptive and inferential statistics are appropriate to use in relation to them.

lurking: the activity of reading and using news groups, bulletin boards, online chat rooms or the like without actively participating. The lurker makes use of the material, and will often need to join the group, but chooses not to participate and remains passive. This can often be an entirely legitimate and reasonable role to play, though it is frequently disparaged as exploitative, or at least as not entering fully into the interactive spirit which such groups foster. Researchers may be lurkers, and many active participants would perceive them as 'malign lurkers'.

measures of central tendency: descriptive measures that summarise how values in a set of data gather centrally. There are three measures available for use: the *mean* (the arithmetic average), the *mode* (the most commonly occurring score) and the *median* (the midpoint between the lowest and highest values). These measures are commonly used in conjunction with **measures of dispersion**.

measures of dispersion: these statistics summarise the degree of spread of values in relation to a variable. A **frequency table**, which shows the proportional distribution of different values, is the only measure of dispersion that can be used on *nominal* data (see **levels of measurement**). The *range* can be used on data that attains the *ordinal* level of measurement or higher, and calculates the difference between the highest and lowest value. The *standard deviation* is widely used to measure dispersion of values that attain the *interval* or *ratio* level of measurement. It calculates the average overall deviation of all values from the mean value of the variable.

metaphor: a figure of speech in which a word is applied to a situation or object not conventionally associated with it. For example, in the figure 'blood-red wine' the word 'blood' is used to enhance the impression of the wine's depth of colour and flavour.

metonymy: a figure of speech closely related to **metaphor**, but one in which part of an object or person is used to signify the whole, or in which an attribute substitutes for the thing itself. An example of this is where the phrase 'the stage' is used metonymically to refer to the theatre as a cultural institution and/or profession.

missing values: either values that have been missed in the data-collection or data-entry processes, or sample units that are logically excluded from the statistical analysis of a variable (because no data is required from them in relation to that variable).

moral panic: the process through which a particular practice, set of beliefs, value system, subculture or social grouping becomes defined as a threat to dominant social interests or what is discursively identified as 'the majority view'. This process involves the mass media in combination with other official bodies and institutions, such as the police, the judicial system and politicians. Moral panics result in what is perceived as a threat or challenge becoming defined as deviant and then being treated as such. (See Cohen 1972; Hall and Jefferson 1976; Hall et al. 1978; Golding and Middleton 1982; and Watney 1989.)

multi-stage cluster sampling: a sampling method that combines elements of **stratified random sampling** and **cluster sampling**. First the researcher decides on salient stratification variables for his or her research (e.g. income factors) and groups clusters in relation to these strata. Random selections of clusters are then made within these strata.

multivariate analysis: analysis of the interaction between three or more variables. This sort of analysis is used to examine in more complex ways how different variables interact and intervene in social and psychological processes.

myth: classically, myths are forms of narrative which are not simply about everyday life, but are concerned with relationships between the commonplace world and uncommon events, the sacred and the profane or the individual and society. Myths are also now often considered more generally as forms of seeing and believing, being composed of elements 'half-way between precepts and concepts' (Lévi-Strauss 1972: 18). Myths can in some ways be compared to dreams, but of course they operate through consciously related narrative or imagery at a social and often public level, rather than within the subconscious mind. At this level, myths are fundamentally concerned with a culture's idea of itself, with its self-definition and identity, and as such they explain the world through the terms of that definition and identity in order to make them seem natural and inevitable. In this way, myth is conceptually close in its modern sense to the term **ideology**. As a form of cultural explanation or understanding operating through narrative, myth is associated most of all with the central preoccupations, values, fears and anxieties of the culture in which it has its genesis and in which it is habitually reproduced.

nominalisation: the transformation of a relatively simple word into an abstract noun. This process is closely allied to **passivisation** in that the more straightforward word is often a verb; and the consequence of nominalisation as a feature of the syntactical transformation is to deactivate or remove a sense of agency from a process or subject. For example, the change to 'the repercussions of yesterday's *killing* have been severe' from 'police *kill* rioters' has the effect of wiping from public view the agents of the killing, those directly responsible for the deaths of the rioters (Trew 1979).

non-random sampling: with this type of sampling, researchers actively select their sample units, rather than leaving the selection to chance. Examples include **quota sampling**, **theoretical sampling**, **snowball sampling** and **convenience sampling**. They do not depend on a sampling frame, and researchers are not able to guarantee that every population unit has had an equivalent chance of inclusion or to calculate the response rate to the research.

non-response: the occasions when no data are gathered from certain sample units. Non-response can be a significant source of **constant error**, and can undermine the representativeness of a sample. When people are being sampled, it can occur because of non-cooperation or confusion on the part of research subjects, or because of administrative failures on the part of the researcher in recording responses. Therefore, when designing research, you should give considerable thought to ways in which you can maximise the motivation and cooperation of your research participants, as well as the accuracy of your data collection.

normal distribution: a bell-shaped distribution (normally rendered as a curved line) that can vary in height and width. It captures the standard distribution of values of many 'naturally occurring' variables (e.g. people's heights and weights) and is widely used in inferential statistics (e.g. see **standard error of the mean**).

open-response formats: used in interviews and self-completion questions to provide people with the opportunity to construct answers in their own terms and their own words. This freedom can produce richer, more sensitive insights into the views and activities of respondents and remove the danger of undermining rapport by inappropriately restricting the nature of people's answers. However, open-response questions place greater demands on the articulacy of respondents (and their literacy, where they have to write their answers down), and the material they generate is less easy to summarise. For these reasons, open-response formats are often used in tandem with **closed-response formats**.

over-lexicalisation: this process involves the accumulation of words or phrases which all mean more or less the same, a proliferation of synonyms referring to a practice or object which closely informs the identity of a particular group or collectivity, or which provides an index to those aspects of their lives that certain groups consider a source of considerable disquiet, anxiety, and so on.

paradigm: a set of units of communication from which selections are made, the selections then being put together in *syntagms*. Selection determines the use of paradigms; combination determines the use of syntagms. The letters of the alphabet are paradigmatic units which are identifiable because they are different. Words are particular patterns of letters brought into syntagmatic conjunction with each other. As such, they acquire an identity because of the paradigmatic units of which they are syntagmatically composed, as for instance in the 1980s neologism 'yuppie' (nakedly careerist and opportunist middle-class financier or executive type), which is also an example of a part-acronym in that it is derived from the initial letters of the description, **y**oung **u**rban **p**rofessional.

parole: the concrete use of language in any communicational and cultural form, as opposed to language as an abstract system of rules and conventions (for which see **langue**). The term originates in Saussurian linguistics. In its subsequently broad adoption, it is generally downgraded in conceptual status and value compared to the theoretically privileged langue, with which, nevertheless, it operates in perennial conjunction. Langue and parole are therefore unequally weighted terms and this has had widespread ramifications in the human sciences.

passivisation: turning active verbs into their passive form, as for example in the sentence from *The Observer* analysed by Fowler and Kress (1979: 209–10): 'US coalminers are expected to return to work tomorrow'. Those who expressed this expectation are concealed by the way the sentence is constructed in the passive rather than the active mode, for to have constructed it in the active mode would have turned those who did expect this outcome into the subjects of the sentence, thus revealing their identity. The effect is similar to that resulting from processes of **nominalisation**: the occlusion of agency and the redirection of decoder attention to other players in the situation being reported.

pilot interview: see **piloting**.

piloting: testing out a research instrument before embarking on full-scale data collection. It is a particularly important step to undertake when using highly formalised research instruments (such as a self-completion questionnaire, **content analysis** coding frame or **standardised interview** schedule), because these methods are not flexible and adaptable and cannot easily be adjusted in the course of the data collection process. Piloting can help to identify any glaring problems in the design of a research instrument, as well as any areas of confusion in the terminology employed. It can also be used productively with less structured research techniques, allowing the researcher to orientate her/himself in the field and to gain a sense of the relevance and validity of their initial research concerns.

plagiarism: the deliberate presentation of someone else's thoughts, ideas or findings as one's own. Research, even the most original, depends to some extent on past work. It is reasonable, indeed desirable, to make such dependency explicit and always acknowledge as accurately and fully as possible the sources for material presented.

polysemy: the multiplicity of meanings associated with cultural **signs**, **texts** and **representations**, particularly across different contexts and circumstances of use and interpretation, and in relation to different subject-positions.

population: sometimes alternatively referred to as the 'universe' of a piece of research, the 'population' of a study is the group that a sample is supposed to represent. Populations are not necessarily made up of people; they can be aggregates of texts, institutions, and so on. The population of a piece of research is defined by the research objectives, and varies from study to study.

positivist: a term used to describe approaches to research that are based on the assumption that social and cultural studies should be modelled on the natural sciences. Like natural scientists, positivists are philosophical realists. They argue that social and cultural life is governed by sets of forces, many of which take the form of cause–effect relations. The aim is to identify these forces and to produce generalisations about the way they work that will produce robust predictions that can be used as a basis for interventions designed to regulate social and cultural life in the interests of 'progress'. It was because they believed in the ability of the social sciences to contribute to a more positive future that the early supporters of this position, in the mid nineteenth century, chose to call themselves 'positivists'. To achieve this aim, they argue, researchers must remain 'objective', not getting involved with the people they study and not allowing their own personal values to influence their professional work. Producing robust generalisations also requires factors that might interfere with the relations under study to be rigorously controlled, and observations to be as precise and unambiguous as possible. As a result, positivism displays a marked preference for *quantitative* (numerical) data, and for experimental methods or research techniques (such as sample surveys) that allow confounding factors to be controlled statistically.

probing: supplementary questions and standard techniques for asking them when informants produce inadequate answers or when further detail is required of informants. In fixed-question surveys, interviewers are generally restricted to stock probes, whereas in non-standardised forms of interviewing they are allowed greater scope for seeking fuller or more nuanced forms of data. However, regardless of the interview format, the same care needs to be taken in probing as in asking the initial questions, for there is no point in avoiding loaded questions in the first instance if such questions are then posed in follow-up requests for further elaboration or clarification.

prompts: see **standardised interviews**.

quota sampling: a form of **non-random sampling** that is widely used in opinion polls and market research. Rather than selecting units randomly from a sampling frame, the method involves deciding on a range of criteria that are likely to be important to the study, and then setting a series of 'quotas' in relation to them that are filled to produce a representative sample. As with proportionate stratified **random sampling**, the size of each quota should be weighted to match with known distributions in the population.

random errors: it is recognised that all sampling techniques will introduce a degree of sampling error into research. By this we mean that the sample findings may differ from the 'true' values of a research population. These errors are not necessarily due to faults in sampling procedures (see **constant errors**), but are the consequence of the variation that you would expect to find when selecting sample units by chance. Various statistical tests exist to estimate the effect that random sampling error may have had on the population estimates of a sample. They provide guidelines, via confidence intervals, that specify the degree of uncertainty that should be attributed to a sample finding (see **standard error of the mean**).

random sampling: sometimes alternatively referred to as probability sampling, random sampling covers all sampling methods that share two attributes. First, the selection of sample units from the sampling frame is left to chance; the researcher has no final control in deciding which sample units are selected. Second, each unit of a research population (as represented by the sampling frame) has an equal and calculable chance of selection.

relexicalisation: a process of transformation in the way someone or something is classified or conventionally described, such as 'greenfield site' for open field, 'coffee without milk' for black coffee or 'challenged' for mentally handicapped. The process has recently become common in relation to the nominalist obsessions associated with 'political correctness', but it is actually a much wider phenomenon, occurring in any sphere where euphemisms are preferred or existing categories have become socially embarrassing or politically damaging.

representation: the general process through which meanings are embodied in specific material forms: speech, written language, visual images, or any combination of these – as, for example, in film and television. It is a more specific sense of the term which is critical for media studies, covering the meanings attached to particular views of given social groups or categories where these mediate public understanding of the actual groups or categories. This entails processes of 'speaking for' or 'speaking of' those who are represented, in images, characterisations, descriptions, and so on, processes which raise important issues not only about the content and form of media representations, but also about those producing them, about public access and denial of public access. Representation thus simultaneously brings into critical question both the mode and degree of typification and representativeness in media texts and images – covering under-representation, over-representation and misrepresentation – and the political economy underpinning the media personnel and organisations involved in media production. Representations are built around group conceptions of other groups; they invariably have 'us' and 'them' implications, and in this way they function as vehicles of ideological transmission.

sampling: the process by which units are selected from a larger population to draw wider conclusions about it. Sampling occurs when researchers do not have the time, opportunity or resources to include every unit of the research population in their study. Most research incorporates some degree of sampling.

sampling frame: the list that supposedly contains all the elements of a research population from which a sample is chosen using random-sampling techniques. In some research books, this list is talked about as if it were itself the research population, but in many studies the sampling frame is really just the best approximation of the population available. (This is because ready-made, comprehensive, accurate and relevant sampling frames are rarely easily to hand.) Any major disparity between a sampling frame and the population that it is taken to represent can introduce **constant errors** into the research process.

semi-structured interviews: in these interviews, the interviewer retains some control over the interview agenda by using an interview guide. This lists the topics and issues that the researcher is interested in examining. However, with this method, there are no restrictions on question rewording or reordering, and the interviewer can explore and elaborate on issues that emerge during the course of the interview. The free format of these interviews also extends to the type of responses elicited from interviewees. Rather than recording answers mainly or solely through closed-format responses (as is the case with **standardised interviews**), these interviews leave the response format open. (In most cases, interviewees' comments are taped and then fully transcribed.) Consequently, these interviews generate a richer type of data and are better suited to dealing with complex and sensitive subjects. However, they make greater demands of both interviewer and interviewee, and are far more time-consuming to conduct and arrange than standardised interviews. Their informality and non-standardised nature can also create difficulties in comparing and aggregating interview data, as well as in processing and analysing the vast amounts of qualitative detail that they generate.

sign: the basic element of communication which refers to something other than itself, and which potentially has an expressive function at the levels of both **denotation** and **connotation**, as for instance with the English word 'dog'. In Saussurian terms, the sign is composed of two constituent units – the *signifier*, the physical form of the sign, and the *signified*, the mental concept to which the sign refers – and operates when these two units are actively combined.

signification: the process by which any media text or discourse acts as a series of messages to produce meanings.

signifier/signified: see **sign**.

simple random sampling: the most basic form of **random sampling**. It involves assigning each unit of a sampling frame a separate number and then selecting random numbers until you have the requisite number of units for your sample.

snowball sampling: a form of **non-random sampling** in which initial sample units are used as contacts to identify other units relevant to the sample. The method is commonly used in sampling populations that are either very informal in structure, very rare or somewhat closed to the outside world.

spiral of silence: a term coined by the German public-opinion theorist and researcher Elisabeth Noelle-Neumann (1984). It describes the social process by which less popular ideas become increasingly silenced and thus unavailable to influence others. The underlying theory assumes that people fear isolation and thus constantly monitor the cultural environment to see whether their opinions are in line with the prevailing climate of ideas. That climate is created significantly by the mass media. Where people perceive ideas to be unpopular, they are reluctant to give voice to them. Conversely, they become more assured about voicing views they perceive to be popular. The term was developed to explain why German public opinion seemed at odds with obvious predictions, a phenomenon explained by the argument that the left-leaning German media were 'misleading' the public about the prevailing currency of popular attitudes. The empirical work and theory behind this concept and its operationalisation have been severely challenged in recent years (see chapter 15).

standard error of the mean: an example of an **inferential statistic** that is used to make 'population estimates' on the basis of sample data. It draws on our knowledge of the mathematical properties of the normal distribution curve and the central limits theorem, which posits that sample means will be normally distributed around the 'true' population mean. The standard error of the mean provides confidence intervals that indicate the probability of where the 'true' population mean lies relative to the sample figure (e.g. we can be 95 per cent certain that the sample mean is within ±1.96 standard errors of the mean of the true population mean). The size of the standard error of the mean is influenced by the size of a sample and the degree of variation in the values of a variable (as measured by the standard deviation). The smaller a sample is and the greater the dispersion of values, the larger the standard error of the mean will be.

standardised interviews: highly structured interviews where interviewers are required to follow strictly standardised procedures in asking questions and eliciting responses. They use a formal interview schedule, which precisely lists the question wording, ordering and response frameworks. Although interviewers are sometimes allowed to use prompts to get interviewees to elaborate their answers or to rectify apparent misunderstandings, these are prescribed at the outset of the research and are designed to be as neutral in tone and detail as possible. The reason for seeking such high standardisation in the conduct of interviews is to minimise the impact of **interviewer bias**, and thereby strengthen the grounds for aggregating and comparing interviews. However, their formality means they are not well suited to dealing with complex or sensitive issues. They are most commonly employed in research that has an extensive, rather than intensive, perspective (e.g. large-scale sample surveys).

statistical significance: a finding derived from a sample is deemed statistically significant if it is calculated that there is an acceptably low chance that it could have emerged by chance. These estimations are expressed as probability statements. Although the researcher should decide on their own significance levels, a convention has emerged which says that findings cannot be deemed statistically significant if there is more than a 1 in 20 chance that they occurred by accident ($p > 0.05$). Statistical significance assumes that 'sample errors' are random and not constant in nature. In other words, it assumes a sample is valid and credible, which may not always be the case. For this reason, 'statistical significance' is not the same as 'sociological significance'. Apparently statistically significant findings can sometimes be an artefact of defects in sample design.

stratified random sampling: with this form of **random sampling**, the sampling frame is ordered into different strata before the random selection begins (e.g. males/females). This provides the researcher with greater control over the final sample composition. With some stratified random sampling, the proportion of units selected for each sample stratum corresponds to known distributions in the research population (proportionate stratified random sampling). However, in some cases, researchers generate *disproportionate* stratified samples to focus on specific sections of the research population that would be marginalised if the sample selection were strictly proportionate.

synchronic: see **diachronic**.

syntagm: see **paradigm**.

systematic sampling: a **random-sampling** method that involves sampling elements of a sampling frame in a repetitive, yet random, way. You first calculate the sampling interval you need to select across all the cases listed on your sampling frame. (You do this by dividing your required sample size into the total number of cases on your sampling list.) Then you randomly select a number between 1 and your sampling interval, which becomes your first sample unit. You use the sampling unit ($\underline{n}$) to select every $\underline{n}$th entry in the sampling frame until you have your requisite number of sample units.

text: formerly confined to written forms of communication, as in a biblical or legal text, this term has now been widely extended to refer to any discrete unit of communication, ranging from a letter arriving in the morning post or a newspaper read over lunch, to a TV programme watched in the evening or an instalment of *Book at Bedtime* listened to on the radio. The range thus covers visual and audio as well as print forms of communication. (Textualism is not unrelated to this considerable expansion of reference, but is in many respects quite different, particularly in its poststructuralist manifestations, with their associated formalism and antirealist implications or avowals.)

thematic structure and **discourse schemas**: a thematic structure is a preoccupying conception or proposition which runs throughout a media text, usually around an initiating topic. It strategically ties together a number of more specific conceptions or statements on the basis of particular social forms of knowledge and social forms of perception and belief. A thematic structure helps to make a media text cohere: it orients a text around a central theme or strand of related themes running throughout a story. Without thematic structures, media texts would be fragmentary and narratively dissolute. Their function is to provide a sense of the overall organisation, hierarchy and relations between different aspects or properties of the text, and between different units of the text, such as sentences and paragraphs. Thematic structures are linked linguistically with discourse schemas. Schemas group information and circumstantial detail into sequentially and hierarchically ordered categories and units of meaning. In news discourse, data are structured in a functional order of narrative disclosure which is specific to its particular mode of storytelling. This entails a patterned movement from the headline and lead paragraphs, through episodes or statements by witnesses and commentators (which are ranked in an implicit order of priority), to the further elaboration of detail and possible extrapolation and evaluation, often coming from key players or accredited sources.

theoretical sampling: a form of **non-random sampling** commonly used in qualitative research. Theoretical sampling jettisons formal concerns about the proportionality and representativeness of a sample. Instead, the sample is constructed directly in relation to the theoretical concerns of the research, and is designed to achieve as much variation and contrast as possible in the sample units selected. This is seen to maximise the opportunities for theoretical development.

tradition: this complex term refers, in its most simple sense, to the process by which ideas, beliefs, values or practices are handed down from one generation to the next, and from one historical period to another. It is also used to refer to the content of what is transmitted across time, and, as the adjective 'traditional', is applied to a given state of mind, an associated mental set, a general cultural orientation or disposition, a distinguishable generic form or an antiquated (sometimes hallowed) practice (e.g. a craft skill or religious ritual).

The adjective has also been used in classical sociology and anthropology to refer to forms of society or culture which are claimed to be diametrically opposite to societies of modernity and the cultural formations of modernity. The tradition/modernity binary is in many ways misconceived. It has also helped to sustain what have become highly contentious programmes of modernisation in so-called undeveloped (i.e. 'traditional') countries. A further difficulty with the term is that the weight and authority attached to tradition is often ideologically hijacked, perhaps especially (but, of course, not invariably) for reactionary political purposes. Against this, we should always remember that – despite any appearances to the contrary – traditions change over time, and their transmission and reception are historically conditioned. The term 'tradition' is best conceptualised today as referring to processes characterised by the tension felt within a social group or collectivity that has been generated as a result of the changed historical conditions and circumstances in which the content and form of traditions are negotiated.

typical-case sampling: a **non-random sampling** method that focuses on specific sampling units that can claim to be 'typical cases' of a wider population. That is, they represent the 'essence' or 'composite ideal' of the topic being investigated. This method is often used in conjunction with more extensive and representative sampling data, which is used to ascertain the criteria for establishing typicality in a given research context.

univariate analysis: the statistical analysis of individual variables. **Frequency tables, measures of central tendency** and **measures of dispersion** are all examples of univariate analysis.

weblog: see **blog**.

Bibliography

10 Downing Street (2005) 'PM's Press Conference – 5 August 2005', http://www.number10.gov.uk/output/Page8041.asp (accessed 8 February 2007).

ALASUUTARI, P. (1995) *Researching Culture: Qualitative Method and Cultural Studies*, London: Sage.

ALTHAUS, S.L. (2003) 'When News Norms Collide, Follow the Lead: New Evidence for Press Independence', *Political Communication*, 20(3): 381–414.

ALTHEIDE, D. and MICHALOWSKI, R.S. (1999) 'Fear in the News: A Discourse of Control', *Sociological Quarterly*, 40(3): 475–503.

ANDERSON, K. and JACK, D.C. (1991) 'Learning to Listen: Interview Techniques and Analyses', in Gluck, S.B. and Patai, D. (eds), *Women's Words: The Feminist Practice of Oral History*, New York and London: Routledge.

ANG, I. (1985) *Watching Dallas: Soap Opera and the Melodramatic Imagination*, London and New York: Methuen.

ANG, I. (1991) *Desperately Seeking the Audience*, London: Routledge.

ANGOLD, A. (2002) 'Diagnostic Interviews with Parents and Children', in Rutter, M. and Taylor, E. (eds), *Children and Adolescent Psychiatry*, London: Blackwell Publishing.

ARGYRIS, C. (1974) *Behind the Front Page: Organisational Self-renewal in a Metropolitan Newspaper*, San Francisco, CA: Jossey-Bass.

ATKINSON, J.A. and HERITAGE, J.C. (eds) (1984) *Structures for Social Action: Studies in Conversation Analysis*, Cambridge: Cambridge University Press.

ATKINSON, M. (1984a) *Our Masters' Voices: The Language and Body Language of Politics*, London: Methuen.

ATKINSON, M. (1984b) 'Public Speaking and Audience Responses: Some Techniques for Inviting Applause', in Atkinson, J.A. and Heritage, J.C. (eds), *Structures for Social Action: Studies in Conversation Analysis*, Cambridge: Cambridge University Press.

ATKINSON, M. (1985) 'The 1983 Election and the Demise of Live Oratory', in Crewe, I. and Harrop, M. (eds), *Political Communications: The General Election Campaign of 1983*, Cambridge: Cambridge University Press.

BANDURA, A. (1965) 'Influence of Model's Reinforcement Contingencies on the Acquisition of Imitative Responses', *Journal of Personality and Social Psychology*, 1: 589–95.

BANDURA, A. and WALTERS, R. (1963) *Adolescent Aggression*, New York: Ronald Press.

BARBOUR, R.S. and KITZINGER, J. (eds) (1999) *Developing Focus Group Research: Politics, Theory and Practice*, London: Sage.

BARKER, M. (2006) *The Story of the Lord of the Rings International Audience Research Project*, Aberystwyth: Department of Theatre, Film and Television Studies, University of Wales Aberystwyth, Departmental Working Paper.

BARKER, M. and EGAN, K. (2006) 'Rings Around the World: Notes on the Challenges, Problems and Possibilities of International Audience Projects', *Participations*, 3(2).

BARKER, M. and PETLEY, J. (eds) (1997) *Ill Effects: The Media/Violence Debate*, London: Routledge.

BARRETT, M. (1980) *Women's Oppression Today*, London: Verso.

BARRIOS, L. (1988) 'Television, Telenovelas, and Everyday Life', in Lull, J. (ed.), *World Families Watch Television*, Newbury Park, CA: Sage.

BARTHES, R. (1973) *Mythologies*, St Albans: Paladin.

BARTHES, R. (1977) *Image, Music, Text*, Glasgow: Fontana/Collins.

BARTON, J.A. (1958) 'Asking the Embarrassing Question', *Public Opinion Quarterly*, 22: 67–8.

BAUMAN, Z. (1987) *Legislators and Interpreters*, Cambridge: Polity Press.

BAUSINGER, H. (1984) 'Media Technology and Daily Life', *Media, Culture and Society*, 6: 340–52.

BEARDSWORTH, A. (1980) 'Analysing Press Content: Some Technical and Methodological Issues', in Christian, H. (ed.), *Sociology of Journalism and the Press*, Keele: Keele University Press.

BEAULIEU, A. (2004) 'Mediating Ethnography: Objectivity and the Making of Ethnographies of the Internet', *Social Epistemology*, 18(2–3): 139–63.

BELL, A. (1991) *The Language of News Media*, Oxford: Blackwell.

BELL, A. (1994) 'Climate of Opinion: Public and Media Discourse on the Global Environment', *Discourse and Society*, 5: 33–63.

BELL, A. (1995) 'News Time', *Time and Society*, 4: 305–28.

BENJAMIN, W. (1970) *Illuminations*, London: Fontana.

BERELSON, B. (1952) *Content Analysis in Communication Research*, New York: Hafner Press.

BERGER, A.A. (1991) *Media Analysis Techniques*, London: Sage.

BERKOWITZ, D. (1992) 'Non-routine News and Newswork: Exploring a What-a-Story', *Journal of Communication*, 42(1): 82–94.

BHASKAR, R. (1989) *Reclaiming Reality: A Critical Introduction to Contemporary Philosophy*, London: Verso.

BILLIG, M. (1995) *Banal Nationalism*, London, Thousand Oaks, CA and New Delhi: Sage.

BILLIG, M. (1999) 'Whose Terms? Whose Ordinariness? Rhetoric and Ideology in Conversation Analysis', *Discourse and Society*, 10(4): 543–58.

BILLS, S. (1988) *Kent State/May 4: Echoes Through a Decade*, Kent, OH: Kent State University Press.

BLAU, J.R. (1992) *The Shape of Culture: A Study of Contemporary Cultural Patterns in the United States*, Cambridge: Cambridge University Press.

BLUMER, H. (1969) *Symbolic Interactionism: Perspective and Method*, Englewood Cliffs, NJ: Prentice-Hall.

BLUMLER, J. and GUREVITCH, M. (1995) *The Crisis of Public Communication*, London: Routledge.

BOELLSTORFF, T. (2006) 'A Ludicrous Discipline? Ethnography and Game Culture?', *Games and Culture*, 1(1): 29–35.

BORN, G. (2004) *Uncertain Vision: Birt, Dyke and the Reinvention of the BBC*, London: Secker & Warburg.

BOURDIEU, P. (1984) *Distinction: A Social Critique of the Judgement of Taste*, London: Routledge.

BOURDIEU, P. (1991) *Language and Symbolic Power*, Cambridge: Polity Press.

BOURDIEU, P. (1996) 'Understanding', *Theory, Culture and Society*, 13(2): 17–36.

BOURDIEU, P. (1998) *On Television and Journalism*, London: Pluto Press.

BRIGGS, A. (1961) *The History of Broadcasting in the United Kingdom, Volume 1: The Birth of Broadcasting*, London: Oxford University Press.

BRIGGS, A. (1965) *The History of Broadcasting in the United Kingdom. Volume 2: The Golden Age of Wireless*, London: Oxford University Press.

British Psychological Society (BPS) (2006) *Code of Conduct, Ethical Principles, and Guidelines*, Leicester: BPS.

British Sociological Association (BSA) (2003) *Guidance Notes: Statement of Ethical Practice*, Durham: BSA, http://www.britsoc.co.uk/equality/60.htm (accessed 8 February 2007).

BRUNT, R. (1990) 'Points of View', in Goodwin, A. and Whannell, G. (eds), *Understanding Television*, London and New York: Routledge.

BRYANT, S. (1989) *The Television Heritage: Television Archiving Now and in an Uncertain Future*, London: British Film Institute.

BRYMAN, A. (2001) *Social Research Methods*, Oxford: Oxford University Press.

BRYMAN, A. (2004) *Social Research Methods*, second edition, Oxford: Oxford University Press.

BRYMAN, A. and CRAMER, D. (2005) *Quantitative Data Analysis with SPSS 12 and 13: A Guide for Social Scientists*, London: Routledge.

BURGELIN, O. (1968) 'Structural Analysis of Mass Communications', in McQuail, D. (ed.), *Sociology of Mass Communications*, Harmondsworth: Penguin.

BURGESS, R.G. (1984) *In the Field: An Introduction to Field Research*, London: Allen and Unwin.

BURNETT, R. (2004) *How Images Think*, Cambridge, MA and London: MIT Press.

BURNS, T. (1977) *The BBC: Public Institution and Private World*, London: Macmillan.

CALDER, A. and SHERIDAN, D. (1984) *Speak for Yourself: A Mass-Observation Anthology, 1937–49*, London: Jonathan Cape.

CAMERON, D. (1995) *Verbal Hygiene*, London and New York: Routledge.

CAMERON, P. (2003) 'Molestations by Homosexual Foster Parents: Newspaper Accounts Versus Official Records', *Psychological Reports*, 93(3): 793–802.

CAPUTO, P. (2005) *13 Seconds: A Look Back at the Kent State Shootings*, New York: Chamberlain Bros.

CAREY, J. (1975) 'Communication and Culture', *Communication Research*, 2: 173–91.

CARRAGEE, K.M. and ROEFS, W. (2004) 'The Neglect of Power in Recent Framing Research', *Journal of Communication*, 54(2): 214–33.

CASCIO, L. (2005) 'Ludology, Narratology, and Simulations as Paradigm', 30 July, http://www.worldchanging.com/archives/003218.html (accessed 8 February 2007).

CATHERWOOD, C. (2004) *Winston's Folly: Imperialism and the Creation of Modern Iraq*, London: Constable.

CAUTE, D. (1988) *Sixty-Eight: The Year of the Barricades*, London: Hamish Hamilton.

CHANEY, D. (1987) 'Audience Research and the BBC: A Mass Medium Comes into Being', in Curran, J., Smith, A. and Wingate, P. (eds), *Impacts and Influences: Essays on Media Power in the Twentieth Century*, London: Methuen.

CHAPMAN, G., KUMAR, K., FRASER, C. and GABER, I. (1997) *Environmentalism and the Mass Media: The North–South Divide*, London: Routledge.

CLARKE, G. (1997) *The Photograph*, Oxford: Oxford University Press.

CLAYMAN, S. and HERITAGE, J. (2002) *The News Interview*, Cambridge and New York: Cambridge University Press.

CLAYRE, A. (1973) *The Impact of Broadcasting, or, Mrs Buckle's Wall is Singing*, Salisbury, Wiltshire: Compton Russell.

CMIEL, K. (1996) 'On Cynicism, Evil, and the Discovery of Communication in the 1940s', *Journal of Communication*, 46(3): 88–107.

COHEN, S. (1972) *Folk Devils and Moral Panics*, Oxford: Martin Robertson.

CONDIT, C. (1989) 'The Rhetorical Limits of Polysemy', *Critical Studies in Mass Communication*, 6(2): 103–22.

CONRAD, P. (2001) 'Genetic Optimism: Framing Genes and Mental Illness in the News', *Culture, Medicine and Psychiatry*, 25(2): 225–47.

CORNER, J. (1995) *Television Form and Public Address*, London, New York, Melbourne and Auckland: Edward Arnold.

CORNER, J. (1996) 'Reappraising Reception: Aims, Concepts and Methods', in Curran, J. and Gurevitch, M. (eds), *Mass Media and Society*, second edition, London: Edward Arnold.

CORNER, J., RICHARDSON, K. and FENTON, N. (1990) *Nuclear Reactions: Form and Response in Public Issue Television*, London: John Libbey.

CULLER, J. (1976) 'Deciphering the Signs of the Times', *Times Higher Educational Supplement*, 24 September, p. 15.

CUMBERBATCH, G. and HOWITT, D. (1989) *A Measure of Uncertainty: The Effects of the Media*, London: John Libbey.

CURRAN, C. (1971) 'Researcher/Broadcaster Co-operation: Problems and Possibilities', in Halloran, J.D. and Gurevitch, M. (eds), *Broadcaster/Researcher Co-operation in Mass Communication Research*, Leicester: Leicester University Press.

CURRAN, J. (1976) 'Content and Structuralist Analysis of Mass Communication', *D305 Social Psychology*, Project 2: Content and Structuralist Analysis, Milton Keynes: Open University.

CURRAN, J., SMITH, A. and WINGATE, P. (eds) (1987) *Impacts and Influences: Essays on Media Power in the Twentieth Century*, London: Methuen.

D'ANGELO, P. (2002) 'News Framing as a Multi-paradigmatic Research Program: A Response to Entman', *Journal of Communication*, 52(4): 870–88.

D'HAENENS, L. and DE LANGE, M. (2001) 'Framing of Asylum Seekers in Dutch Regional Papers', *Media, Culture and Society*, 23(6): 847–60.

DE LAURITIS, T. (1984) *Alice Doesn't*, London: Macmillan.

DE VAUS, D.A. (1990) *Surveys in Social Research*, second edition, London: Unwin Hyman.

DEACON, D. (1996) 'The Voluntary Sector in a Changing Communication Environment: A Case Study of Non-official News Sources', *European Journal of Communication*, 11(2): 173–99.

DEACON, D. (1999) 'Charitable Images: The Construction of Voluntary Sector News', in Franklin, B. (ed.), *Social Policy, the Media and Misrepresentation*, London: Routledge and Kegan Paul: 51–68.

DEACON, D. (2003) 'Holism, Communion and Conversion: Integrating Media Consumption and Production Research', *Media, Culture and Society*, 25(2): 209–31.

DEACON, D. (2007) 'Yesterday's Papers and Today's Technology: Digital Newspaper Archives and "Push Button" Content Analysis', *European Journal of Communication*, 22(1): 5–25.

DEACON, D. and GOLDING, P. (1991) 'The Voluntary Sector in the Information Society: A Study in Division and Uncertainty', *Voluntas: International Journal of Voluntary and Non-profit Organisations*, 2(2): 69–88.

DEACON, D. and GOLDING, P. (1994) *Taxation and Representation: The Media, Political Communication and the Poll Tax*, London: John Libbey.

DEACON, D., WRING, D., DOWNEY, J., GOLDING, P. and DAVIDSON, S. (2005) 'Reporting the 2005 General Election', London: Electoral Commission, http://www.electoralcommission.org.uk/files/dms/MediaReport-160805FINAL_19222-14161__E__N__S__W__.pdf (accessed 8 February 2007).

DESCOLA, P. (1997) *The Spears of Twilight: Life and Death in the Amazon Jungle*, London: Flamingo.

DICK, B.F. (1990) *Anatomy of Film*, second edition, New York: St Martin's Press.

DILMAN, D. (1978) *Mail and Telephone Surveys: The Total Design Method*, New York and Chichester: John Wiley.

DINGWALL, R. (1980) 'Ethics and Ethnography', *Sociological Review*, 28: 871–91.

DOMHOFF, W.G. (1975) 'Social Clubs, Policy-Planning Groups, and Corporations: A Network Study of Ruling-Class Cohesiveness', *The Insurgent Sociologist*, 5(3): 173–84.

DOMINELLI, A. (2003) 'Web Surveys – Benefits and Considerations', *Clinical Research and Regulatory Affairs*, 20(4): 409–16.

DOMKE, D. (2004) *God Willing? Political Fundamentalism in the White House, the War on Terror and the Echoing Press*, London: Pluto Press.

DOWNEY, J. and KOENIG, T. (2006) 'Is there a European Public Sphere? The Berlusconi Case', *European Journal of Communication*, 21(2): 165–87.

DU BOIS, J., SCHEUTZE-COBURN, S., CUMMING, S. and PAOLINO, D. (1993) 'Outline of Discourse Transcription', in Edwards, J. and Lampert, M. (eds), *Talking Data: Transcription and Coding in Discourse Research*, Hillsdale, NJ: Lawrence Erlbaum, pp. 45–89.

DUNAWAY, D.K. and BAUM, W.K. (eds) (1984) *Oral History: An Interdisciplinary Anthology*, Nashville, TN: American Association for State and Local History, and Oral History Association.

DURHAM, F.S. (1998) 'News Frames as Social Narratives: TWA Flight 800', *Journal of Communication*, 48(4): 100–17.

DYER, C. (2006) 'Falconer Accuses US of Affront to Democracy', *The Guardian*, 13 September, p. 5.

EAGLETON, T. (1991) *Ideology*, London: Verso.

EASTHOPE, A. (1991) *Literary into Cultural Studies*, London and New York: Routledge.

EDWARDS, D. and CROMWELL, D. (2004) *Guardians of Power: The Myth of the Liberal Media*, London: Pluto.

Electoral Commission (2003) *The Electoral Registration Process – Report and Recommendations*, London: Electoral Commission.

ELLIOTT, P. (1971) *The Making of a Television Series: A Case Study in the Sociology of Culture*, London: Constable.

ELLIOTT, P. and MATTHEWS, G. (1987) 'Broadcasting Culture: Innovation, Accommodation and Routinization in the Early BBC', in Curran J., Smith, A. and Wingate, P. (eds), *Impacts and Influences: Essays on Media Power in the Twentieth Century*, London: Methuen.

ENTMAN, R. (1993) 'Framing: Towards a Clarification of a Fractured Paradigm', *Journal of Communication*, 43(4): 6–27.

ERICSON, R.V., BARARNEK, P.M. and CHAN, J.B.L. (1987) *Visualizing Deviance: A Study of News Organisation*, Milton Keynes: Open University Press.

ERIKSON, K.T. (1967) 'A Comment on Disguised Observation in Sociology', *Social Problems*, 14: 363–73.

ESSER, F., REINEMANN, C. and FAN, D.P. (2001) 'Spin Doctors in the United States, Great Britain and Germany: Metacommunication about Media Manipulation', *Harvard International Journal of Press/Politics*, 6(1), 16–45.

EVAN, W.M. and MILLER, J.R. (1969) 'Differential Effects on Response Bias of Computer vs Conventional Administration of a Social Science Questionnaire', *Behavioral Science*, 14: 216.

EVANS, H. (1978) *Pictures on a Page*, London: Pimlico.

EYSENCK, H.J. and NIAS, D.K. (1978) *Sex, Violence and the Media*, London: Maurice Temple Smith.

FABER, J. (1978) *Great News Photos and the Stories Behind Them*, second revised edition, New York: Dover Publications.

FAIRCLOUGH, N. (1988) 'Discourse Representation in Media Discourse', *Sociolinguistics*, 17: 125–39.

FAIRCLOUGH, N. (1989) *Language and Power*, London and New York: Longman.

FAIRCLOUGH, N. (1992) *Discourse and Social Change*, Cambridge: Polity Press.

FAIRCLOUGH, N. (1995a) *Media Discourse*, London, New York, Sydney and Auckland: Arnold.

FAIRCLOUGH, N. (1995b) *Critical Discourse Analysis*, London: Edward Arnold.

FAIRCLOUGH, N. (2000) *New Labour, New Language?* London and New York: Routledge.

FAIRCLOUGH, N. (2003) *Analysing Discourse: Textual Analysis for Social Research*, London and New York: Routledge.

FENTON, N., BRYMAN, A. and DEACON, D. (1998) *Mediating Social Science*, London: Sage.

FERGUSON, M. (1983) *Forever Feminine: Women's Magazines and the Cult of Femininity*, London: Heinemann.

FICKLING, D. (2006) 'Falconer Condemns "Shocking" Guantanamo', 13 September, http://www.guardian.co.uk/guantanamo/story/0,,1871628,00.html (accessed 8 February 2007).

FILMER, P. (1972) *New Directions in Sociological Theory*, London: Collier Macmillan.

FINCH, J. (1984) '"It's Great to Have Someone to Talk To": The Ethics and Politics of Interviewing Women', in Bell, C. and Roberts, H. (eds), *Social Researching: Politics, Problems and Practice*, London: Routledge and Kegan Paul.

FINNEGAN, R. (1996) *Oral Traditions and the Verbal Arts*, London and New York: Routledge.

FISHMAN, P. (1990) 'Interaction: The Work Women Do', in McCarl Nielsen, J. (ed.), *Feminist Research Methods: Exemplary Readings in the Social Sciences*, London: Westview Press.

FISKE, J. (1987) *Television Culture*, London and New York: Methuen.

FISKE, J. (1994) 'Audiencing: Cultural Practice and Cultural Studies', in Denzin, N.K. (ed.), *Handbook of Qualitative Research*, London: Sage.

FISKE, J. and HARTLEY, J. (1978) *Reading Television*, London: Methuen.

FOSTER, J. and SHEPPARD, J. (eds) (1995) *British Archives: A Guide to Archive Resources in the UK*, Basingstoke and London: Macmillan (originally published 1982).

FOWLER, R. (1986) *Linguistic Criticism*, Oxford and New York: Oxford University Press.

FOWLER, R. (1993) *Language in the News*, London and New York: Routledge.

FOWLER, R. and KRESS, G. (1979) 'Critical Linguistics', in Fowler, R., Hodge, B., Kress, G. and Trew, T., *Language and Control*, London: Routledge and Kegan Paul.

FOWLER, R., HODGE, B., KRESS, G. and TREW, T. (1979) *Language and Control*, London: Routledge and Kegan Paul.

FREUDENBURG, W.R., COLEMAN, C.L., GONZALES, J. and HELGELAND, C. (1996) 'Media Coverage of Hazard Events: Analyzing the Assumptions', *Risk Analysis*, 16(1): 31–42.

FRICKER, S., GALESIC, M., TOURANGEAU, R. and YAN, T. (2005) 'An Experimental Comparison of Web and Telephone Surveys', *Public Opinion Quarterly*, 69(3): 370–92.

FRITH, S. (1983) 'The Pleasures of the Hearth: The Making of BBC Light Entertainment', in Donald, J. (ed.), *Formations of Pleasure*, London: Routledge and Kegan Paul, pp. 101–23.

GADAMER, H.G. (1975) *Truth and Method*, London: Sheed and Ward.

GANS, H. (1979) *Deciding What's News: A Study of CBS Evening News, NBS Nightly News, 'Newsweek' and 'Time'*, New York: Pantheon Books.

GARCÍA CANCLINI, N. (1995) 'Mexico: Cultural Globalization in a Disintegrating City', *American Ethnologist*, 22(4): 743–55.

GARFINKEL, H. (1967) *Studies in Ethnomethodology*, Englewood Cliffs, NJ: Prentice-Hall.

GARY, B. (1996) 'Communication Research, the Rockefeller Foundation, and Mobilisation for the War on Words, 1938–1944', *Journal of Communication*, 46(3): 124–47.

GATES, B. (1995) *The Road Ahead*, New York: Viking Books.

GEERTZ, C. (1973) *The Interpretation of Cultures: Selected Essays*, New York: Basic Books.

GEERTZ, C. (1983) *Local Knowledge: Further Essays in Interpretive Anthropology*, New York: Basic Books.

GEERTZ, C. (1993) *The Interpretation of Cultures*, London: Fontana.

GERBNER, G. (1969) 'Towards Cultural Indicators: The Analysis of Mass Mediated Public Message Systems', in Gerbner, G., Holsti, O., Krippendorff, K., Paisley, W. and Stone, P. (eds), *The Analysis of Communication Content: Developments in Scientific Theories and Computer Techniques*, New York: John Wiley.

GERBNER, G. (1983) 'The Importance of Being Critical – In One's Own Fashion', *Journal of Communication*, 33(3): 355–62.

GERSTER, G. (2003) *The Past from Above*, London: Francis Lincoln.

GIDDENS, A. (1976) *New Rules of Sociological Method*, London: Hutchinson.

GIDDENS, A. (1984) *The Constitution of Society: Outline of a Theory of Structuration*, Cambridge: Polity Press.

GIDDENS, A. (1990a) *Social Theory and Modern Sociology*, Cambridge: Polity Press (originally published 1987).

GIDDENS, A. (1990b) *The Consequences of Modernity*, Cambridge: Polity Press.

GILLARD, M., FLYNN, S. and FLYNN, L. (1998) 'How Millions Were Fooled', *The Guardian*, 9 June, p. 5.

GITLIN, T. (1978) 'Media Sociology: The Dominant Paradigm', *Theory and Society*, 6: 205–53.

GITLIN, T. (1980) *The Whole World Is Watching*, Berkeley, CA and London: University of California Press.

GITLIN, T. (1983) *Inside Prime Time*, New York: Pantheon.

GLASER, B.G. and STRAUSS, A.L. (1967) *The Discovery of Grounded Theory*, Chicago: Aldine.

Glasgow University Media Group (1980) *More Bad News*, London, Henley and Boston, MA: Routledge and Kegan Paul.

GOFFMAN, E. (1974) *Frame Analysis: An Essay on the Organisation of Experience*, New York: Harper and Row.

GOFFMAN, E. (1981) *Forms of Talk*, Oxford: Basil Blackwell.

GOLAFSHANI, N. (2003) 'Understanding Reliability and Validity in Qualitative Research', *The Qualitative Report*, 8(4): 597–607, http://www.nova.edu/ssss/QR/QR8-4/golafshani.pdf (accessed 8 February 2007).

GOLDING, P. and ELLIOTT, P. (1979) *Making the News*, London: Longman.

GOLDING, P. and MIDDLETON, S. (1982) *Images of Welfare*, Oxford: Martin Robertson.

GORDON, W.A. (1995) *Four Dead in Ohio*, Laguna Hills, CA: North Ridge Books.

GRABER, D. (1989) 'Content and Meaning: What's It All About?', *American Behavioral Scientist*, 33(2): 144–5.

GRAMSCI, A. (1978) *Selections from Prison Notebooks*, London: Lawrence and Wishart.

GREATBATCH, D. (1986) 'Aspects of Topical Organisation in News Interviews: The Use of Agenda-Shifting Procedures by Interviewees', *Media, Culture and Society*, 8(4): 441–55.

GUNTER, B., NICHOLAS, D., HUNTINGTON, P. and WILLIAMS, P. (2002) 'Online Versus Offline Research: Implications for Evaluating Digital Media', *Aslib Proceedings*, 54(4): 229–39.

HALL, S. (1988) *The Hard Road to Renewal*, London and New York: Verso.

HALL, S. (1996) 'Signification, Representation, Ideology: Althusser and the Post-Structuralist Debates', in Curran, J., Morley, D. and Walkerdine, V. (eds), *Cultural Studies and Communications*, London: Edward Arnold.

HALL, S. and JEFFERSON, T. (eds) (1976) *Resistance through Rituals*, London: Hutchinson.

HALL, S., CRITCHER, C., JEFFERSON, T., CLARKE, J. and ROBERTS, B. (1978) *Policing the Crisis*, London: Macmillan.

HALLIDAY, M.A.K. (1970) 'Language Structure and Language Function', in Lyons, J. (ed.), *New Horizons in Linguistics*, Harmondsworth: Penguin.

HALLIDAY, M.A.K. (1973) 'Towards a Sociological Semantics', in *Explorations in the Functions of Language*, London: Edward Arnold.

HALLIN, D. (1986) *The Uncensored War*, Oxford: Oxford University Press.

HALLIN, D. (1992) 'Soundbite News: Television Coverage of Elections 1968–1988', *Journal of Communication*, 42(2): 5–25.

HALLORAN, J.D., ELLIOTT, P. and MURDOCK, G. (1970) *Demonstrations and Communication: A Case Study*, Harmondsworth: Penguin Books.

HAMMERSLEY, M. (1992a) *What's Wrong with Ethnography?*, London: Routledge.

HAMMERSLEY, M. (1992b) 'On Feminist Methodology', *Sociology*, 26(2): 187–206.

HARDT, H. (1979) *Social Theories of the Press: Early German and American Perspectives*, Beverly Hills, CA: Sage.

HARRIS, R. (1983) *Gotcha! The Media, the Government and the Falklands Crisis*, London: Faber and Faber.

HARRIS, S. (1991) 'Evasive Action: How Politicians Respond to Questions in Political Interviews', in Scannell, P. (ed.), *Broadcast Talk*, London, Newbury Park, CA and New Delhi: Sage.

HAWTHORN, J. (1992) *A Concise Glossary of Contemporary Literary Theory*, London, New York, Melbourne and Auckland: Arnold.

HENRY, G. (1990) *Practical Sampling*, New York: Sage.

HERITAGE, J. (1985) 'Analysing News Interviews: Aspects of the Production of Talk for Overhearing Audiences', in van Dijk, T. (ed.), *Handbook of Discourse Analysis*, volume 3, London: Academic Press.

HERITAGE, J. and GREATBATCH, D. (1986) 'Generating Applause: A Study of Rhetoric and Response at Party Political Conferences', *American Journal of Sociology*, 92: 110–57.

HETHERINGTON, A. (1985) *News, Newspapers and Television*, London: Macmillan.

HIGGINS, J. (2003) 'Visual Images in the Press: The Case of the Okinawa G8 Summit', presented at *Knowledge and Discourse: Speculating on Disciplinary Futures*, 2nd International Conference, Web Proceeding July 2003, http://ec.hku.hk/kd2proc/proceedings (accessed 8 February 2007).

HOBSBAWM, E. and RANGER, T. (eds) (1984) *The Invention of Tradition*, Cambridge, London and New York: Cambridge University Press.

HODDER, I. (1994) 'The Interpretation of Documents in Material Culture', in Denzin, N.K. and Lincoln, Y.S. (eds), *Handbook of Qualitative Research*, London: Sage, pp. 393–402.

HOLSTI, O. (1969) *Content Analysis for the Social Sciences and Humanities*, Reading, MA: Addison Wesley.

Home Office (1992) *Research Findings 2*, London: HMSO.

HOROWITZ, I.L. (1967) *The Rise and Fall of Project Camelot*, Cambridge, MA: MIT Press.

HORRIE, C. (2003) *Tabloid Nation: From the Birth of the Daily Mirror to the Death of the Tabloid*, London: Andre Deutsch.

HORTON, D. and WOHL, R.R. (1956) 'Mass Communication and Para-social Interaction', *Psychiatry*, 19: 215–19.

HUANG, H.M. (2004) 'Do Print and Web Surveys Provide the Same Results?', *Computers in Human Behaviour*, 22: 334–50.

HUDSON, D., LEE-HONG, S., HITE, D. and HAAB, T. (2004) 'Telephone Pre-surveys, Self-selection and Non-response Bias to Mail and Internet Surveys in Economic Research', *Applied Economic Letters*, 11: 237–40.

HUDSON, R.A. (1980) *Sociolinguistics*, Cambridge: Cambridge University Press.

HUMPHRIES, S. (1984) *The Handbook of Oral History*, London: Inter-Action Imprint.

HUNTINGTON, S. (1998) *The Clash of Civilizations and the Remaking of the World Order*, London: Touchstone.

HUTCHBY, I. (1996) *Confrontation Talk*, Mahweh, NJ: Lawrence Erlbaum.

HYMES, D.H. (1972) 'On Communicative Competence', in Pride, J.B. and Holmes, J. (eds), *Sociolinguistics*, Harmondsworth: Penguin.

IVES, E.D. (1980) *The Tape-Recorded Interview: A Manual for Fieldworkers in Folklore and Oral History*, Knoxville: University of Tennessee Press.

JEFFERSON, G. (1984) 'On the Organization of Laughter in Talk about Trouble', in Atkinson, J.M. and Heritage, J. (eds), *Structures of Social Action: Studies in Conversation Analysis*, Cambridge: Cambridge University Press, 346–69.

JENSEN, N.E., AARESTRUP, F.M., JENSEN, J. and WEGENER, H.C. (1996) '*Listeria monocytogenes* in Bovine Mastitis: Possible Implication for Human Health', *International Journal of Food Microbiology*, 32(1–2): 209–16.

JOHNSON, C.G. (1982) 'Risks in the Publication of Fieldwork', in Sieber, J.E. (ed.), *The Ethics of Social Research*, New York: Springer-Verlag.

JOHNSON, L. (1988) *The Unseen Voice: A Cultural Study of Early Australian Radio*, London: Routledge.

JOHNSTON, H. (1995) 'A Methodology for Frame Analysis: From Discourse to Cognitive Schema', in Johnston, H. and Klandermans, B. (eds), *Social Movements and Culture*, London: UCL Press, pp. 217–46.

JONES, D. (1942) 'Quantitative Analysis of Motion Picture Content', *Public Opinion Quarterly*, Fall: 411–28.

JORDIN, M. and BRUNT, R. (1988) 'Constituting the Television Audience: A Problem of Method', in Drummond, P. and Paterson, R., *Television and its Audience: International Research Perspectives*, London: British Film Institute.

KEIGHTLEY, E. and PICKERING, M. (2006) 'For the Record: Popular Music and Photography as Technologies of Memory', *European Journal of Cultural Studies*, 9(2): June, 131–47.

KEPPLINGER, H.M. (1997) 'Political Correctness and Academic Principles: A Reply to Simpson', *Journal of Communication*, 47(4): 102–17.

KERR, P.A. and MOY, P. (2002) 'Newspaper Coverage of Fundamentalist Christians', *Journalism and Mass Communication Quarterly*, 79(1): 54–72.

KIESLER, S. and SPROULL, L.S. (1986) 'Response Effects in the Electronic Survey', *Public Opinion Quarterly*, Fall: 402.

KIMMEL, A.J. (1988) *Ethics and Values in Applied Social Research*, Newbury Park, CA: Sage.

KLAEHN, J. (ed.) (2005) *Filtering the New: Essays on Herman and Chomsky's Propaganda Model*, London: Blackrose Books.

KLAPPER, J.T. (1960) *The Effects of Mass Communication*, New York: Free Press.

KNAPP, H. and KIRK, S.A. (2003) 'Using Pencil and Paper, Internet and Touch-tone Phones for Self-administered Surveys: Does Methodology Matter', *Computers in Human Behaviour*, 19: 117–34.

KNOWLES, M. and MOON, R. (2005) *Introducing Metaphor*, London and New York: Routledge.

KOCH, G. (1982) *International Association of Sound Archives: Directory of Member Archives*, Milton Keynes: IASA Special Publications No. 3.

KOENIG, T. (2004) 'Frame Analysis: A Primer', http://www.lboro.ac.uk/research/mmethods/resources/links/frames_primer.html (accessed 8 February 2007).

KOENIG, T. (2004) 'CAQDAS – A Primer', Loughborough: Department of Social Sciences, http://www.lboro.ac.uk/research/mmethods/research/software/caqdas_primer.html (accessed 8 February 2007).

KRACAUER, S. (1952–53) 'The Challenge of Qualitative Content Analysis', *Public Opinion Quarterly*, 16(4): 631–42.

KRAMARAE, C. (1981) *Women and Men Speaking: Frameworks for Analysis*, Rowley, MA: Newbury House.

KRESS, G. (1994) 'Text and Grammar as Explanation', in Meinhof, U. and Richardson, K. (eds), *Text, Discourse and Context: Representations of Poverty in Britain*, London and New York: Longman.

KRESS, G. and FOWLER, R. (1979) 'Interviews', in Fowler, R., Hodge, B., Kress, G. and Trew, T., *Language and Control*, London: Routledge.

KRESS, G. and HODGE, R. (1979) *Language as Ideology*, London: Routledge and Kegan Paul.

KRESS, G. and VAN LEEUWEN, T. (1996) *Reading Images: The Grammar of Visual Design*, London: Routledge.

KRZYWINSKA, T. (2006) 'The Pleasures and Dangers of the Game', *Games and Culture*, 1(1): 119–22.

LABOV, W. (1972a) *Language in the Inner City: Studies in the Black English Vernacular*, Philadelphia: University of Pennsylvania Press.

LABOV, W. (1972b) *Sociolinguistic Patterns*, Philadelphia: University of Pennsylvania Press.

LACAN, J. (1977) *Ecrits*, London: Tavistock.

LANG, G.E. and LANG, K. (1981) 'Watergate: An Exploration of the Agenda-Building Process', in Wilhoit, G.C. and de Bock, H. (eds), *Mass Communication Review Yearbook*, volume 2, Beverly Hills, CA.: Sage, pp. 445–68.

LANG, K. and LANG, G. (1953) 'The Unique Perspective of Television and its Effect', *American Sociological Review*, 18(1): 103–12.

LANG, K. and LANG, G.E. (1984) *Politics and Television Reviewed*, London: Sage.

LAPSLEY, R. and WESTLAKE, M. (2006) *Film Theory: An Introduction*, Manchester: Manchester University Press.

LASSWELL, H. (1936) *Politics: Who Gets What, When, How*, London: McGraw-Hill.

LASSWELL, H. and LEITES, N. (1949) *Language of Politics: Studies in Quantitative Semantics*, Cambridge, MA: MIT Press.

LAZARSFELD, P.F. (1941) 'Administrative and Critical Communications Research', *Studies in Philosophy and Social Science*, 9.

LEACH, E. (1973) 'Anthropological Aspects of Language: Animal Categories and Verbal Abuse', in Maranda, P. (ed.), *Mythology*, Harmondsworth: Penguin.

LEONARD, D. (2006) 'Not a Hater, Just Keepin' it Real: The Importance of Race- and Gender-based Game Studies', *Games and Culture*, 1(1): 83–8.

LERNER, D. (1958) *The Passing of Traditional Society*, Glencoe: Free Press.

LÉVI-STRAUSS, C. (1969) *The Raw and the Cooked*, London: Cape.

LÉVI-STRAUSS, C. (1972) *The Savage Mind*, London: Weidenfeld and Nicolson.

LINCOLN, Y. and GUBA, E. (1985) *Naturalistic Inquiry*, Beverly Hills, CA: Sage.

LINDLOF, T. (1995) *Qualitative Communication Research Methods*, Thousand Oaks, CA: Sage.

LINDNER, R. (1996) *The Reportage of Urban Culture: Robert Park and the Chicago School*, Cambridge: Cambridge University Press.

LIPPMANN, W. and MERZ, C. (1920) 'A Test of the News', *The New Republic*, 23, pt 2(296): 1–42.

LIVINGSTONE, S. (2006) 'Drawing Conclusions from New Media Research: Reflections and Puzzles Regarding Children's Experience of the Internet', *The Information Society*, 22(4): 219–30.

LIVINGSTONE, S. and LUNT, P. (1994) *Talk on Television: Audience Participation and Public Debate*, London: Routledge.

LIVINGSTONE, S., WOBER, M. and LUNT, P. (1994) 'Studio Audience Discussion Programmes: An Analysis of Viewers' Preferences and Involvement', *European Journal of Communication*, 9(4): 355–80.

LODZIAK, C. (1986) *The Power of Television*, London: Frances Pinter.

LOFLAND, J. (1971) *Analysing Social Settings*, Belmont, CA: Wadsworth.

LOTZ, A.D. and ROSS, S.M. (2004) 'Towards Ethical Cyberspace Audience Research: Strategies for Using the Internet for Television Audience Studies', *Journal of Broadcasting and Electronic Media*, 48(3): 501–12.

LUKES, S. (1974) *Power: A Radical View*, London: Macmillan.

LULL, J. (ed.) (1988) *World Families Watch Television*, Newbury Park, CA: Sage, pp. 49–79.

LULL, J. and HINERMAN, S. (1997) *Media Scandals: Morality and Desire in the Popular Culture Marketplace*, Cambridge: Polity Press.

LUMMIS, T. (1987) *Listening to History*, London, Melbourne, Sydney, Auckland and Johannesburg: Hutchinson.

MACDONALD, K. and COUSINS, M. (1996) *Imagining Reality: The Faber Book of Documentary*, London: Faber and Faber.

MACDONALD, K. and TIPTON, C. (1993) 'Using Documents', in Gilbert, N. (ed.), *Researching Social Life*, London: Sage, pp. 187–200.

MACGREGOR, B. and MORRISON, D.E. (1995) 'From Focus Groups to Editing Groups: A New Method of Reception Analysis', *Media, Culture and Society*, 17(1): January, 141–50.

MACMILLAN, K. and KOENIG, T. (2004) 'The Wow Factor: Preconceptions and Expectations for Data Analysis Software in Qualitative Research', *Social Science Computer Review*, 22(2): 179–86.

MACWHINNEY, B. (1995) *The CHILDES Project: Tools for Analyzing Talk*, second edition, Hillsdale, NJ: Lawrence Erlbaum.

MADDEN, P. (ed.) (1981) *Keeping Television Alive*, London: British Film Institute.

MAHER, T. (2001) 'Framing: An Emerging Paradigm or a Phase of Agenda Setting', in Reese, S., Gandy, O. and Grant, A. (eds), *Framing Public Life: Perspectives on Media and Our Understanding of Our Social World*, Mahwah, NJ: Lawrence Erlbaum.

MALABY, T. (2006) 'Parlaying Value: Capital in and Beyond Virtual Worlds', *Games and Culture,* 1(2): April, 141–62.

MALINOWSKI, B. (1922) *Argonauts of the Western Pacific*, London: Routledge and Kegan Paul.

MALINOWSKI, B. (1944) *A Scientific Theory of Culture and Other Essays*, Chapel Hill: University of North Carolina Press.

MANNING, P. (1998) *Spinning for Labour: Trade Unions and the New Media Environment*, Aldershot: Ashgate.

MARCUS, G. and FISCHER, M. (1986) *Anthropology as Cultural Critique*, Chicago and London: University of Chicago Press.

MARWICK, A. (1998) *The Sixties*, Oxford and New York: Oxford University Press.

MASON, J. (1996) *Qualitative Researching*, London, Thousand Oaks, CA and New Delhi: Sage.

MAY, T. (1993) *Social Research: Issues, Methods and Process*, Buckingham, UK and Philadelphia, PA: Open University Press.

MAYKUT, P. and MOREHOUSE, R. (1994) *Beginning Qualitative Research: A Philosophical and Practical Guide*, London: Falmer Press.

MCCHESNEY, R.W. (1993) *Telecommunications, Mass Media and Democracy: The Battle for Control of U.S. Broadcasting, 1928–1935*, New York: Oxford University Press.

MCDONNELL, B. (1998) *Fresh Approaches to Film*, Auckland: Longman.

MCQUAIL, D. (1997) *Audience Analysis*, London: Sage.

MCROBBIE, A. (1996) 'All the World's a Stage, Screen or Magazine: When Culture Is the Logic of Late Capitalism', *Media, Culture and Society*, 18(2): 335–42.

MEEK, J. (2004) 'Get a Life', *The Guardian*, G2, 3 August: pp. 2–4.

MEMRI (The Middle East Media Research Institute) (2004) Special Dispatch Series No. 811 http://www.memri.org/sd.html (accessed 8 February 2007).

MERTON, R. (1956) *The Focused Interview*, New York: Free Press.

MERTON, R. and KENDALL, P. (1956) 'The Focused Interview', *American Journal of Sociology*, 51(6): 541–57.

METZ, C. (1974a) *Film Language*, New York: Oxford University Press.

METZ, C. (1974b) *Language and Cinema*, The Hague: Mouton.

MILLER, T. (2006) 'Gaming for Beginners', *Games and Culture*, 1(1): 5–12.

MILLS, C. WRIGHT (1970) *The Sociological Imagination*, Harmondsworth: Penguin Books.

MITCHELL, W.J. (1994) 'When Is Seeing Believing?', *Scientific American*, February: 44–9.

MOON, Y. (1998) 'Impression Management in Computer-based Interviews: The Effects of Input Modality, Output Modality and Distance', *Public Opinion Quarterly*, 62(4): 610–22.

MOORE-GILBERT, B. (1997) *Postcolonial Theory*, London and New York: Verso.

MOORES, S. (1988) "The Box on the Dresser": Memories of Early Radio and Everyday Life', *Media, Culture and Society*, 10(1): January, 23–40.

MOORES, S. (1993) *Interpreting Audiences: The Ethnography of Media Consumption*, London: Sage.

MORLEY, D. (1980) *The Nationwide Audience*, London: British Film Institute.

MORLEY, D. (1992) *Television, Audiences and Cultural Studies,* London: Routledge.

MORLEY, D. and SILVERSTONE, R. (1991) 'Communication and Context: Ethnographic Perspectives on the Media Audience', in Jensen, K.B. and Jankowski, N.W. (eds), *Handbook of Qualitative Methodologies for Mass Communication Research*, London: Routledge.

MORRISON, D. (1998) *The Search for a Method: Focus Groups and the Development of Mass Communication Research*, Luton: University of Luton Press.

MOSER, C. and KALTON, J. (1971) *Survey Methods in Social Investigation*, London: Heinemann.

MURDOCK, G. (1973) 'Political Deviance: The Press Presentation of a Militant Mass Demonstration', in Cohen, S. and Young, J. (eds), *The Manufacture of News: Deviance, Social Problems and the Mass Media*, London: Constable.

MURDOCK, G. (1997a) 'Reservoirs of Dogma: An Archaeology of Popular Anxieties', in Barker, M. and Petley, J. (eds), *Ill Effects: The Media/Violence Debate*, London: Routledge.

MURDOCK, G. (1997b) 'Thin Descriptions: Questions of Method in Cultural Analysis', in McGuigan, J. (ed.), *Cultural Methodologies*, London: Sage.

MURDOCK, G. and McCRON, R. (1979) 'The Television and Delinquency Debate', *Screen Education*, 30(Spring): 51–67.

MYERS, D. (2006) 'Signs, Symbols, Games, and Play', *Games and Culture*, 1(1): 47–51.

NEGUS, K. and PICKERING, M. (2004) *Creativity, Communication and Cultural Value*, London, Thousand Oaks, CA and New Delhi: Sage.

NIGHTINGALE, V. (1989) 'What's "Ethnographic" about Ethnographic Audience Research?', *Australian Journal of Communication*, 16: 50–63.

NOAKES, J. and WILKINS, K. (2002) 'Shifting Frames of the Palestinian Movement in the News', *Media, Culture and Society*, 24(5): 649–71.

NOBLE, G. (1975) *Children in Front of the Small Screen*, London: Constable.

NOBLE, I. (1992) 'Opinion and the Polls', *The Guardian*, 14 May, p. 18.

NOELLE-NEUMANN, E. (1984) *The Spiral of Silence: Public Opinion, Our Social Skin*, Chicago, IL: University of Chicago Press.

O'CONNELL, D. and KOWAL, S. (1999) 'Transcription and the Issue of Standardization', *Journal of Psycholinguistic Research*, 28(2): 103–20.

O'CONNELL DAVIDSON, J. and LAYDER, D. (1994) *Methods, Sex and Madness*, London: Routledge.

O'MALLEY, T. (2002) 'Media History and Media Studies: Aspects of the Development of the Study of Media History in the UK 1945–2000', *Media History*, 8(2): 155–73.

O'SULLIVAN, T. (1991) 'Television Memories and Cultures of Viewing 1950–65', in Corner, J. (ed.), *Popular Television in Britain: Studies in Cultural History*, London: British Film Institute.

OAKLEY, A. (1981) 'Interviewing Women: A Contradiction in Terms' in Roberts, H. (ed.), *Doing Feminist Research*, London: Routledge and Kegan Paul.

OLIVER, E. (ed.) (1985) *Researcher's Guide to British Film and TV Collections*, London: British Universities Film and Video Council.

PALETZ, D.L. (1994) 'Just Deserts?', in Bennett, W. and Paletz, D.L., *Taken by Storm: The Media, Public Opinion and US Foreign Policy in the Gulf War*, Chicago, IL: University of Chicago Press.

PAN, Z. and KOSICKI, G. (1993) 'Framing Analysis: An Approach to News Discourse', *Political Communication*, 10: 55–75.

PAPE, R.A. (2006) 'Dying to Win: Why Suicide Terrorists Do It: An Extract', *Open Democracy*, http://www.opendemocracy.net/xml/xhtml/articles/3836.html (accessed 8 February 2007).

PAPERNY, D.M., AONO, J.Y., LEHMAN, R.M., HAMMAR, S.L. and RISSER, J. (1990) 'Computer assisted detection and intervention in adolescent high-risk health behaviors', *Journal of Pediatrics*, March: 456.

PARK, J. (2003) 'Contrasts in the coverage of Korea and Japan by U.S. television networks: A frame analysis', *International Communication Gazette*, 65(2): 145–64.

PARKER, L. (1998) 'Professionalisation, Presidentialisation, Americanisation: A Comparison of the BBC and ITN Flagship Evening News Bulletins of the General Elections of 1992 and 1997', BSc dissertation, Loughborough: Department of Social Sciences, Loughborough University.

PARKS, M.R. (1996) 'Making Friends in Cyberspace', *Journal of Communication*, 46(1): 80–97.

PASSERINI, L. (1979) 'Work Ideology and Consensus under Italian Fascism', *History Workshop Journal*, 8: 82–108.

PATERSON, B. (2006) 'Newspaper Representations of Mental Illness and the Impact of the Reporting of "Events" on Social Policy: The "Framing" of Isabel Schwarz and Jonathan Zito', *Journal of Psychiatric and Mental Health Nursing*, 13(3): June, 294–300.

PEARCE, C. (2006) 'Productive Play: Game Culture from the Bottom Up', *Games and Culture*, 1(1):17–24.

PEARSON, A. (1994) 'As Long As It Goes Out Live', *Independent on Sunday*, 30 October.

PERKS, R. (1995) *Oral History: Talking About the Past*, London: Historical Association.

PHILO, G. (1990) *Seeing and Believing: The Influence of Television*, London: Routledge.

PHILO, G. (ed.) (1996) *Media and Mental Distress*, London: Longmans.

PHILO, G. and BERRY, M. (2004) *Bad News from Israel*, London: Pluto Press.

PICKERING, M. (1996) 'The BBC's Kentucky Minstrels, 1933–1950: Blackface Entertainment on British Radio', *Historical Journal of Film, Radio and Television*, 16(2): 161–95.

PICKERING, M. (1997) *History, Experience and Cultural Studies*, Basingstoke and London: Macmillan.

PICKERING, M. (2001) *Stereotyping: The Politics of Representation*, Basingstoke and New York: Palgrave Macmillan.

PICKERING, M. (2007) *Blackface Minstrelsy in Britain*, Aldershot, UK and Burlington, VT: Ashgate.

POLLNER, M. (1987) *Mundane Reason: Reality in Everyday and Sociological Discourse*, Cambridge: Cambridge University Press.

POTTER, J. (1996) *Representing Reality*, London, Thousand Oaks, CA and New Delhi: Sage.

PRESTINARI, P. (1993) 'Structure of the European Audiovisual Sector: Distribution of Ownership and Alliances between Companies – November 1992', in Pilati, A. (ed.), *MIND: Media Industry in Europe*, London: John Libbey.

REID, W.J. and MISENER, E. (2001) 'Social Work in the Press: A Cross National Study', *International Journal of Social Welfare*, 10: 194–201.

REINHARZ, S. (1992) *Feminist Methods in Social Research*, New York and Oxford: Oxford University Press.

RICHARDSON, J.E. (2004) *(Mis)representing Islam: The Racism and Rhetoric of British Broadsheet Newspapers*, Amsterdam and Philadelphia, PA: John Benjamins.

RICHARDSON, J.E. (2006) *Analysing Newspapers*, Basingstoke and New York: Palgrave Macmillan.

RICHARDSON, K. and CORNER, J. (1986) 'Reading Reception: Mediation and Transparency in Viewers' Accounts of a TV Programme', *Media, Culture and Society*, 8(4): 485–512.

RITCHIN, F. (1990) 'Photojournalism in the Age of Computers', in Squires, C. (ed.), *The Critical Image: Essays on Contemporary Photography*, London: Lawrence and Wishart.

ROBERTSON, G. and NICOL, A. (1992) *Media Law*, London: Penguin.

ROBINS, K., WEBSTER, F. and PICKERING, M. (1987) 'Propaganda, Information and Social Control', in Hawthorn, J. (ed.), *Propaganda, Persuasion and Polemic*, London, Victoria and Baltimore, MD: Edward Arnold.

ROEH, I. (1989) 'Journalism as Storytelling, Coverage as Narrative', *American Behavioral Scientist*, 33(2): 162–8.

ROETHLISBERGER, F. and DICKSON, W. (1939) *Management and the Worker*, Cambridge, MA: Harvard University Press.

ROGERS, E.M. (1982) 'The Empirical and Critical Schools of Communications Research', in Burgoon, M. (ed.), *Communication Yearbook 5*, New Brunswick, NJ: Transaction Books.

ROSCOE, J., MARSHALL, H. and GLEESON, K. (1995) 'The Television Audience: A Reconsideration of the Taken-for-Granted Terms "Active", "Social" and "Critical"', *European Journal of Communication*, 10(1): March, 87–108.

ROSENBLUM, B. (1978) *Photographers at Work: A Sociology of Photographic Styles*, New York: Holmes and Meier Publishers.

ROSENGREN, K. (1996) 'Klaus Bruhn Jensen: "The Semiotics of Mass Communication"', *European Journal of Communication*, 11(1): March, 129–41.

SAID, E. (1985) *Orientalism*, Harmondsworth: Penguin.

SARDAR, Z. (1999) *Orientalism*, Buckingham, UK and Philadelphia, PA: Open University Press.

SAUSSURE, F. (1974) *Course in General Linguistics*, Glasgow: Fontana/Collins.

SCANNELL, P. (ed.) (1991) *Broadcast Talk*, London, Newbury Park, CA and New Delhi: Sage.

SCANNELL, P. (1996) *Radio, Television and Modern Life*, Oxford: Basil Blackwell.

SCANNELL, P. and CARDIFF, D. (1991) *A Social History of British Broadcasting. Volume 1, 1922–1939: Serving the Nation*, Oxford: Basil Blackwell.

SCHLESINGER, P. (1980) 'Between Sociology and Journalism', in Christian, H. (ed.), *The Sociology of Journalism and the Press*, Keele: Sociological Review Monograph 29, pp. 341–69.

SCHLESINGER, P. (1989) 'From Production to Propaganda', *Media, Culture and Society*, 11(3): 283–306.

SCHLESINGER, P. and TUMBER, H. (1994) *Reporting Crime: The Media Politics of Criminal Justice*, Oxford: Clarendon Press.

SCHLESINGER, P., MURDOCK, G. and ELLIOTT, P. (1983) *Televising 'Terrorism': Political Violence in Popular Culture*, London: Comedia.

SCHLESINGER, P., TUMBER, H. and MURDOCK, G. (1991) 'The Media Politics of Crime and Criminal Justice', *British Journal of Sociology*, 42(3): 397–420.

SCHLESINGER, P., DOBASH, R.E., DOBASH, R.P. and WEAVER, C. (1992) *Women Viewing Violence*, London: British Film Institute.

SCHOFIELD, W. (1996) 'Survey Sampling', in Sapsford, R. and Jupp, V. (eds), *Data Collection and Analysis*, London: Sage.

SCOLLON, R. (1998) *Mediated Discourse as Social Interaction*, London and New York: Longman.

SCOTT, J. (1986) *Capitalist Property and Financial Power: A Comparative Study of Britain, the United States and Japan*, Brighton: Wheatsheaf Books.

SCOTT, J. (1990) *A Matter of Record*, Cambridge: Polity Press.

SELDON, A. and PAPPWORTH, J. (1983) *By Word of Mouth: Elite Oral History*, London and New York: Methuen.

SILVERMAN, K. (1983) *The Subject of Semiotics*, New York: Oxford University Press.

SIMPSON, C. (1996) 'Elisabeth Noelle-Neumann's "Spiral of Silence" and the Historical Context of Communication Theory', *Journal of Communication*, 46(3): 149–73.

SIMPSON, P.A. (1996) 'The Washington Press Club Foundation's Oral History Project', in Allen, D., Rush, R.R. and Kaufman, S.J. (eds), *Women Transforming Communications: Global Intersections*, Thousand Oaks, CA, London and New Delhi: Sage.

SINGER, J.B. (2005) 'The Political J-blogger: "Normalizing" a New Media Form to Fit Old Norms and Practices', *Journalism*, 6(2): 173–98.

SKILLINGTON, T. (1997) 'Politics and the Struggle to Define: A Discourse Analysis of the Framing Strategies of Competing Actors in a "New" Participatory Forum', *British Journal of Sociology*, 48(3): 493–513.

SMITH, D.E. (1987) *The Everyday World as Problematic: A Feminist Sociology*, Milton Keynes: Open University Press.

SMITH, H.W. (1975) *Strategies of Social Research: The Methodological Imagination*, London: Prentice Hall.

SOOTHILL, K. and GROVER, C. (1997) 'A Note on the Computer Searches of Newspapers', *Sociology*, 31(3): 591–6.

SPIGEL, L. (1992) *Make Room for TV: Television and the Family Ideal in Postwar America*, Chicago, IL: University of Chicago Press.

SUDMAN, S. and BRADBURN, N. (1983) *Asking Questions*, San Francisco, CA: Jossey-Bass.

SVETLIK, I. (1992) 'The Voluntary Sector in a Post-communist Country: The Case of Slovenia', in Kuhnle, S. and Selle, P. (eds), *Governments and Voluntary Organisations*, Aldershot: Avebury.

TANNEN, D. (1990) *You Just Don't Understand: Women and Men in Conversation*, New York: Ballantine.

TAYLOR, L. (2006) 'The Poppy: To Wear or Not to Wear', http://www.channel4.com/apps26/blogs/page/newsroom?entry=the_poppy_to_wear_or (accessed 8 February 2007).

TEO, P. (2002) 'Racism in the News', in Toolan, M. (ed.), *Critical Discourse Analysis*, London and New York: Routledge, pp. 360–403.

THOMPSON, J.B. (1984) *Studies in the Theory of Ideology*, Cambridge: Polity Press.

THOMPSON, J.B. (1990) *Ideology and Mass Culture*, Cambridge: Polity Press.

THOMPSON, P. (1975) *The Edwardians*, London: Weidenfeld and Nicolson.

THOMPSON, P. (1978) *The Voice of the Past: Oral History*, Oxford, London and New York: Oxford University Press.

TOSH, J. (1989) *The Pursuit of History*, London and New York: Longman.

TRACEY, M. (1978) *The Production of Political Television*, London: Routledge and Kegan Paul.

TRACHTENBERG, A. (ed.) (1980) *Classic Essays on Photography*, New Haven, CT: Leete's Island Books.

TRAUGOTT, M. and LAVRAKAS, P. (1996) *The Voter's Guide to Election Polls*, Chatham, NJ: Chatham House.

TREW, T. (1979) 'Theory and Ideology at Work', in Fowler, R., Hodge, B., Kress, G. and Trew, T., *Language and Control*, London: Routledge and Kegan Paul.

TRUDGILL, P. (1974) *The Social Differentiation of English in Norwich*, Cambridge: Cambridge University Press.

TRUDGILL, P. (1978) *Sociolinguistics*, Harmondsworth: Penguin.

TUCHMAN, G. (1972) 'Objectivity as Strategic Ritual: An Examination of Newsmen's Notions of Objectivity', *American Journal of Sociology*, 77: January, 66–70.

TULLOCH, J. and ALVARADO, M. (1983) *Dr Who: The Unfolding Text*, London: Macmillan.

TUNSTALL, J. (1971) *Journalists at Work: Special Correspondents, the News Organisations, News Sources, and Competitor Colleagues*, London: Constable.

TUNSTALL, J. (1977) *The Media Are American*, London: Constable.

TURNER, R. (ed.) (1974) *Ethnomethodology*, Harmondsworth: Penguin.

VAN DIJK, T.A. (1983) 'Discourse Analysis: Its Development and Application to the Structure of News', *Journal of Communication*, 33(2): 20–43.

VAN DIJK, T.A. (1986) 'News Schemata', in Cooper, C.R. and Greenbaum, S. (eds), *Studying Writing: Linguistic Approaches*, Beverly Hills, CA: Sage.

VAN DIJK, T.A. (1988a) *News as Discourse*, Hillsdale, NJ and London: Lawrence Erlbaum.

VAN DIJK, T.A. (1988b) *News Analysis: Case Studies of International and National News in the Press*, Hillsdale, NJ: Lawrence Erlbaum.

VAN DIJK, T.A. (1991) *Racism and the Press*, London and New York: Routledge.

VAN DIJK, T.A. (2000) 'New(s) Racism: A Discourse Analytical Approach', in Cottle, S. (ed.), *Ethnic Minorities and the Media*, Buckingham, UK and Philadelphia, PA: Open University Press.

VAN LEEUWEN, T. (1995) 'Representing Social Action', *Discourse and Society*, 6(1): 81–106.

VAN ZOONEN, L. (1994) *Feminist Media Studies*, London: Sage.

VOLOSINOV, V. (1973) *Marxism and the Philosophy of Language*, New York: Seminar Press.

WATNEY, S. (1989) *Policing Desire: Pornography, Aids and the Media*, Minneapolis: University of Minnesota Press.

WEBB, B. (1950) *My Apprenticeship*, London, New York and Toronto: Longmans Green and Co. (originally published 1926).

WEERASINGHE, L. (ed.) (1989) *Directory of Recorded Sound Resources in the United Kingdom*, London: British Library.

WEISS, R. (1968) *Statistics in Social Research: An Introduction*, New York: John Wiley.

WELSH, T., GREENWOOD, W. and BANKS, D. (2005) *McNae's Essential Law for Journalists*, Oxford and New York: Oxford University Press.

WILLIAMS, A. (1993) 'Diversity and Agreement in Feminist Ethnography', *Sociology*, 27(4): 575–89.

WILLIAMS, D. (2006) 'Why Game Studies Now? Gamers Don't Bowl Alone', *Games and Culture*, 1(1): 13–16.

WILLIAMS, F., RICE, R. and ROGERS, E. (1988) *Research Methods and the New Media*, London and New York: The Free Press.

WILLIAMS, P. and DICKINSON, J. (1993) 'Fear of Crime: Read All About It: The Relationship Between Newspaper Crime Reporting and Fear of Crime', *British Journal of Criminology*, 33(1): 33–56.

WILLIS, P. (1978) *Profane Culture*, London, Henley and Boston, MA: Routledge and Kegan Paul.

WILLIS, P. (1980) 'Notes on Method', in Hall, S., Hobson, D., Lowe, A. and Willis, P. (eds), *Culture, Media, Language*, London: Hutchinson.

WILSON, E. (1992) 'The Invisible Flaneur', *New Left Review*, 191: January/February, 90–110.

WILSON, M. (1996) 'Asking Questions', in Sapsford, R. and Jupp, V. (eds), *Data Collection and Analysis*, London, Thousand Oaks, CA and New Delhi: Sage.

WINSTON, B. (1990) 'On Counting the Wrong Things', in Alvarado, M. and Thompson, J.B. (eds), *The Media Reader*, London: British Film Institute.

WINSTON, B. (1995) *Claiming the Real: The Griersonian Documentary and its Legitimations*, London: British Film Institute.

WITTGENSTEIN, L. (1967) *Philosophical Investigations*, Oxford: Basil Blackwell.

WOLLEN, P. (1972) *Signs and Meanings in the Cinema*, London: Secker and Warburg.

WOOD, F. (1995) *Did Marco Polo Go to China?*, London: Secker and Warburg.

WREN-LEWIS, J. (1983) 'The Encoding/Decoding Model: Criticisms and Redevelopments for Research on Decoding', *Media, Culture and Society*, 5(2): 179–97.

WRING, D. (1998) 'The Media and Intra-party Democracy: "New" Labour and the Clause Four Debate in Britain', *Democratization*, 5(2): 42–61.

YOUNG, R. (1995) *White Mythologies*, London and New York: Routledge.

YTREBERG, E. (2002) 'Erving Goffman as a Theorist of the Mass Media', *Critical Studies in Media Communication*, 19(4): 481–97.

Index